Encyclopedia of Literature and Politics

○○○ ENCYCLOPEDIA OF ○○○
Literature *and* Politics

Censorship, Revolution, and Writing
VOLUME II: H–R

○ ○ ○

Edited by M. Keith Booker

GREENWOOD PRESS
Westport, Connecticut • London

Library of Congress Cataloging-in-Publication Data

Encyclopedia of literature and politics : censorship, revolution, and writing / edited by M.
  Keith Booker.
     p. cm.
  Includes bibliographical references and index.
  ISBN 0–313–32928–1 ((set) : alk. paper)—ISBN 0–313–32939–7 ((vol. 1) : alk. paper)—
  ISBN 0–313–32940–0 ((vol. 2) : alk. paper)—ISBN 0–313–33568–0 ((vol. 3) : alk. paper)
  1. Politics and literature—Encyclopedias. I. Booker, M. Keith.
 PN51.E63 2005
  809'.93358'03—dc22   2005008522

British Library Cataloguing in Publication Data is available.

Library of Congress Catalog Card Number: 2005008522
ISBN 0–313–32928–1 (set)
     0–313–32939–7 (Vol. I)
     0–313–32940–0 (Vol. II)
     0–313–33568–0 (Vol. III)

First published in 2005

Greenwood Press, 88 Post Road West, Westport, CT 06881
An imprint of Greenwood Publishing Group, Inc.
www.greenwood.com

Printed in the United States of America

The paper used in this book complies with the
Permanent Paper Standard issued by the National
Information Standards Organization (Z39.48–1984).

10 9 8 7 6 5 4 3 2 1

For Amy, Adam, Marcus, Dakota, Skylor, and Benjamin

○○○ *Contents* ○○○

Preface ix

Alphabetical List of Entries xi

Categorical List of Entries xix

The Encyclopedia 1

Bibliography 783

Index 873

Notes on Contributors 919

○○○ *Preface* ○○○

During the past few decades, literary studies have come to be dominated by approaches that emphasize the social, historical, and political significance of literary works. This development (after the cold-war decades, in which political approaches to literature were out of favor) reemphasizes the close connection that has existed between literature and politics throughout Western history. This three-volume encyclopedia brings together a wide variety of information on the relationship between literature and politics in a conveniently accessible encyclopedia format.

The encyclopedia is international in scope, covering relevant information from the ancient Greeks forward, though with a necessary emphasis on the modern era (after 1900). Indeed, because the topic of the encyclopedia is so broad, it has been necessary to make a number of choices in emphasis. For example, because the encyclopedia is written in English and because English is expected to be the principal language of most readers, the various entries concentrate especially on American and British literature, with the expectation that this literature will be most relevant to the majority of readers. Secondary emphasis has been given to other Anglophone literatures (from Canada, Australia, the Caribbean, and Africa), while it has been possible only to touch on the highlights of other world literatures (from Latin America, Russia and the Soviet Union, China, Europe, and the Middle East).

The more than five hundred entries in the encyclopedia are of a number of basic types. The most numerous entries are biographical ones, which summarize the careers of important authors, critics, and literary theorists, as well as historical figures who have had an impact on the evolving relationship between literature and politics. There are also a number of entries describing important works of literature, as well as crucial critical nonfiction works and literary journals. A number of broader entries survey national literatures or important literary movements (such as Soviet socialist realism, American proletarian fiction, or postcolonial literature), while others cover broad critical categories, such as Marxist criticism, feminist criticism, or postcolonial studies. Finally, additional entries provide coverage of specific themes, concepts, and genres toward the goal of providing a single reference point for a general approach to the relationship between literature and politics. The various entries are cross-referenced using a system of boldfacing; in any entry, the first mention of an item that is also covered in an entry of its own will be given in boldface.

The entries in the encyclopedia have been written by expert scholars who work in the field to which the entries are relevant. In that sense, the information provided is the best that could be obtained. However, the length restrictions inherent in a work such as this one require that the information included here is merely a starting point and should not be taken as complete and comprehensive. In this sense, readers interested in more complete and detailed information should pay serious attention to the suggestions for further reading that are included at the ends of the entries and should consult the suggested sources for further information.

○○○ *Alphabetical List of Entries* ○○○

Abrahams, Peter
Académie Française
Achebe, Chinua
Adorno, Theodor Wiesengrund
African American Literature
African Literature (Anglophone)
African Literature (Francophone)
Akhmatova, Anna
Albiac, Gabriel
Algren, Nelson
Alienation
Allende, Isabel
Althusser, Louis
Amado, Jorge
America Is in the Heart
American Literature (After 1900)
American Literature (Before 1900)
Anand, Mulk Raj
Les Anciens Canadiens
Anticommunism
Antoni, Robert
Anvil /New Anvil
Anzaldúa, Gloria E.
Apartheid
Aragon, Louis
Arendt, Hannah
Armah, Ayi Kwei
Al-Ashqar, Yusuf Habshi
Asian American Literature
Asturias, Miguel Angel
Attaway, William

Atwood, Margaret
Auden, W(ystan) H(ugh)
Australian Literature

Bakhtin, Mikhail Mikhailovich
Baldwin, James
Balzac, Honoré de
Baraka, Amiri
Barker, Pat
Barthes, Roland
Base and Superstructure
Bates, Ralph
Baudrillard, Jean
Beat Movement
De Beauvoir, Simone Ernestine Lucie Marie
    Bertrand
Beckett, Samuel
The Beggar's Opera
Bei Dao
Beloved
Bely, Andrei
A Bend in the River
Benjamin, Walter
Berger, John
Bildungsroman
Black Arts Movement
Black Nationalism
Bloch, Ernst
Bond, Edward
Bonheur d'occasion
Bourdieu, Pierre

Brathwaite, Edward Kamau
Brave New World
Brazilian Literature
Brecht, Bertolt
Brecht-Lukács Debate
British Immigrant Literature
British Literature (after 1900)
British Novel (Nineteenth Century)
British Working-Class and Socialist
    Literature
Brown, Lloyd L.
Bulgakov, Mikhail
Bulosan, Carlos
Burger's Daughter
Burke, Fielding
Butler, Judith

Calvino, Italo
Canadian Literature (Anglophone)
Canadian Literature (Francophone)
Canons and Canonicity
The Cantos
Čapek, Karel
Cardenal, Ernesto
Caribbean Literature (Anglophone)
Caribbean Literature (Francophone)
Carpentier, Alejo
Carter, Angela
Carter, Martin Wylde
Cather, Willa
The Caucasian Chalk Circle
Caudwell, Christopher
Certeau, Michel de
Cervantes Saavedra, Miguel de
Césaire, Aimé
Chartism
Chernyshevsky, Nikolai
Chinese Literature
Chinese Writers' Association
Churchill, Caryl
Cold War
Coleridge, Samuel Taylor
Commodification
Communist Party
Composition Studies and Literature

Condé, Maryse
Conrad, Joseph
Conroy, John Wesley (Jack)
Creoleness (Créolité)
Cuban Literature
Cuban Revolution
Cultural Studies
Culture Wars
Cunard, Nancy

Al-Daif, Rashid
The Daily Worker
Dalton, Roque
Darío, Rubén
Davis, Jack
Davis, Rebecca Harding
Day Lewis, C(ecil)
De Boissière, Ralph
Debord, Guy
Delany, Samuel R.
Deleuze, Gilles
Derrida, Jacques
Desai, Anita
Detective and Crime Fiction
Devil on the Cross
The Devils
Dick, Philip K(indred)
Dickens, Charles
Dictionaries (English)
Dictionaries (French)
Ding Ling
Doctorow, Edgar Lawrence (E. L.)
Don Quijote
Dos Passos, John
Dostoevsky, Fyodor Mikhailovich
Douglass, Frederick
Dreiser, Theodore
Du Bois, W.E.B.
Duras, Marguerite
Dystopian Literature

Eagleton, Terry
Easter Rising
Eastern and Central European Literature
Eastman, Max Forrester

Eliot, George
Eliot, T(homas) S(tearns)
Ellison, Ralph
English Literature (Medieval)
English Literature (Renaissance)
English Literature (Restoration and Eighteenth
    Century)
English Studies and Politics
Environmentalism
Enzensberger, Hans Magnus
Epic Theater

Fanon, Frantz
Farrell, James T.
Fast, Howard
Faulkner, William
Fearing, Kenneth
Federal Writers' Project
Feminist Criticism and Theory
Fernández Retamar, Roberto
For Whom the Bell Tolls
Fortini, Franco
Foucault, Michel
Fox, Ralph
Frankenstein; or, The Modern Prometheus
Frankfurt School
Freeman, Joseph
French Literature
French Revolution
Fuentes, Carlos

Gao Xingjian
García Lorca, Federico
García Márquez, Gabriel
Gaskell, Elizabeth
Gastonia Mill Strike
Gay and Lesbian Studies
Gender and Literature
General Strike
German Literature
Germinal
Ghosh, Amitav
Gibbon, Lewis Grassic
Gilbert, Kevin
Ginsberg, Irwin Allen

Gladkov, Fyodor Vasilyevich
Glissant, Edouard
Godwin, William
Goethe, Johann Wolfgang von
Gogol, Nikolai Vasilievich
Gold, Michael
Goldman, Emma
Goldmann, Lucien
Gordimer, Nadine
Gorky, Maxim
Gothic Literature
Goytisolo Gay, Juan
Gramsci, Antonio
The Grapes of Wrath
Grass, Günter
Greene, Graham
Guillén, Nicolás

Habermas, Jürgen
Haitian Revolution
Hall, Stuart
Hammett, Dashiell
Haraway, Donna J.
Harlem Renaissance
Harvey, David
Havel, Vaclav
Heart of Darkness
Hegemony
*Hegemony and Socialist Strategy: Towards a
    Radical Democratic Politics*
Heinlein, Robert
Hellman, Lillian
Hemingway, Ernest
Herbst, Josephine Frey
Hernandez, Amado V.
Hernández, Miguel
Heslop, Harold
Heym, Stefan
Hicks, Granville
Hikmet, Nazim
Himes, Chester Bomar
Historical Novel
Holdsworth, Ethel Carnie
Holocaust Literature
How the Steel Was Tempered

Hughes, Langston
Huxley, Aldous

Ibsen, Henrik
Ideology
Indigenismo
Industrial Workers of the World (IWW)
International Literature
Invisible Man
Irish Literature
Isherwood, Christopher
Italian Literature
Iyayi, Festus

James, C.L.R.
James, Henry
Jameson, Fredric
Jewish American Literature
Jews without Money
John Reed Clubs
Johnson, Emily Pauline (Tekahionwake)
Jones, Lewis
Joyce, James

Kane, Sarah
Kataev, Valentin Petrovich
Killens, John Oliver
Kipling, Rudyard
Kiš, Danilo
Kluge, Alexander
Koestler, Arthur
Kollontai, Alexandra Mikhailovna
    Domontovich
Kraus, Karl
Kristeva, Julia
Krleža, Miroslav
Kundera, Milan

La Guma, Alex
Lamming, George
Latin American Literature
Latina/o Literature
Le Guin, Ursula Kroeber
Lefebvre, Henri
Left Review

Lehrstück
Lenin, Vladimir Ilyich
The Leopard
Lermontov, Mikhail Iurevich
Lessing, Doris
LeSueur, Meridel
Let Us Now Praise Famous Men
Levertov, Denise
Levi, Primo
Lewis, Wyndham
Li Ang
Lindsay, Jack
Lippard, George
London, Jack
Looking Backward: 2000–1887
Lorde, Audre
Love on the Dole
Lu Xun
Lukács, Georg
Lumpkin, Grace

MacDiarmid, Hugh
Macherey, Pierre
Madame Bovary
Magical Realism
Mailer, Norman
Malraux, André
Mandel'shtam, Osip Emil'evich
Mann, Thomas
Mao Dun
Mao Zedong
Mariátegui, José Carlos
Martí, José
Marx, Karl
Marxist Criticism
Marxist-Feminism (M-F)
Masses
Matthiessen, Francis Otto
Mayakovsky, Vladimir Vladimirovich
McKay, Claude
McLuhan, Herbert Marshall
Menchú Tum, Rigoberta
Menippean Satire
Midnight's Children
Milosz, Czeslaw

Milton, John

Mir, Pedro

Mo Yan

Modernism

Mohanty, Chandra Talpade

Momaday, N. Scott

Monette, Paul

Moravia, Alberto

Morrison, Toni

Mother

*Mother Courage and Her Children: A Chronicle
    from the Thirty Years War*

Müller, Heiner

Mulvey, Laura

Nabokov, Vladimir

Naipaul, V(idiadhar) S(urajprasad)

Native American Literature

Native Son

Naturalism

Negri, Antonio

Negritude

Neruda, Pablo

New Criticism

New Historicism

New Left Review

New Masses

New York Intellectuals

News from Nowhere

Nexø, Martin Andersen

Ngũgĩ wa Thiong'o

Nigerian Civil War

Nineteen Eighty-Four

Nizan, Paul

Nkrumah, Kwame

O'Casey, Sean

Odets, Clifford

Ohmann, Richard

Olsen, Tillie

Ondaatje, Philip Michael

Oodgeroo

Orientalism

Orwell, George

Osofisan, Femi

Ostrovsky, Nikolai Alekseevich

Owen, Wilfred

Padmore, George

Page, Myra

Paley, Grace

Partisan Review

Pasolini, Pier Paolo

Pavese, Cesare

Peter the First

Pilnyak, Boris Andreyevich

Pinter, Harold

Platonov, Andrei Platonovich

Plenzdorf, Ulrich

La Poesía Sorprendida

Political Unconscious

Polonsky, Abraham

Popular Culture

Popular Front

Postcolonial Literature

Postcolonial Theory and Criticism

Post-Marxism

Postmodernism

Pound, Ezra

Prichard, Katharine Susannah

Prison Literature

Prochain Episode

Proletarian Fiction, American

Pushkin, Aleksandr Sergeevich

Race and Ethnicity Studies

The Ragged Trousered Philanthropists

Realism

Red Letters

Red Love

Reed, John

Reification

The Republic

The Revenge for Love

Revueltas, José

Rickword, Edgell

Ridge, Lola

Robinson, Kim Stanley

Robinson, Lillian S.

Rolland, Romain

Romanticism
Roumain, Jacques
Routinization
Rushdie, Salman
Russ, Joanna
Russian Literature (Nineteenth Century)
Russian Revolution

Said, Edward
San Juan, Epifanio, Jr.
Sartre, Jean-Paul
Sassoon, Siegfried
The Satanic Verses
Scandinavian Literature
Schuyler, George S(amuel)
Science Fiction
Scott, F. R.
Scottish Literature
Sedgwick, Eve Kosofsky
Seghers, Anna
Sembène, Ousmane
Senghor, Léopold Sédar
Serge, Victor
The Seventh Cross
Shakespeare, William
Shaw, (George) Bernard
Shelley, Percy Bysshe
Shen Congwen
Sholokhov, Mikhail
Silko, Leslie Marmon
Sillitoe, Alan
Silone, Ignazio
Sinclair, Upton
Slave Narratives
Slesinger, Tess
Smedley, Agnes
Socialist Realism (Soviet)
Solzhenitsyn, Aleksandr Isaevich
South African Literature
South Asian Literature
Soviet Writers' Congress (1934)
Soyinka, Wole
The Space Merchants
Spanish Civil War
Spanish Literature (Twentieth Century)
Spenser, Edmund

Spivak, Gayatri Chakravorty
Stalin, Joseph Vissarionovich
Stead, Christina
Steinbeck, John
Stevenson, Philip Edward
Stowe, Harriet Beecher
Surrealism
Swift, Jonathan
Swingler, Randall

Taggard, Genevieve
Tagore, Rabindranath
Testimonio
Theater, Political
Third International
Thompson, Jim
Thoreau, Henry David
The Threepenny Opera
Tolstoy, Alexei
Tolstoy, Leo (Lev) Nikolaevich
Toomer, Jean
Traven, B.
Trotsky, Leon
Tsvetayeva, Marina
Turgenev, Ivan Sergeevich

Unamuno, Miguel de
U.S.A. Trilogy
Utopia
Utopian Fiction

Valenzuela, Luisa
Vallejo, César
Vargas Llosa, Mario
Vietnam War Literature
A Vindication of the Rights of Woman
Vizenor, Gerald Robert
Voinovich, Vladimir Nikolaevich

Walker, Margaret
Wang Shuo
Warner, Sylvia Townsend
We
Weatherwax, Clara
Weber, Max
Weiss, Peter

Wells, H. G.
West, Nathanael
West, Rebecca
Whitman, Walt
Wiesel, Elie
Williams, Raymond
Williams, William Carlos
Wolf, Christa
Wollstonecraft, Mary
Woolf, Virginia
World War I

World War II
The Wretched of the Earth
Wright, Richard

Yeats, William Butler
Yezierska, Anzia
Yugoslav Literature

Zamyatin, Evgeny Ivanovich
Zizek, Slavoj
Zola, Émile

⚬⚬⚬ *Categorical List of Entries* ⚬⚬⚬

AUTHORS

Abrahams, Peter
Achebe, Chinua
Akhmatova, Anna
Albiac, Gabriel
Algren, Nelson
Allende, Isabel
Amado, Jorge
Anand, Mulk Raj
Antoni, Robert
Aragon, Louis
Armah, Ayi Kwei
Al-Ashqar, Yusuf Habshi
Asturias, Miguel Angel
Attaway, William
Atwood, Margaret
Auden, W(ystan) H(ugh)

Baldwin, James
Balzac, Honoré de
Baraka, Amiri
Barker, Pat
Bates, Ralph
Beckett, Samuel
Bei Dao
Bely, Andrei
Berger, John
Bond, Edward
Brathwaite, Edward Kamau
Brecht, Bertolt

Brown, Lloyd L.
Bulgakov, Mikhail
Bulosan, Carlos
Burke, Fielding

Calvino, Italo
Čapek, Karel
Cardenal, Ernesto
Carnie, Ethel. *See* Holdsworth, Ethel Carnie
Carpentier, Alejo
Carter, Angela
Carter, Martin Wylde
Cather, Willa
Cervantes Saavedra, Miguel de
Césaire, Aimé
Chernyshevsky, Nikolai
Churchill, Caryl
Coleridge, Samuel Taylor
Condé, Maryse
Conrad, Joseph
Conroy, John Wesley (Jack)
Cunard, Nancy

Al-Daif, Rashid
Dalton, Roque
Darío, Rubén
Davis, Jack
Davis, Rebecca Harding
Day Lewis, C(ecil)
De Boissière, Ralph
Delany, Samuel R.

Desai, Anita
Dick, Philip K(indred)
Dickens, Charles
Ding Ling
Doctorow, Edgar Lawrence (E. L.)
Dos Passos, John
Dostoevsky, Fyodor Mikhailovich
Douglass, Frederick
Dreiser, Theodore
Duras, Marguerite

Eastman, Max Forrester
Eliot, George
Eliot, T(homas) S(tearns)
Ellison, Ralph

Farrell, James T.
Fast, Howard
Faulkner, William
Fearing, Kenneth
Fernández Retamar, Roberto
Fortini, Franco
Freeman, Joseph
Fuentes, Carlos

Gao Xingjian
García Lorca, Federico
García Márquez, Gabriel
Gaskell, Elizabeth
Ghosh, Amitav
Gibbon, Lewis Grassic
Gilbert, Kevin
Ginsberg, Irwin Allen
Gladkov, Fyodor Vasilyevich
Glissant, Edouard
Godwin, William
Goethe, Johann Wolfgang von
Gogol, Nikolai Vasilievich
Gordimer, Nadine
Gorky, Maxim
Goytisolo Gay, Juan
Grass, Günter
Greene, Graham
Guillén, Nicolás

Hammett, Dashiell
Havel, Vaclav

Heinlein, Robert
Hellman, Lillian
Hemingway, Ernest
Herbst, Josephine Frey
Hernandez, Amado V.
Hernández, Miguel
Heslop, Harold
Heym, Stefan
Hicks, Granville
Hikmet, Nazim
Himes, Chester Bomar
Holdsworth, Ethel Carnie
Hughes, Langston
Huxley, Aldous

Ibsen, Henrik
Isherwood, Christopher
Iyayi, Festus

James, Henry
Johnson, Emily Pauline (Tekahionwake)
Jones, Leroi. *See* Baraka, Amiri
Jones, Lewis
Joyce, James

Kane, Sarah
Kataev, Valentin Petrovich
Killens, John Oliver
Kipling, Rudyard
Kiš, Danilo
Kluge, Alexander
Koestler, Arthur
Kollontai, Alexandra Mikhailovna
    Domontovich
Krleža, Miroslav
Kundera, Milan

La Guma, Alex
Lamming, George
Le Guin, Ursula Kroeber
Lermontov, Mikhail Iurevich
Lessing, Doris
LeSueur, Meridel
Levertov, Denise
Levi, Primo
Lewis, Wyndham

Li Ang
Lindsay, Jack
Lippard, George
London, Jack
Lorde, Audre
Lu Xun
Lumpkin, Grace

MacDiarmid, Hugh
Mailer, Norman
Malraux, André
Mandel'shtam, Osip Emil'evich
Mann, Thomas
Mao Dun
Martí, José
Matthiessen, Francis Otto
Mayakovsky, Vladimir Vladimirovich
McKay, Claude
Menchú Tum, Rigoberta
Milosz, Czeslaw
Milton, John
Mir, Pedro
Mo Yan
Momaday, N. Scott
Monette, Paul
Moravia, Alberto
Morris, William. See *News from Nowhere*
Morrison, Toni
Müller, Heiner

Nabokov, Vladimir
Naipaul, V(idiadhar) S(urajprasad)
Neruda, Pablo
Nexø, Martin Andersen
Ngũgĩ wa Thiong'o
Nizan, Paul

O'Casey, Sean
Odets, Clifford
Olsen, Tillie
Ondaatje, Philip Michael
Oodgeroo
Orwell, George
Osofisan, Femi
Ostrovsky, Nikolai Alekseevich
Owen, Wilfred

Page, Myra
Paley, Grace
Pasolini, Pier Paolo
Pavese, Cesare
Pilnyak, Boris Andreyevich
Pinter, Harold
Platonov, Andrei Platonovich
Plenzdorf, Ulrich
Polonsky, Abraham
Pound, Ezra
Prichard, Katharine Susannah
Pushkin, Aleksandr Sergeevich

Revueltas, José
Rickword, Edgell
Ridge, Lola
Robinson, Kim Stanley
Rolland, Romain
Roumain, Jacques
Rushdie, Salman
Russ, Joanna

Sassoon, Siegfried
Schuyler, George S(amuel)
Scott, F. R.
Seghers, Anna
Sembène, Ousmane
Senghor, Léopold Sédar
Serge, Victor
Shakespeare, William
Shaw, (George) Bernard
Shelley, Percy Bysshe
Shen Congwen
Sholokhov, Mikhail
Silko, Leslie Marmon
Sillitoe, Alan
Silone, Ignazio
Sinclair, Upton
Slesinger, Tess
Smedley, Agnes
Solzhenitsyn, Aleksandr Isaevich
Soyinka, Wole
Spenser, Edmund
Stead, Christina
Steinbeck, John
Stevenson, Philip Edward

Stowe, Harriet Beecher
Swift, Jonathan
Swingler, Randall

Taggard, Genevieve
Tagore, Rabindranath
Thompson, Jim
Thoreau, Henry David
Tolstoy, Alexei
Tolstoy, Leo (Lev) Nikolaevich
Toomer, Jean
Traven, B.
Trotsky, Leon
Tsvetayeva, Marina
Turgenev, Ivan Sergeevich

Unamuno, Miguel de

Valenzuela, Luisa
Vallejo, César
Vargas Llosa, Mario
Vizenor, Gerald Robert
Voinovich, Vladimir Nikolaevich

Walker, Margaret
Wang Shuo
Warner, Sylvia Townsend
Weatherwax, Clara
Weiss, Peter
Wells, H. G.
West, Nathanael
West, Rebecca
Whitman, Walt
Wiesel, Elie
Williams, William Carlos
Wolf, Christa
Woolf, Virginia
Wright, Richard

Yeats, William Butler
Yezierska, Anzia

Zamyatin, Evgeny Ivanovich
Zola, Émile

CRITICS AND THEORISTS

Adorno, Theodor Wiesengrund
Althusser, Louis
Anzaldúa, Gloria E.
Arendt, Hannah

Bakhtin, Mikhail Mikhailovich
Barthes, Roland
Baudrillard, Jean
De Beauvoir, Simone Ernestine Lucie Marie
    Bertrand
Benjamin, Walter
Bloch, Ernst
Bourdieu, Pierre
Butler, Judith

Caudwell, Christopher
Certeau, Michel de

Debord, Guy
Deleuze, Gilles
Derrida, Jacques
Du Bois, W.E.B.

Eagleton, Terry
Enzensberger, Hans Magnus

Fanon, Frantz
Foucault, Michel
Fox, Ralph

Gold, Michael
Goldmann, Lucien
Gramsci, Antonio

Habermas, Jürgen
Hall, Stuart
Haraway, Donna J.
Harvey, David

James, C.L.R.
Jameson, Fredric

Kraus, Karl
Kristeva, Julia

Lefebvre, Henri
Lukács, Georg

Macherey, Pierre
Mariátegui, José Carlos
Marx, Karl
McLuhan, Herbert Marshall
Mohanty, Chandra Talpade
Mulvey, Laura

Negri, Antonio

Ohmann, Richard

Reed, John
Robinson, Lillian S.

Said, Edward
San Juan, Epifanio, Jr.
Sartre, Jean-Paul
Sedgwick, Eve Kosofsky
Spivak, Gayatri Chakravorty

Weber, Max
Williams, Raymond
Wollstonecraft, Mary

Zizek, Slavoj

HISTORICAL EVENTS, GROUPS, AND MOVEMENTS

Académie Française
Anticommunism
Apartheid

Black Nationalism
Brecht-Lukács Debate

Chinese Writers' Association
Cold War, The
Comintern. *See* Third International
Communist Party
Cuban Revolution

Easter Rising

Federal Writers' Project
French Revolution

Gastonia Mill Strike
General Strike

Haitian Revolution
Harlem Renaissance

Indigenismo
Industrial Workers of the World (IWW)

John Reed Clubs

McCarthyism. *See* Anticommunism

Nigerian Civil War

Popular Front

Russian Revolution

Soviet Writers' Congress (1934)
Spanish Civil War

Third International

World War I
World War II

HISTORICAL FIGURES

Goldman, Emma

Lenin, Vladimir Ilyich

Mao Zedong

Nkrumah, Kwame

Padmore, George

Stalin, Joseph Vissarionovich

JOURNALS AND NONFICTION WORKS

Anvil/New Anvil

The Daily Worker
Dictionaries (English)
Dictionaries (French)

Hegemony and Socialist Strategy: Towards a
   Radical Democratic Politics

International Literature

Left Review
Let Us Now Praise Famous Men

Masses

New Anvil. See *Anvil/New Anvil*
New Left Review
New Masses

Orientalism

Partisan Review

Red Letters
The Republic

Utopia

A Vindication of the Rights of Woman

The Wretched of the Earth

LITERARY WORKS

America Is in the Heart
Les Anciens Canadiens

The Beggar's Opera
Beloved
A Bend in the River
Bonheur d'occasion
Brave New World
Burger's Daughter

The Cantos
The Caucasian Chalk Circle

Devil on the Cross
The Devils
Don Quijote

For Whom the Bell Tolls
Frankenstein; or, The Modern Prometheus

Germinal
The Grapes of Wrath

Heart of Darkness
How the Steel Was Tempered

Invisible Man

Jews without Money

The Leopard
Life in the Iron Mills. See Davis, Rebecca
   Harding
Looking Backward: 2000–1887
Love on the Dole

Madame Bovary
Midnight's Children
Mother
Mother Courage and Her Children: A Chronicle
   from the Thirty Years War

Native Son
News from Nowhere
Nineteen Eighty-Four

Peter the First
Prochain Episode

The Ragged Trousered Philanthropists
Red Love
The Revenge for Love

The Satanic Verses
The Seventh Cross
The Space Merchants

The Threepenny Opera

U.S.A. Trilogy

We

NATIONAL AND REGIONAL LITERATURES

African American Literature
African Literature (Anglophone)
African Literature (Francophone)
American Literature (after 1900)
American Literature (before 1900)
Anglophone African Literature. *See* African
    Literature (Anglophone)
Anglophone Caribbean Literature. *See*
    Caribbean Literature (Anglophone)
Asian American Literature
Australian Literature

Brazilian Literature
British Immigrant Literature
British Literature (after 1900)
British Literature (Nineteenth Century). *See*
    British Novel (Nineteenth Century);
    Romanticism
British Novel (Nineteenth Century)
British Working-Class and Socialist Literature

Canadian Literature (Anglophone)
Canadian Literature (Francophone)
Caribbean Literature (Anglophone)
Caribbean Literature (Francophone)
Chinese Literature
Cuban Literature

Eastern and Central European Literature
English Literature (Medieval)
English Literature (Renaissance)
English Literature (Restoration and Eighteenth
    Century)
English Studies and Politics

Francophone African Literature. *See* African
    Literature (Francophone)

Francophone Caribbean Literature. *See*
    Caribbean Literature (Francophone)
French Literature

German Literature

Indian Literature. *See* South Asian Literature
Irish Literature
Italian Literature

Jewish American Literature

Latin American Literature
Latina/o Literature

Native American Literature

Postcolonial Literature

Russian Literature (Nineteenth Century)

Scandinavian Literature
Scottish Literature
Socialist Realism (Soviet)
South African Literature
South Asian Literature
Spanish Literature (Twentieth Century)

Yugoslav Literature

PERIODS, GENRES, AND LITERARY MOVEMENTS

Beat Movement
Bildungsroman
Black Arts Movement

Chartism

Detective and Crime Fiction
Dystopian Literature

Epic Theater

Gothic Literature

Historical Novel
Holocaust Literature

Lehrstück

Magical Realism
Menippean Satire
Modernism

Naturalism
Negritude

La Poesía Sorprendida
Postmodernism
Prison Literature
Proletarian Fiction, American
Proletarian Literature. *See* Proletarian Fiction,
   American

Realism
Romanticism

Science Fiction
Slave Narratives
Surrealism

Testimonio
Theater, Political

Utopian Fiction

Vietnam War Literature

THEORETICAL AND CRITICAL CONCEPTS

Alienation

Base and Superstructure

Canons and Canonicity
Commodification

Hegemony

Ideology

Political Unconscious

Reification
Routinization

THEORETICAL AND CRITICAL MOVEMENTS AND APPROACHES

Composition Studies and Literature
Creoleness (Créolité)
Cultural Studies
Culture Wars

Environmentalism

Feminist Criticism and Theory
Frankfurt School

Gay and Lesbian Studies
Gender and Literature

Marxist Criticism
Marxist-Feminism (M-F)

New Criticism
New Historicism
New York Intellectuals

Popular Culture
Postcolonial Studies. *See* Postcolonial Theory
   and Criticism
Postcolonial Theory and Criticism
Post-Marxism

Race and Ethnicity Studies

·H·

HABERMAS, JÜRGEN (1929–). The most important intellectual in postwar Germany, Habermas, a second-generation member of the **Frankfurt School**, has contributed seminally to West German public life in fields ranging from sociology to philosophy to political science. After attending universities in Göttingen and Bonn, he settled in Frankfurt in 1956, where he became an assistant to **Theodor Adorno** at the Institute for Social Research. In 1971, he became director of the Max Planck Institute in Starnberg. From 1983 until his retirement in 1994, he taught in the philosophy department in Frankfurt.

Habermas's *Structural Transformation of the Public Sphere* (*Strukturwandel der Öffentlichkeit*, 1962) aroused considerable interest among literary scholars. The "public sphere" is a realm in which opinions are exchanged between private persons unconstrained by external pressures; open to all citizens, it is the place where something approaching public opinion is formed. Predating the political public sphere is a "literary public sphere," in which men of letters debate matters of public import. Habermas's notion of the commodification of art in the eighteenth century and his discussion of the various institutions in which art and criticism occurred (coffeehouses, moral weeklies) have been suggestive for literary scholars. He also makes important observations on the rise of new genres, pointing out that correspondence as a literary form and the emergence of the psychological novel are reactions to a restructuring of the relationship between author, text, and reader. Intimacy as a matter for public scrutiny in fictional works depends on and fosters the legitimation of the public utterance of private opinions.

Habermas's *Philosophical Discourse of Modernity* (*Philosophische Diskurs der Moderne*, 1985) thrust him into the center of controversy concerning the concepts of modernity and postmodernity. Opposing Jean-François Lyotard's notion of the postmodern condition, Habermas contends that modernity poses for us a task that must still be completed. For Habermas, the constellation among modernity, consciousness, and rationality that crystallized in Hegel's philosophy had three distinct fates in subsequent thought: (1) the progressive neo-Hegelians such as **Karl Marx**, operating with a more modest notion of reason, continued the project of modernity; (2) the new conservatives, who reduced reason (*Vernunft*) to understanding (*Verstand*) and affirmed scientific notions of rationality, jettisoned any critical element in the project; and (3) the young conservative faction, which draws its inspiration from Friedrich Nietzsche and includes most adherents to poststructuralism, abandons reason altogether and falls into nihilism or anarchy. Habermas's contention, therefore, is that those who feel that they have gone beyond the project of modernity are deceiving themselves. There is no escape from the problems raised by subjectivity and enlightenment, only a continuation, a trivialization, or a pseudoradicalization of the initial premises. Instead of proceeding from the isolated subject confronting the objective world, Habermas opts for a model that considers human beings in dialogue with each other to be the foundation for emancipatory social thought.

Selected Bibliography: Bernstein, Richard J., ed. *Habermas and Modernity.* Cambridge, MA: MIT P, 1985; Duvenage, Pieter. *Habermas and Aesthetics: The Limits of Communicative Reason.* London: Polity P, 2003; Habermas, Jürgen. *The Philosophical Discourse of Modernity.* Trans. Frederick Lawrence. Cambridge, MA: MIT P, 1987; Habermas, Jürgen. *The Structural Transformation of the Public Sphere: An Inquiry into a Category of Bourgeois Society.* Trans. Thomas Burger. Cambridge, MA: MIT P, 1989; Habermas, Jürgen. *The Theory of Communicative Action.* Trans. Thomas McCarthy. 2 vols. Boston: Beacon P, 1984, 1987; Holub, Robert C. *Jürgen Habermas: Critic in the Public Sphere.* London: Routledge, 1991; McCarthy, Thomas. *The Critical Theory of Jürgen Habermas.* Cambridge, MA: MIT P, 1978; Thompson, John B., and David Held, eds. *Habermas: Critical Debates.* Cambridge, MA: MIT P, 1982.

Robert C. Holub

HAITIAN REVOLUTION. In 1791, black slaves in the wealthy French colony of St. Domingue (Haiti) revolted against white planters and free mulattoes and successfully proclaimed their own liberation. This utterly remarkable event eventually led to Napoleon's sale of the Louisiana Territory to the United States and triggered a number of major slave revolts in the United States. This event and its leaders, figures such as Toussaint L'Ouverture, Henri Christophe, and Jean Jacques Dessalines, have sparked the imagination of many American (especially African American) writers. The revolt was seemingly successful for a number of years, and in 1804, Haiti proclaimed itself the first black republic in the Western world. However, internal struggles among the leaders led to political unrest and subsequent revolutions, therefore substantially diminishing the initial success of the revolt.

American newspapers reported frequently on the Haitian slave revolt as well as the ensuing struggle for independence from France. Southern plantation owners followed these reports closely, as they were quite nervous about the possibility of this revolt inspiring similar uprisings among their own slaves, which it did in several cases, most notably those led by Gabriel Prosser, Denmark Vesey, and Nat Turner. As the abolitionist movement of the mid-nineteenth century gained momentum, the Haitian slave revolt began to appear as a subject of fiction, poetry, and drama, and Haiti itself was the subject of numerous travel narratives throughout the nineteenth and early twentieth centuries. Since that time, both African American and Euro-American writers have continued to explore various facets of the revolution in their drama and fiction. What tends to make many of these texts politically radical is their dual function, for they often intend to glorify the revolution and its leaders while also providing a critique of American slavery, racism, colonialism, and capitalism.

Poetic tributes to L'Ouverture have included poems by William Wordsworth, Victor Hugo, and John Greenleaf Whittier. Perhaps the earliest appearance of L'Ouverture in American poetry is in Thomas Branagan's 1805 epic poem *Avenia: A Tragical Poem*. From the end of the nineteenth century through the 1940s, the Haitian revolution was depicted primarily in drama, including such plays as William Edgar Easton's *Dessalines* (1893) and *Christophe* (1911), Eugene O'Neill's *Emperor Jones* (1921), and Leslie Pickney Hill's *Toussaint L'Ouverture* (1928). In the 1930s and 1940s, the Federal Theatre Project sponsored several plays that portray various aspects and figures of the revolution. *Black Empire* by Christine Ames and Clarke Painter, *Haiti* by relatively unknown journalist William Du Bois, and *Emperor of Haiti* by **Langston Hughes** are all Federal Theatre Project plays. One of the most talked about plays of the period was Orson Welles's production of a voodoo *Macbeth* in a Harlem theater. Years later, Lorraine Hansberry began a play entitled *Toussaint*, but it was never completed. By the 1940s, the historical novel became the dominant genre for exploring the slave revolt, these novels include Guy Endore's *Babouk* (1934), Arna Bontemps' *Drums at Dusk* (1939), Kenneth Roberts's *Lydia Bailey* (1947), James Jess Hannon's *The Black Napoleon* (1992), and Madison Smartt Bell's first two novels in a planned trilogy, *All Souls' Rising* (1995) and *Master of the Crossroads* (2000).

Selected Bibliography: Dash, J. Michael. *Haiti and the United States: National Stereotypes and the Literary Imagination.* 2nd ed. New York: St. Martin's, 1997; James, C.L.R. *The Black Jacobins: Toussaint L'Ouverture and the San Domingo Revolution.* 1938. New York: Vintage-Random House, 1989.

Angela Albright

HALL, STUART (1932–). Born in Jamaica, Hall has lived in Britain since 1951, originally studying literature at Oxford University as a Rhodes scholar. He is one of the founders of **cultural studies**, an influential political theorist, and a major analyst of the black British experience. He is a public intellectual.

Hall's career can be roughly divided into three phases. The first coincides with his role in founding the British New Left (1956–1962). Hall was among the founders of *Universities and Left Review*, a journal produced by radical Oxford students impatient with existing political orthodoxies and critical of Britain's role in the 1956 Suez crisis. He was the first editor of **New Left Review** and played a primary role in mediating between the rising student generation and older ex-Communists, such as the historian E. P. Thompson. Hall's intellectual work at this time was influenced by **Raymond Williams**'s cultural theory, though he had a higher regard for mass popular culture. *The Popular Arts* (1964), written with Paddy Whannel, is a notable example.

The second phase (1964–1980) involves Hall's role in founding and shaping the Center for Contemporary Cultural Studies at the University of Birmingham, the first institutional site for this interdisciplinary field. Initially as a faculty member and assistant to the founding director, Richard Hoggart, and then as the center's director, Hall helped define the "Birmingham school." The center attempted to fuse "structuralism" and "humanism," drawing on Western Marxism (particularly **Louis Althusser**'s and **Antonio Gramsci**'s thought) and British socialist humanism (Williams's cultural theory and Thompson's historical practice). In collectively produced studies—notably *Resistance through Rituals* (1976), *Policing the Crisis* (1978), *Culture, Media, Language* (1980), and *The Empire Strikes Back* (1982)—it made influential contributions to numerous fields: contemporary media, youth subcultures, working-class life, the modern state, historical theory and the theory of ideology, and the relationship between race, class, and gender.

Since 1980 (in what might be construed as a third phase), Hall has been active on multiple fronts. *Hard Road to Renewal* (1988) established him as a major critic of the British New Right. Drawing on Gramsci's thought, he argued that Thatcherism was a hegemonic project that reconfigured the relationship between public and private, the individual and the state. Correlatively, the Left's renewal depended on articulating cultural and political alternatives. Hall outlined this alternative in the journal *Marxism Today*'s "New Times" project (1990). As part of this rethinking, Hall became increasingly drawn to questions regarding identity, particularly black British identity, which he analyzed in essays on contemporary black photography, cinema, and popular culture. Hall understands black Britons in terms of a postcolonial perspective. He views them as having produced hybrid and marginalized identities that are at the same time culturally central, emblematic of how identity is constructed in the contemporary globalized world. Hall's current position is seemingly a long way from the days of the early New Left, but it fuses a characteristic preoccupation with the analysis of social, political, and cultural changes and the identification of oppositional forces that might potentially reshape them.

Selected Bibliography: Dworkin, Dennis. *Cultural Marxism in Postwar Britain: History, the New Left and the Origins of Cultural Studies.* Durham, NC: Duke UP, 1997; Gilroy, Paul. *The Black Atlantic: Double Consciousness and Modernity.* Cambridge, MA: Harvard UP, 1993; Morley, David, ed. *Stuart Hall: Critical Dialogues in Cultural Studies.* London: Routledge, 1996; Rojek, Chris. *Stuart Hall.* London: Polity P, 2003; Turner, Graeme. *British Cultural Studies: An Introduction.* 2nd ed. London: Routledge, 1996.

Dennis Dworkin

HAMMETT, DASHIELL (1894–1961). One of the most important stylistic innovators in American popular fiction, Hammett drew on his experience as a Pinkerton detective and an advertising copywriter to produce enduring and compelling crime narratives. Hammett's literary career began in the 1920s with *Black Mask*, an H. L. Mencken magazine, and culminated in the 1930s with popular novels like *The Maltese Falcon* (1930) and *The Thin Man* (1934). It was in the late 1930s, after he stopped writing fiction, that Hammett became politically active, especially in support of the republican side in the **Spanish Civil War**. He had served with the Ambulance Corps in **World War I** and also served in **World War II**, stationed in the Aleutian Islands. After the latter war, Hammett actively opposed U.S. antiradical repression, and he served five months in prison for refusing to cooperate with the prosecution of **Communist Party** members. He was blacklisted; he was harassed for back taxes; and, for a while during this period, his books were banned from overseas U.S.

libraries. Increasingly marginalized, Hammett spent the rest of his life in and around New York City, teaching at the party-affiliated Jefferson School of Social Science from 1946 to 1956. Suffering from a host of illnesses, including tuberculosis and venereal disease, he spent the last years of his life being cared for by his longtime companion, playwright **Lillian Hellman**, until his death from lung cancer in 1961.

Hammett was first and foremost a short-story writer, and most of his novels are amalgams of his short fiction. Developing the central character of the "Continental Op," a private investigator who would become the precursor to *The Maltese Falcon*'s Sam Spade, Hammett set out to modernize and Americanize the detective narrative. In his first novel, *Red Harvest* (1929), and others, he rejected, for instance, traditional whodunit plots and the ratiocination of Conan Doyle and Poe in favor of action. His detectives are consummate readers of motive and ambition; rather than deciphering puzzles, they exploit greed, lust, and hypocrisy to provoke narrative resolutions. Hammett's fiction also popularized a striking new literary language, emphasizing objectivity, detachment, and a stylized American vernacular to introduce a new set of themes—alienation, cynicism, and corruption—into the detective narrative. In his novels, Hammett drew equally on working-class style and modernist attitudes to fashion a hard-boiled American masculinity. Hammett also drew on his experience as an ad copywriter and his understanding of the relation between class, consumption, and commodities to fashion a subtle but powerful critique of American capitalism. *The Maltese Falcon*, for instance, can easily be read as a parable of commodity fetishism: the value of the elusive Falcon is the product of competing desires, and these never-satisfied desires succeed only in generating violence and anarchy. Consumers, like romantics and idealists, become saps when they submit to desire, and the detective's ability to resist this desire at all costs shields and alienates him from a dangerous world. Unfortunately and inexplicably, Hammett's literary pursuit of these issues essentially ended in 1931 with the publication of the much under-appreciated *The Glass Key* (1931).

Selected Bibliography: Layman, Richard. *Shadow Man: The Life of Dashiell Hammett*. New York: Manley, 1981; Marling, William. *American Roman Noir: Hammett, Cain, and Chandler*. Athens: U of Georgia P, 1998; Smith, Erin. *Hard-Boiled: Working-Class Readers and Pulp Magazines*. Philadelphia: Temple UP, 2000; Wheat, Edward M. "The Post-Modern Detective: The Aesthetic Politics of Dashiell Hammett's 'Continental Op.'" *Midwest Quarterly* 36.3 (Spring 1995): 237–50.

Larry Hanley

HARAWAY, DONNA J. (1944–).

U.S. academic whose wide-ranging scholarship draws upon feminism, socialism, literary and cultural studies, philosophy, biology, and critical studies of science and technology. Haraway has a Ph.D. in biology from Yale University and is a professor in and a former chair of the groundbreaking History of Consciousness Program at the University of California at Santa Cruz.

Haraway's "A Cyborg Manifesto: Science, Technology, and Socialist-Feminism in the Late Twentieth Century" makes a particularly convincing case for the constitutive force of science and technology in the era of **postmodernism**. One cyborgologist has referred to it as "the founding document of cyborg politics" (Gray, *Cyborg*

Citizen 26). "The Manifesto," which Haraway describes as "an ironic dream of a common language for women in the integrated circuit" (149), is an early example of her penchant for deploying allegorical figures with weirdly unsettled ontologies through which to examine the political implications of contemporary technoscience. Others of these figures include **Joanna Russ**'s "female man" and DuPont's patented transgenic OncoMouse. The "Manifesto" is one of the first, and remains one of the most powerful, statements of a feminism that recognizes technoculture as an ineluctable presence and a crucially shaping force. It has had immense influence on the development of feminist science and technoculture studies, helping to give rise to new critical fields such as "cyberfeminism" and "cyborgology," and to new scholarly work such as the mammoth *Cyborg Handbook*. Haraway's work, especially in the "Manifesto," has also been embraced by many feminist science-fiction scholars, who find in her combination of feminist theory and critical analysis of science, and in her valorization of science-fiction writers such as Joanna Russ, **Samuel R. Delany**, and Octavia Butler as "theorists for cyborgs" (173), an entry into a fully politicized technoscientific postmodernism. For Haraway, scientific theories are also **science fiction**, stories that while claiming the objectivity of the scientific observer are in fact ideologically shaped to respond to the expectations of that observer. These ideas are at the center of her *Primate Visions* (1989) and provide one major strand running through *Modest_Witness* (1997).

Haraway's resonant conclusion to her "Manifesto"—"I would rather be a cyborg than a goddess" (181)—underlines the impossibility of our ever "returning" to some idealized pretechnological state of nature. In September 2000, Haraway was the recipient of the J. D. Bernal Award, the highest honor given by the Society for Social Studies of Science.

Selected Bibliography: Gray, Chris Hables. *Cyborg Citizen: Politics in the Posthuman Age*. New York: Routledge, 2002; Gray, Chris Hables, ed. *The Cyborg Handbook*. New York: Routledge, 1995; Haraway, Donna J. "A Cyborg Manifesto: Science, Technology, and Socialist-Feminism in the Late Twentieth Century." 1985. Rev. *Simians, Cyborgs, and Women: The Reinvention of Nature*. New York: Routledge, 1991. 149–81; Haraway, Donna J. *Modest_Witness@Second_Millennium.FemaleMan ©_Meets_OncoMouse™: Feminism and Technoscience*. New York: Routledge, 1997; Haraway, Donna J. *Primate Visions: Gender, Race, and Nature in the World of Modern Science*. New York: Routledge, 1989; Kirkup, Gill, Linda Janes, Kath Woodward, and Fiona Hovenden, eds. *The Gendered Cyborg: A Reader*. New York: Routledge, 2000; Sofoulis, Zoë. "Cyberquake: Haraway's Manifesto." *Prefiguring Cyberculture: An Intellectual History*. Ed. Darin Tofts, Annemarie Jonson, and Allesio Cavallaro. Cambridge, MA: MIT P, 2002. 84–103.

Veronica Hollinger

HARLEM RENAISSANCE (1919–1929). In the first decades of the twentieth century, a number of important national and international political events and social conditions helped bring about the birth of the New Negro movement, with its marked determination that the old narrative in which black people in the United States had been situated must be challenged in new ways. There also arose a New

Negro movement in arts and letters, which has been regularly referred to as the Harlem Renaissance—especially after John Hope Franklin, in his seminal history *From Slavery to Freedom*, used the term in 1947 to describe the arts and literary activities of the New Negroes. Harlem, with its intense cultural and artistic production, certainly operated as the representative cultural space of the New Negro. However, the aptness of the term "Harlem Renaissance" has been contested, notably in 1955 by Sterling A. Brown, who was in fact a member of this New Negro literary movement.

The peak activity of the movement occurred in the 1920s, when many of the significant writers of the era received their first recognition or publication: Sterling Brown, "When de Saints Go Ma'ching Home" (1927); **Jean Toomer**, *Cane* (1923); Dorothy West, "The Typewriter" (1926); Countee Cullen, *Color* (1925); Nella Larsen, *Quicksand* (1928) and *Passing* (1929); Georgia Douglas Johnson, *The Heart of a Woman* (1918) and *Bronze* (1922). Some New Negro/Harlem Renaissance writers used modernist as well as traditional literary forms to showcase new content, while others employed music, colloquial language, and folk traditions in sophisticated ways, demonstrating a literary **modernism** situated in a New Negro political, social, and aesthetic consciousness. In so doing, they transformed the American and African American literary terrain.

Langston Hughes, a key New Negro era writer, discusses the period as a time "when the Negro was in vogue" because of the wealthy white patrons supporting black writers as well as the large numbers of white customers who frequented clubs and cabarets in Harlem. Hughes, whose interest in ordinary black people was expanded in the 1930s as he became involved in leftist politics, also observed that among the ordinary people in Harlem, the Harlem Renaissance as a literary and arts movement did not exist.

For many, the literature of the New Negro is situated at the turning point into the 1920s with **Max Eastman**'s publication of **Claude McKay**'s poem "If We Must Die" in the July 1919 issue of *Liberator* magazine. Although McKay, who was active in communist and socialist politics during the early part of the twentieth century, later disavowed any connection between this poem and the political events associated with the New Negro in 1919, his poem is consistent with the attitudes of the burgeoning New Negro movement, as black people were beginning to revolt actively against inequitable treatment. This poem and the sentiments that McKay presents in it represent an aspect of the New Negro attitude of resistance, which rejected the old posture of servility and submission.

At the other end of the New Negro literary spectrum is uplift literature, designed to replace negative images of black people with positive representations of black life for white audiences and positive models of black life for their New Negro audiences. Among the prominent advocates of uplift literature was Alain Locke, editor of *The New Negro*, an anthology of writings by and about black people. Locke's anthology, published in 1925, repeats the title from a short-lived (August–October 1919) monthly magazine edited by the radical founder of the New Negro manhood movement, Hubert Henry Harrison. The literary pieces in Locke's book raised the profile of the aspiring New Negro artists and writers, while a number of the essays, including those by Locke and others, argued for a New Negro artistic and literary culture based on African and African American folk culture.

W.E.B. Du Bois also was, in the 1920s, a proponent of uplift, although in the 1930s he, as did Hughes, aligned himself even more strongly with left-wing politics. Du Bois and the New Negro novelist and editor Jessie Fauset were the primary editorial team at the *Crisis*, the official publication of the NAACP, which was begun by Du Bois in 1910. In 1920, James Weldon Johnson, author of *God's Trombones* (1927), became the general secretary of the NAACP and contributed his literary knowledge to its official publishing organ.

The editors of the *Crisis* and *Opportunity*—the official publication vehicle of the Urban League, edited and founded in 1923 by Charles Spurgeon Johnson with Eric Walrond as his associate—sponsored literary contests during the years 1924–1934. The aforementioned publications, along with Marcus Garvey's *Negro World* (1918–1933) and A. Philip Randolph and Chandler Owen's *The Messenger* (1917–1928)—which its labor- and left-influenced founders early on promoted as both the "Only Radical Negro Magazine" and the "Journal of Scientific Radicalism"—were the principal publishing outlets for the New Negro writers, although many of the writers were published in *Liberator,* **New Masses,** *The Nation, American Mercury, Atlantic Monthly*, and other periodicals, as well as in various local newspapers—primarily those operated or owned by African Americans.

In 1926, responding to the impetus toward uplift among the prominent New Negroes, Wallace Thurman, Zora Neale Hurston, Hughes, and others among the younger participants of the era established their own literary magazine, *Fire!!* These writers sought a level of literary freedom that was not afforded them within the confines of uplift. This literary magazine lasted only one issue, but its contents included a story by Hurston on domestic abuse and a story by Bruce Nugent that presents homoerotic themes. These writers sought to present black people as each individual writer saw them rather than as others wished black people to be or as they wished the dominant society to view black people.

The literary activities of the New Negro era were curtailed by the crash of the stock market in 1929 and by the Depression of the 1930s, yet the attitudes and many of the varied aesthetic ideals of the New Negro literary movement continued to influence African American literature throughout the century.

Selected Bibliography: Austin, Addell. "The Opportunity and Crisis Literary Contests." *CLAJ* 32 (1988): 235–46; Baker, Houston A., Jr. *Modernism and the Harlem Renaissance*. Chicago: U of Chicago P, 1987; Brown, Sterling. "The New Negro in Literature (1925–1955)." *The Harlem Renaissance 1920–1940: Remembering the Harlem Renaissance*. Ed. Cary D. Wintz. New York: Garland, 1996. 203–18; Garber, Eric. "A Spectacle in Color: The Lesbian and Gay Subculture of Jazz Age Harlem." *Hidden from History*. Ed. Martin B. Duberman et al. New York: NAL, 1989. 318–31; Huggins, Nathan Irvin. *Harlem Renaissance*. New York: Oxford UP, 1971; Hughes, Langston. *The Big Sea: An Autobiography*. 1940. New York: Thunder's Mouth, 1986; Hutchinson, George. *The Harlem Renaissance in Black and White*. Cambridge, MA: Belknap-Harvard UP, 1995; James, Winston. "Dimensions and Main Currents of Caribbean Radicalism in America: Hubert Harrison, the African Blood Brotherhood, and the UNIA." *Holding Aloft the Banner of Ethiopia: Caribbean Radicalism in Early Twentieth-Century America*. New York: Verso, 1998. 122–84; Lewis, David Levering. *When Harlem Was in Vogue*. 1970. New York: Oxford UP, 1981; Patton, Venetria K., and Maureen Honey, eds. Introduction. *Double-Take: A Revision-*

ist Harlem Renaissance Anthology. New Brunswick: Rutgers UP, 2001; Perry, Jeffrey B., ed. *A Hubert Harrison Reader.* Westport: Wesleyan UP, 2001.

A. Yemisi Jimoh

HARVEY, DAVID (1935–). A graduate of the University of Cambridge (1962), Harvey is a major Marxist geographer whose interdisciplinary work on urbanization, capitalism, social theory, the environment, and modern and postmodern culture has influenced many fields in the humanities and social sciences. His exploration of the relationship between culture and economics has been particularly influential, not only for Marxist cultural theory but also for **cultural studies** in general. During his distinguished career, Harvey has taught at Oxford University, the Johns Hopkins University, the London School of Economics, and the CUNY Graduate Center, and he has received numerous awards, including the Outstanding Contributor Award from the Association of American Geographers (1980), the Anders Retzius Gold Medal from the Swedish Society for Anthropology and Geography (1989), the Patron's Medal of the Royal Geographical Society (1995), and the French Vautrin Lud Prize (1995).

Harvey's best-known work is *The Condition of Postmodernity* (1990), a study of the correlation between cultural and economic changes in the Western world during the twentieth century, with particular attention to post-1972 developments. Harvey sees a fundamental economic transition from Fordism to flexible accumulation—that is, from monopoly capitalism centered on manufacturing to postindustrial finance capitalism, which focuses on investment, information, decentralized work environments, temporary professional labor, and global markets, among other things. Conditioned by this economic transition is a corresponding cultural transition from **modernism** to **postmodernism** that includes cultural changes in the perception of time and space. In studying these transitions, Harvey joins detailed economic analysis with a careful examination of cultural forms, touching on architecture, literature, painting, photography, and literary and cultural theory. A highly regarded instance of committed cultural studies, *The Condition of Postmodernity* can be read productively alongside **Stuart Hall** and Martin Jacques's edited volume *New Times: The Changing Face of Politics in the 1990s* (1990) and Fredric Jameson's *Postmodernism; or, the Cultural Logic of Late Capitalism* (1991).

Harvey's other books include *The Limits of Capital* (1982, 1999), a technical exposition and expansion of Karl Marx's economic theories; *The Urban Experience* (1989), a study of urbanization and its effect on consciousness; and *Justice, Nature and the Geography of Difference* (1996), an extension of Harvey's work to environmental issues. More recently, Harvey has published *Spaces of Hope* (2000), an examination of the relationship between the body and globalization and a defense of "dialectical utopianism"; *Spaces of Capital* (2001), a theoretical step toward a critical geography; *Paris, Capital of Modernity* (2003), a collection of essays on the social, cultural, and economic history of Paris; and *The New Imperialism* (2003), a critical look at the geopolitical influence of the United States.

Selected Bibliography: Harvey, David. *The Condition of Postmodernity: An Enquiry into the Origins of Cultural Change.* Cambridge, MA: Blackwell, 1990; Harvey, David. *Justice, Nature and the Geography of Difference.* Malden, MA: Blackwell, 1996; Harvey, David. *The Limits of Capital.* 1982. New ed. New York: Verso, 1999; Harvey, David. *The New Imperialism.* Oxford: Oxford UP, 2003; Harvey, David. *Paris, Capital of Modernity.* New York: Routledge, 2003; Harvey, David. *Spaces of Capital: Towards a Critical Geography.* New York: Routledge, 2001; Harvey, David. *Spaces of Hope.* Berkeley: U of California P, 2000; Harvey, David. *The Urban Experience.* Oxford: Basil Blackwell, 1989.

Mitchell R. Lewis

HAVEL, VACLAV (1936–), Czech playwright, dissident writer and human rights philosopher, statesman, president of Czechoslovakia, and first president of the Czech Republic. Havel was born into a prominent business family in Prague during the interwar period of Czech independence. When Czechoslovakia came under Soviet domination after 1948, Havel's bourgeois origins barred him from enrolling in a university. From 1960 to 1968, he worked in Prague's famed Theater on the Balustrade, where his most important plays were produced. *The Garden Party, The Memorandum, Largo Desolato*, and three one-act plays featuring the same hapless intellectual Vanek (*Audience, Unveiling,* and *Protest*) all reveal an apathetic pseudo-reality that can only be exploded—and reconnected to genuine meaning—by forcing the audience to confront loss of meaning in the absurd. After Soviet tanks put an end to the process of social regeneration and liberation known as the Prague Spring (1968), Havel's plays were banned. Subsequent essays and analyses delineated a philosophy of dissidence that reflected a fundamental critique of twentieth-century trends in both bourgeois and socialist societies. At the center of Havel's analysis is the idea that something he calls "living in truth" can rupture the dehumanizing force of modern totalitarian and mass consumer societies. According to Havel, "living in truth" is as simple as exercising one's individual responsibility and integrity as a citizen of the planet (not just of one club or country or religion). In the practice of real life, as Havel experienced it first as a victim of one regime and then as the political leader of another, living in truth is an unpredictable and demanding enterprise but one on which his hope for averting the environmental and social destruction of the future rests. His essay "The Power of the Powerless" stands at the center of his thought and as a companion piece to the Charter 77 Human Rights manifesto, which he coauthored in 1977.

In 1979, Havel was arrested and spent almost four years in prison, where he recorded his intellectual and more mundane meditations in a series of intricately structured letters to his wife (*Letters to Olga*). Havel's role as an intellectual and moral leader in the subterranean spread of Czech opposition culminated in the Velvet Revolution of 1989 and Havel's election to the presidency of a newly independent Czechoslovak nation. Under his rule, frequently described as the reign of a "philosopher king," the Czech and Slovak Federation split into two separate countries, and Havel served as first president of the Czech Republic. His speeches and addresses as president and as recipient of many international honors comprise an ongoing series of essays about the relationship between politics and spiritual values in the modern world. His most important writings are edited and translated by Paul Wilson in *Open Letters: Selected Writings, 1965–1990; Summer Meditations; The Art of the Impossible:*

Politics as Morality in Practice; and *Toward a Civil Society: Selected Speeches and Writings, 1990–1994.*

Selected Bibliography: Goetz-Stakiewicz, Marketa, and Phyllis Carey, eds. *Critical Esays on Vaclav Havel.* New York: G. K. Hall, 1999.

Yvonne Howell

HEART OF DARKNESS (1899, 1902)— originally serialized in *Blackwood's* magazine and later published as part of a collection of stories—is **Joseph Conrad**'s best-known and most controversial work. Drawing on protomodernist techniques such as multiple narrators, chronological confusion, and impressionistic narrative, *Heart of Darkness* is based on Conrad's journey to the Belgian Congo in 1890–1891. It tells the story of Charlie Marlow, a sailor who takes a post as captain of a steamship plying the Congo River. Marlow's mission is to pilot the riverboat up to the Inner Station and retrieve an ailing ivory trader named Kurtz. Overcoming many obstacles, Marlow eventually makes it to the Inner Station, where he finds Kurtz installed as a warlord. Corrupted by the power afforded him by his status as a white man and access to firearms, Kurtz has gone morally mad; the local chieftains crawl before him, and he participates in "unspeakable rites" held in his honor. Marlow himself feels the pull of the "dark continent" and nearly gives in to its temptations. Ultimately, his commitment to his work on the boat saves him, and he brings Kurtz safely away from the Inner Station. On the trip back downriver, Kurtz sums up the knowledge he has acquired in the famous whispered cry, "The horror! The horror!" and then dies. Marlow, too, becomes deathly ill but recovers, and in the novel's conclusion, he visits Kurtz's betrothed in Brussels, where he tells her that Kurtz's last words were her name rather than a damning indictment.

In the first six decades after its original publication, *Heart of Darkness* was routinely thought of as a moral tale only, an account of humanity's feral nature and the role culture plays in keeping that nature under wraps. In the wake of the decolonization movements of the 1950s and 1960s, though, literary critics began to reconsider *Heart of Darkness* for its commentary on late-nineteenth-century imperialism. Perhaps the most famous of these reevaluations came in 1975, when Nigerian novelist **Chinua Achebe** called Conrad "a bloody racist." Achebe charged that *Heart of Darkness* is a racist text because it minimizes African culture and reduces Africa to a backdrop against which the implicitly more important drama of European consciousness happens. Other critics, such as **Edward Said**, took a more moderate view, arguing that while there are certainly racist moments in *Heart of Darkness*, these are not reason to ban it from university English courses. Still other critics maintain that *Heart of Darkness* is a damning critique of European imperialism, and that it should be celebrated for its effort to point out the rapacious brutality of the 1890s "scramble for Africa." The debate has spawned many variations on these basic positions, and the question remains open, though no one is likely again to mistake *Heart of Darkness* for a pure psychological novel that holds itself distant from questions of political engagement.

Selected Bibliography: Achebe, Chinua. "An Image of Africa." *Research in African Literatures* 9.1 (1978): 1–15; Firchow, Peter Edgerly. *Envisioning Africa: Racism and Imperialism in Conrad's "Heart of*

Darkness." Lexington: UP of Kentucky, 1999; Parry, Benita. *Conrad and Imperialism: Ideological Boundaries and Visionary Frontiers.* London: Macmillan, 1983; Said, Edward. *Joseph Conrad and the Fiction of Autobiography.* Cambridge, MA: Harvard UP, 1966.

Stephen Ross

HEGEMONY. Hegemony seems to have first entered Marxist politics and theory by way of the **Russian Revolution**, when **Lenin** and Bukharin used the term to describe the political leadership of the proletariat within a revolutionary class alliance. Its fuller development is associated with the Italian Communist and theoretician **Antonio Gramsci**. In Gramsci's view, the dense civil society and cultural, social, and geographical complexities of modern nation-states prevented the "war of maneuver" that had allowed the Russian Communists to sieze state power so quickly. The different conditions of industrialized, modern nations required a "war of position," in which revolutionaries battled for power along a variety of fronts and within shifting alliances of classes and class fractions. For Gramsci, hegemony thus named "a continuous process of formation and superseding of unstable equilibria between the interests of the fundamental groups [or classes] and those of the subordinate groups" (*Gramsci Reader* 6). Hegemony entailed more than simple domination, or what Gramsci described as "coercion." Because it worked by drawing together social groups into "historic blocs," it also required the securing of "consent." Here, **ideology** plays a key role, for it functions as the "social glue" that binds these blocs together. Finally, as Gramsci's language indicates, hegemony was a process, not a state; the formation and maintenance of ruling blocs was always partial, contingent, and historical.

Hegemony's most significant entrance into cultural criticism came through the work of the Birmingham Centre for Contemporary Cultural Studies in the 1970s. Because it stressed both containment and resistance, Gramsci's hegemony allowed the Birmingham critics to add in power and domination to a native Marxist tradition pioneered by E. P. Thompson and **Raymond Williams**; but because it also stressed resistance, it enabled these critics to inject struggle and history into the more structuralist Marxism of **Louis Althusser** and other continental Marxists. Hegemony thus became a way of mediating these two powerful currents in contemporary Marxism, producing a very exciting and theoretically flexible Marxist **cultural studies**.

By the mid-1980s, however, the rise of poststructuralism across academic disciplines posed major challenges to Marxist criticism. The publication of Ernesto Laclau and Chantal Mouffe's *Hegemony and Socialist Strategy: Towards a Radical Democratic Politics* (1985) marks the peak of hegemony's currency within Marxist criticism and cultural studies. Laclau and Mouffe presented a thoroughly poststructuralized version of Gramsci's hegemony, one premised on "the precarious character of every identity and the impossibility of fixing the sense of the 'elements' [of any identity] in any ultimate literality" (96). All social relations are reduced to "discursivity," and there is "no necessary correspondence" between social relations and politics. In one of the most important if underappreciated essays in contemporary Marxism—"The Problem of Ideology: Marxism without Guarantees"—**Stuart Hall** defended a specifically Marxist version of hegemony while appropriating much of the poststructuralist embrace of indeterminacy and antiessentialism. Indeed, Hall's work on the rise of Thatcherism in Britain and the politics of "nation" and "national identity" produced a plethora of exciting and influential theoretical insights often referred to as "articulation theory." In this view, ideologies work to articulate or link together representations, signs, and symbols. Hegemony then describes the process of naturalizing or enforcing these articulations.

While this reworking of Gramsci's ideas was intellectually breathtaking, the translation of "hegemony" through poststructuralism also helped to unmoor the term from its original class and Marxist contexts. As a result, within cultural criticism today, "hegemony" and "hegemonic" typically function as somewhat vague metaphors for domination.

Selected Bibliography: Gramsci, Antonio. *An Antonio Gramsci Reader*. Ed. David Forgacs. New York: Schocken Books, 1988; Hall, Stuart. "The Problem of Ideology: Marxism without Guarantees." *Stuart Hall: Critical Dialogues in Cultural Studies*. Ed. David Morley and Kuan-Hsing Chen. New York: Routledge, 1996. 25–46; Laclau, Ernesto, and Chantal Mouffe. *Hegemony and Socialist Strategy: Towards a Radical Democratic Politics*. London: Verso, 1985.

Larry Hanley

HEGEMONY AND SOCIALIST STRATEGY: TOWARDS A RADICAL DEMOCRATIC POLITICS (1985).

Work by Ernesto Laclau and Chantal Mouffe around which one might say the project of **post-Marxism** consolidated itself. The book claims to stand in the Marxist tradition, yet deconstructs the fundamental concepts of that tradition, sometimes rearticulating them as part of a "radical democratic" project. Laclau and Mouffe claim that this deconstruction was undertaken by Marxism itself, that the history of Marxist discourse is the history of its self-dissolution. For them, the fundamental principles of Marxism—class, class interest, capital's laws of motion, the vanguard party as representing a preexisting interest—are undermined by the manifest noncorrespondence between class interest and political reality, base and superstructure. Traditional Marxism, they claim, has failed because of its reliance on closed, totalized, necessary, objective, a priori, teleological systems.

For Laclau and Mouffe, politics has no foundation in any nondiscursive class interest. Politics—always contingent, unfixed, temporarily sutured—goes all the way down. Their rejection of class as foundational to the political project goes along with their rejection of a realist epistemology as they announce that the era of normative epistemology has passed.

Laclau and Mouffe argue that the failure of the Marxist narrative brings in its wake the displacement of the working class as the principal agent of liberation. The working class is either a barrier to radical democratic projects or, at best, one movement among a proliferating plurality of new social movements, rooted in irreducible social logics. With criteria of validity internal to each discourse (antiracist, feminist, queer), the plurality of these logics seems to be almost a good in itself. It is important to stress that these autonomous movements cannot be understood as closed or fixed; they cannot stand alone but must link with other movements—a possibility that is accounted for by what the authors call "the logic of equivalence." What keeps this equivalence from becoming reified is overdetermination and ultimately "the impossibility of the social, the antagonism or negativity which guarantees the necessary failure of all social relations, the irreducible contingency and precariousness of all (sutured) subject positions."

The Marxist rebuttal has been fierce. Critics see the presumed deconstruction of class and class interest as resting on two main prongs: attributing to Marxists both an economic or technological (productive forces) determinist interpretation of Marx and a naive realist epistemology, featuring one-to-one correspondences and "transparency," which most philosophers of science, many of them prominent Marxists, haven't held in fifty years. The discursive construction of interests leaves little room to account for real material interests, for the genuine difference between slave and slave owner, between worker and capitalist. Meanwhile, Laclau and Mouffe make much of the noncorrespondence between presumed working-class interests and actual politics but do not, interestingly, suggest that ruling-class interests in profit maximization are discursive. Finally, their antirealism, responding to a caricature of realism, renders their discourse thoroughly incoherent. Oppression is an irreducibly normative concept, something Laclau and Mouffe recognize but cannot explain.

Selected Bibliography: Bhaskar, Roy. *Reclaiming Reality: A Critical Introduction to Contemporary Philosophy.* London: Verso, 1989; Eagleton, Terry. *Ideology: An Introduction.* London: Verso, 1991; Laclau, Ernesto, and Chantal Mouffe. *Hegemony and Socialist Strategy: Towards a Radical Democratic Politics.* London: Verso, 1985; Miller, Richard. *Analyzing Marx.* Princeton: Princeton UP, 1984; Wood, Ellen Meiksins. *The Retreat from Class: A New True Socialism.* London: Verso, 1986.

Gregory Meyerson

HEINLEIN, ROBERT (1907–1988). Heinlein described having three lives: as a naval officer, a politician, and a writer of **science fiction** and fantasy—both for adults and for children. His first career ended after he attended the Naval Academy and served as an officer in the U.S. Navy from 1929 to 1934, when he was invalided out with tuberculosis. His second was shorter still and ended with his 1938 unsuccessful campaign for the California Assembly as a candidate endorsed by **Upton Sinclair**'s progressive EPIC (End Poverty in California) Democratic Party organization. As a writer of thirty-two novels and many short stories, Heinlein found his success as the "dean" of American science-fiction writers.

In the tradition of science fiction, many of Heinlein's stories resemble "thought experiments," a considerable number of which concern a wide range of imagined governments and political structures. Nevertheless, some attitudes are consistently and repeatedly emphasized, especially through normative characters such as Professor Bernardo de la Paz in Heinlein's most fully developed political novel *The Moon Is a Harsh Mistress* (1966, Hugo Award winner). Throughout his fiction and public pronouncements, Heinlein stressed the value of minimal government, the ill effects of government spending ("the socialist disease," as one character puts it) and of governmental regulations on producing wealth, the value of personal freedom, and the value of science as a human activity that frees characters. Celebrating the military's virtues, Heinlein adamantly championed patriotism but opposed conscription; he also opposed any limitations on nuclear testing and was a firm defender of gun rights. He alienated some conservative readers, however, with his interest in alternatives to traditional monotheism, the nuclear family, and monogamy.

Thus, the unconventional ideas expressed in *Stranger in a Strange Land* (1961) made Heinlein a favorite of the 1960s counterculture, while also reportedly providing some of the inspiration for the killing sprees of Charles Manson and his followers. On the whole, the political attitudes expressed in Heinlein's novels have made him a darling of the Libertarian Party and gained him a reputation as an extreme right-winger—a reputation enhanced by the rabid **anticommunism** of *The Puppet Masters* (1951) and the unapologetic militarism of *Starship Troopers* (1959). Nevertheless, Heinlein also has a reputation as perhaps the first truly accomplished *writer* to be devoted almost exclusively to the writing of science fiction. He and his work have received extensive critical attention and are the subjects of a dedicated journal (*the Heinlein Journal*) and a semischolarly society (the Robert Heinlein Society).

Selected Bibliography: Dolman, Everett Carl. "Military, Democracy, and the State in Robert A. Heinlein's *Starship Troopers.*" *Political Science Fiction*. Ed. Donald M. Hassler and Clyde Wilcox. Columbia: U of South Carolina P, 1997. 196–213; Erisman, Fred. "Robert A. Heinlein's Primers of Politics." *Extrapolation* 38.2 (Summer 1997): 94–101; Franklin, H. Bruce. *Robert A. Heinlein: America as Science Fiction*. New York: Oxford UP, 1980; Panshin, Alexei. *Heinlein in Dimension*. Chicago: Advent, 1968.

Keith W. Schlegel

HELLMAN, LILLIAN (1905–1984). The only child of middle-class Jewish parents in New Orleans, Hellman later became not only the premier American woman playwright but one of the most politically engaged playwrights in the history of the American theater. There was little indication of this engagement in her first play, *The Children's Hour* (1934), loosely based on an actual charge of lesbianism between two Scottish schoolteachers made by a malicious student. Hellman's next play, *Days to Come* (1936), is less well known but far more representative of her work as a whole. Set in the Depression in the midst of a strike at a Midwestern brush factory, it anatomizes industrial relations and anticipates widespread corruption in the American labor movement nearly a generation before such corruption became headline news across the United States.

Two plays based on Hellman's own family—*The Little Foxes* (1939) and *Another Part of the Forest* (1946)—present an excoriating view of postbellum Southern capitalism, while Hellman deepened her critique of the American way of life with *Watch on the Rhine* (1941) and *The Searching Wind* (1944). In the earlier play, American indifference to the onslaught of European Fascism is scrutinized as a German American couple seeks to acquire funds to assist Germans wishing to flee Nazi tyranny. Ostensibly a diatribe against American appeasement of the Hitler regime, the play really assails the apolitical nature of American life by offering up a contrasting view of family life shaped by political events. What is important here is not the struggle against Fascism but the implicit naiveté with which Americans are shown to conduct their lives. This theme is given even wider expression in *The Searching Wind*, in which the broad scope of American foreign policy is criticized through the attitude and conduct of a career diplomat on duty in Italy, then Germany, between the world wars. His son's clarion indictment—"I don't want any more of Father's mistakes, because I think they do [the nation] harm"—can serve as the underlying epigraph for most of Hellman's plays.

Hellman also produced a number of screenplays, including somewhat depoliticized adaptations of several of her own plays. Though she was never formally a member of the **Communist Party**, her unabashed sympathies for the Soviet Union led her to script *The North Star* (1943), one of several pro-Soviet films to emerge from American studios during World War II. Though such films were actively encouraged by the American government during the war, *The North Star* was a central reason that Hellman was called to testify before the House Un-American Activities Committee in 1952. (*See* **Anticommunism**.) There, she refused to testify and defended herself with the declaration, "I cannot cut my conscience to fit this year's fashions." Her experiences before the committee (and her subsequent blacklisting from Hollywood) form the subject matter of *Scoundrel Time* (1976), the last of her three volumes of memoirs.

Selected Bibliography: Dick, Bernard F. *Hellman in Hollywood.* Rutherford, NJ: Fairleigh Dickinson UP, 1982; Estrin, Mark W. *Lillian Hellman: Plays, Films, Memoirs. A Reference Guide.* Boston: G. K. Hall, 1980; Lederer, Katherine. *Lillian Hellman.* Boston: Twayne, 1979; Moody, Richard. *Lillian Hellman, Playwright.* New York: Pegasus, 1972; Wright, William. *Lillian Hellman: The Image, the Woman.* New York: Simon and Schuster, 1986.

James MacDonald

HEMINGWAY, ERNEST (1899–1961).

Hemingway's feelings toward the tumultuous politics of the first half of the twentieth century were a combination of two significant and often contradictory factors. The first was his upbringing in a relatively conservative Midwestern family that valued duty and idealistic service to one's country. The second was his personal experience during and immediately after **World War I**. Hemingway's service as an ambulance driver on the Italian front and his journalistic observations in Europe during the postwar period contributed to a disillusionment with politics that informs such early novels as *The Sun Also Rises* (1926) and *A Farewell to Arms* (1929). Unlike his friend and contemporary **John Dos Passos**, Hemingway avoided overt engagement with politics in both his personal life and his writing for nearly fifteen years after the war—often openly scorning activist writers.

In the mid-1930s, however, Hemingway returned to the United States from self-imposed expatriation, subsequently becoming prominent in support of the republican forces during the **Spanish Civil War**. He also engaged in debates on domestic politics, as in a 1935 article—provocatively entitled "Who Murdered the Vets?"—that he was commissioned to write by *New Masses*, a publication that had previously been outspokenly critical of Hemingway's lack of political engagement. This brief piece chronicled the plight of unemployed veterans, hundreds of whom had been killed in a hurricane in September 1935, working in Civilian Conservation Corps (CCC) camps in the Florida Keys. Hemingway accused the government of direct complicity in the veterans' deaths and insinuated that the whole New Deal was just another political sham.

Although Hemingway frequently stated that his support was for the Spanish Republic generally rather than the ideology of the Communists who were fighting to defend it, he had to fend off charges of Stalinist sympathies from the late 1930s onward because of his deep personal involvement in the Spanish Civil War. Like **George**

Orwell, Hemingway traveled to Spain in 1937 as a war correspondent. Unlike Orwell, he did not himself take up arms, but he did begin funding a number of pro-Loyalist causes, including the production of a propaganda film entitled *The Spanish Earth* (on which Dos Passos also worked). While in Madrid, he wrote a play entitled *The Fifth Column*, a melodrama centering on a group of Loyalist fighters. He followed this up with a series of short stories about the civil war (these were posthumously collected in a single volume along with *The Fifth Column*), all of which led prominent leftist critics such as **Michael Gold** and **Granville Hicks** to attribute a newfound political consciousness to Hemingway. Such attitudes were quickly undermined when Hemingway published *For Whom the Bell Tolls* in 1940. Though generally still sympathetic to individual Loyalist soldiers, Hemingway heaps scorn on the tactics and pettiness of the ideologues he saw leading the anti-Fascist forces. The novel is more of a tribute to individuals willing to sacrifice their lives for liberty than a statement of affinity with any particular political ideology. Though Hemingway continued his anti-Fascist journalism throughout **World War II**, his direct engagement with politics waned considerably after 1939 and remained, as Stephen Cooper wrote, "a subordinate, although often important and interesting, subject."

Selected Bibliography: Baker, Carlos. *Ernest Hemingway: A Life Story.* New York: Scribner, 1969; Cooper, Stephen. *The Politics of Ernest Hemingway.* Ann Arbor, MI: UMI Research, 1987; Hemingway, Ernest. "Who Murdered the Vets?" *New Masses* 16 (September 1935): 9–10; Meyers, Jeffrey. *Hemingway: A Biography.* New York: Harper and Row, 1985; Reynolds, Michael S. *The Young Hemingway.* New York: Basil Blackwell, 1986.

Derek C. Maus

HERBST, JOSEPHINE FREY (1892–1969). Growing up in Iowa listening to her mother's tales about family fortune seekers venturing across America's vast continent, Herbst seemed destined to narrate history. Always in tune with the political movements of her time—feminism, Marxism, anti-imperialism—she was an accomplished journalist and novelist whose writing career spanned almost half a century, from modernism to New Journalism. Herbst's last book, an elegant social history and biography of the naturalists John and William Bartram, heralded the beginning of the ecology movement. Her perceptive eye for the quirky details of desire, labor, and politics incorporated modernist stylistics into sharp observations, forging a unique blend of personal memoir, political commentary, and historical narrative. Using her family's saga as the basis for her 1930s Trexler trilogy—*Pity Is Not Enough* (1933), *The Executioner Waits* (1934), and *Rope of Gold* (1939)—Herbst tracked the rise and fall of America's middle class, as she followed generations of adventurers from speculating for gold in South Dakota to fighting Fascism in Spain.

Graduating from the University of California at Berkeley in 1919, Herbst moved to New York to pursue her writing. She traveled in Europe, where she met her future husband, John Hermann, settling in Paris in 1924. Her evocative 1960s memoirs of this period, "Yesterday's Road" and "A Year of Disgrace," recall their purchase of **James Joyce**'s *Ulysses* (which they smuggled back with them when they later returned to the United States) and detail the rise of Nazism in Germany as seen from the bleary eyes of expatriate bohemia. Witnessing the birth of these two episodes—

modernism and Fascism—became the source for her entire literary career. A journalist who reported on the Kharkov writer's convention, farm foreclosures in the Midwest, the sugar monopoly in Florida, the Scottsboro trial in Alabama, revolutionary uprisings in Cuba, the **Spanish Civil War** (which was described in her incredible essay, "The Starched Blue Sky of Spain"), and Nazi street violence, Herbst developed a style of first-person reportage to convey the immediacy of the experience. Her astute ability to synthesize personal and psychic dramas with public and historical panoramas—to understand marriage, divorce, pregnancy, and abortion as sites of political struggle between men and women that are often caused by or even effect larger social forces—forged a powerful materialist-feminist critique.

During the 1930s, the Herbst-Hermann farm in Erwinna, Pennsylvania, became a center for a remarkable group of left-wing writers—**Michael Gold**, **Nathanael West**, and James Agee were among those who lived and wrote in the vicinity, often meeting up at the Erwinna house. After her divorce from Hermann in 1940, Herbst remained in Erwinna and wrote two more novels, a novella, and her double biography of the Bartrams, as well as the personal essays that were to become her posthumously published memoir, *The Starched Blue Sky of Spain* (1991). Here again, she pioneered the genre of memoir as a form of political analysis. Nevertheless, just as Herbst was vague about her **Communist Party** affiliation during the 1930s, she kept her long-standing lesbian love affair with WPA muralist Marion Greenwood closeted.

Selected Bibliography: Bevilacqua, Winifred Farrant. *Josephine Herbst.* Boston: Twayne, 1985; Browder, Laura. *Rousing the Nation: Radical Culture in Depression America.* Amherst: U of Massachusetts P, 1998; Hapke, Laura. *Daughters of the Great Depression: Women, Work, and Fiction in the American 1930s.* Athens: U of Georgia P, 1995; Herbst, Josephine. *The Starched Blue Sky of Spain.* 1991. Boston: Northeastern UP, 1999; Langer, Elinor. *Josephine Herbst: The Story She Could Never Tell.* Boston: Little, Brown, 1984; Rabinowitz, Paula. *Labor and Desire: Women's Revolutionary Fiction in Depression America.* Chapel Hill: U of North Carolina P, 1991; Rideout, Walter B. *The Radical Novel in the United States, 1900–1954.* Cambridge: Harvard UP, 1956; Roberts, Nora Ruth. *Three Radical Women Writers: Class and Gender in Meridel Le Sueur, Tillie Olsen, and Josephine Herbst.* New York: Garland, 1996.

Paula Rabinowitz

HERNANDEZ, AMADO V. (1903–1970). By general consensus, Hernandez is the most serviceable Filipino revolutionary artist of the twentieth century. His poetry, fiction, and plays in Filipino (the national language of 80 million Filipinos) continue to inspire the popular struggle for national democracy and genuine independence against U.S. imperialism.

Born in Tondo, Manila, on September 13, 1903, Hernandez began his career in journalism in the 1920s when the initial massive Filipino resistance against U.S. military rule had declined. He became editor of the Manila daily *Mabuhay* from 1932 to 1934. In 1939, he won the Philippine Commonwealth Award for a nationalist historical epic, *Pilipinas*; in 1940, his collection of mainly traditional poems, *Kayumanggi*, won a Commonwealth Award. During the Japanese occupation of the Philippines (1942–1945), Hernandez served as an intelligence officer for the underground guerilla resistance, an experience reflected in his major novel of neocolonial dependency and revolt, *Mga Ibong Mandaragit*.

After the war, Hernandez assumed the role of public intellectual. He organized the Philippine Newspaper Guild in 1945, and he spoke out on national issues as an elected councilor of Manila in 1945–1946 and 1948–1951. It was during his presidency of the Congress of Labor Organizations (1947)—the largest federation of militant trade unions in the country—that Hernandez graduated from the romantic reformism of his early years to become a national-democratic militant. Meanwhile, the establishment of a U.S. neocolony in the Republic of the Philippines in 1946 extended the cold war into the repression of local nationalist, progressive movements. It intensified the feudal landlord exploitation of the peasantry and reinforced the impoverishment of workers and middle strata, leading to the communist-led Huk uprising in the late 1940s and early 1950s. An allegorical representation of the sociopolitical crisis of the country from the 1930s up to the 1950s can be found in Hernandez's realistic novel *Luha ng Buwaya* and his epic poem of class struggle *Bayang Malaya*, for which he received the prestigious Balagtas Memorial Award.

Owing to his anti-imperialist work, Hernandez was arrested on January 26, 1951, and accused of complicity with the Huk uprising. While imprisoned in various military camps for five years and six months, Hernandez wrote the pedagogical drama *Muntinlupa* and most of the satiric, agitational poems in *Isang Dipang Langit*. His singular achievement is what might be called the invention of the Filipino "concrete universal"—the dialectical representation of socially typical situations that project the contradictions of ordinary life in a neocolonial formation, with its peculiar idioms and idiosyncratic nuances. Stories like "Langaw Sa Isang Basong Gatas" (see San Juan, *Introduction*) and poems like "Mga Muog ng Uri," "Bartolina," "Ang Dalaw," and "Kung Tuyo na ang Luha Mo" exemplify this dialectical poetics in the service of what **Mao Zedong** calls in the Yenan Forum on Literature and Art the twin tasks of partisan art: the uplifting of standards and the popularization of revolutionary ideas.

From 1956 to 1960, Hernandez wrote numerous stories under various pseudonyms for the leading weekly *Liwayway*; he also wrote columns for the daily *Taliba* and edited the radical newspapers *Ang Makabayan* (1956–1958) and *Ang Masa* (1967–1970). But it was his participation in the Afro-Asian Writers' Emergency Conference in Beijing, China, in June–July 1966, followed by his active intervention in the International War Crimes Tribunal (organized by Bertrand Russell, **Jean-Paul Sartre**, and others) in November 1966, that demonstrated Hernandez's renewed commitment to the advance of the internationalist struggle against global capitalism. His numerous honors culminated in the Republic Cultural Heritage Award (1962) and the National Artist Award, given posthumously in 1973—a recognition of his life-long service to the cause of liberatory poetics and social justice. Up to the day (March 24, 1970) he died, Hernandez was involved as a leading protagonist in mass rallies both against imperialism, feudalism, and bureaucratic capitalism, and for democratic socialism and national independence.

Selected Bibliography: Malay, Rosario S. "*Mga Ibong Mandaragit* and the Second Propaganda Movement." *General Education Journal* 17 (1969–1970): 107–17; San Juan, E., Jr. *Ang Sining ng Tula*. Quezon City: Alemar-Phoenix Publishing House, 1975; San Juan, E., Jr. *Introduction to Modern Pilipino*

Literature. New York: Twayne, 1974; San Juan, E., Jr. *Only by Struggle: Reflections on Philippine Culture, Politics and Society*. Quezon City: Giraffe Books, 2002; San Juan, E., Jr. *Toward a People's Literature*. Quezon City: U of the Philippines P, 1984.

Epifanio San Juan Jr.

HERNÁNDEZ, MIGUEL (1910–1942), acclaimed as one of the greatest Spanish poets of all time, is also one of the most important literary and political icons of twentieth-century Spain. Born into a peasant family in the village of Orihuela, in the eastern province of Alicante, he was forced to abandon his formal schooling at the age of fifteen in order to join his father in the rearing of cattle. He pursued his own education by reading classic poets and by the age of twenty had published his first poems locally. Despite his humble origins and his lack of formal education, Hernández wrote his early poetry under the influence of the Spanish classicism of the golden age, a deep Catholic feeling, and a taste for classic religious drama.

Soon after the proclamation of the Second Republic in 1931, Hernández started a series of journeys to Madrid, where he came into contact with some of the leading members of the so-called Generation of 1927, including Rafael Alberti, **Federico García Lorca**, Pedro Salinas, and Vicente Aleixandre. He borrowed from them a playful infatuation with the classic poet Luis de Góngora, together with a move toward surrealist aesthetics. More importantly, life in the capital opened Hernández up to a greater social and political awareness, leading him toward a political, intellectual, and emotional commitment he would keep for the rest of his life.

After the first of these trips, and while temporarily back in Orihuela, he published his first book, *Perito en lunas* (An Expert on Moons, 1933), in which his early and recent influences came to the fore. A few years later, in *The Unending Lightning* (*El rayo que no cesa*, 1936), he revealed his deep obsession with love, life, and death, all while foregrounding a passionate sense of tragedy and producing a poetic style that kept him firmly attached to the land and to the physical world—a purely original style that is recognized today as *hernandiano*.

Soon after the outbreak of the **Spanish Civil War** (1936–1939), Hernández joined the Fifth Regiment of the Popular Republican Army as a volunteer, and was made cultural commissar of the battalion "El Campesino." He combined his duties as a soldier and as a commissar with his work as a poet, participating actively in the creation of the landmark "Romancero de Guerra" (War Poetry)—a body of poetry written by professional poets, soldiers, and workers so that it could be recited on the front lines, written and distributed in leaflets and postcards, broadcast by radio, or published in improvised newsletters and magazines. His landmark *Vientos del Pueblo* (Winds of the People, 1937) is one of the best examples of war poetry, singing to the courage of a people in arms while making explicit the commitment of poets and intellectuals to the victory of the people. No one like Hernández, the peasant poet, could embody the union of the intellectuals and the people and symbolize the quasi-mythical status it was given during the Spanish Civil War.

After the end of the war, Hernández was taken to prison and sentenced to death, though his punishment was later commuted for thirty years. While in jail, he wrote his last book of poems, *Cancionero y romancero de ausencias* (A Songbook of Absences,

1940), and died of tuberculosis two years later, at the age of thirty-one. Hernández was reclaimed both as a political icon and as a poet by the young generations who led the transition to democracy in Spain after 1975. For them, the poet was the best symbol of the purest social and political commitment, as exercised by a man who was truly "of the people" and who committed his intellect and his heart to the cause of social justice, political freedom, and the representation of the dispossessed.

Selected Bibliography: Nichols, Geraldine Cleary. *Miguel Hernández*. Boston: Twayne, 1978.

Mayte Gómez

HESLOP, HAROLD (1898–1983). Son of a Durham miner who became a colliery manager, Heslop's grammar-school education was interrupted at the age of thirteen by a family move, after which he left school and started work in the pit. Subsequent education was largely through the National Council for Labour Colleges (NCLC); in 1923, Heslop won a Durham Miners' Association scholarship to the Central Labour College in London, where **Lewis Jones** was also a student. He later led classes in Marxism and economics.

Heslop's political career started early; by the age of sixteen, he was an active member of the Durham Miners' Association and a branch secretary of the Independent Labour Party. The degree of Heslop's association with the **Communist Party** is unclear. He was a friend of many prominent party members, including Harry Pollitt, but he may not have been a member later than 1927 (possibly for reasons of poverty rather than belief). After the **General Strike**, Heslop was involved in the minority movement, which aimed to turn the trade-union movement away from "class collaboration" and work for the "overthrow of the capitalist system."

Heslop's first novel was published in the Soviet Union as *Pod Vlastu Uglya* in 1926, eight years before it appeared in England as *Goaf* (1934). The Russian publication came at the instigation of an editor who saw the work; it was highly successful, selling half a million copies in paperback, and was praised in *Isvestia*. Heslop's first novel to be published in England was *Gate of a Strange Field* (1929), which was also published in the Soviet Union and the United States. Between the mid-1920s and the mid-1940s, Heslop published a range of writings, including journalism for Communist Party publications and a successful (and class conscious) crime fiction novel, *The Crime of Peter Ropner* (1934). His final published novel (many of his works were never published) was *The Earth Beneath* (1946)—set in the nineteenth century in the Durham coalfields, with the Hartley Colliery disaster at its center.

In November 1930, Heslop visited Kharkov in Russia as a delegate to the Second Conference of Proletarian and Revolutionary Writers. Comments in his autobiography *Out of the Old Earth* (1994) indicate an uneasiness with aspects of the Soviet Union, generated in part by his meeting with **Evgeny Zamyatin**. However, his speech and comments closer to the event suggest an enthusiasm for all that he saw, from the embalmed corpse of **Lenin** to the political trial at which five men were sentenced to death. This is apparent in his best-known novel, *Last Cage Down* (1935), an account of life and political struggles around a nearly exhausted seam of coal. The novel uses Russia as its model for what can be achieved through political struggle and contrasts a disciplined, Marxist approach to industrial action with less effective, emotionally charged protests.

Selected Bibliography: Bell, David. *Ardent Propaganda: Miners' Novels and Class Conflict 1929–39.* Uppsala: Swedish Science P, 1995; Klaus, H. Gustav. "Harold Heslop: Miner Novelist." *The Literature of Labour: Two Hundred Years of Working-Class Writing.* Ed. H. Gustav Klaus. New York: St. Martin's, 1985. 89–105.

Kathleen Bell

HEYM, STEFAN (1913–2001). Born into a Jewish family in Chemnitz as Helmut Flieg, Heym changed his name after fleeing Germany for Czechoslovakia in 1933, retaining it during further exile in the United States (1935–1950) and in East Berlin (from 1951), where he was to remain for the rest of his life. Each of Heym's early pieces was inspired by a sense of social or political injustice. His first poem, published when he was only sixteen, was pacifist; that for which he was forced out of his school, at age eighteen, was a satirical attack on the German army; and his first newspaper article (1932) was devoted to the plight of unemployed buskers in Berlin. For the rest of his career, Heym dealt principally with problems surrounding Fascism, revolution, idealistic intellectuals, anti-Semitism, the structures and problems of socialist governments, and, above all, Stalinism and its legacy.

In the United States, Heym studied at the University of Chicago, eventually becoming an American citizen and serving with considerable distinction as an anti-Nazi propagandist for the U.S. Army in **World War II**. During early exile, he wrote numerous political poems, dramas, and short stories, and edited a German-language antifascist newspaper in New York. His breakthrough came with his first work in English, *Hostages* (1942)—a thriller about resistance in Nazi-occupied Czechoslovakia—followed in 1948 by his second best-seller, *The Crusaders*, based on his experiences in psychological warfare with the U.S. Army in Europe. In both novels, he is concerned with elements of the fascist personality, an issue also explored with reference to striking individuals—on both the Left and the Right—in numerous later novels. Driven back to Germany from the United States by McCarthyism, Heym dealt in his next novels with the way in which politics impinge on the lives of ordinary workers, the constant threat of right-wing activity, and the hope offered by Socialism. Although this optimism remained for his first years in the German Democratic Republic (GDR), by the mid-fifties, he had encountered frequent difficulties through his independent views and fearless journalistic campaigns against government failings. Having experienced the East German uprising of June 1953, he began work on a novel that aroused the cultural politicians' displeasure and that was not completed until 1958–1959 (and only published—as *Five Days in June* in the West—in 1974). From then on, historical subjects featured regularly in his work, partly as a means of evading censorship. For example, *Lenz* (1965) deals ostensibly with the 1848 revolution in South Germany; *Lassalle* (1969) portrays the founder of the German Workers' Union, in whose megalomania Heym identified the seeds of "cult of personality" in socialist societies; and the allegorical *King David Report* (1973) brilliantly evokes political conflicts in ancient Israel and the issue of historiography in a repressive state. He continued to write in English until the early 1970s.

Heym bitterly attacked the popular move toward capitalism after the collapse of the GDR in 1989, but as the mood swung against Western "colonization," he successfully stood for parliament in 1994, becoming its oldest member. He continued to write extensively, his most significant achievement being *Radek* (1995), a historical novel that deals with postrevolutionary power struggles in the Soviet Union and the problems of the intellectual under Communism.

Selected Bibliography: Hutchinson, Peter. *Stefan Heym: The Perpetual Dissident.* Cambridge: Cambridge UP, 1992.

Peter Hutchinson

HICKS, GRANVILLE (1901–1982). The son of a New Hampshire foundry manager and a mother active in the Unitarian Church in Exeter, New Hampshire, Hicks was a full-fledged product of Yankee New England. As such, Hicks embodied—according to Daniel Aaron—Communist leader Earl Browder's proclamation that "Communism is twentieth-century Americanism." This role Hicks ratified in 1938 in a **Popular Front** manifesto entitled *I Like America*. Hicks also lived out this role from 1932 to 1978 in the rural village of Grafton, New York. Hicks graduated from Harvard in 1923, but later dropped out of its theological seminary, finding the ministry an inadequate way to help overcome social and economic inequality. He returned to Harvard in 1928 to earn a master's degree in English.

In 1925, Hicks wed his high school friend Dorothy Dyer and began teaching English at Smith College. Upon completing his graduate studies at Harvard, Hicks joined the faculty at Rensselaer Polytechnic Institute. While at Rensselaer, Hicks began his long association with the Yaddo artists' colony, where he would serve as director in 1970. During the Rensselaer years, Hicks and his wife also bought a Grafton farmhouse, which became their lifelong home. In 1935, Rensselaer fired Hicks for his radical politics. Hicks's increasing prominence on the left resulted from his becoming an editor at *New Masses* in 1934, and his joining the **Communist Party**, coediting *Proletarian Literature in the United States*, and publishing *One of Us*—a popular illustrated hagiography of the American Bolshevik martyr **John Reed**—in 1935. Hicks's full-fledged biographical homage, *John Reed: The Making of a Revolutionary*, followed a year later. Though widely and favorably reviewed and still regarded as both readable and solidly scholarly, *John Reed* disappointed the Communist Party leadership because of its candor about Reed's changing views of the **Russian Revolution**.

Hicks's reputation as a literary Marxist rests on his most influential work, *The Great Tradition*. Published in 1933, this Marxist interpretation of American literature since the Civil War examined literary responses to industrialization, praising such writers as **Whitman**, Howells, **Dreiser**, and **Dos Passos** for their efforts to address this transformation. Hicks followed up *The Great Tradition* six years later with a companion volume on British literature, *Figures of Transition*. The young Alfred Kazin seized on this pair of books as symptomatic of everything wrong with "overreaching"—"earnest but essentially unimaginative"—thirties Marxist criticism, which, in Kazin's estimate, "mechanically ignores the writer in favor of the broad social design." In 1939, Hicks broke with the party over the Molotov-Ribbentrop pact. Hicks's efforts as a leading "Red Decade" aesthetician and arbiter marked the peak of his long career. After leaving the party, Hicks published his first novel, *The First to Awaken* (1940)—a futurist utopian novel (reminiscent of Edward Bellamy's **Looking Backward**)—and went on to write several books about his adopted hometown, Grafton: a memoir-manifesto entitled *Small Town* (1946) and three novels: *Only One Storm*, *Behold Trouble*, and *There Was a Man in Our Town*.

Hicks wrote two memoirs treating his intellectual development, especially his engagement with Communism: *Where We Came Out* (1954) and *Part of the Truth* (1965). The first book was in part an apologia for his cooperative testimony in 1952 and 1953 before the House Un-American Activities Committee, during which Hicks fully informed the committee about his comrades and his activities as a Communist during the thirties. Hicks produced two anthologies that aimed to illustrate the state of American fiction mid-century, *The Living Novel* (1957) and *Literary Horizons* (1970). For over half a century, Hicks was steadily prolific as a reviewer and cultural commentator, producing articles for such magazines and quarterlies as *New Masses*, the *New Republic,* the *New York Times Book Review*, **Partisan Review**, *College English*, the *Sewanee Review*, *Commentary*, the *Saturday Review*, and *Harper's*. In his last two decades, Hicks befriended and championed younger writers such as Bernard Malamud, Wright Morris, Herbert Gold, and Mark Harris.

Selected Bibliography: Aaron, Daniel. *Writers on the Left: Episodes in American Literary Communism.* New York: Harcourt, Brace and World, 1961; Levenson, Leah, and Jerry H. Natterstad. *Granville Hicks: The Intellectual in Mass Society*. Philadelphia: Temple UP, 1993; Long, Terry. *Granville Hicks*. Boston: Twayne, 1981; Long, Terry. "Interview with Granville Hicks." *Antioch Review* 33 (Summer 1935): 93–102.

James D. Bloom

HIKMET, NAZIM (1902–1963), a Turkish poet who combined political courage with artistic creativity, even under prison conditions. Born in Salonika, he was descended from a cosmopolitan Ottoman family. The turmoil of **World War I** and the Allied occupation of Istanbul inspired him to start writing poetry, and after escaping to Ankara at the age of nineteen to join the anti-imperialist Resistance, he was advised by Mustafa Kemal (Atatürk) to write "poetry with a purpose." But it was in Moscow during the 1920s that he found his mission, drawing inspiration from the artistic experiments of **Vladimir Mayakovsky** and Vsevolod Meyerhold as well as the political vision of **Vladimir Lenin**. Returning to Istanbul in 1928, Hikmet became the charismatic leader of the Turkish avant-garde. His informal style of poetry marked a radical break from Ottoman tradition, developing a language that combined colloquial idioms with a strong sense of rhythm and folk tradition. Between 1929 and 1938, he published an exhilarating series of poems, polemics, plays, and film scenarios. He was not only a Communist committed to revolution, but a romantic who was passionately in love: with his country and his people, with nature and the women to whom he dedicated his finest poetry. Repeatedly arrested for his political beliefs, he was sentenced in 1938 to twenty-eight years imprisonment on trumped-up charges of organizing a revolt in the Turkish armed forces. His epic poem *Human*

Landscapes from My Country was written in Bursa Prison, from which he was released in 1950 under an amnesty.

The anticommunist climate of the **cold war** led Hikmet to fear further imprisonment, and in 1951 he fled to the Soviet Union. During the following decade, he used his literary prestige to campaign against the spread of nuclear weapons, sharing a platform with **Jean-Paul Sartre** and **Pablo Neruda**, Ilya Ehrenburg, and **Louis Aragon**. In exile, he remained remarkably creative, his new relationships finding their echo in poignant lyrics and love letters, and producing political poetry of great imaginative power. He campaigned against Western imperialism, especially in his radio broadcasts, but he also became widely known through his writing for the theater, including *Ivan Ivanovich*, a satire on Stalinism. Hikmet's health had been undermined by long years in prison, and his late poetry is permeated by reflections on the anguish of exile and the approach of death. By giving voice to the experiences of the oppressed, his work has not only become extremely popular in modern Turkey but also acquired a global appeal, enhanced by many fine translations and evocative musical settings. He died in Moscow in June 1963 and is buried in Novodevichi cemetery alongside Chekhov, **Gogol**, and Mayakovsky.

Selected Bibliography: Göksu, Saime, and Edward Timms. *Romantic Communist: The Life and Work of Nazim Hikmet.* London: Hurst, 1999; Hikmet, Nazim. *Poems of Nazim Hikmet.* Trans. Randy Blasing and Mutlu Konuk. New York: Persea Books, 2002; Turgut, Erhan, ed. *Nazim Hikmet: Biographie et Poèmes* (Turkish, English, and French parallel texts). Paris: Turquoise, 2002.

Saime Göksu and Edward Timms

HIMES, CHESTER BOMAR (1909–1984). The son of an African American teacher of industrial arts in primarily black institutions in the South, Himes began writing short fiction and articles while incarcerated from 1928 to 1936 for armed robbery in the Ohio state prison system, during which time he began to write. His first published novel, *If He Hollers Let Him Go*, appeared in 1945 and was prompted by the discrimination he experienced working in the defense plants in California during **World War II**. By the late 1940s, Himes was thoroughly disillusioned about the possibilities of American society due to his ongoing poverty and the treatment he received as a black man. Increasingly inspired by the writing of **Richard Wright**, Himes published in rapid succession a series of semiautobiographical protest novels—*Lonely Crusade* (1947), *Cast the First Stone* (1952), *The Third Generation* (1954), and *The Primitive* (1955)—which made him one of the more celebrated black writers in America.

In 1953, Himes moved to Europe, living first in Paris, where he associated with the expatriate Negro community. Except for a few brief visits to the United States, Himes remained abroad for the rest of his life, finally settling in Spain, where he died in 1984. For the French publishing house Gallimard's *Série Noire*, he produced a series of detective novels featuring two black police detectives, Coffin Ed Johnson and Grave Digger Jones. Toward the end of his life, he wrote a two-volume autobiography, which if not wholly accurate about his life is nevertheless engaging as a testament of the survival of a black artist struggling to make his voice heard.

Himes's Harlem novels deal with the poverty, discrimination, and exploitation experienced by those living in New York City's African American neighborhoods, and remain his most popular works of fiction. However, Himes's reputation as an author of angry protest novels was established in his earlier fiction, in which he created many-faceted black characters and reflected the ambivalence of living in an American society full of contradictions and insecurities. Unlike Wright, Himes never belonged to any left-wing political parties, although he did see himself as Wright's successor in the fight against black oppression. He never formulated a doctrine or proclaimed any political agenda for remedying these wrongs, but using his own experiences as a model, he fashioned in his impassioned prose a clear indictment against American society for its discriminatory treatment of its black citizens. Through his writing, Himes struggled to come to grips with the racist American society into which he was born and lived, and to realize his place in that society as a black man and an artist.

Selected Bibliography: Fabre, Michel, and Robert Skinner, eds. *Conversations with Chester Himes.* Jackson: UP of Mississippi, 1995; Lundquist, James. *Chester Himes.* New York: Ungar, 1976; Margolies, Edward, and Michel Fabre. *The Several Lives of Chester Himes.* Jackson: UP of Mississippi, 1997; Milliken, Stephen F. *Chester Himes: A Critical Appraisal.* Columbia: U of Missouri P, 1976; Sallis, James. *Chester Himes: A Life.* New York: Walker and Co., 2001; Silet, Charles L. P., ed. *The Critical Response to Chester Himes.* Westport, CT: Greenwood, 1999; Skinner, Robert E. *Two Guns from Harlem: The Detective Fiction of Chester Himes.* Bowling Green, OH: Bowling Green State U Popular P, 1989.

Charles L. P. Silet

HISTORICAL NOVEL. The historical novel is a relatively new form in the Western literary tradition. As **Georg Lukács** pointed out in his masterful study *The Historical Novel* (1937), in its authentic form, the historical novel emerged at the beginning of the nineteenth century, more precisely around the time of the debacle of Napoleon's great army. Walter Scott, the founder of the genre, published his first *Waverley* novel in 1814. Most critics would agree with Lukács on his choice of Scott as the inventor of the genre but may disagree with his genealogy, which conforms to a Hegelian, Marxist conception of historical forms. According to this paradigm, all prior historical fictions—such as seventeenth-century novels with a historical theme by Georges de Scudéry or La Calprenède, or eighteenth-century **gothic** novels such as Horace Walpole's *Castle of Otranto* (1764)—fall into the pre-history of the genre. In these fictional works, the historical scenery is a mere backdrop for a more or less improbable plot in which the characters resemble their contemporary audience. Walter Scott, according to Lukács, represents a clear departure from this practice.

In Lukács's scheme, Scott embodies not only the origins of the genre but also its climax. Scott's novels are truly historical because the psychology of the characters is derived from the historical specificity of the period in which they are set. Characterization is, in fact, crucial to the historicity of the novels. Scott, according to Lukács, is able to connect the private and the public and to "give living embodiment to historical-social types" (35), creating "typical" characters who "in their psychology and destiny always represent social trends and historical forces" (34).

For Lukács, Scott's novels also epitomize the historical novel as a genre because of their sense of an organic connection between the past and the present, and because of their ability to depict societies as totalities in which all elements (including private and public experience) are interrelated. Moreover, Scott's novels, in their depiction of the destruction of older forms of social organization by the coming of modernity, derive their energies from actual historical forces. The novels, in their acceptance of the possibility of genuine historical transformation, have a strong utopian dimension that reflects the new progressive conception of history that arose in Europe at the beginning of the nineteenth century due to recent events such as the **French Revolution** and the Napoleonic wars.

Subsequent writers, such as **Honoré de Balzac** and **Leo Tolstoy**, are also praised by Lukács, but for him, the historical novel begins a general decline from Scott onward. In particular, the growing decadence of bourgeois society itself contributes to a loss of historical sense and an inability to conceive of society as a totality. As a result, the historical novel lapses into inauthentic forms, dominated by antiquarian or modernizing impulses. The year 1848—the year when the once-radical European bourgeoisie showed their new conservative nature by opposing (and helping to defeat) the wave of revolutions that swept Europe—represents a particular landmark in this growing decadence. It is not surprising, therefore, that in Lukács's account, historical novels produced after 1848, such as Gustave Flaubert's *Salammbô* (1862), should be viewed as corrupt versions of the classical archetype created by Scott. In spite of Flaubert's painstaking reconstruction of ancient Carthage, the action and characters are but lurid projections of the author's mind. Flaubert's disgust with the mediocre bourgeois reality that surrounds him permeates the archaic atmosphere he so laboriously describes.

Importantly, Lukács saw the early bourgeois historical novel (before its period of decadence) as a valuable model for writers of the 1930s who wished to create works that would contribute to the coming of a world socialist revolution. Indeed, the historical novel became one of the most dynamic genres of Soviet **socialist realism**, with writers such as **Mikhail Sholokhov** and **Alexei Tolstoy** producing important historical fiction. However, this particular focus of Lukács's work makes his comments on the historical novel appear a bit dated. In addition, his exclusive focus on the European tradition as a privileged site for the emergence of nationalism and historical consciousness seems, in our contemporary global context, provincial and out of date. In recent decades, the historical novel has reemerged with a new vitality and variety in the works of numerous non-Western writers. For example, the historical novel has been particularly important to African writers such as **Ousmane Sembène** and **Ngũgĩ wa Thiong'o**, who have used the genre to contest colonialist versions of African history. Meanwhile, novelists such as the Colombian **Gabriel García Márquez**, the Indian-born **Salman Rushdie**, and the Nigerian Ben Okri have used the mode of magical realism in constructing historical novels that reflect the sometimes fantastic texture of reality and history in the non-Western world.

Other developments subsequent to Lukács's work include the rise of **postmodernism**, which has had a powerful impact on the evolution of the historical novel. For Marxist critics such as **Fredric Jameson** (heavily influenced by Lukács), the erosion of the boundary between fact and fiction—a central characteristic of post-modernist culture—is a sign of a growing loss of historical sense that essentially extends the arc of decadence earlier described by Lukács. For a critic like Linda Hutcheon, on the other hand, the self-consciously fictionalized histories embedded in the novels of writers such as Rushdie, García Márquez, and **Günter Grass** bespeaks the rise of a new, potentially critical genre Hutcheon calls "historiographic metafiction," which calls attention to the constructed (and potentially biased) nature of all historical accounts.

Selected Bibliography: Booker, M. Keith, and Dubravka Juraga. "The Reds and the Blacks: The Historical Novel in the Soviet Union and Postcolonial Africa." *Socialist Cultures East and West: A Post–Cold War Reassessment*. Ed. Dubravka Juraga and M. Keith Booker. Westport, CT: Praeger, 2002. 11–30; Carnes, Mark, ed. *Novel History: Historians and Novelists Confront America's Past (and Each Other)*. New York: Simon and Schuster, 2001; Henderson, Harry B. *Versions of the Past: The Historical Imagination in American Fiction*. New York: Oxford UP, 1974; Hutcheon, Linda. *A Poetics of Postmodernism: History, Theory, Fiction*. New York: Routledge, 1988; Lukács, Georg. *The Historical Novel*. Trans. Hannah Mitchell and Stanley Mitchell. Lincoln: U of Nebraska P, 1983; Orel, Harold. *The Historical Novel from Scott to Sabatini*. New York: St. Martin's, 1995; Rance, Nicholas. *The Historical Novel and Popular Politics in Nineteenth-Century England*. New York: Barnes and Noble, 1975; Sheppard, Tresidder Alfred. *The Art and Practice of Historical Fiction*. London: Humphrey Toulmin, 1930; Sommer, Doris. *Foundational Fictions: The National Romances of Latin America*. Berkeley: U of California P, 1991.

Alina Clej and M. Keith Booker

HOLDSWORTH, ETHEL CARNIE (1886–1962).

Born into a radical weaving family in Lancashire, Holdsworth started part-time work in a cotton mill at age eleven and was in full-time employment from the age of thirteen. In her later articles for the *Woman Worker*, she described her experience as "slavery"—a view of working-class life that runs through her writing. From her first publications in the *Blackburn Weekly Telegraph*, she quickly achieved a wider audience, publishing her first book of poems, *Rhymes from the Factory*, in 1907. She attracted the notice of Robert Blatchford, proprietor of the *Clarion*, who encouraged her to write articles and poems for his weekly paper, the *Woman Worker*, which she edited in London for six months in 1909. The experience seems to have increased her radicalism, as demonstrated in her second book of poems, *Songs of a Factory Girl* (1911).

Holdsworth's output also includes novels and children's stories as well as a third collection of poems, *Voices of Womanhood* (1914), which is probably her most accomplished. She combined writing with a variety of jobs and political campaigning; during **World War I**, she protested against the introduction of conscription, and during the 1920s, she edited the *Clear Light*—an antifascist journal—with her husband, Alfred Holdsworth. During this period, she also published a series of sonnets in the anarchist journal *Freedom*, protesting at the imprisonment of anarchists in Soviet jails.

At its best, Holdsworth's poetry illuminates the gap between working-class people's desire for liberty, often evident in their imaginative capacity, and the constraints and suffering of their lives. Her children's story "The Blind Prince" (in *The Lamp Girl and Other Stories*, 1913) uses its palace setting to uncover the cruelty and oppression by which beauty and luxury have been achieved. Her novels often use popular genres to raise political and class-based questions, attacking the status quo. *This Slavery* (1925), her best-known novel, published by the Labour Publishing Co., combines a treatment of industrial conflict with a focus on women. Questions of poverty and oppression are elucidated by their contrast with conventions from romantic fiction and through melodramatic devices. Holdsworth's final novel, *All on Her Own* (1929), was published in a series of romantic fictions for women, but the work and its characters remain politically aware.

Holdsworth's work was popular for a while; the suffragette and composer Ethel Smyth included two of her poems in a song cycle (*Three Songs*, 1913) that premiered in London, and her novel *Helen of Four Gates* (1917) was made into a film in 1920. During her career, she published under both Ethel Carnie and Ethel Holdsworth. Unfortunately, there is no record of her writing in the last thirty years of her life.

Selected Bibliography: Alves, Susan. " 'Whilst working at my frame': The Poetic Production of Ethel Carnie." *Victorian Poetry* 38.1 (Spring 2000): 77–93; Booker, M. Keith. *The Modern British Novel of the Left: A Research Guide*. Westport, CT: Greenwood, 1998; Fox, Pamela. *Class Fictions*. Durham: Duke UP, 1994. Frow, Ruth, and Edmund Frow. "Ethel Carnie: Writer, Feminist and Socialist." *The Rise of Socialist Fiction, 1880–1914*. Ed. H. Gustav Klaus. Brighton: Harvester, 1987. 251–56.

Kathleen Bell

HOLOCAUST LITERATURE. The always powerful stories of individuals affected by the collapse of society into war have acquired an unparalleled poignancy in the literature of the Holocaust. So unprecedented was the assault on human values by Nazi Germany and its supporters in the systematic persecution and attempted destruction of whole peoples in concentration and death camps during the dark period between 1933 and 1945 that influential critics such as George Steiner have proclaimed it the end of culture. Art, as the supreme articulation of what it means to be human, must, by this argument, stand mute in the face of man's most inhuman chapter. And literature, to the extent that it attempts to render the Holocaust aesthetically, must inevitably debase art or at least call into question those principles of aesthetics on which our Western culture is founded. To write poetry after Auschwitz, **Theodor Adorno** famously mused, would be barbaric.

Despite these dicta, a slow trickle of memoirs, diaries, and autobiographical narratives has grown into a torrent of fiction, nonfiction, poetry, drama, television melodrama, and film that seems increasingly attractive year after year to popular and serious artists alike. This seems nowhere more clear than in America, where films such as Steven Spielberg's *Schindler's List*, Roberto Benigni's *Life Is Beautiful*, and Roman Polanski's *The Pianist* have received multiple Academy Awards in the past decade. In elite literary circles, this influence is equally palpable, as seen by the frequency with which authors drawn to Holocaust themes have received the Nobel Prize for Literature (eight times since the prize—suspended between 1939 and 1944—was resumed). The works of these authors, from Albert Camus in 1957 to Nelly Sachs in 1966 to Imre Kertész in 2002, not only demonstrate that the Holocaust can be approached in literature but contribute to a growing consensus that it must if literature is to be more than an ornament in a cultured life.

The moral imperative to teach and learn about the Holocaust, or *Shoah*, is felt and met in extraliterary dimensions as well, most notably in the proliferation of Holocaust memorials, museums, and days of remembrance in North America, Europe, and Israel. Specifically in literature, this imperative has traditionally been met by the introduction of key texts to young readers in school, and then more recently by the creation of dedicated courses on the literature of the Holocaust in college and university curricula. The most widely used of these texts is Anne Frank's *The Diary of a Young Girl*, first published in Holland in 1947, then in English translation in 1952. Anne's confessional diary of the years spent hiding in the "secret annexe" of her father's Amsterdam factory is often paired with **Elie Wiesel**'s haunting story of his own deportation and nightmare pilgrimage through Auschwitz and Buchenwald, *Night* (translated into English in 1960). Together, these accounts introduce readers to most of the themes that resonate through memoir after memoir: the interruption of adolescence, the rupture of the family, Pan-European anti-Semitism, the power (or impotence) of faith, survivor guilt, resistance, and the courage of those who risked their lives for others.

These themes and dozens of others are developed in a corpus that has become huge, sometimes contradictory, and always complex. The most recent compendium, *Holocaust Literature: An Encyclopedia of Writers and Their Work*, introduces over three hundred authors from countries in North and South America, Europe, and Israel. While most of these are first-generation writers—their stories driven by the credibility of personal experience—new work is increasingly coming from the second, and even the third, generation. As the events of this freighted chapter grow more remote in historical terms, the challenge to literature is to remain responsive to the mandate of memory—to keep the lessons fresh for new generations of readers and viewers, and to do so without succumbing to what Art Spiegelman (author of the graphic novel *Maus*) calls "holokitsch."

Selected Bibliography: Adorno, Theodor W. "Engagement." *Noten zur Literatur*. Vol. 3. Frankfurt: Suhrkamp, 1963; Bloom, Harold, ed. *Literature of the Holocaust*. Philadelphia: Chelsea House, 2004; Kremer, Lillian S. *Women's Holocaust Writing*. Lincoln: U of Nebraska P, 1999; Kremer, Lillian S., ed. *Holocaust Literature: An Encyclopedia of Writers and Their Work*. New York: Routledge, 2003; Langer, Lawrence. *The Holocaust and the Literary Imagination*. New Haven: Yale UP, 1975; Rosenfeld, Alvin. *A Double Dying: Reflections on Holocaust Literature*. Bloomington: Indiana UP, 1980; Skloot, Robert. *The Darkness We Carry: The Drama of the Holocaust*. Madison: U of Wisconsin P, 1988; Steiner, George. *In Bluebeard's Castle*. New York: Atheneum, 1971; Steiner, George. *Language and Silence: Essays on Language, Literature, and the Inhuman*. New York: Atheneum, 1967.

Mark E. Cory

HOW THE STEEL WAS TEMPERED (*KAK ZAKALYALAS' STAL'*, 1932–1934), an important, largely autobiographical **bildungsroman** written in a mode of **socialist realism** by **Nikolai Ostrovsky**. In addition to protagonist Pavel Korchagin (modeled on Ostrovsky), many characters are modeled on people Ostrovsky knew. Although the focus of the novel is on Pavel, Ostrovsky pays close attention to current contexts of the **Russian Revolution**, the civil war, and the postrevolutionary period of the establishment of Soviet power. His goal is to depict the hardships of the working class and their struggles and contributions to the revolution.

Pavel and his poor family live in the small Ukrainian railroad town of Shepetovka. He is expelled from school in the third grade for questioning his religious teacher. From then, Pavel's life is a series of hardships: he works in a railroad restaurant, where he witnesses young girls forced into prostitution; he works in an electric company and at a railroad shop. Offended by the injustices around him, Pavel joins the revolution. While portraying Pavel's life, Ostrovsky also gives a vivid picture of the time, drawing on real events in Ukraine as the Soviets battle various forces, including the Germans, Petlyura and his Ukrainian bourgeois nationalistic SR forces, and a pogrom of Jews in Pavel's town.

The civil war rages on, and Pavel's hometown is the scene of fierce battles. While the white Ukrainians are in power, Pavel is imprisoned and tortured; released by mistake, he leaves for the front to fight, where he is wounded several times. Ostrovsky vividly portrays the chaotic aftermath of the civil war as well, as workers struggle to build a socialist society amid food shortages, counterrevolutionary violence, border disputes, and murders and robberies by roving gangs.

Pavel is completely dedicated to the success of the revolution, but his health fails rapidly. Like Ostrovsky himself, in addition to injuries sustained during the war, Pavel contracts typhus, rheumatic fever, and arthritis, and is rapidly becoming an invalid. But Pavel's greatest desire is to contribute to the building of the new Soviet society. Unable to work in a railroad shop, he focuses on political and propaganda work for Komsomol and the **Communist Party**. After the civil war, Pavel goes to a village at the Soviet-Polish border to help stabilize the situation there, then goes back to Kiev, still hoping to work in a railroad shop. But his health is failing more and more, and he is eventually declared an invalid.

Pavel's life is always narrated within its historical context. In 1924, Pavel is a political worker in Kiev at the time of Lenin's death and the debates with Trotsky groups. Two years later, his condition worsens even more, and he has to move to Crimea for his health. Constantly searching for ways to contribute to the fight for the better, socialist society, Pavel struggles to educate himself, but soon goes blind. Nevertheless, he manages to write a novel—the story of his life and of the establishment of Soviet power. His indomitable spirit overcomes his failing physical condition when his manuscript is approved for publication: "His cherished dream was realized! The steel bonds have been burst, and now, armed with a new weapon, he had returned to the fighting ranks and to life."

Selected Bibliography: Luker, Nicholas. *From Furmanov to Sholokhov.* Ann Arbor, MI: Ardis, 1988.

Dubravka Juraga

HUGHES, LANGSTON (1902–1967). Born James Mercer Langston Hughes in Joplin, Missouri, Hughes is best known for accessible, evocative, oft-anthologized poems such as "Harlem," "I, Too," and "Theme for English B." He was an enormously prolific, versatile writer, producing volumes of poems and short fiction, two novels, plays, opera libretti and musical plays, translations, a screenplay and television scripts, works for children and young adults, two autobiographies, and edited anthologies. His *Collected Works* run to sixteen volumes.

Hughes was, in one sense, a political writer almost from the beginning because of his affinity for working people and his awareness of the plight of African Americans. His essay "The Negro Artist and the Racial Mountain" (1926) urges young black writers to write about, to, and for African Americans instead of trying to adhere to white middle-class aesthetic strictures. A participant in the **Harlem Renaissance** of the 1920s, Hughes knew **W.E.B. Du Bois**, Alain Locke, and other renaissance architects. He embraced the culture of the blues and had a lifelong love of Harlem, but he was also an inveterate traveler, who developed a keen sense of global politics. In 1940, Hughes collaborated with James P. Johnson (composer of the song "Charleston") on a blues opera about the labor movement, *De Orgnizer*. Throughout his career, he published in politically attuned magazines, including the *Crisis, Opportunity*, the *Messenger, Fire!!*, **New Masses**, and the *Chicago Defender*. In the 1930s, he produced unabashedly Marxist-influenced poems and drama. He wrote about and helped rally support for the Scottsboro Boys—eight black youths whose false arrest, unfair trial, and conviction for rape in Alabama (1931) drew national attention. Hughes also covered the **Spanish Civil War** for the *Baltimore Afro-American* newspaper (1937). Although he drifted from Marxist thought and wrote in support of U.S. involvement in **World War II**, Hughes leftist politics caused him to be summoned to appear before Senator Joseph McCarthy's Permanent Sub committee on Investigations in 1953; Hughes defended his views but mentioned no other individuals. He never lost his affinity for working people, nor did he relent in his critique of American racism. The last volume of poems published in his lifetime was *The Panther and the Lash* (1967), with reference to the Black Panther Party, and the last poem he published before his death was "The Backlash Blues," referring to the reaction against advances in protecting the civil rights of African Americans. Throughout his writings—published over five decades—readers will encounter critiques of capitalism, racism, the abuse of women, lynching, Jim Crow laws, restrictive real-estate covenants, colonialism, Fascism, and most especially the contrast between American democratic ideals and America's problems with racism and economic inequity. Hughes's reputation has continued to grow since his death.

Selected Bibliography: Berry, Faith, ed., *Good Morning Revolution: Uncollected Writings of Social Protest by Langston Hughes*. New York: Citadel P, 1973; De Santis, Christopher. *Langston Hughes and the Chicago Defender: Essays on Race, Politics, and Culture, 1942–62*. U of Illinois P, 1995; Ostrom, Hans. *A Langston Hughes Encyclopedia*. Westport, CT: Greenwood, 2002; Rampersad, Arnold. *The Life of Langston Hughes*. 2 vols. New York: Oxford UP, 1986, 1988.

Hans Ostrom

HUXLEY, ALDOUS (1894–1963) was born into a family of prominent British intellectuals in Godalming, Surrey, on July 26, 1894. His grandfather was Thomas Henry Huxley, a physiologist and close collaborator of Charles Darwin, and his granduncle was Matthew Arnold, the Victorian poet. Leonard Huxley, Aldous's father, was the editor of a literary magazine, the *Cornhill*, but his sons enjoyed even greater success. Aldous became a renowned novelist and essayist; Julian, Aldous's elder brother, became an influential biologist, knighted by the queen; and Andrew, Aldous's half brother, won the Nobel Prize in Physiology.

Aldous Huxley attended Eton and Balliol College, Oxford, where he had hoped to study science, but after a severe eye infection robbed him of half his eyesight, he settled on a literary career. In 1919, he became a columnist for the London *Athenaeum*, and in 1921, he published a short novel, *Crome Yellow*, which became an immediate sensation. Now able to support himself through writing, Huxley traveled around the world and wrote several cynical and satirical novels, including his most important, *Point Counterpoint* (1928). During this period, he made friends with D. H. Lawrence, and the two men remained close until Lawrence's untimely death in 1931. Together they complained of the moral and spiritual destitution of the Western world and hoped to find new foundations for meaning and values to replace those eroded by the scientific and industrial revolutions. Aldous, specifically, worried that if the grounds of human purpose were reduced to what science can quantify, then life becomes a search for only comfort and pleasure. Aldous found this vulgar, and in **Brave New World** (1931), he presented a cautionary tale against such a possible future—and a satire of what he believed was already happening.

In 1937, Huxley immigrated to the United States, accompanied by his close friend and fellow writer Gerald Heard. Heard's interest in Asian mysticism was taken up by Huxley and together they saw in the ideal of spiritual enlightenment and self-actualization the possible cure for the vacuity and materialism of modern society. This interest in mysticism culminated in *The Perennial Philosophy* (1945), outlining Huxley's view of a primordial religion underlying all the world's wisdom traditions.

During the 1950s, Huxley was a columnist for *Esquire* magazine, writing important early warnings on the dangers of population growth and environmental degradation. From 1959 to 1963, he was a visiting professor at several institutions, including Berkeley and the Massachusetts Institute of Technology, both of which gave him honorary doctoral degrees. For his eleven novels, Huxley received important literary awards, but he wrote nearly fifty books altogether; today he is remembered for his social criticism and moral philosophy as much as for his literary output. He died of throat cancer on November 22, 1963—the day President Kennedy was shot.

Selected Bibliography: Bedford, Sybille. *Aldous Huxley*. New York: Harper and Row, 1974; Dunaway, David King. *Huxley in Hollywood*. New York: Harper and Row, 1989; Huxley, Laura Archera. *This Timeless Moment*. New York: Farrar, Straus and Giroux, 1968; Sawyer, Dana. *Aldous Huxley: A Biography*. New York: Crossroad Publishing, 2002; Smith, Grover, ed. *The Letters of Aldous Huxley*. New York: Harper and Row, 1969.

Dana Sawyer

I

IBSEN, HENRIK (1828–1906), Norwegian playwright and poet who has gained worldwide recognition as the father of modern drama. Various political groups, whether socialists, anarchists, or feminists, claimed him as their spokesman. A well-known cartoon that shows him lashing out first at the conservatives and then at the liberals perfectly captures his politics; he abhorred conservative values and attitudes, but was equally outraged by liberals who failed to defend their beliefs.

In the 1870s, contact with the radically progressive Danish writer Georg Brandes, who felt that modern literature should address contemporary problems, led to Ibsen's political and literary awakening. He abandoned verse for prose; set his plays in contemporary middle-class life; and dealt with problems of gender, culture, and society. Like most of the radical thinkers of his time, Ibsen advocated revolution—but spiritual and moral, not political. He followed closely the politics of his time and especially of his country. A passionate advocate of Pan-Scandinavianism, he was appalled by Norway's failure to help Denmark in the war over Schleswig-Holstein in 1864 and moved to Italy, where he wrote *Brand* (1866) and *Peer Gynt* (1867), the latter an implicit criticism of Norway's moral weakness in the war. He continued living abroad for a total of twenty-seven years, moving from Italy to Germany and producing his great "social problem" plays.

Although Ibsen's social dramas are set in small towns in provincial Norway, they resonate across cultures and periods. Nora's decision to leave her family at the end of *A Doll's House* (1879) in order to question society's way of educating women sent shock waves not just through Norway but everywhere it was published and performed. Ibsen answered the outrage with another provocative work, *Ghosts* (1881), which attacks the institutions of marriage and the church, showing the tragedy of a woman who remains in a loveless marriage for the sake of appearances. Utterly condemned by the critics, Ibsen wrote *An Enemy of the People* (1882), his most overtly political drama, about a doctor castigated by his community for his discovery that the town spa, its main source of income, is contaminated. Doctor Stockmann is reviled by the mayor (his own brother) and the so-called liberal newspapermen who, in the interests of self-preservation, side with the mayor and refuse to publish Stockmann's findings. True to form, Ibsen did not adopt an entrenched and predictable position; *The Wild Duck* (1884) shows the tragic consequences of an idealism that is too unbending.

Ibsen's increasingly radical portrayals of women are perhaps his greatest dramatic and political legacy. *Rosmersholm* (1886) and *The Lady from the Sea* (1888) mark a renewed engagement with feminist ideas that intensifies in *Hedda Gabler* (1890) and *The Master Builder* (1892). In general, despite their remote settings and topical themes, Ibsen's social plays have lost none of their forcefulness, continuing to provoke audiences to a greater awareness of the social and cultural forces that shape their political consciousness.

Selected Bibliography: Downs, Brian W. *Ibsen: The Intellectual Background.* New York: Octagon, 1969; McFarlane, James, ed. *The Cambridge Companion to Ibsen.* Cambridge: Cambridge UP, 1994; Meyer, Michael. *Henrik Ibsen.* 3 vols. London: Rupert Hart-Davis, 1971; Shepherd-Barr, Kirsten. *Ibsen and Early Modernist Theatre, 1890–1900.* Westport, CT: Greenwood, 1997; Templeton, Joan. *Ibsen's Women.* Cambridge: Cambridge UP, 1997; Van Laan, Thomas F. "Generic Complexity in Ibsen's *An Enemy of the People.*" *Comparative Drama* 20 (Summer 1986): 95–114.

Kirsten Shepherd-Barr

IDEOLOGY. One of the most complex and vaguely defined concepts in all of social and political science, *ideology* can be roughly defined as a particular view of the world, informed by a specific social and political perspective. In the tradition of **Marxist criticism**, ideology has often carried negative connotations as a distortion of reality, or "false consciousness," through which the bourgeoisie maintain dominance over the proletariat in a capitalist society. On the other hand, much recent Marxist criticism, influenced especially by the work of the French Marxist theorist **Louis Althusser**, has seen this opposition between ideology and reality as simplistic. For Althusser and those influenced by him, human consciousness is itself a product of ideology, and all perceptions of reality are influenced by one kind of ideology or another.

Althusser famously defines ideology as the individual's "imaginary relationship . . . to his or her real conditions of existence." Elaborating this point of view, Althusser develops the notion of the "ideological state apparatus" (ISA), or the complex of institutions such as schools, churches, and families that operate to disseminate the dominant ideology in a given culture. Indeed, in a process that Althusser refers to as "interpellation," Althusser argues that individuals are not simply influenced by ideology; they are, in fact, constructed by it. As the dominant ideology in a given culture will play the leading role in this construction, then that ideology will inherently seem more natural, thus making it easier for the dominant group associated with this ideology to maintain its power.

Terry Eagleton, a Marxist critic influenced by Althusser, indicates the complexity of this new, more nuanced vision of ideology when he sets out to give a basic definition of the term in *Ideology: An Introduction* and finds that he must list sixteen different definitions, just as a start, ranging from the classic negative view of ideology as "false ideas which help legitimate a dominant political power" to neutral views such as "the process of production of meanings, signs and values in social life" (*Ideology* 1). This situation was complicated even more during the **cold-war** years, when

Western anticommunist rhetoric attempted to reverse the traditional negative Marxist definition of ideology by associating the term with a distorted view of the world attributed to Communism. Thus, Daniel Bell's now-classic work *The End of Ideology* (1960) was largely a declaration of the defeat of Socialism as an alternative to capitalism.

Whatever view one takes of ideology, it is clear that ideology operates in the realm of ideas, or in the realm of the "superstructure" in the conventional Marxist **base and superstructure** model of society. One could, in fact, define ideology as the basic network of ideas and attitudes around which the superstructure is formed. As such, ideology has a powerful impact on such superstructural phenomena as literature and culture. In fact, as explained in such fundamental works as **Fredric Jameson**'s *The Political Unconscious*, the principal activity of most Marxist literary critics is "ideological analysis," that is, the process of carefully decoding literary works in order to determine the ideological roots that lie behind them. This process is particularly important when applied to bourgeois literature, given that bourgeois ideology by its nature tends to operate in disguise, presenting itself as common sense or scientific truth rather than politically motivated opinion. Moreover, as argued especially by **Pierre Macherey**, a protégé of Althusser, literature is a particularly important focus for ideological analysis because literary language makes visible ideological orientations that might remain hidden in the world at large.

Given that most of what has been regarded as literature in the modern Western tradition has been produced within capitalist societies dominated by bourgeois ideology, it should come as no surprise that most Western literature is dominated by bourgeois ideology. Understanding the ideological basis of such literature provides important insights not only into individual texts but into broader phenomena such as **canons and canonicity**, indicating that the process of canon formation is not merely a matter of selecting key texts based on their aesthetic merit but of selecting texts that most effectively convey the dominant ideology. Indeed, as Eagleton has demonstrated in *The Ideology of the Aesthetic*, aesthetic criteria are themselves highly ideological, even though a key characteristic of bourgeois aesthetics is to regard aesthetic criteria as absolute and universal.

Selected Bibliography: Althusser, Louis. *Lenin and Philosophy and Other Essays.* Trans. Ben Brewster. London: Monthly Review P, 1971; Bell, Daniel. *The End of Ideology: On the Exhaustion of Political Ideas in the Fifties.* 1960. Cambridge, MA: Harvard UP, 1988; Eagleton, Terry. *Ideology: An Introduction.* London: Verso, 1991; Eagleton, Terry. *The Ideology of the Aesthetic.* Oxford: Blackwell, 1990; Jameson, Fredric. *The Political Unconscious: Narrative as a Socially Symbolic Act.* Ithaca, NY: Cornell UP, 1981; Macherey, Pierre. *A Theory of Literary Production.* Trans. Geoffrey Wall. London: Routledge and Kegan Paul, 1978; McLellan, David. *Ideology.* Milton Keynes, UK: Open UP, 1986.

M. Keith Booker

INDIAN LITERATURE. *See* SOUTH ASIAN LITERATURE.

INDIGENISMO. A Latin American literary and artistic movement, mainly of the early twentieth century, addressing the problems of the indigenous peoples, their contribution to the national cultures, and their integration into the modern nation-state.

This movement corresponded to the social and agrarian reforms implemented in the region, such as the postrevolutionary government of Lázaro Cárdenas in Mexico (1934–1940) and the socialist APRA (Alianza Popular Revolucionaria Americana/Popular American Revolutionary Alliance) movement in Peru.

Indigenist writers such as Peruvian **José Carlos Mariátegui** expressly sought to distance themselves from both the savage image and the exotic, idealized image of the Indian produced by Europeans and Creoles (Europeans born in America), scientific travelers, romantic writers, and others since the turn of the sixteenth century. Instead, indigenist writers addressed the problems of contemporary indigenous societies and sought the political involvement of its readers in the cause. Indigenist writers like the Ecuadorian Jorge Icaza or the Guatemalan Miguel Angel Asturias were mainly urban intellectuals—Creoles and mestizos (those of mixed blood) whose view of indigenous society was mainly from the "outside" and from the vantage point of the state and the hegemonic society. In other words, indigenismo's assimilation politics basically tended to offer no alternative to the framework of the nation-state and the telos of modernity.

Viewed in a broader sense, indigenista literature can range from the colonial writings of Bishop Fray Bartolomé de las Casas (1474–1566) and el Inca Garcilaso (1539–1616) to the revolutionary communiqués of Sub Commandant Marcos in Chiapas, Mexico, in the 1990s. Manuel González Prada's *"Discurso en el Politeama"* (Politeama Hall Lecture, 1888) and Clorinda Matto de Turner's novel trilogy *Aves sin nido* (*Birds without a Nest*, 1889), *Indole* (1891), and *Herencia* (1895) are some classical examples of early indigenismo. Other indigenista works are *Raza de bronce* (1919) by Alcides Arguedas, *El mundo es ancho y ajeno* (*Broad and Alien Is the World*, 1941) by Ciro Alegría, *Yawar fiesta* (1941) and *Los ríos profundos* (*Deep Rivers*, 1961) by José María Arguedas, and *Balún Canán* (*The Nine Guardians*, 1957) and *Oficio de tinieblas* (1962) by Rosario Castellanos. Indigenismo in other media include the murals of José Orozco, Diego Rivera, and David Alfaro Siqueiros in Mexico; in film, an illustrative example is Jorge Sanjinés'neorealist work *Yawar Mallku* (*Blood of the Condor*, 1969).

In contrast to indigenismo, in Latin America there are Indianism and indigenous literatures. Indianism is the idealized view of indigenous peoples, such José León Mera's *Cumandá* (1871) and Manuel de Jesús Galván's *Enriquillo* (*The Cross and the Sword*, 1882). Colonialism did not erase indigenous literatures completely, and there are a number of extant works, such as the Mayan *Popol Vuh*. In the late twentieth century, from numerous cultural revitalization movements across the Americas started to emerge a growing corpus of indigenous literatures written by indigenous writers themselves—some in Amerindian languages, such as the fifteen-volume collection *Letras mayas contemporáneas*, edited by Carlos Montemayor in Mexico.

Suggested Bibliography: Cornejo Polar, Antonio. *Escribir en el aire*. Lima: Horizonte, 1994; Foster, David William. "Bibliografía del indigenismo hispanoamericano." *Revista iberoamericana* 50.127 (1984): 587–620 (especial issue on indigenismo); Lienhard, Martin. *La voz y su huella*. Hanover, NH: Ediciones del Norte, 1990; Moraña, Mabel, ed. *Indigenismo hacia el final del milenio*. Pittsburgh: Instituto Internacional de Literatura, 1998; Prieto, René. "The Literature of Indigenismo." *Cambridge History of Latin American Literature*. Vol. 2. Ed. Roberto González Echeverría and Enrique Pupo Walker. Cambridge: Cambridge UP, 1996. 138–63; Rabasa, José. "Pre-Columbian Pasts and Mexican Presents in Mexican History." *Colonialism Past and Present*. Ed. Alvaro Felix Bolaños and Gustavo Verdesio. Albany: SUNY P, 2002. 51–78.

Luis Fernando Restrepo

INDUSTRIAL WORKERS OF THE WORLD (IWW). When two hundred men and women convened on June 27, 1905, to found the Industrial Workers of the World (IWW), the United States was still freshly emerged from its status as a frontier nation but about to become a world power. William D. Hayward brought the convention to order by stating, "Fellow workers, this is the Continental Congress of the working class." The program that came to be associated with the IWW was a unique blend of trade union and radical ideology. The IWW preamble, destined for endless reprintings, stated that the working class and the employing class had nothing in common. The solution to economic and social injustice was the creation of a worker-controlled "industrial democracy." The IWW mandate was to create industrial unions that would fight for gains in the present system while gaining experience for a general strike that would culminate in the industrial unions taking over all economic enterprises and government institutions. The means of production would then operate to satisfy social needs rather than private profit. This peaceful and democratic revolution via a general strike would also serve as a model for workers everywhere in the world to do likewise.

Not least of the IWW's distinguishing features was that in an age characterized by hostile feelings to the foreign born, ethnic minorities, and the rights of women, the IWW insisted that every American would have an equal place in its unions. This included integrated unions of lumber workers in the South, Asian agricultural workers on the West Coast, and Spanish-speaking maritime workers along the Atlantic coast. Women such as Elizabeth Gurley Flynn, Matilda Rabinowitz, and Marie Equi had prominent roles in the IWW.

The IWW was to pass through stages that flowed into one another rather than emerging abruptly. From 1905 to 1911, it forged its distinctive ideas and tactics. Beginning with a series of sensational but short-lived victories in the textile industry that improved the lives of a quarter million American workers in 1912–1913, the IWW was increasingly effective as an organizer of harvest workers, lumberjacks, mariners, miners, and longshoremen. Having surged to a formal membership of approximately 100,000, the IWW came under federal and state persecution in 1917. The supposed offense was the IWW's opposition to **World War I**, but at the core of the repression was the desire of establishment forces to destroy an organization offering a fundamental challenge to capitalist notions of governance and economics. Following an ideological schism in 1924, the IWW entered what became a permanent decline despite occasional upsurges in specific locales. The IWW lost its last industrial units in the 1950s. Since that time, a skeletal IWW with pronounced anarchist views has largely functioned as an educational and historical institution.

The Wobblies, as the IWW members were termed, believed that workers were most powerful at the point of production, where they could use "direct action." Using the ballot box for social change was not attractive to them at a time when women, racial minorities, migratory workers, and other large sections of the working class had no vote. Exactly what direct action entailed differed from place to place, but it always meant the assertion of worker power in the workplace. Slowdowns and strikes were the most common direct action, but the IWW also spoke of sabotage, which could signify anything from damaging equipment to what was termed "the conscious withdrawal of efficiency." In fact, IWW actions in general were remarkably nonviolent. The Wobblies understood that violence would immerse them in a judicial system in which employers had a decided advantage. They were particularly wary of provocateurs.

Belief in direct action lead to the IWW's most problematic policy: opposition to written contracts. The IWW thought gains won through direct action were best safeguarded by the militancy that had won them. Having no contractual obligations left them free to take further actions as soon as they were strong enough. In practical terms, however, no contracts made the daily operation of any local union cumbersome. Even collecting dues became a time-consuming effort.

By far the most spectacular form of direct action was the IWW's massive civil disobedience to unjust laws. In an age when soapbox oratory was a major means of mass communication, employers often convinced city officials to arrest Wobblies who spoke in public places such as street corners or parks. The IWW responded by calling for sympathizers to flock to any such city to flood the jails, rendering such persecutions financially and politically untenable. More than a score of free-speech fights occurred between 1909 and World War I, earning the IWW the respect of many Americans not otherwise supportive of the IWW program.

Physical harassment had always been the lot of IWW organizers. As the IWW grew more effective, the anti-Wobbly violence escalated. A symbolic turning point came in 1914 when organizer Joe Hill was executed for the supposed murder of two grocers in a case that drew international protest. In the following years, local sheriffs, patriotic groups with names like the Knights of Liberty, and company gunman would beat and kill numerous IWW rank-and-file members as well as famous organizers, such as Frank Little. What proved an organization deathblow were the federal and state indictments brought against virtually every IWW official.

The IWW experience is the historic link to the successes of the Congress of Industrial Organizations (CIO) in the 1930s. That "Solidarity Forever," a song composed for the IWW by Ralph Chaplin, became the national anthem of organized labor is not a matter of happenstance. IWW history became a living legacy in works by writers as varied as Eugene O'Neill, **Dashiell Hammett**, **John Dos Passos**, and James Jones. A song celebrating Joe Hill became a mass hit in the 1930s and again in the 1960s.

Seen strictly as a trade-union movement, the IWW was in the mainstream of industrial unions for more than two decades. Just as importantly, within a radical movement plagued by authoritarianism, the IWW was a beacon of leftist practice and theory rooted in democracy. The IWW remains emblematic of a time when many Americans did not accept the existence of giant corporations as essential for their economic and social welfare.

Selected Bibliography: Bird, Stewart, Dan Georgakas, and Deborah Shaffer, eds. *Solidarity Forever: An Oral History of the IWW.* Chicago: Lake View P, 1985; Dubofsky, Melvyn. *We Shall Be All: A History of the Industrial Workers of the World.* Ed. Joseph Anthony McCartin. Updated ed. Urbana: U of

Illinois P, 1988; Foner, Philip S. *The Industrial Workers of the World, 1905–1917.* New York: International Publishers, 1965; Kornbluh, Joyce, ed. *Rebel Voices: An IWW Anthology.* Ann Arbor: U of Michigan P, 1972; Renshaw, Patrick. *The Wobblies: A History of the IWW and Syndicalism in the United States.* Updated ed. Chicago: Ivan R. Dee, 1999.

Dan Georgakas

INTERNATIONAL LITERATURE, a highly influential monthly cultural journal published from 1932 through 1945 as the official organ of the International Union of Revolutionary Writers—an organization sponsored by the Comintern. Separately published in English, Russian, French, and German editions, *International Literature* contained a variety of materials that made it a central locus for leftist debates about cultural issues during the years of its publication. In addition to contemporary statements about literature and culture, the journal also included such content as translations of some of the important writings of Marx and Engels on art and literature. While the journal was intended, among other things, to give guidance to committed leftist writers, the lively debates contained within the pages of *International Literature* make clear the inaccuracy of the commonly held notion of a single, officially enforced "**Communist Party** line" on matters of literature and culture.

International Literature continued the earlier journal, *Literature of the World Revolution.* Beginning in 1946, *International Literature* was succeeded by *Soviet Literature*, which continued publication until 1990.

Selected Bibliography: Foley, Barbara. *Radical Representations: Politics and Form in U.S. Proletarian Fiction, 1929–1941.* Durham, NC: Duke UP, 1993; Murphy, James F. *The Proletarian Moment: The Controversy over Leftism in Literature.* Urbana: U of Illinois P, 1991.

M. Keith Booker

INVISIBLE MAN (1952), novel by **Ralph Ellison.** Published in 1952 and garnering the National Book Award in 1953, *Invisible Man* is widely recognized as one of the most important novels of the twentieth century and one of the two or three most important works of African American literature. The experiences of the novel's nameless hero constitute an allegorical chronicle of black historical experience in the United States. Beginning in the Jim Crow South, the picaresque narrative follows the naive hero's attempts to ingratiate himself with the white power structure and model himself on Booker T. Washington. Expelled from a college closely resembling Washington's Tuskegee Institute by its president A. Hebert Bledsoe—a vicious proponent of "Negro uplift" kowtowing to the will of the white trustees—the invisible man travels north, only to encounter exclusion from the worlds of Wall Street and modern industry. Disillusioned, he becomes involved with the Brotherhood—an interracial organization closely resembling the **Communist Party** that is involved in fighting evictions and battling the influence of Ras the Exhorter, a figure based on various 1930s Garveyites. Eventually discovering that even among the Brotherhood his humanity is denied, he enters epistemological chaos and, in the context of a riot closely resembling the Harlem riot of 1943, descends through the sewers to a basement from which, surrounded by 1,369 lights, he writes the story of his life. In the epilogue, he affirms ambiguity and absurdity, ponders the nation's "diversity" and the need to re-vive its democratic traditions, and famously muses, "Who knows but that on the lower frequencies, I speak for you?"

Drawing on a broad range of literary influences—**Fyodor Dostoevsky**, Lord Raglan, Kenneth Burke, **T. S. Eliot**, **James Joyce**, James Weldon Johnson, **Frederick Douglass**, **André Malraux**, **William Faulkner**, **Richard Wright**—*Invisible Man* is structured through a series of recurrent symbols and motifs. Blindness and invisibil-ity figure prominently, as do white women (as false symbols of democracy) and pieces of paper supplying the protagonist with identities and instructions to "keep him run-ning." The effect of this patterning is to establish thematic equivalences among the invisible man's enemies. The white supremacism and paternalism of Jim Crow racists and Northern monopoly capitalists are repeated among the radicals, whose hypo-critical pretensions to egalitarianism make them the most repellent antagonists of all. Well established in the first half of the novel, the repeated motifs enable the text to run on automatic in the second half, with the result that classroom teachers seeing themselves simply rendering the text in its own terms can end up reproducing its ide-ological presuppositions without interrogation.

Invisible Man is a **cold-war** text in which formal seamlessness reinforces anticom-munist politics, and the celebration of "diversity" reinforces U.S. patriotism. Some critics have noted a disjunction between the transracial claims to universal identity in the epilogue and the portrait of pervasive white racism in the preceding narrative. Others have commented on Ellison's historical distortions of both communist and black nationalist theory and practice. Most significant for an understanding of pol-itics and form in the novel, however, is a comparison between the published text and Ellison's many notes and earlier drafts. Originally Ellison contemplated a still more harsh commentary on the southern college, proposing that Bledsoe had handed over to vigilantes a black sharecropper organizer seeking refuge on the campus. Ellison also at first contemplated having the invisible man, after his expulsion from college, become a southern organizer of poor whites and blacks modeled on the Communist Angelo Herndon. Earlier versions of the New York material have the invisible man staying in a Harlem boardinghouse, where the Brotherhood's activities are routinely discussed over the dinner table, and where the protagonist's room was formerly oc-cupied by one Leroy, an organizer for an interracial maritime workers' union who was murdered for his activism. The Brotherhood is also more sympathetically por-trayed in the drafts. Brother Jack, its leader, is far less demonic, and the climactic "eye scene"—in which, as Jack chastises the hero for lack of "discipline," his glass eye pops out—was added only late in the composition. Moreover, where in the published text the hero's sexual encounters are limited to two nymphomaniac white women seeking "primitive" thrills, in the drafts the hero has intimate relationships with Cleo, an African American woman at the boardinghouse, and Louise, a white Brotherhood member. The effect of these changes is to make the invisible man more alienated from other African Americans than he was in the drafts and to toxify the portrayal of interracial sexual relationships on the Left. The terms in which *Invisible Man* has been valorized by the literary establishment have shifted over the decades. The plau-dits originally accorded to the text's existentialist universalism, integrationism, and explicit **anticommunism** have more recently been rearticulated as admiration for the text's grasp of the fluidity, hybridity, and linguistically constructed nature of identity. However, the novel's portrayal of the Left as repressive, monologic, and inhospitable to racial/ethnic diversity remains central to its rhetoric. The role played by Ellison's 1952 novel in discouraging exploration of alternatives to capitalism remains as powerful as ever.

Selected Bibliography: Foley, Barbara. "From Communism to Brotherhood: The Drafts of *Invisible Man.*" *Left of the Color Line: Race, Radicalism, and Twentieth-Century Literature of the United States.* Ed. Bill Mullen and James Smethurst. Chapel Hill: U of North Carolina P, 2003. 163–82; Schaub, Thomas Hill. *American Fiction in the Cold War.* Madison: U of Wisconsin P, 1991; Wolfe, Jesse. "'Ambivalent Man': Ellison's Rejection of Communism." *African American Review* 34 (Winter 2000): 621–38.

Barbara Foley

IRISH LITERATURE of the twentieth century represents an attempt to come to terms with the nationalist discourses that had dominated the island's cultural imagination during the modern era. The key figure here is the writer and activist **W. B. Yeats**, who over the course of a long and prolific career was successful in his bid to place issues of national identity and ethnic inheritance at the heart of Irish literary discourse. To the degree that it engages with these issues, all subsequent Irish writing may be described as in some sense post- or sub-Yeatsian.

In common with many "modernist" writers of the earlier twentieth century (**Ezra Pound** and **T. S. Eliot** may be the most obvious examples), Yeats's vision was clearly animated by right-wing perspectives. As a number of critics have pointed out, however, most of the writers who make up the pantheon of modern Irish literature professed socialist sympathies that were at odds with Yeats's authoritarianism, and which they deployed in various ways to mitigate his influence. While some (Wilde, **Shaw**, and Synge, for example) disdained Yeats's example on a variety of philosophical-aesthetic grounds, others (including **O'Casey**, Behan, and a number of "minor" writers such as Liam O'Flaherty) had a much more politicized sense of the limitations of Irish nationalism—a discourse that, in line with classic Marxian theory (as professed by James Connolly, one of the leaders of the 1916 **Easter Rising**) they perceived as a reactionary bourgeois program precipitated during the latter half of the eighteenth century by the economic limitations of the ancien régime.

The most sustained challenge to Yeats's dominance, however, was provided by **James Joyce**. Some seventeen years the younger, Joyce was (among other things) a modernizing internationalist whose disdain for traditional forms of authority—especially Catholicism and nationalism—made him a hero of the twentieth-century liberal intelligentsia but left him more or less entirely alienated from his Irish contemporaries. Joyce's regard for Ireland was no less sincere than Yeats's, but in books such as *Dubliners* (1914) and *Ulysses* (1922), his support was filtered through a merciless deconstruction of revolutionary rhetoric and nationalist bad faith. Insofar as modern Ireland has evolved into an increasingly secular, postnationalist formation, Joyce's anti-Yeatsian vision remains seminal. Much of the force of Joyce's critique of Ireland was lost, however, when the study of Irish literature became dominated after mid-century by Anglo-American critics and theorists for whom Irish literature was "political" to the extent that it articulated (or not) a sense of national identity defined in terms of certain stereotypical values and attributes.

This situation was reinforced with the advent of the so-called "Troubles" in Northern Ireland toward the end of the 1960s, a development widely understood (even by Marxists) as a struggle between communities that could be identified with reference to competing nation-states (Great Britain and the Republic of Ireland). A recognizable, pan-generic "Troubles literature" began to emerge, linked to earlier articulations of Ireland's troubled history but oriented toward the exigencies of the current conflict. The issues faced by the writer in the face of politically motivated violence—even those writers who refuse to engage with it—are perhaps most fully explored in the work of the Nobel Prize–winning poet Seamus Heaney.

The nationalistically determined model of Ireland's literary history persisted until a range of new cultural theories and concerns began to impact on the study of Irish writing in the latter decades of the century. As the "Troubles" began to rage in Northern Ireland, the equation of identity with nationality or ethnicity began to come under pressure from feminists. The debate came to a head with the appearance of *The Field Day Anthology of Irish Writing* (1991), a massive, three-volume undertaking edited by writer-critic Seamus Deane. The controversy—sparked by what feminists regarded as the patriarchal and masculinist assumptions informing the project—resulted in the commissioning and publication of two more volumes dedicated to women's contributions to the history of Irish writing.

In the meantime, nationalism as an analytical paradigm was overtaken by a growing emphasis on **postcolonial literature** and politics in literary studies. Again, this new turn has generated intense controversy, as critics and theorists have debated widely as to the political provenance of colonialism as a critical model, and its potential for the analysis of Irish culture. This debate has cross-fertilized with two related issues: historical revisionism and the Irish diaspora. With regard to the first, postcolonialism has been dismissed as inappropriate by those who claim that Ireland was never a colony in any meaningful sense of the term, but also by those who claim that treatment of Irish culture within the context of postcolonialism is part of a wider revisionist front determined to eradicate the nationalist struggle from Irish history. With regard to the second, the question of Irish identity has been much influenced in recent years by the recognition of an enormous Irish diaspora—in some accounts, upwards of forty million—in various parts of the world, and by the growing realization that a great deal of what counts as "Irish" activity (including writing and other cultural pursuits) actually takes place at a significant geographical remove from the motherland.

Perhaps the greatest challenge to established discourses of Irish culture, however, has emerged in recent years in the wave of immigration the island has experienced in the wake of its economic success (the so-called Celtic Tiger). Traditionally disposed to consider itself an exotic, romantic "other" vis-à-vis dominant Anglo-American culture, Irish society has not responded particularly well to the appearance of economic migrants and political refugees, a development all the more questionable when the island's history as one of the most energetic modern exporters of people is considered.

Like the best of their predecessors, the best contemporary Irish writers have taken up the challenge of engaging with all the issues mentioned here. Working in a range of genres and styles, contemporary writers such as John Banville, Eavan Boland, Marina Carr, Brian Friel, John McGahern, and Paul Muldoon continue to produce writing that manages to reflect the wider social and political landscape while at the same time questioning the mission—and in certain instances the possibility—of a "political literature."

Selected Bibliography: Berresford Ellis, Peter. *A History of the Irish Working Class.* 1972. London: Pluto P, 1996; Deane, Seamus. *A Short History of Irish Literature.* London: Hutchinson, 1986; Kiberd, Declan. *Inventing Ireland: The Literature of the Modern Nation.* London: Jonathan Cape, 1995; Lloyd, David. *Anomalous States: Irish Writing and the Post-Colonial Moment.* Dublin: The Lilliput P, 1993; Smyth, Gerry. *Decolonisation and Criticism: The Construction of Irish Literature.* London: Pluto P, 1998.

Gerry Smyth

ISHERWOOD, CHRISTOPHER (1904–1986). Born into an upper-class English family, Isherwood spent much of his life rebelling against Victorian sensibilities. Perhaps his most flagrant rebellion was leaving England in 1929. First, he went to Berlin, which to him "meant boys" (*Christopher* 2), and then, after much world traveling throughout the 1930s, he went to the United States. He became an American citizen in 1946 and lived with his lover, the artist Don Bachardy, in Santa Monica, California, for the rest of his life.

Isherwood witnessed the end of Weimar Germany. As a writer and an outsider, he was uniquely positioned to become one of that era's best documentarians. His *Berlin Stories* (a volume that includes the novels *The Last of Mr. Norris* and *Goodbye to Berlin*) chronicle the rise of Hitler and the Nazis while lamenting the death of bohemian life in Berlin. The famous opening passage of *Goodbye to Berlin* has led to a misunderstanding of Isherwood's role as writer-observer: "I am a camera with its shutter open, quite passive, recording, not thinking. . . . Some day, all this will have to be developed, carefully printed, fixed." Of course, Isherwood was more engaged than that. He saw the heightened anti-Semitism, witnessed the conflicts between the Nazis and Communists, recognized the changing climate at the boy bars, and worried over—and wrote about—the ambivalence he felt in many Germans as these developments arose.

For Isherwood, the political was always defined by the personal, as the final passage in *Goodbye to Berlin* demonstrates: "The sun shines, and Hitler is master of this city. . . . [D]ozens of my friends . . . are in prison, possibly dead. . . . I am thinking of poor Rudi . . . the Nazis will play with him. . . . Perhaps at this very moment Rudi is being tortured to death" (*Berlin* 207). Rudi, Isherwood revealed in *Christopher and His Kind* (1976), was based on his lover, Heinz. In that memoir—a retelling of the Berlin years—Isherwood, now out of the closet and active in the American gay movement, made clear that his love for Heinz moved him to pacifism.

Unlike some of his friends, Isherwood never joined the **Communist Party**; he felt that the antihomosexual policies under Stalin were inexcusable and hypocritical in a party ostensibly devoted to justice. Isherwood's shift toward gay activism dominated his politics for the remainder of his life and career. Isherwood wrote about openly gay characters and issues as early as the 1950s. His underrated novel *The World in the Evening* (1954) features a gay couple, Charles and Bob, and shows Bob railing against the military's antigay policy. In his finest novel, *A Single Man* (1965), Isherwood follows a gay professor through one day. George, the protagonist, talks to his students about minority politics, drawing connections between racial and other forms of discrimination while also pointing out rivalries among minorities and critiquing banal liberalism.

Isherwood made important contributions recording and commenting on political and social matters throughout much of the twentieth century. Like his mentor, E. M. Forster, Isherwood practiced a personal politics based in justice and love, not power and might.

Selected Bibliography: Berg, James, and Chris Freeman, eds. *Conversations with Christopher Isherwood.* Jackson: UP of Mississippi, 2001; Isherwood, Christopher. *The Berlin Stories.* 1935. New York: New Directions, 1954; Isherwood, Christopher. *Christopher and His Kind.* New York: Farrar, Straus and Giroux, 1976; Summers, Claude J. *Christopher Isherwood.* New York: Ungar, 1980.

Chris Freeman

ITALIAN LITERATURE. The literary achievement of Dante Alighieri (1265–1321) in Italian and Latin has overshadowed the Paduan prehumanist Albertino Mussato (1261–1329), who wrote in Latin. Mussato was awarded the laurel crown (1315, the first since classical times) for his *Historia Augusta* (1311–1313), about the Emperor Henry VII, and for his tragedy *Ecerinis* (another modern first), which was performed annually by the citizens of Padua to celebrate the overthrow of the bloody tyrant Ezzelino d'Este and their own liberty, in thinly veiled allegory aimed at the contemporary despot Cangrande of Verona, who was again threatening Mussato's town.

Dante—like Mussato, a soldier and politician as well as a writer and intellectual—attempts in his *Comedia* to reverse the course of history and quell the challenge of the papacy, in league with the mercantilist city-states against feudal and imperial power. The political dimension of the poem is inseparable from its theological, psychological, and other dimensions, and had been prepared in Dante's Latin treatise *Monarchia*, on universal monarchy. The *Comedia* projects the turbulent politics of Dante's native Florence, of Italy, and of contemporary Christendom in a perspective that sees human history within eternity, and his use of his native vernacular was itself a decisive political choice.

Criticism of papal power and ecclesiastical corruption became endemic among Italian writers right up to the Counter-Reformation. The two great writers of the generation after Dante, however—Petrarch (Francesco Petrarca, 1304–1374), who received the laurel crown on the Roman Capitol in 1341, and Giovanni Boccaccio (1313–1375)—did not address overtly political themes. They were important politically in two other ways: first, for their revival of classical literature, ultimately subverting Christian values and church authority, and second, for establishing literary brilliance as an end in itself, in the service either of political power or of a nascent reading public. Their sonority, rather than Dante's directness, became the model for literary excellence. Style itself became an implicit political act, marking distinctions between vindication and critique of existing hierarchies, as Luigi Pirandello (1867–1936) was to recognize early in the twentieth century in associating the eloquence of a Gabriele D'Annunzio (1863–1938) with the Petrarchan tradition, and the gritty realism of a Giovanni Verga (1840–1922) with the line extending from Dante.

Renaissance Italy was the intellectual and literary powerhouse of Europe from the fourteenth to the sixteenth century; numerous writers, using Latin, addressed the figure of the ideal prince or mode of government. The reality of power politics, however, broke this mindset, with foreign invasions—beginning in 1494—that eventually left Italy divided, subjected, and impotent. Writers now turned to Italian. Niccolò Machiavelli (1469–1527) famously imagined what a real leader for Italy would be like in *Il principe* (*The Prince*), and drew lessons from the Roman Republic in his *Discourses* on Livy's history. In his history of Florence, Machiavelli also revolutionized historiography from the providential Christian mode to that of the structural analysis of cause and effect. This was carried still further by his fellow Florentine, Francesco Guicciardini (1483–1540), not only in his own history of Florence and treatises on its government but more especially in his massive *Storia d'Italia* (1561–1564), which displays the history of Italy in terms of the psychology of the actors and a whole host of other factors, providential designs being systematically displaced.

Domination by Spain, in alliance with the Counter-Reformation church, progressively quelled effective inquiry into political issues. The epic poem *Gerusalemme liberata* (Jerusalem Delivered, 1581), by Torquato Tasso (1544–1595), dramatizes the primacy of religion in politics and the need for monarchy, and mobilizes Christendom against Ottoman expansion, yet its author rewrote it in an even more orthodox and moral vein as *Gerusalemme conquistata* (1593). Federico Della Valle's deeply religious tragedy *La Reina di Scozia* (The Queen of Scotland, 1591), on the execution of Mary Stuart in 1587, also valorizes divine-right monarchy, but does not deny a plausible voice to Elizabeth's Protestant cause, and its author was condemned to obscurity. While Giordano Bruno, whose dialogue *La cena delle ceneri* (The Ash-Wednesday Dinner, 1584) totalizes a Copernicanism philosophically well ahead of and beyond Galileo's, and whose *Lo spaccio della bestia trionfante* (The Expulsion of the Triumphant Beast, 1584) subverts all ideological hierarchies, was condemned to the stake by the Roman Inquisition in 1600. And another Dominican monk, Tommaso Campanella (1568–1639), set up a utopia in 1599, based on humanist communism and astrological eugenics—expounded in his dialogue *City of the Sun*—but spent some thirty years in dungeons and was subjected seven times to torture by the Holy Inquisition before ending his life as a favorite of Louis XIV of France, having produced an astounding philosophical output and propounded a universal Christian state.

If, up to 1600, Italy's literary politics concerned divine-right monarchy, theology, and natural philosophy, from the eighteenth century, the values of the Enlightenment become the points of conflict. The comedies of the prolific Carlo Goldoni (1707–1793) ridicule Italy's ossified and caste-ridden society and genially celebrate the emergence of a more industrious class, while in the nineteen tragedies and several comedies of the one-man Sturm und Drang, Vittorio Alfieri (1749–1803), what is to be one political imperative of the nineteenth century finds an intensely dramatic focus: the libertarian revolt against what are perceived as the murderous compulsions of all forms of tyranny. Alfieri's diverse oeuvre also includes an eloquent discursive indictment of absolutism and a vindication of the writer's role as champion of liberty.

With the new century, writers wedded these motifs to the new idea of an Italian nation, producing a spate of odes and verse epics, heroic tragedies, and historical novels drawing on the Greek, Roman, and Italian past to construct a tradition of libertarian nationalism, which was transformed into a religion in the life and writings—amounting to a hundred volumes—of the revolutionary nationalist Giuseppe Mazzini (1805–1872). The heroic cult of the nation was carried on after the unification (1860) by the poet Giosuè Carducci (1837–1907, 1906 Nobel Prize winner), the versatile D'Annunzio, and the futurist leader F. T. Marinetti (1876–1944), though it was increasingly problematized by other writers, as in Italo Svevo's sly novel *La coscienza di Zeno* (*Confessions of Zeno* / *Zeno's Conscience*, 1923), in which the Great War and Italy's intervention in it are emptied of rationality.

Fascist rule (1922–1945) was less successful in producing a fascist literature than an antifascist literature, implicitly including Alberto Moravia's first novel, *Gli indifferenti* (*A Time of Indifference*, 1929). This was one of the first twentieth-century novels of alienation and, of course, could not contain any explicit political critique, any more than Elio Vittorini's highly allusive and emblematic *Conversazione in Sicilia* (1941). From exile, **Ignazio Silone** was able to write openly about fascist repression of the peasantry. The Resistance struggle is more or less fictionally documented in the neorealist vein of narratives by writers such as Moravia and Vittorini, but also **Italo Calvino, Cesare Pavese**, and Beppe Fenoglio. This received further impetus from the posthumous publication after the liberation of the prison notebooks of Communist leader **Antonio Gramsci**, which attributed central political importance to culture. Neorealism rarely produced anything politically sharper than a vague humanism and, especially in the novels and stories of Vasco Pratolini, wavered between politically marked **socialist realism** and sentimental melodrama. The politics of neorealism were comically inverted in the hugely popular "Don Camillo" books by Giovanni Guareschi, in which a village parish priest and the local communist mayor fight out in miniature the political issues of the day but are soul brothers under the skin.

The conventions of realism were challenged in the 1950s by the appalling reality of **Primo Levi's Holocaust** testimony, the appalling ultrarealism of **Pier Paolo Pasolini**'s Roman narratives, and the return in subversive mode of the historical novel in Tomasi di Lampedusa's *Il gattopardo* (***The Leopard***, 1958), all carrying strong political implications. Subsequently, neoexperimentalists, including Pasolini, and the neo-avant-garde, including the Gruppo '63, challenged capitalist **hegemony** by deconstructing the means of signification down to language itself, but with narrower impact than the revival of popular theater by 1997 Nobel Prize winner Dario Fo (1926–), or the multifarious and provocative docufictions of Oriana Fallaci (1930–). A satirical genre of *fantapolitica* (political fantasy) arose after 1968, exemplified in Guglielmo Zincone's *Vita, vita, vita!* about a Papal coup d'état (1985), but more surrealistically and metaphysically in Ugo Terruggi's unjustly neglected *Luisa e il presidente* (1972), and with unnerving plausibility in Leonardo Sciascia's *Il contesto* (*Equal Danger*, 1971).

Selected Bibliography: Brand, C. P., and Lino Pertile. *Cambridge History of Italian Literature*. Cambridge: Cambridge UP, 1997; Dotti, Ugo. *Storia degli intellettuali in Italia*. 3 vols. Rome: Editori Riuniti, 1997, 1998, 1999; Gatt-Rutter, John. *Writers and Politics in Modern Italy*. London: Hodder and Stoughton, 1978; Goudet, J. *Dante et la politique*. Paris: Aubier, 1959; Gramsci, Antonio. *Prison Notebooks*. 2 vols. Ed. and trans. Joseph A. Buttigieg. New York: Columbia UP, 1992, 1996; Rühle, J. "Italy between Black and Red." Trans. J. Steinberg. *Literature and Revolution*. London: Pall Mall, 1969.

John Gatt-Rutter

IYAYI, FESTUS (1947–). Important Nigerian fiction writer, economist, and political scientist. Born in Benin City, Iyayi was educated in Nigeria, the Soviet Union, and England, where he received his doctorate from the University of Bradford. Iyayi is a committed Socialist whose application of Marxist ideas to an African context is often reminiscent of the ideas of **Frantz Fanon**. His first novel, *Violence* (1979), is often considered the first Nigerian **proletarian novel**. It relates the travails of a young Nigerian couple, Idemudia and Adisa, as they attempt to make a life for themselves in a modern Lagos dominated by the corrupt manipulations of politicians and businesspeople. In particular, this working-class couple is structurally opposed to Obufun and Queen, a rich couple whose activities dramatize the exploitation of the Nigerian people by a corrupt postcolonial comprador bourgeoisie. Narrated in a straightforward, down-to-earth style that should make its message accessible to large numbers of Nigerian readers, *Violence* addresses a number of crucial issues, including the exploitation of workers by dishonest bosses and the poor functioning of public services, such as hospitals, because of corruption and incompetence among administrators and managers.

Iyayi's next novel, *The Contract* (1982) is another searching Fanonian critique of postcolonial corruption in Nigeria. With the publication of *Heroes* in 1986, Iyayi became a major figure in Nigerian literature, winning the Commonwealth Writers' Prize. This novel focuses on the bloody **Nigerian Civil War** of 1967 to 1970. Of the numerous novels that deal with the war (one might cite Buchi Emecheta's *Destination Biafra* [1982] and Isidore Okpewho's *The Last Duty* [1976] as prominent examples), *Heroes* is the one that treats the war most trenchantly from a leftist perspective. The central point made by Iyayi in the book is a simple one: the intertribal warfare that informed the civil war was instigated by a few powerful leaders on both sides who stood to gain both power and wealth from the war. Meanwhile, the common soldiers who fought on both sides were being manipulated by these leaders into slaughtering one another when in fact their real enemies were not the soldiers on the other side but the generals and politicians instigating the war from both sides. Among other things, *Heroes* deconstructs myths of heroism in war, so that its title is largely ironic. But the book is far from a sentimental cry for peace and universal brotherhood. In fact, the book, which at one point quotes **Mao Zedong**'s dictum that political power grows out of the barrel of a gun, is a direct Fanonian call for class warfare, in which all the common people of Nigeria would unite to destroy the ruling class that has oppressed them since the beginning of independence in 1960.

In 1996, Iyayi published *Awaiting Court Martial*, a collection of fifteen short stories that won the All-Africa Christopher Okigbo Prize and helped Iyayi himself win the first Nigerian Author of the Year award. Though his radical political views have sometimes interfered with the progress of his academic career, Iyayi is also an important figure in Nigerian academic circles. At this writing, he serves as a don at the University of Benin.

Selected Bibliography: Amuta, Chidi. *Towards a Sociology of African Literature.* Oguta, Nigeria: Zim Pan, 1986; Booker, M. Keith. "Writing for the Wretched of the Earth: Frantz Fanon and the Radical African Novel." *Rereading Global Socialist Cultures after the Cold War: The Reassessment of a Tradition.* Ed. Dubravka Juraga and M. Keith Booker. Westport, CT: Praeger, 2002. 27–54; Ni Chreachain, Firinne. "Festus Iyayi's *Heroes*: Two Novels in One?" *Research in African Literatures* 22.1 (1991): 43–53; Udenta, Udenta O. *Revolutionary Aesthetics and the African Literary Process.* Enugu, Nigeria: Fourth Dimension, 1993; Wendt, Albert. "An Interview with Festus Iyayi." *Landfall* 44.4 (1990): 412–22.

M. Keith Booker

J

JAMES, C.L.R. (1901–1989). The son of a schoolteacher and a convent-educated housewife in British colonial Trinidad, James would successively become a unique regional novelist, an outstanding scholar of black history, a political activist and theoretician, a sports historian, and in old age, the last of a generation of great Pan-Africanists. A promising lad with a broad-jump record for his island, James disappointed his parents terribly by shunning classes for the cricket field. Likewise, and unlike many other regional intellectuals of high caliber, he did not leave for schooling in the United Kingdom, but instead stayed to become a secondary-school teacher and a sometime cricket commentator. During the 1920s, drawn at once by the nationalist-radical movement of Captain Cipriani and by the desire to help create a distinctive new literature, James and close friends launched two short-lived cultural journals. By the time he left for the United Kingdom in 1931, he had completed *Minty Alley*, one of the very earliest English-language novels of the region.

James's British sojourn (1931–1939) plunged him into sports journalism (he became a cricket commentator for the *Manchester Guardian*), anticolonial activism, and political Trotskyism. Venturing to Paris archives, he gathered materials for the publication of *The Black Jacobins* (1939), a novelistic treatment of the successful Haitian revolt, ultimately considered—with W.E.B. Du Bois's *Black Reconstruction*—one of the classics of the day and not only for Africans of the New World. Disappointed in political prospects of the tiny British Trotskyist movement, he shifted operations to the United States as the European war neared, met **Trotsky** in Mexico for discussions on the "Negro question," and became active in America under a series of pseudonyms. Soon he had acquired intimate collaborators (especially Grace Lee and Raya Dunayevskaya) and a microfaction within Trotskyism, arguing that Russian society had become "state capitalist," and that only workers fighting free of bureaucratic union control could revolutionize the West. This antibureaucratic position placed him firmly outside Trotskyism (whose chief historical-theoretical text, after Trotsky's own work, he had penned in the United Kingdom as *World Revolution*). He and his group of fifty or so therefore departed into splendid isolation from the rest of the Left but firmly entrenched themselves (at least in their view) into the daily life of working-class Detroit.

James soon suffered incarceration and expulsion due to the political atmosphere of McCarthyism, but in the stressful moments of the later 1940s and early 1950s, he had completed several of the works important to his own development: *State Capitalism and World Revolution* (1950), a group statement about resistance to bureaucracy; *Notes on Dialectics* (1949, issued in mimeographed form until publication in 1984), a political mediation on Hegel; and *Mariners, Renegades and Castaways* (1953), a unique analysis of Herman Melville and *Moby-Dick* as reflecting American conditions and *mentalite*. He did not complete the document that he called "Notes on American Civilization"—a wider interpretation following the Melville study—due to his personal situation but perhaps also to the difficulty of the task. Unbeknownst to him, however, his 1940s documents on black radicalism had deeply influenced a young, imprisoned Malcolm X, and his work exerted a quiet influence on many civil rights leaders, including Martin Luther King Jr.

Back in the United Kingdom, James set to work writing about cricket again and within a decade completed *Beyond a Boundary* (1963)—regarded as the finest cricket study and one of the best sports histories written. Eventually, British audiences who knew little about the old man's politics regarded him as the black savant who spoke frequently on television during test matches.

Beyond a Boundary raised up the cricket play of colonial subjects as demonstrating their societies' readiness for independence and a distinctive contribution to world society. James took part in the political side when Trinidad moved toward independence and the former schoolboy taught by James, Dr. Eric Williams, invited his sometime teacher to become editor of the independence party's weekly newspaper. Regarded with great hostility by the congealing party bureaucracy, James left Trinidad after eighteen months in 1961, but left behind a movement on several islands dedicated to his vision of anticolonialism from the grass roots, and popular rule without neocolonial economics or bureaucratic political machinery.

From the middle 1960s to the end of his long life, James divided his time between the Caribbean, the United Kingdom, Canada, and the United States, where he was readmitted in 1969, and taught at Federal City College of Washington, D.C., for several years when not traveling and speaking at campuses far and wide. As an aged, jet-black militant with oratorical power and a delightful, humorous self-presentation, James drew crowds of devotees. The U.S. New Left journal *Radical America*, which published a selection of his writings in 1970, served as a beacon for his views, and the League of Black Revolutionary Workers drew inspiration from him, while Caribbean activists at home, in the United States, and in Canada imbibed his persona as well as his arguments. In his lifetime, he became known in some circles as the Black Plato because of the scope of his interpretations. Meanwhile, Walter Rodney (the Guyanese political thinker assassinated in 1979), Stokely Carmichael, Tim Hector (leader of the Antiguan opposition), **George Lamming**, and the membership of the Oil Field Workers Trade Union of Trinidad and Tobago, among many others in the region, regarded him as the foremost moral and intellectual force for a Caribbean federation.

Resettled in London during his declining years, he found himself unable to complete his memoirs, but three volumes of selected works appeared (*The Future in the Present*, 1977; *Spheres of Existence*, 1980; and *At the Rendezvous of Victory*, 1984) along with *Notes on Dialectics* (1980), the anthological *Cricket* (1986), and his searing critique of African revolutions gone wrong, *Nkrumah and the Ghana Revolution* (1977). Shortly before his death, the authorized biography, *C.L.R. James: The Artist as Revolutionary*, was published. The years since have seen many new studies; the semiannual appearance of the *CLR James Journal* by the CLR James Society, based at Brown University; and a global conference on the occasion of his centenary in 2001, at the University of West Indies campus in Trinidad, where a major selection of his personal papers have been gathered.

Selected Bibliography: Bogues, Anthony. *C.L.R. James and Marxism.* London: Pluto, 1993; Buhle, Paul, ed. *C.L.R. James: The Artist as Revolutionary.* London: Verso, 1988; Henry, Paget, and Paul Buhle, eds. *C.L.R. James's Caribbean.* Durham, NC: Duke UP, 1992.

Paul Buhle

JAMES, HENRY (1843–1916). Born in New York City, the son of a prominent intellectual, James—brother of the philosopher William James—spent most of his adult life in Europe. This cosmopolitan perspective is reflected in his numerous novels, the most important of which include *The Portrait of a Lady* (1881), *The Ambassadors* (1903), and *The Golden Bowl* (1904). James is often considered an apolitical figure, but he did address political questions directly in two novels, *The Bostonians* (1886) and *The Princess Casamassima* (1886). Both dramatize the compelling emotional power of the notion of revolutionary upheaval, but both also suggest that that power derives more from romantic illusions than from concern for the well-being of humanity. In *The Bostonians*, the angry revolutionary feminist Olive Chancellor yearns for martyrdom. She desires a cataclysmic transformation that will not only benefit women but also punish men for their brutality and exploitation. Significantly, none of the other women in the novel, including other feminists, share Olive's revolutionary zeal. Mrs. Farrinder, for example, is a pragmatic reformer who campaigns for Prohibition and women's suffrage but is suspicious of Olive's romantic philosophy. Mary Prance practices medicine despite the prejudice against women physicians, but she is uninterested in political rhetoric. Most importantly, Verena Tarrant, the young girl Olive Chancellor makes her disciple, eventually discovers that her commitment to Olive's revolutionary feminism was not based on her own deepest feelings. Verena comes to realize that she has joined with Olive because of personal loyalty rather than any belief in the cause itself.

Hyacinth Robinson, the protagonist of *The Princess Casamassima* (set in London), joins a revolutionary terrorist group in a moment of excitement but comes to recognize that the equality desired by the revolutionaries is not inspired by anything nobler than jealousy of those more fortunate than themselves. Still sympathizing with the misery of the many, Hyacinth nevertheless comes to feel that any revolutionary correction of this misery would be so damaging to civilization as we know it that human life as a whole might be worse rather than better. Hyacinth's mentor, Mr. Vetch, seems to embody hard-won wisdom when he realizes the impossibility of great fundamental changes in human relationships. The insistence of the princess of the title on smashing selfishness is impressive, but Hyacinth eventually senses that she is more dedicated to helping herself than helping others.

Though both novels suggest that revolution is an impractical and undesirable way to solve social problems, nobody in either novel convincingly defends the justice of current social arrangements. In both *The Bostonians* and *The Princess Casamassima*, James succeeds in revealing the folly of revolutionary fervor without committing himself to an unqualified endorsement of the political and economic system the revolutionaries opposed.

Selected Bibliography: Fetterley, Judith. *The Resisting Reader: A Feminist Approach to American Fiction.* Bloomington: Indiana UP, 1978. 101–53; Seaton, James. "Henry James's *The Princess Casamassima:* Revolution and the Preservation of Culture." *The Moral of the Story: Literature and Public Ethics.* Ed. Henry T. Edmondson. Lanham, MD: Lexington Books, 2000. 15–25; Trilling, Lionel. *The Liberal Imagination: Essays on Literature and Society.* 1950. New York: HBJ, 1979.

James Seaton

JAMESON, FREDRIC (1934–), American literary and cultural critic, generally considered to be one of the foremost contemporary practitioners of **Marxist criticism** writing in English. Jameson has published a wide range of works analyzing literary and cultural texts and developing his own neo-Marxist theoretical position. A prolific writer, he has assimilated an astonishing number of theoretical discourses into his work and has intervened in many contemporary debates while analyzing a diversity of cultural texts, ranging from the novel to video, from architecture to **postmodernism.**

In his first published book, Jameson analyzed the literary theory and production of **Jean-Paul Sartre.** Written as a doctoral dissertation at Yale University, *Sartre: The Origins of a Style* (1961) was influenced by Jameson's teacher Erich Auerbach and by the stylistics associated with Leo Spitzer; it focuses on Sartre's style, narrative structures, values, and vision of the world. The book is devoid of the Marxist categories and political readings characteristic of Jameson's later work, but read in the context of the stifling conformism and banal business society of the 1950s, Jameson's subject matter (Sartre) and his intricate literary-theoretical writing style (already the notorious Jamesonian sentences appear full-blown) can be seen as revealing an attempt to create himself as a critical intellectual against the conformist currents of the epoch. One also sees him already turning against the literary establishment and the dominant modes of literary criticism and seeking alternatives. Indeed, Jameson's work as a whole constitutes critical interventions against the hegemonic forms of literary criticism and modes of thought regnant in the Anglo-American world.

After intense study of Marxist literary theory in the 1960s, when he was influenced by the New Left and the antiwar movement, Jameson published *Marxism and Form* (1971), which introduced a tradition of dialectical Marxist literary theory to the English-speaking world. Since articulating and critiquing the structuralist project in *The Prison-House of Language* (1972), Jameson has concentrated on developing his own literary and cultural theory in works such as *Fables of Aggression: Wyndham Lewis, the Modernist as Fascist* (1979), *The Political Unconscious: Narrative as a Socially Symbolic Act* (1981), and *Postmodernism, or The Cultural Logic of Late Capitalism* (1991). *Late Marxism* (1990), a study of **Theodor Adorno,** and *Brecht and Method* (1998), on **Bertolt Brecht,** continue Jameson's intensive work in Marxist theory and aesthetics. *A Singular Modernity* (2002) engages the debates over the postmodern through critical analysis of discourses of modernity and modernism.

Jameson has characteristically appropriated into his theory a wide range of positions, from structuralism to poststructuralism and from psychoanalysis to postmodernism, producing a highly eclectic and original brand of Marxist literary and cultural theory. Marxism remains the master narrative of Jameson's corpus, a theoretical apparatus and method that used a dual hermeneutic that critiques the ideological components of cultural texts while setting forth their utopian dimension, and that helps produce criticism of existing society and visions of a better world. Influenced by Marxist theorist **Ernst Bloch**, Jameson has thus developed a hermeneutical and utopian version of Marxist cultural and social theory.

Dialectical criticism, for Jameson, involves thinking that reflexively analyzes categories and methods while carrying out concrete analyses and inquiries. Categories articulate historical content and thus must be read in terms of the historical environment out of which they emerge. For Jameson, dialectical criticism involves thinking that reflects on categories and procedures while engaging in specific concrete studies; relational and historical thinking, which contextualizes the object of study in its historical environment; utopian thinking, which compares the existing reality with possible alternatives and finds utopian hope in literature, philosophy, and other cultural texts; and totalizing, synthesizing thinking, which provides a systematic framework for cultural studies and a theory of history within which dialectical criticism can operate. All these aspects are operative throughout Jameson's work, the totalizing element coming more prominently (and controversially) to the fore as his work evolved.

From the 1970s to the present, Jameson has published an increasingly diverse and complex series of theoretical inquiries and cultural studies. One begins to encounter the characteristic range of interests and depth of penetration in his studies of science fiction, film, magical narratives, painting, and both realist and modernist literature. One also encounters articles concerning Marxist cultural politics, imperialism, Palestinian liberation, Marxist teaching methods, Chinese literature and culture, and the revitalization of the Left. Many of the key earlier essays have been collected in two volumes in *The Ideologies of Theory* (1988), which provide the laboratory for the theoretical project worked out in *The Political Unconscious, Fables of Aggression,* and subsequent texts. These studies should be read together as inseparable parts of a multilevel theory of the interconnections between the history of literary form, modes of subjectivity, and stages of capitalism.

Jameson's theoretical synthesis is presented most systematically in *The Political Unconscious.* The text contains an articulation of Jameson's interpretive method, a systematic inventory of the history of literary forms, and a hidden history of the forms and modes of subjectivity itself, as it traverses through the field of culture and experience. Particularly important here is Jameson's notion that texts need to be interpreted simultaneously on multiple levels: political, social, and historical—or, events, social class, and mode of production. Jameson boldly attempts to establish Marxist criticism as the most all-inclusive and comprehensive theoretical framework, as he incorporates a disparate set of competing approaches into his model. He provides an overview of the history of the development of cultural forms and concludes with his clearest articulation of the above dual hermeneutic as the properly Marxist method of interpretation.

Jameson employs a historical narrative inspired by the work of **Georg Lukács** to tell how cultural texts contain a "**political unconscious**"—buried narratives and social experiences, which require sophisticated literary hermeneutics in order to be deciphered. One particular narrative of *The Political Unconscious* concerns, in Jameson's striking phrase, "the construction of the bourgeois subject in emergent capitalism and its schizophrenic disintegration in our own time" (9). Key stages in the odyssey of the disintegrating bourgeois subjectivity are articulated in George Gissing, **Joseph Conrad**, and **Wyndham Lewis**—a story that will find its culmination in Jameson's account of postmodernism.

Indeed, Jameson's studies on postmodernism are a logical consequence of his theoretical project. Within his analysis, Jameson situates postmodern culture in the framework of a theory of stages of society—based on a neo-Marxist model of stages of capitalist development—and argues that postmodernism is part of a new stage of capitalism. Every theory of postmodernism, he claims, contains an implicit periodization of history and "an implicitly or explicitly political stance on the nature of multinational capitalism today" (*Postmodernism*, 3). Following Ernest Mandel's periodization in his book *Late Capitalism* (1975), Jameson argues in *Postmodernism* that "there have been three fundamental moments in capitalism, each one marking a dialectical expansion over the previous stage. These are market capitalism, the monopoly stage or the stage of imperialism, and our own, wrongly called postindustrial, but what might better be termed multinational, capital" (35). To these forms of society correspond the cultural forms **realism**, **modernism**, and postmodernism.

No early/late dichotomy in Jameson's publications presents itself as a viable hermeneutical device for interpreting his works as a whole, other than the obvious distinction between his pre-Marxist text *Sartre* and his later writings. Rather, what is striking are the remarkable continuities in Jameson's works. One can pick up his articles or books from the early 1970s through the late 1980s and discover strong similarities in their concerns, style, and politics. One gets the feeling in reading *The Ideologies of Theory* that the essays could have all been written yesterday, yet as Jameson notes in the introduction to these essays, they do seem collectively to show a gradual

> shift from the vertical to the horizontal: from an interest in the multiple dimensions and levels of a text to the multiple interweavings of an only fitfully readable (or writable) narrative; from problems of interpretation to problems of historiography; from the attempt to talk about the *sentence* to the (equally impossible) attempt to talk about *modes of production*. (xxix)

Still, this shift in emphasis also points to continuities in Jameson's work, for from the late 1960s to the 1990s, he has privileged the historical dimension of texts and political readings, bringing his critical practice into the slaughterhouse of history, moving critical discourse from the ivory tower of academia and the prison house of language to the vicissitudes and contingencies of that field for which the term "history" serves as marker.

Jameson emerges as a synthetic and eclectic Marxist cultural theorist who attempts to preserve and develop the Marxist theory while analyzing the politics and utopian moments of a stunning diversity of cultural texts. His work expands literary analysis to include popular culture, architecture, theory, and other texts, and thus can be seen as part of the movement toward cultural studies as a replacement for canonical literary studies. Jameson is a master of the essay form, and many of his works over the past decades bring together essays of the era. *Signatures of the Visible* (1992) and *The Geopolitical Aesthetic* (1992) collect studies of film and visual culture, while *The Cultural Turn* (1998) presents a *selection of writings on the postmodern.*

For his work over the past two decades, Jameson is probably best known on a global scale as one of the major theorists of the postmodern. The important essay "The Existence of Italy" (in *Signatures of the Visible*) develops this problematic, as do the studies in *Postmodernism*, *The Cultural Turn*, and *A Singular Modernity*. In the latter book, Jameson analyzes discourses of modernity, modernism in the arts, and the pathos of the modern with the same intensity, depth, and originality that he engages the family of postmodern concepts. He notes the somewhat surprising "return of the modern" in a variety of fields in recent years and attempts to delineate the construction of various concepts of modernity and the modern in rhetorical and narrative contexts.

The title "a singular modernity" is partly ironic, since one of Jameson's strongest arguments is that there is no singular modernity but a variety of narratives of modernity, modernism, and the modern, which serve varied ideological purposes. Nevertheless, he finds that the prime rhetorical gesture and defining feature of the **ideology** of modernism is belief in the autonomy of art, and Jameson provides analysis of the rise of varied modernist discourses in France, Germany, and the United States after **World War II**. Jameson is critical of the aestheticist and antipolitical conceptions of art that underlie most modernist practice but believes that these ideologies can be highly revealing. In particular, Jameson thinks that critically reading the ideology of modernism helps us grasp the structure of modernity and the modern as attempts to produce the new, as ruptures and breaks that produce constant innovation, but without collective projects to fundamentally change the system and thus ultimately serve as ideologies that legitimate the system of capitalism, with its own emphasis on innovation. Rather than a theory of modernity or the modern, Jameson concludes, we need an ontology of the present that grasps the past and future in the present. More specifically, "What we really need is a wholesale displacement of the thematics of modernity by the desire called Utopia" (215). For Jameson, past, present, and future coexist in a problematic that systematically grapples with the past as it attempts to understand the present and move toward a better future.

Selected Bibliography: Anderson, Perry. *The Origins of Postmodernity.* London: Verso, 1998; Best, Stephen, and Douglas Kellner, *Postmodern Theory: Critical Interrogations.* New York: Guilford P, 1991; Burnham, Clint. *The Jamesonian Unconscious: The Aesthetics of Marxist Theory.* Durham: Duke UP, 1995; Dowling, William C. *Jameson, Althusser, Marx: An Introduction to the Political Unconscious.* Ithaca: Cornell UP, 1984; Hardt, Michael, and Kathi Weeks, eds. *The Jameson Reader.* Oxford: Blackwell, 2000; Homer, Sean. *Fredric Jameson: Marxism, Hermeneutics, Postmodernism.* New York: Routledge, 1998; Jameson, Fredric. *Brecht and Method.* London: Verso, 1998; Jameson, Fredric. *The Cultural Turn: Selected Writings on the Postmodern, 1983–1998.* London: Verso, 1998; Jameson, Fredric. *Fables of Ag-*

gression: Wyndham Lewis, the Modernist as Fascist. Berkeley: U of California P, 1979; Jameson, Fredric. The Geopolitical Aesthetic: Cinema and Space in the World System. Bloomington: Indiana UP, 1992; Jameson, Fredric. Late Marxism: Adorno; or The Persistence of the Dialectic. London: Verso, 1990; Jameson, Fredric. Marxism and Form: Twentieth-Century Dialectical Theories of Literature. Princeton, NJ: Princeton UP, 1971; Jameson, Fredric. The Political Unconscious: Narrative as a Socially Symbolic Act. Ithaca, NY: Cornell UP, 1981; Jameson, Fredric. Postmodernism, or The Cultural Logic of Late Capitalism. Durham, NC: Duke UP, 1991; Jameson, Fredric. The Prison-House of Language: A Critical Account of Structuralism and Poststructuralism. Princeton, NJ: Princeton UP, 1972; Jameson, Fredric. Sartre: The Origins of a Style. New Haven, CT: Yale UP, 1961; Jameson, Fredric. Signatures of the Visible. New York: Routledge, 1992; Jameson, Fredric. A Singular Modernity: Essay on the Ontology of the Present. London: Verso, 2002; Kellner, Douglas, ed. Postmodernism/Jameson/Critique. Washington, DC: Maisonneuve P, 1989; Roberts, Adam. Fredric Jameson. New York: Routledge, 2000.

Douglas Kellner

JEWISH AMERICAN LITERATURE. Although this literary phenomenon has flourished in the twentieth century, the origin of Jewish American writing has its roots decisively in the nineteenth-century immigrant experience of European Jewry. After the collapse of the Moorish empire in medieval Spain (1492), there were reports of a modest Jewish population in America, which steadily grew throughout the seventeenth and eighteenth centuries. By 1881, there were a quarter of a million Jews already living in America before the mass exodus of some three million Eastern European Jews (of which nearly two million settled in the United States) from widespread persecution and pogroms executed by Tsar Alexander III in Russia, Romania, and Hungary.

In America, the religious and cultural diversity of Jewish settlers was marked. Whereas the eighteenth-century German Jewry had instigated the liberal theology of Reform Judaism influenced by the Enlightenment (*Haskallah*), those of Eastern European descent emphasized the centrality of traditional Yiddish and folklore to Jewish identity. Many thousands of Jews who fled Europe in the 1880s and the early part of the twentieth century eked out a poverty-stricken existence in New York's Lower East Side, living in tenements supported by Jewish charities. Jewish American writing of this period—including Abraham Cahan's *Yekl: A Tale of the New York Ghetto* (1896), Rose Cohen's *Out of the Shadow: A Russian Jewish Girlhood on the Lower East Side* (1918), and **Anzia Yezierska**'s *Salome of the Tenements* (1923)—testifies to the process of social, economic, and cultural transition with, as Stephen Wade observes, a "basis of emotional belonging in the 'old country'" and an emphasis on "learning, growth and change in the individual consciousness" (*Jewish*, 33). In recording the communal and individual consequences of the cultural transition from European *shtetl* to American ghetto, this first generation of Jewish American writers appreciated the private and public pressures exerted on Jewish identity from without—by the materialist aspirations of the secular capitalist economy into which many desired integration—and from within—by a commitment to traditional spirituality, religious practice, and Talmudic scholarship that renounced worldly gain. Cahan's novel *The Rise of David Levinsky* (1917) perfectly captures this dualistic aspect of what it is to be Jewish in the New World, as the protagonist of the title becomes an entrepreneur in the capitalist system through the manufacture of cloaks (themselves an emblem of duplicity), only to become aware that his successful business venture is modeled on the homespun industry of his former Eastern European village, Antomor. Such historical reminders of the past perpetually alert David to an inner sense of vacancy at variance with his ostensible commercial triumph and caused by his apparent inability to live a worthwhile inner spiritual life.

Throughout the 1930s, Jewish American fiction continued to explore the tension between old and new modes of existence but, gradually, offered a reassessment of the first-generation Jewish immigrant experience in America and explored issues of assimilation, embracing the individual liberties and opportunities offered by secular society and culture. In this respect, Yiddish American modernist poets—such as Moyshe-Leyb Halpern (*In New York*, 1919), Jacob Glatshteyn (*Yiddish Meanings*, 1937), and Kudya Molodowsky (*In the Country of My Bones*, 1937)—increasingly found themselves solitary and marginal voices because of their artistic choice to employ Yiddish as their linguistic medium and their often critical attitudes toward America as the Promised or Golden Land. Prose writing of this period, however, galvanized the philosophical speculation of European and Yiddish traditions into an intellectualism that defined Jewish identity in the New World by depicting protagonists—as, for example, in **Michael Gold**'s *Jews without Money* (1930), Henry Roth's *Call It Sleep* (1934), Tess Slesinger's *The Unpossessed* (1934), Delmore Schwartz's *In Dreams Begin Responsibilities* (1937), and **Nathanael West**'s *The Day of the Locust* (1939)—who were self-conscious journalists, writers, thinkers, and political activists with socialist sympathies akin to those of the Jewish Literary Left (including Cahan, Yezierska, and Gold). To varying degrees, these prose works critiqued the anachronism of Eastern European Jewish folklore, criticized the vacuity of **popular culture**, and satirized the urban intellectual and political movements in modern America. In the next decade, this satirical element is still evident in **Norman Mailer**'s stringent Marxist analysis of capitalist economics and outright condemnation of the futility of war, *The Naked and the Dead* (1948), and also in two plays of the same era by Arthur Miller, *All My Sons* (1947) and *Death of a Salesman* (1949).

In *Death of a Salesman*, Biff's diagnosis of his father's "phony dream" (106) indicates an intellectual crisis over the disjuncture between self and world, private sentiment and public obligation, and reaffirms intellectualism as a prevalent characteristic of Jewish American literary identity before and after **World War II** and the catastrophic events of the *Shoah* (**Holocaust**). This cataclysmic occurrence determined the elegiac voice present in Jewish American poetry of the postwar era and is detectable in poetic collections as diverse as *Howl and Other Poems* (1956) by **Allen Ginsberg**, *Poems of a Jew* (1958) by Karl Shapiro, and *When We Dead Awaken* (1971) and *Diving into the Wreck* (1973) by Adrienne Rich. In postwar fiction, Saul Bellow became the most prominent novelist to translate the spatial sphere of physical action into a psychic arena of intellectual and existential angst. Invariably, the protagonists of Bellow's fiction are men of letters, verbal eloquence, and philosophy, who derive a fundamental sense of being in the world—as well as a vantage point from which to scrutinize postwar American culture—from their intellectual and literary sensibilities. Joseph, the central character in Bellow's first novel, *Dangling Man* (1944), explicitly rejects the mode of physical activity preferred by those heroes of **Ernest**

Hemingway (1898–1961), claiming that "[t]he hard-boiled are compensated for their silence; they fly planes or fight bulls or catch tarpon, whereas I rarely leave my room" (10). Bellow's inward psychic turn is a response to American urban culture, anti-Semitism, and the threatened loss of unique identity in a pluralistic society where total assimilation is the perceived goal. These individual questions about ethical behavior and communal responsibility are frequently universalized in Bellow's work to the wider philosophical issue of humanity's chaotic, fragmentary, and disjointed perception of reality and advocacy of a self-reliance close in conception to **Jean-Paul Sartre**'s existentialism in *Being and Nothingness* (1943). Consequently, those central characters of Bellow's early fiction, such as Asa (*The Victim*, 1947), Augie (*The Adventures of Augie March*, 1953), Tommy (*Seize the Day*, 1956), Henderson (*Henderson the Rain King*, 1959), Moses (*Herzog*, 1964), and Artur (*Mr. Sammler's Planet*, 1970), are acutely attuned to the unreality of their own states of being, the contingent nature of their socially constructed selves, and how their self-imposed alienation from community is a fictional defense against their own human shortcomings and absurdities that they recognize in others. From his earliest to his most recent fiction, *Ravelstein* (1999), Bellow's esoteric meditations on the nature of Jewish identity constitute alternative responses to the devastation of the Holocaust and invariably advocate an intellectual humanism.

Philip Roth adapts such intellectualism to a highly satirical mode of first-person narrative, as in *The Professor of Desire* (1977) and most recently in *The Human Stain* (2000), to examine the complexities of what it means to be Jewish and living the suburban life of middle-class comfort and relative financial security. Roth's debut novella, *Goodbye, Columbus* (1959), is acutely sensitive to the various manifestations of Jewishness, including a sympathetic intellectual sensibility, an insular narrow-mindedness, a practical hard-work ethic, and finally a projected future liberal consciousness receptive to secular society. This commitment to secular America becomes blasphemous in Roth's infamously graphic portrayal of Portnoy's neurotic psychosis, with its origins in the emotional trauma of his childhood and pubescent sexual awakening. Framed as a confessional exchange between the central character and his psychiatrist, Portnoy's unfolding account of his life, irreverently, sketches and ridicules Orthodox practices and institutions (*Portnoy's Complaint*, 1969).

Other Jewish American literature of the twentieth century valorized the traditional rituals, beliefs, and lifestyle. Written originally in Yiddish (and translated by Bellow), a seminal short story, "Gimpel the Fool," by Isaac Bashevis Singer illustrates how the institutional rules of Judaism are exercized by rabbis with discretion and compassion, when Gimpel's wayward wife is forgiven and left unpunished. In a manifesto entitled "The Problems of Yiddish Prose in America" (1943), Singer advocated that all Jewish American writers should write in Yiddish, which, for him, was inextricable from Jewishness itself. Singer's novels *Shadows on the Hudson* (1957, 1998) and *Enemies: A Love Story* (1966, 1972) were serialized in Yiddish in the *Jewish Daily Forward*, founded in New York (1897), and later translated—with authorial involvement—for a wider reading public. His fiction often blends a modern cityscape with a hauntingly lyrical nostalgia for the past world of Eastern European Jewry. In the English-speaking world, the work of Bernard Malamud reverberates with the historical consciousness of the Holocaust (*The Fixer*, 1966) and is closest to the artistic concerns and method of Singer's work. Malamud's first collection of short stories, *The Magic Barrel* (1958), investigates, through the eyes of the Old World and a literary mode bordering on **magical realism**, the Jewish condition in terms of guilt, expiation, and suffering, exemplified by the tragicomic tale "The Jewbird." His first novel, *The Assistant* (1957), similarly derives its mythic grandeur from its evocation of the moral conscience of those first Jewish immigrants but, with its tale of intermarriage, transcends social, racial, and religious division. A short-story collection by **Grace Paley**, *The Little Disturbances of Man* (1959), also broaches these issues of social justice and political activism but scales down weighty topics to their local, intimate, and human aspect by narrating events through a series of distinct multiple voices. Paley's second volume of stories, *Enormous Changes at the Last Minute* (1974), again employs a succession of narrators that, ironically, examine the condition of the Jewish family in modern urban environs.

Using American history as a backdrop for his novels, **E. L. Doctorow** addresses many of these same sociopolitical concerns and attendant ethical questions in a vivid panoramic evocation of the past with his creative coalescence of fact and fiction. His widely acclaimed *The Book of Daniel* (1971) is an imaginative reworking of the events surrounding the Rosenberg spy case that strikingly captures the atmosphere and sentiments of a bygone historic era. Subsequent novels by Doctorow recapture a variety of historical epochs: American society at the beginning of the twentieth century (*Ragtime*, 1975); 1930s New York (*World's Fair*, 1985, and *Billy Bathgate*, 1989); and late nineteenth-century New York (*The Waterworks*, 1994). Doctorow's historical fiction provides cultural barometers of particular historical moments rather than an accurate record of actual events, and the cinematic quality of his writing has produced several screen and stage adaptations of his work. Doctorow's latest novel, *City of God* (2000), adopts an unconventional, fragmentary exposition of narrative (raising important aesthetic, scientific, moral, and historical questions for our own time) to gauge the cultural and intellectual milieu of the twenty-first century. At the turn of the twentieth century, Jewish American writers were still as prolific as ever. Roth published four books in the 1990s (*Patrimony* [1991], *Operation Shylock* [1993], *Sabbath's Theater* [1995], and *American Pastoral* [1997]); Henry Roth's *Mercy of a Rude Stream* appeared along with Tony Kushner's *Angels in America* (both 1994); Erica Jong launched her autobiographical *Fear of Fifty* (1995); Paul Auster's *Ground Work* (1996) went on sale; and Bellow completed a novella, *The Actual* (1997). A *Norton Anthology of Jewish American Literature* was issued in 2001. At the start of the twenty-first century, the continued significance, importance, and interest in Jewish American literature as a major contributor to the past and contemporary literary culture of the United States is assured for generations to come.

Selected Bibliography: Bucher, Irving H. *Isaac Bashevis Singer and the Eternal Past.* New York: New York UP, 1968; Clayton, John Jacob. *Saul Bellow: In Defense of Man.* Bloomington: Indiana UP, 1968; Fowler, Douglas. *Understanding E. L. Doctorow.* Columbia: South Carolina UP, 1992; Fuchs, Daniel. *Saul Bellow: Vision and Revision.* Durham, NC: Duke UP, 1984; Isaacs, Neil David. *Grace Paley: A Study of the Short Fiction.* Boston: Twayne, 1990; Kraemaer, Michael, and Hana Wirth-Nesher. *Cambridge Companion to Jewish-American Literature.* Cambridge: Cambridge UP, 2003; Lee, Hermione. *Philip Roth.* London: Methuen, 1982; Malin, Irvin. *Critical Views of Isaac Bashevis Singer.* New York: New York UP, 1972; Morris, Christopher D. *Models of Misrepresentation: On the Fiction of E. L. Doctorow.*

Jackson: UP of Mississippi, 1991; Ochshorn, Kathleen G. *The Heart's Essential Landscape: Bernard Mala-mud's Hero*. New York: Lang, 1990; Taylor, Jacqueline. *Grace Paley: Illuminating the Dark Lives*. Austin: U of Texas P, 1990; Wade, Stephen. *The Imagination in Transit: The Fiction of Philip Roth*. Sheffield: Sheffield UP, 1996; Wade, Stephen. *Jewish American Literature since 1945: An Introduction*. Edinburgh: Edinburgh UP, 1999.

Mark Sandy

JEWS WITHOUT MONEY (1930), an important proletarian novel by the American leftist writer, editor, and activist **Michael Gold**. The novel is an autobiographical **bildungsroman** whose protagonist, Mikey Gold, seems transparently modeled after Gold himself. Yet the book is more the story of the East Side tenements in which Gold grew up than of Gold himself. Gold's evocation of the poverty and misery that surround life in this neighborhood is powerful and convincing. Some critics have described *Jews without Money* as a crude work of propaganda, and it certainly formed an important part of Gold's campaign to promote the development of **proletarian literature** in America. Yet the language of the book is intense, passionate, and sometimes quite literary, leading James D. Bloom to note that "readers conditioned by misrepresentations of Gold as a crude anti-intellectual hack" might be quite surprised by his "playful feel for the spoken word and his savoring of it throughout" the book (21). Indeed, Bloom concludes that "if a noncanonic program such as proletarian fiction can be said to have produced any classics, then Gold's single novel is its classic, not just a classic of proletarian fiction but of American protest writing" (16).

Jews without Money is actually quite subtle in its critique of capitalism. It does not lecture on the evils of capitalism directly but simply sprinkles its account of childhood in the tenements with numerous descriptions of injustice and intolerance, leaving it to readers to connect these episodes with the effects of the capitalist system. Meanwhile, Gold does not directly apotheosize proletarian class consciousness but counters instances of ethnic intolerance (such as battles among ethnic street gangs) with episodes of collective solidarity, as when neighboring mothers band together to beg door-to-door to help families that have been evicted. Gold does provide some specifically anticapitalist rhetoric, as when the admirable Dr. Isidore Solow advises a sick man that the only medicine he needs is to join a labor union to fight for fair treatment on the job (233). The main activist figure in the text, however, is Mikey's mother, who engenders rent strikes and other forms of resistance, though with very little theoretical consciousness of the implications of her activities. The book's most bitter and impassioned criticisms of capitalism are left to Mikey's father, Herman, a great proponent of the capitalist system but a consistent victim of its inequities. Herman Gold realizes that "one has to be selfish in America. . . . It is dog eat dog over here" (162). But his undeveloped political consciousness does not permit him to envision a viable alternative to the capitalist system in which he finds himself entrapped.

Gold also pays a great deal of attention to the ideological practices used by the American capitalist system to win the willing obedience of the immigrants in the book, even though they are mired in dismal poverty and enjoy few of the benefits of capitalism. For example, religion, in its role as opiate, serves to offer false hopes of salvation that deflect attention from politics. **Popular culture**, meanwhile, offers important visions of escape that tend to discourage political action in the real world.

Jews without Money ultimately points toward a genuine way out of the degradation of the tenement by introducing Mikey to leftist politics in the closing scene, in which he encounters a street-corner orator who proclaims a coming world revolution that will abolish the poverty of workers. While some critics have seen this ending as a sudden, unanticipated quasi-religious conversion, the salvation adduced by Gold at the end of *Jews* has been carefully prepared by the gradual development of Mikey's experiences and by the book's engagement with religion throughout. Mikey's final conversion to revolutionary activism is in fact the very antithesis of religious conversion, offering a better life not in the next world but in this one.

Selected Bibliography: Bloom, James D. *Left Letters: The Culture Wars of Mike Gold and Joseph Freeman*. New York: Columbia UP, 1992; Booker, M. Keith. "Mike Gold or James Joyce? The Literature of Politics and the Politics of Literature." *Socialist Cultures East and West: A Post–Cold War Reassessment*. Ed. Dubravka Juraga and M. Keith Booker. Westport, CT: Praeger, 2002. 81–99; Dickstein, Morris. "Hallucinating the Past: *Jews without Money* Revisited." *Grand Street* 9.2 (Winter 1989): 155–68; Folsom, Michael Brewster. "The Book of Poverty." Review of *Jews without Money* by Michael Gold. *Nation*, 28 February 1966, 242–45; Gold, Michael. *Jews without Money*. 1930. New York: Carroll and Graf, 1984.

M. Keith Booker

JOHN REED CLUBS. Named after the leftist writer **John Reed**, these organizations were the most prominent attempt by the **Communist Party** of the United States (CPUSA) to produce **proletarian literature**. Inspired by similar attempts to mobilize art in the service of communist ideology in the Soviet Union, the John Reed Clubs only lasted from 1929 until 1935, but they nevertheless supported and facilitated the development of a number of prominent leftist writers, including **Nelson Algren**, **Jack Conroy**, **Joseph Freeman**, **Michael Gold**, **Meridel LeSueur**, **Tillie Olsen**, and **Richard Wright**.

Although at their peak there were more than thirty John Reed Clubs in the United States, the New York club was by far the most influential. Founded in 1929, the group's membership quickly grew to more than fifty (including Whittaker Chambers, who two decades later would be the prime government witness against Alger Hiss). In November 1930, the New York club sent delegates to an international conference on proletarian literature in the Ukrainian city of Kharkov. Upon returning, many of these delegates—Freeman perhaps most notable among them—spearheaded the movement to expand the John Reed Clubs around the nation. When the first national congress of John Reed Clubs was held in Chicago in May 1932, there were established clubs in nineteen cities, and the group claimed more than eight hundred individual members, including the young Wright—a new member of the Chicago chapter. Wright would later negatively recount his experiences at this congress and with the John Reed Club in general in a 1944 essay entitled "I Tried to Be a Communist," which he later incorporated into his autobiography, *Black Boy (American Hunger)*. A second congress was held in September 1934, again in Chicago, and this meeting represented the high point of the organization, both in terms of membership and influence.

The John Reed Clubs provided professional mentoring and ideological instruction for young, politically engaged writers, thereby putting the clubs' motto of "Art Is a Class Weapon" into practice. They sponsored lectures by prominent leftist thinkers and conducted workshops on writing techniques and Marxist philosophy. Many of the chapters published their own journals, including *Left Front* in Chicago, *Left Review* in Philadelphia, and the *Partisan* in California. Perhaps the most influential of all these was *Partisan Review*—the house organ of the New York chapter—which drifted away from its communist origins and eventually became a rival to the more established communist publication, *New Masses*.

In part because of this potential schism among "literary workers" but also because of the increasingly vigorous opposition from the political right, the John Reed Clubs were disbanded not long after the Chicago meeting. In their place, the League of American Writers was formed in April 1935 to correspond more closely with the new **Popular Front** policy of incorporating all leftist revolutionary views, not just those of the Communists.

Selected Bibliography: Foley, Barbara. *Radical Representations: Politics and Form in U.S. Proletarian Fiction, 1929–1941.* Durham, NC: Duke UP, 1993; Hemingway, Andrew. *Artists on the Left: American Artists and the Communist Movement, 1926–1956.* New Haven, CT: Yale UP, 2002; Homberger, Eric. *American Writers and Radical Politics: Equivocal Commitments, 1900–39.* New York: St. Martin's P, 1989; Rideout, Walter B. *The Radical Novel in the United States, 1900–1954.* Cambridge: Harvard UP, 1956.

Derek C. Maus

JOHNSON, EMILY PAULINE (TEKAHIONWAKE) (1861–1913).

A Mohawk poet and recitalist, Pauline Johnson was a celebrity artist in English Canada at the turn of the twentieth century, who strove for recognition of First Nations' cultural integrity and political aims. Her poetry, collected in *Flint and Feather* (1912), ranges from romantic and aestheticist lyrics, to popular narratives based on regional legends, to political poems intended to combat popular prejudices regarding Aboriginal peoples. Born on the Six Nations Reserve in Ontario, she grew up committed both to the Loyalist heritage of her mother (a relative of William Dean Howells) and the Iroquois heritage of her father and grandfather (the latter a wampum keeper responsible for tribal histories, from whom she took her Mohawk name). Educated mostly by her mother, Johnson began publishing poetry in the 1880s, and in the 1890s began performing recitals on stage. By 1909, she had toured Canada extensively, as well as the United States and Britain.

In London in 1894, Johnson met the Squamish Chief Su-á-pu-luck (Joe Capilano), the most prominent First Nations activist in British Columbia, who was seeking the support of the Crown against his provincial government. When she settled in Vancouver in 1909, she renewed her bonds with him. After his death in 1910, she helped Su-á-pu-luck's son continue his father's struggles, and crafted a series of heritage stories told to her by Su-á-pu-luck and his wife, Líxwelut (Mary Agnes), in *Legends of Vancouver* (1911). The latter stories blend Johnson's characteristic poetic style with multiple narrative frames and perspectives, explicitly if gently critiquing a history of Aboriginal dispossession from an Aboriginal and maternal feminist perspective.

Selected Bibliography: Keller, Betty. *Pauline.* Vancouver: Douglas and McIntyre, 1981; Strong-Boag, Veronica, and Carole Gerson. *Paddling Her Own Canoe: Times and Texts of E. Pauline Johnson (Tekahionwake).* Toronto: U Toronto P, 2000.

Glenn Willmott

JONES, LEROI. *See* BARAKA, AMIRI.

JONES, LEWIS (1897–1939). The illegitimate child of a domestic servant, Lewis Jones was born in Clydach Vale, South Wales, and started work in the pit at age twelve. He briefly studied to be a mining engineer, then, in 1923, he gained a scholarship to attend the Central Labour College, where he became friendly with the writer Jack Jones (one of his models for the character of Len in his two novels). **Harold Heslop** was another fellow student. In that same year, Jones joined the **Communist Party**, remaining a member until his death despite some criticism of his lack of discipline.

In 1925, Jones returned to Wales and took work as a checkweighman at the Cambrian Colliery in Clydach Vale, where he remained until 1930. However, in 1926 he was imprisoned for three months in Swansea jail for sedition after making speeches in support of the **General Strike**. He appeared in court on several subsequent occasions for "inciting disorder."

Lewis Jones's job ended when he refused to work with scab labor; he became unemployed and active in the Unemployed Workers' Movement, organizing and leading hunger marches, including a 1936 march to London. In 1935, Jones visited the Soviet Union for the Seventh World Congress of the Communist International; he was uneasy with the cult of leadership and reportedly refused to clap or stand at **Stalin**'s name. In 1936, he was elected as one of two Communist Party county councillors for Glamorgan. In addition to his council duties, the last years of Jones's life were occupied with campaigning on behalf of the republican side in the **Spanish Civil War.** He died during the week that Franco's Fascists took Barcelona, after addressing thirty street meetings in a day.

Jones's career as a writer began in 1932 when he began to submit short stories to the *Daily Worker.* He also wrote two pamphlets supporting hunger marchers. However, Jones's reputation as a writer derives from two novels: *Cwmardy* (1937) and *We Live* (1939). Both are set in a Rhondda mining community, offering fictionalized versions of real events and taking industrial and political struggle as their focus. *Cwmardy* covers the period from the 1890s to the end of the First World War while *We Live* includes the General Strike and the Spanish Civil War. A third projected novel would have shown the triumphant return of the International Brigade, sparking a popular revolutionary movement in Britain. The novels are notable for including individuals who resist convention (especially strong women) and scenes of collective action; they also indicate and support a move from old style trade-union activism to the discipline of the Communist Party.

Selected Bibliography: Bell, David. *Ardent Propaganda: Miners' Novels and Class Conflict 1929–39.* Uppsala: Swedish Science P, 1995; Booker, M. Keith. *The Modern British Novel of the Left: A Research Guide.* Westport, CT: Greenwood, 1998; Smith, David. *Lewis Jones.* Cardiff: U of Wales P, 1982.

Kathleen Bell

JOYCE, JAMES (1882–1941). Joyce was born in Rathgar, a fairly well-to-do suburb of Dublin. As the eldest and most promising child, at the age of six he was sent to Clongowes Wood College, a Jesuit-run preparatory school in County Kildare with a good reputation, attended mostly by children of the rising Catholic middle class. Within a few years, his father was no longer able to pay the tuition, as he had been pensioned off from his sinecure at the Office of the Collector of Rates after the fall of the politician Parnell, whom he had vigorously supported. As his family sank into poverty, Joyce attended the less expensive Belvedere College, and was then admitted to University College Dublin, which itself had been handed over to the Jesuits to manage.

During his university years, Joyce was exposed to the Irish nationalist movement, which encouraged an interest in Irish sports and the Irish language; he had little enthusiasm for either of these, although he resented the colonial status of Ireland. The young Joyce was enthusiastic about the poetry of **W. B. Yeats**, although he opposed most of the principles on which Yeats and George Russell were establishing the Irish literary revival, especially their stress on the peasantry as a repository of virtue and wisdom. Despite the traditional university curriculum, Joyce became aware of contemporary European writing at the turn of the century, and distinguished himself as an undergraduate by publishing a laudatory essay on "**Ibsen**'s New Drama" in the *Fortnightly Review*.

In 1904, Joyce left Ireland with Nora Barnacle, a hotel maid, without benefit of marriage as a protest against both church and state. They lived first in Pola and then in Trieste, where Joyce taught at the Berlitz school and attempted to publish his collection of rather naturalistic short stories entitled *Dubliners*. Two years after that book finally appeared in 1914, Joyce's innovative autobiographical novel *A Portrait of the Artist as a Young Man* was published with the encouragement of Ezra Pound. Although some English reviewers noted that the young men in the book all seemed to share an antipathy and distrust for England, the book's protagonist Stephen Dedalus rejects his friend Davin's call to join his group of nationalists, and when the other UC students protest Yeats's play *Countess Cathleen* as a libel on Irish womanhood, Dedalus alone opposes them in the name of artistic freedom.

Begun in Trieste and finished in Paris, *Ulysses*, published in 1922, brought Joyce international fame and was quickly accepted as a central text of modernism, though it was also controversial, banned in the United States as pornographic until 1934. An unapologetically difficult book, formally complex and self-referential, *Ulysses* was for many years taken as proof that Joyce, like the other major modernist authors, was apolitical; it was taken to be art for art's sake, a word world that anticipated the even more hermetic and inscrutable *Finnegans Wake* (1939). Joyce's writing was routinely attacked by Marxist critics as an example of bourgeois self-involvement and aesthetic mystification. Joyce claimed to be baffled by this dismissal, and pointed out that virtually all his characters were lower middle class.

While psychological, mythic, and aesthetic approaches to Joyce's work dominated the 1940s through the 1960s, by the 1980s, a few critics—including Joyce's biographer Richard Ellmann and Dominic Manganiello—pointed out that Joyce's Trieste library had included a great deal of political writing, traces of which could easily be found in *Ulysses* and even *Portrait*. In early letters, Joyce claimed to be a Socialist, and his early reading included work by the American anarchist Benjamin Tucker. As politically oriented criticism became increasingly acceptable in the academy, more critics began to find that *Ulysses* was seriously concerned with Dublin's colonial (and, by 1922, its postcolonial) condition, not to mention with Irish anti-Semitism, which Joyce portrays as an obvious distraction from real conditions of oppression. Vincent Cheng's *Joyce, Race, and Empire* (1995) explored these and other themes, finding an abiding political concern throughout Joyce's work, including *Finnegans Wake*. Trevor Williams helps articulate the current-consensus notion of Joyce in showing him to be, like Woolf, a subscriber to the left-wing, "progressive" wing of modernism.

A branch of poststructuralist criticism adopted Joyce as an example of writing that through its very violation of literary and linguistic norms constitutes a protest more fundamental than what Socialism offers; Colin MacCabe is probably the best early example of this, while Patrick McGee's *Paperspace* is a well-developed reading of *Ulysses* along those lines. Meanwhile, feminist critics explored Joyce's sexual politics, some of them arguing that his work shows a misogyny typical of the time, while others, including Marilyn French, insist that Joyce carefully highlighted sexual inequalities through the limitations of his protagonist Stephen Dedalus. Exploring some of the same concerns, Richard Brown's *James Joyce and Sexuality* shows the connection between Joyce and turn-of-the-century writers on sexuality and politics such as Havelock Ellis, while Katherine Mullin's recent work portrays Joyce as consciously engaged in a cultural and political struggle with the "social purity" movement.

Selected Bibliography: Booker, M. Keith. Ulysses, *Capitalism, and Colonialism: Reading Joyce after the Cold War.* Westport, CT: Greenwood, 2000; Brown, Richard. *James Joyce and Sexuality.* Cambridge: Cambridge UP, 1985; Cheng, Vincent. *Joyce, Race, and Empire.* Cambridge: Cambridge UP, 1995; Ellmann, Richard. *The Consciousness of Joyce.* Oxford: Oxford UP, 1977; French, Marilyn. *The Book as World.* Cambridge, MA: Harvard UP, 1975; Gibson, Andrew. *Joyce's Revenge: History, Politics and Aesthetics in "Ulysses."* Oxford: Oxford UP, 2002; Kershner, R. Brandon. *Joyce, Bakhtin, and Popular Literature.* Chapel Hill: U of North Carolina P, 1989; MacCabe, Colin. *James Joyce and the Revolution of the Word.* London: Macmillan, 1978; Manganiello, Dominic. *Joyce's Politics.* London: Routledge and Kegan Paul, 1980; McGee, Patrick. *Paperspace.* Lincoln: U of Nebraska P, 1988; Mullin, Katherine. *James Joyce, Sexuality and Social Purity.* Cambridge: Cambridge UP, 2003; Nolan, Emer. *James Joyce and Nationalism.* London: Routledge, 1995; Scott, Bonnie Kime. *Joyce and Feminism.* Bloomington: Indiana UP, 1984; Williams, Trevor. *Joyce's Politics.* Gainesville: UP of Florida, 1997.

R. Brandon Kershner

◦ K ◦

KANE, SARAH (1971–1999). Despite the brevity of her career (she committed suicide after a long bout with depression), Sarah Kane managed, in her drama, to bring controversy back to the English Stage Company (ESC) in the 1990s. Inaugurating what has retrospectively been dubbed "the New Brutalism" and "In-Yer-Face Theater," Kane's five plays show a distinct development from something akin to social realism in *Blasted* (1995) to a full-fledged absurdism in *4.48 Psychosis* (2000). Throughout, however, an Artaudian strain of cruelty, prevalent also in the works of **Edward Bond** and Howard Brenton, links her drama to the ESC's fifty-year tradition of political theater. In *Blasted*, the distant brutalities of compartmentalized contemporary military atrocity make themselves uncannily, graphically, and inexplicably felt in a Leeds hotel room, where a reporter has just raped a mentally handicapped young woman. The play, in its abrupt temporal shifts, links the apparently local, isolated, domestic brutality of rape to the recognizably global atrocities of genocide and torture. Kane's *4.48 Psychosis*, produced and published posthumously, marks the distance her dramaturgy traversed in less than a decade. The text—a series of disjointed reflections, rants, narratives, reminiscences, and enactments of and about depression and anxiety—dispenses with set and character, leaving itself radically open to interpretation. The resulting play of signifiers—at times, sequences of numbers or patterned repetitions of verbs—suggests a posthumanist concept of identity that resists depth reading and instead embraces a model of identity and agency more closely aligned with postmodern techniques of bricolage and pastiche. The politics of her works range from representations of military and social atrocity to Foucaultian investigation of the social constructions of abnormality, deviance, and madness.

Selected Bibliography: Cohn, Ruby. "Sarah Kane: Architect of the Theater." *Cycnos* 18.1 (2001): 39–49; Rabellato, Dan. "Sarah Kane: An Appreciation." *New Theatre Quarterly* 15 (1999): 280–81; Saunders, Graham. *Love Me or Kill Me: Sarah Kane and the Theatre of Extremes.* Manchester: Manchester UP, 2002; Sellar, Tom. "Truth and Dare: Sarah Kane's *Blasted.*" *Theater* 27.1 (1997): 29–34.

Craig N. Owens

KATAEV, VALENTIN PETROVICH (1897–1986). Born in Odessa, Kataev published his first poem in 1910, foreshadowing the considerable contribution he would make to Soviet literature in the form of poetry, drama, and prose. He began writing stories in 1916. After the **Russian Revolution** of 1917, Kataev moved to Moscow and worked for the newspaper *Gudok*. His early style is easily recognizable with its specific romantic flavor, characteristic of the southern Odessa school. During the relatively relaxed literary atmosphere of the New Economic Policy (NEP) period, Kataev wrote a novel, *The Embezzlers* (1926), and a play, *Squaring the Circle* (1927). The novel is a comic tale of two employees of a Moscow trust who embezzle some money and go on a merry romp in search of "high society." The play is a comedy based on the housing shortage in Moscow during the 1920s, and deals with the new morality of a new regime. Until the 1960s, Kataev was known mostly for his works of this period and, to a lesser degree, for his two novels written in the 1930s: *Time Forward* (1932), a novel about the building of an industrial complex at Magnitogorsk during the first Five-Year Plan, and *The Lone White Sail* (1936), a book that gave him a reputation as a writer of children's books.

During the Great Patriotic War (1941–1945), Kataev served as a correspondent at the front for the newspapers *Pravda* and *Krasnaia Zvezda*. The war impressions became the basis of his novel *Son of the Regiment* (1945). Another novel, *For the Power of the Soviets* (1949), is a portrayal of the underground activities of partisans in Odessa during **World War II**.

In the 1950s and 1960s, Kataev was the editor of the journal *Youth*, where he oversaw publications of young writers such as Aksenov, Gladilin, and Yevtushenko. A turning point in Kataev's literary career was his *The Little Iron Door in the Wall* (1964), a subjective account of **Vladimir Lenin** and his life on Capri and in Paris. The book brought forth negative responses from Soviet critics, who accused Kataev of letting his own personality dominate that of Lenin. In 1966, the literary magazine *Novy mir* published *The Holy Well*, a remarkable lyrical-philosophical account of dreams experienced while the narrator is under anaesthesia for surgery. Clearly reflecting the influence of Proust, **Joyce**, and Kafka, Kataev weaves scenes of his family, friends, and lovers, events of Soviet history, and his travels in America into a kind of stream-of-consciousness autobiography. Kataev's relentless imagination, sensitivity, and originality made him one of the most distinguished Soviet writers. Other volumes of reminiscences include *The Grass of Oblivion* (1967), *A Mosaic of Life; or, The Magic Horn of Oberon* (1972), *The Cemetery at Skuliany* (1975), *My Diamond Crown* (1978), *Werter Has Been Written* (1980), and *The Adolescent's Novel* (1983).

Selected Bibliography: Borden, Richard C. *The Art of Writing Badly: Valentin Kataev's Mauvism and the Rebirth of Russian Modernism.* Evanston, IL: Northwestern UP, 1999; Russell, Robert. *Valentin Kataev.* Boston: Twayne, 1981; Szarycz, Ireneusz. *Poetics of Valentin Kataev's Prose of the 1960s and 1970s.* New York: Peter Lang, 1989.

Ireneusz Szarycz

KILLENS, JOHN OLIVER (1916–1987). Raised in a politicized, intellectual, and relatively comfortable home in Macon, Georgia, Killens attributed much of his inspiration as a writer to his great-grandmother's memories of slavery. Recalling her declaration that "the half ain't never been told," Killens committed himself to telling that half. His fiction, drama, and essays eloquently document the struggles and triumphs of African Americans faced with innumerable manifestations of racism. Reflecting on his political development near the end of his life, Killens elaborated on his lineage: "philosophically speaking, **Du Bois** was my grandfather, Robeson was my father, and Malcolm was my brother" (296).

After attending several colleges, Killens abandoned his pursuit of a law degree and instead worked for the National Labor Relations Board and the Congress of Industrial Organizations as a labor organizer and served in the military during **World War II**. Killens's first novel, *Youngblood* (1954), was the pioneer publication of the Harlem Writers Guild, which he helped to found in 1950. The story of an African Ameircan family's travails in a Georgia town, *Youngblood* contains many of the themes that would characterize most of Killens's work: positive representations of African American men and women who often move from individual to collective struggle; the varied forms of racism and resistance; an astute analysis of racialized capitalism and social class; and the unifying role of African American expressive and persuasive traditions, including spirituals, sermons, folklore, and humor. His Pulitzer Prize–nominated second novel about an African American army unit's fight for double victory within the segregated military during World War II, *And Then We Heard the Thunder* (1962), drew more directly on his own experiences as a soldier and an emergent, politically committed writer. Despite the accolades Killens would earn (including a second Pulitzer Prize nomination for his 1971 *Cotillion: One Good Bull Is Half the Herd*), some literary critics have charged that his writing is often "flat" or "didactic." Such critiques usually also take issue with Killens's incisive portrayal of racist violence—a feature of his writing that others venerate.

During the 1960s, Killens was a vocal participant in the civil rights and black power movements. Though respectful of his friend Martin Luther King Jr.'s nonviolent philosophy, Killens advocated self-defense and questioned the feasibility of integration. A contributor to the composition of Malcolm X's Organization of Afro-American Unity charter, Killens was committed to Pan-Africanism and the building of economic, cultural, and community institutions as empowerment strategies. His political views and artistic accomplishments made him a central figure for the **black arts movement**. In addition to his fiction, dramas, screenplays, and essays, Killens's contribution to radical literature and politics can be measured by the conferences he organized, furthering his influence on younger writers and the evolution of a politically committed African American literature.

Selected Bibliography: Gayle, Addison, Jr. *The Way of the World: The Black Novel in America*. Garden City, NY: Doubleday, 1975; Gilyard, Keith. *Liberation Memories: The Rhetoric and Poetics of John Oliver Killens*. Detroit: Wayne State UP, 2003; Killens, John Oliver. "The Half Ain't Never Been Told." *Contemporary Authors: Autobiography Series*. Vol. 2. Ed. Adele Sarkissian. Detroit: Gale, 1985; Lehman, Paul R. *The Development of the Black Psyche in the Writings of John Oliver Killens (1916–1987)*. Lewiston, NY: Edwin Mellon, 2003.

Rachel Peterson

KIPLING, RUDYARD (1865–1936). Kipling was the first major English author to receive renown from tales about India. He was born in the coastal city of Bombay (now Mumbai) to expatriate English parents. His father, John Lockwood Kipling, was a teacher of sculpture and the director of the Lahore Museum. Kipling went to England at a rather early age and completed his college education in 1882. He returned to India the same year to work as a journalist for the *Civil and Military Gazette*, located in Lahore. Meanwhile, he was publishing poetry and fiction, and several pieces appeared in the *Gazette* and other journals. He eventually returned to England and also spent a number of years in the United States, possibly at the behest of his American wife, whom he married in 1892. They returned to England a few years later and settled in Sussex. *Kim*, Kipling's best-known work, was published in 1901. Other works followed *Kim*, firmly establishing his reputation as an author. He was awarded the Nobel Prize for Literature in 1907, becoming the first Englishman to win the distinction.

Adored by his admirers, Kipling was prolific. Particularly in the genre of colonial writing, he was seen as the author who possessed an insider's knowledge of the natives, because the Englishmen he creates in his fiction display remarkable understanding of the complexities of native cultures. His reputation, on the other hand, declined over time—even during his lifetime. His jingoism seemed extreme even to some of his right-wing contemporaries. His "White Man's Burden," the poem he wrote to assert the supremacy of white males, testifies to his undisguised chauvinism. As it heaps lavish praise on imperial ventures of all sorts, investing them with high moral missions, it declares all nonwhites to be "Half devil and half child."

Kipling's short stories, written primarily for young readers, earned huge popularity. His long fictions, on the other hand, were less successful, with the exception of *Kim*. Though unequivocal in its faith in the salubrious effect of British rule in India, this novel draws on Kipling's full powers as a storyteller. It describes the life of Kim, an Irish boy orphaned in childhood in India. Kim grows up as a street urchin in the city of Lahore; such is his assimilation into Indian culture that he is regarded as one of the natives. At an early age, Kim becomes the disciple of a Tibetan lama who has come to India on a holy quest. Circumstances change when Kim draws the attention of Colonel Creighton, an anthropologist secretly running the British intelligence service in India known as "the Great Game," which is primarily designed to prevent Russian expansion, to preempt a rival imperial threat that India's perilous northern border makes distinctly viable. Trained in the art of the Game, Kim provides valuable services to the empire. The story ends when he and his Tibetan guru successfully foil a Russian move to instigate rebellion among northern rajas.

Selected Bibliography: Lycett, Andrew. *Rudyard Kipling.* London: Weidenfeld and Nicolson, 1999; McBranty, John. *Imperial Subjects, Imperial Space: Rudyard Kipling's Fiction of the Native-Born.* Columbus: Ohio UP, 2002; Moore-Gilbert, B. J. *Kipling and "Orientalism."* New York: St. Martin's, 1986; Randall, Don. *Kipling's Imperial Boy: Adolescence and Cultural Hybridity.* London: Palgrave, 2000.

Farhad B. Idris

KIŠ, DANILO (1935–1989) was one of the most celebrated cultural icons of post–**World War II** Yugoslavia. Despite his relatively brief oeuvre, his literary work as well as his theoretical and political polemics addressed issues crucial to the Yugoslav cultural scene. Kiš was born in Subotica, of a Jewish father and Montenegrin Serb mother. His father, an inspector of the Yugoslav railways, was deported to a concentration camp, where he perished during the war. Kiš's own family background is crucial to his "family cycle" novels, which include *Bašta, pepeo* (*Garden, Ashes*, 1965), *Rani jadi* (*Early Sorrows,* 1969), and *Peščanik* (*Hourglass*, 1972). Lyrically detached, these works depict the chaos of postwar Europe, the loss and disorientation of its people, and their overwhelming sense of alienation and solitude. Kiš received the prestigious NIN literary award for *Peščanik.*

In addition to their ironic and lyrical quality, Kiš's early novels contain central elements that will significantly inform his later works, particularly the intertwining of factual and fictional elements in order to create a fantastic, parallel universe, and a documentary style imposed on a world of literary imagination. While his early novels borrowed facts from his family life, Kiš utilizes facts from world history and politics in his later works. His most famous novel—*Grobnica za Borisa Davidoviča* (*A Tomb for Boris Davidovich*, 1976)—is written as a closely interconnected collection of stories with characters resurfacing in different stories. The novel focuses on the fate of Russian and European revolutionaries at the hands of the Stalinist Comintern in the 1930s. Borrowing from historical and biographical works of other authors, Kiš weaves a nightmarish picture of the 1930s Soviet landscape.

Although Kiš received the Vjesnik Award for the novel, its publication was a major scandal in Yugoslavia, even though Yugoslavia and its Stalinist past are never mentioned explicitly. Kiš's specific engagement with the historical reality of Stalinism adds a great deal of substance to his text, but it seems safe to assume that the novel is not so much a historical analysis of Stalinism as a cautionary tale about the potential horrors of an ideology that still posed a threat to his own contemporary Yugoslavia. However, presumably ignoring these political implications of the novel, a number of critics attacked Kiš for his aesthetic principles and accused him of plagiarism. This battle went on until 1978, when Kiš seemed to settle the account with the publication of his theoretical tour de force *Čas anatomije* (Anatomy Lesson). Modeling his book on **Miroslav Krleža**'s *Dijalektički antibarbarus*, Kiš attacked his opponents for their ignorance and incompetence, critically dissecting their own aesthetic views. He brilliantly exposed the hollowness of their arguments and their shortcomings as literary theoreticians and critics.

As a consequence of this controversy, Kiš moved to France, where he spent the rest of his life, visiting Yugoslavia only sporadically. He taught Serbo-Croatian and Yugoslav literature at the Universities of Strasbourg, Bordeaux, and Lille. While in exile, Kiš published *Enciklopedija mrtvih* (*Encyclopedia of the Dead,* 1985), his last major work for which he received the Ivo Andrić Award. Heavily influenced by Jorge Luis Borges, the novel's main theme is death and its metaphysical variations. Aware of his fast spreading lung cancer, Kiš uses the novel to meditate on human mortality. Despite his life being cut so short, he remains one of the most influential Yugoslav writers. Controversies surrounding his name and work influenced many Yugoslav authors from mid-1970 onward, and enabled the younger generation to question issues of ideology, history, and politics that were unchallenged until then. Together with **Milan Kundera**, György Konrád, and **Czeslaw Milosz**, Danilo Kiš belongs to a circle of central European writers who defined the cultural horizon of that region during the second part of the twentieth century.

Selected Bibliography: Birnbaum, Marianna D. "History and Human Relationships in the Fiction of Danilo Kiš." *Cross Currents* 8 (1989): 346–60; Juraga, Dubravka, and M. Keith Booker. "Literature, Power, and Oppression in Stalinist Russia and Catholic Ireland: Danilo Kiš's Use of Joyce in *A Tomb for Boris Davidovich.*" *South Atlantic Review* 58.4 (November 1993): 39–58; Longinović, Tomislav. "Danilo Kiš" in *Dictionary of Literary Biography: South Slavic Writers since World War II.* Detroit: Gale Research, 1997; Matvejević, Predrag. "Danilo Kiš: *Encyclopedia of the Dead.*" *Cross Currents* 7 (1988): 337–49.

Dubravka Juraga

KLUGE, ALEXANDER (1932–). Born the son of a doctor in Halberstadt; schooled in Berlin, Marburg, and Frankfurt; and recipient of a doctorate in law in 1956, Kluge has gone on to become one of the most visible and prolific cultural figures of post– **World War II** Germany. Describing himself as the "rear guard of **modernism,**" he has worked with eminent personalities from the first two-thirds of the twentieth century in nearly every artistic field: filming with Fritz Lang, advising the Institute for Social Research (**the Frankfurt School**) on legal affairs, and reading regularly for the literary elite of the Gruppe 47. Better known to English-speaking audiences as a film-maker and critical theorist who first came to prominence in the early 1960s, Kluge is also, perhaps above all, a writer, who published his first collection of stories, *Lebensläufe,* in 1962. These "case histories" often reappeared as parts of films: most famously, "Anita G." became the basis for *Abschied von gestern* (Yesterday Girl, 1966)—one of the inaugural films of the New German Cinema, of which Kluge was a prime mover, both artistically and institutionally. Since the mid-1980s, he has shifted from making feature-length films to working in mainstream television, re-defining the viewing possibilities of cultural-magazine, documentary, and "talking-head" programming. Kluge has steadily published film books, works of social philosophy (often authored in collaboration with Oskar Negt), and literature while pursuing his activities in the visual media, and in 2003 garnered Germany's most coveted literary award, the Georg-Büchner-Preis.

Central to all of Kluge's endeavors are concepts taken from and advancing the ideas of seminal modernists of the Left such as **Theodor Adorno, Walter Benjamin,** and **Bertolt Brecht,** who were concerned (albeit differently) with the aesthetic politics of representation after the advent of mass culture. His literature is marked by multi-plicity and fragmentation in narrative perspective, and by a rejection of narrow his-torical teleology and simplistic causalities that paint coincidence as fate. Especially characteristic is the montage of different forms—images, graphs, documentary ma-terials, footnotes, and fiction—that stresses textual gaps in order to give room to the conscious and unconscious fantasy of the audience. The aim is to help foster a *Gegenöffentlichkeit* (counter public sphere), where bourgeois institutions and modes of channeling experience no longer hold sway over thought and desire.

Selected Bibliography: Hansen, Miriam. "Alexander Kluge, Cinema and the Public Sphere: The Con-struction Site of Counter-History." *Discourse: Journal for Theoretical Studies in Media and Culture* 6 (Fall 1983): 53–74; Hansen, Miriam. "Unstable Mixtures, Dilated Spheres: Negt and Kluge's *The Public*

Sphere and Experience, Twenty Years Later." *Public Culture* 5.2 (Winter 1993): 179–212; Hansen, Miriam, ed. Special Issue on Alexander Kluge. *New German Critique: An Interdisciplinary Journal of German Studies* 49 (Winter 1990); Kluge, Alexander. *Chronik der Gefühle*. Vol. 1: "Basisgeschichten"; vol. 2: "Lebensläufe." Frankfurt am Main: Suhrkamp Verlag, 2000; Kluge, Alexander. *Die Wächter des Sarkophags: 10 Jahre Tschernobyl*. Hamburg: Rotbuch, 1996; Kluge, Alexander. *Gelegenheitsarbeit einer Sklavin: Zur realistischen Methode*. Frankfurt am Main: Suhrkamp Verlag, 1975; Kluge, Alexander. *In Gefahr und grösster Not bringt der Mittelweg den Tod: Texte zu Kino, Film, Politik*. Berlin: Vorwerk 8, 2002; Kluge, Alexander. *Schlachtbeschreibung*. Frankfurt am Main: Suhrkamp Verlag, 1964, 1978, 1983; Kluge, Alexander, and Oskar Negt. *Geschichte und Eigensinn*. Vols. 1–3. Frankfurt am Main: Suhrkamp Verlag, 1981; Kluge, Alexander, and Oskar Negt. *Öffentlichkeit und Erfahrung; zur Organisationsanalyse von bürgerlicher und proletarischer Öffentlichkeit*. Frankfurt am Main: Suhrkamp Verlag, 1972; Lutze, Peter. *Alexander Kluge: The Last Modernist*. Detroit: Wayne State UP, 1998; Muller, Harro. "In solche Not kann nicht die Natur bringen': Stichworte zu Alexander Kluges Schlachtbeschreibung." *Merkur:-Deutsche-Zeitschrift-fur-europaisches-Denken* 36.9 (Sept. 1982): 888–97; Schulte, Christane, and Winfried Siebers, eds. *Kluges Fernsehen: Alexander Kluges Kulturmagazine*. Frankfurt am Main: Suhrkamp, 2002.

John E. Davidson

KOESTLER, ARTHUR (1905–1983). Born in Budapest, Koestler was the only son of Austro-Hungarian Jewish parents. Although best remembered as the author of *Darkness at Noon*, Koestler shaped the political world more deeply than in this one powerful depiction of Stalinist terror. From 1922 until 1926, he studied science at the polytechnic in Vienna, where he became a devoted Zionist. He left the university before graduation to go to Palestine. His experiences there served as inspiration for his first novel, *Thieves in the Night* (1946). He left Palestine in 1927 after being hired by Ullstein's, a German newspaper concern. He first worked for them as a correspondent in Paris. In 1930, he moved to Berlin, where he became science editor of the *Vossische Zeitung* and foreign editor of the *Berliner Zeitung am Mittag*.

In 1931, Koestler joined the German **Communist Party**. Within a year, he left his position with Ullstein's and toured the Soviet Union in order to study that nation's Five-Year Plan. In 1933, he moved to Paris, where he worked for three years for the **Comintern**. At the outbreak of the **Spanish Civil War** (1936–1939), Koestler volunteered to go to Spain as a spy for the Comintern. After several such trips, he was arrested by the nationalists and sentenced to death. Due to public pressure in England, however, he was released. He wrote of his experiences in prison in *Spanish Testament* (1938), later revised as *Dialogue with Death* (1942). An important period of his life ends in 1938 with his resignation from the Communist Party, disillusioned with Stalinism and the Moscow show trials. His signature work, *Darkness at Noon*, was first published in 1940. With this book, his reputation was established, and Koestler became one of the principal spokesmen among anticommunist intellectuals.

In 1939, the French imprisoned him as a suspicious foreigner. This incarceration became the subject of an autobiographical work, *Scum of the Earth* (1941). After his release, Koestler joined the French foreign legion and eventually escaped to England, where he spent 1941 and 1942 in the British Pioneer Corps. In *The God That Failed* (1950), Koestler wrote of his personal disillusionment with Communism. This book contains similar testimonies from other ex–fellow travelers such as André Gide, Stephen Spender, **Richard Wright**, and Ignazio Silone. In 1955, Koestler announced in *The Trial of the Dinosaur and Other Essays* (written 1945–1954) that he was through with political writing.

In 1959, Koestler began a new phase in his writing career with a history of astronomy, *The Sleepwalkers: A History of Man's Changing Vision of the Universe*. Other notable books from this period include two volumes on the psychology of creativity, *The Act of Creation* (1964) and *Ghost in the Machine* (1967). In 1965, Koestler married Cynthia Jefferies. They lived in London, where he wrote numerous books and essays on a number of topics, until they both committed suicide on March 3, 1983.

Selected Bibliography: Cesarani, David. *Arthur Koestler: The Homeless Mind*. New York: Free P, 1998; Hamilton, Iain. *Koestler: A Biography*. London: Macmillan, 1982; Koestler, Cynthia. *Stranger on the Square*. Ed. Harold Harris. London: Hutchinson, 1984.

Andrea Tyndall

KOLLONTAI, ALEXANDRA MIKHAILOVNA DOMONTOVICH (1873–1952)

was born into a Russian aristocratic family of Finnish descent. In 1893, she married Vladimir Kollontai, an engineer. While observing his professional work, she had an opportunity to see the deplorable conditions of the Russian working class. This had a major impact on her, and she became involved in lifelong political work centered on the improvement of these conditions. She began to study Marxism and, in 1899, leaving her husband and her son behind, went to Zurich to study political economy and Marxism, eventually becoming a leading figure in Soviet politics. Her main focus was the improvement of women's social and political status.

A skilled orator, Kollontai was often sought to speak at public meetings or to workers in factories, to write speeches, and to do propaganda work. She also used her public skills abroad, most often in Western Europe. In 1907, she participated in the international conference of socialist women in Germany. In 1909, she joined the German Social Democratic Party; in 1910, she participated at the 8th Congress of the Second International. In 1915, Kollontai, a Menshevik, joined the Bolshevik faction of the Social Democrats in support of their antiwar position. A productive writer, she wrote pamphlets, essays, speeches, lectures, and books.

During the **Russian Revolution** and the years that followed, Kollontai was politically active on many different fronts. In 1917, she was the only woman elected to the Central Committee and the first commissar of social welfare. In 1919, she became the commissar of propaganda and agitation of the Ukraine, but by the end of the year, she refocused her attention on women's issues and the Zhenotdel, the department dealing with these issues.

Kollontai was instrumental in changing marriage and family laws after the revolution, as well as a variety of other social and welfare legislation. She emphasized the need to involve women in political life and argued that women's issues had to be addressed at the same time as other political and economic issues. Her often misunderstood radical views concerned sexual politics; personal relations; and marriage, love, and sexuality unfettered by bourgeois property relations. In all her writings, political as well as fictional, she emphasized the importance of women's emancipation, especially their economic independence. A striking woman of great beauty and charm, with a flamboyant lifestyle reflecting her ideas, she was often regarded critically by her comrades.

Kollontai's prolific oeuvre includes "The Social Basis of the Woman's Question" (1909), "The New Morality and the Working Class" (1918), "The Family and the Communist State," "Women Workers Struggle for their Rights" (1919), "The Working Woman and the Peasant Woman in Soviet Russia," "Prostitution and Ways of Fighting It" (1921), "Make Way for the Winged Eros" (1923), and "About the New Law on the Family and Marriage" (1926). Her major fictional works include the trilogies *A Great Love* (1927) and *Love of Worker Bees* (1923). The story "Vasilisa Malygina" from the latter trilogy is known as ***Red Love*** in its English translation. *The Autobiography of a Sexually Emancipated Woman* (1920) examines the ways an emancipated and independent woman addresses issues of sexuality and love.

During 1920, she supported the Workers' Opposition faction of the Bolshevik Party, which criticized the party for its lack of democracy and increasing bureaucratization. As a consequence, the post of advisor to the Soviet legation in Norway, which came in 1922, was a diplomatic way of removing her from political activity in the Soviet Union. From then on, her career was in the field of diplomacy: she served as an ambassador to Norway and Sweden, a trade delegate to Mexico, and a delegate to the League of Nations. She was an advisor to the Soviet Ministry of Foreign Affairs when she died of a heart attack in 1952.

Selected Bibliography: Clements, Barbara Evans. *Bolshevik Feminist: The Life of Aleksandra Kollontai.* Bloomington: Indiana UP, 1979; Ebert, Teresa L. "Left of Desire." *Cultural Logic* 3.1 (Fall 1999–Spring 2000) http://eserver.org/clogic/3-1%262/ebert.html; Farnsworth, Beatrice. *Aleksandra Kollontai: Socialism, Feminism, and the Bolshevik Revolution.* Stanford, CA: Stanford UP, 1980; Holt, Alix, ed. *Alexandra Kollontai: Selected Writings, with an Introduction and Commentaries by Alix Holt.* New York: Norton, 1977; Ingermanson, Birgitta. "The Political Function of Domestic Objects in the Fiction of Aleksandra Kollontai." *Slavic Review* (Spring 1989): 71–82.

Dubravka Juraga

KRAUS, KARL (1874–1936), editor of the Austrian satirical magazine *Die Fackel* (The Torch), which he founded in 1899, was a pioneering critic of militarism and the media. At the outbreak of **World War I**, he delivered a speech entitled "In These Great Times," challenging the propaganda of the belligerent nations. "How is the world governed and how do wars begin?" he asked, in a cryptic aphorism, and provided his own reply: "Diplomats tell lies to journalists and believe them when they see them in print." He continued to campaign against militarism throughout the war, circumventing censorship by means of ingenious quotations contrasting official communiqués with snippets of information revealing the true face of modern warfare. This documentary technique underlies his masterpiece, *The Last Days of Mankind* (1919), a dramatic panorama of the folly and cruelty of war. Government officials and newspaper reporters are condemned to regurgitate their own platitudinous words in a grotesque sequence of scenes that culminates in a vision of the end of the world. The view that the capitalist world is incurably militaristic led the satirist to foresee a clash of civilizations from which China might emerge as the one power capable of establishing peace on earth. The tragic chorus consists of dialogues between the Optimist and the Grumbler, which expose the "technoromantic adventure" of modern warfare: heroic metaphors used to justify the use of poison gas and euphemisms to legitimate the bombing of civilian targets. The play shows how inhuman events are converted into "shows" and "stories" through slick interviews, saturation press coverage, and the tendentious use of newsreel cameras.

Kraus was among the first to identify the hypnotic capacity of the modern media to create a world in their own image, insisting that "the report *is* the reality." Press reports about supposed atrocities provoke readers to commit actual atrocities. He approached politics through language, combining a Wittgensteinian sensitivity to conceptual muddles with a Popperian hostility to ideological thinking. The absurdities of propaganda are exposed by highlighting clichés like "standing shoulder to shoulder," while his deconstruction of plausible neologisms like "military justice" and "protective custody" reveals the brutal practices of the modern state. The close focus on language makes it difficult to translate his dense and allusive German style, which combines the playfulness of Austrian popular comedy with the radicalism of Orwell's attack on double-speak. He identified what we now call "spin" as an insidious means of converting news into propaganda, arguing that the vacuous "chatter" of peacetime journalism renders public opinion vulnerable to more malign forms of propaganda. He did not live to witness the emergence of media-generated "virtual reality" in the television age, but his ideas have been taken up by more recent critics of the nexus between mass communications, global corporations, and the military-industrial complex.

Kraus was actively involved in the campaign for sexual liberation that originated in Freud's Vienna and culminated in the work of Wilhelm Reich, but he distanced himself from the therapeutic claims of psychoanalysis, which he defined as "the disease which it purports to cure." Where Freud interpreted childhood memories of being beaten as fantasies, Kraus saw battered children as victims of the social violence that pervaded the patriarchal family and authoritarian forms of education. After the collapse of the Hapsburg Empire in 1918, he supported the Austrian Republic, especially the innovative policies of Red Vienna, but he became disillusioned with the Social Democrats, not least because of their German nationalist tendencies. He admired the radicalism of Rosa Luxemburg, with whom he shared both a hatred of war and a love of animals. Implacably opposed to nationalism in all its forms, he supported Masaryk's Czechoslovakia as an experiment in multicultural democracy, but he remained hostile to the liberal conception of "freedom of the press," which he saw as the source of pervasive mystification.

To counteract what he saw as a journalistic civilization, Kraus took to the public platform, giving a total of seven hundred recitals over a period of twenty-five years. In addition to his own satirical poetry and polemical prose, he recited works by a range of other authors, including **Goethe** and **Shakespeare**, **Gogol**, Offenbach, Wedekind, and **Brecht**. This enabled him to mobilize a revitalized form of "cultural memory" against both shallow modernists and benighted nationalists, using music to heighten the effect of his performances. He responded to political crises by citing prophetic passages from the Bible, although his attitude toward religion was ambivalent. Renouncing his Jewish origins, he criticized what he saw as excessive Jewish influence in the press and show business, but conversion to Catholicism did not inhibit him from satirizing the obscurantism of the churches. His imagination was shaped by biblical myths, from the Creation to the Apocalypse, and his Judaic heritage found secularized expression in a commitment to the rule of law that led him to fight innumerable court cases against ideological opponents.

The focus on propaganda provides the link between Kraus's satire on the decadence of the Hapsburg Empire and his critique of the rise of National Socialism. He identified the dangers of "creeping Fascism" long before Hitler's seizure of power, and went on to expose the duplicity of Nazi propaganda in *Third Walpurgis Night*, a prophetic analysis written during the summer of 1933. Unlike other antifascist authors who relied on a black-and-white schema, he argued that Nazism was not the opposite of liberal democracy but an extension of the oppressive potential that lies at the heart of Western civilization, with its reliance on mass communications and military power. He supported the last-ditch attempts of the government of Engelbert Dollfuss to defend the independence of Austria against the Nazi threat. Kraus died of natural causes, leaving his polemic against the Third Reich unpublished (the manuscript of *Third Walpurgis Night*, smuggled out of Germany to the safety of the United States, was published in 1952). His intellectual legacy still reverberates through the political theater of Bertolt Brecht and **Peter Weiss**, the cultural theory of **Theodor Adorno** and **Walter Benjamin**, and the media criticism of Jacques Bouveresse and **Jean Baudrillard**.

Selected Bibliography: Kraus, Karl. *Half Truths and One-and-a-Half Truths: Selected Aphorisms.* Ed. and trans. Harry Zohn. New York: Carcanet P, 1986; Kraus, Karl. *The Last Days of Mankind.* Abridged and ed. by Frederick Ungar. Trans. Alexander Gode and Sue Ellen Wright. New York: Frederick Ungar, 1974; Timms, Edward. *Karl Kraus—Apocalyptic Satirist.* Vol. 1: *Culture and Catastrophe in Habsburg Vienna.* New Haven, CT: Yale UP, 1986. Vol. 2: *The German-Jewish Dilemma between the World Wars.* New Haven, CT: Yale UP, 2004; Zohn, Harry, ed. *In These Great Times: A Karl Kraus Reader.* Trans. Joseph Fabry, Max Knight, Karl F. Ross, and Harry Zohn. Montreal: Engendra P, 1976.

Edward Timms

KRISTEVA, JULIA (1941–). First coming to notice with the emergence of poststructuralism in the mid-1960s and early 1970s, the Bulgarian-born Kristeva was among writers such as **Roland Barthes, Jacques Derrida,** and **Michel Foucault** associated with the seminal journal *Tel Quel.* Her contribution to literary and cultural theory perhaps fulfills more influentially than any other that journal's ambitious aim to combine theories of language (from linguistics, semiotics, formalism, and structuralism), subjectivity (from psychoanalysis), and political economy (from Western Marxism) in an effort to understand the social and psychological bases of power as domination, and to rethink revolutionary social change. Her work is important to both feminist and Marxist politics of literature.

In *Revolution in Poetic Language* (1974, English trans. 1984), Kristeva both draws on and challenges Lacanian psychoanalysis with a theory of a pre-Oedipal realm of signification associated with the mother, which she calls *semiotic,* whose irruptions within the symbolic order convey a persistent, destructive threat to the symbolic workings of patriarchy and capitalism. Her key development is a view of the individual as a speaking body, constructed by and in language, but also by prelinguistic structures that paradoxically both give rise to and work against language and the normative self. Only by tapping into this latter, formative layer will hope for radical political change be found.

In subsequent writings such as *Powers of Horror* (1980, English trans. 1982), Kristeva introduces new concepts and structures built on this basis, and continues to be fascinated by the importance of maternal relationships in the constitution of language and self; by the reservoirs of political subversion (both progressive and reactionary) revealed in primal psychological structures; and, especially, by their expression in avant-garde literature. The political register in this work is spun out of her attention to individual subjectivity rather than to social forms.

In the late 1980s and1990s, the more direct political engagement that marked her work in the 1960s returns in essays devoted to nationalism, multiculturalism, and what she calls the necessity of *revolt* to psychic well-being. Her works during this period—*Strangers to Ourselves* (1989, English trans. 1991), *Nations without Nationalism* (1990, English trans. 1993), *New Maladies of the Soul* (1993, English trans. 1995), *The Sense and Non-Sense of Revolt* (1996, English trans. 2000), and *Intimate Revolt* (1997, English trans. 2001)—are also informed by her psychoanalytic practice, which provides her with instances of the xenophobia, alienation, and depression produced by modern life. The ethics in psychoanalysis, she insists, implies a politics; and her work as an analyst, she notes in an interview, is political work. The above writings strive to articulate the dialectical relationship between the personal and the political with the aim of effecting change in both realms: the subject becomes a microcosm and locus of social relations (*Strangers to Ourselves*) just as *revolt* is, in that locus, necessary to the constitution and happiness of the subject (*Sense and Non-Sense of Revolt*).

Selected Bibliography: Guberman, Ross Mitchell, ed. *Julia Kristeva Interviews*. New York: Columbia UP, 1996; Kristeva, Julia. *Powers of Horror: An Essay in Abjection*. Trans. Leon S. Roudiez. New York: Columbia UP, 1982; Kristeva, Julia. *Revolution in Poetic Language*. Trans. Margaret Waller. New York: Columbia UP, 1984; McAfee, Noëlle. *Julia Kristeva*. London: Routledge, 2004; Moi, Toril, ed. *The Kristeva Reader*. New York: Columbia UP, 1986; Oliver, Kelly, ed. *The Portable Kristeva*. Updated ed. New York: Columbia UP, 2002.

Glenn Willmott and Yaël R. Schlick

KRLEŽA, MIROSLAV (1893–1981) is generally considered one of the greatest Yugoslav intellectuals and writers of the twentieth century. Krleža was born in Zagreb (then Austria-Hungary). From the early beginnings of his literary career, his political views significantly informed his literary output even though he always insisted on the separation of artistic creation from political commitment. Fiercely disappointed by **World War I**, the Balkan Wars of 1910–1911, and their underlying ideology of bourgeois nationalism, Krleža espoused communist ideas and welcomed the **Russian Revolution** as the best alternative for the world's poor and underprivileged. In his collection of essays *Izlet u Rusiju* (An Excursion to Russia, 1926), he discusses the Soviet society he then visited. During 1920–1940, Krleža worked as an editor for a number of literary journals frequently banned by the police. In those journals, he also fought ideological battles on many sides. His superb polemics against bourgeois nationalistic writers collected in *Moj obracun s njima* (My Conflict with Them, 1932) provide some of the finest Yugoslav examples of literary and cultural polemics. Krleža attacked Croatian bourgeois intellectual and religious leaders for their endorsement of the perpetuation of capitalist exploitation and social misery in Croatia. His literary output, such as the play cycle about the family Glembay—*Gospoda Glembajevi* (*The Noble Glembays,* 1928), *U agoniji* (In Agony, 1931), and *Leda* (Leda, 1930)— as well as the collection of poems *Balade Petrice Kerempuha* (Ballads of Petrica Kerempuh, 1936), the collections of essays *Deset krvavih godina* (Ten Bloody Years, 1937), and *Eppur si muove: studije i osvrti* (Eppur Si Muove: Studies and Reflections, 1938), also condemned the decadent and sterile Croatian bourgeoisie.

Krleža's novels also strongly support his political views. He fiercely criticizes the decadent and reactionary ideology of Croatian bourgeoisie in his *Povratak Filipa Latinovića* (*The Return of Philip Latinovicz,* 1932) and *Na rubu pameti* (*On the Edge of Reason,* 1938). In the nightmarish phantasmagoria *Banket u Blitvi* (A Banquet in Blitva, 1938–1939), he warns that a dystopian terror will be a realistic outcome of a military dictatorship supported by decadent bourgeoisie. In these novels, as in his later play *Aretej* (Areteus, 1959), Krleža is particularly interested in the relationship of intellectuals and power.

In addition to the debates with bourgeois intellectuals, Krleža actively participated in the 1930s polemics on the Left about the relationship between aesthetic values and political commitment, particularly with regard to **socialist realism**. Krleža supported the view that argued for the separation of art from political activism. He is often pointed out as the writer who almost single-handedly defeated the writers who insisted on the importance of political views for creative output and on adherence to the principles of socialist realism. His essays in *Dijalektički antibarbarus* (Dialectical Antibarbarian, 1939) address this literary agenda. However, at the end of his career, in his perhaps finest though unfinished novel *Zastave* (Banners, 1967), he returns to the principles of socialist realism, ultimately proving that it is possible to create a superb literary artifact while following the principles of socialist realism.

Krleža was also the chief editor of the first Yugoslav encyclopedia *Enciklopedija Jugoslavije* (1955–1971). His essays and diaries *Davni Dani* (Days Long Gone, 1956) and *Dnevnik* (Diaries, 1977) are excellent documents about the cultural and political climate of Yugoslavia in the twentieth century.

Selected Bibliography: Bogert, Ralph. *The Writer as Naysayer: Miroslav Krleža and the Aesthetic of Interwar Central Europe.* Columbus, OH: Slavica, 1991; Juraga, Dubravka. "Miroslav Krleža's *Zastave:* Socialism, Yugoslavia, and the Historical Novel." *South Atlantic Review* 62.4 (Fall 1997): 32–56; Kadić, Ante. "Miroslav Krleža." *Dictionary of Literary Biography: South Slavic Writers before World War II.* Detroit: Gale Research, 1995; Krtalić, Ivan. *Krleža, za i protiv (1914–1927).* 2 vols. Zagreb: Komunist, 1988.

Dubravka Juraga

KUNDERA, MILAN (1929–). Milan Kundera was born in Brno, Czechoslovakia. His first novel, *The Joke,* was published in Czech in 1967. After the 1968 Russian invasion, his works were banned; Kundera eventually immigrated to France, where he became a citizen in 1981. Although Kundera has rightly protested that the meaning of his fiction is not exhausted by its political message, his critique of the Czech communist regime in particular is both powerful and unique. Kundera's fiction does not make a straightforward moral condemnation of the tyranny of Stalinist-era Communism but instead dramatizes the often comic gap between the romantic illusions sponsored by Communism and the prosaic reality of everyday life. In doing so, Kundera is carrying on what he sees as the great tradition of the novel inaugurated by **Cervantes** in **Don Quixote**. The main character of *The Joke* wants to be a loyal Communist but discovers that the revolution, while demanding that its followers be joyful, has no toleration for humor, satire, or jokes. Deprived of the insight humor can provide, true believers like Helena are able to convince themselves that their devotion to the party is simple idealism. *Life Is Elsewhere* (1969) explores the political irresponsibility inherent in lyric poetry's expression of personal emotion alone. Jaromil, the young protagonist of the novel, writes surrealistic love poetry without having any sexual experience, and celebrations of revolution while lacking any political understanding. According to Kundera, the novel was prompted by the willingness of the poet Paul Éluard to write poetry in honor of the communist regime even as personal friends were being condemned to death in show trials.

The seven stories that make up *The Book of Laughter and Forgetting* (1979) powerfully indict the 1968 communist invasion of Czechoslovakia and the regime it installed, but Kundera never descends to a melodramatic portrayal of heroes and villains. His dissenters, like Mirek in the first story "Lost Letters," are capable of nobility but also pettiness and meanness. Mirek condemns the regime for rewriting history, but he himself wants to rewrite his own past by destroying old love letters to a woman he now considers embarrassingly unattractive. In an autobiographical section, Kundera describes how he himself was suddenly seized by a desire to rape a woman who was risking prison to help him avoid the police.

Kundera's targets include not only Communism but also the kind of "progressivism" whose primary function is to proclaim one's own moral goodness. The members of the Clevis family in "The Border," the last story in *The Book of Laughter and Forgetting*, are all careful to hold opinions that are provocative enough to be certified as progressive but also popular enough to be safe. Franz, in *The Unbearable Lightness of Being* (1984), believes in the "Grand March," a view of history whose kitschy appeal depends on seeing history as progress from revolution to revolution without detours or reversals. Kundera's fiction ridicules the illusions of the Right as well as the Left, but his most immediate and most vulnerable target is the utopian romanticism associated primarily with the Left.

Selected Bibliography: Banerjee, Maria Nêmcová. *Terminal Paradox: The Novels of Milan Kundera.* New York: Grove Weidenfeld, 1990; Misurella, Fred. *Understanding Milan Kundera: Public Events, Private Affairs.* Columbia: U of South Carolina P, 1993; Petro, Peter, ed. *Critical Essays on Milan Kundera.* New York: G. K. Hall, 1999; Seaton, James. "Milan Kundera vs. Richard Rorty." *South Carolina Review* 29.1 (Fall 1996): 211–17.

James Seaton

∘ L ∘

LA GUMA, ALEX (1925–1985) was born into a politically active family in Cape Town's District Six. His father, Jimmy La Guma, was a member of the executive of the Industrial and Commercial Workers Union of Africa, and by the time Alex was one year old, his father was on the central committee of the **Communist Party** of South Africa. Jimmy La Guma went on to become the secretary of the Western Cape African National Congress (ANC). It was into this politically charged environment that Alex was thrust at an early age and from which he attempted, in the 1930s and early 1940s, both to join the International Brigade to fight the fascists in the **Spanish Civil War** and to enlist in the army to fight in **World War II**; both offers were refused. In 1947, he became a member of the Young Communist League, although he had to strategically distance himself from the movement after three years, when it decided to disband rather than be banned by the national party.

Alex La Guma was a politically active writer fully committed to the anti-**apartheid** struggle. His credentials as an activist were impeccable: he was a member of the executive committee of the South African Coloured People's Organisation in 1954 and its chairman in 1955, and later that year, he was elected to lead a delegation to the Congress of the People in Kliptown, Johannesburg. La Guma was a staunch opponent of the racist government of South Africa, and as such, his life was at risk several times: an assassination attempt was made in 1958, and he was one of the 155 charged in the infamous treason trial of 1956–1961. Several further spells of imprisonment and house arrest culminated in his leaving the country of his birth in 1966 on a one-way exit permit. He spent a brief period of time in Britain before moving to Cuba, where he was the ANC's Caribbean spokesperson until his death in 1985. La Guma's keen political sense would pervade the journalism with which he started his writing career, and his eclectic and resourceful comprehension of South African struggles would underpin the contexts he went on to create in his novels.

As well as being a journalist, La Guma was an accomplished cartoonist, having created the character Little Libby, whose adventures were featured in *New Age*. La Guma wrote five novels: *A Walk in the Night* (1962), *And a Threefold Cord* (1964), *The Stone Country* (1967), *In the Fog of the Seasons' End* (1972), and *Time of the Butcherbird* (1979). *In the Fog of the Seasons' End* has received considerable international critical attention, and the evocative *A Walk in the Night*, which recounts the turbulent events of a single evening in District Six, is a remarkable novel that—although banned when it was first published, has found a place on South African curricula. La Guma is heralded as one of Africa's best novelists.

Selected Bibliography: Abrahams, Cecil A. *Alex La Guma.* Boston: Twayne, 1985; Asein, Samuel. *Alex La Guma: The Man and His Work.* Ibadan: New Horn/Heinemann, 1987; Balutansky, Kathleen. *The Novels of Alex La Guma: The Representation of a Political Conflict.* Boulder, CO: Lynne Rienner, 1990; Chandramohan, Balasubramanyam. *A Study in Trans-Ethnicity in Modern Africa: The Writings of Alex La Guma.* Lampeter: Mellen Research UP, 1992; Odendaal, Andre, and Roger Field, eds. *Liberation Chabalala: The World of Alex La Guma.* Bellville: Mayibuye Books, 1993; Yousaf, Nahem. *Alex La Guma: Politics and Resistance.* Portsmouth, NH: Heinemann, 2001.

Nahem Yousaf

LAMMING, GEORGE (1927–). Born in obscure Carrington's Village near Bridgetown, Barbados, George Lamming shot to international fame and canonical status in modern Anglophone Caribbean literature with his first novel, *In the Castle of My Skin* (1953). Like G., the first-person narrator in the novel, who says that it was "my mother who really fathered me," Lamming grew up in a struggling, single-parent household and eventually migrated to Trinidad in search of employment. Initially known for his short stories and poems, he left for England in 1950 with plans for his first novel already germinating; he published his remaining novels in a span of about twenty years before returning to Barbados, where he is now based. While Lamming's decision to return to his native island is unusual among most Caribbean writers who migrated to the United Kingdom, the United States, and later Canada, he shares with them common themes, even if his poetic style and political positions bear his distinct, often uncompromising stamp. His first collection of essays, *The Pleasures of Exile* (1960), can be read as a literary treatise on what he considers to be the major preoccupations of modern Caribbean writing in English: the apparent inevitability of exile from islands with an economically and artistically impoverished heritage; the importance of black peasant life in Barbados; the struggle to find a national language and identity that would break free from centuries of slavery and inherited colonial traditions; the gradual establishment of a regional affiliation; the internal tensions of a multiracial and multiethnic Caribbean; the hope and failure of independence. His famous revisionist reading of **Shakespeare**'s Caliban in *Pleasures*, where he claims a heroic, revolutionary role for the slave and makes Prospero instead the "monster," sets the tone for Lamming's fierce challenges to white, middle-class, Euro-American notions of cultural and moral superiority, and for his passionate commitment to forging an ethical if combative Caribbean politics.

Lamming's novels—for all their dense prose, fragmented voices, and diffuse plots—make a surprisingly coherent and compact statement on colonial and postcolonial Caribbean history, although not in strictly chronological order. His first novel deals with the impact of colonial education, the rise of the nationalist movement, and the influence of the 1930s labor riots on the latter. *The Emigrants* (1954) is set in the 1950s mass migration to England and broodingly explores the dilemmas of black migrants in a hostile "mother country." *Of Age and Innocence* (1958) literally returns to the Caribbean from England through the failed messianic leader, John Isaac Shephard, and introduces the imaginary San Cristobal, which Lamming uses in later novels as a typical Caribbean island. It also deepens the foreboding tone of earlier novels and foretells troubled times for the postindependence period and ethnic electoral politics—a historically accurate prediction in the case of British Guiana and Trinidad. *Season of Adventure* (1960) is arguably anomalous in the oeuvre, with a more (for Lamming) optimistic view and a central female character. But even here, a brief people's revolution, modeled along the initial hopes of revolutionary Haiti and, later, Cuba, is not uniformly triumphant. *Water with Berries* (1971) shifts between England and San Cristobal and, continuing the explosive challenge to the Prospero-Caliban-Miranda triad of Shakespeare's *The Tempest*, suggests a **Fanon**esque violence, both internecine and anticolonial. Lamming's last novel, *Natives of My Person* (1972), is an allegorical representation of the first slaving and settlement expeditions that repopulated the Caribbean, virtually exterminated the native populations, and refashioned the islands into plantations. Now followed by a new generation of writers, many of them women, Lamming occupies the status of respected elder in the Anglophone Caribbean, where he has left an enduring literary legacy.

Selected Bibliography: Da Silva, A. J. Simoes. *The Luxury of Nationalist Despair: George Lamming's Fiction as Decolonizing Project*. Atlanta, GA: Rodopi, 2000; Lamming, George. *The Pleasures of Exile*. 1960. Ann Arbor: U of Michigan P, 1992; Nair, Supriya. *Caliban's Curse: George Lamming and the Revisioning of History*. Ann Arbor: U of Michigan P, 1996; Paquet, Sandra Pouchet. *The Novels of George Lamming*. London: Heinemann, 1982.

Supriya Nair

LATIN AMERICAN LITERATURE. There exists a widespread idea, at least on the Left, according to which literature and politics achieve a kind of synthesis in Latin America that has eluded the rest of the world. Where the linking of political and literary avant-gardes once envisioned, say, by communists and constructivists in the early days of the Soviet Union or by surrealists and Marxists in pre–**World War II** Paris soon come to grief, whether at the hands of Zhdanovism or of petty bourgeois individualism or aestheticism, Latin America offers us the synthetic avant-gardism of the unflinchingly communist-cum-surrealist **Pablo Neruda**, or the doubly revolutionary filmmaking of Cuban director Tomás Gutiérrez Alea. A more sweeping version of this idea extends the successful union of the avant-gardes to the third world generally, but its Latin American variation probably gets the most play, because it was the generation of Latin American writers and critics who were to gain the first genuinely world audience for Latin American literature, the "boom" generation, that presented *itself* to the world this way. In the historic prologue (1949) to the first edition of his novel on the Haitian Revolution—*The Kingdom of This World* (*El reino de este mundo*)—the Cuban novelist **Alejo Carpentier** evoked ethnographic concepts of popular culture and religion to account for this synthetic possibility: because the experience of day-to-day life in Latin America was itself still mediated by the premodern and in effect pre-"realist" narratives of tribalist and peasant societies, the merely private and self-induced defamiliarizations of Parisian surrealists and of the metropolitan avant-garde generally could find—say, in Haiti or Cuba—a public and spontaneous soil in which to take root. The writer or artist had only to situate him- or herself at the dialectical intersection of these two disparate worlds—hypermodern and premodern—for the new literary possibility to burst forth.

As the formula for what, following Francophone currents, Carpentier would refer to in Spanish as the "*real maravilloso*" (the "*réel merveilleux*" or "marvelously real"), this same idea could more directly take on political articulations as well. Indeed, the hypothetical possibilities set forth by the great Peruvian Marxist **José Carlos Mariátegui** and other *indigenistas* in the 1920s of an "Incan socialism" (rooted here in the purportedly still viable institution of the *ayllu*, or indigenous village commune) already foresaw something akin to this, even if Mariátegui remained skeptical, failing the revolution itself, of its literary possibilities. The art of the Mexican muralists Diego Rivera, David Siqueiros, and José Clemente Orozco in the 1930s and 1940s— seemingly realist, modernist, and popular all at once—also partook, both objectively and subjectively, in this dialectic, though, curiously, such revolutionary painting had as yet no (Mexican) literary equivalent. But by the time the *real maravilloso* morphed into **magical realism**—after the Cuban revolution of 1959 and the literary revolution unleashed by **Gabriel García Márquez**'s novel *One Hundred Years of Solitude* (*Cien años de soledad*, 1967)—the fairy-tale marriage of literature and (revolutionary) politics had come to seem almost as typically Latin American as guitars or volcanoes. The earlier, path-breaking work of Latin America's great revolutionary poets—above all, that of Neruda, heretofore largely unknown outside the Spanish-speaking world—rode the crest of the boom into the tastes of a cosmopolitan, Left public sphere.

To pronounce all of this a myth has now, nevertheless, become almost as much an article of accepted wisdom as the idea of a revolutionary literary-political synthesis itself. For one thing, of course, the latter leaves out of the picture three rather large pieces of Latin American literary history: (1) those major modern Latin American writers, such as Jorge Luis Borges and the later **Mario Vargas Llosa**, whose literary avant-gardism is either resolutely nonpolitical or linked to right-wing politics; (2) almost all of pre-twentieth-century Latin American literary history, especially that of the nineteenth century, during which period the vaunted literary-political synthesis often failed and, when it succeeded, produced distinctly dystopian results; and (3) the radically changed and itself much more dystopian contemporary literary-political scene in Latin America. A theory of the literary-political relation able to encompass both these, so to speak, utopian and dystopian moments within the full expanse of Latin American literature and history must, in fact, begin on a deeper, less obvious plane. This is the plane on which the vaunted happy union of Latin American literature and politics is revealed as simply one perhaps serendipitous variation on a more fundamental relation: the chronic impossibility of their divorce.

The colonial period in Latin America already, in effect, betrays the presence of this relation of the "nondivorcible" in the very fact that, formally speaking, it contains no Latin American literature at all. What passes for literature in the eyes of the Spanish colonial regime is really just derivative and second-rate Spanish literature, as in the case of Alonso de Ercilla's Virgilian epic of the Spanish conquest of Chile, *La araucana*. The only works produced in Latin America during just over three centuries (the sixteenth through the eighteenth) of colonial rule that evoke a literary response beyond the confines of the vice-royal courts or their decrepit remains are, technically, nonliterary. These are, above all, the many so-called chronicles of conquest and colonization, whether authored by subaltern conquistadores such as Bernal Díaz del Castillo or by quasi-assimilated, high-ranking native supplicants such as the minor Incan nobleman Guamán Poma de Ayala. They are, almost invariably, political works, here for the simple reason that they are addressed to a public still understood in its royal, courtly form. Even the greatest of these, "el Inca" Garcilaso de la Vega's *Royal Commentaries* (*Comentarios reales*, 1609), which incorporates preconquest Incan legend into its history of the conquest of Peru, obeys a preeminently political imperative: to plead indirectly the case for acceptance and integration of middle-ranking mestizos such as the author within Spanish imperial society. And because this society both exercises a monopoly on the literary itself and works to exclude noncourtiers, Garcilaso's only viable claim to recognition is—in early-modern terms—also a political one: the certification of a parallel Incan courtly lineage. From this standpoint, the considerable literary, quasi-epic qualities of the *Royal Commentaries* are collateral, even accidental, benefits. The case of Sor Juana Inés de la Cruz, colonial Mexico's great, late-baroque poetess, is roughly analogous. Her poetry, superlative as it often is, requires the metropolitan courtly seal. Without this *political* license, no literature—and therefore no non-Spanish, Latin American literature—is possible. Or rather, the latter *is* possible, but only if the absolute political constraints placed on the literary are abrogated, as they are in Sor Juana's most widely read work: the so-called "Letter of Reply to Sister Filotea" ("Carta de respuesta a Sor Filotea," 1691), in which, threatened with official censure, the poetess drops the sanctioned persona of the baroque court and the convent and, however briefly and unconsciously, invents a seventeenth-century avant-garde.

The formal end of colonial rule that marks the early nineteenth century in Latin America obviously supplies the precondition for the autonomizing of literature, its "divorce" from the rigid, directly political constraints of the colonial regime. But the immediate result of independence is the even greater exacerbation of a *political* overdetermination of all other social spheres, here brought on by civil wars and the generalized social violence of new state and class formation. The modern intellectual division of labor that delineates "politics" and "literature," although present in ideal form in Latin America with the first incursions of liberal ideology, must nevertheless continuously break down in the face of the continuous states of exception that turn most nineteenth-century Latin American novels (e.g., José Mármol's *Amalia*, 1851) into fictionalized propaganda. But it is the same historical conditions that likewise transform such tracts as Sarmiento's *Facundo* (1845)—a biography-cum-travelogue written in exile for the immediate purpose of denouncing the latter's political enemies—into one of nineteenth-century Latin America's most remarkable works of literature, and perhaps yet another unwitting, even unwilling form of avant-gardism, one that has in some sense moved beyond conventional fictional form.

And it is in fact this ideally affirmed but socially deferred division of intellectual labor between the poet and the politician—what the Brazilian critic Roberto Schwarz would call a "misplaced idea"—out of which the modern, romanticized figure of the Latin American writer-revolutionary itself develops. Despite the fact that Sarmiento—

once he puts down the pen to pick up the sword of politics itself—becomes more the immediate ancestor of a Pinochet than of a Che, the formal gesture of a politically overdetermined resort to literary activism makes him the ancestor of a Jorge Amado or of an **Ernesto Cardenal** as well. Even with the birth of the literary movement known as *modernismo* at the end of the nineteenth century—a movement of French symbolist-influenced poets, whose central figure, **Rubén Darío**, a social conservative and intimate of dictators, is probably Latin America's first *orthodox* vanguardist writer—the forced marriage of literature to politics merely changes form. In content, for the most part, a pastiche of the *Parnassian*, Darío's poetry achieves a revolution in form that is in every sense politically overdetermined: it makes it possible for Latin American writers to produce, in Spanish, a *style* from which all traces of colonial tutelage have been expunged. Meanwhile, Darío's master and the other great figure of *modernismo*, **José Martí**—a poet and martyr of Cuban national liberation—turns newspaper prose, the art of the pamphlet, and old-fashioned political oratory into an unheard of form of vanguard prose-poetry. The most famous of these writings, "Nuestra América," Latin America's ur-manifesto, somehow combines pre-Raphaelite-like preciosity and imagistic clutter with rhetorical bombast to produce political-aesthetic intensities that have never since been equaled and that have yet to be adequately theorized.

These, at any rate, are the kinds of historical configurations that, once the Latin American bourgeoisies have exhausted their last remaining revolutionary energies in directly political exploits on the order of the Mexican Revolution and Peronism, position the novelists and poets of **cold-war** Latin America to mount the barricades of national liberation and anti-imperialism with words as well as guns. The self-interested mythologies of the boom and magical realism aside, there is no question that the recent tradition of revolutionary poetry in Central America—Cardenal, **Roque Dalton**, Otto René Castillo, Daisy Zamora—represents a synthesis of revolutionary literature and politics that a country like the United States is totally incapable of producing. And the same can probably be said for the even more recent phenomenon of so-called **testimonio** literature, catapulted into world notoriety first by the new, plebeian social realism of the **Cuban Revolution**; later by the narratives emerging from human-rights campaigns under the "dirty war" regimes in Chile, Argentina, and Uruguay; and most recently by the extraordinary story of Guatemala's **Rigoberta Menchú**.

Still, the question remains: With what may be the effective defeat of the radical social movements of the cold-war period in Latin America, will the "marriage of the avant-gardes"—or, rather, their chronic failure to divorce—finally give way to the reifying division of intellectual labor that has long since turned experimental novelists into academics and poets into insurance company executives (and vice versa) in countries like the United States? Judging from the apparent stagnation of much recent Latin American literature, this may be the trend. Yet to suppose so would be to suppose that the social modernization proclaimed but never quite obtained by Latin America's ruling elites since the days of Sarmiento, whether of the Right or the Left, had finally arrived, bringing with it the end of literature's messy overdetermination by the political. But the most recent social crises in Latin America may in fact mark the definitive failure, not the belated success, of (capitalist) modernization. If so, then the forever divorcing but chronically overdetermined inseparability of literature and politics in Latin America may be in the process of entering still another, unscripted phase.

Selected Bibliography: Beverley, John, and Marc Zimmerman. *Literature and Politics in the Central American Revolutions.* Austin: U Texas P, 1990; Larsen, Neil. *Determinations: Essays on Theory, Nation and Narrative in the Americas.* London: Verso, 2001; Larsen, Neil. *Reading North by South.* Minneapolis: Minnesota UP, 1990; Monsiváis, Carlos. *Amor Perdido.* Mexico City: Biblioteca Era, 1978; Rama, Angel. *La ciudad letrada.* Hanover, NH: Ediciones del Norte, 1984; Schwarz, Roberto. *Misplaced Ideas: Essays on Brazilian Culture.* London: Verso, 1992.

Neil Larsen

LATINA/O LITERATURE. A widely varied field of literature published in the United States that is as much a creation of publishers looking to publicize and categorize writers in order to sell books as it is of writers who are actually producing similar texts. Authors grouped in this way range from **Isabel Allende**, who writes in Spanish and is from Chile, and Native American activist **Rigoberta Menchú** (also writing in Spanish, from Guatemala) to Chicana, Puerto Rican, and Cuban American writers like Ana Castillo, Sandra Cisneros, Alejandro Morales, Judith Ortiz Cofer, Cristina Garcia, and Oscar Hijuelos, who all write in English with Spanish mixed in.

Latina/o literature can be considered to begin in the nineteenth century with the Treaty of Guadalupe-Hidalgo that ended the Mexican-American War (1846–1848) and ceded the northern half of what was then Mexico to the United States. While texts have been written since then, the true bloom of this writing came in the late 1960s and early 1970s. Writers such as Tomás Rivera, Rudolfo Anaya, Rolando Hinojosa-Smith, and Pedro Juan Soto; critics such as Luis Dávila and Nicolás Kanellos; and publishing house Quinto Sol began telling stories from the *barrio*, as well as stories from rural Texas, the Island (Puerto Rico), and *Nueva Yol* (New York). Infusions of Cuban exiles followed after Fidel Castro's takeover in 1959, adding a critical mass to earlier Cuban immigrants. These three groupings—Mexican Americans, Puerto Ricans, and Cubans (in exile or Cuban Americans)—are the main subsets that originally produced much of the Latina/o literature, but they have been joined by exiles, immigrants, and their children from all over Latin American, including writers such as Allende (Chile), Julia Álvarez (Dominican Republic), Alicia Partnoy (Argentina), and Ariel Dorfman (Chile).

While these subcategories are often quite dissimilar, some general characteristics are spread across the works, particularly those that are written in a mix of English and Spanish from the 1980s and later. Language and culture go hand-in-hand, and as cultural critic **Gloria Anzaldúa** has noted, there are multiple levels of Spanish within the United States—depending not only on the original nationality of the immigrant parents but also on their socioeconomic status, what sort of community they live in, and where that community is located. As the protagonist of Garcia's *Dreaming in Cuban* (1992) notes: "I envy my mother her Spanish curses sometimes. They make my English collapse in a heap." Such linguistic anxiety is common, and a point of separation between Latinas, especially, as each judges and is judged for "authenticity."

Another common concern is the struggle to fit into the Anglocentric U.S. culture while still holding on to a semblance of autonomous identity that is not dictated by either a culturally dominant (and often patriarchal) Anglo society or a patriarchal Latina society. Novels such as Cisneros's *The House on Mango Street* (1984), Castillo's *So Far from God* (1993), Garcia's *Dreaming*, Ortiz Cofer's *The Line of the Sun* (1989), and María Amparo Escandón's *Esperanza's Box of Saints* (1999) all feature women who must make their way in an Anglo man's world.

Castillo's vision is by far the darkest, for the four sisters of her novel are all killed by that world—the eldest as a newscaster in Iraq; the second poisoned in a chemical factory and then blamed by her Anglo bosses for misusing the chemicals (when in actuality the men gave them to her in exchange for a pay raise); the third disappears in midair after jumping off a cliff (following her rape and mutilation at the hands of an anonymous man), and the last dies of AIDS, but a virgin. The common factor between them is that all are killed following their contact with men—often Anglo men, but also Latino and Native American men—and by venturing into the public men's world outside the home. This vision of Anglos as deadly can be traced back to Rivera's *. . . And the Earth Did Not Devour Him* (*. . . y no se lo tragó la tierra*, 1970), where Anglos are, in turn, a child killer, bullies, racists, liars, friends to a Latino couple that murders and robs illegal immigrants, unfaithful, and irreligious. Going even further, Anzaldúa symbolizes death using Anglo culture and the color white in her seminal *Borderlands/La Frontera* (1987), and in Cisneros's story collection *Woman Hollering Creek* (1991), Anglos are seducers, liars, and cheats, and other men are abusive and unfeeling or incapable of expressing positive emotions.

The men who write Latina/o literature tend to portray a darker vision of the world also. This is evidenced in the early work by Rivera, as well as works by Gary Soto, Morales, Luis Valdez (particularly in his earlier *El Teatro Campesino* years), and even in Hijuelos's Pulitzer Prize—winning *The Mambo Kings Play Songs of Love* (1989). It is here that we see a pair of Cuban brothers, musicians, on their way up in the New York music scene. They meet Desi Arnaz and play on the *I Love Lucy* show, gain some popularity, then lose everything as one brother dies and the other loses his heart because of it. The story is told as reminiscences of the surviving brother, drinking himself to death in the ironically named Hotel Splendor while listening to the records of his youth. Following his brother's death, he abandoned his musical dreams and became a handyman and then a building superintendent. His nephew, a bitter and withdrawn young man, eventually follows in his father's footsteps and meets Arnaz, now very old. Both feel a sense of loss for the period of the 1950s when Mambo was king, and Cubans in the United States were not yet in exile. There is a longing for this lost past—as a child longs for a lost parent, so too does a culture of Cubans in exile long for a more certain time—where social and gender roles are easy and clear. Living "life on the hyphen," as critic Gustavo Pérez Firmat notes, is about translation and transition. Those who are between cultures live on the hyphen in "Cuban-American" and are at once familiar with and not at home in both cultures. The past is inaccessibly remote, with its old strictures, but the present and future are almost as isolated because of the need to abandon that past to join mainstream Anglo culture; spiritual or economic death seem to be the only options open, whether the men are Chicano, Puerto Rican, or Cuban.

While men such as Hijuelos have played and continue to play an important role in the Latina/o literary movement, particularly in the early years, women have become much more widely marketed and read since the 1980s and 1990s, particularly with the appearance of Cisneros. Her success opened the way for other female authors, and their success can be attributed in part to the fact that women are readers much more than men are, but an equally strong cultural reason for the success can be explained by the ways in which cultures interact. Dominant cultures do not merely shape minority cultures but are shaped in turn. This absorption of culture can be seen not only in the popularity of Latina/o literature (and other ethnic/minority writings) in the United States but also in the fact that women from other cultures are viewed as exotic, alluring, often sensual—"a hot tamale," as Ortiz Cofer notes of her own personal experience, where she has been importuned by drunken Anglos singing sexually explicit songs to her in public. These women are objects of sexual desire and conquest; their absorption is viewed by dominant cultures as a way of taming the "other" and demonstrating cultural (and patriarchal) power. In direct opposition to this, the males of minority cultures are demonized and represented as dangerous by the dominant culture. The subordinate males are represented as oversexed, subhuman monsters incapable of holding true humanity or forming part of civilized society. Thus, while male authors continue to produce texts, it is their female counterparts who receive contracts from major publishing houses and greater financial rewards. This tension is suggestive of yet another point of commonality among writers classified as Latina/o authors—that of a social, cultural, and political struggle for recognition and acceptance on their own terms.

Suggested Bibliography: Álvarez Borland, Isabel. *Cuban-American Literature of Exile: From Person to Persona.* Charlottesville: UP of Virginia, 1998; Augenbraum, Harold, and Margarite Fernández-Olmos, eds. *U.S. Latino Literature: A Critical Guide for Students and Teachers.* Westport, CT: Greenwood, 2000; Christian, Karen. *Show and Tell: Identity as Performance in U.S. Latina/o Fiction.* Albuquerque: U of New Mexico P, 1997; Flores, Ángel. "Magical Realism in Spanish American Fiction." *Hispania* 38.2 (May 1955): 187–92; Gracia, Jorge J. E. *Hispanic/Latino Identity: A Philosophical Perspective.* Oxford: Blackwell, 2000; Horno Delgado, Asunción. *Breaking Boundaries: Latina Writing and Critical Readings.* Amherst: U of Massachusetts P, 1989; Kafka, Phillipa. *"Saddling la Gringa": Gatekeeping in Literature by Contemporary Latina Writers.* Westport, CT: Greenwood, 2000; Kanellos, Nicolás, ed. *The Hispanic Literary Companion.* Detroit: Visible Ink P, 1997; McCracken, Ellen. *New Latina Narrative: The Feminine Space of Postmodern Ethnicity.* Tucson: U of Arizona P, 1999; Ortiz Cofer, Judith. "The Myth of the Latin Woman: I Just Met a Girl Named María." *Boricuas.* Ed. Roberto Santiago. New York: Ballantine Books, 1995. 102–8; Pérez Firmat, Gustavo. *Life on the Hyphen: The Cuban-American Way.* Austin: U of Texas P, 1994.

Jason G. Summers

LE GUIN, URSULA KROEBER (1929–). Prominent writer of **science fiction** (SF), best known for the novels *The Left Hand of Darkness* (*LHD,* 1969) and *The Dispossessed* (1974). The first represents Le Guin's earliest sustained exploration of gender as a cultural construct. In it, an envoy, Genly Ai, visits the planet Gethen seeking its inclusion in a loose federation of worlds, the Ekumen. Ai, a human male, finds that the human inhabitants of Gethen have evolved into physical androgyny, briefly becoming either male or female once monthly to engage in sexual activity. Ai, attempting to navigate a complex mesh of local politics while completing his mission, eventually finds himself with an exiled royal advisor, forced to journey across an arctic wasteland. Though the novel won both Hugo and Nebula awards from the SF community, indicating both popular and critical success, critics took issue with the Gethenians' general masculinity and an apparent disconnect between *LHD*'s plot and theme. In her many essays (*Dancing at the Edge of the World* [1989]), Le Guin has shown herself to be dialectically open to the arguments of feminism, and the progression of her novels reflects constant engagement with gender questions.

The Dispossessed is Le Guin's most overtly political work. **Fredric Jameson** calls it "the most important **utopia** since Skinner's *Walden Two*" (221). A portion of the planet Urras' population removes itself to the moon Annares, where a socialist community is set up, though still tied economically to the warring capitalist and **Stalin**ist nations of Urras. After two hundred years, a brilliant Annaresti scientist seeks to meet with scientists on Urras. The novel traces his journey up to the point of the departure and, in alternating chapters, his travels in Urras. The contrast of the two planets, through the eyes of the utopian character, results in a novel portrayal of the ugliness and brutality of consumer capitalism and Soviet-style communism on Urras. Le Guin avoids idealism with Annares. In her vision of Socialism, a state structure emerging from within is always a possibility and a threat. While left-oriented critics tend to praise the novel, some point out that the barrenness of Annares deliberately undercuts the effectiveness of the socialist utopia, creating a forced ambiguous utopia, which has further led to criticism of Le Guin's failure to commit herself politically. However, as Darko Suvin and others have shown, Le Guin's politics are hardly ambiguous. Although she cites influences ranging from **Dostoevsky** to Kropotkin to Lao Tzu to **Marx**, her work is consistently critical of the destructive effects of capitalism on human community, that of **alienated** labor and social relations. Indeed, much of her later work explores the idea of humans working for one another rather than against one another (see especially *Always Coming Home* [1985]). Le Guin's fantasy, the *Earthsea* novels in particular, and her largely ignored historical stories (*Malafrena* [1979]) reflect the same political concerns as her SF novels and short stories.

Selected Bibliography: Jameson, Fredric. "World-Reduction in Le Guin: The Emergence of Utopian Narrative." *Science Fiction Studies* 2 (1975): 221–30; Le Guin, Ursula K. *Dancing at the Edge of the World.* New York: Grove, 1989; Olander, Joseph, and Martin Harry Greenberg, eds. *Ursula K. Le Guin.* New York: Taplinger, 1979; White, Donna R. *Dancing with Dragons: Ursula K. Le Guin and the Critics.* Columbia, SC: Camden House, 1999.

David Leaton

LEFEBVRE, HENRI (1901–1991). Born in the south of France and devoutly Catholic in his youth, Lefebvre rejected religion while a young philosophy student in Paris. Amid the intellectual agitation of the interwar years, he evidenced a decided taste for the avant-garde, embracing both **surrealism** and Marxism in the 1920s. His adherence to the French **Communist Party** toward the end of that decade began a long and often uneasy relationship with orthodox Stalinist thought. After publishing a handful of philosophical works in the 1930s (and being instrumental in the translation of Marx's early writings into French) and serving with the French Resistance during **World War II**, Lefebvre published his first major book, the *Critique of Everyday Life*, in 1947. Marked by the disappointed hopes of the liberation from German occupation, it analyzed daily life in dialectical terms as a site of alienation and the potential space for liberation. Its unconventional theses earned him a censure from the party, with which he would definitively break following the Hungarian Uprising of 1956. Everyday life and its transformations in the postwar world continued to be of interest into the 1960s, and there was significant mutual influence between Lefebvre's thought and that of **Guy Debord** concerning the emergence of a "consumer society" or "society of the spectacle." By the end of the 1960s, Lefebvre increasingly turned to analyses of the city as the physical setting for everyday life, work that culminated in what many consider his greatest contribution, *The Production of Space* (1974). Altogether, he authored more than sixty books.

Lefebvre's specifically literary studies are concentrated during a brief period in the mid-1950s, and are strongly marked by his ambivalent embrace of orthodox Stalinism at this moment. Books on Musset and Rabelais (both 1955) were part of a concerted effort by the party to appeal to a wider intellectual audience using a somewhat diluted materialist approach to literature. Following the contemporary work of **Lucien Goldmann**, Lefebvre rejects "subjective" methods of analysis in favor of a "science of letters" that sought to link culture to its "objective historical base," or the economic and social base. Yet he was also at pains to distinguish his studies from "any vulgar 'sociologism,' any simplified Marxist schema," by insisting on the indirect links between base and superstructure. What was perhaps most forward looking in these works was their insistence that the writer did not passively "express" his or her lived experience, but that the work was an active attempt to resolve social conflicts encountered therein. This, as well as his insistence on the avant-garde role of the intelligentsia and youth regarding **romanticism**, would inform his writings of the 1960s on what he called "revolutionary romanticism" and the utopian currents then stirring French politics and letters.

Selected Bibliography: Lefebvre, Henri. *Alfred de Musset: Dramaturge*. Paris: L'Arche, 1955; Lefebvre, Henri. *Introduction to Modernity*. Trans. John Moore. London: Verso, 1995; Lefebvre, Henri. *The Production of Space*. Trans. Donald Nicholson-Smith. Oxford: Blackwell, 1991; Lefebvre, Henri. *Rabelais*. Paris: Les Éditeurs français réunis, 1955; Shields, Rob. *Lefebvre, Love and Struggle: Spatial Dialectics*. London: Routledge, 1999.

Tom McDonough

LEFT REVIEW. Published monthly between October 1934 and May 1938, *Left Review* was the first English journal of **Marxist criticism** and cultural studies and an interesting experiment in cultural democracy. During its brief run, the journal published a body of innovative criticism that still retains analytical value and introduced Marxist literary theory to Britain. It also gained credibility from the appearance in its pages of some of the most respected names of the British cultural scene, such as **Edgell Rickword**, **C. Day Lewis**, Winifred Holtby, **Hugh MacDiarmid**, Stephen Spender, Herbert Read, and Eric Gill.

Left Review was founded by Writers' International, an organization of writers associated with the **Third International**, explicitly anti-fascist, pro-Soviet, and willing to take part in "the struggle of the working class for a new socialist society." Throughout, it was Communist-dominated, but this was before a communist political line on literature had been developed in England, which meant that writers had to derive conclusions for themselves, and that those who offered slogans instead of concrete argument were subject to sharp criticism. There was the excitement of discovery and creation; in the absence of established Marxist principles, many contributors were developing revolutionary critical theory. A range of articles of great imagination resulted. Alick West's examination of the development of the detective story explained the social basis of a change in genre; Edgell Rickword's treatment of literary history argued that a mechanical treatment ran counter to a Marxist approach; C. Day Lewis developed an extraordinary explanation of the basis of poetry's social force, which had a fundamental influence on **Christopher Caudwell**'s theory.

Left Review was informed by a strong sense that the world could be changed by individuals who retained their independent judgment while participating in the collective purpose. This sense of the potential in ordinary individuals was particularly obvious in *Left Review*'s literary competitions, in which readers were invited to produce their own work on a particular topic. Without indulging in the egalitarian sentimentality that anyone can do anything, the competitions, under the direction of Amabel Williams Ellis, propagated the view that material from the lives of individuals can provide a meaningful basis for understanding—and judging—the world. Gradually, however, the demand for professionalism, for experts, surfaced first in the competitions and then throughout *Left Review*. The 1934 **Soviet Writers Congress** declared positions that could be made into a line, and slogans sometimes began to be given as much prominence as concrete argument.

But the democratic spirit remained sufficiently in evidence to cause unease among the leadership of the **Communist Party**. The closing of *Left Review* was announced in the penultimate number, in order, it was said, to pursue a more ambitious and more popular project. The project never materialized, and whether one was in fact ever intended is open to question. With increasing tensions between the genuinely popular character of the **Popular Front** and loyalty to the Soviet Union, the leadership of the party may have felt that they could no longer risk the creative Marxism of *Left Review*.

Selected Bibliography: Clark, Jon, et al. *Culture and Crisis in Britain in the Thirties.* London: Lawrence and Wishart, 1979; Margolies, David, ed. *Writing the Revolution: Cultural Criticism from "Left Review."* Chicago: Pluto, 1998.

David Margolies

LEHRSTÜCK. Mainly formulated and designed by **Bertolt Brecht** between 1929 and 1933, the *Lehrstück* (learning play) was an attempt to establish a radical form of political theater. Brecht's revolutionary starting point was to abolish the division between the actor and the audience, creating what Augusto Boal would later call the spectactor. The *Lehrstücke* written in this period (such as *The Baden-Baden Lehrstück on Consent, The Measures Taken,* and *The Horatians and the Curiatians*) tend to contrast the will and desires of the individual with those of the collective. Individual actors are set against a sea of choral voices. Questions of identity and identification pervade the dramas, and are often couched in innovative dramaturgies that play with the conventional mapping of one actor onto one role and flit between time levels to enhance the cleavage of immediate performance and considered deliberation. In the most controversial of the plays, *The Measures Taken*, a Young Comrade agrees to his own execution at the hands of four other communist agitators because his heart has led him down a path of short-term reformism while his head should have been holding him back for the revolution. Yet the Young Comrade has already been killed when the play opens and so he has to be represented by his four companions in a series of plays-within-a-play before the Control Chorus. Each agitator thus has the opportunity to play the flawed activist and to compare their experience of the role with their feelings of disappointment when the others take their turn to play the same figure. Members of the Chorus both witness the performance of individualism and experience the collective delivery of tendentious text. That the episodes of weakness are told in the past and that they follow similar, almost ritualistic patterns indicates Brecht's formal debt to Japanese Noh. In general, the *Lehrstück*'s pedagogic thrust is that actors learn through experiencing and then reflecting on the carefully articulated contradictions of the plays. Verse is used extensively to construct meaning through rhythm, and music often accompanies the texts not only to aid the delivery of choral text but also to suggest dialectical counterpoints to the words themselves. Brecht also advocated the intervention of those involved to question and to alter the texts.

For many years, the *Lehrstück* was the whipping boy of Brecht's *oeuvre*; the plays were dismissed either as mere propaganda pieces (by such luminaries as Adorno) or as cold treatises on political submission. The uncovering of Brecht's theoretical fragments on the *Lehrstück* in the early 1970s by Rainer Steinweg led, however, to a new critical engagement with the form, and theater practitioners and scholars started to grasp the dynamics of the plays. The political lessons of the plays rarely come without (sometimes fatally) damaging the body, and the rhythms and cadences of the texts suggest a far more sensual relationship between speaker and spoken. Brecht described the *Lehrstück* in 1930 as "major pedagogy," which "changes the function of performing completely." The abolition of the actor/audience divide meant that there was no simple consumption of the *Lehrstück* as such; its productive value lay as a site for learning through continued rehearsal rather than in a finished production.

Selected Bibliography: Boal, Augusto. *Theater of the Oppressed.* London: Pluto, 1979; Jameson, Fredric. *Brecht and Method.* London: Verso, 1998; Nägele, Rainer. "Brecht's Theatre of Cruelty." *Reading after Freud: Essays on Goethe, Holderlin, Habermas, Nietzsche, Brecht, Celan, and Freud.* New York: Columbia UP, 1987; Steinweg, Rainer. *Das Lehrstück: Brechts Theorie einer politisch-ästhetischen Erziehung.* 2nd ed. Stuttgart: Metzler, 1976; Wirth, Andrzej. "The *Lehrstück* as Performance." *Drama Review* 43.4 (1999): 113–21.

David Barnett

LENIN, VLADIMIR ILYICH (1870–1924). Born Vladimir Ilyich Ulyanov at Simbirsk, Lenin went on to become a leading figure in the radical Russian Social Democratic Labor Party. By 1903, when that party split into two factions, Lenin became the leader of the Bolshevik faction, remaining as such until the October Revolution of 1917, in which he was the most important figure. Lenin subsequently became the head of the new Soviet government, a position he officially held until his death, though his activities were seriously curtailed after a series of strokes in 1922 and 1923. During his brief rule, he placed great emphasis on industrialization, electrification, and general economic development as he sought to make his backward country genuinely modern, though his plans were hampered in the first years by an ongoing postrevolutionary civil war. He remained a semilegendary hero of the revolution throughout the years of the Soviet Union, his body preserved in state for permanent public viewing in Red Square in Moscow.

One of the most important political leaders of the twentieth century, Lenin was also a major Marxist intellectual who made a number of important theoretical contributions to the Marxist tradition. For example, his first major study, *The Development of Capitalism in Russia* (1899), is an impressive and painstaking work of sociopolitical analysis. On the other hand, his influential early pamphlet "What Is to Be Done" (1902) is more closely related to his ultimate role as revolutionary, serving as a blueprint for the later Bolshevik-led October Revolution. Other theoretical writings, such as *Imperialism: The Highest Stage of Capitalism* (1915), greatly advanced Marxist understanding of the phenomenon of capitalism while extending and globalizing **Marx**'s own theories of history. Literature was certainly not at the center of Lenin's concerns, but he did insist that culture, by representing the lives of ordinary people, could be an important tool for organizing the masses in the struggle for socialism. On the other hand, he was suspicious of attempts to create an entirely new workers' literature and felt that socialist writers should draw on the bourgeois cultural heritage. His comments on literature (rejecting **modernism**, he was a great supporter of **realism** and an admirer of **Leo Tolstoy**) had an impact on the later development of **Soviet socialist realism**, though Lenin's worldwide reputation made his views on literature influential abroad as well. For example, some of his ideas were printed in the journal *New Masses*, where they were presented as advice for writers in the **American proletarian literature** movement of the 1930s.

During the Stalinist period, Lenin was generally treated with great reverence in Soviet literature, though the representation of Lenin was sometimes more complex than has been generally recognized in the West. For example, Mikhail Zoshchenko's series of twelve "Stories about Lenin" (1939–1940) can be read as iconographic apotheoses of Lenin, intended to instill good socialist values in Soviet children. But it is also quite possible to read the Lenin stories as a sly satirical assault on the Soviet "cult of personality" that tended to deify leaders like Lenin and **Stalin**.

Selected Bibliography: Harding, Neil. *Leninism.* Durham, NC: Duke UP, 1996; Lenin, Vladimir Ilyich. "The Collapse of the Second International." *Collected Works.* Vol. 21. Moscow: Progress Publishers, 1980. 207–59; Lenin, Vladimir Ilyich. *Collected Works of V. I. Lenin.* New York: International Publishers, 1927; Lenin, Vladimir Ilyich. "Opportunism, and the Collapse of the Second International." *Collected Works.* Vol. 21. Moscow: Progress Publishers, 1980. 438–53; Pomper, Philip. *Lenin, Trotsky, and Stalin: The Intelligentsia and Power.* New York: Columbia UP, 1990; Tucker, Robert C., ed. *The Lenin Anthology.* New York: Norton, 1975; Tumarkin, Nina. *Lenin Lives! The Lenin Cult in Soviet Russia.* Enlarged ed. Cambridge, MA: Harvard UP, 1997; Williams, Beryl. *Lenin.* New York: Longman, 2000.

M. Keith Booker

THE LEOPARD (*IL GATTOPARDO*, 1958), historical novel by Giuseppe Tomasi di Lampedusa (1896–1957), translated into English by Archibald Colquhoun. The novel—based on the life of Lampedusa's grandfather, a Sicilian prince at the time of Sicily's unification with Italy in 1860—was rejected for publication (partly because it was read as a nostalgic apology for aristocracy) until after the author's death. Hugely successful both in Italy and internationally, it was dismissed by most of the Italian literary establishment as a mere best-seller and a narcissistic and cynically reactionary rejection of Italian nationhood and political progress. **Louis Aragon** (in *Lettres françaises*, December 1959 and February 1960) pointed out, however, that the work is powerfully structured as a partly unconscious self-critique of his own class by Prince Fabrizio—who is the main center of consciousness within the novel—and as a fully conscious critique of Fabrizio and of the unification process generally by the author. Lampedusa centers two chapters on other characters: the prince's chaplain, who muses on the continued disenfranchisement of the peasantry; and the prince's now aged daughters, whom he has betrayed. The novel presents moments from 1860 to 1910, long after the prince's death, which show a rapacious new bourgeoisie and a conservative church dominating the island. This reflects on the political situation at the time of the book's composition and publication, a period of Christian democrat domination in Sicily and Italy as a whole. *The Leopard* thus furnishes a classical case study not only in the literature of politics (in terms of its subject matter) but also in the politics of literature (in its stylistic and narrative structure).

Selected Bibliography: Cainen, Brian. *Study Guide to Tomasi di Lampedusa's "Il gattopardo."* Market Harborough, UK: Troubadour, 2003; Gilmour, David. *The Last Leopard: A Life of Giuseppe di Lampedusa.* New York: Pantheon, 1988.

John Gatt-Rutter

LERMONTOV, MIKHAIL IUREVICH (1814–1841), short-lived but seminal Russian author of poetry, plays, and prose fiction, who embraced romantic ideals of individual autonomy, artistic creativity, and social justice without clearly translating those ideals into a political philosophy. Reared on a small estate in central Russia, and inspired by the daring poems of his older Russian contemporary **Aleksandr Pushkin** and by the rebellious image of Lord Byron, Lermontov began writing lyric and narrative poetry in adolescence. After studying literature in Moscow, he entered a St. Petersburg military academy, aspiring to a Byronic life of adventure—partly to compensate for his social alienation. Commissioned a hussar in 1834, he continued to write poetry, often expressing resentment of social inequities, but it went unpublished. He also failed to gain approval from tsarist censors for his play *Masquerade* (*Maskarad*, 1836), a scathing portrayal of a vicious aristocratic society.

In 1837, Lermontov won sudden public acclaim for a clandestinely circulated poem, "The Death of a Poet" ("*Smert' poeta*"), which angrily blamed envious Petersburg courtiers for Pushkin's fatal duel and prompted Lermontov's arrest and sentencing to military service in the Caucasus. Pardoned the next year, Lermontov returned to St. Petersburg an esteemed poet, who now had entrée to the highest social circles, despite his antagonism toward aristocracy. But only two years later he was rearrested, this time for dueling, and sent back to military duty in the Caucasus, where he was killed in yet another duel, fought over an affront to his romantic sense of honor.

Before his rearrest, Lermontov wrote his most famous literary creation, the novel *A*

Hero of Our Time (*Geroi nashego vremeni*, 1840), often considered the first work of Russian psychological realism. This novel probes the ambiguous character of a highly intelligent, sensitive, and self-conscious army officer, Pechorin, who seduces young women and exploits friendships while condemning society for its hypocritical moralism. The novel ignited intense controversy: leftist critics extolled Lermontov's depiction of an authentic hero corrupted by the decadent society that had bred him; conservative critics complained that the novel praised a selfish immoralist who unrepentantly violates societal norms. Lermontov responded that he was simply portraying the "disease" of his "hero" and his society, concluding: "God alone knows the cure." An astute diagnostician of his times, Lermontov implied that the illness afflicting contemporary Russian society was less a loss of political legitimacy than an erosion of cultural values that lend structure to individual lives and impart discipline and direction to society overall.

Selected Bibliography: Golstein, Vladimir. *Lermontov's Narratives of Heroism.* Evanston, IL: Northwestern UP, 2000; Kelly, Laurence. *Lermontov: Tragedy in the Caucasus.* New York: George Braziller, 1978; Ripp, Victor. "*A Hero of Our Time* and the Historicism of the 1830s: The Problem of the Whole and the Parts." *Modern Language Notes* 92 (1977): 969–86; Todd, William Mills, III. *Fiction and Society in the Age of Pushkin: Ideology, Institutions, and Narrative.* Cambridge, MA: Harvard UP, 1986.

Elizabeth Cheresh Allen

LESSING, DORIS (1919–). Over an extremely prolific fifty-plus-year writing career, Doris Lessing has gone from being an active Communist to a follower of Sufi mysticism while always remaining a maverick. Born of British parents in Persia (now Iran) and raised on an isolated farm in southern Rhodesia (now Zimbabwe), she became a communist in 1940s Rhodesia because it seemed to be the only group that cared about the "Native question." While becoming disillusioned with communism in 1950s London after learning of **Stalin**'s atrocities, she continued to struggle with her Marxist identification into the early 1960s. Her involvement with communism and socialism is fully described in her two volumes of autobiography, *Under My Skin* (1994) and *Walking in the Shade* (1997).

Declaring in 1957 that her novels study "the individual conscience in relation to the collective," Lessing reveals this artistic creed most fully in her five-volume **bildungsroman** series *Children of Violence* (1952–1969) ("The Small Personal Voice," 14). The first four volumes trace the growth from adolescence to maturity of her autobiographical protagonist, Martha Quest, against the background of an astutely analyzed white-settler community in Zambesia, a fictionalized Rhodesia. The last volume—*The Four-Gated City* (1969), set in London—stretches Lessing's earlier political vision to embrace psychological and Sufi interests, including the need to investigate altered states of consciousness.

Between the third and fourth volumes of *Children of Violence*, Lessing took a break from the series to write what is probably her best known novel, *The Golden Notebook* (1962). Her central character, Anna Wulf, a writer suffering from writer's block, not only details the emotions and thoughts accompanying her break with communism but also portrays the difficult relations between men and women and the exploration of madness as a means of breaking through psychic sterility and fragmentation. Her depiction of thoughtful, independent women daring to talk together about their often unsatisfactory relations with men, as well as about politics, children, and work, made Lessing one of the heroines of early feminism.

Following a five-volume **science fiction** series, *Canopus in Argos: Archives* (1979–1983), Lessing returned to fictional realism, writing, among other novels, *The Good Terrorist* (1985), a darkly satirical look at not only emotionally unstable amateur terrorists but also an England where the "dispossessed are the norm" (Greene 207). Lessing's latest novel, *The Sweetest Dream* (2002), written in lieu of volume three of her autobiography, casts a satirical look back at left-wing politics in the 1960s.

Selected Bibliography: Greene, Gayle Jacoba. *Doris Lessing: The Poetics of Change.* Ann Arbor: U of Michigan P, 1994; Kaplan, Carey, and Ellen Cronan Rose, eds. *Doris Lessing: The Alchemy of Survival.* Columbus: Ohio UP, 1988; Lessing, Doris. "The Small Personal Voice." 1957. *A Small Personal Voice: Essays, Reviews, Interviews.* Ed. Paul Schleuter. New York: Vintage, 1975. 3–21; Rubenstein, Roberta. *The Novelistic Vision of Doris Lessing: Breaking the Forms of Consciousness.* Urbana: U of Illinois P, 1979; Sprague, Claire, and Virginia Tiger. *Critical Essays on Doris Lessing.* Boston: Hall, 1986.

Phyllis Perrakis

LESUEUR, MERIDEL (1900–1996). Born with the century in the middle of the American continent to Midwestern socialists, Meridel LeSueur embodied a native rebellious dynamism that sent her hitchhiking to Hollywood with her cousin (who became the star Joan Crawford) in the 1920s, picketing with women on the breadlines during the 1930s, writing children's books while blacklisted throughout the 1950s, only to be resurrected as a feminist legend in the 1970s. Between the 1930s and 1950s, LeSueur wrote novels, poems, stories, reportage, and children's fiction; she taught writing to workers, recorded the stories of homeless women, edited radical magazines, organized the unemployed, and raised two daughters while living in the Twin Cities with Robert Brown, a painter. Her early stories and poems, and her 1939 novel, *The Girl* (which was rejected by publishers until 1978), limned women's desire for sex, for female companionship, for children as the basis for a new kind of political association and activism. LeSueur's gift for listening to the underlying sounds of daily life transcribed the speech of working-class women into a poetic account of suffering and struggle caused by men and capitalism. *The Girl*, for instance, relies on the heist plot popularized by early 1930s Hollywood gangster films but instead of following the rise and fall of the immigrant hustler focuses on his farm-bred moll—a St. Paul bar girl—and the other waitresses and streetwalkers left destitute by the Depression.

LeSueur was acutely aware of the complexities of writing across class and gender divides. Her 1935 essay for **New Masses**, "The Fetish of Being Outside," presents a cogent argument for what **Antonio Gramsci** called the "organic intellectual." In this early piece of materialist-feminist critique, LeSueur theorizes about the gendered dynamics of class positions and worries over the plight of the unaligned intellectual. She further developed these ideas in her pamphlet written while teaching creative writing for the Works Progress Administration (WPA), "Worker Writers," which summarizes her pedagogical belief in a people's culture voiced through the authentic rendering of workers' own language. Her introspection, in which her theoretical discussion rests on her own self-revelation, became a model for later academic feminists.

This grounding in experience and self-disclosure marked the hallucinatory prose of her stories and reportage from the 1930s. "Annunciation" expresses the inner consciousness of a young pregnant woman whose dreamy sense of her body's physicality supplants her day-to-day existence; "I Was Marching" traces the development of a middle-class woman, moved by the scenes of massive demonstrations during the Minneapolis truckers' strike of 1934, from observer (looking at the strike) to participant (marching on the picket line). At once lyrical and polemical, LeSueur's prose unsettles the genre distinctions separating reportage and fiction. Even her children's books—such as the biography of Nancy Hanks, Lincoln's mother, and that of Davy Crockett, *Chanticleer of Wilderness Road*, written for Knopf while she was blacklisted during the "dark years," as she called them—are full of wonderful historical detail wrapped in a sensuous prose style. The recovery of LeSueur's works by Feminist Press and West End Press in the 1970s revived her influence on another generation of women and working-class writers. She lived to see her work—once scorned, trivialized, and censored—become the subject of scholarship as well as inspiring song, theater, and poetry.

Selected Bibliography: Browder, Laura. *Rousing the Nation: Radical Culture in Depression America.* Amherst: U of Massachusetts P, 1998; Coiner, Constance. *Better Red: The Writing and Resistance of Tillie Olsen and Meridel Le Sueur.* New York: Oxford UP, 1995; Hapke, Laura. *Daughters of the Great Depression: Women, Work, and Fiction in the American 1930s.* Athens: U of Georgia P, 1995; Rabinowitz, Paula. *Labor and Desire: Women's Revolutionary Fiction in Depression America.* Chapel Hill: U of North Carolina P, 1991; Roberts, Nora Ruth. *Three Radical Women Writers: Class and Gender in Meridel Le Sueur, Tillie Olsen, and Josephine Herbst.* New York: Garland, 1996; Schleuning, Neala. *America, Song We Sang without Knowing: The Life and Ideas of Meridel LeSueur.* Mankato, MN: Little Red Hen P, 1983.

Paula Rabinowitz

LET US NOW PRAISE FAMOUS MEN **(1941),** by poet and journalist James Agee and photographer Walker Evans, is an account of the lives of three poverty-stricken families in rural Alabama in 1936. Some scholars have argued that *Let Us Now Praise Famous Men* is the single most important book-length documentary about American underclass life in the twentieth century. Certainly, it was a book well ahead of its time.

Famous Men began as a six-week assignment from *Fortune* magazine (where Agee was associate editor) to produce a photojournalistic record of three tenant-farmer families. Evans's austere and beautifully composed photographs of the families and their surroundings fulfilled this task. But Agee's highly digressive text posed problems: it included anecdotes about Agee's own clumsiness as a reporter; it mocked and parodied New Deal efforts to improve tenant-farmer life; it described every last item in the tenants' homes in excruciating detail; it included awkward confessions about Agee's marital difficulties and his attraction to the tenant women; and it was written in a highly poetic and deeply personal style. In short, Agee's report was as much (if not more) about Agee as it was about tenant farmers. Unsurprisingly, *Fortune* rejected it.

After Agee substantially revised and expanded his report into a book, publishers also turned him down. Finally, years after it was completed, Houghton Mifflin brought out the book, but sales were abysmal. By 1941, the United States was engaged in a world war against fascism; contemporary concerns utterly eclipsed interest in Agee's idiosyncratic account from the depths of the Great Depression. The book fell quickly out of print.

In the 1960s and 1970s, however, Agee's self-critical mode of documentary reportage acquired a fervent new following. For all its flaws (and these are numerous), *Famous Men* has more recently been recognized as a contentious, if also brilliant, meditation on how to—*and* how *not* to—do ethnographic or journalistic fieldwork among the impoverished and dispossessed. It foregrounds the power imbalance between author, subjects, and readers, and the difficulty of representing lived reality without being complicit in its distortion. "As a matter of fact," Agee wrote memorably in *Famous Men*, "nothing I might write could make any difference whatsoever."

In *Famous Men*, Agee calls himself "a Communist by sympathy and conviction," but the text of *Famous Men* suggests little in the way of a direct political or social reformist impulse. Rather, *Famous Men* is an anarchic and angry book that above all seeks urgently to make its subjects' pain and dignity palpable to its readers. It rages against the idea that the human beings it describes might be interpreted as abstractions or objects of pity, "as 'tenant' 'farmers,' as 'representatives' of [a] 'class,' as social integers in a criminal economy" (100). At the same time, it does so with full foreknowledge that it would inevitably fail in its goal. Today, *Famous Men* remains a crucial—if too often unheeded—cautionary tale about the limits of participant observation as a method and the inherent inadequacy of any ethnography or documentary that claims to have captured the "real" experiences of "others."

Selected Bibliography: Reed, T. V. "Unimagined Existence and the Fiction of the Real: Postmodernist Realism in *Let Us Now Praise Famous Men*." *Representation* 24 (Fall 1988): 156–76; Staub, Michael E. *Voices of Persuasion: Politics of Representation in 1930s America*. New York: Cambridge UP, 1994; Stott, William. *Documentary Expression and Thirties America*. Chicago: U of Chicago P, 1973.

Michael E. Staub

LEVERTOV, DENISE (1923–1997).

LEVERTOV, DENISE (1923–1997). Born in Ilford, England, Levertov immigrated to the United States in the late 1940s after marrying the American writer Mitchell Goodman; she adopted U.S. citizenship in 1955. At the time of her death from cancer, she was widely recognized as one of America's foremost poets. A leading campaigner in the international peace movement, Levertov's outspoken opposition to military action in Vietnam, El Salvador (her oratorio *El Salvador* was first performed in 1983), and the first Gulf war reflected a broader, left-leaning commitment to social justice fueled by suspicion of capitalism and the globalization of U.S. commerce. Fervently antinuclear, she was also a committed environmentalist.

A late protégée of the poet **William Carlos Williams**, Levertov is often grouped with the Black Mountain writers, primarily through her friendship with the poets Robert Creeley (a college friend of Goodman's) and Robert Duncan. Coming, like them, to poetic prominence in the highly charged political atmosphere of the 1960s and 1970s, she was partly radicalized by student activism on the university campuses in New York and California where she taught. However, her compassionate humanitarian politics, underpinned by the seam of spirituality that prevails in later works, can be traced to a childhood spent watching her father (a Russian Jew who converted to become an Anglican clergyman), mother, and older sister Olga protesting various causes (as an eleven-year-old, she sold the *Socialist Worker*). Levertov's appearances and speeches at anti–Vietnam War rallies and demonstrations across the country made her a household name. Controversially, the blending of poetry and politics caused her no difficulty: "there is no abrupt separation between so-called political poetry and so-called private poetry in an artist, who is in both cases writing out of his own inner life" (Brooker 31. See also the essays of *The Poet in the World*, 1973; *Light Up the Cave*, 1981; *New and Selected Essays*, 1992).

Earlier works like the elegaic sequence "Olga Poems," "The Pulse," and "Life at War" (*The Sorrow Dance*, 1967) and "Advent 1966" (*Relearning the Alphabet*, 1970) refract the sociocultural tensions of a period during which Levertov cofounded "Writers and Artists Protest against the War in Vietnam" (1965) and helped launch the antiwar movement RESIST (1967). Some argue that the sharper note of *To Stay Alive* (1971) and *Footprints* (1972), which records the trip she made to Hanoi, North Vietnam, with the poet Muriel Rukeyser, becomes more refined and persuasive in *The Freeing of the Dust* (1975), especially "The Pilots." Although claimed by feminists for poems like "Song for Ishtar," "Hypocrite Women" (*O Taste and See*, 1964), and "The Mutes" (*The Sorrow Dance*), Levertov always rejected the separatism of feminist ideology and was impatient of attempts to gender her political views.

Selected Bibliography: Brooker, Jewel Spears, ed. *Conversations with Denise Levertov.* Jackson: UP of Mississippi, 1998; Gelpi, Albert, ed. *Denise Levertov: Selected Criticism.* Ann Arbor: U of Michigan P, 1993; Sakelliou-Schulz, Liana. *Denise Levertov: An Annotated Primary and Secondary Bibliography.* New York: Garland, 1988; Wagner, Linda, ed. *Denise Levertov: In Her Own Province.* New York: New Directions, 1979; Wagner-Martin, Linda. *Critical Essays on Denise Levertov.* Boston: G. K. Hall, 1990.

Alice Entwistle

LEVI, PRIMO (1919–1987) was a nonreligious Italian Jew from Turin and an Auschwitz survivor whose *Se questo è un uomo* (*Survival in Auschwitz*, 1947) is one of the most respected works of **Holocaust literature**. Its perspective is broadly humanistic rather than specifically Jewish, and Levi strives for objectivity. As a scientist trained in a humanistic tradition, Levi documents the systematic nature of the extermination camp and of its dehumanization of both captors and captives, as signaled in his title. Levi's book was little noticed at first, having been rejected by the prestigious publisher Einaudi, which, however, published a second edition in 1958. His second book, *La tregua* (*The Reawakening*, 1963), carries on the inquiry to the liberation of the Auschwitz survivors by the Red Army and their months of journeying around Eastern Europe and, for Levi, back to Italy during 1945. Issues of what is ultimately political morality are strongly implied in both these works, as in his only novel, *Se non ora, quando?* (*If Not Now, When?* 1982), about Jewish Zionist Resistance fighters toward the end of **World War II**, as well as in several other literary works of memory and inquiry into the role of science and industry in relation to humanity written during his career as an industrial chemist, which have no direct link to the Holocaust or Jewishness. Some of the issues related to Levi's

Auschwitz experience—on the nature of evil, the gray area of moral indeterminacy, the unreliablity of memory, the difficulty of bringing home the enormity to others— are discursively treated in *I sommersi e i salvati* (*The Drowned and the Saved*, 1986). His best known work in the English speaking world is probably *Il sistemo periodico* (*The Periodic Table*, 1975), a collection of highly literary meditations on the human condition.

Selected Bibliography: Belpoliti, Marco, and Robert S. C. Gordon, eds. *The Voice of Memory: Primo Levi—Interviews 1961–1987*. Cambridge: Polity, 2001; Cicioni, Mirna. *Primo Levi: Bridges of Knowledge*. Oxford: Berg, 1995; Gordon, Robert S. C. *Primo Levi's Ordinary Virtues: From Testimony to Ethics*. Oxford: Oxford UP, 2001; Thomson, Ian. *Primo Levi*. London: Hutchinson, 2002.

John Gatt-Rutter

LEWIS, WYNDHAM (1882–1957). Born in Canada but a product of the British educational system, the Slade School of Art in London, and several years of *ad hoc* education in Paris, Lewis was first a revolutionary artist and then became—at least by reputation—the most reactionary of all the high modernists. Recognition of Lewis's interest in anarchism and Marxism has recently led to his political writings being understood as an ideological critique of the cultural consequences of capitalism. He wrote as early as 1926 that "the *capitalist state* is . . . an *educationalist state*" (*Art of Being Ruled*, 106). Subtle use of the terms **ideology** and **hegemony** here and in *Time and Western Man* (1927) suggest the beginnings of a critique consistent with later developments in **cultural studies**.

In 1908, Lewis began *Tarr* (1918, rev. 1928), a novel about artists in Paris, in parallel with his work as an artist. He led the radical art movement vorticism (1913–1915), which reacted against futurism and attempted to absorb the lessons of cubism while insisting on the importance of content. Lewis's experience as a gunner in **World War I** was the long-term cause of his postwar social and political critiques. *The Childermass* (1928) is an intensely imaginative fiction of the afterworld, dealing with contemporary philosophical problems of time and process. *The Apes of God* (1930) satirizes London literary life and the Sitwell family (not the Bloomsbury group, as is often thought). In 1931, Lewis published *Hitler*, the first of a number of ill-judged political books; all damaged his reputation, but he repudiated them and adopted a philosemitic position before 1939. *The Revenge for Love* (1937) is a political work of poise, intelligence, and sympathy. Lewis's reputation as an antifeminist is contradicted by his positive characterizations of women, notably Anastasya in *Tarr*, Margot in *The Revenge for Love*, and Hester in *Self Condemned* (1955).

Lewis and his wife spent 1939–1945 in the United States and Canada in an unhappy venture that bore fruit in *Self Condemned*, set in a fictionalized Toronto. He met **Marshall McLuhan**, who later noticed the phrase "now that the earth has become one big village" in Lewis's *America and Cosmic Man* (1949) and adapted it into "the global village." Lewis became blind in 1951 but continued to write, adding two volumes to *The Childermass* to make, in *The Human Age* trilogy (1955), an unsparing examination of the difficulties of the intellectual in the twentieth century.

Selected Bibliography: Edwards, Paul. *Wyndham Lewis: Painter and Writer*. New Haven: Yale UP, 2000; Jameson, Fredric. *Fables of Aggression: Wyndham Lewis, the Modernist as Fascist*. Berkeley: U of California P, 1979; O'Keeffe, Paul. *Some Sort of Genius: A Life of Wyndham Lewis*. London: Cape, 2000.

Alan Munton

LI ANG (1952–). Li Ang (pen name of Shih Shu-tuan) was born in Lu-kang, a coastal town in central Taiwan, famous for its unique architectural style and rich Taiwanese tradition, from which Li drew inspiration for her earlier works, such as "Flower Season" ("Hua ji," 1968). From 1975 to 1977, she studied at the University of Oregon and earned a master's degree in drama. After returning to Taiwan, Li published novels, short stories, and numerous essays on Taiwan's social and cultural issues, primarily in relation to gender politics. Always a controversial figure, Li attracted critical attention and rancorous criticism for her short novel, *The Butcher's Wife* (*Sha fu*, 1983), a tale of sex and power.

In spite of severe criticism, Li Ang has mercilessly indicted the patriarchal Taiwanese society for its hegemonic power over women and its regressive attitude toward women and sexual liberation. In the late 1980s, Li Ang was drawn into opposition politics, attending political rallies organized by the then illegal Democratic Progressive Party (DPP). Her political activities made her even more keenly aware of the complex interplay between sex and political power, as she was one of a handful of female activists in a predominately male arena. The experience steered her toward an exploration of women and power via four linked stories entitled *Everyone Got to Stick an Incense in the Beigang Burner* (*Beigang xianglu renren cha*, 1997). A huge scandal ensued when the director of public relations for the DPP was identified as the purported real-life model for the female protagonist, who sleeps her way to power. Li Ang was sued by the director, and many in the opposition camp attacked her for painting such a negative picture of women in politics. The controversy turned a serious exploration of women's accessibility to power into a sensational catfight between two women. Undaunted, Li Ang went on to write another political novel, *Autobiography: A Novel* (*Zizhuan de xiaoshuo*, 1999), which narrates the life of a legendary female member of the Taiwanese **Communist Party**, Xie Xuehong. It is also an examination of women in politics, as well as a study of women and writing/reading. It is an ambitious work that seeks to rewrite, re-present, and reinterpret women in modern Taiwanese history.

As a political activist/feminist/writer, Li Ang attempts to create a dialogue between life and art, bridging the gap between reality and fiction. The election of Annette Hsiu-lien Lü as Taiwan's first female vice president best illustrates the great strides Taiwanese women have taken toward increased political power, which is an uncanny reflection of the central theme of Li Ang's many works.

Selected Bibliography: Goldblatt, Howard. "Sex and Society: The Fiction of Li Ang." *Worlds Apart: Recent Chinese Writing and Its Audience*. Ed. Howard Goldblatt. Armonk, NY: M. E. Sharpe, 1990. 150–65; Haddon, Rosemary. "From Pulp to Politics: Aspects of Topicality in Fiction by Li Ang." *Modern Chinese Literature and Culture* 13.1 (2001): 36–72; Ng, Sheung-Yuen Daisy. "Feminism in the Chinese Context: Li Ang's *The Butcher's Wife*." *Gender Politics in Modern China: Writing and Feminism*. Ed. Tani E. Barlow. Durham, NC: Duke UP, 1993. 266–89; Ng, Sheung-Yuen Daisy. "Li Ang's Experiments with the Epistolary Form." *Modern Chinese Literature* 3.1–2 (1987): 91–106; Yeh, Michelle. "Shapes of Darkness: Symbols in Li Ang's Dark Night." *Modern Chinese Women Writers: Critical Appraisals*. Ed. Michael S. Duke. Armonk, NY: M. E. Sharpe, 1989. 78–95.

Sylvia Li-chun Lin

LIFE IN THE IRON MILLS. *See* DAVIS, REBECCA HARDING.

LINDSAY, JACK (1900–1989). An Australian who lived most of his life in England, Lindsay was an erudite and eclectic writer whose major works bear a strong imprint of his socialist convictions. He was the oldest son of the celebrated illustrator and cartoonist Norman Lindsay. Though denigrated by much of the art establishment, Norman Lindsay was the best-known Australian artist in the early decades of the twentieth century, and remains a popular figure. Jack's parents separated when he was a child. He spent an unhappy adolescence in Brisbane, where he studied classics at the university. Drawn to his father's bohemian world, Lindsay abandoned a promising academic career to move to Sydney and live by his pen. Throughout the 1920s, he was an enthusiastic advocate of his father's philosophy of exalting art and sex. In 1926, he traveled to London to establish a small publishing house and became a figure in the London literary world.

This phase of Lindsay's life ended with the Depression, which coincided with the bankruptcy of his business and a deep personal crisis. Instead of returning to Australia, he broke decisively with his father and withdrew to the English countryside, living in great poverty and refashioning himself as a novelist. His struggle to understand and write imaginatively about the past (as in *Rome for Sale*, 1934) prepared him for Marxism, at a time when many of his former associates were shifting to the right. Becoming a Communist at the beginning of 1936 triggered a creative outpouring almost manic in its intensity. In the following years, he did some of his best and most characteristic work: a study of John Bunyan (1937) that foreshadows recent **cultural studies** in its melding of Marxism, psychoanalysis, and textual criticism; a trilogy of novels about revolutionary periods of English history, beginning with *1649: A Novel of a Year* (1938); propaganda performance poems written for troupes at political rallies; and an attempt to explain his social philosophy in *A Short History of Culture* (1939, rev. 1962).

Immediately after the war, Lindsay was politically active, but by the early fifties, he had left London and settled in an Essex village. Beginning with *Betrayed Spring* (1953), he wrote nine novels about the class politics of contemporary Britain; sales were modest, however, and in his last decades, he concentrated on writing books about aspects of the ancient world and biographies of artists noteworthy for their rich social backgrounds and attention to the role of political ideas and events in artistic creation, including *J.M.W. Turner* (1966), *Cézanne* (1972), and *William Morris* (1979). During these years, he also found time to write three wonderful volumes of autobiography, probably his magnum opus (republished as *Life Rarely Tells: An Autobiography in Three Volumes*, 1982).

Lindsay's vast and fascinating output was uneven, and his idiosyncratic Marxism, drawing heavily on early twentieth-century anthropology, has attracted little interest.

Nevertheless, his influence has been greater than his slight fame might suggest. He was a noteworthy presence in a wide range of fields and specialties: the social life of Roman Egypt, seventeenth- and eighteenth-century English history, Australian poetry, French art, British socialist realism—the list goes on. Furthermore, despite living in impoverished and somewhat isolated circumstances for much of his life, he met and maintained an extensive correspondence with significant writers and intellectuals around the world. After many years of marginalization in Australia, he is finally winning acceptance there as an important figure in its cultural history.

Selected Bibliography: Gillen, Paul. *Faithful to the Earth: A Jack Lindsay Compendium.* Sydney: Collins/Angus and Robertson, 1993; Smith, Bernard, ed. *Culture and History.* Sydney: Hale and Iremonger, 1984.

Paul A. Gillen

LIPPARD, GEORGE (1822–1854). Born on a modest Pennsylvania Dutch homestead near the Wissahickon River outside Philadelphia, close to the site of a vanished utopian colony, young Lippard traveled to the big city to make his fortune as a journalist. There he learned rapidly by writing fiction for the "story papers," weekly tabloids that relied on melodrama and served as popular entertainment for the literate working classes. Struck by the juxtaposition of wealth and poverty in this first heavily industrialized zone of the new nation—home to a near general strike in 1825, and to virtual ethnic-religious warfare between Irish and English-born residents in later decades—Lippard turned radical with a vengeance.

The approximate American counterpart of Eugene Sue, the immensely popular French radical novelist, Lippard delivered in *The Quaker City, or Monks of Monk Hall* (1845) an exposé of the moral corruption of the financial class and, most especially, their preying on innocent girls of the working class (as Lippard feared for his younger sister, also drawn to the city, impoverished and perhaps tempted by prostitution). *Quaker City* sold some sixty thousand copies, followed by more than a dozen other volumes and hundreds of short stories in his short life. *New York: Its Upper Ten and Lower Million* (1853) once more showed upper-class corruption, while *Washington and His Generals* (1847) emphasized the patriotism of idealists, and *Paul Ardenheim, the Monk of Wissahickon* (1848) cast light on Lippard's own self-assessment as the scribe of German American pietists.

An acquaintance of Edgar Allan Poe, Lippard drew more on the British traditions of **gothic literature**, with political interpretations closely etched on scenes of sometimes unearthly horror. Ardently patriotic, Lippard could at times become militantly antiracist, embracing African Americans, Native Americans, and those of all ethnic types. He could also envision an imagined, secret international brotherhood of workers, essentially a literary precursor to the International Workingmen's Association led by **Karl Marx** shortly after Lippard's demise.

In the few years before his death, Lippard had become a noted lecturer and political activist, launching the Brotherhood of the Union in 1849, a protolabor movement with its own organ (*The White Journal,* for which Lippard wrote most of the contents) and secret ritual. The Brotherhood survived in various forms for a century, mainly in Pennsylvania, becoming essentially an insurance cooperative; among its early members was Uriah Stephens, founder of the Knights of Labor, who clearly drew examples from the Brotherhood. A victim of tuberculosis ("the shop disease," as Jewish Socialists would call the illness common to urban working classes), Lippard drew crowds of radical craftsmen to his funeral, demonstrating one final time that the poor and exploited had possessed a champion of their own.

Selected Bibliography: Reynolds, David S. *Beneath the American Renaissance: The Subversive Imagination in the Age of Emerson and Melville.* Cambridge, MA: Harvard UP, 1988; Reynolds, David S. *George Lippard.* Boston: Twayne, 1982; Reynolds, David S., ed. *George Lippard, Prophet of Protest: Writings of an American Radical, 1822–1854.* New York: Peter Lang, 1986.

Paul Buhle

LONDON, JACK (1876–1916). The foremost "adventure" novelist in early twentieth-century America and over the next half century the most widely read American author around the globe, London was a socialist enigma. The working-class revolutionist who could not accept his own celebrity, he was also the social Darwinist and racial fatalist who chose personal escape to places far from an overcivilized culture. Born in Oakland, California, London was significantly the son of a troubled relationship (and nonmarriage) between a local spiritualist and an astrologer. He grew up along the docks; called to the water, he was arrested as a teenager for raiding the oyster beds owned by the railroad trust. Harried by police, he headed for the Alaska Territory and the gold rush. Unsuccessful in this venture and more interested in the human element of the north country, he returned to Oakland and wrote the adventure fiction *Call of the Wild* (1901), which captured the attention of readers across the world. Here and in several other works (including an extended novel from the perspective of an Alaskan husky), London drew a portrait of the freedom of the wild—unbounded, virile, death-dealing, but also symbolic of the basics of existence. Committed to the socialist movement from the early years of the century, and especially beloved by the members and followers of the **Industrial Workers of the World (IWW)**, London was also a melancholy dreamer, alcohol abuser, and compulsive writer, who spent his energies on stories and novels for publication while falling frequently into depression and bouts of heavy drinking. A founder of the Intercollegiate Socialist Society, which urged educated young people to move leftward, London portrayed in *Martin Eden* (1909) a desperately sad writer of proletarian origins who becomes successful but also frustrated by his own success, certain that he is being personally transformed into something commercial and artificial. The novel's protagonist throws himself overboard to drown—a more than symbolic suicide, as the author sank further into drink. *The Iron Heel* (1911), an important and influential work of **dystopian literature**, foresaw something very much like fascism, including the willingness, almost eagerness, of most Americans to accept the crushing of idealists. "The Dream of Debs," published after his early death, offered a vision of redemption led by the most Christlike of American radicals until the emergence of Martin Luther King Jr. London met the outbreak of **World War I** with personal confusion and a craving to escape its complications. His literary representation of nature as a war of all versus all had reinforced a youthful prejudice against Asians at large, and he first construed the war as a crusade of Aryan civilization. On the other hand, enraged by capitalism's depredations, he supported the IWW with speech and check-book, certain that one day workers would literally take the industries from their en-emies. By the 1920s and 1930s, translations of London into Russian made him, in remarkable ways, one of the favorite modern "Russian" authors, attuned to the mix-ture of idealism and fatalism, melancholy and romance, perhaps more suited to So-viet readers than their American counterparts. As the next century turned, London continued to find new generations of readers, perhaps previewing interest among those who viewed society as once again in desperate straits.

Selected Bibliography: Labor, Earle. *Jack London.* New York: Twayne, 1974; London, Jack. *Jack London, American Rebel: A Collection of His Social Writings.* New York: Citadel, 1947; London, Joan. *Jack London and His Daughters.* San Bernardino, CA: Borego P, 1995; Sinclair, Andrew. *Jack: A Biography of Jack London.* New York: Harper and Row, 1977.

Paul Buhle

***LOOKING BACKWARD: 2000–1887* (1888).** A best-selling and vastly influential utopian novel of the late nineteenth century, *Looking Backward* was one of the lead-ing works of utopian literature of its time. This romantic narrative was the genius child of journalist-turned-novelist Edward Bellamy (1850–1898). It influenced a gen-eration of radicals and of doubters in the emerging industrial capitalism and remained on the shelves of readers deep in the nation's heartland for a generation or more, a reminder that the American Dream enjoyed by the powerful also contained large el-ements of nightmare for those less fortunate.

Author Bellamy, born in Chicopee, Massachusetts, attended Union College, stud-ied law, and then abandoned it to become a successful newspaper and short-story writer. From early on, he leaned toward a kind of early **science fiction**, the imagina-tive fiction perhaps best exemplified in Nathaniel Hawthorne but adopted by many radical critics during the 1870s–1890s. Bellamy's fantasy tales, often satirical, dealt with all manner of abnormal psychology, and provided a searing critique of the de-struction of the natural environment for an ugly capitalist culture of acquisitiveness.

These writings prepared Bellamy for *Looking Backward*, the tale of a sleeper who awakens in the year 2000 and discovers around him a society that has made rational decisions to become cooperative, friendly to nature, but also highly productive, with most necessary labor conducted by safe and clean machinery. Government itself has been reduced to the absolute minimum, and there is no need for lawyers, politicians, police, or jails, any more than slums, advertising, a standing army, or sexism.

Bellamy's warm endorsement of women's equality was among the most remarkable elements of his work, inspiring women reformers such as Women's Christian Tem-perance Union leader Frances Willard to embrace its "Christian socialist" vision. Bel-lamy Clubs formed by the dozens, a most remarkable phase of political and intellectual life in the fin de siècle period. Such noted reformers as Civil War hero Thomas Went-worth Higginson, Madame Blavatsky (representing a wing of theosophists who adopted the novel as their own), putative baseball founder Abner Doubleday, future socialist leader (then Professsor at Columbia) Daniel DeLeon, and Newport socialite Maude Howe Elliott (daughter of Julia Ward Howe) found their inspiration in it.

Enthusiasts published their own journal, the *Nationalist*, while Bellamy himself launched the *New Nation*, both widely read. Meanwhile, the novel spawned a new phase of intended utopian colonies, mostly in the West. Only a few of these survived their opening years, but the theosophist Kaweah (outside present-day San Diego) lasted for decades. Bellamy had himself joined the populist cause, and near the end of his short life, he endorsed political Socialism.

Although often unfavorably compared with the better literary style and less regimented descriptions of future society in William Morris's *News from Nowhere* (written partly in response to Bellamy), *Looking Backward* was perfectly suited for an American society out of kilter and ready to reconsider its basic assumptions. It also influenced any number of subsequent visions of the future, including the more modern socialistic response of Mack Reynolds's *Looking Backward, from the Year 2000* (1973).

Selected Bibliography: Morgan, Arthur. *Edward Bellamy.* New York: Columbia UP, 1944; Patai, Daphne, ed. *Looking Backward 1988–1888: Essays on Edward Bellamy.* Amherst: U of Massachusetts P, 1988; Rosemont, Franklin, ed. *Apparitions of Things to Come: Edward Bellamy's Tales of Mystery and Imagination.* Chicago: Charles H. Kerr Co., 1990.

Paul Buhle

LORDE, AUDRE (1934–1992). The daughter of Caribbean immigrants to the United States, Audre Lorde achieved international stature as a poet and social activist. Growing up in New York City in the 1940s and 1950s, Lorde negotiated the particularly vehement racism and xenophobia faced by migrating southern blacks and Caribbean immigrants in the northern United States at that time. She completed her B.A. at Hunter College in 1959 and her M.L.S. at the Columbia University School of Library Science in 1961. She began her teaching career as poet-in-residence at Tougaloo College in 1968, eventually holding the Thomas Hunter Chair at Hunter College. Her first books of poetry—*The First Cities* (1968), *Cables to Rage* (1970), *From a Land Where Other People Live* (1973), and *New York Head Shop and Museum* (1974)—were published by small presses, and her poetry was identified with both the **black arts movement** and the feminist movement, whose adherents provided the main audience for writers who challenged the apolitical aesthetics of mainstream publishing. Initially, however, even these allies on matters of race and gender responded to the representation of lesbian sexuality in her poetry with homophobia. When *From a Land Where Other People Live* was nominated for the National Book Award, Lorde's work began to find a broader audience, and ultimately she became a model for writers of the gay movement. Politicizing the intimate, the familial, and the erotic, Lorde's poetry renders exceptionally nuanced connections among gender, sexuality, class, race, health, ability, and nation, complicating its seamless appropriation by any group defined by a singular identity. Her use of the enjambed free-verse line to create, question, and revise meaning provides formal complexity consonant with the multiplicity she asked her audiences to acknowledge within and among themselves and across the world. Lorde's direct address and challenge to her audiences made her readings unforgettable demonstrations of the power of poetry. Later books, especially *The Black Unicorn* (1978) and *Our Dead Behind Us* (1986), establish her link to the African diaspora. Exclusively published by small presses, Lorde's prose also broke thematic and formal ground. *The Cancer Journals* (1980) chronicles her battle with breast cancer and mastectomy; her "biomythography" *Zami* (1982) provides a fictionalized account of the first twenty years of her life; and *Sister Outsider* (1984) collects key essays. Lorde was the recipient of numerous awards and honors, including two National Endowment for the Arts grants and the Walt Whitman citation of merit. In 1991, she was named poet laureate of New York State. In 1992, having made her home on the island of St. Croix and taken the African name Gamba Adisa, Lorde died of liver cancer.

Selected Bibliography: De Veaux, Alexis. *Warrior Poet: A Biography of Audre Lorde.* New York: W.W. Norton, 2004; Hall, Joan Wylie, ed. *Conversations with Audre Lorde.* Jackson: UP of Mississippi, 2004; *A Litany for Survival: The Life and Work of Audre Lorde.* Dir. Ada Gay Griffin and Michelle Parkerson. Third World Newsreel, 1996.

Zofia Burr

LOVE ON THE DOLE (1933). Walter Greenwood's *Love on the Dole* was one of the most important of a number of novels focusing on working-class life that appeared in Great Britain in the early 1930s. It presents a vivid account of the tribulations of the working-class inhabitants of the impoverished Hanky Park district of the town of Pendleton, based on Greenwood's own Salford, near Manchester. The book focuses primarily on the Hardcastle family and the increasing hardships they suffer in the course of the book. It opens in 1923 as young Harry Hardcastle, sixteen, completes his schooling and manages to obtain a seemingly desirable position as an apprentice machinist in Marlowe's Engineering Works, one of the largest local employers. Harry soon realizes that Marlowe's is pursuing a policy of employing as many apprentices as possible because of their low wages and then dismissing them when their seven-year apprenticeship is finished. By the time Harry himself is dismissed, the English economy has taken an overall downturn, and the entire family is plunged into hardship.

In the course of the book, Harry becomes engaged to Helen Hawkins and is forced to marry her after she becomes pregnant. This pregnancy leads to a violent confrontation between Harry and Mr. Hardcastle, and Harry and Helen are forced to live in squalid conditions on their own. Harry quickly deteriorates both physically and emotionally. Sally, his beautiful sister, falls in love with Larry Meath, a local worker who provides the book's principal political consciousness. Meath is clearly set apart from the other locals by his superior sensitivity and intelligence, but his efforts to educate his fellow workers in social ideas meet with very little success. Already frail, Meath dies of pneumonia after being beaten by police, and Sally, driven to desperation, eventually becomes the mistress of the disreputable bookmaker Sam Grundy, whose continuing success suggests that, in these conditions, only criminals prosper.

Historian A.J.P. Taylor has called *Love on the Dole* "one of the few genuinely 'proletarian' novels written in English," going on to suggest that Greenwood's novel is rivaled only by Robert Tressell's **The Ragged Trousered Philanthropists** as a British proletarian novel (352). Greenwood's novel was probably the most prominent of the numerous examples of British working-class fiction that were produced in the 1930s, becoming a popular play (first performed in 1934) and eventually a successful commercial film (in 1941).

The success of the book, however, may have partly had to do with the fact that it was unthreatening to middle-class readers in its failure to suggest radical political solutions to the problems it describes. Thus, Carole Snee argues that Greenwood's novel is "a cry of outrage, but the rage is impotent, for his own ideological position is essentially that of the liberal reformer" (171). On the other hand, Ramón López Ortega finds in the book's language an effective representation of working-class consciousness, while Roger Webster makes an extended argument that the book actually manages to subvert bourgeois literary conventions.

Selected Bibliography: Constantine, Stephen. "*Love on the Dole* and Its Reception in the 1930s." *Literature and History* 8.2 (1982): 232–47; López Ortega, Ramón. "The Language of the Working-Class Novel of the 1930s." *The Socialist Novel in Britain: Towards the Recovery of a Tradition.* Ed. H. Gustav Klaus. New York: St. Martin's, 1982. 122–44; Snee, Carole. "Working-Class Literature or Proletarian Writing?" *Culture and Crisis in Britain in the Thirties.* Ed. Jon Clark, Margot Heinemann, David Margolies, and Carole Snee. London: Lawrence and Wishart, 1979. 165–91; Taylor, A.J.P. *English History 1914–1945.* Oxford: Oxford UP, 1992; Webster, Roger. "*Love on the Dole* and the Aesthetic of Contradiction." *The British Working-Class Novel in the Twentieth Century.* Ed. Jeremy Hawthorn. London: Edward Arnold, 1984. 49–62.

M. Keith Booker

LU XUN (1881–1936), pen name of Zhou Shuren, born in Shaoxing, in the southeastern-seaboard province of Zhejiang. Lu Xun achieved prominence by the early 1920s as the author of modern short stories, while his stature as an essayist and social critic continued to grow into the 1930s when he became the chief intellectual spokesman for the opposition—first to the warlords and then, after 1927, to the one-party rule of the nationalists, or Kuomintang. By the early 1930s, he became associated with the **Communist Party**—then an illegal underground oppositional organization—although he never joined it officially.

The Zhou clan were scholar-gentry, but fell on hard times after a scandal involving Lu Xun's grandfather and the premature death of Lu Xun's father. Lu Xun went on government scholarship to Japan in 1902 to study Western medicine, hoping to do something to alleviate the suffering of victims like his father, thereby promoting the cause of reform at home. But his interests turned more and more toward literature, and he eventually gave up the study of medicine. Returning to China in 1909, Lu Xun taught in academic institutions until 1927 (and also worked in the newly founded Ministry of Education of the Republic). His disappointment at the failure of the 1911 revolution to make genuine changes in Chinese society is reflected in his satiric novella *The True Story of Ah Q* (1921), which uses black humor to point out the foibles in the character of Ah Q, a hapless coolie who is bullied by others and in turn bullies the weak. Though a bully, Ah Q is not without a sympathetic side, and this leads us to the perception of an injustice when he is arrested, tried, and wrongfully shot as a looter by the new order. A film version of Ah Q was released in 1981, with a fairly faithful screenplay adaptation by Chen Baichen.

Lu Xun's *Diary of a Madman* (1918) is often regarded as the first "modern" Chinese short story. This has to do not only with its unconventional use of the vernacular language but, more importantly, with its innovative style (it is presented by the narrator in the form of a real diary by an alleged madman) and sensational content (it indicts the old order as "cannibalistic"). *The New-Year Sacrifice* (1924), the tragic story of a twice-widowed woman taken into service by a gentry family, was adapted into a film with the same title in 1956 by the communist playwright Xia Yan.

Lu Xun also composed a collection of acclaimed prose poetry reminiscent of Baudelaire, published in 1927 under the title *Wild Grass*. In his final years, he devoted himself almost exclusively to polemical articles for journals and short essays critical of the right-wing Kuomintang government. He continued to write classical-style poetry until 1935, the year before his death.

Selected Bibliography: Hsia, T.A. *The Gate of Darkness: Studies on the Leftist Literary Movement in China*. Seattle: U of Washington P, 1968; Kowallis, Jon Eugene von. *The Lyrical Lu Xun: A Study of His Classical Style Verse*. Honolulu: U of Hawaii P, 1996; Lee, Leo Ou-fan. *Voices from the Iron House: A Study of Lu Xun*. Bloomington: Indiana UP, 1987; Lee, Leo Ou-fan, ed. *Lu Xun and His Legacy*. Berkeley: U of California P, 1985; Lyell, William A. *Lu Hsün's Vision of Reality*. Berkeley: U of California P, 1976; Prusek, Jaroslav. *The Lyrical and the Epic*. Bloomington: Indiana UP, 1985.

Jon Eugene von Kowallis

LUKÁCS, GEORG (1885–1971). The son of a Jewish Hungarian banker, Lukács grew up to become an important, many-sided cultural figure, comparable in range and achievement to such other major twentieth-century intellectual figures as **Jean-Paul Sartre** and Bertrand Russell. He also played a leading role in the Hungarian communist movement. Lukács, who was bilingual in Hungarian and German, wrote mainly in German. He was also something of a prodigy, helping to organize the Thalia Theater in his native Budapest while still a teenager. His huge corpus, which began when he was only seventeen, continued in an immense outpouring in such fields as literary criticism, literary theory, history of literature, Marxism, and aesthetics.

Lukács's intellectual itinerary is inseparable from the events of his time. Before **World War I**, he studied in Heidelberg, where he became acquainted with **Max Weber**, attempting unsuccessfully to write a second doctoral dissertation under his direction, and came under the influence of the important neo-Kantian Emil Lask. Lukács subsequent career divides neatly into two main parts, a shorter pre-Marxist period, ending with a sudden, unexpected conversion to Marxism in December 1918, and a much longer, exceptionally convoluted Marxist period extending over more than five decades. His long Marxist period is marked by a continuous but continually unsuccessful effort to be politically orthodox, which led him to perform public acts of self-criticism and to renounce some of his most important works almost as soon as they were published.

Lukács's published output was enormous. His first important book, *Soul and Form* (1910), often regarded as an early existentialist work, appeared when Lukács was only twenty-five. Before he turned to Marxism, he also produced two interesting studies of basic aesthetics. His *Heidelberg Philosophy of Art* (1912–1914), which anticipates the problems he later took up in writings on aesthetics during his Marxist period, employs a neo-Kantian approach—strongly influenced by Lask—for the study of the aesthetic object. Lukács here develops a type of aesthetic phenomenology in the study of values. His *Heidelberg Aesthetic*, which was written slightly later (1916–1918), appeared only posthumously. This work studies the autonomy of the art object on the basis of Kant's third *Critique* and Lask's views. Lukács's still residual Kantianism is evident on the first page of the book in the claim that any aesthetics must begin with the Kantian question of the possibility of works of art. This study is further important for an early indication of Lukács's later strong interest in G.W.F. Hegel. During this early period, Lukács also produced *The Theory of the Novel* (1915), a study of the genre that is still influential today.

Lukács is mainly known today as a many-sided, brilliant Marxist thinker. In virtue of the depth and originality of his philosophical insights, Lukács ranks as perhaps the most important among the many Marxist philosophers of the twentieth century. Unlike most Marxists, who tend to make sweeping pronouncements about what they call bourgeois philosophy, by the standards of the day, Lukács was thoroughly trained in philosophy, particularly in German idealism and German neo-Kantianism. His most important Marxist work is the seminal, highly influential collection of essays *History and Class Consciousness: Studies in Marxist Dialectics,* which appeared in 1923. The overall aim of this work can be described as an effort to produce a philosophical justification of bolshevism through an examination of related themes. In comparison to other Marxist authors, this book is distinguished by a strong emphasis on Hegel. With Karl Korsch, another Marxist philosopher, Lukács is responsible for creating Hegelian Marxism. One of the most important aspects of *History and Class Consciousness* is Lukács's attention to the relation of **Karl Marx** and Hegel, hence the importance of the latter for understanding the former. Throughout his long Marxist period, he is constantly concerned with understanding Marx in terms of Hegel and Hegel in terms of Marx.

In *History and Class Consciousness*, Lukács examines a number of themes from an orthodox and even sometimes unorthodox Marxist perspective. Lukács suggests that orthodox Marxism concerns only a particular approach, that is, historical materialism, as opposed to any single doctrine. And he suggests the need to transform historical materialism into an authentic method for concrete historical research. His account of class consciousness focuses attention on this concept, which is central to the early Marx's view of social change.

The long central essay in this book, "Reification and the Class Consciousness of the Proletariat," has been very influential. Lukács here calls attention to the category of the whole, or totality in Hegel and Marx. He brilliantly rediscovers Marx's concept of **alienation** at a time when Marx's early writings had not yet been published. The fact that Lukács tends to conflate alienation and objectification under the single heading of **reification**, a mistake he later corrected, does not detract from the importance of this discovery. He further departs from Marxist orthodoxy in criticizing Friedrich Engels while improving on the latter's contention that Marxism, which he understands as continuous with Marx, solves the main problems of German idealism. In the same essay, Lukács famously criticizes Engels, whose grasp of philosophy was precarious, for basic misunderstandings of Kant, especially as concerns the "thing in itself." According to Lukács, beginning in Kant and ending in Hegel, classical German philosophy tries to solve the problem of knowledge of the thing in itself. This unsuccessful effort culminates in Hegel's mythological theory of history. The problem is only later solved by Marx in his discovery of what Lukács, in a Hegelian turn of phrase, calls the identical subject-object.

This brilliant text called attention to Lukács as a leading Marxist intellectual. Yet since Lukács desired to adhere to Marxist orthodoxy, he immediately abandoned his very interesting philosophical approach to Hegelian Marxism, including rescinding his criticism of Engels and hence orthodox Marxism. When in 1924 **Vladimir Lenin**'s *Materialism and Empiriocriticism* (1908)—in comparison to Lukács's writings an inferior work of philosophical scholarship—became known in the West, Lukács simply renounced his work and rescinded his criticism of Engels.

In writings after *History and Class Consciousness*, Lukács considerably reinforces his emphasis on Hegel. During the late 1930s and early 1940s, Lukács spent considerable time abroad, mainly in the Soviet Union. During this period, he produced a number of significant studies. Marxists, including Lukács, have often taken a reductive approach to literature, which they label as good or bad in terms of its adherence to social realism, which they routinely take as the only style adequate to providing a faithful depiction of the social world. In a detailed study of *The Historical Novel* (1937), Lukács breaks with this simplistic conception of literature through a rich account of the historical novel against the background of the historical context. He argues that the historical novel only became possible after the **French Revolution**, and further argues that it belongs to the progressive forces linked to the realization of all that is best in human beings. In his preface to the English translation, **Fredric Jameson** calls *The Historical Novel* "perhaps the single most monumental realization of the varied program and promises of a Marxist and a dialectical literary criticism." Lukács's study of the historical novel formed part of his general advocacy of realism as the appropriate mode for socialist writers. In the **Brecht-Lukács debate**, Lukács upheld this view in opposition to **Bertolt Brecht**, who advocated modernism—a mode Lukács saw as symptomatic of bourgeois decadence.

At the same time, Lukács was continuing and deepening his research on Hegel. In *The Young Hegel*, which was completed in 1938 but only appeared in 1947, Lukács provides the first and only full-length Marxist study of Hegel's thought. This book centers on the relation of Marx and Hegel as viewed through the lens of the concept of alienation. Lukács here provides the first detailed account from any angle of vision of the relation of philosophy and economics in Hegel's position.

Due to his desire to be politically orthodox, Lukács was never able to isolate himself from political currents, such as Stalinism. *The Young Hegel* belongs to the early phase of Lukács's Stalinist period; *Existentialism or Marxism?* (1948) and *The Destruction of Reason* (1962) both belong to the later phase. The book on existentialism and Marxism is a short, polemical work, growing out of a series of lectures presented shortly after **World War II**. It is meant to compare and contrast the two leading contenders for philosophical supremacy at the time. From the vantage point of his commitment to Marxist orthodoxy, Lukács here argues that existentialism is a form of idealism and that there is no third way between idealism and materialism.

The very long and detailed account of reason continues the analysis of the intrinsic irrationality of non-Marxist philosophy in tracing the rise of irrationalism from Schelling's middle period through Schopenhauer and Kierkegaard, then through Nietzsche to National Socialism. In the study of reason, the emphasis shifts from the need to choose between one of only two alternatives to the social consequences of idealism. Through his discussion in this book of Germany's path to Hitler, Lukács hopes to enable Germany to understand and hence to overcome the possibility of a revival of the fascism that arose within its borders. In arguing that irrationalism, defined as the alternative to Marxism, in some sense leads to fascism, Lukács implies clearly but unconvincingly that fascism is the consequence of the failure to opt for philosophical materialism.

Shortly before his death, Lukács was at work on two huge, unfinished studies: *The Specific Nature of the Aesthetic* (1962) and *The Ontology of Social Being* (1971). The two-volume work on aesthetics is the major aesthetic treatise of Lukács's Marxist period, though Lukács completed only approximately the first third of the planned study. Gone at this point is Lukács's earlier Kantianism, which is replaced by his characteristic Hegelian Marxism, in this case a detailed effort to apply the Hegelian category of specificity (*Besonderheit*) to aesthetic phenomena. Lukács here argues that form, which is determined by content, constitutes an ever more concrete objective totality through a developmental process. According to Lukács, an artwork presents the objective unity of subjective and objective elements. As in his writings on literary theory and literary criticism, Lukács is interested less in problems of beauty than in those of truth.

Lukács's enormous study of ontology, which was originally intended as a prolegomenon to a Marxist theory of ethics, later grew into a separate work, which runs to the almost fantastic length of 1,457 pages. Here, at the end of his long Marxist itinerary, Lukács returns to many of his early Marxist themes in a discussion that is no longer orthodox in any recognizable sense. This multifaceted work includes a greater appreciation of non-Marxist thought on its own merits, and a view of Marx's position as continuous with but going further than the preceding philosophical tradition. Lukács, who now moves away from a strictly economic interpretation of Marx, reinterpets the latter's position as a new philosophy of history. He follows Marx in envisioning ontology as a philosophy based on history, more specifically an ontology of social being. He also appropriates ontological insights from Nikolai Hartmann, a non-Marxist German philosopher.

In his study of social ontology, Lukács returns once again to Hegel on the basis of the traditional Marxist claim for the priority of being to thought. From this vantage point, he now detects an unresolved dualism including false and true ontologies in Hegel's thought. Hegel's false ontology lies in the view that authentic ontological relations initially receive their appropriate conceptual expression in the form of logical categories. His true ontology is the ontological view in which logical categories are understood not as pure moments of thought but as the dynamic constituents of the essential movement of reality itself. Here, at the end of Lukács's lengthy Marxist itinerary, the standard Marxist critique of Hegel as an idealist from the materialist perspective is no longer accepted. The supposed reversal of Hegel's thought in Marx's position is not a simple inversion; it is rather Marx's rejection of one strand of Hegel's thought in favor of another.

Selected Bibliography: Lukács, Georg. *The Destruction of Reason*. 2 vols. Trans. Peter Palmer. Atlantic Highlands, NJ: Humanities P, 1981; Lukács, Georg. *Die Eigenart des Ästhetischen*. 2 vols. Berlin: Aufbau-Verlag, 1987; Lukács, Georg. *Existentialisme ou marxisme?* Trans. E. Kelemen. Paris: Nagel, 1948; Lukács, Georg. *Heidelberger Ästhetik (1916–1918)*. Ed. György Márkus and Frank Benseler.

Darmstadt: Luchterhand, 1975; Lukács, Georg. *Heidelberger Philosophie der Kunst (1912–1914)*. Ed. György Márkus and Frank Benseler. Darmstadt: Luchterhand, 1974; Lukács, Georg. *The Historical Novel*. Trans. Hannah Mitchell and Stanley Mitchell. Lincoln: U of Nebraska P, 1983; Lukács, Georg. *The Ontology of Social Being*. Trans. David Fernbach. London: Merlin, 1980; Lukács, Georg. *Realism in Our Time: Literature and the Class Struggle*. Trans. John Mander and Necke Mander. New York: Harper and Row, 1964; Lukács, Georg. *Soul and Form*. Trans. Anna Bostock. Cambridge, MA: MIT P, 1974; Lukács, Georg. *The Young Hegel: Studies in the Relation between Dialectics and Economics*. Trans. Rodney Livingston. Cambridge, MA: MIT P, 1975; Lunn, Eugene. *Marxism and Modernism: An Historical Study of Lukács, Brecht, Benjamin, and Adorno*. Berkeley: U of California P, 1982; Rockmore, Tom. *Irrationalism: Lukács and the Marxist View of Reason*. Philadelphia: Temple UP, 1992.

Tom Rockmore

LUMPKIN, GRACE (1891–1980). Author of **proletarian fiction** focusing on industrialization and race relations in the South. She was born to a family of the fallen southern aristocracy in Milledgeville, Georgia, the daughter of a Confederate veteran. Her family moved to South Carolina around 1900 to try to recoup its financial standing (her sister Katherine would eventually become a prominent sociologist, and her brother, a U.S. Senator). In 1910, the family established a farm on which Grace first came into contact with white and African American sharecroppers. She attended Brenau College in Gainesville, Georgia, to become a teacher; as a teacher, she started a night school for farmers, and spent summers living with mill workers and sharecroppers in the North Carolina mountains. She worked for the YWCA in France for a year; in 1924, she went to New York, where she worked for the *World Today*—a Quaker publication—and studied journalism at Columbia University. She became involved in pacifist and socialist movements in New York, and eventually joined the **Communist Party.**

Lumpkin was prominent in radical literary circles of the 1930s. She published the novel *To Make My Bread,* based on the **Gastonia Mill Strike**, in 1932 and *A Sign for Cain*, based on the Scottsboro Boys case, in 1935, after which she became anticommunist. Her third novel, *The Wedding* (1939), was personal and nonpolitical. In later life she turned reactionary, testifying before a Senate subcommittee in the 1950s and naming names of her radical former friends. She also became quite religious, and returned to Columbia, South Carolina. Her final novel, *Full Circle* (1962), portrays a protagonist who leaves the church, becomes a communist, then returns to the church. She died in 1980.

Selected Bibliography: Cook, Sylvia Jenkins. "Gastonia: The Literary Reverberations of the Strike." *Southern Literary Journal* 7.1 (1974): 49–66; Foley, Barbara. *Radical Representations: Politics and Form in U.S. Proletarian Fiction, 1929–1941*. Durham, NC: Duke UP, 1993; Hapke, Laura. *Daughters of the Great Depression: Women, Work, and Fiction in the American 1930s*. Athens: U of Georgia P, 1995; Lumpkin, Katharine Du Pre. *The Making of a Southerner*. 1946. Athens: U of Georgia P, 1992; Sowinska, Suzanne. "Writing across the Color Line: White Women Writers and the 'Negro Question' in the Gastonia Novels." *Radical Revisions: Rereading 1930s Culture*. Ed. Bill Mullen and Sherry Lee Linkon. Urbana: U of Illinois P, 1996. 120–43.

Renny Christopher

M

MACDIARMID, HUGH (1892–1978). This major poet of twentieth-century Scotland was christened Christopher Murray Grieve and began using the name Hugh MacDiarmid in 1922. Politically active throughout his adult life, he became a founding member of the National Party of Scotland (NPS) in 1928. The NPS merged with the Scottish Party to become the Scottish National Party (SNP) in 1934, and MacDiarmid was the official SNP candidate in the 1945 election in Kelvingrove (Glasgow). He also became a member of the **Communist Party** of Great Britain in 1934, though his relationship with the party was troubled due to his advocacy of Scottish separatist self-determination without reference to party directives. On the other hand, he explained in his autobiography, *Lucky Poet* (1943), his view that "Scottish separation is part of the process of England's imperial disintegration and is a help towards the ultimate triumph of the workers of the world." Finally expelled from the party in 1939, he was readmitted in 1957 after the Soviet suppression of the Hungarian Uprising, and remained a member until his death. He stood as a Communist Party candidate against the Conservative prime minister Sir Alec Douglas-Home in the general election of October 15, 1964, in the constituency of Kinross and West Perthshire, a farming area. The publicity generated by a subsequent court case that raised the question of equal broadcasting rights for minority parties was a triumph for the Communist Party and MacDiarmid.

MacDiarmid's relationship with Ireland is also important. In an interview the year before his death, he recalls that he was in barracks in Sheffield when the **Easter Rising** in Ireland took place in 1916, and if it had been possible, he would have deserted the British Army and joined the Irish. He claims to have taken a very active part subsequently in gunrunning for the Irish. In 1928 he visited Ireland, meeting **W. B. Yeats**, AE (George William Russell), Oliver St. John Gogarty, and Eamon de Valera; he and **Sean O'Casey** became good friends. MacDiarmid's drive toward an independent Scottish republic was encouraged by his idealized vision of Ireland.

MacDiarmid's early poetry is in English, but in 1922, he began publishing poetry in Scots, the ancient tongue of William Dunbar and Robert Burns. His early lyrics are intense, densely packed imagist masterpieces, including "The Bonnie Broukit Bairn," in which a Dickensian picture of a neglected child looking in on a high-class soiree of well-dressed sophisticates is metaphorically seen as earth among the constellation of unpopulated planets and an inhuman universe. Human life and expressivity is at the center of these poems, along with a sense of human potential—whether wasted in the apocalypse of **World War I** or still to be developed in unforeseeable ways. The book-length *A Drunk Man Looks at the Thistle* (1926) includes "Ballad of the General Strike" and other explicitly political passages. Formally, MacDiarmid's poetry reclaims distinctive Scottish idioms and often uses ballad meters. In the 1930s, he wrote "The Seamless Garment" and three "Hymns to Lenin" in which he calls for ruthlessly practical socialist commitment to be brought to bear on Scotland. The "Third Hymn" is dedicated to the American poet Muriel Rukeyser, who responded enthusiastically.

In 1939, in response to Roy Campbell's profascist poem *Flowering Rifle*, MacDiarmid wrote a long poem called *The Battle Continues* (which remained unpublished till 1957). Passages in praise of Spain—salutations to the Spanish poet **Federico García Lorca** and the International Brigade—were given dramatic performance in the early 1940s by Joan Littlewood and Ewan MacColl in Manchester's Round House Theatre as part of their "Living Newspaper" project. One sequence—beginning, "Fascists, you have killed my comrades"—proved immensely powerful in the theatrical context. In the 1960s, MacDiarmid translated **Bertolt Brecht**'s *Threepenny Opera* and the Swedish poet Harry Martinson's post-nuclear **science-fiction** poem *Aniara* and was a member of Bertrand Russell's antinuclear Committee of 100.

Explicitly anti-British, anti-imperialist poems written during **World War II** were collected and published posthumously to some controversy in *The Revolutionary Art of the Future* (2003), including "On the Imminent Destruction of London, June 1940." MacDiarmid's later work extended his political vision through explorations of questions of political authority, artistic experimentalism, and the varieties of language in the world. In the great long poem *In Memoriam James Joyce* (1955), MacDiarmid calls for an end to all forms of imperialism, including linguistic imperialism, which he describes as a summation of all the others—an assertion that effectively encapsulates his contradictory, regenerative beliefs about poetry and politics.

Selected Bibliography: Bold, Alan. *Hugh MacDiarmid: Christopher Murray Grieve: A Critical Biography.* Rev. ed. London: Paladin, 1990; Gish, Nancy K. *Hugh MacDiarmid: The Man and His Work.* London: Macmillan, 1984; Glen, Duncan. *Hugh MacDiarmid and the Scottish Renaissance.* Edinburgh: W.R. Chambers, 1964; MacDiarmid, Hugh. *Collected Works.* Gen. ed. Alan Riach. Manchester: Carcanet, 1992–ongoing; McCulloch, Margery Palmer, ed. *Modernism and Nationalism: Literature and Society in Scotland 1918–1939. Source Documents for the Scottish Renaissance.* Glasgow: Association for Scottish Literary Studies, 2004; Riach, Alan. "The Idea of Order and 'On a Raised Beach': The Language of Location and the Politics of Music." *Terranglian Territories.* Ed. Susanne Hagemann. Frankfurt am Main: Peter Lang, 2000. 613–29; Riach, Alan. *The Poetry of Hugh MacDiarmid.* Glasgow: Association for Scottish Literary Studies, 1999.

Alan Riach

MACHEREY, PIERRE (1938–). Pierre Macherey is a French philosopher whose early writings on literature revitalized New Left literary theory well beyond the borders of France. His *Pour une théorie de la production litteraire* (1966)—translated as

A Theory of Literary Production (1978)—drew on **Louis Althusser**'s essay "A Letter on Art in Reply to André Daspre" (1966) and is as much a critique of dominant Marxist accounts of literature as it is of traditional literary criticism, for if the latter speaks of a mystical literary "creation" and locates the reader as the "consumer" of the text's intended meaning, then the former tends either to reduce literature to ideology or to see it as providing a mimetic knowledge of history.

Macherey positions the critic as (Marxist) scientist seeking to identify the autonomous "laws of literary production." However, the text can never be a self-sufficient totality because literature bears a complex but identifiable relationship with ideology, which is as it were the "raw material" transformed by the specific processes of literary production. For Macherey as for the early Althusser, ideology is by definition invisible and "formless," as it has been naturalized into common sense. Moreover, an ideology must be limited or incomplete, since there are certain ideas about which it must remain silent (the colonial discourse of the "civilizing mission" cannot speak about its superexploitation of the native), but this is typically papered-over to offer a self-representation of a harmonious totality at one with reality itself. Nevertheless, "it exists because there are things which must not be spoken of." It is above all also silent about its own limitations, its incompleteness, and its absences.

By working on ideology, the literary text congeals it into a specific form, and thus turns ideology into a "visible object": what precisely is revealed by the text is its ideological *unconscious*, "what it *cannot say*." The text pushes ideology to the point where its erstwhile hidden fault lines—its silences, gaps, contradictions, incompletenesses—become exposed. Against the grain of its manifest (and ideological) intention to produce a coherent and unified fictional world, the literary text succumbs to a "determinate disorder" and, in so doing, lets slip the limits of its ideology. The task of literary criticism is not to fill in these gaps in order to complete the text, but to theorize the necessity of these absences and thus to enable an emancipatory critique of ideological subjection.

The influence of Althusser's essay "On Ideology and Ideological State Apparatuses" (1969), which emphasized the institutional materiality of ideology in the production of compliant subjects, led to Macherey's "On Literature as an Ideological Form" (1974) with Etienne Balibar, in which literature was now seen rather reductively as functioning within the French educational apparatus to reproduce the dominant ideology.

Still, Macherey's reputation in the English-speaking world rests largely on *A Theory of Literary Production*, which was the only one of his books to appear in English before 1995, though he published several important works (especially on the philosophy of Spinoza) in France during that time. In 1995, the English translation of *À quoi pense la littérature?* (1990; translated into English as *The Object of Literature*) appeared, marking another important engagement with literary questions, especially in relation to philosophy. In 1998, *In a Materialist Way*—a collection of essays written by Macherey over a period of almost thirty years—was published in English.

Selected Bibliography: Althusser, Louis, and Etienne Balibar. *Reading Capital*. London: Verso, 1970; Belsey, Catherine. *Critical Practice*. London: Methuen, 1980; Eagleton, Terry. *Criticism and Ideology: A Study in Marxist Literary Theory*. London: NLB, 1976; Macherey, Pierre. *In a Materialist Way: Selected Essays*. Ed. Warren Montag. London: Verso, 1998; Macherey, Pierre. *The Object of Literature*. Cambridge: Cambridge UP, 1995; Macherey, Pierre. *A Theory of Literary Production*. Trans. Geoffrey Wall. London: Routledge and Kegan Paul, 1978; Macherey, Pierre, and Etienne Balibar. "On Literature as an Ideological Form." Trans. I. McCleod, J. Whitehead, and A. Wordsworth. *Oxford Literary Review* 3 (1978): 4–12.

Jean-Philippe Wade

MADAME BOVARY (1857, SERIALIZED 1856). Gustave Flaubert's novel of the desires and final disillusionment and suicide of a Normandy farmer's daughter is set during the Second Empire of Napoleon III—a period of intense political suppression and great financial and industrial expansion following the February Revolution of 1848 and the proclamation of the Second Republic. The tale of Emma Bovary's marriage to a country doctor and her search for romantic love and material goods—displayed for her periodically by the pernicious salesman, Lheureux—reveals not Emma's vice but the pitfalls of a bourgeois society where seduction—romantic and economic—rouses desires that it cannot satisfy. Emma's descent into debt and her reckless pursuit of material and sensual pleasure reveal the interconnectedness of the economic and romantic plots of the novel as well as their similar, exploitative nature. Her ruin is depicted as her failure both to fulfill desire and to find a means of authentic expression. And the novel, too, battles to find an authentic language in a corrupt world, a language that, despite the ugliness it portrays, might nonetheless achieve beauty. "Human speech," writes Flaubert in the novel, "is like a cracked kettle on which we tap crude rhythms for bears to dance to, while we long to make music that will melt the stars." Herein lies Flaubert's identification with his heroine, his famous line: "Madame Bovary, c'est moi."

The novel scandalized many, not merely for its portrayal of immorality in the form of adultery but for its mingling of religion with erotic and commercial desire. The town priest, for example, is a dirty and petty man, who not only fails to offer Emma consolation but uses the churchyard for growing potatoes. Further, the scene of Emma's last rites, which was particularly offensive to clergy and officialdom, fuses erotic and religious language. Flaubert was charged in December 1856 for offenses against public and religious morals and prosecuted. He was acquitted in February 1857 with a reprimand: "the mission of literature," said the court, "must be to embellish and refresh the mind by raising the understanding and refining morals, more than to impart disgust with vice by offering a picture of the disorders which may exist in society." Even Sainte-Beuve, an eminent critic of the time who praised the novel's "stern and pitiless truth," regretted its lack of consolation, saying "Good is too absent, no one represents it." Indeed, the novel does not spare us in its realism or in its thorough critique of the bourgeoisie. We see the black liquid pouring out of the dead Emma's mouth "like vomit" and are delivered the coup de grace in the form of the rise to success of the deceitful and conniving apothecary, Monsieur Homais. And yet the novel appeals implicitly to the existence of both beauty and sincerity in life and art through its relentless critique of a world that fails to nurture or realize these ideals.

Selected Bibliography: Culler, Jonathan. *Flaubert: The Uses of Uncertainty.* Ithaca, NY: Cornell UP, 1974; Heath, Stephen. *Madame Bovary.* Cambridge: Cambridge UP, 1992; LaCapra, Dominick. *Madame Bovary on Trial.* Ithaca: Cornell UP, 1982.

Yaël R. Schlick

MAGICAL REALISM. Term first applied to Latin American writers such as Jorge Luis Borges and **Alejo Carpentier**, more specifically linked to 1960s boom authors, including Julio Cortázar, **Carlos Fuentes**, **Mario Vargas Llosa**, and **Gabriel García Márquez**, whose *One Hundred Years of Solitude* (*Cien años de soledad,* 1967) is for many the signature text of the movement. Magical realism has also been employed by post-boom writers such as **Isabel Allende**. The term was originally used by art critic Franz Roh to denominate a painting style of the early twentieth century, but was applied to literature by Ángel Flores in 1955. His basic argument was that the mixture of the magical and realism have existed throughout Latin American writing, with "the magical, writ large from the earliest" (189). Magical realism as practiced in the 1940s and 1950s "is predominantly an art of surprises. From the very first line the reader is thrown into a timeless flux and/or the unconceivable, freighted with dramatic suspense" (190).

As magical realism has continued in use, it has entered into various formations and even what could be termed "popular literature," which Flores disparaged as "flatulence." Magical realism is more than just fantasy, because it is not an unusual occurrence that bursts into the ordinary world but merely one more element of the world that characters simply take in stride. Irony is a basic requirement—magic is made ordinary, while the quotidian is transformed into something that seems unreal within the text, which leads to a sense of wonder—yet at the same time, the reader knows that this is artifice. The idea that magical realism is an attempt to present a perspective of the world that centers on popular, traditional, rural culture is just that—an idea. Worse, we can argue that the idea is actually built by outside, dominating forces attempting to transform a real lifestyle into a mythical cultural construct for their own ends. This has been one of the main criticisms leveled at the boom writers from the 1960s, who are most identified with magical realism in recent critical studies.

Isabel Allende's *The House of the Spirits* (*La casa de los espíritus,* 1982) is one text of the Latin American post boom that demonstrates the lessening influence of magical realism. In the early part of the novel, the protagonist is Clara, a girl who speaks to spirits, performs telekinesis, and stops speaking for twelve years. But as the novel progresses from the late 1800s to the 1970s, the magic disappears, and the brutal reality of social inequality and Pinochet's military coup in Chile take over. Magical realism has been taken up, however, by writers in other places, especially in **Latina/o literature**, where writers like Ana Castillo, Cristina Garcia, and Judith Ortiz Cofer present an amazing view of reality: where a child can return from the dead, fly, and smell the scent of hell on people, but not be thought very unusual. The style is not limited to the Americas, however; writers such as **Günter Grass**, **Salman Rushdie**, **Amitav Ghosh**, Ben Okri, and B. Kojo Laing have also incorporated it.

Suggested Bibliography: Angulo, María-Elena. *Magic Realism: Social Context and Discourse.* New York: Garland, 1995; Faris, Wendy B. *Ordinary Enchantments: Magical Realism and the Remystification of Narrative.* Nashville, TN: Vanderbilt UP, 2004; Flores, Ángel. "Magical Realism in Spanish American Fiction." *Hispanía* 38.2 (May 1955): 187–92; Monet-Viera, Molly. "Post-Boom Magical Realism: Appropriations and Transformation of a Genre." *Revista de estudios hispánicos* 38.1 (January 2004): 95–117; Parkinson Zamora, Lois, and Wendy B. Faris, eds. *Magical Realism: Theory, History, Community.* Durham, NC: Duke UP, 1995; Swanson, Philip. *The New Novel in Latin America: Politics and Popular Culture after the Boom.* Manchester: Manchester UP, 1995.

Jason G. Summers

MAILER, NORMAN (1923–). Born in New Jersey, Mailer grew up in Brooklyn and attended Harvard University before serving in the U.S. Army in the Pacific campaign of **World War II.** This experience provided the material for his first novel, *The Naked and the Dead* (1948), still widely regarded as one of the finest novels to have come out of the war. It is a powerful and compelling war novel that narrates in vivid naturalistic detail the successful assault of the fictional Japanese-held island of Anopopei by a large U.S. force. However, the book emphasizes the horror of war rather than its glory, depicting the realities of jungle combat in ways that not only undermine any notion that World War II was glorious and romantic but also strikingly anticipate the later U.S. experience in the **Vietnam War.** The victory is achieved more by chance than by heroism or brilliant strategy and tactics, in addition, the book refuses to characterize the combat in terms of good versus evil. The Japanese are consistently depicted as human beings who suffer and die just like the Americans, which adds a chilling note to the fact that after winning the victory, the American forces coldly massacre the remaining Japanese because it is too much trouble to take prisoners. Meanwhile, the book suggests that figures such as the neofascist Cummings represent a dangerous element that threatens to ride the military victory in World War II to power in postwar America.

Barbary Shore (1951), Mailer's second novel, has the most openly leftist content of any of his numerous books. The book is very much a philosophical novel in which various characters debate the relative merits of different political philosophies (especially Marxist ones), while using these philosophies to provide perspectives on historical events in the twentieth century. Though critical of the Stalinist Soviet Union as a bureaucratic nightmare dominated by state capitalism, the book eschews the usual **cold-war** oppositions by suggesting that the United States is also drifting toward bureaucratic tyranny and that ultimately the two states will probably become indistinguishable.

Mailer's long and varied career has included the writing of dozens of books of both fiction and nonfiction, including several—such as the Pulitzer Prize–winning works *The Armies of the Night* (1968) and *The Executioner's Song* (1979), and the less successful *Oswald's Tale* (1996)—that blur the boundary between fact and fiction in rich and suggestive ways. His more purely fictional novels range from realistic works, such as *The Naked and the Dead* and *The Deer Park* (1955); to more experimental, sometimes fantastic fictions, such as *An American Dream* (1965) and *Why Are We in Vietnam?* (1967); to massive late works, such as *Ancient Evenings* (1983) and *Harlot's*

Ghost (1991). Along the way, Mailer has complemented this vast and varied fictional opus with essays, commentary, and autobiography, becoming a highly visible (and often controversial) public intellectual.

Selected Bibliography: Dearborn, Mary V. *Mailer: A Biography.* Boston: Houghton Mifflin, 1999; Ehrlich, Robert. *Norman Mailer: The Radical as Hipster.* Metuchen, NJ: Scarecrow P, 1978; Gutman, Stanley T. *Mankind in Barbary: The Individual and Society in the Novels of Norman Mailer.* Hanover, NH: UP of New England, 1975; Leigh, Nigel. *Radical Fictions and the Novels of Norman Mailer.* New York: St. Martin's, 1990; Merrill, Robert. *Norman Mailer Revisited.* New York: Twayne, 1992.

M. Keith Booker

MALRAUX, ANDRÉ (1901–1976). Georges André Malraux was born November 3, 1901, in Paris. He attended the École Turgot until July 1918 at which time he terminated his formal education. In 1923, he set off for Indochina with wife Clara and friend Louis Chevasson, where they took part in an expedition to the Cambodian temple of Banteaï-Srey, from which they removed valuable statues and bas-reliefs. Subsequently, Malraux and his companions were tried and later acquitted for the theft of the precious art objects. In 1925, he returned to Indochina, where he launched two short-lived newspapers that criticized French colonialist practices.

Having returned to Paris after his Asian sojourn, Malraux published the epistolary work *Temptation of the West* (*La Tentation de l'Occident*). In 1928, *The Conquerors* (*Les Conquérants*), his first authentic novel, was published. In 1930, Grasset published his *The Royal Way* (*La Voie royale*). After visiting China in 1931, he began working on the novel that would win him the prestigious Goncourt literary prize in 1933, *Man's Fate* (*La Condition humaine*). During the 1930s, Malraux became a champion of left-wing political causes without formally joining the **Communist Party**. His antifascist political involvement culminated in the publication of *Days of Wrath* (*Le Temps du mépris*) in 1935. A year later, Malraux was busy organizing an air squadron, which he later commanded in support of the embattled Spanish Republic. His **Spanish Civil War** novel, *Man's Hope* (*L'Espoir*), appeared in December 1937, when there was still a glimmer of hope that a democratic Spain might triumph over the mechanized armies of General Franco. He also wrote, directed, and produced his only film, *Sierra de Teruel.* When Nazi Germany invaded France in 1940, he was taken prisoner but later escaped. In 1941, he began working on *The Walnut Trees of Altenburg* (*Les Noyers de l'Altenburg*) and on a biography of T. E. Lawrence. By 1943, Malraux had made contact with French Resistance groups, and in 1944, he assumed command of the Alsace-Lorraine brigade, one year before he met Charles de Gaulle, an encounter that would change his life.

After the war, Malraux channeled his creative energy into a series of brilliant studies on the metamorphosis of art over time and space. When not working on what he termed his "imaginary museum" of art masterpieces, he served intermittently in de Gaulle's cabinets. His highest political post was that of minister of cultural affairs, which he held from 1959 until de Gaulle's resignation in 1969. During the remaining seven years of his life, Malraux underwent a kind of artistic resurrection, personified by the biblical character Lazarus—the title he in fact later gave to an autobiographical account of his near fatal illness in 1972. Malraux's death in 1976 was marked by an outpouring of obituaries, editorials, and eulogies in literary journals.

Selected Bibliography: Cate, Curtis. *André Malraux: A Biography.* London: Hutchinson, 1995; Frohock, Wilbur M. *André Malraux and the Tragic Imagination.* Stanford UP: Stanford, 1967; Lacouture, Jean. *Malraux, une vie dans le siècle.* Paris: Seuil, 1976; Larrat, Jean-Claude. *André Malraux.* Paris: Librairie Générale Française, 2001; Madsen, Axel. *André Malraux: A Biography.* New York: William Morrow, 1976.

John B. Romeiser

MANDEL'SHTAM, OSIP EMIL'EVICH (1891–1938). Born in Warsaw, Mandel'shtam became one of the most important and influential Russian poets of the twentieth century. After a brief fling with symbolism, Mandel'shtam joined Nikolai Gumilev's anti-symbolist, St. Petersburg-based *Poets' Guild* and initiated, together with Gumilev, **Anna Akhmatova**, and Sergei Gorodetskii, the acmeist movement in Russian literature (1912–1913), which was—unlike symbolism—emphatically concerned with this life and this world. His poetry (from *Stone* [*Kamen'*, 1913] through *Tristia* [1922] to the late *Voronezh Notebooks* [1935–1937]) and prose (from the autobiographical *The Noise of Time* [*Shum Vremeni*, 1925] to the essayistic masterpiece *Conversation about Dante* [*Razgovor o Dante*, 1933]) set unprecedented poetic standards, whose force and reach would be felt by such diverse successors across the globe as Paul Celan, Robert Lowell, and Joseph Brodsky. Two aspects of Mandel'shtam's poetics in particular stand out among the voices of literary modernism (in and out of Russia): his twofold conception of poetry as (1) a breathing, living body analogous to what he perceived to be the living spirituality of Gothic architecture *and* (2) inherently dialogic, as addressed especially to an interlocutor in the future, like a message in a bottle. It was not Mandel'shtam's poetic genius alone, however, that made for his status as a literary legend. Mandel'shtam's biography—certainly, in part, a function of his avowed experience of a fundamental lack of fit between himself and his world ("I have never been anybody's contemporary," Mandel'shtam wrote in 1924)—equally facilitated his accession to the pantheon of poets from Ovid to Pushkin who fell afoul of the powers-that-be and became grist for the mills of totalitarianism. Neither at home in what he called the "Judaic chaos" of his cultural-religious background (as a result of which he converted to Protestantism in 1911) nor in the new Soviet order, the erstwhile supporter of the Bolshevik Revolution saw his attempts at making a decent living as a writer and translator thwarted most infamously in the so-called Eulenspiegel affair (1929–1930), during which he was accused of plagiarism. Rather than playing along with the new regime, Mandel'shtam chose to resist its grip. Both the polemical *Fourth Prose* (*Chetvertaia Prosa*, 1929–1930) and the famous anti-Stalinist verses of 1933 saliently attest to the antitotalitarian thrust of Mandel'shtam's project. In 1934, the poet was arrested and sentenced to three years in internal exile, spent in Cherdyn and Voronezh, where the majority of his late poetry was created (and recorded by his wife, Nadezhda). After returning to Moscow in 1938, the prematurely aged Mandel'shtam was again arrested and sentenced—on the trumped-up charge of counter-revolutionary activity—to five years of forced labor in the Siberian far east. Before reaching his final destination, Mandel'shtam died, aged forty-seven, of "paralysis of the heart" (thus the official diagnosis) in the transit camp Vtoraja Rechka, near Vladivostok.

Selected Bibliography: Brown, Clarence. *Mandelstam.* Cambridge: Cambridge UP, 1973; Cavanagh, Clare. *Osip Mandelstam and the Creation of Modernist Tradition.* Princeton, NJ: Princeton UP, 1995; Harris, Jane Gary. *Osip Mandelstam.* Boston: Twayne, 1988; Mandel'shtam, Osip. *Sobranie sochinenii* [Collected Works]. Ed. Pavel Nerler et al. 4 vols. Moscow: Art-Biznes-Tsentr, 1993–1997.

Michael Eskin

MANN, THOMAS (1875–1955). Born of patrician parents in the North German commercial port city of Lübeck, Mann achieved financial independence and critical acclaim with his first novel, *Buddenbrooks* (1901). The theme of the incompatibility of the artistic temperament with a successful integration into bourgeois society and a style characterized by skillful use of the literary leitmotif would become hallmarks of Mann's prodigious output. With a sophisticated, ironic virtuosity, Mann developed a series of successful short stories ("Tristan," "Tonio Kröger"), culminating in 1912 with the long novella *Death in Venice.* The explorations of sensitive men—some young, some not—contending with passions that pushed them to the margins of the very society whose center they craved might have defined and at the same time exhausted Mann's creativity, had Germany not gone twice to war.

Although exempted from military service for physical reasons, Mann embraced the patriotic fervor of **World War I.** His essay "Reflections of an Unpolitical Man" (1918) was anything but apolitical, and his second novel, *The Magic Mountain* (*Der Zauberberg,* 1924), concludes with its young protagonist bravely entering the fields of death on the western front. When Mann was awarded the Nobel Prize in 1929, it was explicitly for the early *Buddenbrooks,* but already in *The Magic Mountain* and certainly by "Mario and the Magician" (1930) there is a softening of the patriotic reflex in favor of a troubled, questioning uncertainty. By the assumption of power in 1933 by the National Socialists under Adolf Hitler, Mann had become an unabashed supporter of the Weimar Republic and opponent of fascism. He took his family into exile, eventually to settle in the United States, and was stripped of his German citizenship.

While in the United States, Mann held visiting lectureships and ultimately a chair at Princeton. In 1941, he moved to Pacific Palisades, where he became the acknowledged representative of the "good German." He concluded a vast tetralogy, *Joseph and His Brothers* (*Joseph und seine Brüder,* 1933–1943); wrote extensively on the legacy of German idealism in the works of Goethe; recorded a series of anti-Hitler broadcasts for the BBC; and began his last great work, *Dr. Faustus.* This massive novel, completed in 1947, attempts to explain the collapse of hallowed idealism into the perversions of National Socialism by invoking the legend of a German scholar with overreaching ambitions who sells his soul to the devil in return for extraordinary powers. Mann "takes back" Goethe's classic and redemptive version of the same legend in a vision of Germany as Faust, damned perhaps forever.

An American citizen since 1944, Mann returned to postwar Germany only briefly, but also elected not to remain in an America plagued by McCarthyism. He died in Switzerland in 1955.

Selected Bibliography: Heilbut, Anthony. *Thomas Mann: Eros and Literature.* London: Macmillan, 1996; Kurzke, Hermann. *Thomas Mann: Life as a Work of Art. A Biography.* Trans. Leslie Willson. Princeton, NJ: Princeton UP, 2002; Minden, Michael, ed. *Thomas Mann.* New York: Longman, 1995; Reed, T. J. *Thomas Mann: The Uses of Tradition.* Oxford: Clarendon P, 1974, 1996; Robertson, Ritchie, ed. *The Cambridge Companion to Thomas Mann.* Cambridge: Cambridge UP, 2002.

Mark E. Cory

MAO DUN (1896–1981). Pen name of Shen Yanbing—Chinese critic, editor, novelist, and short-story writer noted for his commitment to communism. Born in Tongxiang, Zhejiang Province, he was admitted to Peking University in 1913, though he did not graduate. Inspired by the **Russian Revolution** of 1917, he took part in the May Fourth Movement in China and became one of the founders of the Chinese **Communist Party** in 1921. Between 1921 and 1932, he was one of the chief editors of China's foremost literary journal, *Xiaoshuo yuebao* (Fiction Monthly). He went into exile in Japan in 1928 to take refuge from Nationalist Party attacks on Communists. After his return to China in 1930, he helped organize the League of Left-Wing Writers. He was active in the War of Resistance against Japan beginning in 1937, working in the meantime to promote the development of a new literature that was both revolutionary and distinctively Chinese in nature. After the Chinese Revolution established a communist government in China, Mao, a close associate of **Mao Zedong**, served as minister of culture from 1949 to 1965.

Writing in a mode of **naturalism** that nevertheless shows some of the sweep of the great works of Western **realism** (he was an admirer of writers such as **Leo Tolstoy**), Mao produced a number of novels depicting life in China in great detail, always placing the experiences of his characters within the context of the historical sweep toward communism in China. Many of his best-known works have been translated into English, including his greatest work, *Midnight* (*Zi ye*, 1933)—a long urban novel set in Shanghai, which quickly received international recognition as a work of revolutionary literature, with translations into Russian and German as well. Other works translated into English include *Rainbow* (*Hong*, 1929), which focuses on a young Shanghai woman who escapes from her bourgeois family to join the revolutionary May Thirtieth Movement, and the rural trilogy *Spring Silkworms* (*Chun can*, 1932–1933).

In the 1970s, Mao edited a magazine of children's literature and started to write his memoirs, which were serialized in the Communist Party quarterly *Xinwenxue Shiliao* (Historical Materials on New Literature), but which were left unfinished at his death.

Selected Bibliography: Chen Yu-Shih. *Realism and Allegory in the Early Fiction of Mao Dun.* Bloomington: Indiana UP, 1986; Gálik, Marián. *Mao Tun and Modern Chinese Literary Criticism.* Wiesbaden: F. Steiner, 1969; Hsia, C. T. *A History of Modern Chinese Fiction.* New Haven, CT: Yale UP, 1961; Wang Dewei. *Fictional Realism in Twentieth-Century China: Mao Dun, Lao She, Shen Congwen.* New York: Columbia UP, 1992.

M. Keith Booker

MAO ZEDONG (1893–1976). Influenced by anarchist and socialist ideas in the late 1910s, Mao converted to Marxism in 1920 and was a founding member of the

Chinese **Communist Party** (CCP) in 1921. During the late 1920s, Mao developed a revolutionary strategy carried out in China's rugged countryside and based on China's peasants, although led by the working class and its vanguard, the CCP. This latter point is essential to an understanding of Mao's thought, for though he respected and relied on the revolutionary potential of the peasants, he was not a classic peasant revolutionary. His vision of China's future incorporated themes of industrialization, modernization, and an independent and powerful Chinese nation-state. The objective of the Chinese Revolution, as Mao saw it, was the overthrow of the reactionary classes—the comprador bourgeoisie and landlords—and the Nationalist (Kuomintang) government that represented their interests, and the establishment of a modern socialist society dedicated to the interests of China's "masses."

Mao's thought incorporated many themes drawn from European and Soviet Marxism, particularly the concepts of class and class struggle, and the idea that the interests of economic classes are reflected in and fought over in the realm of the political-ideological superstructure. He has often been criticized, from both the Right and the Left, for putting excessive emphasis on struggles in the superstructure, although many of these criticisms ignore the contextual and contingent nature of the campaigns that Mao initiated. His political thought remained underpinned by an economic reading of history, one to which the concept of class was central.

However, while Mao drew core themes from European and Soviet Marxism, he was very conscious of the need to adapt these to Chinese conditions and the requirements of the Chinese Revolution. This process—described as the "Sinification of Marxism"—became an increasing preoccupation from the late 1930s as Mao struggled to seize control of the CCP from those he believed dogmatically applied Marxism in China without sufficient attention to China's particular characteristics. His ultimate success in the early 1940s allowed him to establish his thought as the party's leading ideology at the CCP's Seventh Party Congress in 1945, and it remained a vital ideological ingredient in China's politics up to Mao's death in 1976 and beyond.

This amalgam of classic Marxist ideas adapted to Chinese conditions—particularly the conditions of class and class struggle in China—is central to Mao's views on art and literature. Mao had a well-developed sense of the importance of art and literature to the prosecution of China's revolutionary struggles; he also had a deep aesthetic appreciation of literature, particularly poetry. Mao was himself an accomplished poet, leaving a corpus of over eighty poems, written in the classical Chinese style, which are highly regarded in both China and the West. When Mao spoke on the theme of art and literature, he thus did so with authority and a strong sense of the way in which the political and aesthetic functions of literature should be combined. This is clearly reflected in a number of his authoritative statements on art and literature. Without doubt, the best known of these is his "Talks at the Yan'an Forum on Literature and Art" of May 1942 (first published in 1943 and to be found in volume 3 of *Selected Works of Mao Tse-tung*). In these "Talks," Mao insists that art and literature do not exist in a social vacuum and that there is no "art for art's sake." All art and literature reflect the interests of particular economic classes, and it was a failing of many writers in the revolutionary ranks that they did not recognize that their artistic and literary creations must serve either the interests of the Chinese "masses"— the workers, peasants, and soldiers—or the interests of the exploiting classes.

The question of "class stand" is thus the basic premise for all work in the cultural sphere. Revolutionary writers have to consciously recognize their class position and write appropriately for their class audience; it is of no value to write and perform "high-brow" works of culture if workers and peasants cannot understand them. The responsibility is thus on revolutionary writers to know their audience, indeed to live with and study the lives of China's ordinary people. Mao thus endorses "popularization," the creation of works of art and literature that not only had meaning for China's "masses" but revealed to them the dark side of Chinese society and inspired them to change it. Art and literature thus have an explicitly political function but should also be aesthetically pleasing. The criterion for the aesthetic quality of art and literature is inevitably political, but derives also from the lived (class) experiences of the audience.

While Mao endorsed popularization of art and literature as a means of mobilizing China's masses to support the revolution, he also believed in the importance of raising cultural standards. He recognized that there was a tension between these two objectives, one that could only be reconciled through a sensitive recognition of the cultural limits of the audience. During the revolutionary period, however, popularization was the dominant imperative.

Mao's views on art and literature were to have a dramatic impact on cultural policy following the victory of the revolution in 1949. Art and literature that extolled the virtues of life in a socialist society proliferated, and during the Cultural Revolution (1966–1976), the idea of proletarian literature was taken to extreme lengths, with only a handful of approved operas and writings permitted. Whether this cultural policy actually conformed to Mao's insistence on both popularization and raising standards is debatable, however, and there was a general relaxation in the cultural realm following Mao's death, although the CCP continues to this day to be influenced by his views on art and literature.

Selected Bibliography: Boorman, Howard L. "The Literary World of Mao Tse-tung." *China Quarterly* 13 (January–March 1963): 15–38; Dirlik, Arif, Paul Healy, and Nick Knight, eds. *Critical Perspectives on Mao Zedong's Thought*. Atlantic Highlands, NJ: Humanities P, 1997; Kim Chung-ryol. "Mao Tse-tung's Views of Revolutionary Literature." *Journal of Asiatic Studies* 24.1 (1981): 69–84; Mao Zedong. "Talk to Music Workers." *Mao Tse-tung Unrehearsed*. Ed. Stuart R. Schram. Harmondsworth: Penguin, 1974. 84–90; McDougall, Bonnie S. *Mao Zedong's "Talks at the Yan'an Conference on Literature and Art": A Translation of the 1943 Text with Commentary*. Ann Arbor: U of Michigan P, Michigan Papers in Chinese Studies, no. 39, 1980; Schram, Stuart R. *Mao Tse-tung*. Harmondsworth: Penguin, 1966; Wang Hsueh-wen. "Mao Tse-tung's Thought on Literature and Art and the Maoist Struggle between the Two Lines in Literature and Art." *Issues and Studies* 10 (June 1974): 46–56.

Nick Knight

MARIÁTEGUI, JOSÉ CARLOS (1894–1930). A journalist and socialist militant in his native Peru, Mariátegui was a pioneering figure in the development of an independent Latin American tradition of Marxist political theory and social analysis. Of poor health from birth, his untimely death at the height of his activity has perhaps enhanced the aura surrounding his contributions. Among other milestones, Mariátegui established the Peruvian Socialist Party (PSP) in 1928 and organized the

Peruvian Trade Union Congress (CGTP) in 1929. He also founded and sustained as editor from 1926 until his death the Peruvian journal *Amauta*, arguably the most vibrant and vital of several quality Latin American avant-garde reviews that circulated in the 1920s and 1930s and kept the region conversant with the latest cultural and political developments. Mariátegui's prolific writings, most produced under deadline for immediate consumption, include essays in Peruvian historical and sociopolitical analysis, literary criticism, articles on world politics and current events, and several poems and short stories from his early years. His seminal work, however, was the essay collection *Seven Interpretative Essays on Peruvian Reality* (*Siete ensayos de interpretación de la realidad peruana*, 1928), one of only two book-length volumes printed during his lifetime.

Mariátegui himself always divided his life into his youthful and "mature" phases, separated by his residence in Europe from 1919 until 1923. He termed the early period his "Stone Age," though scholars recognize many continuities between the two phases. A completely self-made intellectual of humble origins, Mariátegui took his first job in 1909 as a typesetter for a Lima daily, and soon rose to become a reporter for a variety of publications. When his articles took on an increasingly pro-labor slant, the government of Augusto Leguía arranged to send Mariátegui to Europe as a "cultural attaché." During the next four years, mostly in Italy, Mariátegui imbued himself in the socialist theories and politics of postwar Europe, and returned to Peru in 1923 an admitted (but by no means orthodox) Marxist. His remaining years in Peru were ones of fervent political activity and intellectual productivity, and his home in Lima became a gathering place for workers, artists, and intellectuals of many stripes.

Mariátegui made no apologies for the European origins of his Marxist views; Croce, Sorel, and **Gramsci** are considered key influences. But the *Siete ensayos* argued, in Leninist fashion, that revolutionary strategies should fit local circumstances and national conditions. While his analyses prioritized the economic base—he saw the "Indian problem" in Peru as a class-based rather than a racial issue—he resisted the strict determinisms of historical materialism and favored a voluntaristic building of revolutionary spirit among workers, peasants, and Indians. Mariátegui's attitude toward Peru's indigenous communities was far from paternalistic; however, like many enlightened Latin American intellectuals at the time, he held a rather utopian view of the Incan past and he considered it a potential model for modern socialism in Peru. Perhaps the distinctive characteristic of Mariátegui's heterodox approach— clearly anticipating the later spread of liberation theology across Latin America—was the amalgamation of his Catholic roots and his Marxist convictions.

Selected Bibliography: Becker, Marc. *Mariátegui and Latin American Marxist Theory*. Athens: Ohio University Center for International Studies, 1993; Chang-Rodríguez, Eugenio. *Poética e ideología en José Carlos Mariátegui*. Madrid: José Porrúa Turanzas, 1983; Mariátegui, José Carlos. *Seven Interpretive Essays on Peruvian Reality*. Trans. Marjori Urquidi. Austin: U of Texas P, 1989; Vanden, Harry E. *National Marxism in Latin America: José Carlos Mariátegui's Thought and Politics*. Boulder: Lynne Rienner, 1986.

Steven M. Bell

MARTÍ, JOSÉ (1853–1895). Renowned for his role as leader and martyr of the Cuban insurrection against Spanish colonialism and as a critic of U.S. imperialism,

José Martí offers a defining example of the revolutionary poet in **Latin American literature**. Although known primarily as Cuba's founding father until the mid-twentieth century, Martí helped to found Latin American **modernism**, invented a new literary genre—the modern *crónica*—and wrote and spoke tirelessly as a prescient public intellectual and cultural critic.

Born to Spanish and Canary Islander immigrants in Havana, Cuba, and coming of age during the 1868–1878 civil war in Cuba, Martí criticized governments that restricted self-determination throughout his life. As a result, Martí lived and wrote mostly in exile. Deported from Cuba to Spain at age eighteen (after serving six months of chain-gang labor at the age of fifteen) for his political views, Martí studied law and literature in Spain. Deported from Cuba a second time in 1878, he worked as a journalist, translator, and political organizer in New York City, after sojourns in Mexico, Guatemala, Cuba, and Venezuela. Martí's writing informed his political action and vice versa, in guarded praise and ironic criticism of the United States, Europe, and Latin America; in outspoken rejection of James Blaine's proposal to Latin American republics to adopt a single currency throughout the Americas in 1889–1891; and in his grassroots mobilization of tobacco workers in Florida and elsewhere between 1892 and 1895.

His most widely read literary texts—*Simple Verses* (*Versos sencillos*, 1891) and "Our America" ("Nuestra América," 1891)—respond to the failure of Latin American republics to perceive U.S. imperial designs on his America. In simple, musical rhymes, *Simple Verses* shows him taking stock of his life at the moment before he will dedicate himself to waging war. "Our America" calls for unity and self-critique in the definition of a collective response to the advances of the lascivious United States. Using dense, hermetic metaphors, Martí wrote hundreds of journalistic essays (1880–1892) that interpret the "wrinkled underside" of the "monster" in which he lived for readers scattered throughout the Americas. In addition to chronicles about Europe and Latin America, this North American collection of literary reportage marvels at Coney Island's mass culture, the life-consuming construction of the Brooklyn Bridge, voyeuristic responses to a Chinatown funeral in New York, and whites who burned an African American at the stake in Texarkana in 1892. His literary manifesto, a prologue to Venezuelan poet Juan Antonio Pérez Bonalde's *Poem of Niagara Falls* (*Poema del Niágara*, 1882), and his posthumously published *Versos Libres* (*Free Verses*, 1913) and *Diarios de campaña* (*War Diaries*, 1940, 1996) reveal the marks of **postcolonial** ambivalence and modernity on his poetics.

Laura Lomas

MARX, KARL (1818–1883). Nineteenth-century German philosopher, political economist, political and social theorist, and revolutionary socialist. The influence of Marx's work in economics, philosophy, and political science has been inestimable. In addition, many elements of Marx's work point to the importance of literature and culture in human society, and the entire field of **Marxist criticism** has taken its inspiration from his ideas, even if often moving away from or beyond those ideas in important ways.

Working primarily in England, Marx was closely associated for some four decades with Friedrich Engels, another German-born nineteenth-century revolutionary socialist and thinker. Engels, who was from a wealthy background, helped Marx pay his bills, collaborated with him on many political projects, and helped work out many of Marx's basic ideas. Engels, working after Marx's death, can be said to be the founder of Marxism as a political and intellectual movement. However, the legacy of Marxism is extremely varied, and it is a simplification to see a seamless continuity between Marxism and Marx. To understand Marx, it is important to both identify and criticize the main aspects of the Marxist view of the identity of Marx and Marxism.

Marx began his intellectual career as a student in philosophy, in which he took a Ph.D. in 1841 at a time when philosophy in Germany was still dominated by the work of G.W.F. Hegel. Marx was decisively influenced by Hegel as well as the leftist "young Hegelians." This movement included such figures as Engels and Ludwig Feuerbach, who later became known as a theologian. After receiving his doctorate, Marx found work as a journalist at the same time as he began to write. In 1843, a year before he came into contact with Engels, Marx began to criticize Hegel in two texts, which laid the foundations of his life's work.

Marx's relation to Hegel is central to understanding his own theories. Marx's interest was a strong element in his doctoral dissertation, which presents a Hegelian analysis of the difference of ancient theories of nature. Marxists have routinely but incorrectly linked the difference between Marx and Hegel with the further difference between materialism and idealism. The Marxist approach to the relation of Marx to Hegel is based on a passage found in the second afterword to *Capital*. Marx here says he found the dialectic on its head in Hegel and set it on its feet. Many Marxists interpret this passage as authorizing a break between Marx and Hegel, which they understand as that between materialism and idealism, or again as that between Marx's position—however understood—and philosophy.

In fact, all important thinkers differ from their predecessors. Marx should be understood as claiming to provide a new position, relevantly different from Hegel's, as concerns dialectic. Marx's position—which differs from Hegel's, as the latter's differs from Kant's—belongs to classical German philosophy, that movement running from Kant through Fichte, Schelling, and Hegel, and leading to Marx.

Marxists have frequently viewed Marx as a political economist, while Engels has been seen as a philosopher. In fact, Engels, who was self-taught in philosophy, was at best an amateur in that domain, while Marx was fully trained as a professional philosopher. Though the claim is controversial, Marx is best seen as presenting a philosophical position with important economic ramifications, which originates in an important criticism of Hegel. In the *Philosophy of Right*, in which Hegel presents his theory of the state, he takes a juridical, or legal, approach to property. The very young Marx, at a time when he had not yet undertaken his economic studies, adopts an economic approach to property. On that basis, he develops a philosophical critique of Hegel, a rival philosophical theory with special attention to the nature of modern industrial society, and a critique of orthodox, or so-called bourgeois, political economy.

Marx's philosophical position begins to emerge in his early writings on Hegel. In "Contribution to the Critique of Hegel's Philosophy of Right" (1843), Marx for the first time speaks of the proletariat, going on to suggest that Hegel's philosophy has failed to grasp what he calls the real man. Marx, in pointing toward philosophical anthropology, insists that the root of humanity is the physical human being rather than any sort of abstract superhuman concept. And he famously says that religion is the opium of the people, to which philosophy might serve as an antidote. For Marx, the goal is not simply to understand society but to change it.

Marx begins to work out the position to which this approach points in a series of texts, variously known as the "Paris Manuscripts," the "Manuscripts of 1844," or the "Economic and Philosophical Manuscripts" (1844). In a little more than a hundred pages, Marx presents a theory of modern economic society in terms of the categories of capital, rent and work, or labor (*Arbeit*). Marx argues that, by definition, the worker under capitalism becomes increasingly impoverished, hence pushed toward revolutionary action. He brilliantly analyzes the types of **alienation** resulting from the normal functioning of capitalism, which he defines as a system based on the private ownership of the means of production. Marx goes on to sketch a conception of communism, which cannot be reduced to any single historical example, and which he intends as the goal to be reached by going beyond capitalism. He subjects Hegel to additional criticism.

Marx's "Theses on Feuerbach" cover less than three pages in a text he composed in 1845 but which only appeared after his death. Marx here takes his distance from Feuerbach, as well as all merely contemplative approaches. In the eleventh thesis on Feuerbach, he remarks that the problem is not to interpret reality but to change it.

The German Ideology, written jointly by Marx and Engels, was finished in 1846 but only published after Marx died. The polemical text is especially important for the theory of **ideology**. Marx and Engels treat consciousness as a social product in relating it to economic conditions. A system such as capitalism, where the conditions of life are distorted, leads to false consciousness of oneself and one's surroundings. Marx and Engels also provide an account of the emergence of modern industrial society—based on the private ownership of the means of production—from ancient Greek society through a series of intermediate stages. Capitalism is only another transitory stage. It is sometimes argued that in Marx's later writings, and specifically in this text, there is a discernible break with his earlier writings; yet there is no break, only further development, since the idea that consciousness is a product of, and hence depends on, the economic dimension of the social context is already clearly stated in several of Marx's earlier texts.

As someone who valued practice over theory, Marx was closely interested in political events. In 1848, as revolutionary fervor was sweeping Europe, he wrote with Engels "The Communist Manifesto," one of the most famous of all political writings. The short but brilliantly written text ends with a famous call to arms, in effect a battle cry, inviting workers of all countries, who have nothing to lose but their chains, to unite in the revolutionary battle against capitalist exploitation. On the other hand, this text shows a great deal of admiration for the historical accomplishments of the bourgeoisie, even as it happily envisions their coming demise.

From the time he wrote the "Paris Manuscripts," Marx was at work supplementing his philosophical background through economic studies. These studies resulted in the composition of a series of "critiques of political economy," which were in fact steadily more focused critiques of modern industrial society, or capitalism. The first such study is the vast series of manuscripts, including over 1,100 pages, known as *Grundrisse: Foundations of the Critique of Political Economy* (completed in 1857); originally intended to contain six volumes, it was published long after Marx's death. Generally speaking, this book provides the key elements leading to Marx's masterwork *Capital*, for which this unfinished outline offers a wider framework. It continues Marx's intention, as early as the "Paris Manuscripts," to provide a detailed picture of modern industrial society. Marx here analyzes such categories as production, consumption, and exchange. The introduction is especially important for a series of remarks on method. In taking up the problem of the relation of categories to content, which is central to German idealism since Kant, Marx suggests the need to begin with simple conceptions, such as labor, in order to reach abstract conceptions, such as class. Marx is claiming that we cannot grasp economic phenomena directly but through the economic categories used in modern political economy—in a word, against the background of a categorial framework.

A Contribution to the Critique of Political Economy, a short work of some 150 pages, appeared in 1859. In the famous preface, Marx concisely states the main elements of his position. His position originates in the insight that legal relations and the forms of the state are rooted in material conditions. He clearly says that the anatomy of civil society is to be sought in political economy, and that in social production, men enter into definite relations independent of their will. He further depicts consciousness as a product in claiming that it depends on social existence and must be explained on the basis of economic contradictions. Marx here elaborates the **base and superstructure** model of society.

Marx's literary production comes to a peak and an end in the first volume of *Capital: A Critique of Political Economy* (1867), the only volume published during his lifetime. The second and third volumes as well as *Theories of Surplus Value* (in four volumes) were all quarried from manuscripts he left unfinished at his death. Volume one of *Capital* is widely regarded as Marx's masterpiece. Marx begins by sketching a theory of **commodification**, implicit in previous writings. A commodity (*die Ware*) is a tangible material object that satisfies a human need of some kind. In this connection, Marx now introduces a distinction, already known to Aristotle, between use-value, or the purpose served by a thing, and exchange-value, or that variable value that can be had for a thing in the marketplace. Marx follows Locke, Hegel, and others in arguing that labor confers value on products. Value is calculated as a multiple of what Marx calls average labor power. This is an application of the Hegelian view that the work of individuals is objectified, or crystallized, in what they make. In a brilliant section on the fetishism of commodities, Marx describes the way in which social relations between individuals appear in capitalism as a relation between things.

Capital is a long and complex book that cannot be described in a few lines. Aristotle was already aware that the circulation of money through commodity exchange leads to riches. Marx, who introduces a distinction between the worker, or laborer, and labor-power, considers the latter with respect to use-value. He suggests that surplus value is the result of the difference between the sum paid for labor-power, which creates use-value in producing a commodity, and its exchange value. On this basis, he further analyzes the main features of modern industrial society. Especially noteworthy is a very long chapter on machinery and modern industry in which Marx hammers away at the point that the progress of modern industrial society is dearly paid for in the sacrifice of workers who literally give up the good life and life itself in pursuit of capital. He closes his great book in affirming that the basic condition of the accumulation of capital in modern industrial society lies in the expropriation of the worker.

Selected Bibliography: Berlin, Isaiah. *Karl Marx: His Life and Environment.* 4th ed. New York: Oxford UP, 1996; Marx, Karl. *Capital: A Critique of Political Economy.* Vol. 1. Trans. Samuel Moore and Edward Aveling. Ed. Frederick Engels. New York: International Publishers, 1967; Marx, Karl. *A Contribution to the Critique of Political Economy.* Trans. S. W. Ryazanskaya. Ed. Maurice Dobb. New York: International Publishers, 1970; Marx, Karl. *Grundrisse: Foundations of the Critique of Political Economy.* Trans. Martin Nicolaus. Harmondsworth: Penguin, 1973; Marx, Karl. *Karl Marx: Early Writings.* Trans. and ed. T. B. Bottomore. New York: McGraw-Hill, 1964; Rockmore, Tom. *Marx after Marxism: The Philosophy of Karl Marx.* Oxford: Blackwell, 2002.

Tom Rockmore

MARXIST CRITICISM. It would at first seem unlikely that a doctrine that legendarily synthesizes English economics, French utopian socialism, and German philosophy should have so profoundly excited so many writers of literature and literary criticism; however, any intuitive sense of surprise about the impact Marxism has had may be tempered by the consideration that the young **Karl Marx**'s most fervent ambition was to be a poet and that, once he had changed course, he did not omit to indicate the implications of his theory for the realm of aesthetics. In what is usually taken to be the *locus classicus* of historical materialism—the elaboration of the base/superstructure distinction found in Marx's preface to *A Contribution to the Critique of Political Economy* (1859)—the "aesthetic" is designated (along with the other examples of law, politics, religion, and philosophy) as one of the "ideological forms in which men become conscious" of the conflict between "the material productive forces of society" and "the existing relations of production" and "fight [the conflict] out." In other words, the basic economic forces at work in society "determine" the superstructural forms of consciousness (including literature) rather than the reverse.

Much of the debate that has raged around this fundamental proposition concerns the weight that is to be given to the notion of "determination." The German verb in Marx's original text, *bedingen,* ranges considerably in nuance, so that his "*bedingt*" could conceivably be translated as "presupposes," "causes," "necessitates," "conditions," or "determines." Depending on the chosen inflection, the passage can be used to imply either (1) a strongly deterministic theory in which literature is seen as being wholly preordained by the economic context within which it is produced or consumed—in fact, is virtually reducible to it—and thus plays a negligible role in "real" historical processes; or (2) a theory in which, although ultimately dependent on and influenced by economic forces, art and literature have a variable freedom (or "relative autonomy") from the economic system within which they arise, to the extent that they cannot be explained only by reference to it and indeed may even influence its course—for example, by promoting ideas, emotions, or actions that amount to an intervention in the prevailing economic order (either to change or to uphold it).

It is obviously conceivable that one may concur with position (1) and deny that literature has any social value or importance beyond the merely aesthetic, spiritual, or ideological satisfactions it may in itself give; many art-for-art's-sake writers and readers have done so. It is also possible to deny (1) from a somewhat different but paradoxically related position; thus the banning of **James Joyce**'s *Ulysses*, the persecution of Soviet literary dissidents, or the *fatwa* pronounced against **Salman Rushdie** after the publication of *The Satanic Verses* may all be used to demonstrate the social change that those in authority perceive literature to be supremely capable of bringing about. Yet both views share idealist assumptions that are anathema to Marxism, and it is therefore unlikely that Marx, though himself a passionate *literatus*, would have espoused either. The likelihood is that he did not consider so many writers and readers (or governments and censors) to have been wildly deluded in adjudging literature to potentially be a somewhat influential factor in social and historical development. Unfortunately, unlike his great antagonist Hegel (the combat with whom probably provoked the starkly differentiating formulations of the quoted preface), Marx did not leave any substantial material on aesthetic questions from which we can draw unified conclusions. His comments and reflections on such matters were so incidental, brief, and scattered that they offer little to make his theoretical stance on the aesthetic unambiguously clear. Nonetheless, virtually all subsequent literary and critical work of a Marxist tinge has predictably assumed one or other variant of position (2).

It is little acknowledged that it is Marx's friend and collaborator Engels—most often thought of as the popularizer or editor of the former's work—who is responsible for what today are understood to be the main aesthetic emphases of "classic Marxism." A glance at Baxandall and Morawski's anthology, *Karl Marx and Frederick Engels on Literature and Art* (1973), shows that it was Engels rather than Marx who tended to offer detail, exemplary cases, and quasi-theoretical elaboration. For example, while both men shared the same enthusiasm for the work of Balzac, it was Engels who more forcefully celebrated, on more than one occasion, the "revolutionary dialectic" inherent in the historical novels of this ostensibly most conservative writer, his compulsion "to go against his own class sympathies and political prejudices" in delineating the decadence and downfall of the French nobility, as Engels put it in a key letter to Margaret Harkness in April 1888. Thus Engels undermined in advance the later (Stalinist) heresy that a Marxist sense of the value of a writer was to be seen as coextensive with his or her class origins or expressed affinity with or conscious attempt to promote a socialist politics. In the same letter, furthermore, he explicitly comes out against the "tendency novel," whose author is avid to convey a particular set of ideological precepts by resorting to the vehicle of fiction ("the more the opinions of the author remain hidden, the better for the work of art") and offers an observation on his own and Marx's much-favored narrative form ("**Realism**, to my mind, implies, besides truth of detail, the truthful reproduction of typical characters under typical circumstances"), which was to form the foundation for the development of Marxist criticism of the novel for the next half century. It is not hard, for example, to see **Georg Lukács**'s well-known essay of 1936, "Narrate or Describe? A Preliminary Discussion of Naturalism and Formalism," with its similar evaluative slighting of post-1848 novelists such as **Émile Zola**, as simply a more discriminating and somewhat more contentious advocacy of classic realism.

Undoubtedly the richest resource Engels offered to those keen to provide Marxist answers to aesthetic questions was the concept we now know as "mediation." In a letter to Franz Mehring on July 14, 1893, Engels offered a more nuanced version of historical materialist doctrine than that found in Marx's preface of 1859. Here, as a counterweight to the blunt notion of literature (as well as other ideological phenomena and activity) being derived in reality "from basic economic facts," Engels addresses the "false consciousness" of the "so-called thinker" who does not perceive this derivation: "He works with mere thought material, which he accepts without examination as the product of thought, and does not investigate further for a more remote source independent of thought; indeed this is a matter of course to him, because, as all action is mediated by thought, it appears to him to be ultimately based upon thought." The attempt to define this awareness as "false consciousness" is actually eclipsed by the refreshingly candid acknowledgment that "all action is mediated by thought" because, whatever the truth of such a claim, it unquestionably restores social agency and purposiveness to ideology, which, even if it can still be said to be only instrumental, is nonetheless now seen as indispensable. In this formulation, ideology is the very element in which humans socially exist, rather like the air that sustains biological life: by breathing alone, we achieve very little, but without it, we can achieve nothing at all. It is a short step from this insight to a near *bouleversement* of the more mechanically deterministic reading of the theory. Far from being rather negligible epiphenomena, ideological forms (including literature) have suddenly become indissociable from historical agency. Engels's insistence on "false consciousness" has long since been abandoned, and the concept of mediation has occasionally been problematized by later Marxists, but the possibility that literature can be one means of thought through which historical action is enabled has not been lost. Thus, Marxist materialism legitimately lays claim to being "dialectical," and its use-value to writers and critics is definitively restored.

However, to speak of "using" Marxism is in itself potentially treacherous. A critic does not work with it the way a structuralist works with structuralism or a deconstructionist with deconstruction, nor does a creative writer employ it the way a surrealist may turn to automatic writing or a sonneteer choose between Petrarchan, Shakespearean, or Spenserian models. Unlike certain other isms, Marxism is not merely an intellectual method and even less an artistic technique. To use it or work with it is inevitably to subordinate one's work to, or at least to integrate it with, either the political commitments Marxism implies in a particular instance or the system of ideological beliefs it propounds in general, or both, with the intention that these shall be furthered in the world outside the text. This truth remains undeniable despite the prescriptivist atrocities (the Stalinist doctrine of **socialist realism** has often been seen in this way) that are the outcome of ultradogmatic interpretations of it. Marxist writers or critics are not Marxists unless they are in one way or another demonstrably partisan in favor of a particular kind of socialism. In this respect alone, they have more in common with, for example, avowedly Christian writers and critics than they do with avant-garde concrete poets or semioticians decoding the commodity branding strategies within advertisements. The poet and the semiotician may well be Marxists, but not by virtue of their technique or their object of analysis. Nor does partisanship on its own—in the form, say, of a generalized sympathy with the downtrodden, poor, and oppressed, or in the expression of a wish that the social world ought to be more equitable, just, and fair—mark the Marxist. A grasp of the more systematic and philosophical dimensions of the Marxist critique of capitalism, and an understanding of what this requires by way of *praxis* in any "real world" conjuncture would both need to be seen before one might consider the textual producer Marxist. Many so-called Marxist English poets of the 1930s, for example, lacked the former; a number of "armchair Marxist" critics are likewise rather deficient when it comes to the latter. (These observations imply nothing, one should insist, about the aesthetic value of their poetry or the intellectual worth of their criticism, respectively.) In short, there are arguably no "Marxist" texts at all in the sense that Marxism always implies an additional interventionist orientation along certain ideological lines, but varying in respect to the specific nature of any historical moment—to the "real" world of contingent social relations, conflicting economic interests, and uneven distribution of power that lies outside any text. But such texts may well be part of a wider social project that is identifiably Marxist.

In 1996 **Terry Eagleton** proposed a useful charting of four broad "regions" in the history of Marxist criticism. The terms he uses to designate these currents of inquiry are "anthropological," "political," "ideological," and "economic." With the exception of the last, which is not summarized here in any detail (it describes the field traditionally known as the sociology of literature, containing relatively circumscribed studies of the economic and legal context in which literature is socially distributed and consumed), Eagleton's categories are largely chronological phases. (For a comparable three-phase categorization, see Mulhern.) The anthropological perspective within Marxist criticism is that to which Marx's own occasional reflections frequently belong, in that they often try to define art in relation to the functions it fulfills within what Marx termed the "species being" of humanity, or what more traditional thinkers may envisage to be human nature. The questions addressed within this tradition seldom attract the contentious and tendentious political discourse that constitutes the common badge of Marxist debate, concerned as they are with fundamental issues: What is the function of art within social evolution? What are the material and biological bases of "aesthetic" capacities? What are the relations between art and human labor? How does art relate to myth, ritual, religion, and language, and what are its social functions? From the middle of the nineteenth to the end of the first third of the twentieth century, such inquiries are common in works by writers such as William Morris, Antonio Labriola, Franz Mehring, Karl Kautsky, and Georgei Plekhanov (the five immediate post-Marx/Engels figures anthologized in Solomon's voluminous anthology). This strand within aesthetic Marxism virtually dries up with **Christopher Caudwell**'s *Illusion and Reality* (1937), although it enjoys its last postwar gasps of vitality in George Thomson's two studies of ancient Greek society, *The Prehistoric Aegean* (1954) and *The First Philosophers* (1955), and in Ernst Fischer's *The Necessity of Art* (1959). As Eagleton points out, the transhistorical nature of the "anthropological" perspective contrasts markedly with subsequent developments in Marxist criticism, which have tended to place literary texts within more precise and, indeed, ever increasingly specific and localized historical moments (usually of their production or, less frequently, their consumption), implicitly placing much greater stress on historical contingency and change than persistence and continuity. No doubt the positivist scholarly bent of the "anthropological" approach made it difficult to sustain in the twentieth century, when there were titanic issues of contemporary global politics that could clearly not, furthermore, be met by its agenda.

"Political" criticism arose to meet this challenge with something of a vengeance, perhaps inaugurated by **Lenin**'s articles on **Tolstoy** (1908–1911), in which, in a manner reminiscent of Marx and Engels on **Balzac** and **Goethe**, he argues that Tolstoy transcended the limitations of his own class ideology by transferring his loyalty to the Russian peasantry in the revolution of 1905. The sharp contemporaneousness of Lenin's focus is an obvious point of contrast with "anthropological" criticism, as is the alignment of aesthetic judgments with fairly immediate political purposes. The dangers of this contiguity come to the fore most strongly in Lenin's essay "Party Organisation and Party Literature" (1905), which does not renounce the liberality that permits that "everyone is free to write and say whatever he likes, without any restrictions," but reserves the right to expel from the Bolshevik Party those whose exercise of this freedom brings them into conflict with the party line. (It is clear in the essay that Lenin's remarks may apply to creative writers as well as commentators on politics.) Lenin justified such a policy because the party was a "voluntary association" whose ideological integrity needed to be protected if it was to achieve its historical aims. Once it had done so and actually become the governing party in 1917—a little later making itself indissociable from the state—such a policy applied to literature was indisputably repressive.

Yet it is perfectly clear that the evaluation of literature according to its political tendency was never originally intended by culture-inclined Bolsheviks to preclude other kinds of evaluation or to necessitate what eventually took place under **Stalin**— intensifying censorship, rigid prescriptivism for writers prepared to toe the line, and systematic liquidation of those who did not. The high point of "official" Soviet literary criticism is undoubtedly **Leon Trotsky**'s *Literature and Revolution* (1923), in which all the best possibilities of artistic tolerance were promoted alongside the recognition that "it is silly, absurd, stupid to the highest degree, to pretend that art will remain indifferent to the convulsions of our epoch." Unreservedly suspicious of philistine attempts to reject the achievements of bourgeois art, to implement a "proletarian culture" in its place, and to impose widespread repression in the cultural field, Trotsky undertook a vigorous and trenchant survey of the contemporary state of Russian literature from his undeniably partisan position as one of the architects of the revolution. Insofar as government was concerned, he stated, "Our policy in art, during a transitional period, can and must be to help the various groups and schools of art which have come over to the Revolution to grasp correctly the historic meaning of the Revolution, and to allow them complete freedom of self-determination in the field of art, after putting before them the categorical standard of being for or against the Revolution." The position is characteristically contradictory. Once writers have "come over to the Revolution," and once they have been helped to "grasp correctly" its historic meaning, they will be allowed "complete freedom of self-determination." But what if they do not "come over," or what if they do but fail to "grasp correctly," or, even if they do both, what if their allegiance to and "correct" understanding of the revolution later flags or is otherwise found wanting by those who consider themselves empowered to judge? The implications are obviously anxiety provoking to liberal democratic sentiment. Yet Trotsky's position goes to the heart of the debate about literature and politics. If literature has no political effectivity but is merely a concern of hobbyists, then it can be left alone by the state. But if it does indeed have an appreciable role in shaping a society, it would be a foolish government that did not keep an eye on and attempt to control its workings—and, indeed, many liberal democratic governments have imposed censorship and repression precisely out of a recognition of literature's perceived social effectivity. If it happens that the best known cases in the "free world" are to do with the sexual rather than the political content of literary texts—from the bowdlerization of **Shakespeare** to the banning of *Lady Chatterley's Lover*—all that is demonstrated is that liberal governments have considered public discussion or dramatization of sexual mores to be a powerful social force requiring their vigilant control in much the same way as the Soviets came to consider expressions of political "deviance" a threat to the goals of the **Russian Revolution**. Inimical as all writers understandably are to such control, where it is present, it is clear that literature is not politically underestimated.

It is then something of an irony to come to understand that many of the advances in Marxist criticism were made by those who had temporarily or permanently turned away from engagement in direct political activity. Trotsky's composition of *Literature and Revolution* has often been considered a grotesque political irresponsibility, a cultural distraction that, among others, prevented him from properly ensuring his place as Lenin's successor, in which case the nightmare of Stalinism might not have followed. Because of that very nightmare, Lukács turned from political activism to the "safer" arena of literary criticism, and some of the best remembered political novels of the century, at least in the West, are devastating satires on the Soviet system and its self-declared identity with Marxism (**Zamyatin**'s *We*, **Koestler**'s *Darkness at Noon*, **Orwell**'s *Animal Farm*, and **Nabokov**'s *Bend Sinister*).

Antonio Gramsci, incarcerated by Mussolini, could no longer agitate in the factory movement of Turin, and instead penned his prison notebooks, in which he adumbrated his theory of "cultural **hegemony**." **Walter Benjamin**, exiled in Paris and unable to return to Hitler's Germany, wrote his important texts on the city's nineteenth-century culture, literary and otherwise. His **Frankfurt School** colleagues, such as **Bloch**, **Adorno**, and Horkheimer, similarly relocated to New York, where they concentrated entirely on academic research, which attempted to keep utopian and "high" cultural dreams alive. In the period of the **cold war**, the only Marxist writer and critic of international repute who seemed to find the Eastern bloc congenial was **Bertolt Brecht**. Otherwise, the main center of gravity of Marxist cultural work shifted, paradoxically, to the capitalist West, where it became mainly the preserve of critics and theorists, and only infrequently the resort of creative writers.

The paradox is not new within Marxism: Marx himself, after the political disappointments of 1848, retreated to the British Library to write *Capital*. Likewise, the postwar period of "ideological" criticism was marked by tremendous theoretical advance and elaboration—especially in France, in the hands of expressly or implicitly Marxist theorists such as **Jean-Paul Sartre**, **Lucien Goldmann**, **Louis Althusser**, **Pierre Macherey**, **Roland Barthes**, Etienne Balibar, and **Pierre Bourdieu**. The price paid was an increasing academization (and, thus, neutralization of the political effectivity) of the field, aided by the correspondingly intensifying rebarbativeness and obfuscation in the discourse employed by many of these scholars. The experience of reading any of the critics named above can hardly be said to be easy or straightforward; the level of education and degree of wider philosophical and theoretical knowledge required for their understanding are taxing. These factors served to widen the gulf between this scholarly and analytic Marxist aesthetic and that to which Marxist artists might actively subscribe (the chances of another Brecht who might convincingly combine theory and creative practice became more and more remote) and the remnants of the committed "political" criticism that persisted (cheerfully untheoretical British texts like **John Berger**'s *Ways of Seeing* [1972] or Paul O'Flinn's *Them and Us in Literature* [1975] now seem rather vulgar and populist by comparison). Consequently, fierce internecine debates erupted from time to time. The growing influence of Althusser in particular drew a rhetorically memorable but overweeningly hostile reaction from the English humanist Marxist historian E. P. Thompson in *The Poverty of Theory* (1978) and a less fêted critique, Terry Lovell's *Pictures of Reality: Aesthetics, Politics and Pleasure* (1980), which calmly excoriated Althusserianism, but only to prescribe a return to a largely Brechtian aesthetics, which by now seemed entirely of its moment and unresurrectable in the dawning of a period to be dominated by the New Right. French Marxism had itself already been thrown into disarray by the political downturn following May 1968, shortly after which Althusser, in his most famous (or notorious) essay, "Ideology and Ideological State Apparatuses" (1969), implicitly abandoned the hope of any significant social change coming from within the ideological sphere. Indeed, it was not even that literature was no longer envisaged to have much potential for socialist radicalism; as Macherey and Balibar were to argue at greater length after him, Althusser now envisaged the teaching of literature by the modern state within its educational institutions as a powerfully reactionary force to which all-too-optimistic Marxists had been blind. It was one of the many hegemonic ideological means whereby the state persuaded its citizens to adopt a value system that ensured resignation to the world-as-it-is rather than agitation to create the world-as-it-could-be.

Nonetheless, theses, anthologies, and monographs in Marxist aesthetics continued to pile up with impressive plenitude throughout the cold-war and Thatcher/Reagan periods in the liberal democracies in which the actualization of Marxism, or even its slightest demonstrable effect on official political policy, seemed something one would have been foolhardy to have gambled on. One can certainly trace its influence in every other theoretical trend, especially those with an implied or explicit political agenda, such as **postcolonial theory and criticism** and **feminist criticism and theory**, which could eclectically adopt Marxist ideas and strategies without having to deal, as Marxism itself did, with the political embarrassment of something known as "actually existing socialism." The critique of the education system under capitalism, and of the specific role of literature within that system, was variously embellished, most often in relation to the literary classics, and frequently (especially in Britain) under the rubric of "cultural materialism"—a term proposed by **Raymond Williams** in *Marxism and Literature* (1977) in a bid to advance Marxist aesthetics beyond the limiting concepts of reflection and mediation. But paradoxically, Marxist theory itself seemed to have less direct political impact the more intellectually redistributed and reformulated it became. In the absence of any evident political use-value, it nonetheless did acquire an obvious exchange-value within the academic publishing and employment markets. In certain situations, it seemed unperturbed that it could take a detour around political questions entirely. **Fredric Jameson**'s *Marxism and Form* (1971), the first of his many volumes that eloquently reconfigured Marxist aesthetic thinking, declared itself to be a "general introduction" to "a relatively Hegelian kind of Marxism," within a tradition he described as "a mixture of political liberalism, empiricism and logical positivism which we know as Anglo-American philosophy and which is hostile at all points to the type of thinking outlined here," and he was thus able to bypass entirely the distractions of "vulgar" Marxist political positions, which had never made any serious impression on American intellectual life in the first place. Jameson's work, whose main themes have changed little in over thirty years, is perhaps the most supple, elegant, and influential contribution made to Marxist aesthetics yet, but again at serious cost, for it has arguably refined and adjusted the intellectual methods of Marxism in its application to the arts in an exclusively contemplative mode, all the while neglecting to address the issue of what this means for actual political practice.

But this is a standard that Marxism has, uniquely among critical theories, exacted from itself, ever since the eleventh and most famous of Marx's "Theses on Feuerbach," concerning philosophers before him who only interpreted the world: "the point, however, is to *change* it." A deconstructionist, for example, may happily dismantle the opposition between "interpretation" and "change" and hold that an interpretation, if it gains general consent, *is* a change, because the intellectual work of analyzing society is integral to the process of transforming it. For a Marxist to do so would willfully constitute an evasion of Marx's basic point, which is that interpretation on its own is never enough (a point that takes us back to the dialectical model of base/superstructure relations). It remains the case, however, if the resourcefulness and survivability of capitalism is a touchstone, that Marxist intellectual theory has more evidently allowed us to interpret the world anew rather than manifestly changed the relations of production—and this truth seemed ineluctable when the "actually existing socialism" of the Eastern bloc crumbled in the late 1980s and the historic changes made in the name (if not the spirit) of Marxism went into dramatically rapid reversal.

One other truth seems to be that Marxism has consistently been more potent as a critique than as a program. During the international oil crisis of the 1970s, when capitalism entered one of the periodic slumps that Marx diagnosed as the inevitably recurring outcome of its systemic contradictions, and one might have expected a widespread turn to Marxist explanatory models and political action, **Jean Baudrillard**'s *The Mirror of Production* (1975) simultaneously threw down the gauntlet of **postmodernism** to most fundamental Marxist tenets. Baudrillard was closely followed by Jean-François Lyotard, who attacked all "grand narratives" (including Marxism) in *The Postmodern Condition* (1979). It is undeniably the case, over the next quarter century, that postmodernism became the ascendant philosophy in the aesthetic sphere. While one struggles to name significant contemporary writers who can be unequivocally designated as Marxist, a simple perambulation around any literary bookstore will now yield dozens who are undeniably postmodernist. In the critical sphere, attempts to integrate postmodernism (and/or poststructuralism) with traditional Marxism resulted in the oddly termed (and contestably conceived) "post-Marxism" (see, for example, Tony Bennett's *Outside Literature* [1990]), but mainstream Marxism has proved generally more resilient than other "grand narratives" to such incursions and, in books like **David Harvey**'s *The Condition of Postmodernity* (1980) and Jameson's *Postmodernism, or The Cultural Logic of Late Capitalism* (1991), produced the finest intellectual responses to the postmodernist challenge. The latter—almost certainly the most talked-about academic text of the 1990s—read postmodernism as a response to the changed nature of capitalism, which, Jameson argued, has been transformed, particularly in the post–**World War II** period, from being the sum total of a number of similar systems of state and/or monopoly capitalism operating within distinct national boundaries and under markedly differing degrees and kinds of legal and governmental regulation, to a more unified system organized on a global scale, by and around multinational corporations whose activities transcend and shatter the older national divisions. Both philosophical and literary postmodernism, for Jameson, ultimately do little more than oil the wheels of this system in the cultural realm. They attempt to normalize the new world order with its relativizing discourses that propose to abolish the "master narratives"—such as Freudian psychoanalysis, Marxism, and scientific rationalism—which had been held up to explain the old order. All the while, they ignore the "master code," which continues to determine everything—including those relativizing discourses themselves—namely the newly configured ("late" or "advanced") capitalism. Thus, Jameson brought Marxism thudding back onto the table—in the intellectual sphere at least—with a classically Marxist argument, engaging with contemporary thought and society, and demonstrating the role of ideology, art, and immanent critique to the preservation of, developments within, and challenges to the economic order. The enterprise convinced many that whatever emerges from the post-post-everything epoch within which all cultural discourse seems now to be conducted, the waning flame of Marxism—under whatever name and in whatever form—is unlikely to be extinguished, and will have much more to say about literature and the social processes that engender it and in which, in turn, it modulates.

Selected Bibliography: Baxandall, Lee, and Stefan Morawski, eds. *Karl Marx and Frederick Engels on Literature and Art.* New York: International General, 1973; Craig, David. *Marxists on Literature: An Anthology.* Harmondsworth: Penguin, 1975; Eagleton, Terry, and Drew Milne, eds. *Marxist Literary Theory: A Reader.* Oxford: Blackwell, 1996; Haslett, Moyra. *Marxist Literary and Cultural Theories.* Basingstoke: Macmillan, 2000; Jay, Martin. *The Dialectical Imagination: A History of the Frankfurt School and the Institute of Social Research, 1923–1950.* London: Heinemann, 1973; Lunn, Eugene. *Marxism and Modernism: An Historical Study of Lukács, Brecht, Benjamin, and Adorno.* Berkeley: U of California P, 1982; Mulhern, Francis, ed. *Contemporary Marxist Literary Criticism.* Harlow: Longman, 1992; Prawer, S.S. *Karl Marx and World Literature.* Oxford: Oxford UP, 1976; Solomon, Maynard, ed. *Marxism and Art: Essays Classic and Contemporary.* New York: Knopf, 1973.

Macdonald Daly

MARXIST-FEMINISM (M-F) is an umbrella term that denotes a variety of feminist theories that, despite their differences, have in common a solid grasp of the relevance of Marx's work for feminist theory and politics. Though M-F is sometimes used interchangeably with terms such as socialist-feminism, the latter is more properly seen as a dual-system perspective for which the oppression of women is a product of the interaction between two distinct systems, capitalism and patriarchy. M-F, however, seeks the foundations of gender inequality in the very functioning of capitalism.

The theoretical point of departure for M-F is Engels's 1884 treatise, *The Origin of the Family, Private Property, and the State*, which begins with the postulate that the determining factor in history is the production and reproduction of the essentials of life. Production, in turn, comprises both the production of material things (i.e., "the economy," in commonsense language) and the production of human beings themselves (i.e., "the family"). This is the basis for the M-F contention that the roots of gender inequality, as a key structure of capitalist societies, are to be found in the relationship between the capitalist mode of production and the capitalist mode or network of social relations (Gimenez calls it the "mode of reproduction") in which human beings and their characteristics and abilities are reproduced. The concepts of "mode" (or form) of production and reproduction, unlike the more common terms "economy" and "family," call attention to the historically specific variations in how the production of things and the reproduction of life are organized and interconnected within different modes of production, such as capitalism, feudalism, and hunting and gathering. Under capitalism, the economic survival of everyone who is neither an owner of capital nor economically self-sufficient depends on the sale of labor power in exchange for wages or salaries. Unemployment, however, is endemic in the system, and the number of workers is always in excess of the demand for labor. Individual workers can pool resources to improve their living standards. Historically, the most widespread form this strategy takes is family formation; marriage and kinship allow children, those unable to work, and the unemployed to have a legitimate claim on the earnings of the employed.

The capitalist organization of production pits individual workers against each other in the market, where men and women compete for jobs in a sex-segregated occupational structure where higher male wages are typically justified on the grounds that men need to support families. But not all men have families to support, while many single women do have families that need their earnings. A "family wage," however, has never been available to all workers, and most working families today rely on two incomes to keep above the poverty line.

M-F identifies the objective foundations for the oppression of women in the complex articulation between the organization of production (which fosters competition and inequality among individual working men and women) and the organization of reproduction, where, in households of various types (such as extended, nuclear, or single-parent families; one or two paycheck families; or households formed by same-sex partners), the primary responsibility for domestic work and child care is left to women.

From the standpoint of M-F, then, the oppression of women is the outcome of the inherent, systemic inability of capitalism to offer full employment and pay a living wage to all workers. While the reproduction of the present and future generations of workers is left to the ability of the workers themselves, households' stability and well-being, parents' ability to care for and educate their children, women's ability to care for their families, and so on depend on the employment and earnings of households' adult members. Unequal earnings and unequal opportunities result in men's and women's unequal power and unequal responsibilities in the home. While most men support themselves through paid employment, paid work is often insufficient to support women, so women are better off, economically, by combining paid work outside the home with unpaid domestic work in the home. This situation, which entails a burden of time commitments and responsibilities from which most men are free, is a key barrier to women's equality under capitalism.

M-F theories vary according to the emphasis given to different aspects of this complex interconnection between production and reproduction. Important points of emphasis include the exploitation of women's unpaid domestic labor by capitalists (who can pay lower wages to male workers) and by the males in their families, who appropriate the products of their labor; the collusion between male employers and male workers to exclude women from well-paid jobs; and the privatized nature of reproduction under capitalism, which renders problematic the provision of social services (such as universal entitlements to subsidized quality child care and elderly care) that would put an end to women's "double shift." M-F also places great importance on the dominant ideologies and state policies that reinforce the capitalist organization of production and reproduction through the dominant discourses about masculine and feminine identity and family roles propagated by the media, and through policies, such as welfare reform, that intensify the problems facing most working people who must cope with the demands of work and family with hardly any social supports.

Literary critics well versed in M-F theory are likely to examine how fiction deals with the ideologies and social forces that shape women's and men's lives in capitalist societies, interrogating texts to discover whether, for example, they challenge or reinforce ideologies about love and femininity that contribute to disempower women, or whether they illuminate or overlook the relationship between men's work experience and their understanding of women's needs and yearning for autonomy. M-F theory sensitizes the student of literature to the ways fiction may contribute to the oppression of women or may raise women's consciousness about the sources of their oppression.

Selected Bibliography: Brenner, Johanna. *Women and the Politics of Class.* New York: Monthly Review P, 2000; Engels, Friedrich. *The Origin of the Family, Private Property, and the State.* 1884. New York: International Publishers, 1972; Gimenez, Martha. "The Mode of Reproduction in Transition: A Marxist-Feminist Analysis of the Effects of Reproductive Technologies." *Gender and Society* 5.3 (Fall 1991): 334–50; Vogel, Lise. *Marxism and the Oppression of Women: Toward a Unitary Theory.* New Brunswick, NJ: Rutgers UP, 1983.

Martha E. Gimenez

MASSES. Self-described as "a revolutionary magazine directed against rigidity and dogma," *The Masses* was published from 1911 to the end of 1917, after which it was succeeded by the *Liberator* and then eventually *New Masses* in 1926. Founded in New York by Dutch immigrant and socialist Piet Vlag, the magazine supported such issues as workmen's compensation, safe working conditions for miners and other workers, women's suffrage, the right to birth control, and world peace. The magazine included a wide variety of fiction, poetry, political articles, and artwork. After an initial lack of success, the magazine gained momentum in 1912 when **Max Eastman** assumed the editorship, broadening the magazine's political stance beyond socialism to include a range of leftist positions. *The Masses* was buoyed by contributors such as **John Reed**, who joined the staff of the magazine in 1913. Well-known writers eventually to be published in the magazine included Mary Heaton Vorse, Sherwood Anderson, **Upton Sinclair**, Carl Sandburg, and Amy Lowell. Though the circulation never exceeded 25,000, the magazine was influential, gaining a reputation for both literary quality and controversial points of view.

During **World War I**, Eastman's strong antiwar stance caused the U.S. postmaster general to revoke the magazine's mailing license under the Espionage Act of 1917. Eastman, Reed, and others were tried on criminal charges of "conspiracy against the government," though their trials ended in hung juries and they were never convicted. Government pressure continued to keep the magazine out of the mail (and, largely, off the newsstands), leading to the demise of the magazine in December 1917.

Selected Bibliography: Fishbein, Leslie. *Rebels in Bohemia: The Radicals of "The Masses," 1911–1917.* Chapel Hill: North Carolina UP, 1982; Zurier, Rebecca. *Art for the Masses: A Radical Magazine and Its Graphics, 1911–1917.* Philadelphia: Temple UP, 1988.

M. Keith Booker

MATTHIESSEN, FRANCIS OTTO (1902–1950).

One of the twentieth century's most influential scholar-critics of American literature, F. O. Matthiessen was born in Pasadena, California; grew up near LaSalle, Illinois; and was an undergraduate (1919–1923) at Yale. After two years in Europe as a Rhodes scholar at New College, Oxford, he attended Harvard for his master's (1926) and doctoral (1927) degrees. Matthiessen began his career as an instructor at Yale (1927–1929), but soon returned to Harvard, where he was a challenging, inspiring teacher and advisor (1929–1950).

As a critic, Matthiessen stressed close attention to the text. He insisted, however, that each text be examined within its social and political contexts, and he showed a passionate concern for the contemporary impact of the literature of America's past. He argued that the insights into the national character articulated by Emerson, **Whitman**, **Thoreau**, Hawthorne, and Melville, and the ideals of freedom and equality they affirmed, provide a "literature for our democracy." These words appear in the preface to Matthiessen's *American Renaissance* (1941), the book that, as the literary historian Sacvan Bercovitch has said, "reset the terms for the study of American literary history; it gave us a new canon of classic texts; and it inspired the growth of American Studies in the United States and abroad."

Matthiessen's personal, professional, and political interests and loyalties were complex and precariously balanced. He was a nationally known scholar, a homosexual, a devout Christian, a socialist, and a radical who celebrated "the **Russian Revolution** as the most progressive event of our century," even as he wrote highly favorable studies of two masters of elite art, **T. S. Eliot** (1935, rev. 1947) and **Henry James** (1944). Matthiessen was a believer in the primacy of high artistic standards whose final book, *Theodore Dreiser* (1951), focused on an author noted for stylistic clumsiness; he was a fervent advocate of equality and inclusiveness who wrote rarely about women authors and not at all about African American authors. His book *From the Heart of Europe* (1948) describes his social and political views, dealing in particular with his period as a teacher and lecturer, summer–fall 1947, at the Salzburg (Austria) Seminar on American Civilization and at Charles University in Prague.

Matthiessen committed suicide in Boston on April 1, 1950. In a note he explained: "I am exhausted. I have been subject to so many severe depressions during the past few years that I can no longer believe that I can continue to be of use to my profession and my friends. . . . How much the state of the world has to do with my state of mind I do not know. But as a Christian and a socialist believing in international peace, I find myself terribly oppressed by the present tensions." Matthiessen's death was a tragic loss for American literary scholarship, but he left behind an extraordinary body of work. He was the author of ten books, the editor of five books, and the writer of more than 150 essays and reviews.

Selected Bibliography: Bercovitch, Sacvan. "The Problem of Ideology in American Literary History." *Critical Inquiry* 12.4 (Summer 1986): 631–53; Cain, William E. *F. O. Matthiessen and the Politics of Criticism.* Madison: U of Wisconsin P, 1988; Gunn, Giles. *F. O. Matthiessen: The Critical Achievement.* Seattle: U of Washington P, 1975; Matthiessen, F. O. *American Renaissance: Art and Expression in the Age of Emerson and Whitman.* New York: Oxford UP, 1941; Matthiessen, F. O. *The Responsibilities of the Critic: Essays and Reviews.* Ed. John Rackliffe. New York: Oxford UP, 1952; Stern, Frederick. *F. O. Matthiessen: Christian Socialist as Critic.* Chapel Hill: U of North Carolina P, 1981; Sweezy, Paul M., and Leo Huberman, eds. *F. O. Matthiessen (1902–1950): A Collective Portrait.* New York: Monthly Review Press, 1951; White, George Abbott. "Ideology and Literature: *American Renaissance* and F.O. Matthiessen." *Literature and Revolution,* special issue of *TriQuarterly* 23/24 (Winter/Spring 1972): 430–500.

William E. Cain

MAYAKOVSKY, VLADIMIR VLADIMIROVICH (1893–1930). Although his aesthetic innovations alone would reserve him a place in Russian literary history, Mayakovsky is perhaps second only to **Maxim Gorky** as a literary figure associated with the **Russian Revolution**. Mayakovsky joined the outlawed Russian Social Democratic Party at fourteen and was arrested three times before his sixteenth birthday, resulting in a six-month prison term in 1909. Upon his release, he gained admission to a prestigious art school in Moscow, where he met many of the innovators of the burgeoning Russian modernist avant-garde in both visual art and poetry. The painter-poet David Burliuk took Mayakovsky under his wing, and it was through his influence that Mayakovsky was invited to publish several poems as part of the futurist manifesto/almanac *A Slap in the Face of Public Taste* in 1912. Not only did the futurists—especially the cubo-futurists with whom Mayakovsky was associated—reject traditional artistic forms, but their work also echoed (albeit not always explicitly) the revolutionary political philosophy of Bolshevik leaders like **Lenin** and **Trotsky**.

Mayakovsky established himself as the leader among the cubo-futurists, but the onset of **World War I** shifted the nation's attention away from experimental literature. Not long after the February 1917 revolution had toppled the Romanov dynasty, Mayakovsky seized the opportunity to publish such poems as "Revolution: A Poetic Chronicle," which declared that this event was only a precursor to the Bolshevik Revolution. So prominent was his agitation that the sailors who overthrew Alexander Kerensky's provisional government in October 1917 were singing one of Mayakovsky's revolutionary songs as they marched on the Winter Palace in St. Petersburg.

After the Bolsheviks assumed power, Mayakovsky remained a vocal proponent of revolutionary ideals. He produced a copious stream of propagandistic verses and illustrations about the progress of the Russian civil war for the Soviet-run telegraph agency. He also began creating literary works that were meant to reinforce the spirit of the revolutionary age. His play *Mystery Bouffe* (1918)—a satirical retelling of the biblical flood story from a Bolshevik perspective—was first staged on the first anniversary of the October revolution. Similarly, his lengthy poem *150,000,000* (1918) depicts the entire population of the Soviet Union as a mythic hero engaging in battle against Woodrow Wilson. Mayakovsky attempted to define the role of the artist as an indispensable ideological worker in the new Soviet state. Toward this end, he helped found the Left Front of Art (LEF) collective in 1922. LEF tried to establish a broad set of futurist aesthetics as the truest means of artistically expressing revolutionary ideas, and its members committed themselves to making art serve social and political ends.

Ultimately, Mayakovsky's efforts failed, mostly because of increasing hostility toward experimental art in the Soviet Union. After Lenin's death in 1924, the insistence on genuinely "proletarian" art saw more avant-garde groups like LEF condemned as bourgeois holdovers. Mayakovsky wrote a pair of plays in the late 1920s—*The Bedbug* (1929) and *The Bathhouse* (1930)—that satirized the decline of revolutionary idealism, but neither play received popular or critical acclaim. Mayakovsky committed suicide on April 14, 1930. In 1935, **Stalin** posthumously declared him "the best and most talented poet of our Soviet era," even though many of his later works were still banned.

Selected Bibliography: Brown, Edward J. *Mayakovsky: A Poet in the Revolution*. Princeton, NJ: Princeton UP, 1973; Markov, Vladimir. *Russian Futurism: A History*. Berkeley: U of California P, 1968; Terras, Victor. *Vladimir Mayakovsky*. Boston: Twayne, 1983; Woroszylski, Wiktor. *The Life of Mayakovsky*. Trans. Boleslav Taborski. New York: Orion, 1970.

Derek C. Maus

McCARTHYISM. *See* ANTICOMMUNISM.

McKAY, CLAUDE (1889–1948). Born near Kingston, Jamaica, poet and novelist Claude McKay grew up reading **Shakespeare**, **Dickens**, and mid-nineteenth-century popular romances and science books. His mentor, the English expatriate and garden enthusiast Walter Jekyll, instilled in him a love of culture, gardening, and philosophy. McKay was also influenced by Sydney Olivier, an English radical and governor of Jamaica from 1907 until 1913, whose brand of Fabian socialism, transplanted to the colonies, impressed the young poet.

McKay's first published poem, entitled "Hard Times" (1907), is a critique of the social and economic conditions in Jamaica. He would go on to publish two volumes of poetry before leaving his homeland: *Songs of Jamaica*, about peasant folkways, and

Constab Ballads, which chronicled his experiences as a Kingston police cadet. The young poet—expected to follow in the family tradition of farming—attended Tuskegee Institute, then Kansas State College in 1912.

Neither Tuskegee nor Kansas appealed to McKay, and he moved to New York City in 1914. "If We Must Die," a poem written during the "Red Summer" of 1919, appeared in the *Liberator*'s July issue, and reappeared a few months later as the *Messenger*'s lead editorial in its September "Riot" issue, a call-to-arms for black resistance. While the poem established McKay as a powerful poetic voice of the emerging **Harlem Renaissance**, it created such a stir among government officials that it was read into the *Congressional Record* as an example of subversive literature, prompting McKay to consider leaving the country.

In September, with a letter of introduction from the English poet Walter Fuller, McKay set off for England, where he published *Spring in New Hampshire*, the first collection of poems published in England by a black Jamaican. Two years later, with New York editor Max Eastman's help, it would be expanded and retitled *Harlem Shadows*. During this time, from 1919 to 1922, McKay was also a contributor and later an editor of the *Liberator* and Sylvia Pankhurst's *The Workers' Dreadnought*, periodicals with strong ties to international feminism and pacifism.

Although he delighted in referring to his unsophisticated roots, McKay was an erudite intellectual, fluent in Spanish and French. He became an expert on African American literature as well, and devoted a lengthy section to it in his critical study *Negroes in America*, which was commissioned by **Vladimir Lenin** after the poet's charismatic appearance at the Third International in 1922. Unable to return to the United States because of his connections to Russian Communists, McKay eventually settled in the industrial port city of Marseilles, where he completed the novel *Home to Harlem* (1928), a signature text of the Harlem Renaissance. His second novel, *Banjo* (1929), set in Marseilles and first published in French, would inspire **Francophone** writers of Africa and the Caribbean. After some difficulties with French authorities, McKay decided to move to the outskirts of Tangiers, on a small farm near an Arab village, which he purchased with royalties from *Home to Harlem* and *Banjo*. There, he completed two other works—*Gingertown* (1932), a collection of short stories, and *Banana Bottom* (1933), a novel set in the Jamaican countryside and dedicated to his childhood mentor, Jekyll. McKay eventually returned to the United States and died in Chicago in 1948, having been a U.S. citizen for the last eight years of his life.

Selected Bibliography: Cooper, Wayne F. *Claude McKay: Rebel Sojourner in the Harlem Renaissance*. Baton Rouge: Louisiana UP, 1987; Cooper, Wayne F., ed. *The Passion of Claude McKay*. New York: Schocken Books, 1973; Gayle, Addison, Jr., ed. *Claude McKay: The Black Poet at War*. Detroit: Broadside P, 1972; Giles, James Richard. *Claude McKay*. Boston: Twayne, 1976; Maxwell, William J. *New Negro, Old Left*. New York: Columbia UP, 1999; Tillery, Tyrone. *Claude McKay: A Black Poet's Struggle for Identity*. Amherst: U of Massachusetts P, 1992.

Josh Gosciak

McLUHAN, HERBERT MARSHALL (1911–1980). Marshall McLuhan's *The Mechanical Bride* (1951) is the ur-text of cultural studies in North America (preceding

Roland Barthes' *Mythologies* by six years), and his *The Gutenberg Galaxy* (1962) and *Understanding Media* (1964) established him as one of the most widely influential intellectuals of the late twentieth century. In *The Mechanical Bride*, McLuhan reproduced a series of visual "exhibits" drawn from the mass media of the 1930s and 1940s, including advertisements, cartoon strips, pulp-fiction series, and film icons. Each exhibit was then accompanied by a rapid-fire, densely allusive, and wide-ranging commentary in an experimental critical style influenced by modernist montage. A conservative critic of modern capitalist culture, McLuhan was here concerned with revealing the unconscious programming of mass society by the commercially rather than morally driven fantasy and dream productions of a culture industry that erotically fetishizes death and violence. These concerns quietly persist in the less overtly political media theory of his later books, which explore the structural powers and limits imposed by communications media as the bases of social organization. In his now-cliché notion of the "global village," McLuhan sought to understand not only the new creative potentials but also the new unconscious vulnerabilities and social conflicts that arise with an electronically and digitally mediated planet. McLuhan is also significant as a public intellectual who attempted both to work within the culture industry, as a media celebrity and icon of late twentieth-century modernity, and to find new forms of radical pedagogy and public discussion based on collective, participatory dialogue.

Selected Bibliography: Cavell, Richard. *McLuhan in Space: A Cultural Geography.* Toronto: U Toronto P, 2002; Grosswiler, Paul. *The Method Is the Message: Rethinking McLuhan through Critical Theory.* Montreal: Black Rose, 1998; Marchand, Philip. *Marshall McLuhan: The Medium and the Messenger. A Biography.* Toronto: Vintage Canada, 1998.

Glenn Willmott

MENCHÚ TUM, RIGOBERTA (1959–). Awarded the Nobel Peace Prize in 1992 for defending indigenous rights, Rigoberta Menchú Tum is a Quiché-Maya from Uspantán, Guatemala, who gained international recognition with *I, Rigoberta Menchú, an Indian Woman from Guatemala* (*Me llamo Rigoberta Menchú y así me nació la conciencia,* 1983), a testimonial narrative that tells "from below" the story of the Guatemalan civil war during the 1980s. *I, Rigoberta*, based on interviews by anthropologist Elizabeth Burgos Debray, is a powerful first-person *testimonio* narrating how Menchú, her family, and numerous indigenous towns became the target of a brutal counter-insurgency campaign called *tierra arrasada* (leveled ground), which killed hundreds and forced thousands into exile. Several family members of Menchú, including her parents and a brother, were killed by Guatemalan security forces. In her account, Menchú also tells how indigenous peoples, peasant organizations such as the Comité de Unidad Campesina (Committee for Peasant Unity), workers' unions, Catholic catechists, and the armed Left (the Guerrilla Army of the Poor and later the Guatemalan National Revolutionary Unity) came together to oppose the government.

In 1999, U.S. anthropologist David Stoll published a book that questioned the truthfulness of *I, Rigoberta*, disputing Menchú's statements on her experience as a farm worker, her education, her family land struggles, and her witnessing the death of family members. For Stoll, Menchú's text is more a literary rendition of Guatemalan history—like an epic—than it is objective truth. Menchú has publicly rejected Stoll's accusations, and the debate that ensued has raised several issues on Guatemalan history, such as the distance between the Left and the indigenous population, as well as a debate on more general issues, such as historical truth and the validity of eyewitness accounts.

In 1998, with the editorial aid of Italian journalist Giani Minà and the Guatemalan writer Dante Liano, Menchú published *Crossing Borders* (*Rigoberta: La nieta de los mayas*). Whereas in *I, Rigoberta*, Menchú had little say in the editorial process, in this second book, she revised and approved every sentence. Closer to the memoir genre than to the *testimonio, Crossing Borders* narrates in detail Menchú's human-rights activism from Guatemala to the United Nation's corridors. Speaking from the vantage point of a Nobel Prize winner, *Crossing Borders* advocates for the specificity of indigenous peoples' rights and condemns the prevailing racism that even Menchú and her family still experience when traveling.

After winning the Nobel Prize, Menchú funded the Rigoberta Menchú Tum Foundation for promoting indigenous rights internationally. She was an outspoken critic of the 1992 celebration of the quincentennial anniversary of the "discovery" of the "New World." As a response, she organized two world summits of indigenous peoples. In 1993, she was the United Nations goodwill ambassador for the International Year of Indigenous Peoples. In 1996, she was nominated goodwill ambassador for UNESCO. She has received several honorary doctoral degrees and other international recognitions, including the French Legion of Honor distinction (1996) and the Spanish Principe Asturias Prize (1998).

Suggested Bibliography: Arias, Arturo, ed. *The Rigoberta Menchú Controversy.* Minneapolis: U of Minnesota P, 2001; Beverley, John. *Against Literature.* Minneapolis: U of Minnesota P, 1993; Fundación Rigoberta Menchú Tum. http://www.frmt.org. Accessed April 5, 2004; Liano, Dante. "La génesis de *Rigoberta, La nieta de los mayas." La memoria popular y sus transformaciones.* Ed. Martin Lienhard. Madrid: Iberoamericana, 2000. 209–19; Stoll, David. *Rigoberta Menchú and the Story of All Poor Guatemalans.* Boulder: Westview P, 1999.

Luis Fernando Restrepo

MENIPPEAN SATIRE is named after the third century B.C.E. Greek philosopher Menippus of Gadara, who was a student of the cynic Metrocles. His name characterizes satire that mocks institutions, professions, orthodox social conventions, and philosophical credulousness. Though none of his writings are extant, Menippus is credited with introducing three innovations to satire. First, he treated serious philosophical issues in a comic manner. Second, he combined prose and poetry. Third, Menippus wrote for a broader audience than was normally the practice, with work treating philosophical themes. Such claims to originality are problematic, however, because all three "innovations" were present hundreds of years earlier in Greek drama, and arguably trace further back to the dawn of literacy—such practices being standard forms of expression in Bacchic festivals, in which verse and drama are brought together to celebrate the bounty of the harvest. Works of Menippean satire have also been called "anatomies," after Robert Burton's *Anatomy of Melancholy* (1621).

Some of the definitive authors and titles associated with the genre include Aristophanes' *The Clouds* (fourth–fifth century B.C.E.), Petronius's *Satyricon* (first century C.E.), Lucian's *Dialogues* (second century C.E.), Rabelais' *Gargantua and Pantagruel* (1532, 1534), **Swift**'s *Tale of a Tub* (1704) and *Gulliver's Travels* (1726), Voltaire's *Candide* (1759), Carlyle's *Sartor Resartus* (1836), Melville's *Moby-Dick* (1851) and *The Confidence-Man* (1857), and Lewis Carroll's *Alice's Adventures in Wonderland* (1865) and *Through the Looking-Glass* (1872). More recent work in the Menippean vein includes **Aldous Huxley**'s *Antic Hay* (1923) and *Point Counterpoint* (1928); the terrifying **dystopian literature** of **Karel Čapek**, such as *R.U.R.* and *War with the Newts*; and the cosmopolitan phantasms of **Vladimir Nabokov**, such as *Lolita* (1955) and *Pale Fire* (1962). There are also strong Menippean elements in such modern classics as **James Joyce**'s *Ulysses* (1922) and Thomas Pynchon's *Gravity's Rainbow* (1973).

Menippean satire has proven to be a fertile field for theoretical activity. Northrop Frye's characterization of Menippean satire spotlights the encyclopedic nature of the genre, emphasizing the farrago of voices that animate the text, as well as the "magpie instinct" of authors who are as much compilers and redactors as they are literary artists. After Frye, much of the interest in Menippean satire has been generated by the late-twentieth-century century vogue of **Mikhail Bakhtin**, who saw the form as a "dialogic" arena in which archetypical notions of social class and gender—incumbent on their relative sub-genres, dialects, and languages—struggle with each other between the covers of a single volume. More recent work has identified important affinities with Ludwig Wittgenstein and analytic philosophy, describing the genre as a technical process of philosophical analysis that uses allegory, parody, and grammatical precision as a supple and adaptive framework for exposing the significance, the truth, the application, and the relevance of scientific and philosophical propositions.

Selected Bibliography: Bakhtin, Mikhail M. *The Dialogic Imagination: Four Essays by M. M. Bakhtin.* Ed. Michael Holquist. Trans. Caryl Emerson and Michael Holquist. Austin: U of Texas P, 1981; Bakhtin, Mikhail M. *Problems of Dostoevsky's Poetics.* Ed. and Trans. Caryl Emerson. Minneapolis: U of Minnesota P, 1984; Blanchard, W. Scott. *Scholar's Bedlam: Menippean Satire in the Renaissance.* London: Associated UP, 1995; Frye, Northrop. *Anatomy of Criticism.* Princeton, NJ: Princeton UP, 1957; Kaplan, Carter. *Critical Synoptics: Menippean Satire and the Analysis of Intellectual Mythology.* Madison: Fairleigh Dickinson UP, 2000; Kirk, Eugene P. *Menippean Satire: An Annotated Catalogue of Texts and Criticism.* New York: Garland, 1980; Relihan, Joel C. *Ancient Menippean Satire.* Baltimore: Johns Hopkins UP, 1993.

Carter Kaplan

MIDNIGHT'S CHILDREN (1981). Winner of Britain's prestigious Booker Prize in 1981 and later of the special Booker of Bookers Prize, an honor awarded to the best novel among the twenty-five that had won the prize since 1969, *Midnight's Children* is widely regarded as a masterpiece of world literature. The novel has been translated into more than a dozen languages, and it is widely regarded as the best work of its author, **Salman Rushdie**. *Midnight* is a complex and lengthy novel that tells the tale of Saleem Sinai, the narrator-protagonist, whose Indian Muslim family migrates to Pakistan after the independence of the Indian subcontinent and its partition into two countries along religious lines in 1947. At the same time, it is a **historical novel** that narrates the entire process of Indian independence, using complex, ironic techniques typical of works of **postmodernism**.

Midnight begins with Aadam Aziz, Saleem's maternal grandfather, who has returned from Germany with a medical degree. Contrasting with Aadam's knowledge of modern science is the traditional wisdom of Tai, Aadam's childhood mentor. Tai, a boatman, represents age-old India, frozen in time and unchanging in its habits. Aadam tries to remain true to the values of his family in which religion occupies a central role. His medical training, on the other hand, forces him to question many of his assumptions. The seeking of two opposites, those of Islam and modernity, plagues him with a fragmented self throughout his life, a problem that many other characters in the novel experience as well.

Rushdie's narrative strategy creates profound ambiguity regarding the events in *Midnight*. While the work is a political allegory, it establishes and, at the same time, undermines many of the actions it recounts, thus raising historiographic issues. Born at the exact moment of India's independence, Saleem feels he is "mysteriously handcuffed to history." His account is not India's only history; other histories with other perspectives compete with Saleem's master narrative, and the reader is made aware of the complexity in the task of identifying a dominant identity in the extremely pluralistic nation that is India.

An influential text in **postcolonial literature**, *Midnight* has generated substantial critical attention. It is a work that rewards the scholar who wants to study Rushdie's intertextual strategies or his allegory or his concerns for historiography. The text lends itself also to postmodern studies. *Midnight's* ability to tell an Indian tale so effortlessly in English have led some scholars to examine the text's oral elements, and attempts to place the work in an Indian/Middle Eastern tradition of storytelling are many. Other scholars see the text as an exemplary work of postmodernism, following in a long Western tradition of nonlinear writers, such as Laurence Sterne and **James Joyce**.

Selected Bibliography: Booker, M. Keith, ed. *Critical Essays on Salman Rushdie*. New York: G. K. Hall, 1999; Brennan, Timothy. *Salman Rushdie and the Third World: Myths of the Nation*. London: Macmillan, 1989; Cundy, Catherine. *Salman Rushdie*. Manchester: Manchester UP, 1996; Fletcher, M. D., ed. *Reading Rushdie: Perspectives on the Fiction of Salman Rushdie*. Amsterdam: Rodopi, 1995; Harrison, J. *Salman Rushdie*. New York: Twayne, 1992.

Farhad B. Idris

MILOSZ, CZESLAW (1911–). Polish poet, essayist, novelist, and public intellectual in his reconstituted native land, to which he returned from exile in the early 1990s. Milosz's personal history mirrors the twists and turns of twentieth-century European history. His "native realm," now in Lithuania, has been reconstituted geographically as well as politically some half dozen times since his birth; he was a citizen of Poland, living in his beloved Wilno (now Vilnius) only during the two interwar decades. Milosz lived through **World War II** in occupied Warsaw; his writings from that time express his anguished contemplation of the collapse of a European civilization abandoned by God.

Milosz's hastily written first novel, *The Seizure of Power* (1953), records the political anxieties and confusions during the war's endgame, as Poland teetered between its German occupiers and its Soviet "liberators." Seeing no plausible third path, he chose to side with the new communist authorities, serving as Warsaw's cultural attaché in New York and Washington (1946–1950). Posted to Paris, he defected in 1951, citing his writer's obligation to protect his moral and aesthetic freedom from the demands of the state, as encoded in the theory and practice of **socialist realism**. *The Captive Mind* (1953), the most explicitly political of Milosz's writings, is a subtle and devastating exploration of the many reasons why dialectical materialism, buttressed by Soviet power, proved so attractive to East European intellectuals in the immediate postwar years. Milosz had already described this attraction as a moral collapse in several scathing poems, including the cycle *A Moral Treatise* (1947).

After his defection, Milosz settled uncomfortably in France, where he was scorned by left-wing intellectuals. (America's **cold-war** anxieties barred this "Communist" from immigrating until the University of California at Berkeley appointed him to its faculty in 1960.) Banned from overt participation in Polish intellectual life until his Nobel Prize for Literature, awarded in 1980, made it too awkward for the communist government to pretend he did not exist, Milosz used his occasional political essays to denounce the xenophobic nationalism of certain émigré factions. Returning to Poland in the 1990s, he undertook one more major act of political "correction": a thick, annotated collection of long-forgotten documents and propagandistic texts from the interwar decades, intended to counter an emerging nostalgia for the precommunist "good old days" of 1930s Poland (*Wyprawa w dwudziestolecie* [Excursion into the Interwar Decades], 1999).

However, Milosz is not primarily a political writer. He is a contemplative poet obsessed with transience, an ecstatic poet delighting in God's and man's world; he is also, by historical accident, a poet from "the other Europe," fated to bear witness to the horrors of the twentieth century, but one "whose true vocation," as he states in his Nobel lecture, "is to contemplate Being."

Selected Bibliography: Cuddihy, Michael, ed. *Czesław Miłosz: A Special Issue. Ironwood* 18 (1981); Fiut, Aleksander. *The Eternal Moment: The Poetry of Czeslaw Milosz.* Trans. Theodosia S. Robertson. Berkeley: U of California P, 1990; Milosz, Czeslaw. *Native Realm: A Search for Self-Definition.* Trans. Catherine S. Leach. Garden City, NY: Doubleday, 1968; Milosz, Czeslaw. *Nobel Lecture.* New York: Farrar, Straus and Giroux, 1981; Milosz, Czeslaw. *The Witness of Poetry.* Cambridge, MA: Harvard UP, 1983; Możejko, Edward. *Between Anxiety and Hope: The Poetry and Writing of Czesław Miłosz.* Edmonton: U of Alberta P, 1988; Nathan, Leonard, and Arthur Quinn. *The Poet's Work: An Introduction to Czeslaw Milosz.* Cambridge, MA: Harvard UP, 1991.

Madeline G. Levine

MILTON, JOHN (1608–1674). Born into London's middle class during King James's reign, Milton went to Cambridge and then persuaded his father, a scrivener, to let him spend a further six years at home reading. Afterwards, he traveled for a year in Italy—meeting scholars and apparently visiting Galileo while the astronomer was under house arrest—before returning to London to become a tutor. In 1641, he began publishing political tracts, some supporting the Puritan cause (*Eikonoklastes*, *The Tenure of Kings and Magistrates*) and some addressing such issues as divorce (*The Doctrine and Discipline of Divorce*, *Tetrachordon*), censorship, and individual freedom (*Areopagitica*). In 1649, Oliver Cromwell's Commonwealth government made him secretary for foreign tongues.

Milton's early poetry includes major lyrics such as "Ode Upon the Morning of Christ's Nativity" and "Lycidas," as well as a masque, *Comus*. He wrote his most ambitious works after becoming blind about 1651, dictating to his daughters and requiring them to read aloud to him. The publication of *Paradise Lost* in 1667, followed in 1671 by *Paradise Regained* and *Samson Agonistes*, brought him literary fame, and it was not until long after his death that scholars fully understood that these two epics and this closet drama investigate theological ideas that many of Milton's contemporaries would have found heretical if they had recognized them.

Milton's theology and politics were fiercely idiosyncratic, despite his working for the Commonwealth. He was not Trinitarian, believed in God's foreknowledge but not strictly in predestination, admired Copernican cosmology, speculated that the earth might not be the only inhabited planet, was uncomfortable with the paradox of the Incarnation because of its emphasis on Jesus' meekness, and believed that Adam and Eve would have had prelapsarian sexual intercourse. Because of his disastrous marriage to the royalist Mary Powell, Milton advocated the legalization of divorce on the grounds of incompatibility, and his pamphlets on the subject drew public invective from all sides. Recent analyses of his work have focused on his attitudes toward republicanism, colonization, and revolution; on the sexual politics of his Eden; on his unprecedentedly complex deployment of iambic pentameter; and on his quirky humor, which often depends on etymological puns. He was not as naively Byronic as Blake later believed him to be ("of the Devil's party without knowing it"), but Milton's belief that reason was empowered by a titanic inspiration made him profoundly unlike the next generation of poets, who admired him rather as they might admire an avalanche: glad to keep their civilized distance.

Selected Bibliography: Achinstein, Sharon. *Milton and the Revolutionary Reader*. Princeton, NJ: Princeton UP, 1994; Evans, J. Martin. *Milton's Imperial Epic: "Paradise Lost" and the Discourse of Colonialism*. Ithaca, NY: Cornell UP, 1996; Fish, Stanley Eugene. *How Milton Works*. Cambridge, MA: Harvard Belknap, 2001; Lieb, Michael. *Milton and the Culture of Violence*. Ithaca: Cornell UP, 1994; Silver, Victoria. *Imperfect Sense: The Predicament of Milton's Irony*. Princeton, NJ: Princeton UP, 2001; Turner, James. *One Flesh: Paradisal Marriage and Sexual Relations in the Age of Milton*. Oxford: Clarendon P, 1987; Walker, Julia M., ed. *Milton and the Idea of Woman*. Urbana: U of Illinois P, 1988.

Dorothy Stephens

MIR, PEDRO (1913–1999), Dominican poet, fiction writer, historian, journalist, and literary theorist, recognized in Latin America as a major progressive writer deeply committed to the welfare of the working classes of the Caribbean and Latin America. In 1982, the Dominican Congress designated Mir as the national poet. In 1993, he was awarded the prestigious National Prize for Literature in the Dominican Republic. Mir published seven volumes of poetry, three works of fiction, five historical studies, and four books on aesthetics.

Mir first published his poems in newspapers and journals in the late 1930s and was singled out by friends and foes as a significant social poet. Under threat of the dictatorship of Rafael Trujillo, Mir fled the Dominican Republic for Cuba in 1947. There he wrote and published one of his most admired volumes of poetry, *Hay un país en el mundo* (There Is a Country in the World, 1949), which laments the domination of the Dominican Republic by U.S. capital and its internal representatives, implicating the Trujillo dictatorship. The poet envisions, however, the day when the workers and farmers will overthrow the tyranny of the dollar and build a "constructive peace" (27).

In 1952, Mir published his second book of poetry in Guatemala, one now counted as a major poetic work. His epic poem *Countersong to Walt Whitman (Song of Ourselves)* is a poetic conversation with **Whitman**'s democratic ethos and telos. The transcendental and democratic inclusivity of Whitman's self and song holds great promise for Mir because it represents the historical emergence of the modern proletariat on the world's stage and the possibility of building a "giant nation" for the working people (69). However, the realization of a democratic America is thwarted by the development of the capitalist world market; the hope of a liberating possessive individualism is shattered, for now the only truly possessive individuals are ruling classes who steal the labor and lands of the working class. Mir's response to this crisis of history and representation is to call forth a "countersong" that arises as the dialectical counterpart of imperialism. Mir's key concept for the emergent new working-class subjectivity is the collective *nosotros* (we), not the ideological *yo* (I) of the bourgeoisie. While separated by occupations, the international working class is united by common conditions of exploited work, oppression, and hope. Mir envisions the establishment of worker's power throughout the Americas.

Until his death, Mir continued to write in multiple genres on the dialectic of both oppression and resistance in the Dominican Republic and in other parts of Latin America. When he returned to his homeland in the 1960s after the assassination of Trujillo, he was so admired by workers, farmers, and intellectuals that they memorized and recited his poetry. He stands next to the other great Latin America poets, such as **Nicolás Guillén**, **Pablo Neruda**, and **Ernesto Cardenal**, whose poetry is on the side of the working class.

Selected Bibliography: Conway, Christopher. "Of Subjects and Cowboys: Frontier and History in Pedro Mir's 'Countersong to Walt Whitman.'" *Walt Whitman Quarterly Review* 15.4 (Spring 1998): 161–71; Laguna, Elpidio. "Social Genesis and Historical Understanding in the Works of Pedro Mir." *Revista canadiense de estudios hispánicos* 15.2 (Winter 1991): 235–50; Sommer, Doris. "History and Romanticism in Mir's *Cuando amaban las tierras comuneras*." *Revista de Estudios Hispánicos* 6 (1979): 219–48; Torres-Saillant, Silvio. *Caribbean Poetics: Toward an Aesthetic of West Indian Literature*. Cambridge: Cambridge UP, 1997.

Anthony Dawahare

MO YAN (1955–).

Born Guan Moye, Mo Yan won his fame with *Red Sorghum* (*Hong gaoliang*, 1986), a series of novellas adapted in 1987 into a successful film. He was a central figure in the shift to radically experimental prose, away from the "scar literature" and "root-seeking literature" that explored the aftermath of the Cultural Revolution (1966–1976). Together with Yu Hua, Su Tong, Ye Zhaoyan, and other writers slightly younger than himself, Mo Yan established avant-garde fiction as the major literary trend in the People's Republic of China from the late 1980s to the mid-1990s. Influenced by **William Faulkner** and **Gabriel García Márquez**, Mo Yan's works combine down-to-earth local flavor with gruesome images and black humor. His works include both crisp descriptions of concrete social issues and surprising forays into surreal fantasy.

Born to a peasant family in Gaomi County, Shandong, Mo Yan would continue to set his plots in the backwater villages of Gaomi. He was sent to the countryside during the Cultural Revolution, joined the People's Liberation Army (PLA) in 1976, and entered the PLA Art Academy in 1984. Mo Yan started publishing in 1981 and rose to national prominence after the appearance of his short story *A Transparent Carrot* (*Touming de hongluobo*, 1984). *Red Sorghum* describes the resistance against Japanese invaders in 1939, yet unlike previous accounts of the war, the novel does not depict unmitigated heroism. Instead, the characters are humanly fallible, and the narrative is ironic and self-mocking. *The Garlic Ballads* (*Tiantang suantai zhi ge*, 1988) is set in a contemporary, reform-era village and explores the corruption of petty officials; the theme is brought to the absurd in *The Republic of Wine* (*Jiu guo*, 1993), in which a drunken detective finds out—or hallucinates—that local cadres serve him the flesh of a human child. The epic concerns of *Red Sorghum* are taken up in *Big Breasts and Wide Hips* (*Feng ru fei tun*, 1995), which spans the twentieth century in a rural community, and *Sandalwood Torture* (*Tanxiang xing*, 2001), set against the Boxer Rebellion of 1900. His ninth novel, *Forty-one Bombs* (*Sishiyi pao*, 2003), returns to the 1990s and weaves a tale of revenge by a mentally challenged youngster who goes after the village head. Mo Yan's criticism of local politics, disregard of Maoist historiography, and brazen depictions of sex have often triggered official disapproval. Even though, contrary to speculations, the Nobel Prize has so far eluded Mo Yan, his prolific writing and constant search for new literary forms—in voluminous novels, short stories, and essays—place him as one of China's leading authors.

Selected Bibliography: Lu Tonglin. "*Red Sorghum:* Limits of Transgression." *Politics, Ideology, and Literary Discourse in Modern China: Theoretical Interventions and Cultural Critique.* Ed. Liu Kang and Tang Xiaobing. Durham, NC: Duke UP, 1993. 188–208; Wang Jing. *High Culture Fever: Politics, Aesthetics, and Ideology in Deng's China.* Berkeley: U of California P, 1997.

Yomi Braester

MODERNISM. The mood attending the advent of literary modernism in the United States and on the continent was far from uniform, hardly optimistic, and often downright despairing over the contemporary state of arts and letters and, by extension, of the world at large (for the former was understood by many modernist writers not as a symptom but as a direct cause of the latter). Certainly **Virginia Woolf**'s dramatic 1923 assertion "that on or about December, 1910, human nature changed" (194) constitutes one attempt to chronicle the birth of literary modernism and even to greet this change with some degree of excitement over emerging and innovative practices for representing human character and subjectivity. For Woolf, this change in human nature resulted from progressive developments that altered all kinds of social relationships.

The relief expressed here for social transformations, whether actual or not, that promised to inaugurate more egalitarian social relationships, especially for women, was countered by grief and anxiety in others. **James Joyce**'s fiction and his supposed desire to escape the "nightmare of history" are at best ambivalent (critics like **Georg Lukács** have felt that Joyce retreated irresponsibly into subjectivism, disarming meaningful historical intervention), and **W. B. Yeats**'s famous lines "Things fall apart; the centre cannot hold; / Mere anarchy is loosed upon the world" from his 1919 poem "The Second Coming" suggest far less than an optimistic attitude toward changes in the world that held out the prospect of the displacement of established orders not just by the chaotic events of **World War I** but perhaps by the socialist revolutions in Russia, Germany, and Italy.

Many modernists echoed this vision of a world in a profound state of crisis, while also believing that culture could make a crucial contribution to the resolution of this crisis. The increasing fragmentation of the world intensified by the war, as well as the alienating effects of urban industrial capitalism that eroded the organicism of the pastoral past, had much to do with the overwhelming of civilized values by collective society and mass culture, and the purity of language and sanctity of received tradition—**T. S. Eliot** and the modernist New Critics believed—had to be sustained against these developments. Modernists such as **Ezra Pound**, in fact, held the litterati directly responsible for the fate of civilization through its guardianship of language and expression.

From this point of view, whatever capitalism, tyranny, aggressive human nature, or the world war might have contributed to the current crisis, these apparent possible causes were but symptoms of the more fundamental dissolution in language usage. Certainly, then, the cure to contemporary ills resided in the restoration of a proper cultural discipline. Thus, the practitioners of literary modernism would develop a range of techniques to go about the project of cultural salvation. Following developments in anthropological discourse, represented iconically by Sir James Frazer's *The Golden Bough*, modernism would seek to find order amid the chaos of the modern world via the "mythic method," whereby authors would seek to find the underlying original myth that bound us all together in a common cultural discourse. In *The Man Who Died*, for example, D. H. Lawrence blends the myths of Osiris and Jesus Christ in weaving an allegory of the erotic death and resurrection of civilization through a peasant or lower-class sensuality, highlighting what he takes to be the identity of these myths as they sprang from a common source. Additionally, the modernists put a premium on tradition, and this importance manifests itself formally in the dense allusiveness of many modernist works, most famously Joyce's *Ulysses* and Eliot's *The Waste Land*, which enact through their many references and cultural layerings the recovery of a lost tradition, even as, at least in the case of *Ulysses*, they often challenged the authority of that tradition. If the elitist modernists have hope, they generally find it by embracing cyclical conceptions of history that posit that no matter how decayed and lifeless contemporary culture and civilization might seem, this culture too will die and pave the way for a wholly new culture to spring forth.

Hence, the first part of *The Waste Land*, "The Burial of Dead," is a ritualistic gesture adapted from the burial service of the Anglican Church, which in this instance is meant to enact the burial of the lifeless contemporary culture so something new might be born.

The generally despairing assessments of the contemporary political scene cited above, at times political and at times poetical, ally, it must be noted, with a certain segment of elite modernist writers and intellectuals who were in the midst of a trauma brought on not just by the unexpected and unimaginable horrors of the unprecedented carnage of World War I, which would have been enough perhaps to shake anyone's faith in civilization, but also by the threats of democratic and particularly socialist development. Yet while modernism in its origins was certainly linked in sensibility to an endangered aristocratic sensibility and even to fascism (Eliot voiced a preference for fascism over communism, and Pound's admiration for Mussolini is well known), the avante-garde formal revolutions in modernism held an attraction for writers from a range of ideological persuasions, from right to left. Many writers on the left did not ignore the vibrant experiments of modernism but tried to adapt them to more consciously social and political ends. Certainly intellectuals and writers on the left shared the elite modernists' disdain for industrial capitalism and its commercial culture, but they rejected the elitist dismay and gloom toward the world and its democratic prospects. While the elite modernists worried over preserving their cultural traditions against the postwar tide of immigrants, people of color, and "Bolsheviks," it was precisely writers associated with these groups who appropriated modernist critical practice to challenge the racist class structure from the left, as we will see below. Nonetheless, as the terms of the so-called **Brecht-Lukács debate** demonstrate, modernism still remained a source of critical conflict on the left, subject to charges from critics such as Lukács that its representational practices, particularly its extreme subjectivism, prevented an adequate comprehension of the relationship between individual consciousness and history. Brecht would argue that the doctrines of **realism** were outdated and needed to be supplanted by modernist techniques that more deftly allowed for the grasping of new historical and social conditions, producing a new and heightened form of realism.

In any case, modernism became nothing less than an intense battlefield, the contestations over which bore complex relationships to struggles and power dynamics going on elsewhere in society, as writers fought over the meaning of culture itself and by extension their right to be counted among the human and to participate in the production of society.

Culture Wars

Political issues in the modernist period often found themselves cast as, even sublimated into, aesthetic and narrowly literary frameworks. For example, **Anzia Yezierska**, in her novel *Salome of the Tenements* (1923), dramatizes the translation of the dominant culture's social anxieties over the incursion of the working-class and racialized "other" as a concern over the preservation of a cultural tradition; one might, in fact, characterize the anxiety as a concern over the very preservation of civilization.

Indeed, in the pages of Eliot's *Criterion* in 1926, one would find Henri Massis expressing the same concern in identical rhetoric, worrying in his essay "Defense of the West" that the colored nations of Asia and Africa, "united by Bolshevism," were ranging themselves against Western civilization (see Klein 6)—the very rhetoric Yezierska echoes in her novel. These, too, were the concerns of Yeats, anxious about the spread of socialism in Europe and, closer to home, about the fact that the leaders of the 1916 **Easter Rising** in Dublin—Connolly and Pearse—were both Socialists, igniting perhaps Yeats's fearful sense of coming apocalyptic violence in "The Second Coming" (1922), a poem that stands as one of the central statements of the modernist sense of contemporary cultural crisis.

Obviously, as such cases exemplify, the elite modernists, while translating sociopolitical and economic concerns into cultural terms, were not bashfully masking their convictions as to the modes of social organization, such as racial and class hierarchies, that would be required to preserve culture in its proper status against the barbarians at the gate. In this sense, the project of a modernist such as Joyce—who might otherwise appear elitist but who is himself, as an Irish Catholic and former Socialist, one of these very barbarians—is set apart from that of Eliot or the Anglo-Irish Yeats. In their own rhetoric, however, the concerns and critical pronouncements of the elite modernists, while perhaps ultimately containing implicit political advocacy for one type of society over another, were first and foremost over issues of culture. Eliot, for example, in the introduction to his 1949 collection of essays—*Notes towards the Definition of Culture*—states, in outlining the social conditions requisite for the proper cultivation of culture, "The first of these is organic (not merely planned, but growing) structure, such as will foster the hereditary transmission of culture within a culture: and this requires a persistence of social classes" (13). But while he is clear about the necessity of class structure for the growth and survival of culture, he does not pretend to make an argument for any set of political convictions or against, say, a Marxism committed to the abolition of classes but simply for the conditions culture requires for existence. "What I try to say is this," he writes, "here are what I believe to be essential conditions for the growth and for the survival of culture. If they conflict with any passionate faith of the reader—if, for instance, he finds it shocking that culture and equalitarianism should conflict, if it seems monstrous to him that anyone should have 'advantages of birth'—I do not ask him to change his faith. I merely ask him to stop paying lip-service to culture" (14–15). Thus, Eliot, in a gesture typical of elite modernist posturing, at once resituates class struggle in the sphere of culture and declares this sphere immune to and free from political investment. The battle between left and right, radicalism and conservatism, would, for the moment, be lifted off the street and into the polite realm of culture, where the outcome of the battle was foregone since leftist radicalism and social democracy were by definition incompatible with culture, as defined by Eliot. To be for culture, one must be prepared to surrender any attachments to or desires for a democratic egalitarian culture and instead accept the necessity of an aristocratic hierarchy characterized by the hereditary transmission of privilege. Such is the version of tradition Eliot's cultural project was to underwrite, which became the site of intense contestation.

Tradition

We can clearly see that in the modernist rhetorical framework, political issues would be resolved through the struggle of various groups—from various political perspectives—to define culture. In particular, "tradition"—how it would be defined and constructed—became the terrain of fervent contestation and also a chief formal feature of modernist literary practice, as evidenced paradigmatically in such works as Eliot's *The Waste Land* or in his essay "Tradition and the Individual Talent." The contestations over tradition and over literary form, however, were simultaneously ideological struggles over, among other issues, the racial and class content and structure of civilization.

The crisis of World War I that had shaken Western civilization to its roots—and, the modernists stridently forwarded, from its roots—was the condensation of a host of social and historical developments linked most generally to the rise of capitalism and commercialism that corroded social values by privileging the accumulation of wealth over family, breeding, and education. A figure such as F. Scott Fitzgerald's Gatsby registers this cultural dissolution, evidenced by the drunk's comments at Gatsby's party at his mansion early in the novel: expressions of shock that the books are real but of smug validation that they clearly haven't been read. Business interests and their values had become dominant, pervading cultural and social institutions. The university, for example—once the refuge where a Brahmin class received its classical education prior to assuming its role as social and cultural vanguard—became the training ground for a new managerial class, a transition again registered in *The Great Gatsby* (1925) in the character of Nick Carraway, who comes from an old family and yet seeks new money in the financial markets of developing capitalism, holding classical learning and business knowledge in precarious juxtaposition. Just as the mode of life dominated by "profit and loss" had struck down Eliot's Phlebas the Phoenician and his society as represented in *The Waste Land*, industrial and commercial capitalism and its attendant cultural developments, or more properly dissolutions, had been responsible for the mass and inhuman destruction of the first mechanized war, and not the least reason for the cultural decline brought on by capitalism was its disregard for the Western cultural tradition and the civilizing values of classical education. Once again, in diagnosing the crisis of civilization, culture is foregrounded.

Moreover, the fallout from the war's ravaging of Europe resulted in a substantial rise in immigration to the United States, and the lack of a properly hierarchical order to contain this "barbarian invasion"—a lack created by capitalism—threatened the cultural foundations of those remaining fragments of civilization. This perceived threat often translated into racist terms, especially anti-Semitic ones. Eliot, for example, argued that in order for a stable cultural tradition to thrive, "[t]he population should be homogeneous; where two or more cultures exist in the same place they are likely either to be fiercely self-conscious or both to become adulterate. What is still more important is unity of religious background; and the reasons of race and religion combine to make any large number of free-thinking Jews undesirable (Klein 15).

This modernist rendering would establish the framework for cultural and political debate that some of the "barbarians" on the left would take up. While many writers on the left held fast to the realist forms traditionally valorized in left-wing critical circles, many also picked up the gauntlet thrown by Eliot and others and responded in his terms. Hence, in *Salome of the Tenements*, Yezierska buys into the modernist framing of the debate but attempts to reverse the valuations of the terms of that frame; that is, she represents the racialized working-class character of Sonya as the source of life and cultural vibrancy, creativity, and renewal while characterizing Manning—with his Puritan ancestry, breeding, and refined cultural tradition—as in fact sterile and moribund. Additionally, Yezierska's conception of artistic practice directly challenges the characteristic ethos of high modernist practice, which, from its inception, rather than addressing the oppressed classes tended to be directed at refining the sensibilities of an intellectual elite in ways simply not available to the working classes. As a fashion designer and seamstress, Sonya believes in what she calls the "democracy of beauty" and, at the end of novel, intends to open a shop that would serve the people of the ghetto in an attempt to extend an aesthetic sensibility to those typically culturally disenfranchised, so to speak, and to incorporate the beautiful into the utilitarian.

Similarly, **W.E.B. Du Bois**, in his 1928 novel *Dark Princess,* adopts the terms of modernist persuasion and implicitly argues that civilization's salvation lies not in the cultures of the elite classes but in the cultures of the working classes, including the spirituals of African American working-class culture. In this novel, the protagonist Matthew Towns, after giving up on his desire to practice medicine because of the racial discrimination he endures, travels through Europe supporting himself as laborer, where he happens to meet the title character, who is part of a world committee composed of elite representatives of "the darker peoples" of the world. While putatively committed to ending oppression, this group of Asian and African aristocrats replicates the elitist rhetoric of high modernist intellectuals with the difference that they identify themselves as the superior representatives of civilization, arguing that the "superior races" are "yellow and brown." This aristocracy even marks Matthew as inferior, deeming African Americans to be a degraded people bereft of culture. In a scene that recalls Du Bois's valorization of the spirituals from his earlier *Souls of Black Folk* (1903), Matthew, as a response to this indictment of African American culture, sings a spiritual in deep, rich tones for the princess, convincing her of his conviction that culture can be attained by common people and not just the elite.

Finally, as both Matthew and the princess return to the United States, become laborers, and join the labor movement, the novel valorizes the working classes as the ultimate producers of culture because they concretely build up and remake the material world day after day and have a fuller and more intricate understanding of the operations of this world precisely because of their participation in its production. Du Bois's portrayal and definition of culture here sharply critiques and stands against the high modernist racist and class-bound dismissals of **Marx** by writers such as John Gould Fletcher, who wrote in the *Criterion* in 1929 that "the reason for Marx's naive dismissal of man's finest achievements" was a function of "his own peculiar racial psychology." His "confusion of thought, that of the wage-earning class with the producing class," is a product of "specifically Jewish psychology" (Klein 6).

Thus, in these examples, Yezierska and Du Bois effectively engage in a racial class struggle on the terrain of modernist discourse, challenging the terms of high modernism's cultural elitism and trying to wrest the very concept of culture away from its elitist moorings and to extend its use and application democratically. Against Eliot, Pound, and other writers of the "lost generation," such as Fitzgerald, **Ernest Hemingway**, Gertrude Stein, Wallace Stevens, E. E. Cummings, **William Faulkner**, and Marianne Moore, who, Marcus Klein notes, were all of "old American stock" and "were with remarkable uniformity of a certain class, one which might well think of itself as a dispossessed *social* aristocracy" (Klein 11), Yezierska and Du Bois were just two among many writers with left-wing associations who, challenging Eliot's definition of culture as requiring a society of classes and hereditary transmission of social advantages, located the production of meaningful culture not just among the laboring classes but in the act of labor or work itself. The values informing this culture are decidedly those of democracy and equality achieved—the narratives of these novels suggest—through class struggle, with the ultimate objective of the abolition of classes.

While these works engage modernist aesthetics perhaps more in terms of the cultural content and thematics they address than the formal techniques and stylistic devices they deploy, they focus the ideology of high modernism through their dialogic engagements with modernist narratives and forms. Particularly, Du Bois and Yezierska highlight the aristocratic antidemocratic politics of high modernist form and its cultural critique in their response to what Walter Benn Michaels has identified as the nativist cultural logic of literary modernism. While the elite modernists such as Fitzgerald, Faulkner, and Eliot often engaged in cross-class critique of society as a whole, the underlying solution was for the best of society, the elite class with family histories, to regain its convictions and position of cultural leadership. In the second section of *The Waste Land*, "A Game of Chess," Eliot moves from the upper-class boudoir to the working-class pub, critiquing the malaise and the lack of creativity, erotic connection, and purpose characterizing each; yet we know that the cure for this situation lies finally with the poet—the intellectual aristocracy—who can shore the fragments of our cultural tradition against our ruin. The density of the allusiveness of the poem and the erudition the poem requires to comprehend it already separates its readership into classes of the culturally capable and classically educated and those who must look to others for cultural leadership. Similarly, in *The Great Gatsby*, when Nick first visits Tom and Daisy Buchanan, Fitzgerald represents this set as constantly yawning, without aims, having little sense of purpose or direction, and largely devoid of passion for life. Yet at the end of the novel, the commoners Gatsby and Myrtle Wilson, each represented as passionate and vital, are dead, and Tom and Daisy, each of old family stock, survive, left to rekindle their "natural affection" for another and to regain their lost conviction, that "irrecoverable football game" Tom seeks. Both Du Bois and Yezierska, on the other hand, while not rejecting tradition, do reject the privileging of family ancestry and heritage, which constitutes something of the Eliotic ideal order, in favor of materialist historical identities rooted in the concrete practices of labor.

Technique

While in Du Bois and Yezierska we see an engagement with the class and racial logics of elite modernism from a generally radical left perspective, the left cultural milieu was divided and not immediately receptive to works that relied on and experimented with the innovative avant-garde formal techniques and stylistic devices of literary modernism. The publication, for example, of Henry Roth's tour de force proletarian modernist epic *Call It Sleep* (1934), a work obviously and admittedly very much influenced by Joyce's *Ulysses,* inspired heatedly conflicting reviews in left literary circles. The critical divisions were shaped largely by differing judgments as to the effectiveness of modernist representational practice to grasp society historically. Despite the novel's application of the technique of fragmentation and intense stream-of-consciousness to dramatize the organic reconstruction of the various immigrant voices into a collective, polyglot working-class consciousness (as would Pietro Di Donato's 1939 proletarian modernist tour de force novel *Christ in Concrete*) and in general to comprehend the social totality in the novel, negative reviews excoriated what they viewed primarily as the excessive Freudianism of the novel and its subjective impressionism, criticizing the novel as too introspective and basically balking at the novel's symbolic and experimental techniques, partly inspired by such modernist icons as Eliot, Joyce, and Freud. Meanwhile, a work such as **John Dos Passos's** *U.S.A.* **trilogy** (1930–1936) employs a panoply of Joycean modernist narrative techniques in the interest of a leftist assault on the values of modern consumer capitalist society only to collapse into a final despair, almost as if Dos Passos's modernist techniques are unable to bear the weight of leftist critique.

Deploying the stream-of-consciousness narration advocated by Woolf in her essay "Modern Fiction" (1919) and most notably used by Joyce, the novel fell subject to critical debates exemplary of the Left's divided assessment of literary modernism, particularly of the positions represented by the Marxist philosopher Georg Lukács and the Marxist playwright **Bertolt Brecht**. Long favoring a realist practice that represented people, practices, and things as the effects or embodiments of larger historical processes, Lukács charged that modernism was merely a decadent genre that, like the naturalist fiction of which it was an offspring, perceives reality in its factual immediacy divorced from objective reality of society, which is a historically changing social totality. Whether describing objects or the sense-data of psychological experience, the representations are effectively static, abstracted from historical process and thus incapable of providing insight into our own ability to participate in the production and transformation of reality. While for the realist the "goal is to penetrate the laws governing objective reality and to uncover the deeper, hidden, mediated, not immediately perceptible network of relations that go to make up society" (Taylor 38), the modernist only captures the surface perceptions divorced from these governing laws. Hence, Lukács levels the following much-debated critique against Joyce's *Ulysses*: "The perpetually oscillating patterns of sense- and memory-data, their powerfully charged—but aimless and directionless—fields of force give rise to an epic structure which is *static*, reflecting a belief in the basically static character of events" (Lukács 18). Hence, the subjectivism of Joyce—for Lukács, a position that has generated much controversy—constitutes a flight from history into abstract psychology and sense perception.

Brecht, however, defended the experimental techniques of modernism and argued that formalistic experimentation could be used to explode the reified illusions of capitalist ideology and, by estranging or alienating the audience from the taken-for-granted structures of their everyday life, provoke the audience into self-conscious reflection on existing social arrangements and, perhaps, even to action. He argued that the social reality had changed since the age of realism Lukács valorizes and hence new methods are necessary: "Reality changes; in order to represent it, modes of representation must also change" (Taylor 82). Lukács's method called for representing people as organically integrated into the social totality in order to challenge the illusions that foster a sense of alienation from historical process. Brecht, however, felt that such representation reconciled contradictions and promoted an illusion of harmony that would allow for a catharsis in his audience. Indeed, Brecht wanted a realism that captured the totality but argued that certain kinds of modernist practice, like the montage, might be better suited to representing the increasingly complex world of developing capitalism.

This debate regarding the ideology of modernism is far from settled and has no easy answer, requiring perhaps text-specific study. In addition, there is the problem of separating the ideologies of the modernists from those of critics who have been responsible for the formation of our perceptions of modernism. For example, modernism was first institutionalized as the paradigm of high culture in the West during the 1950s, when proponents of the **New Criticism**, themselves highly conservative, saw in the work of modernists such as Joyce and Eliot a reflection of their own reactionary horror at the dehumanizing consequences of modern industrial society. In addition, they saw in the work of such writers an attempt to establish, through an escape out of history and into aesthetics, an alternative vision of order that could stand against the confusion of contemporary reality, pointing the way toward a more genteel future based on the past. Given the institutional power of the New Criticism in the United States in the 1950s, this vision became the dominant view of modernism for decades. Meanwhile, though the principal New Critics were themselves almost as appalled by capitalism as they were by communism, this New Critical view was conscripted in the interest of Western **cold-war** propaganda, making modernism the epitome of aesthetic sophistication and integrity, as opposed to the supposedly debased art of the Soviet Union, presented in this propaganda as shackled in the service of communist ideology. Thus, as Andreas Huyssen notes, modernism was "domesticated" for just such purposes in the 1950s and "turned into a propaganda weapon in the cultural-political arsenal of Cold War anti-communism" (190).

Huyssen himself agrees that many modernist writers were elitists, who fought to preserve genuine high art as opposed to the debased popular art of the marketplace. On the other hand, he acknowledges that modernists such as Brecht were involved in quite different egalitarian projects. Meanwhile, beginning with the rediscovery of the work of Woolf by the emerging feminist criticism of the 1960s and 1970s, many modernist writers formerly regarded as elitist aestheticists have been reread as engaged artists who mounted, through their writing, subversive challenges to the prevailing bourgeois order. Joyce, here, is the paradigmatic case. Much admired by the New Critics, Joyce had formerly been regarded as the epitome of the artist who seeks to create his works within a purely aesthetic realm, free of all contaminating truck with the real. In recent decades, however, critics have paid increasing attention to Joyce's interest in radical politics, while Joyce himself has more and more come to be seen as an important forerunner of **postcolonial literature**, whose challenges to Catholic propriety and repression were at least matched by his anticolonial assaults on British bourgeois rule in Ireland.

Selected Bibliography: Booker, M. Keith. Ulysses, *Capitalism, and Colonialism: Reading Joyce after the Cold War.* Westport, CT: Greenwood, 2000; Eagleton, Terry. *Exiles and Emigres: Studies in Modern Literature.* New York: Schocken, 1970; Eliot, T. S. *Notes towards the Definition of Culture.* New York: Harcourt, Brace, 1949; Filreis, Alan. *Modernism from Right to Left: Wallace Stevens, the Thirties, and Literary Radicalism.* New York: Cambridge UP, 1994; Huyssen, Andreas. *After the Great Divide: Modernism, Mass Culture, Postmodernism.* Bloomington: Indiana UP, 1986; Klein, Marcus. *Foreigners: The Making of American Literature, 1900–1940.* Chicago: U of Chicago P, 1981; Levenson, Michael, ed. *The Cambridge Companion to Modernism.* Cambridge: Cambridge UP, 1999; Lucas, John. *The Radical Twenties: Writing, Politics, and Culture.* New Brunswick: Rutgers UP, 1999; Lukács, Georg. *Realism in Our Time: Literature and the Class Struggle.* Trans. John Mander and Necke Mander. New York: Harper and Row, 1964; Lunn, Eugene. *Marxism and Modernism: An Historical Study of Lukács, Brecht, Benjamin, and Adorno.* Berkeley: U of California P, 1982; Michaels, Walter Benn. *Our America: Nativism, Modernism, and Pluralism.* Durham: Duke UP, 1995; Nelson, Cary. *Repression and Recovery: Modern American Poetry and the Politics of Cultural Memory, 1910–1945.* Madison: U of Wisconsin P, 1989; Nicholls, Peter. *Modernisms: A Literary Guide.* Berkeley: U of California P, 1995; Taylor, Ronald, ed. *Aesthetics and Politics.* London: NLB, 1977; Williams, Raymond. *The Politics of Modernism: Against the New Conformists.* London: Verso, 1989; Woolf, Virginia. *The Virginia Woolf Reader.* New York: Harcourt, 1984.

Tim Libretti

MOHANTY, CHANDRA TALPADE (1955–).

A South Asian American who lived in India until she was twenty-one, Mohanty centers her work around transnational feminist theory, antiracist education, and immigrant and third-world political activism. Born in Mumbai, India, Mohanty taught high school in Lagos, Nigeria, for a year before moving to the United States to earn her M.A. in the teaching of English and her Ph.D. in education at the University of Illinois. Dedicated to exploring the intersections between pedagogy, scholarship, and community service, Mohanty teaches as professor of women's studies and Dean's Professor of the Humanities at Syracuse University; lectures and publishes regularly on topics integral to understanding the complicated relationships between imperialism and feminism; and contributes to the political education of grassroots community organizations that serve local populations in both India and the United States. While she realizes that "it is [not] easy to bridge the gap between the academy and activism," Mohanty believes that "the academy provides both a very contradictory and productive base for thinking about fundamental issues of democracy, social justice and citizenship . . . [that can help to promote] activist work, such as mobilizing resistance" ("Transnational" 74) to institutional power, including higher education itself. Mohanty's writings, which have been translated into several European and Asian languages, continue to focus on what she terms "cartographies of struggle," or the complex global affiliations between colonialism, capitalism, and the Eurocentric conceptualizations of both feminism and third-world women.

In her often anthologized essay "Under Western Eyes: Feminist Scholarship and Colonial Discourses" (1984), Mohanty cautions against Western feminism's tendency to present "a homogeneous notion of the oppression of women as a group . . . which, in turn, produces the image of an 'average Third World woman' . . . [who is] . . . ignorant, poor, uneducated, tradition-bound, religious, domesticated, family-oriented, victimized, etc." (*Feminism* 22). Although Mohanty wants to demonstrate how West-

ern feminism can thus deny third-world women their agency by ironically perpetu-
ating their objectification, critics such as Sara Suleri have asked, "How will the ethnic voice of womanhood counteract the cultural articulation that Mohanty too easily
dubs as the exegesis of Western feminism?" (759). Mohanty responds to such criticism in her essay " 'Under Western Eyes' Revisited" (2003), in which she underscores
the critical importance for feminist theory to recognize the ways in which women
around the globe experience different material, historical, and cultural conditions.

In attempting to build coalitions and solidarities across (global) boundaries, Mohanty has been reaching out to multiple audiences for decades not only through her
teaching career but by assisting grassroots organizations in India, North Carolina,
and New York City that aid poor, working-class populations; by advising the Center for Women Policy Studies in Washington, D.C.; and by serving on several editorial advisory boards of international scholarly journals. Whether she is discussing
third-world women's films, Native American literature and history, immigrant rights,
or the impact of colonial imperialism on feminist studies, Mohanty's critical acumen
speaks to Western and non-Western communities alike.

Selected Bibliography: Alexander, M. Jacqui, and Chandra Talpade Mohanty, eds. *Feminist Genealo-
gies, Colonial Legacies, Democratic Futures.* New York: Routledge, 1997; Mohanty, Chandra Talpade.
Feminism without Borders: Decolonizing Theory, Practicing Solidarity. Durham: Duke UP, 2003; Mohanty, Chandra Talpade. "Transnational Pedagogy: Doing Political Work in Women's Studies: An Interview with Chandra Talpade Mohanty." *Atlantis* 26.2 (Spring/Summer 2002): 66–77; Mohanty,
Chandra Talpade, Ann Russo, and Lourdes Torres, eds. *Third World Women and the Politics of Feminism.* Bloomington: Indiana UP, 1991; Suleri, Sara. "Woman Skin Deep: Feminism and the Postcolonial Condition." *Critical Inquiry* 18.4 (1992): 756–69.

Bruce G. Johnson

MOMADAY, N. SCOTT (1934–).

MOMADAY, N. SCOTT (1934–). Born in Lawton, Oklahoma, N. Scott Momaday spent his youth on reservations in the Southwest, where his Cherokee mother
and Kiowa father worked. At Stanford University, he studied poetry and completed
a Ph.D. in English. In 1968, Momaday published his first novel, *House Made of
Dawn*, which received the Pulitzer Prize and ushered in a renaissance in American
Indian literature in the midst of Red Power. The novel announced a spirited departure from previous American Indian novels, in a hopeful vision of a reclaimed indigenous culture, land, and identity, as well as in unprecedented modernist prose that
melds together ritual, history, and landscape in elegant lyricism. Such literary qualities set a new standard for American Indian writers.

House Made of Dawn charts the struggle of the protagonist Abel to regain his Jemez
culture and lands. On his return from **World War II**, he murders an albino man, is
imprisoned, and is later deposited in Los Angeles. The novel delivers an unparalleled
portrayal of American Indians enduring federal programs to forcibly relocate them
to cities, but redeems Abel through a friendship with a Navajo man who sends Abel
home, where he awakens to his culture in a ritual race at dawn. Momaday continues such life-affirming portrayals of Native people in his 1969 essay "The Man Made
of Words," in which he presents his views on language and imagination. Exemplifying this process is the mixed-genre work *The Way to Rainy Mountain* (1969), in which

the narrator returns to his Kiowa lands and engages mythic, ethnographic, and familial voices to recover his sense of place. Momaday enacts a similar but more autobiographical journey in *The Names* (1976). In *The Ancient Child* (1989), Momaday's protagonist is a Kiowa artist, who, adopted by white parents, returns to his homeland, where he discovers romance with a Kiowa-Navajo woman healer. Like his lyrical prose, Momaday's poetry is full of sharp sound and color, as displayed in *The Gourd Dancer* (1976).

Selected Bibliography: Allen, Paula Gunn. "Bringing Home the Fact: Tradition and Continuity in the Imagination." *Recovering the Word: Essays on Native American Literature.* Ed. Brian Swann and Arnold Krupat. Berkeley: U of California P, 1987. 563–79; Evers, Lawrence J. "Words and Place: A Reading of *House Made of Dawn.*" *Critical Essays on Native American Literature.* Ed. Andrew Wiget. Boston: G. K. Hall, 1985. 211–30; Landrum, Larry. "The Shattered Modernism of Momaday's *House Made of Dawn.*" *Modern Fiction Studies* 42 (1996): 763–86; Woodard, Charles L. *Ancestral Voice: Conversations with N. Scott Momaday.* Lincoln: U of Nebraska P, 1989.

Sean Teuton

MONETTE, PAUL (1945–1995).

MONETTE, PAUL (1945–1995). From working-class beginnings in Andover, Massachusetts, Paul Monette went on to a Yale education and careers as a teacher, poet, novelist, and memoirist. He left Boston for Los Angeles in 1977, dreaming of show business success. He spent the next few years as a frustrated screenwriter.

Like so many gay men of his generation, Monette's life was transformed by AIDS. Until the mid-1980s, he had been "political" only in the sense of his visibility as a gay writer and supporter of gay causes in Los Angeles, not as a writer. When his lover of over a decade, Roger Horwitz, was diagnosed with AIDS in 1985, everything changed. Monette dedicated the ten remaining years of his life to AIDS writing and activism and to celebrating and articulating gay and lesbian lives in his time.

In 1988, Monette published two groundbreaking books centering on the personal story of AIDS from inside a gay man's life. *Love Alone* is a collection of raw, apparently unstructured poetry about his lover's death. In his polemical preface, Monette wrote, "The story that endlessly eludes the decorum of the press is the death of a generation of gay men." *Borrowed Time: An AIDS Memoir* points toward Monette's shift to nonfiction as a form. Well aware of Randy Shilts's journalistic account of AIDS, *And the Band Played On*, Monette saw *Borrowed Time* as a personalized version of the story of AIDS. He then went back to fiction writing, publishing two novels with AIDS at their center: *Afterlife* (1990) and *Halfway Home* (1991).

Monette's blend of the personal and political is exemplified in his second memoir, *Becoming a Man: Half a Life Story* (1992), which won a National Book Award. The book's tone was politically influenced by Monette's lover, Stephen Kolzak, whose AIDS-related illnesses forced him into early retirement from a successful career in Hollywood (he is most well known for casting "Cheers"). Kolzak's life was fully devoted to ACT-UP (AIDS Coalition to Unleash Power) and other forms of activism, and as Monette has said, "Stephen was an education in politics for me" (Bramer). *Becoming a Man* is both confrontational (Monette quotes Stephen saying "rub their faces in it, Paulie. Nobody told us anything. You tell them") and revealing, as it tells the story of Monette's life in the closet and his struggle to come out.

In 1994, Monette published *Last Watch of the Night*, a collection of eleven essays representing his most explicitly political writing. By then something of a celebrity, Monette used his status as best he could, in print and in public appearances, to spread his message. Perhaps his point of view is best captured in his closing remarks upon receiving an honorary doctorate, charging his audience to "go without hate, but not without rage—heal the world."

Selected Bibliography: Bramer, Monte, director. *Paul Monette: The Brink of Summer's End.* Home Box Office, 1997; Cady, Joseph. "Immersive and Counterimmersive Writing about AIDS: The Achievement of Paul Monette's *Love Alone.*" *Writing AIDS: Gay Literature, Language and Analysis.* Ed. Timothy Murphy and Suzanne Poirier. New York: Columbia UP, 1993. 244–64; Clum, John M. "'The Time Before the War': AIDS, Memory, and Desire." *American Literature* 62.2 (1990): 648–67; Eisner, Douglas. "Liberating Narrative: AIDS and the Limits of Melodrama in Monette and Weir." *College Literature* 24.1 (1997): 213–26.

Chris Freeman

MORAVIA, ALBERTO (1907–1990), prolific Italian novelist and essayist, born Alberto Pincherle. Moravia's first novel, *Gli indifferenti* (*The Time of Indifference*, 1929), was a tragicomic portrait of a Roman family that was seen as an indictment of the fascist elite, but the author maintained it was an honest portrait "from within" his own world. The work depicts that world in a spare, acrid prose, unforgiving in its depiction of mediocrity and indifference to the higher values of humanistic culture.

The best-selling Italian author of his generation, Moravia was a master of the novel and short story. His characters are embroiled in problems of money and sex—issues interrelated in ingenious plots that reveal the moral weakness of ordinary people caught in predicaments of their own making. At the same time, there are protagonists who evoke empathy and admiration, such as the first-person narrator of *La Romana* (*The Woman of Rome*, 1947), a prostitute during the fascist era struggling against all odds. The short novels *Luca* and *Agostino* (in *Two Adolescents*, 1944) explore the theme of civic and psychosexual awakening in two overprotected lads of the Roman bourgeoisie.

Spied on by the fascists (his father was Jewish), Moravia and his wife, Elsa Morante, spent 1943–1945 in the mountains southeast of Rome, living in a sheepherder's cabin. The novel *La ciociara* (*Two Women*, 1957) was conceived at this time and functions as a political allegory in which the leading character, her daughter, and a partisan fighter named Lazarus represent the grassroots hopes of Italians to reform their society amid grave internal dangers. Moravia's novels are paradigmatic in this sense, representing common elements in the society at large. When a fashion for existentialism coincided with the advent of consumerism in Italy, Moravia wrote *La noia* (*The Empty Canvas*, 1960), a portrait of an alienated artist that one can read as a portrait of collective middle-class neurosis.

The brand of humanism Moravia advocates is explicated in his essays of the 1940s and 1950s, collected in English in *Man as an End* (1965). The essays affirm the secular and humanistic roots and motivations of civil society; provide a critical reference point for other artists and intellectuals; and suggest to a new generation of readers a broader, more ecumenical view of Italian culture than had been tolerated during the years of fascism. Ever prepared to intervene on matters of the day, Moravia's prose—cosmopolitan yet accessible, ethical but not moralistic—left no doubt as to the need for civil culture to embrace a progressive politics, always in defense of the individual.

Selected Bibliography: Capozzi, Rocco, and Mario Mignone, eds. *Homage to Moravia.* Stony Brook, NY: Forum Italicum, 1993; Moravia, Alberto. *Man as an End.* Trans. Bernard Wall. London: Secker and Warburg, 1965; Moravia, Alberto, and Alain Elkann. *Vita di Moravia.* Rome: Bompiani, 1990; Paris, Renzo. *Alberto Moravia.* Florence: Nuova Italia, 1991; Peterson, Thomas E. *Alberto Moravia.* New York: Twayne, 1996; Rebay, Luciano. *Alberto Moravia.* New York: Columbia UP, 1970.

Thomas E. Peterson

MORRIS, WILLIAM. *See NEWS FROM NOWHERE.*

MORRISON, TONI (1931–). Born Chloe Anthony Wofford in Lorain, Ohio, Morrison grew up in a tight-knit African American family and was the first woman in her family to attend college. After earning B.A. and M.A. degrees in English from Howard University (1953) and Cornell University (1955) respectively, she taught briefly before entering the publishing industry. Rising to the position of senior editor, she worked, among other things, to launch African American writers such as Toni Cade Bambara and Gayl Jones and thus, in this editorial capacity, has had a hand in shaping and diversifying American literature. Morrison's own first novel, *The Bluest Eye*, was published in 1970, and she has subsequently published seven more novels: *Sula* (1973), *Song of Solomon* (1977), *Tar Baby* (1981), *Beloved* (1987), *Jazz* (1992), *Paradise* (1997), and *Love* (2003). Morrison received the 1988 Pulitzer Prize for *Beloved* and was awarded the 1993 Nobel Prize for Literature. She is the first African American and first American woman to win the Nobel Prize, and this international recognition has solidified the place of her novels and, simultaneously, of the African American experience within the canon of American literature.

Because all of her novels focus on and engage the complexities of African American existence within a nation built on the contradictions of freedom and racism, her texts are necessarily political. Moreover, as her Nobel Prize lecture reveals, she views writing as praxis, with narrative as "one of the principle ways in which we absorb knowledge" (7) and "language . . . as agency—as an act with consequences" (13). Indeed, Morrison takes her position as a writer extremely seriously. She does not shy away from difficult topics and questions as her novels confront—and force readers to confront—the ways in which race has structured and continues to structure American thought and life for *all* people living in the United States. Although, as she argues in her nonfictional *Playing in the Dark*, "American Literature" has always been "shaped" by "its encounter with racial ideology" (16), her novels are distinguished in that they explore from an African American perspective the psychic and material effects of racial ideologies on African Americans and their communities. In addition, Morrison's novels pay careful attention to the ways in which racism intersects with ideologies of class and gender.

That Morrison views writing as a way to engage culture is further evidenced in her nonfiction writing. Not only has *Playing in the Dark* become a key text within literary criticism, but her decision to edit and contribute to two volumes engaging the two national public spectacles of the 1990s that brought race to the forefront— the Thomas-Hill Congressional hearings (*Race-ing Justice, En-gendering Power*, 1992) and the O. J. Simpson court case (*Birth of a Nation'hood*, 1997)—demonstrates the possibility of and Morrison's commitment to intellectual engagement with the politics of race in the United States.

Selected Bibliography: Gates, Henry Louis, Jr., and K. A. Appiah, eds. *Toni Morrison: Critical Perspectives Past and Present*. New York: Amistad, 1993; McKay, Nellie Y., and Kathryn Earle, eds. *Approaches to Teaching the Novels of Toni Morrison*. New York: MLA, 1997; Morrison, Toni. *The Nobel Lecture in Literature, 1993*. New York: Knopf, 1997; Morrison, Toni. *Playing in the Dark: Whiteness and the Literary Imagination*. New York: Vintage, 1992; Peterson, Nancy J., ed. *Toni Morrison: Critical and Theoretical Approaches*. Baltimore: Johns Hopkins UP, 1997.

Magali Cornier Michael

MOTHER (1906–1907), a novel on the emergent revolutionary forces in Russia by the prominent writer **Maxim Gorky**. The novel depicts the conditions that helped inspire antigovernment activism among the workers—in particular, the harsh factory work that left employees exhausted and mired in poverty—but the focus is on the growing revolutionary consciousness within the laboring class. Nearly three decades after it was composed, *Mother* became an exemplar of **socialist realism**, the doctrine promulgated under **Stalin** that served as the officially approved method of writing for Soviet writers. With its focus not necessarily on the world as it is but on the world as it should be, socialist realism can paradoxically assume a romantic or even a mythic quality. The characters become more archetypes than individualized figures, and the plot, less realistic than didactic. Such is the case with *Mother*. Pelagaia Nilovna Vlasova, the title figure, is a politically naive individual who becomes fervently dedicated to revolutionary activity after her son's arrest; Pavel Vlasov, the son, is a single-minded and heroic revolutionary. Each represents a type that many Soviet writers were to emulate. The story, in keeping with the goal to instruct and inspire, maintains an underlying optimism. Even though during much of the novel Pavel is in prison, and Nilovna (as she is called throughout) is arrested at the end, the novel conveys a strong sense that their cause will triumph.

While *Mother* was written shortly after the revolutionary upheavals of 1905 in Russia, the actual event that inspired Gorky was a May Day demonstration in 1902 at a shipbuilding plant near his hometown of Nizhniy Novgorod. His characters were similarly modeled on real people. Gorky composed much of the novel, which appeared first in English, during his 1906 stay in the United States. He had made some major revisions by the time *Mother* was published in Russian, so that the version familiar to most Americans differs in significant detail from that known to Russians (though the revised version was eventually translated into English as well, by Margaret Wettlin).

Still, in either version, it is possible to detect a more nuanced narrative than is evident from concentrating exclusively on the main figures. For instance, several secondary characters offer variants on Pavel's **Lenin**-like devotion to the proletariat. Andrei Nakhodka, an acquaintance of Pavel, openly expresses doubts about carrying out violent acts in order to further the revolutionary cause. Although a longtime activist, he tempers his ideology with a concern for individuals, and seems closer to Nilovna than does her own son. The most complex figure in the novel is arguably Mikhail Rybin, the consummate outsider, who comes to represent the darker and more instinctual forces found in rural Russia, as opposed to the ideologically driven urban activism of Pavel.

A surprising feature for a novel in which Bolshevik ideals are so prominent is the prevalence of references to religion. Nilovna remains a firm believer in Christ even as she grows more distant from the church, which she sees as part of the oppressive regime. Even Pavel hangs on the wall of his room a picture of Christ after the Resurrection, while Rybin talks of the need to invent a new faith. Gorky at the time was becoming interested in efforts to combine Marxism and religion; here he suggests a link between certain aspects of Christ's teachings and the goals of his revolutionaries, while also implying that the fervor of religious belief resembles the zeal needed for revolutionary activism.

Selected Bibliography: Clark, Katerina. *The Soviet Novel: History as Ritual.* Chicago: U of Chicago P, 1985; Dinega, Alyssa W. "Bearing the Standard: Transformative Ritual in Gorky's *Mother* and the Legacy of Tolstoy." *Slavic and East European Journal* 42.1 (1998): 76–101; Freeborn, Richard. *The Russian Revolutionary Novel: Turgenev to Pasternak.* Cambridge: Cambridge UP, 1982. 39–52; Scherr, Barry P. "Shadow Narratives and the Novel: The Role of Rybin in Gorky's *Mother.*" *Twentieth-Century Russian Literature: Selected Papers from the Fifth World Congress of Central and East European Studies.* Ed. Karen L. Ryan and Barry P. Scherr. London: Macmillan, 2000. 25–41.

Barry P. Scherr

MOTHER COURAGE AND HER CHILDREN: A CHRONICLE FROM THE THIRTY YEARS WAR (1939)

was written by **Bertolt Brecht** at the beginning of **World War II**. Set in Europe in the first half of the seventeenth century, it has been one of Brecht's most controversial plays ever since its premiere in Zurich, Switzerland, in 1941. Unlike previous major historical dramas, it does not explore the role of the rich and the powerful or the great and the mighty, but concentrates instead on the lower orders of society. The play's central character, Mother Courage, is a trader struggling to survive economically and physically, who wishes to protect her children from the ravages of war. But Brecht felt that productions of the play in Western Europe had misconstrued the role of Mother Courage and misunderstood the play. While Brecht sought to emphasize the socioeconomic basis of war, audiences persisted in seeing the events depicted as being determined by fate. Similarly, whereas Brecht wished to underline the contradiction between Mother Courage's maternal duties and her role as a trader—her business success would entail the destruction of her children—audiences focused on her motherly qualities and saw the destruction of her family and her personal devastation as tragic. One important reason for such discrepancies was that prior to Brecht's own production of the play in East Berlin in

1949, directors had been either ignorant of or hostile to the principles of **epic theater** and presented the play as traditional dramatic theater.

Mother Courage and Her Children systematically undermines the view that the causes of war are religious or ideological. The primary motivation of all parties, from kings and commanders down to private soldiers and prostitutes, is economic. Throughout the play, conventional notions of morality and civilization are overturned as the world of war—and early capitalism—is presented as a world upside down, dominated by constant reversals of fortune, contradictions, and inversions. History is rewritten with a focus on the history of the common people, and all events, even the most trivial, are contextualized in terms of the war, a point ironically underscored by the caption to scene 5: "In 1631, Tilly's victory at Magdeburg costs Mother Courage four officers' shirts." Brecht insists that history is not driven by unchanging, universal features of human nature but by specific social circumstances, just as Mother Courage's personal situation is determined not by vengeful gods or arbitrary fate but by the fact that she must trade in order to survive—even if this destroys her very humanity.

The only redeeming feature in this bleak and harrowing play is the humanitarian altruism of her abused daughter Kattrin, who is shot as she tries to save the besieged citizens of Halle from being massacred. But even the intense emotion generated by Kattrin's death is curtailed by the play's final scene, in which Mother Courage rejoins the war, seeing no alternative but perpetual struggle. From a Marxist viewpoint, this could be seen as the play's weakness: it is quite unclear how the topsy-turvy world of nascent militaristic capitalism is to be overturned and by whom, so that it is ultimately not surprising that audiences have perceived Mother Courage's final devastation as tragic and irreparable.

Selected Bibliography: Bryant-Bertail, Sarah. "Women, Space, Ideology: *Mutter Courage und ihre Kinder.*" *Brecht Yearbook* 12 (1983): 43–61; Leach, Robert. "*Mother Courage and Her Children.*" *The Cambridge Companion to Brecht.* Ed. Peter Thomson and Glendyr Sacks. Cambridge: Cambridge UP, 1994; Speirs, Ronald. *Bertolt Brecht.* London: Macmillan, 1987.

Steve Giles

MÜLLER, HEINER (1929–1995). The son of a socialist functionary who was jailed by the Nazis and then privileged (before being denounced) in the German Democratic Republic (GDR), Müller rose above the hardships of "life in two dictatorships" (the subtitle of his autobiography, *War without Battle* [*Krieg ohne Schlacht*, 1992]) to become the most important dramatist produced by the GDR. His early dramas—for which the East German regime honored him—were relatively naturalistic treatments of industrial workers' problems, which continued the topical dialectical tradition of **Brecht**'s Berliner Ensemble. In 1961, however, Müller was expelled from the GDR Writers' Union for a play that spoke too frankly about land reforms and, in 1965, was denounced by Erich Honecker for a play critical of industrial planning. Sporadic production and publication bans followed, during which he turned to adaptation of classics and counterplays to Brecht's **Lehrstück** as veiled modes of political critique. Driven in part by frustration with political stagnation in the GDR during the 1970s and 1980s, Müller went on to develop a highly idiosyncratic bricolage-dramaturgy of literary fragments in plays such as *Hamletmachine* (*Hamletmaschine*, 1977) and *Germania Death in Berlin* (*Germania Tod in Berlin*, 1956/1971), which attracted enormous interest in the West. Faced with the fait accompli of his international avant-garde stardom, the GDR government embraced him as a national hero in the 1980s.

Müller held solidly Marxist convictions and remained loyal to his country in his sardonic fashion, but he was also a notoriously provocative public commentator and a cynical hoaxster in the vein of Andy Warhol. His mature works are difficult, sometimes infuriating, and frequently susceptible to accusations of evasion, circumlocution, and disingenuousness. Müller challenges received notions of originality as well as the basic strategy of all parable theater based on Brecht. The politics of his drama rests not on current events or topical surfaces but on implicit critiques of the historical ideology and modes of representation found in the source works Müller so liberally adapted. His is a politics of dialogism embedded in points of cultural-historical friction with prominent figures such as **Shakespeare**, Kleist, **Mayakovsky**, **Brecht**, **Beckett**, and Genet. Müller can also be read politically through the lens of Foucault, as a canny analyst of immanent power, or through Artaud, as a deconstructor of the death-of-the-author myth. His political thought is too complex to be reduced to ideological formulas. The book-length interviews he gave on the state of world affairs after the fall of the Berlin wall—*On the State of the Nation* (*Zur Lage der Nation*, 1990), *Beyond the Nation* (*Jenseits der Nation*, 1991), *I Owe the World a Corpse* (*Ich schulde der Welt einen Toten*, 1995), and *I Am a Land Surveyor* (*Ich bin ein Landvermesser*, 1996)—are among his most sophisticated and penetrating creations.

Selected Bibliography: Case, Sue-Ellen. "Developments in Post-Brechtian Political Theater: The Plays of Heiner Müller." Diss. University of California, Berkeley, 1981; Eke, Norbert Otto. *Heiner Müller: Apokalypse und Utopie*. Paderborn: Ferdinand Schöningh, 1989; Kalb, Jonathan. *The Theater of Heiner Müller*. Rev. and enl. ed. New York: Limelight Editions, 2001; Schulz, Genia. *Heiner Müller*. Stuttgart: Metzler, 1980; Teraoka, Arlene Akiko. *The Silence of Entropy or Universal Discourse: The Postmodernist Poetics of Heiner Müller*. New York: Peter Lang, 1985.

Jonathan Kalb

MULVEY, LAURA (1941–). English cultural critic, associated with the alternative film journal *Screen*. Mulvey became well known as a film critic with the 1975 publication (in *Screen*) of her essay "Visual Pleasure and Narrative Cinema" and its objective of "break[ing] with normal pleasurable expectations in order to conceive a new language of desire" (*Visual* 16). In this text, Mulvey applies psychoanalytical theory to dissect how the dominant patriarchal order and the social unconscious influence the male spectator's visual interpretation of gendered film roles. She initially organizes her argument around the connection between scopophilia (the pleasurable perception of another individual as a sexual object) and narcissism (the identification with one who is similar to oneself). Mulvey goes on to explain how, in the film-viewing experience, the male spectator inevitably risks seeing the on-screen woman as representative of sexual difference, a discovery that jeopardizes the film's diegetic integrity. As a result, the male spectator actively fetishizes the woman's passive image by viewing the female character's on-screen beauty as pure spectacle, the surface object of his gaze, in order to distract him from the threat of castration. In addition, the male spectator may attempt, perhaps through identification with the film's male character, to watch the woman's image voyeuristically and to investigate, even punish and rescue, her representation with his oppressive look. Mulvey concludes by recommending that in cinema, the looks of the camera and the audience be explicitly separated from the look of the (male) character.

Feminist film theorists still consistently cite "Visual Pleasure and Narrative Cinema," despite the criticism it has received for its focus on a strictly male spectator. In 1981, in response to questions regarding this issue, Mulvey published "Afterthoughts on 'Visual Pleasure and Narrative Cinema' inspired by King Vidor's *Duel in the Sun* (1946)," in which she extends her earlier essay by considering the female film-viewing experience. Here, Mulvey offers a theory of "trans-sex identification" whereby both female spectator and female character understand, if only temporarily, a greater sense of agency in the film's narrative through a process of masculine identification.

Mulvey has continued to write about fetishism, and she often evaluates cinematic texts as clue-embedded enigmas waiting to be deciphered by their audiences. Not surprisingly, she also frequently parallels psychoanalytical theory with insights from Marxism, specifically its concepts of commodity fetishism and the concealment of production processes. Mulvey has written extensively on *Citizen Kane* and the films of Jean-Luc Godard, numerous non-Western films such as **Ousmane Sembène**'s *Xala*, and various areas of film theory including melodrama and the avant-garde. She has also written on sculpture, art, and photography. Mulvey's essays are collected in *Visual and Other Pleasures* (1989) and *Fetishism and Curiosity* (1996).

Selected Bibliography: Mulvey, Laura. *Fetishism and Curiosity*. Bloomington: Indiana UP, 1996; Mulvey, Laura. "Some Thoughts on Theories of Fetishism in the Context of Contemporary Culture." *October* 65 (1993): 3–20; Mulvey, Laura. *Visual and Other Pleasures*. Bloomington: Indiana UP, 1989; Suárez, Juan, and Millicent Manglis. "Cinema, Gender, and the Topography of Enigmas: A Conversation with Laura Mulvey." *Cinefocus* 3 (1995): 2–8.

Leigh Pryor

N

NABOKOV, VLADIMIR (1899–1977). Received opinion is that the Russian-born Nabokov's aesthetic is narcissistic and contemptuous not just of politics but of the entire modern world and events in it. As his biographer Brian Boyd records, in Saint Petersburg in October 1917 (in the midst of the **Russian Revolution**), the young Nabokov was writing verse one evening and merely noted "fierce rifle fire and the foul crackle of a machine gun" in the street outside. The author himself, in the 1963 introduction to *Bend Sinister* (1947), contentedly proposed that "the influence of my epoch on my present book is as negligible as the influence of my books, or at least of this book, on my epoch." Yet the novel itself—beginning with its cunning title, combining the notion of lineal illegitimacy with that of a swerve to the left—is essentially an idiosyncratic satire on the Bolshevik upheaval.

Nabokov's father, a leader of the Kadet Party, was notable enough to be scathingly portrayed throughout **Trotsky**'s *The History of the Russian Revolution* (1932–1933). The advent of the Soviets dispossessed Nabokov of an inheritance worth two million pounds and caused him, before he reached the age of twenty, to embark on a life that was largely spent in exile and in relative poverty in France, England, and the United States. Other novels to which this personal legacy is constitutive are *Invitation to a Beheading* (1938) and *Pale Fire* (1962), whose modernist (or postmodernist) distantiation from the politics their protagonists cannot escape is, despite their author's ambiguous disavowals, a demonstrably ideological choice. In addition, Nabokov's best-known and most critically respected novel, *Lolita* (1956), can be read both as a scathing satire of American consumer culture and as an ambiguous indictment of the aestheticism of its narrator, Humbert Humbert.

Selected Bibliography: Boyd, Brian. *Vladimir Nabokov: The American Years.* Princeton, NJ: Princeton UP, 1991; Boyd, Brian. *Vladimir Nabokov: The Russian Years.* Princeton, NJ: Princeton UP, 1990; Sharpe, Tony. *Vladimir Nabokov.* London: Edward Arnold, 1991.

Macdonald Daly

NAIPAUL, V(IDIADHAR) S(URAJPRASAD) (1932–). V. S. Naipaul was born in Trinidad to Brahman Hindu parents. They were members of Trinidad's Indian community who had come to the Caribbean Islands as indentured laborers to work the sugar fields owned primarily by British landlords. According to family tradition, Naipaul's father was slated to be a Brahman priest but could not bear the rigors of apprenticeship and chose secular education instead. Seepersad Naipaul pursued a variety of careers, including stints as a news reporter and writer, but failed to secure a stable financial future for himself or his family. However, he inspired his children to obtain a fine education in Trinidad's British school system. (Naipaul recounts his father's life through the portrait of Mr. Biswas in the 1961 novel *A House for Mr. Biswas*.) The family's emphasis on education motivated Naipaul to do well in school, and he earned a prestigious scholarship to study English literature at University College, Oxford. After graduation, while working for the Caribbean service of the British Broadcasting Corporation in the late 1950s, he began writing, and has been writing ever since. Naipaul lives in England with his second wife.

Spanning nearly four decades, Naipaul's writing career has been prolific. He has authored books of fiction, travel narrative, and autobiography, some of them splendidly combining all three genres. In addition, Naipaul has edited several books, one of which is a collection of short stories by his father. Winner of the Nobel Prize for Literature in 2001, Naipaul nevertheless remains a controversial author because of his conservative views on many issues. His writing on third world and Islamic countries has generated intense resentment among some readers who think his characterization of these nations—generally unfavorable—is biased. Many, for example, were offended by his depiction of Indian squalor in the travelogue *An Area of Darkness* (1964). Even in fiction dealing with decolonized societies—such as ***A Bend in the River*** (1979)—Naipaul appears keener on blaming the victim than the behind-the-scene-forces inimical to the interests of postcolonial nations. Indeed, in diagnosing the ills of third-world nations, Naipaul dismisses virtually all of them as imperfect attempts to join the "universal civilization," a Naipaulian notion of a world civilization based on the affluent West.

Other postcolonial authors have joined Naipaul's detractors. Derek Walcott, another Caribbean Nobel laureate, humorously describes Naipaul as "V. S. Nightfall" in "At Last," a poem. **Chinua Achebe**'s strong dislike of Naipaul appears in many of his critical writings. Indeed, to Achebe, Naipaul's Africa in *A Bend in the River* misrepresents the continent in a much worse way than does **Conrad**'s *Heart of Darkness* (87–91).

Over the years, though, Naipaul has softened his views. His *India: A Million Mutinies Now* (1990) is a travelogue with a difference. In it, the traveler-author recedes into the background, allowing the people he encounters voices of their own. *The Enigma of Arrival* (1987), a much more complex work, appears at times as a travel narrative, as fiction, as autobiography, and as all three. It comes as no surprise that the Nobel committee mentioned this work in particular and praised Naipaul's mastery of his materials in its award citation.

Selected Bibliography: Achebe, Chinua. *Home and Exile*. New York: Oxford UP, 2000; Hayward, Helen. *The Enigma of V. S. Naipaul: Sources and Contexts*. New York: Palgrave Macmillan, 2002; Mustafa, Fawzia. *V. S. Naipaul*. Cambridge: Cambridge UP, 1995; Nixon, Rob. *London Calling: V. S. Naipaul, Postcolonial Mandarin*. New York: Oxford UP, 1992; Weiss, Timothy. *On the Margins: The Art of Exile in V. S. Naipaul*. Amherst: U of Massachusetts P, 1992.

Farhad B. Idris

NATIVE AMERICAN LITERATURE. Long before Europeans arrived in North America, indigenous peoples melded literature and politics in *The Great Law of Peace* to end wars and ensure democracy among Indian nations. In this epic, Peacemaker and his student, Hiawatha, unite several tribes in the Iroquois Confederacy.

Upon European invasion, indigenous writings become increasingly political, as American Indians resisted conquest, presented their own histories, and affirmed treaties, such as in the translated protest speeches of Powhatan (1609), Tecumseh (1811), and Seattle (1887). Also translated and recorded throughout the nineteenth century, American Indian autobiographies—such as those of Black Hawk (1833), Pretty Shield (1932), and Black Elk (1932)—challenge dominant narratives of America's manifest destiny.

As early as 1654, American Indians at Harvard wrote protest literature in English. By the eighteenth century, Mohegan minister Samson Occom, in *A Sermon Preached at the Execution of Moses Paul* (1772), and Pequot minister William Apess, in *The Experience of Five Christian Indians* (1833), deployed Christian arguments to decry the treatment of Indian lives and land. In the early nineteenth century, Indians such as the Cherokee writer Elias Boudinot, in *An Address to the Whites* (1826), publicly rejected U.S. representations of Indian civilizations. Native authors by the mid-nineteenth century also appropriated European genres for political ends. In the first novel by an American Indian, *The Life and Adventures of Joaquín Murieta* (1854), Cherokee author John Rollin Ridge chronicled the unrelenting pursuit of a Mexican Indian man expelled from his land by white miners during the California gold rush.

Indian writers entered the twentieth century in the unlikely protest genres of lyric performance and satirical journalism. Mohawk poet **E. Pauline Johnson** began her literary career in 1892 with "A Cry from an Indian Wife," an Indian account of the Métis' 1869 armed resistance to the Canadian government. In 1910, Creek journalist Alexander Posey began his voluminous Fus Fixico Letters series in newspapers across Indian Territory, in which he lampooned white settlers, bureaucrats, and businessmen eager to disband tribal governments and obtain Indian lands; Posey's colloquial speech and oblique political humor prefigured those of later Cherokee humorist Will Rogers.

American Indian emancipation autobiography peaked in Sarah Winnemucca's *Life among the Piutes* (1883). Winnemucca's appeal to protect Indian women from aggressive miners and settlers, and to educate Indian children, inspired the era's growing women's movement. After this sentimental work, early-twentieth-century Indian writers composed direct challenges to the U.S. mainstream in their life writing. Sioux writer Charles Eastman's *From the Deep Woods to Civilization* (1916) questions Western education and solves the contradiction between U.S. Christianity and capitalism with tribalism. One of the first American Indians to graduate from the notoriously cruel Carlisle Indian boarding school, Sioux writer Luther Standing Bear, in *My People the Sioux* (1928), critiques U.S. "civilization," and validates indigenous history and society.

During the 1930s, Native writers conducted politics in the novel, but often presented hopeless Indian-white relations, in which U.S. laws crushed Indian resistance or blocked cultural understanding. John Joseph Mathews's *Sundown* (1934) portrays insidious U.S. attacks on traditional life and pressure to assimilate during the 1920s

Osage oil boom. Salish writer D'Arcy McNickle's *The Surrounded* (1936) concerns the struggle of a young Indian man to come home and recover a tribal culture beset by white settlers and politicians.

After a dormant period, red-power protest awakened American Indian literature. In 1969, Kiowa writer N. Scott Momaday won the Pulitzer Prize for *House Made of Dawn*, a novel in which the protagonist escapes oppressive white institutions to recover his Jemez culture. Other authors from this literary revival, such as James Welch, Simon Ortiz, and Dallas Chief Eagle, advocated colonial resistance. Exemplary is Laguna writer Leslie Marmon Silko's novel *Ceremony* (1977), which explains the cultural healing of its protagonist and confronts the global threat of nuclear weapons.

The 1980s saw the full emergence of Indian women writers and poets, such as Paula Gunn Allen, whose novel *The Woman Who Owned the Shadows* (1983) envisions a feminist return to her Pueblo homelands. In *She Had Some Horses* (1983), Muskogee poet Joy Harjo also considers indigenous women and politics. Louise Erdrich's novel *Tracks* (1988) portrays an Ojibway community enduring famine and confiscation of tribal lands after the 1887 Dawes Act. Despite the conservative Reagan years, Native theorists contributed to a body of Indian writing dedicated to Native treaty rights to lands and worship. Indian intellectuals such as Ward Churchill, in his book *Marxism and Native Americans* (1984), and Jack Forbes, in *Native Americans and Nixon* (1981), demand U.S. recognition of Indian nationhood.

At the turn of the twenty-first century, Native writers engaged politics on both a hemispheric and a community level. While Silko's novel *Almanac of the Dead* (1991) imagines the fulfillment of an indigenous prophecy to expel Europeans, Meskwaki poet Ray Young Bear's verse novel *Black Eagle Child* (1992) and Choctaw writer LeAnne Howe's novel *Shell Shaker* (2001) address local tribal politics. In the novel *Drowning in Fire* (2001), Craig Womack explores a gay Muskogee man's identity. Today, Indian theorists such as Anishinaabe scholar Gerald Vizenor, in *Manifest Manners* (1994), Sioux intellectual Elizabeth Cook-Lynn, in *Anti-Indianism in Modern America* (2001), and Osage scholar Robert Allen Warrior, in *Tribal Secrets* (1995), organize these writings. Native political writing matures with Comanche intellectual Paul Chaat Smith and Robert Allen Warrior's *Like a Hurricane* (1996), a narrative history of the Indian movement during the 1970s to give indigenous people a moment of political reflection—one text among many to serve the cause for Native American rights.

Selected Bibliography: Deloria, Vine, Jr. *Spirit and Reason: The Vine Deloria, Jr., Reader.* Golden, CO: Fulcrum, 1999; Jaimes, M. Annette, ed. *The State of Native America: Genocide, Colonization, and Resistance.* Boston: South End P, 1992; Konkle, Maureen. *Writing Indian Nations: Native Intellectuals and the Politics of Historiography, 1827–1863.* Chapel Hill: U of North Carolina P, 2004; Weaver, Jace. *That the People Might Live: Native American Literatures and Native American Community.* New York: Oxford UP, 1997; Womack, Craig C. *Red on Red: Native American Literary Separatism.* Minneapolis: U of Minnesota P, 1999.

Sean Teuton

NATIVE SON (1940). *Native Son* is **Richard Wright**'s masterpiece of social protest, one of the most important proletarian novels of the Depression era and a key text of the **Popular Front** period, when leftist culture enjoyed a moment of unparalleled ascent, including support by the **Communist Party**. "The day *Native Son* appeared, American culture was changed forever" the critic Irving Howe later wrote. *Native Son* was intended to alienate and challenge almost everyone who read it. Protagonist Bigger Thomas is a bright but estranged teenager wracked and warped by poverty and racism on Chicago's south side. He is remote from his own family: his mother, a domestic whose work shames him, and his brother and sister, with whom he shares no love. The novel begins with Bigger killing a rat running loose in their tenement apartment, an ironic foreshadowing of his own fate. Pressured by his mother, he accepts a job as chauffeur to the Dalton family, a rich white real-estate clan that owns the building the Thomas family lives in. On his first assignment, Bigger is asked to drive for the Dalton daughter Mary and her boyfriend, a Communist named Jan. After a night of drinking they return to the Dalton home, where Bigger dutifully carries a drunken Mary up the stairs to her bedroom. In a scene of masterful ambiguity, dread, and desire, they kiss. Bigger, terrified by the sight of the blind Mrs. Dalton passing the bedroom, covers Mary's face with a pillow to keep her quiet, in the process smothering her, though the book leaves Bigger's confused intentions in the act ambiguous. Terrified further, he burns her body in the basement furnace and flees into the snowy night. He then rapes and kills his girlfriend Bessie and tries to pin the Dalton murder on Communists. All his plans fail. Bigger is arrested, then defended in court by a communist lawyer named Boris Max. He is convicted of raping and murdering Mary Dalton and sentenced to death.

Wright based *Native Son* in part on the case of Robert Nixon, a young black man accused of murdering a white woman in the course of a robbery in Chicago in 1938. Wright's fictional story was a testing ground for a number of political ideas. In "How Bigger Was Born," an essay written after the book's publication and appended to subsequent editions, Wright described Bigger as symbolic of the Depression era international proletariat. Bigger was a "native son of this land" who "carried within him the potentialities of either Communism or Fascism" (521). Bigger also represented the consequences of modernity and migration for millions of southern blacks heaved into the urban North by the great migration after slavery's end. In *12 Million Black Voices*, a photodocumentary book of Chicago's South Side published one year after *Native Son*, Wright described the black migrant, once subject to the "Lords of the Land" under Queen Cotton, now tenants to the "Bosses of the Buildings"—like the Daltons—in the urban North. Wright's representation of communism as an antidote to these ills is at best ambivalent in *Native Son*, despite Wright's membership in the party when he wrote the book. Jan, for example, appears somewhat opportunistic and patronizing in his sympathies for Bigger, who in turn opportunistically seizes on knee-jerk American **anticommunism** in trying to blame the party for his murders. Boris Max's defense of Bigger against false rape charges is meant to recall the role of the International Labor defense in the Scottsboro case of 1932, yet as numerous critics have noted, Max's defense uses explanatory strategies a good communist lawyer would not. His argument is more social determinist than historical materialist, and he falls into sentimental appeal that Wright makes clear will do Bigger no good. Max's speech, and Bigger's silence in the trial, have led many critics to conclude that it is the failures, not the successes, of communist interracial struggle that Wright underscores. Hence, the book ignited serious debate on the left. *New Masses* reviewer Samuel Sillen praised the book's revolutionary vision, but others noted its bleak and nihilistic ending as anything but revolutionary. *Native Son*'s legacy is broad, divisive, and mixed. However, the book itself remains the most commercially and critically successful novel written by an American Communist.

Selected Bibliography: Baldwin, James. "Everybody's Protest Novel." *Notes of a Native Son.* Boston: Beacon P, 1984. 13–23; Howe, Irving. "Black Boys and Native Sons." *Richard Wright's "Native Son": A Critical Handbook.* Ed. Richard Abcarian. Belmont, CA: Wadsworth, 1970. 135–42; Mootry, Maria K. "Bitches, Whores, and Woman Haters: Archetypes and Typologies in the Art of Richard Wright." *Richard Wright: A Collection of Critical Essays.* Ed. Richard Macksey and Frank E. Moorer. Englewood Cliffs: Prentice-Hall, 1984. 117–28; Sillens, Samuel. Review of *Native Son. Richard Wright's "Native Son": A Critical Handbook.* Ed. Richard Abcarian. Belmont: Wadsworth, 1970. 49–52; Wright, Richard. *12 Million Black Voices.* New York: Thunder's Mouth P, 1988.

Bill V. Mullen

NATURALISM. A trend in late-nineteenth-century fiction especially prominent in France and the United States, naturalism in literature was a distinct mode often seen as evolving from **realism**. Naturalism, however, departs from realism in important ways, even though many important naturalist writers considered themselves practitioners of realism. For example, a character in *New Grub Street* (1891) by George Gissing, one of the few important British naturalist writers, takes pride in the fact that he is a "realist" writer, though what he produces is obviously naturalist fiction. Though remaining a prominent movement in itself only shortly into the twentieth century, naturalist elements have continued to appear in subsequent fiction, including a certain resurgence of naturalism in U.S. fiction of the 1930s in the work of such writers as **Richard Wright**.

The movement of naturalism began in France, inspired by the work of **Émile Zola**, whose cycle of the *Rougon-Macquart* novels (1871–1893) excoriated the crass commercialism in French bourgeois society. In two essays, "Naturalism in the Theater" and "The Experimental Novel," Zola promoted a "scientific" theory of realism and argued that humanity possesses no freedom of choice, that evolutionary forces guide human behavior, and that heredity and environment predetermine all aspects of the human condition. This sense of determinism pervades Zola's fictions and is one of the crucial factors that distinguishes naturalism from realism. Other leading naturalist novelists include George Moore, **Theodore Dreiser**, Frank Norris, Stephen Crane, and **Jack London**; dramatists such as **Henrik Ibsen** and Eugene O'Neill wrote in a naturalist mode as well. Authors not known as strict naturalists but occasionally showing naturalist tendencies include Gustave Flaubert, Thomas Hardy, and John Millington Synge.

Naturalism was influenced in obvious and important ways by Darwin's theory of evolution and other nineteenth-century scientific discoveries that placed human history in the context of geological instead of biblical time. Naturalism projects literary characters in a circumscribed world where opportunities are few, human interactions rarely occur, diseases ravage, and events lead to disaster. Believing heredity to be the prime mover of humanity, naturalists deny their characters free will and present them as acutely vulnerable to environmental pressures, thus illustrating the Darwinian notion of a diminished world where only the fittest survive.

Naturalist authors aspire toward authenticity of representation; not surprisingly, naturalism is obsessed with documentation. The narrow focus that the naturalist adopts forces the narrative to dwell on excessive details, which merely provide a lifeless background to the characters. The attempt is to create a sense of history through minute details, but what is lost in the process is the dialectical awareness of society as a totality that is crucial to the best realist fiction. **Georg Lukács**, whose insights on both naturalism and realism are extremely valuable in studying these modes, observes that while realism creates an interconnected world in which characters develop emotionally as well as materially and interact with each other with feeling and warmth, naturalism constructs a fragmentary world inhabited by characters that are self-absorbed and ruled by instincts and passions. This gloomy view of the world, according to Lukács, originated in the disillusionment in Europe following the failed revolution in 1848. According to Lukács, the trend marks the decadence of bourgeois society in the late nineteenth century.

The emergence of naturalism in cultural productions, it is useful to note, closely reflects the onset of another trend in Western society of the time—that of reification, the notion that Lukács developed to describe the objectification of human relations in a society given to commodification. In *History and Class Consciousness*, Lukács argues that in a capitalist society, the fetishism of commodity permeates all social dynamics, which, because of the estrangement of labor and its product, acquire a spectral objectivity of their own. An inevitable result of this process is the absorption of the individual as an atomized unit into a vast dehumanized network of exchange. Naturalist characters fail to connect to each other, and the world appears chaotic to them—patent aspects of their reified existence.

In this sense, much naturalist fiction can be taken as a critique of the dehumanizing consequences of capitalism. Indeed, naturalism often takes a strongly critical stance toward modern society as a whole, largely because of the perception that modern society forces human beings to live in conditions that are contrary to human nature. On the other hand, Lukács argues that Zola, despite his overt critique of capitalism, was never able to transcend his own bourgeois worldview. Similarly, Walter Benn Michaels has recently argued that American naturalist writers such as Dreiser remained thoroughly inscribed within the logic of the capitalist system they sought to criticize. **Fredric Jameson**, on the other hand, has seen much of critical value in the work of naturalist writers, especially Dreiser, whose work he sees as dramatizing and critiquing the tawdriness of the commodified capitalist society he saw around him.

Selected Bibliography: Jameson, Fredric. *The Political Unconscious: Narrative as a Socially Symbolic Act.* Ithaca, NY: Cornell UP, 1981; Lukács, Georg. *The Historical Novel.* Trans. Hannah Mitchell and Stanley Mitchell. Lincoln: U of Nebraska P, 1983; Lukács, Georg. *History and Class Consciousness: Studies in Marxist Dialectics.* Trans. Rodney Livingstone. Cambridge, MA: MIT P, 1971; Lukács, Georg. *Studies in European Realism: A Sociological Survey of the Writings of Balzac, Stendhal, Tolstoy, Gorky, and Others.* Trans. Edith Bone. New York: Fertig Howard, 2002; Michaels, Walter Benn. *The Gold Standard and the Logic of Capitalism: American Literature at the Turn of the Century.* Berkeley: U of California P, 1987; Pizer, Donald. *American Literary Naturalism: Recent and Uncollected Essays.* Bethesda,

MD: Academic P, 2002; Rea, Michael. *World without Design: The Ontological Consequence of Naturalism*. New York: Oxford UP, 2002.

Farhad B. Idris

NEGRI, ANTONIO (1933–). Born in Padua, Italy, Negri was professor of state doctrine (1956–1979) and director of the Institute of Political Science (1967–1973) at the University of Padua. He is currently an independent writer and critic living in Rome. Negri is the author of over thirty books of political theory, philosophy, history of philosophy, and literary criticism, including most famously *Marx beyond Marx* (1979), *The Savage Anomaly* (1981), *Insurgencies* (1992), and, in collaboration with American Michael Hardt, *Labor of Dionysus* (1994) and *Empire* (2000). During the 1960s and 1970s, Negri was a leading organizer of Potere Operaio (Workers' Power) and Autonomia Operaia (Workers' Autonomy), major groups of the Italian extraparliamentary left; at the same time, he emerged as an influential theorist of the new conditions of revolutionary struggle under late capitalism. This unusual combination of roles led ultimately to groundless, politically motivated accusations that he was the leader of the Red Brigades and the mastermind behind the kidnapping and murder of former Italian prime minister Aldo Moro. These accusations and others like them kept Negri in prison awaiting trial for over four years (1979–1983), until his surprise election to parliament resulted in his release. Faced shortly thereafter with the prospect of returning to prison, he fled to France, where he lived in exile until he voluntarily returned to Italy and to prison in 1997.

Negri's early works focus on the metaphysical and juridical legitimation of the modern capitalist state. His first major contribution to contemporary political debates lies in his revival of the theory of revolutionary subjectivity that had been discredited by modernist and postmodernist critics such as **T. W. Adorno** and Jean-François Lyotard. He argues that the subjective composition of the opposition to capital has changed several times in the course of the twentieth century, from the highly skilled "professional workers" of the pre–**World War I** period, through the deskilled but highly organized "mass workers" of the interwar and immediate post–**World War II** period, to the increasingly autonomous and dispersed "socialized workers" of the contemporary period. Different forms of organization and struggle correspond to each form of worker: the centralized Leninist party expresses the struggle of the professional worker; the national trade union represents the mass worker; and the decentered communicative alliance links socialized workers into a global network. Negri's second major contribution follows from this last stage of subjective development: his formulation of a sophisticated and influential model of globalization, detailed primarily in *Empire*. He and Hardt argue that empire must be understood as a structure of global governance and economic exploitation that, unlike older forms of imperialism and colonialism, has no center, not even the United States as sole superpower. Empire transcends and subordinates nation-states, transforming them by means of antidemocratic commercial/financial organizations like the World Trade Organization and the International Monetary Fund into administrative districts that compete for mobile capital investment. This increasingly frictionless mobility of capital is matched by a parallel mobility of goods and laboring bodies across national borders. The mobility of bodies, coupled with the rapid and complex information flow required by transnational economic production, gives rise to new forms of community and new possibilities of struggle. Negri has also published important studies of the Italian romantic poet Giacomo Leopardi and the biblical Book of Job.

Selected Bibliography: Hardt, Michael, and Antonio Negri. *Labor of Dionysus: Critique of the State-Form.* Minneapolis: U of Minnesota P, 1994; Hardt, Michael, and Antonio Negri. *Empire.* Cambridge, MA: Harvard UP, 2000; Negri, Antonio. *Insurgencies: Constituent Power and the Modern State.* 1992. Trans. M. Boscagli. Minneapolis: U of Minnesota P, 1999; Negri, Antonio. *Il Lavoro di Giobbe.* Milan: SugarCo, 1990; Negri, Antonio. *Lenta ginestra: Saggio sull'ontologia di Giacomo Leopardi.* Milan: SugarCo, 1987; Negri, Antonio. *Marx beyond Marx: Lessons on the "Grundrisse."* 1979. Trans. H. Cleaver et al. New York: Autonomedia, 1991; Negri, Antonio. *Revolution Retrieved: Selected Writings.* Trans. E. Emery. London: Red Notes, 1988; Negri, Antonio. *The Savage Anomaly: The Power of Spinoza's Metaphysics and Politics.* 1981. Trans. M. Hardt. Minneapolis: U of Minnesota P, 1991.

Timothy S. Murphy

NEGRITUDE. A mid-twentieth-century political and cultural movement, dominated by writers and thinkers from Francophone Africa and the Caribbean, in which a variety of black intellectuals sought to express their distinctive racial and cultural identities apart from the identities formerly imposed on them by their European (especially French) colonial rulers. The term *negritude* first appeared in 1939 in the long poem *Cahier d'un retour au pays natal,* by **Aimé Césaire,** who would go on to become one of the key figures in the movement. Louis Gontras Damas from French Guiana was also an important figure in the movement. In the 1940s, negritude gained force among African and Caribbean intellectuals living in Paris, though it had important precedents dating back to the 1920s. Perhaps the single most influential figure in the movement was the Senegalese poet **Léopold Senghor,** partly because ideas associated with negritude strongly informed the political program that eventually brought Senghor to the presidency of Senegal from 1960 to 1980. The movement also featured numerous other important figures, as well as a variety of perspectives, though individuals associated with the movement were united in their attempts to further a sense of black racial pride, thereby revising colonialist histories and overcoming the historical experience of racial denigration and discrimination.

Because of its emphasis on distinctively black modes of expression, negritude was an important force in the rise of African literature in the 1950s and 1960s, though many felt that the movement relied far too heavily on European precedents such as surrealism in its quest for alternative aesthetic models. Indeed, the negritude movement has had numerous critics among postcolonial intellectuals, who have variously charged it with merely replicating ideas derived from French intellectuals, failing to break free of the colonial past, and relying on simplistic and essentialist notions of racial identity. Anglophone African writers and intellectuals have been among the strongest critics of negritude, as when **Wole Soyinka** famously remarked (at an important congress of African writers held at Kampala's Makerere University in 1962) that a tiger does not need to proclaim its tigritude.

Selected Bibliography: Irele, Abiola. *The African Experience in Literature and Ideology.* London: Heinemann, 1981; Kesteloot, Lilyan. *Black Writers in French: A Literary History of Negritude.* Philadelphia:

Temple UP, 1974; Markovitz, Irving Leonard. *Léopold Sédar Senghor and the Politics of Negritude.* New York: Atheneum, 1969.

M. Keith Booker

NERUDA, PABLO (1904–1973). Chilean poet, born Neftalí Ricardo Reyes Basoalto on July 12, 1904, in the small town of Parral, in Chile, where his father worked for the railroad and his mother—who died soon after he was born—was a teacher. Encouraged by the Chilean poet Gabriela Mistral, who befriended him very early, he was writing poetry by the time he was twelve. When he was sixteen, some of his poems appeared in the journal *Selva Austral* (Southern Jungle), where he first published under the pen name Pablo Neruda, at the same time linking himself to the Czech poet Jan Neruda, whom he admired, and avoiding a conflict with his father, who was not pleased with his son's desire to be a poet. Neruda's first book, *Crepusculario*, appeared in 1923, as he began his studies in French and pedagogy at the University of Chile in Santiago.

His early interest in government and politics led to his appointment—over a period of eight years beginning in 1927—as honorary consul to Ceylon, Singapore, Java, Madrid, and other stations. Toward the end of these appointments, he published *Residencia en la Tierra*, the collection that clearly established him as a major poet. His next book—published in 1937, after the death of his friend **Federico García Lorca** in the **Spanish Civil War**—was marked by a strong shift in concern from the personal to the political. He resigned his post in Spain at this time because he was openly on the side of the republicans, opposed to Franco and his fascists.

With his appointment as consul general in Mexico in 1939, Neruda began a major revision of his earlier collection *Canto General de Chile*, titling it now simply *Canto General.* This collection met with almost immediate acceptance throughout the Spanish-speaking world and soon throughout most of the rest of the world, as it was translated into a dozen or so languages. By the time Neruda returned from Spain to Chile later that year, he was beginning to realize a considerable amount in royalties from the sale of his increasingly popular books—poetry collections, though they were. He invested the royalties in a home in the peninsular village of Isla Negra.

In 1943, he married one of his several romantic interests, Delia del Carril, who strongly encouraged him to become more politically involved. That year, as a member of the **Communist Party**, he was elected to the Chilean senate. In 1947, his protests against the Chilean government's repression of striking miners forced him into hiding until he went into exile in 1952; he was allowed to return home within a few months. Much of what he wrote while all this was going on is deeply political in its intent. In 1953, he was awarded the Stalin Prize in Literature. He was awarded the Nobel Prize for Literature in 1971. Two years later, he died of leukemia at his home in Santiago.

To say that Neruda's poems became seriously political—that is, public—is not to say that they became preachy or even very direct. He was always a poet of indirection, so that what a reader takes from a Neruda poem is nearly always an impression rather than instruction; Neruda was never on a soapbox, despite his strong political beliefs and commitments.

Selected Bibliography: O'Daly, William. *Pablo Neruda.* Port Townsend, WA: Copper Canyon P, 1984; Reiss, Frank. *The Word and the Stone.* Oxford: Oxford UP, 1972; Teitelboim, Volodia. *Neruda: An Intimate Biography.* Austin: U of Texas P, 1991; Torres-Rioseco, Arturo. *New World Literature: Tradition and Revolt in Latin America.* Berkeley: U of California P, 1949.

Miller Williams

NEW ANVIL. See ANVIL.

NEW CRITICISM, term associated with the work of a group of literary critics who inaugurated in the 1930s a shift in academic literary scholarship toward the interpretation and evaluation of works of literature themselves through close reading, and away from the previously dominant modes of biography, history, philology, and "appreciation." The New Criticism became the dominant form of literary analysis in the American academy from the 1950s to the 1970s. The term is now most frequently associated with the work of John Crowe Ransom (1888–1974), Cleanth Brooks (1906–1994), William K. Wimsatt (1907–1975), Renée Wellek (1903–1995), and a variable host of other critics, including luminous eccentrics William Empson (1906–1984) and Kenneth Burke (1897–1993), as well as R. P. Blackmur (1904–1965), Allen Tate (1899–1979), and Yvor Winters (1900–1968). They were strongly influenced by two earlier critics: **T. S. Eliot** (1888–1965), who insisted on the unique significance of poetry in general and the metaphysical poets in particular, and I. A. Richards (1893–1979), whose quasi-scientific methods encouraged them to find more sophisticated and rigorous ways of talking about poems.

Although their answers often differed significantly, the New Critics agreed on the fundamental questions; in this sense, the New Criticism was more a research program than a unified theory of literature or school of thought. One central question concerns the relation between poems and everyday uses of language; although the two seem worlds apart, and no one who was just trying to communicate information would use so impractical a mode as poetry, poems are also not sheer meaningless noise. Given this, it is difficult to talk about literature in terms of its moral or political "message" because its basic meaning is elusive. The New Critics' favored categories—"paradox," "ambiguity," "irony" and "complexity"—all testify to their interest in the enigmatic character of poetry.

One cannot get around this enigmatic character by focusing on the background of the work instead of the work itself; as Wimsatt and Beardsley argued in "The Intentional Fallacy" and "The Affective Fallacy," the intentions of the author or the subjective responses of the reader may tell us something about the author or reader, but we can only understand the poem by studying the poem (Wimsatt 3ff.). Moreover, as Cleanth Brooks argued in "The Heresy of Paraphrase," any paraphrase, any reduction of a poem to its "prose meaning," will simplify, distort, or simply miss the poem itself (in part because of the poem's enigmatic character). As Brooks acknowledges, we cannot help using paraphrases when we talk about a poem's meaning, but they are just tools that allow us to understand the unique experience that only the poem, just as it is, brings into being. Accordingly, Brooks claims that "poetry as such indulges in no ethical *generalizations,*" but poems do present us with ethical *problems* by dramatizing specific human situations (258). Good poems make us think without telling us *what* to think.

Another paradoxical aspect of poems, which Ransom discusses in "Wanted: An Ontological Critic" and which Wimsatt discusses in "The Concrete Universal," is that they are particular and individual but seem to point toward the universal and general. In Ransom's view, poems have two main aspects: "structure," which is the logical content of the poems (what could be extracted in a paraphrase), and "texture," which is everything else (280–81). Ransom differentiates poetry from scientific discourse based on the importance of "texture": scientific thinking sets out to arrange all the individual things in the world into broader categories (all of the muffins under the category "muffin"), but in doing so, it leaves out everything unique (*this* especially crumbly blueberry muffin with its slightly elliptical cap). Scientific thinking thus erases all of the specific, particular things in our experience, reducing objects to the common denominator of *specimens.* Ransom conceives the study of poetry as a defense of the particularity of human experience against scientism.

In this regard, the New Criticism coincides with many left critiques of scientific and instrumental rationality (**Theodor Adorno** even published three essays in Ransom's *Kenyon Review*), and the New Critics shared an intense resistance to the bureaucratizing, soul-destroying forces of modernity and the inequity they bring in their train. On the other hand, they had little sympathy with the Marxist critics who were gaining prominence in the 1930s, both because they felt that **Marxist criticism** was dogmatic and because they were generally unsympathetic with the Marxist political project (even more so as the **cold war** heated up). Ransom and Tate were suspicious of urban egalitarianism, and participated in the ill-fated agrarian movement, an attempt to save the rural values of the "old South" (including segregation) from the industrial culture of the North. Wimsatt, on the other hand, being keenly aware of poetry's enigmatic character, rarely made explicit political statements, apart from expressing reticence about violent solutions to political problems and insisting on critical reflection, both deeply linked to his understanding of Christianity. As a result of the New Critics' wariness about anything potentially dogmatic, the explicitly politicized forms of criticism that came to the fore in the 1970s often positioned themselves in opposition to the New Critics, whom they accused unjustly of narrow formalism, of believing that literature was absolutely untouched by history and unsullied by political or ethical significance, and of being reactionary merely by virtue of being Christian, as well as (more justly) of generally neglecting works by women and minorities. Some more recent scholars have accused the New Critics of promoting quietism in the guise of aesthetic disinterestedness or of outright complicity with authoritarian politics (see Eagleton 46–51 for an exemplary instance; see Wellek 144–58 for a more sympathetic account). But for many years, the New Critical tenets, especially as systematically elaborated in Wellek and Warren's *Theory of Literature* (1948), remained the basis of graduate training in the discipline. In that work, one can already see intimations of structuralism, and most of the central concerns of the New Criticism reappeared later—with a formidable philosophical apparatus—in deconstruction.

Many New Critical theoretical positions have since become naturalized (the intentional and affective fallacies, the importance of linguistic nuances, the danger of assuming too transparent a relationship between literature and history or politics or morality), but their influence is most evident in the persistence of close reading. Both as a method of teaching and as a method of scholarly work, close reading has survived in its most general form: the obligation to inspect the language of the text itself carefully and sensitively. This fundamental method is—and is likely to remain—the bedrock of literary study.

Selected Bibliography: Brooks, Cleanth. *William Faulkner: The Yoknapatawpha Country.* New Haven, CT: Yale UP, 1963; Eagleton, Terry. *Literary Theory: An Introduction.* 1983. 2nd ed. Minneapolis: U of Minnesota P, 1996; Graff, Gerald. *Professing Literature: An Institutional History.* Chicago: U of Chicago P, 1979; Ransom, John Crowe. *The New Criticism.* Norfolk, CT: New Directions, 1941; Wellek, Renée. *American Criticism, 1900–1950.* Vol. 6 of *A History of Modern Criticism: 1750–1950.* London: Jonathan Cape, 1986; Wellek, Renée, and Austin Warren. *Theory of Literature.* 3rd ed. San Diego: Harcourt Brace Jovanovich, 1977; Wimsatt, William K. *The Verbal Icon.* Lexington: UP of Kentucky, 1954.

Robin J. Sowards

NEW HISTORICISM. New Historicist criticism represents one of the most important trends in literary study in the last decades of the twentieth century, while New Historicist scholarship, such as Stephen Greenblatt's readings of **Shakespeare**, has introduced important new insights and innovations to readings of literary texts. Like traditional historical scholars, New Historicists accept the basic importance of historical context in the reading of literary works. But the New Historicism departs from traditional historical scholarship in important and crucial ways, especially in its suspicion of conventional Enlightenment notions of historical truth.

New historicists understand that history is complex and multiple and that any reading of it privileges certain interpretations at the expense of others. Influenced by the "thick descriptions" practiced by cultural anthropologist Clifford Geertz, New Historicists attempt to describe the workings of particular phenomena in a specific historical context but do not, in general, attempt to construct narrative models of historical change. In addition, New Historicist scholars are intensely aware that their own decisions concerning the focus of their investigations and the kinds of information to employ in pursuing their conclusions have a powerful impact on the resulting historical visions they produce. They extend their recognition of the importance of historical context to their own activities, understanding that their own situation in contemporary culture exerts a powerful influence on the ways they view other cultural contexts.

New Historicist criticism derives from a number of important influences and participates in a quite broad turn toward social, political, and historical concerns in recent literary criticism. The New Historicist emphasis on material practices in society bears obvious affinities to the historical materialism of **Karl Marx**, and New Historicist analysis in general often recalls the cultural criticism of Marxist critics such as **Raymond Williams**. However, the most important theoretical influence on the New Historicism is poststructuralism, especially the work of **Michel Foucault**, who insists that history is too complex to be understood completely and that the events of history are driven by interrelationships far too complicated to be described in terms of simple sequences of cause and effect. He thus eschews the grand historical narratives often produced by traditional historians, insisting that his own interpretations are partial and provisional.

New Historicist scholarship has been criticized by traditionalists for its lack of respect for conventional notions of historical truth; it has been criticized by Marxists and others on the left for its inability to describe historical change and for its consequent inability to envision successful action to force such change. Nevertheless, its emphasis on the importance of historial context to the understanding of literary texts is surely salutary, as are its reminder that interpretations of history are conditioned by the point of view of the interpreter, and its recognition of the relevance of a wide variety of texts to historical analysis.

Selected Bibliography: Brannigan, John. *New Historicism and Cultural Materialism*. London: Palgrave Macmillan, 1998; Cox, Jeffrey N., and Larry J. Reynolds, eds. *New Historical Literary Study: Essays on Reproducing Texts, Representing History*. Princeton, NJ: Princeton UP, 1993; Gallagher, Catherine, and Stephen Greenblatt. *Practicing New Historicism*. Chicago: U of Chicago P, 2001; Greenblatt, Stephen. *Shakespearean Negotiations: The Circulation of Social Energy in Renaissance England*. Berkeley: U of California P, 1988; Veeser, H. Aram, ed. *The New Historicism*. New York: Routledge, 1989.

M. Keith Booker

NEW LEFT REVIEW. Since it was founded in 1960, *New Left Review* (*NLR*) has been among the most prominent left-wing intellectual journals in the world. It was created from a merger of two journals: the *New Reasoner* and *Universities and Left Review*. The *New Reasoner*, edited by the historians E. P. Thompson and John Saville, was produced by ex-Communists who left the party following the Khrushchev speech and the Soviet invasion of Hungary in 1956. *Universities and Left Review was* created by a group of Oxford students active in the opposition to British involvement in the 1956 Suez crisis; the cultural theorist **Stuart Hall**, the historian Raphael Samuel, and the philosopher Charles Taylor were among its founders. *NLR* originally served as a forum for the first British New Left (1956–1962), a small political and intellectual network organized into a national network of clubs and held together by participation in the first Campaign for Nuclear Disarmament.

Over the years, *NLR* has undergone a number of shifts, in large part reflecting changes in the larger intellectual and political climate. Hall, who sought to appeal to the New Left's various constituencies, was the first editor. The journal originally consisted of an eclectic mix of New Left news, cultural and literary criticism, and political analysis. The journal provided a focal point for the emerging field of cultural studies in articles on the mass media and contemporary popular culture.

Perry Anderson became *NLR*'s editor in 1962, and except for the period 1983–1999, when Robin Blackburn edited the journal, he has remained so ever since. Under Anderson, *NLR* committed itself to a theoretical orientation that drew on continental social theory and Western European Marxism. It sought to stimulate interest in and critical reflection on Marxist theorists virtually unknown in the English-speaking world, including **Theodor Adorno**, **Louis Althusser**, and **Antonio Gramsci**. *NLR* made the thought of these and other related thinkers accessible in translations and critical evaluations in both the journal and a book series, which eventually became the publisher Verso. The intellectual transformation of *NLR* was accompanied by solidarity with the political liberation movements of the third world and support for the growing radical student movement that boiled over in 1968. Over time, *NLR* became increasingly drawn to **Trotsky**ism, particularly as espoused by the Belgian Trotskyist Ernest Mandel. This proved a controversial stance that eventually produced a major split in the editorial board in the early 1980s, leading to the departure of several longtime contributors.

NLR has continued to intervene in political and theoretical debates, yet it is not the central reference point that it once was. This is due in part to the left's continued fragmentation. Most important, *NLR* has failed to adequately respond to the emerging cultural politics of identity and difference. In 2000, *NLR* redefined itself, launching a new series designed to confront the political challenges of the new millennium. Whatever its future, *NLR*'s place in twentieth-century left-wing intellectual culture is secure, as it played a central role in defining and expanding Marxist and socialist intellectual culture.

Selected Bibliography: Dworkin, Dennis. *Cultural Marxism in Postwar Britain: History, the New Left and the Origins of Cultural Studies.* Durham, NC: Duke UP, 1997; Eliot, Gregory. *Perry Anderson: The Merciless Laboratory of History.* Minneapolis: U of Minnesota P, 1999; Kenny, Michael. *The First New Left: British Intellectuals after Stalin.* London: Lawrence and Wishart, 1995.

Dennis Dworkin

NEW MASSES. Shortly before its demise in 1948, the *New Masses* vaunted the many years it had "fought the money-lords, the fascists and fakers, the corruptors of literature and art" with its fiction and poetry, art, reportage, essays, and editorials. It is precisely this commitment to struggle that has made some dismiss *New Masses*' contents as vulgar Proletcult expressions of art-as-weaponry and others celebrate its courageous and eclectic combination of ferocity and wit. In any case, it was singular in its capacity to be both an art and a political journal that drew readers and contributors from the upper echelons of the literary world as well as from the working class it sought to venerate. Indeed, during the height of its influence, it became, as its editor Joseph North noted, "the conscience of the literary world at that time."

When *New Masses* appeared as a monthly in 1926, it retained much of the vitality and breadth of previous magazines on culture and politics, such as *Liberator* and *Masses*, and was distinctive in its open engagement with the **Communist Party** of the United States' interpretations of art, literature, and politics. This association has led some critics to underestimate the autonomy of the journal's attempt to forge a **proletarian literature** authentic to the United States, though most agree that *New Masses* published some of the most original, spirited, and committed creative work of its era.

The role of noncommunist writers in *New Masses* is central to its uniqueness. Under the editorship of **Michael Gold**, *New Masses* also solicited work from nonprofessional writers. In his appeal, Gold insisted, "Your life in the mine, mill and farm is of deathless significance in the history of the world." Through this effort and the support of **John Reed Clubs** throughout the country, *New Masses* cultivated new talent, including **Richard Wright** and Ben Field, while also publishing the work of established figures like Sherwood Anderson, **Howard Fast**, and **Ernest Hemingway**.

Though *New Masses* was frequently charged with placing politics before aesthetics, its pages reveal charged debates about radical literature and calls for greater dimension and diversity from its contributors.

The journal published the works of well-known authors more frequently after becoming a weekly in 1934. The **Popular Front** organization League of American Writers and the skilled editor **Granville Hicks** helped popularize it among increasingly radicalized literati. Such a range enabled *New Masses* to develop a distinctive style of reportage of the labor and civic upheavals that marked domestic politics and analyzed world events (with particular attention to the rise of fascism). Contributions from Erskine Caldwell, **Meridel LeSueur**, Dorothy Parker, and **Agnes Smedley** convey its signature commitment to journalistic integrity and ardent realism. In original illustrations and cartoons, Irene Goldberg, William Gropper, and Art Young created striking interpretations of world events. The journal became an arbiter of cultural production during this time, reaching a readership of 25,000 in 1935. Disillusionment and anticommunism diminished *New Masses*' popularity throughout the 1940s, leading to the journal's demise.

Selected Bibliography: Denning, Michael. *The Cultural Front: The Laboring of American Culture in the Twentieth Century.* New York: Verson, 1996; Foley, Barbara. *Radical Representations: Politics and Form in U.S. Proletarian Fiction, 1929–1941.* Durham, NC: Duke UP, 1993; Murphy, James F. *The Proletarian Moment: The Controversy over Leftism in Literature.* Urbana: U of Illinois P, 1991; North, Joseph. *New Masses: An Anthology of the Rebel Thirties.* New York: International Publishers, 1969; Peck, David. "The Tradition of American Revolutionary Literature: The Monthly *New Masses*, 1926–1933." *Science and Society* 42 (Winter 1978–1979).

Rachel Peterson

NEW YORK INTELLECTUALS. Collective designation of a loosely associated group of critics, writers, and thinkers centered in the city of New York. The leading New York intellectuals were born around **World War I**, came into association mainly through the *Partisan Review* during the 1930s, and maintained a distinctive project into the 1970s, though they were at the peak of their influence in the 1950s and 1960s. The most important *literary* critics among several dozen intellectuals were Irving Howe, Alfred Kazin, Philip Rahv, and Lionel Trilling, and leading writers included Saul Bellow, Mary McCarthy, Delmore Schwartz, and Susan Sontag. Older by a decade, Edmund Wilson served as a model for them. Because many of the New York intellectuals were Jewish (usually secularized), the group was sometimes characterized as a Jewish clique. The critics started out as radical literary journalists, first writing for *Partisan Review*, the *New Republic*, and the *Nation*, and later for *Commentary*, *Dissent*, and the *New York Review of Books*, and ended up as respected liberal university professors who still preferred literary journalism to academic scholarship, writing essays, reviews, and eventually memoirs. They maintained a critical view of the university as well as of popular and middlebrow culture, functioning as one of the last of the modern elitist avant-gardes.

As described by Howe in a 1968 retrospective in *Commentary*, the New York intellectuals, alienated from mainstream society, approximated a bohemian intelligentsia; they were democratic (not revolutionary) socialists early opposed to **Joseph**

Stalin's totalitarianism; they denounced the mystique of the proletariat promoted by the **Communist Party**; they focused on nineteenth- and twentieth-century canonical European and American literature, embracing the modernist avant-garde as well as Marxian theory, thereby uniting cosmopolitanism and radical politics; they criticized mass culture from an elitist perspective; they became in the early **cold-war** period liberal (versus right-wing) anticommunists and later occasionally neoconservatives; and in the 1960s and 1970s, they opposed the New Left, the beats, and **postmodernism**, cutting themselves off from younger generations of radicals.

In the early 1930s, the thinkers who became the New York intellectuals were radicals aligned with the Communist Party. In an early piece in *New Masses*, "The Literary Class War" (August 1932), Rahv, longtime coeditor with William Phillips of *Partisan Review*, urged intellectuals to master Marxian theory, defend the Soviet Union, and become part of the proletariat. However, by 1937, Rahv was critical not only of Soviet totalitarianism and Stalin, but of the proletarian program for literature as well as the Communist Party's new program for a **Popular Front**. The intellectuals, importantly influenced by **Leon Trotsky**, became increasingly anti-Stalinist in subsequent years. However, for Rahv and the New York intellectuals, the issue was neither Marxism per se nor the linkage of culture to politics, but the need for freedom of thought and expression—values characteristic of the independent socialism and liberalism adopted by the group during its dramatic deradicalization and mutation from revolutionary vanguard to cold-war establishment. The argument for liberalism was famously crystallized by Lionel Trilling in *The Liberal Imagination* (1950), consisting characteristically of essays—a third of which appeared earlier in *Partisan Review*.

Unlike the formalist literary critics triumphant in the United States during the middle third of the twentieth-century—notably the **New Critics**, who advocated academic criticism focused solely on the complex aesthetic features of literary texts, discounting authors' intentions, readers' responses, and influences from society—the New York critics promoted an eclectic style of social criticism. They blended biography, moral evaluation, sociology, and history with analysis of genre and style. Economics and politics played a part, as did Freudian psychoanalysis. For them, the function of literary criticism was not aesthetic appreciation but secular social engagement, providing ideas central to political action and moral behavior with an eye to the prospects for society.

The literature most admired by the New York intellectuals was modernist fiction blending the realist and naturalist with symbolist traditions, especially novels that overcame nihilism and solipsism. Among poets, they most appreciated **T. S. Eliot** for his critical theory and diagnoses of social problems, but not for his mid-career turn to right-wing politics and anti-Semitism. They championed complex, serious, difficult (though not radically experimental) works, in particular novels by **Dostoevsky**, **James**, Proust, Kafka, Lawrence, **Faulkner**, and **Joyce**. They brought modernist literature into American Marxism.

In his *Politics and the Novel* (1957), Howe asserted revealingly, "The criteria for evaluating a political novel must finally be the same as those for any other novel: how much of our life does it illuminate? How ample a moral vision does it suggest?" (24). Representative of the New York intellectuals, this theory applied a version of the recurring realism-symbolism dialectic: the political novel creates a dramatic world of real social conditions, human motives, and actions set against an ideal world of political goals and ideologies. A similar dialectic appeared earlier in Rahv's landmark essay on American literature, "Paleface and Redskin" (1939), in which he sketched two antithetical positions affecting national literary tradition. "Redskins" are writers like **Walt Whitman**, Mark Twain, **Theodore Dreiser**, and **Ernest Hemingway**—energetic and boisterous plebeian mystics, greedy for experience, materialistic and hedonistic, in tune with the environment and the rabble of the frontier and city, and given to lowbrow forms of realism. "Palefaces" are authors like Nathaniel Hawthorne, Henry James, Emily Dickinson, and **T. S. Eliot**—patrician intellectuals prone to solitude and a tragic sense of life (derived from Puritan religion), characterized by estrangement from reality, devotion to highbrow tradition, respect for disciplined modes of life, and attracted to allegorical symbolic forms of literature. In his *On Native Grounds: An Interpretation of Modern American Prose Literature* (1942), Kazin portrayed the struggle during the 1930s between doctrinaire Communists and literary formalists as a wasteful battle between sociology and aesthetics, propaganda and academicism, and Stalinism and fascism, with the New York intellectuals occupying a sane and saving middle ground.

Given the triumph of New Criticism in the 1950s, the rapid enclosure of intellectual life inside the postwar university, and the red scares and conformism provoked by McCarthyism during the early cold war, the New York intellectuals appeared in the 1950s and thereafter increasingly antiquated, the last of the independent literary journalists and modernist avant-gardes now themselves ironically warehoused, often as anticommunist celebrities, in the university. Rahv, maintaining his Marxist allegiances to the end, labeled this the "*embourgeoisement* of the American intelligentsia," and in his *A Margin of Hope: An Intellectual Autobiography* (1982), the lifelong democratic socialist Howe observed that "the New York literary life had crumbled into success" (289).

Selected Bibliography: Bloom, Alexander. *Prodigal Sons: The New York Intellectuals and Their World.* New York: Oxford UP, 1986; Cooney, Terry A. *The Rise of the New York Intellectuals: "Partisan Review" and Its Circle.* Madison: U of Wisconsin P, 1986; Jumonville, Neil. *Critical Crossings: The New York Intellectuals in Postwar America.* Berkeley: U of California P, 1991; Teres, Harvey M. *Renewing the Left: Politics, Imagination, and the New York Intellectuals.* New York: Oxford UP, 1996; Wald, Alan M. *The New York Intellectuals: The Rise and Decline of the Anti-Stalinist Left from the 1930s to the 1980s.* Chapel Hill: U of North Carolina P, 1987; Wilford, Hugh. *The New York Intellectuals: From Vanguard to Institution.* Manchester: Manchester UP, 1995.

Vincent B. Leitch

NEWS FROM NOWHERE (1890), a socialist work of **utopian fiction** by the English author, interior designer, and political activist William Morris (1834–1896), first published in weekly installments of the Socialist League newspaper *Commonweal* and then in book form in 1891. The narrator, the nineteenth-century socialist William Guest, wakes up in a transfigured future London where a class society has long since been abolished, work is pleasurable rather than dehumanizing, and human relationships are neighborly rather than oppressive. He explores the new, green, and unstressed London, learns of the history and principles of the postrevolutionary society from the "old man Who knew everything" (to borrow a term from **H. G. Wells**), and then travels by boat up the river Thames into Oxfordshire to explore socialist rural life. He finally returns involuntarily to his own epoch, grief stricken to have lost the new perfect world but strengthened in his resolve to start building it in his own time.

News from Nowhere was written by Morris partly as a riposte to Edward Bellamy's *Looking Backward* (1888). Where Bellamy's postcapitalist economy is a relentlessly centralized one, Morris's Nowhere is a thoroughly decentralized world, both politically and economically. Where Bellamy's new society valorizes intellectual pursuits above all, Morris's more holistic utopia (strongly influenced by John Ruskin) celebrates handicrafts as the ultimate aesthetic value in the new world. And where Bellamy's transfigured Boston projects an ideal of urban living *News from Nowhere* vividly stresses the natural environment, both in a London that has become a spacious garden city and in the Thames valley countryside of its later chapters.

Morris's utopia is a remarkably attractive world, both in its genial human relations and in the sensuous particularity of its imagery and writing; it is far removed from the abstract geometrical blueprint of the classical utopia. Yet some critics have found it to be too static, too pastoral, too regressive in its dismissal of science and formal education. It is therefore crucial to note that *News from Nowhere* contains not one but two journeys, and not one but two utopias. Guest first time-travels to the new London, which is a vast improvement over the Victorian slums of his own epoch; but he later sets off on a second major journey, up the Thames, as if toward another utopia. As he does so, he meets the character Ellen, a vivid, energetic, intensely enigmatic figure, who does indeed make the people he met in London look static by comparison.

In the figure of Ellen, *News from Nowhere* adumbrates a second utopia, a more dynamic, self-transformative society than the pleasantly pastoral world we saw earlier in the book. Morris's utopia thus anticipates its critics and answers their objections in advance, producing in the process a sensuous ecotopian vision that will be inspiring to both Greens and socialists for a long time to come.

Selected Bibliography: Coleman, Stephen, and Paddy O'Sullivan, eds. *William Morris and "News from Nowhere": A Vision for Our Time*. Bideford, UK: Green Books, 1990; Meier, Paul. *William Morris: The Marxist Dreamer*. Trans. Frank Gubb. 2 vols. Brighton: Harvester P, 1978.

Tony Pinkney

NEXØ, MARTIN ANDERSEN (1869–1954), who experienced both urban and rural poverty during his childhood, moved with his family from Copenhagen to the island of Bornholm. He uses his childhood fictionally in *Pelle the Conqueror* (*Pelle Erobreren*, 1906–1910), the novel sequence that was his international breakthrough. It records Pelle's harsh life on a farm, his apprentice years as a shoemaker in a small town, and his rise as a labor organizer in the capital of Denmark. A rousing socialist **bildungsroman**, *Pelle* was immensely popular. Previous to Nexø's finding himself politically, he published five introverted novels and collections of short stories that offer a grim view of everyday life among the poor in Denmark; those stories are vivid in their unsentimental portrayal of the proletariat.

Pelle established Nexø as a major voice on the left. His novel sequence *Ditte: Child of Man* (*Ditte Menneskebarn*, 1917–1921) tells the story of a young proletarian girl who grows up in the countryside, then moves to the city where she experiences dire poverty, and eventually dies. The masses, who see her child—a boy accidentally killed while trying to fetch coals to heat their miserable apartment—as a victim of capitalist society, march in the streets as the novel concludes. Pelle appears in this novel as a political hack. Nexø felt that simple reform would not do. Having witnessed the **Russian Revolution**, he hoped for a similar upheaval in Scandinavia.

In *Morten the Red* (*Morten hin røde*, 1945–1957), Morten, who was a friend of Pelle and Ditte, assumes center stage; as a Marxist, he rejects any compromises with the moderate workers' movement and despises Pelle. Nexø's changing view of Pelle demonstrates his own move toward the left. Unfortunately, this novel lacks the narrative power and emotional zest of the former two, as does *In an Age of Iron* (*Midt in en Jœrntid*, (1929), in which Nexø deals with the profiteering spirit during **World War I**. Luckily, Nexø decided to record his early years in four volumes of memoirs (1932–1939), which recall the past with veneration, humor, and whimsy. In addition, he composed some travel accounts, one volume of poetry, one drama, and numerous political articles. Often criticized as an author who let his political tendentiousness stand in the way of his artistic acumen—perhaps true in *Morten*—Nexø's social indignation was an immensely inspirational and powerful force in the Pelle and Ditte narratives.

Selected Bibliography: Ingwersen, Faith, and Niels Ingwersen. *Quests for a Promised Land: The Works of Martin Andersen Nexø.* Westport, CT: Greenwood, 1984; Slochower, Harry. *Mythopoesis: Myth Patterns in Literary Classics.* Detroit: Wayne State UP, 1973.

Faith Ingwersen and Niels Ingwersen

NGŨGĨ WA THIONG'O (1938–). Born in 1938 in Kamiriithu, Limuru, part of the Gikuyu homeland—a rural area outside of Nairobi, Kenya—Ngũgĩ is one of the twenty-eight children of peasant and tenant farmer Thiong'o wa Nduucu, who had four wives, including Wanjiju wa Ngũgĩ, Ngũgĩ's mother. Despite his taking the name James Ngũgĩ in his childhood, his family was not Christian but practiced traditional Gikuyu beliefs. Ngũgĩ's family circumstances—landlessness, polygamy, and religious difference from the colonizers—plunged him into a politically confrontational existence from birth. As a child, he attended a missionary school, where students were punished for speaking English, then a Gikuyu Independent school, dedicated to preserving the Gikuyu language and cultural traditions. Many of the repeated themes of his writing stem from schoolday experiences, especially his understanding that language carries culture and his controversial decision at the end of 1977 that African writers should write in African languages. The physical violence of colonialism hit home when, in the mid-1950s, Ngũgĩ's deaf-and-dumb stepbrother was shot dead by British soldiers, an event the author re-creates in *A Grain of Wheat* (1967). Moreover, his elder brother, a carpenter, became a member of the Land and Freedom Fighters (called "Mau Mau" by the colonizers) and fought in the forest for two years during Kenya's Emergency Period. From the prestigious Alliance High School, Ngũgĩ went to Makerere University College in Kampala, Uganda, graduating with honors in 1964. It was during postgraduate work at the University of Leeds in England, studying with the Marxist scholar Arnold Kettle, that he began reading **Karl Marx**, as well as the works of such Marxist thinkers as **Vladimir Lenin** and **Frantz Fanon**—an important intellectual and political influence that remains with him.

After becoming the first African member of the University of Nairobi's English department in 1967, he and other colleagues successfully replaced it with the Department of Literature in 1968, also adding a new Department of Linguistics and African Languages. He resigned his position in 1969 in protest against the university and government's violations of academic freedom and harsh punishment against striking students. After teaching at Northwestern University in the United States in 1970, he returned to Kenya an even more committed socialist and used his voice and pen against the corruption of the black bourgeoisie (who came to power after Kenyan independence in 1963) and their foreign allies.

Returning to the University of Nairobi in 1973, Ngũgĩ became head of the Department of Literature, becoming that institution's first African department head. His novel *Petals of Blood* (1977) and play of the same year, *Ngaahika Ndeenda* (*I Will Marry When I Want*), commissioned by the Kamiriithu Community Educational and Cultural Centre and written and produced in collaboration with villagers and colleagues from the university, led to his arrest on New Year's Eve and detention at Kamiti Maximum Security Prison, allegedly for possessing eighteen banned books. His detention occasioned widespread local, regional, and international protests and petitions for his release. Although never officially charged, he was held prisoner for almost a year, during which he wrote (on toilet paper) the first modern novel in Gikuyu, *Caitaamo Muitharaba-ini* (1980, English translation *Devil on the Cross*, 1982), and parts of his prison diary, *Detained* (1981).

After his release in December 1978, Ngũgĩ and his family received constant death threats and official harassment, while in March 1982, the Kamiriithu cultural center was razed by the government, all of which events Ngũgĩ discusses in his essays. While in London for the publication of *Devil on the Cross* in 1982, Ngũgĩ was warned that he would be arrested upon his return to Kenya and, therefore, began his present life of exile. In 1986, he published his second novel written in Gikuyu, *Matigari*, which draws on the legacy of the Mau Mau rebellion as a source of oppositional energies in Kenya.

While away from his homeland, Ngũgĩ has continued his professional and artistic careers. However, he continues to suffer from the suspicion of the Kenyan government, which has accused him of leading a clandestine oppositional political group and has continued to ban his books, removing them from school reading lists. In response, to continue reaching young people, he has been writing a series of children's books, the first of which is *Njamba Nene na Mbaathi I Malhagu* (*Njamba Nene and the Flying Bus*, 1986).

In 1992, he accepted the Erich Maria Remarque Chair of Comparative Literature at New York University in the United States and began editing *Mutiiri*, a literary and cultural journal in Gikuyu. Since July 2002, he has been Distinguished Professor and first director of the International Center for Writing and Translation at the University of California in Irvine and has completed a 1,200-page novel, *Murogi wa Kagogo* (*The Wizard of the Crow*). Ngũgĩ has held academic positions and been invited to speak at many distinguished institutions worldwide and has received numerous awards, including the 1986 Fonlon-Nichols Prize and the 2001 Nonino International Prize.

Selected Bibliography: Gikandi, Simon. *Ngugi wa Thiong'o*. New York: Cambridge UP, 2001; Jeyifo, Biodun. *Ngugi wa Thiong'o*. London: Pluto, 1990; Killam, G. D. *An Introduction to the Writings of Ngugi*. London: Heinemann, 1980; Ngũgĩ wa Thiong'o. *Barrel of a Pen: Resistance to Repression in Neo-Colonial Kenya*. London: Heinemann, 1983; Ngũgĩ wa Thiong'o. *Decolonising the Mind: The Politics of Language in African Literature*. London: James Currey, 1986; Ngũgĩ wa Thiong'o. *Detained: A Prison Diary*. London: Heinemann, 1981; Ngũgĩ wa Thiong'o. *Moving the Centre: Struggle for Cultural Freedoms*. London: James Currey, 1993; Ngũgĩ wa Thiong'o. *Penpoints, Gunpoints and Dreams: Towards a Critical Theory of the Arts and the State of Africa*. New York: Oxford UP, 1998; Sicherman, Carol. *Ngugi wa Thiong'o: The Making of a Rebel*. London: Hans Zell, 1990.

Arlene (Amy) Elder

NIGERIAN CIVIL WAR. Conflict between the secessionist state of Biafra and federal Nigeria, also known as the Biafran War and the Nigeria-Biafra War. Following the establishment of the Igbo-dominated secessionist Republic of Biafra in May 1967, the Nigerian federal government responded with sanctions designed to force Biafra to rejoin Nigeria. By July 1967, the tensions between Nigeria and Biafra led to an all-out war, in which it was clear early on that the conflict was one-sided, since the federal government had overwhelming advantages in terms of men, weapons, money, and other resources. The conflict lasted until January 1970, when the original boundaries of Nigeria were restored.

During the civil war, Nigerian writers were profoundly stimulated by the challenges of the new political situation. Previously assumed priorities were reconsidered, alliances were shattered, and the assumptions about "Nigerian national literature" were questioned. As violence spread during 1967, the established novelist **Chinua Achebe** felt forced to leave his post in the federal capital for his hometown in what was then Biafra. During the war, he traveled widely, making appeals to the international community on behalf of suffering Biafrans and the secessionist government. The writing from this period that survived the destruction of his home includes moving poems, some of them occasioned by particular events (*Christmas in Biafra and Other Poems*, 1973), and resonant short stories (*Girls at War and Other Stories*, 1973). While Achebe has not produced an extended fictional treatment of the struggle, other Igbo-born writers have, securing a victory on the page that was denied them in the field. These writers include Elechi Amadi, Cyprian Ekwensi, Chukwuemeka Ike, Eddie Iroh, and Okechukwu Mezu.

As the storm clouds gathered, the intensely individual poet Christopher Okigbo felt drawn to his Igbo roots. His poetry became more public ("Path of Thunder"), and in the months following secession, he worked idealistically and passionately with Achebe to establish a Biafran-based publishing house. Okigbo became a major in the Biafran army and was killed defending Nsukka (1967).

Wole Soyinka, who, as a Yoruba, might have been expected to take the federal line, was detained without trial by Nigerian security forces after a visit to the Biafran enclave and after writing provocatively about the conduct of the federal operations. In his "prison notes," *The Man Died*, he responds to his imprisonment and to the civil war in general, which also influenced his subsequent dramatic novel *Season of Anomy* (1973), in which Soyinka presents the war as a confusing and chaotic event in which there are no clear heroes and villains. An even stronger denunciation of the war appears in **Festus Iyayi**'s *Heroes* (winner of the Commonwealth Writers' Prize in 1986), which rejects the ethnic terms of the conflict as misguided, seeing instead class inequality as the crucial social phenomenon dividing Nigerian society.

In Ken Saro-Wiwa's *Sozaboy* (1985) can be heard a voice hailing from Ogoniland, part of the oil-rich territory that the Igbos initially claimed as part of Biafra. Subtitled "a novel in rotten English," the novel presents a view of the tribulations of war by a writer who belonged to a "micro-nation" whose fragile ecosystem had been ravaged to fill the federal coffers and was fought over by "ignorant armies." *Sozaboy* is a leading contender for the title of "Great Civil War Novel"—terrible events sometimes produce profound literature. Saro-Wiwa later authored an important history of the civil war. In 1995, Saro-Wiwa, who had been branded a secessionist, was executed on the orders of a brutal military regime as a grim postscript to the civil war.

For younger generations of Nigerian writers, the war means different things. For those in their forties who suffered in Biafra, it remains a harrowing memory, and for younger Igbo-speakers, the experience remains only a little less intense for being secondhand. Though there are exceptions, such as Ben Okri's "Laughter beneath the Bridge," writers from other parts of the federation often present the civil war as very remote. The regional and ethnic fault lines along which secession took place were indeed deep and remain real, just as the sufferings of the war were intense and often prolonged. They have not been forgotten and it is often rightly observed that the divisions that open up in debates between Nigerian writers of all ages reflect those along which the civil war was fought.

Selected Bibliography: Ekwe-Ekwe, Herbert. *The Biafra War: Nigeria and the Aftermath*. Lewiston, NY: Mellen, 1990; Ezenwa-Ohaeto. *Chinua Achebe: A Biography*. Bloomington: Indiana UP, 1997; Madiebo, Alexander A. *The Nigerian Revolution and the Biafran War*. Enugu, Nigeria: Fourth Dimension Publishers, 1980; Ravenscroft, Arthur. "The Nigerian Civil War in Nigerian Literature." *Commonwealth Literature and the Modern World*. Ed. Hena Maes-Jelinek. Bruxelles: Librairie Marcel Didier, 1975. 105–13; Saro-Wiwa, Ken. *On a Darkling Plain: An Account of the Nigerian Civil War*. London: Saros International, 1989.

James Gibbs

NINETEEN EIGHTY-FOUR (1949), by the English socialist writer **George Orwell**, was an international publishing phenomenon that became a founding work of modern **dystopian literature**. It influenced world politics during the **cold war** through its devastating portrait of England as Airstrip One, a province of the totalitarian state of Oceania, which is controlled by the Ingsoc (English socialism) Party. Indebted to **Evgeny Zamyatin**'s *We* (1924), *Nineteen Eighty-Four* tells the story of Winston Smith, a balding, unhealthy Outer Party man who works in the Records

Department of the Ministry of Truth, rewriting old news stories—and thus the past—to fit the whims of the dictator, Big Brother. The novel tells the story of his futile rebellion against the state, which begins with his decision to keep a diary; leads to a forbidden and passionate affair with a young party member, Julia; and ends in Room 101 of the Ministry of Love, where he is tortured by the Inner Party leader O'Brien until he finally denounces Julia and learns to love Big Brother. At the book's end, the only hope for England lies with the Proles, an underclass still capable of spontaneous song and thus, supposedly, revolution.

To anyone living in England at the end of the 1940s, the physical world of *Nineteen Eighty-Four* was instantly recognizable. The shortages, the rationing, the broken lifts—all suggest that Orwell did not aspire to create a futuristic fantasy in the tradition of **Aldous Huxley**'s *Brave New World* (1932), but rather a satire of life in bombed out, postwar London. One of Orwell's few indulgences in futuristic invention is the telescreen, which keeps its ubiquitous eye on Oceania's citizens in order to detect any suspicious acts. Yet even the telescreen cannot detect the most dangerous crime of all, thoughtcrime, to which Winston increasingly falls prey before he is arrested with Julia by the Thought Police.

Orwell's appendix to *Nineteen Eighty-Four* explains that thoughtcrime will become impossible once all citizens are fluent in Newspeak, an invented language that will supersede Oldspeak (Standard English) by 2050. Newspeak will "not only provide a medium of expression for the world-view and mental habits proper to the devotees of Ingsoc, but make all other modes of thought impossible." It will eliminate the need for doublethink (accepting contradictory facts as true to maintain political orthodoxy) by suppressing undesirable words such as "justice" and "democracy" and by stripping remaining words of forbidden meanings.

Big Brother, Thought Police, Newspeak, doublethink: these words are *Nineteen Eighty-Four*'s greatest legacy to English language and literature. The book's political reputation is less certain. There is evidence that Orwell wanted the book to be interpreted as a warning about the totalitarian tendencies of all ideologies, but it was read by the mainstream media as an attack on socialism. Received as dire prophecy, it was used for decades to fan the fires of antisocialist and anticommunist sentiment in England and America.

Selected Bibliography: Chilton, Paul, and Crispin Aubrey, eds. *"Nineteen Eighty-Four" in 1984: Autonomy, Control and Communication.* London: Comedia, 1983; *George Orwell and "Nineteen Eighty-Four": The Man and the Book.* Washington, DC: Library of Congress, 1985; Howe, Irving, ed. *Orwell's "Nineteen Eighty-Four": Text, Sources, Criticism.* New York: Harcourt, Brace and World, 1963; Lutz, William, ed. *Beyond "Nineteen Eighty-Four": Doublespeak in a Post-Orwellian Age.* Urbana, IL: National Council of Teachers of English, 1989.

Kristin Bluemel

NIZAN, PAUL (1905–1940). In his brief and tragic life, Paul Nizan became one of the most prolific and contentious intellectuals associated with the French **Communist Party.** Son of a man of provincial peasant stock whose struggle for social advancement was brutally thwarted, and brought up with the painful family memory of a sister who died very young, Nizan was haunted by the fear of failure and the presence of death. In Paris, alongside his friend **Jean-Paul Sartre**, Nizan was a brilliant student whose intellectual ambitions led him to turn against bourgeois culture. In his essays *Aden-Arabie* (1931) and *Les Chiens de garde* (1932), he attacked the establishment that had tried to condition and indoctrinate him and others. Nizan seemed to find his political and existential home in the French Communist Party, which he joined in 1927 during the most extreme and sectarian period of the **Third International**.

Nizan became a journalist for the communist daily newspapers *L'Humanité* and *Ce Soir*, where he chronicled international and domestic events as well as the cultural production of the time. He was one of the first to review the work of Jacques Lacan and, of course, Sartre. Nizan was never completely at ease in a communist movement that was self-consciously working class and distrustful of intellectuals, but he was a faithful Communist; a year spent in the Soviet Union in 1934 nuanced but did not fundamentally shake his attachment to the young revolutionary state.

In his novels, Nizan attempted to give expression to his political and personal concerns. *Antoine Bloyé* (1933) returns to the paternal experience of ruined ambition in the capitalist system. *Trojan Horse* (*Le Cheval de Troie*, 1935) is a socialist realist narrative that portrays, in a flawed yet interesting fashion, reality in its revolutionary development, as well as showing Nizan's obsession with death. His last published novel—*The Conspiracy* (*La Conspiration*, 1939), a tale of naive idealism, espionage, and treachery—deals with bourgeois students tempted by the adventure of communism in late 1920s Paris.

It was the Nazi-Soviet nonaggression pact of August 1939 that led Nizan to break publicly with the party; antifascism, he felt, had been betrayed by Stalin's cynicism and a slavish and incompetent French Communist Party leadership. In May 1940, near Dunkirk, Nizan the soldier was killed by a stray bullet. Days before, he had buried in an unmarked place the manuscript of his unfinished novel, *La Soirée a Somosierra*. Since then, Nizan's reputation has become a battlefield. For the French Communist Party, during the war and early **cold-war** years, he was a "renegade" and "police spy"; Louis Aragon and Henri Lefebvre actively contributed to this view. For Sartre, his friend had been a dissident Communist and precursor of the New Left. For others still, including Nizan's wife, he was an "impossible" Communist.

Selected Bibliography: Cohen-Solal, Anne, and Henriette Nizan. *Paul Nizan, Communist Impossible.* Paris: Grasset, 1980; Redfern, W. D. *Paul Nizan: Committed Literature in a Conspiratorial World.* Princeton, NJ: Princeton UP, 1972; Sartre, Jean-Paul. *Oeuvres romanesques.* Paris: Gallimard, 1981. 1461–1534; Scriven, Michael. *Paul Nizan: Communist Novelist.* London: Macmillan, 1988; Steele, James. *Paul Nizan, un révolutionnaire conformiste?* Paris: Presses de la Fondation Nationale des Sciences Politiques, 1987; Suleiman, Susan. *Authoritarian Fictions: The Ideological Novel as a Literary Genre.* New York: Columbia UP, 1983. 102–18; Thornberry, Robert S. *Les Ecrits de Paul Nizan (1905–1940): Portrait d'une époque. Bibliographie commentée suivie de textes retrouvés.* Paris: Honoré Champion, 2001.

Gavin Bowd

NKRUMAH, KWAME (1909–1972). A leading figure in the Pan-African movement and the first premier of decolonized Ghana, Nkrumah was born in the Gold Coast, a British colony, on September 21, 1909. He trained as a teacher before leaving for the United States in 1935 to study economics and sociology; he eventually obtained a doctorate from Lincoln University in Pennsylvania. A talented scholar, between 1939 and 1945 he taught Negro history at Lincoln and founded both the African Studies Association and the African Students Association of America and Canada. In 1945, he relocated to Britain, where he came into contact with a number of radical figures, such as **George Padmore** (who became a close friend and loyal ally), **C.L.R. James**, and Ras Makonnen, together with whom he furthered the realization of his vision of Pan-African federation, on which the future of a decolonized Africa might rest. A passionate advocate of Pan-Africanism, Nkrumah was a key figure at the Sixth Pan-African Congress held in Manchester, England, in 1945, where he met future African leaders such as Jomo Kenyatta and influential thinkers such as **W.E.B. Du Bois**. He became vice president of the West African Students Union (WASU) in London in 1947, the year he wrote *Towards Colonial Freedom* (eventually published in 1957).

Returning to the Gold Coast, Nkrumah formed the Convention People's Party (CPP) in 1948—its motto was Self-Government Now—and agitated for independence from British colonialism. In 1950, Nkrumah was imprisoned by the colonial authorities due to his advocacy of anticolonial nonviolent protest, yet the chain of events put in place by his activism proved unstoppable. He was freed the following year, after the CPP's landslide election victory, and formed a new government. He became the prime minister of the newly independent Ghana in March 1957 and, during this year, also published his autobiography.

Nkrumah's initial years in government proved popular; however, after a series of economic difficulties in the early 1960s, Nkrumah's style of leadership became increasingly dictatorial. In 1964, he declared himself president for life, imposed a one-party state, and pursued tyrannical forms of power, imprisoning thousands of Ghanaians and challenging the authority of tribal chiefs. In 1966, he was ousted by a coup while on a trip to Beijing and Hanoi; he lived the rest of his life in exile, mostly in Guinea. During the 1960s, he also wrote a series of books that were both influential in the Pan-Africanist debates of the day and indicative of Nkrumah's increasing self-regard and attempt to conjure a quasi-mystical cult of personality. These included *Africa Must Unite* (1963), *Neo-Colonialism: The Last Stage of Imperialism* (1965), *Dark Days in Ghana* (1968), and *Class Stuggle in Africa* (1970). Nkrumah died of natural causes while on a visit to Romania on April 27, 1972. He was buried three months later in Ghana.

Selected Bibliography: Davidson, Basil. *Black Star: A View of the Life and Times of Kwame Nkrumah.* London: Allen Lane, 1973; Geiss, Imanuel. *The Pan-African Movement.* Trans. Ann Keep. London: Methuen, 1974; Hadjor, Kofi Buenor. *Nkrumah and Ghana: The Dilemma of Post-Colonial Power.* London: Kegan Paul International, 1988; James, C.L.R. *Nkrumah and the Ghana Revolution.* London: Allison and Busby, 1977; Nkrumah, Kwame. *The Autobiography of Kwame Nkrumah.* London: Panaf, 1973; Nkrumah, Kwame. *Neo-Colonialism: The Last Stage of Imperialism.* London: Nelson, 1965.

John McLeod

O'CASEY, SEAN (1880–1964). Irish playwright, born John Casey in Dublin. He adopted the name Sean O'Cathasaigh, finally calling himself Sean O'Casey. His father died when he was six, causing financial hardship for the family. As a result, O'Casey's schooling suffered (he always claimed that he couldn't read until he was sixteen). He joined the Irish Citizen Army in 1913, resigning in 1914. After writing plays for amateur productions, he submitted plays to the Abbey Theatre, where he met Lady Gregory and **W. B. Yeats.** His early efforts were rejected, but in 1922, the theater accepted *The Shadow of the Gunman*, the first of three O'Casey plays (crucial to his literary reputation) the Abbey premiered, including *Juno and the Paycock* (1924) and *The Plough and the Stars* (1926). *The Plough and the Stars* sparked nationalist riots but was vigorously defended by Yeats. O'Casey's loyalty was with the working class, and he was no mere propagandist for Irish nationalism, which he saw as potentially inimical to the interests of workers.

O'Casey moved to England after the controversy over *The Plough and the Stars*. In 1928, the Abbey rejected *The Silver Tassie*, leading to a bitter split between O'Casey and the theater. The play premiered the following year at the Apollo Theatre in London. Controversy constantly followed O'Casey's work. *Within the Gates*, which premiered in New York (1934), was banned in Boston in 1935. A self-professed Communist, O'Casey became a member of the advisory board for the *Daily Worker* in 1940—although he never officially joined the **Communist Party**—and published *The Star Turns Red* that same year. *The Green Crow* (1956)—a collection of essays—was seized by Irish customs in 1957 and unofficially banned. His play *The Drums of Father Ned* (1957) was accepted by the Dublin Tostal Council for their 1958 International Festival but was withdrawn after the archbishop of Dublin objected to the play. As a result, O'Casey banned the performance of all of his plays in Ireland, a ban he eventually lifted in 1964.

O'Casey's early plays were realistic portrayals of Dublin tenement life. His later plays would move away from the realistic style in an effort to tackle, more symbolically, the two forces—which, for O'Casey, often merged into one—that oppressed Ireland, namely capitalism and the Catholic Church. His anticlericalism, a constant source of resentment in Ireland, stemmed from his belief that the church encouraged the working class to accept existing working conditions, blunting any desire for real social change. O'Casey published six volumes of autobiography, beginning with *I Knock at the Door* (1939) and ending with *Sunset and Evening Star* (1954).

Selected Bibliography: Hunt, Hugh. *Sean O'Casey.* Dublin: Gill and Macmillan, 1998; Krause, David. *Sean O'Casey: The Man and His Work.* New York: Macmillan, 1960; Krause, David, and Robert G. Lowery, eds. *Sean O'Casey: Centenary Essays.* Totowa, NJ: Barnes and Noble, 1980; McDonald, Ronan. *Tragedy and Irish Literature: Synge, O'Casey, Beckett.* New York: Palgrave, 2002; O'Connor, Garry. *Sean O'Casey: A Life.* New York: Atheneum, 1988.

Steve Cloutier

ODETS, CLIFFORD (1906–1963). Born in Philadelphia and raised in New York, Odets made an indelible mark on the American dramatic landscape. His plays summed up the spirit of the Depression era and gave dramatic resonance to its dilemmas of class struggle and political upheaval. His career peaked in 1935, when four of his plays were produced on Broadway: *Awake and Sing! Till the Day I Die, Paradise Lost,* and the archetypal piece of agitprop, *Waiting for Lefty*—his best-known play.

Odets found his way to playwriting through acting. Working in small companies in New York and Philadelphia, Odets became interested in writing for radio and completed two radio plays, *Dawn* and *At the Waterline,* between 1925 and 1927. In 1931, Odets joined the Group Theatre, where he came under the influence of John Howard Lawson, a successful communist playwright who influenced Odets to look for his material in the working-class experience and the ethnic Jewish American neighborhoods that he knew so well.

Odets succeeded in translating the vital street energy and household language of the working class to the stage for the first time outside the Yiddish theater tradition. When *Waiting for Lefty* opened to tumultuous audience approval on January 5, 1935, the New York theater world woke up to learn that a new playwright of the proletariat was blooming in their midst. Ending in a rousing call for "strike" and filled with topical allusions to the labor struggles of the tabloids, the new drama filled a political need and challenged old dramatic formulas. It not only seemed to speak for an emerging and empowered American working class, but also launched a new dramatic structure. Such playwrights as Eugene O'Neill, **Samuel Beckett**, Jack Gelber, **Harold Pinter**, and August Wilson would copy the dramatic situation of characters waiting for something or someone that might or might not appear.

A handsome and vital man, Odets was lionized as a kind of embodiment of the socialist life force. In such plays as *Golden Boy* (1938), and *Rocket to the Moon* (1938), he found riveting dramatic analogues for a powerful critique of the stifling impact of capitalism and profit seeking on human potential. Odets sought inspiration in the dynamic Americanism of **Walt Whitman**'s poetry, and he dramatized that egalitarian promise for all citizens. Deploring elitism, Odets was drawn to the mass media of the movies and went to Hollywood to pursue a career in film.

Golden Boy was made into a successful film in 1939. Working as a script doctor, Odets anonymously improved many scripts, including Alfred Hitchcock's *Notorious* (1946). Some of his own best-known movie scripts are *None But the Lonely Heart* (1944), *Deadline at Dawn* (1946), *Humoresque* (1947), and *The Sweet Smell of Suc-*

cess (1957). In his Hollywood years, he also completed two significant plays—*The Big Knife* (1948) and *The Country Girl* (1950)—which were made into successful films in the 1950s.

Odets remained ambivalent about his own success in Hollywood, and his career was further complicated when he appeared as a friendly witness before the House Un-American Activities Committee in 1952. However, Odets's great achievement remains unmarred by his later defection. What he dramatized in his work was the impact of class struggle on the daily lives of Americans, and what he dared to show on stage for the first time was the slangy, quirky idiom of working-class American speech and the unquenchable vitality and high democratic aspirations of the American dreamers that populate all his plays.

Selected Bibliography: Benman-Gibson, Margaret. *Clifford Odets, American Playwright.* New York: Atheneum, 1982; Weales, Gerald. *Odets the Playwright.* London: Methuen, 1985.

Norma Jenckes

OHMANN, RICHARD (1931–). It would be hard to overemphasize the influence of Richard Ohmann on the left in the field of English, and especially on the generation of scholars and teachers who were graduate students in the 1960s and 1970s. His first book, *Shaw: The Style and the Man* (1962), is a study in linguistic stylistics that suggests the breadth of his interests; Ohmann has also remarked that it was Shaw's arguments that made him a socialist. Educated at Oberlin and Harvard, Ohmann spent his entire career at Wesleyan University, where he was for a time a vice provost. He was also editor of the influential journal *College English* from 1967 to 1975. Best described in his mature work as a **Gramsci**an Marxist, Ohmann's writing is almost unique for its combination of theoretical sophistication and clarity of style. Among major figures on the left, only **Terry Eagleton** and **Raymond Williams** come to mind as his peers in this regard.

It was *English in America: A Radical View of the Profession* (1976) that established Ohmann's reputation. *English in America* codified many of the insights of the radicals of the 1960s in English studies. It is irreverent toward many of the values, rituals, and contradictions of English, such as publication (Ohmann points out that one of the main problems is that the profession placed too much value on publication and not enough on teaching, and that published work should focus on theoretical or other issues of broad concern in the field, and not just on narrow specialization); the relation of **composition studies** to literature (Ohmann argues that composition was more central to the role of the English department than literary studies, although literature is given much higher prestige); and the relation of English studies to society (although many in English professed liberal and even left-wing values, the practices of English studies helped sort students in ways that reaffirmed their class position, and the way composition was taught tended to acclimatize students to writing in the vast bureaucratic institutions of corporate capitalism). *English in America* is an important contribution to social-reproduction theory, which analyzes the ways in which the U.S. educational system and other social institutions reproduce the inequality of U.S. society.

Ohmann's contribution to the understanding of **English studies and politics** has continued in other important books, including *Politics and Letters* (1988) and *The Politics of Knowledge* (2003). In these works, especially the latter, Ohmann points out that the English profession, like others in the United States, grew with the development of industrial capitalism to both serve society and protect the interests of professionals. English professors may have radical beliefs, but they often act as *professionals* in a profession that reinforces social inequality, and—like other professions—English studies is in decline as a new form of global capitalism develops. In *Politics and Letters*, Ohmann also began to write about the politics of mass culture and the development of the professional-managerial class in the late nineteenth century, as advertising and mass-marketed consumer magazines developed. This analysis is further developed in *Selling Culture: Magazines, Markets, and Class at the Turn of the Century* (1996), a major work in the study of mass culture.

Selected Bibliography: Ohmann, Richard. *English in America: A Radical View of the Profession.* New York: Oxford UP, 1976; Ohmann, Richard. *Politics and Letters.* Middletown, CT: Wesleyan UP, 1988; Ohmann, Richard. *The Politics of Knowledge: The Commercialization of the University, the Professions, and Print Culture.* Middletown, CT: Wesleyan UP, 2003; Ohmann, Richard. *Selling Culture: Magazines, Markets, and Class at the Turn of the Century.* London: Verso, 1996; Ohmann, Richard. *Shaw: The Style and the Man.* Middletown, CT: Wesleyan UP, 1962.

Raymond A. Mazurek

OLSEN, TILLIE (ca. 1912–), U.S. fiction writer, poet, literary critic, and theorist. The daughter of Russian immigrants who participated in the 1905 revolution and later became Socialist Party members in the United States, Olsen first published as a member of the Young Communist League during the Great Depression. During the 1940s and 1950s, Olsen was largely occupied with raising a family, working, and engaging in political activism and did not publish again until the late 1950s. In 1961, she published *Tell Me a Riddle*—a collection of short stories whose title novella won the First Prize O Henry Award, and whose stories are often anthologized. In 1978, Olsen published a highly influential collection of Marxist-feminist literary critical and theoretical writings entitled *Silences*.

Olsen published her first story, "Iron-Throat," in the ***Partisan Review***—then the literary magazine of the **Communist Party**–led New York **John Reed Club**—in 1934. The story instantly established her as one of the more talented proletarian writers of the 1930s. It was drawn from a novel-in-progress entitled *Yonnondio*, which she later published incomplete in 1974, and which is now considered a classic of **proletarian literature**. Both "Iron-Throat," whose title refers to a coal mine that swallows miners' lives, and the novel present powerful narratives that center on an American migrant family, the Holbrooks, who move from city to farm in search of non-exploitative work and stable family life. Olsen's depiction registers the brutalizing effects of economic exploitation and patriarchal ideology on an American working-class family. Yet it equally documents the irrepressible desire of working people to resist their brutalization in a spontaneous manner. To compensate for the historically specific lack of political education of her characters (the novel is set in the 1920s and in the absence of a visible left-lead labor movement), Olsen weaves throughout the text a socialist authorial voice that places the Holbrooks' lives in perspective and imagines the day when a united working class could "wipe out" capitalism and "a human could be a human for the first time on earth" (64).

Tell Me a Riddle is Olsen's second major work to depict working-class people in the grips of the repressive social and economic forces of capitalism. Olsen sets the stories in mid-century America and specifically in suburban locales ringed by **cold-war** conformity and nuclear fears. Many of her characters, and several who traverse the stories, participated in revolutionary struggles in either pre-Soviet Russia or Depression-era America, and now find themselves living in tension with the present and feeling politically isolated. The stories movingly address both the loss of and desire for mass movements of progressive change, and for "*that joyous certainty, that sense of mattering, of moving and being moved, of being one and indivisible with the great of the past, with all that freed, ennobled*" ("Tell Me a Riddle" 113). Like *Yonnondio, Tell Me a Riddle* is particularly sensitive to the lives of working-class women and mothers who struggle with the weight of household labor, child rearing, and sometimes wage labor, and who want so much more out of life—and not only for themselves.

Olsen's last major work, *Silences*, helped establish her as a foremost contemporary Marxist and feminist literary critic and theorist. As the title suggests, Olsen is mainly concerned with the silences of writers and of literary history itself due to unfavorable social circumstances that confront working-class and female writers. The book encapsulates her lifelong commitment of giving voice to the voiceless and of making visible what she called "the not yet in the now"—glimmers of the human capacity for creating a world based on egalitarianism and compassion.

Selected Bibliography: Coiner, Constance. *Better Red: The Writing and Resistance of Tillie Olsen and Meridel LeSueur*. New York: Oxford UP, 1995; Dawahare, Anthony. "'That Joyous Certainty': History and Utopia in Tillie Olsen's Depression-Era Literature." *Twentieth Century Literature* 44.3 (Fall 1998): 261–75; Rosenfelt, Deborah. "From the Thirties: Tillie Olsen and the Radical Tradition." *Feminist Studies* 7 (Fall 1981): 371–406; Staub, Michael E. *Voices of Persuasion: Politics of Representation in 1930s America*. New York: Cambridge UP, 1994.

Anthony Dawahare

ONDAATJE, PHILIP MICHAEL (1943–). Poet, novelist, filmmaker, scholar, Michael Ondaatje produces literary work distinctive for its powerfully poetic engagement—via a range of experimental and generic forms—with suppressed or forgotten histories. "Never again will a single story be told as though it were the only one," reads an epigraph (quoting the leftist writer John Berger) to his first novel, *In the Skin of a Lion* (1987), about the growth of a metropolis as an immigrant community with multiple histories and collective political struggles. These concerns underlie his Booker Prize–winning novel set in wartime Europe and Africa, *The English Patient* (1992), whose title character pastes documents of his own enigmatic life into the pages of Herodotus' histories, and whose Indian character, Kip, has been read as a figure of imperialist critique. Violent social conflict again provides the setting for the novel *Anil's Ghost* (2000), in which a foreign forensic scientist is paired with an anthropologist to investigate the corpses—ancient and contemporary—unearthed in war-torn Sri Lanka.

Ondaatje himself was born in Sri Lanka, but moved to London in 1954 and on to Canada in 1962. In addition to his novels, he has produced an important body of poetry. Two of Ondaatje's earlier long poems (which include prose and illustration) explore the social laws and perceptual norms that condemn but fail to capture individual lives: those of the exterminated outlaw Billy the Kid, in *The Collected Works of Billy the Kid* (1970), and the institutionalized jazz musician Billy Bolden, in *Coming Through Slaughter* (1976). The more recent *Handwriting* (1998) complements *Anil's Ghost* as a more personal excavation of Sri Lankan history in the form of lyric sequences.

Selected Bibliography: Jewinski, Ed. *Michael Ondaatje: Express Yourself Beautifully*. Toronto: ECW Press, 1994; Smythe, Karen, ed. Special Michael Ondaatje issue of *Essays on Canadian Writing* 53 (Summer 1994).

Glenn Willmott

OODGEROO (1920–1993). Publishing her work initially under the name Kath Walker, indigenous Australian poet Oodgeroo of the Noonuccal tribe adopted her new name, meaning "paperbark tree," as a protest again the celebration in 1988 of the bicentenary of the European occupation of Australia. Born on Stradbroke Island, near Brisbane, Queensland, she received little formal education, becoming a domestic servant—then the usual fate of Aboriginal and mixed-race girls—at the age of thirteen. During **World War II**, she served in the Australian Army and, in 1942, married a childhood friend, Bruce Walker. In the 1960s, she became heavily involved in the civil rights and Aboriginal activist movements that led to the 1967 referendum through which indigenous Australians were granted full citizenship rights for the first time. She also took a leading role in many organizations, such as the National Tribal Council, the Aboriginal Arts Board, and the Aboriginal Advancement League.

Oodgeroo's groundbreaking collection of poems, *We Are Going* (1964), inaugurated the contemporary phase of Aboriginal literature and was a best-seller, although dismissed by many white critics at the time as "mere protest writing." The title poem, which has been the most widely anthologized, laments the destruction of indigenous culture since 1788, but others call Aboriginal people to action or angrily address the white oppressors. Oodgeroo's use of traditional verse forms and simple but highly emotive language made her poems readily accessible to readers. Later collections include *The Dawn Is at Hand* (1966) and *My People* (1970). Also a pioneer in Aboriginal education, Oodgeroo devoted her later years to making traditional cultures better known to both Aboriginal and non-Aboriginal children by setting up educational camps, and by writing and illustrating children's books, including *Father Sky and Mother Earth* (1981) and *Australian Legends and Landscapes* (1990).

Selected Bibliography: Mudrooroo. *Writing from the Fringe: A Study of Modern Aboriginal Literature*. Melbourne, Victoria: Hyland House, 1990; Oodgeroo. *Stradbroke Dreamtime*. Sydney: Angus and Robertson, 1972; Shoemaker, Adam, ed. *Oodgeroo: A Tribute*. St. Lucia: U of Queensland P, 1994; Van

Toorn, Penny. "Indigenous Texts and Narratives." *The Cambridge Companion to Australian Literature.* Ed. Elizabeth Webby. Cambridge: Cambridge UP, 2000. 19–49.

Elizabeth Webby

ORIENTALISM (1978). Edward Said's groundbreaking theoretical text, *Orientalism* has shaped and defined **postcolonial studies** unlike any other. Using the works of Vico, **Gramsci**, and **Foucault**, Said shows in *Orientalism* how a variety of discourses developed in post-Enlightenment Europe to represent the Orient. These discourses created a vast body of knowledge, generated key cultural texts, and authorized an image of the Orient. While the objective of Orientalism was to complement imperialism, it in fact served and continues to serve a more basic need: that of fashioning a self-image for Western civilization. The identity that Orientalism constructs for the West derives from the notion that the Orient is its "other" and that the Orient possesses qualities that oppose Western culture. The Orient, in this equation, is passive, feminine, childlike, lascivious, and mute—qualities contrasting the values and dynamics of Western civilization. An additional quality, the Orient's inability to express itself, permits Orientalist discourse to appropriate the moral authority to speak for the Orient.

Said's study is well researched and establishes its thesis through an enumeration of historical and cultural texts. Orientalist discursive formations, Said demonstrates, have led to the growth of a number of humanistic disciplines ("discourses of power"), such as literature, history, linguistics, anthropology, and archaeology—all of which fed Western imperialism in the nineteenth and early twentieth centuries. In two later works, *The World, the Text, the Critic* (1983) and *Culture and Imperialism* (1993), Said develops his exposé of Orientalism further, clarifying the role of the humanistic scholar in modern times and illustrating subtle links between Orientalism, imperialism, and well-known literary works. Meanwhile, Western domination of many non-Western regions of the world continues politically, economically, militarily, and culturally, making Said's work as relevant and important as ever.

Without doubt, *Orientalism* has turned out to be a primary theoretical text in postcolonial studies, rivaled in importance only by **Frantz Fanon**'s *The Wretched of the Earth* as a founding text in the field. Using Said's insight, scholars have examined similar discourses about other regions of the world. For instance, Christopher Miller explores representations of Africa or the "Africanist" discourse in *Blank Darkness: Africanist Discourse in French* (1985), while Ronald Inden probes into "Indology"—the genre of Orientalism dealing specifically with India—in *Imagining India* (2001).

Said is not without his detractors, however. Some scholars have pointed out that he grants the Orientalist discourse a totalizing power that ignores all oppositional voices. Others have pointed out that he overstates Orientalism's romanticizing of the Orient. Said's lack of interest in the gender aspects of Orientalism concerns some feminists. A harsh reproach of Said, interestingly enough, comes from non-Western scholars who accuse him of being rooted too much in the Western humanistic tradition.

Regardless of the censures it draws, Said's critique of the Orientalist discourse remains an indispensable text at the center of postcolonial studies, a field that has been crucially shaped by its engagement with Said's work. Said's theory allows scholars to approach the complexities of contemporary literary study with sophisticated theoretical self-awareness, and enables them to do so with a broader view of the making of global culture.

Selected Bibliography: Ansell-Pearson, Keith, et al., eds. *Cultural Readings of Imperialism: Edward Said and the Gravity of History*. New York: St. Martin's, 1997; Ashcroft, Bill, and Pal Ahluwalia. *Edward Said: The Paradox of Identity*. New York: Routledge, 1999; Bové, Paul A., ed. *Edward Said and the Work of the Critic: Speaking Truth to Power*. Durham, NC: Duke UP, 2000; Kennedy, Valerie. *Edward Said: A Critical Introduction*. Malden, MA: Polity, 2000; Sprinker, Michael, ed. *Edward Said: A Critical Reader*. Oxford and Cambridge: Blackwell, 1992.

Farhad B. Idris

ORWELL, GEORGE (1903–1950). In his 1946 essay "Why I Write," George Orwell reflected, "What I have most wanted to do throughout the past ten years is to make political writing into an art." In that same essay, he also noted, "Every line of serious work that I have written since 1936 has been written, directly or indirectly, *against* totalitarianism and *for* democratic Socialism, as I understand it." These two statements define his importance for **British working-class and socialist literature** and twentieth-century English literature more generally. Most famous for his last, immensely influential works—the satire *Animal Farm* (1945) and dystopia *Nineteen Eighty-Four* (1949), which made him the darling of the new, anti-Soviet cold warriors—Orwell is remembered most fondly by leftists for his 1930s documentaries of working-class life and his protest novels. He is also celebrated for his delightful essays on popular culture, including "Boys' Weeklies," "Good Bad Books," and "Raffles and Miss Blandish," which form early contributions to **cultural studies**.

Orwell was born (as Eric Arthur Blair) in Motihari, India, into an Anglo-Indian family with ties to the Far East that extended several generations. He grew up with his mother and two sisters in what he famously described as a "lower upper middle class" household. His father, a minor official in the Opium Department, remained for seven years in India while the rest of the family lived in the charming English town of Henley-on-Thames. At age eight, Orwell was sent on scholarship to St. Cyprian's School, where he was successfully crammed for a scholarship to Eton, but was so traumatized by the experience that his memoir of his prep-school days, "Such, Such Were the Joys" (1953), could only be published after his death due to fears of libel.

Orwell's years at Eton were unexceptional, politically and academically, and at their end, he chose to go into the Indian Imperial Police. At age nineteen, he arrived in Mandalay and then Mulmein, Burma, where the routine work of upholding "the machinery of despotism" transformed him into a fierce opponent of British colonialism. He retired from the service after five years, much to the dismay of his family, and began the series of domestic adventures that led to the publication of his first major work, *Down and Out in Paris and London* (1933), a documentary of his journeys into the underworlds of Parisian slums and English lodging houses. *Burmese Days* (1934), a bitter satire of British imperialism, followed quickly.

In 1936, the editors of the Left Book Club commissioned Orwell to write an account of unemployment in the distressed areas of the industrial North. The result was *The Road to Wigan Pier* (1937), half powerful documentary of working and living conditions of Wigan's miners, half blistering critique of socialism and the "cranks" that supported it. Before leftists had time to digest Orwell's diatribe in *Wigan Pier* against English Socialists, Orwell had left England to fight Fascists in the **Spanish Civil War**. Exhilarated by the egalitarian society that greeted him in Barcelona, where his equally committed wife, Eileen O'Shaughnessy, joined him, he fought bravely on the Aragon front, leading a group of P.O.U.M. (*Partido Obrero de Unificación Marxista*) anarchists until being shot through the throat. He heroically returned to service only to find that all the members of his division were in danger of capture, torture, and execution by their one-time allies, the Communists. His book *Homage to Catalonia* (1938) is a piercing, partisan account of what Orwell experienced as a Soviet betrayal of the anarchists and republicans in Spain.

His novels of the late 1930s, *Keep the Aspidistra Flying* (1936) and *Coming Up for Air* (1939), are humorous, somewhat despairing protests against capitalist development in England. Although Orwell still called himself a Socialist, only at the extraordinary moment of national unity inspired by Dunkirk could he bring himself to advocate radical political change, arguing in *The Lion and the Unicorn* (1941) that war would facilitate a socialist "bloodless revolution."

Rejected from military service because of the lung disease that would eventually kill him, Orwell spent the years of **World War II** in London, working as a talks producer for the BBC. He resigned from that job, frustrated with censorship originating with the Ministry of Information, and plunged into journalism full time. His regular "London Letter" to the American *Partisan Review* extended his influence, as did his "As I Please" columns for the leftist weekly *Tribune*, for which he worked as literary editor. During these same years, he crafted *Animal Farm*, though publication was delayed because he could not find a sympathetic editor. It was eventually published in 1945 by the leftist Frederick Warburg, who anticipated that the book would be interpreted as an attack on Socialists everywhere, but understood the power of the fable and the necessity of its publication.

Animal Farm became an international sensation, and financed Orwell's retreat to the Hebrides island he had often fantasized about. Now a widower, Orwell wrote most of his last, most famous book, *Nineteen Eighty-Four*, on Jura, amid conditions that some of his friends considered suicidal. Published by Warburg in 1949, it made Orwell wealthy. Yet wealth came too late, since Orwell's failing lungs required him to exchange his remote island for a bed in London University Hospital. There Orwell suffered uncomplainingly, his life enlivened only by visits from friends and his courtship of Sonia Brownell, whom he married three months before he died.

Orwell's legacy is, from the perspective of English Socialists, a mixed one; intellectuals on the right and left have tried to lay claim to his reputation as England's and America's most "honest," "decent," "plain-speaking" political writer, creating in the process an "Orwell myth" that continues to serve politicians as much as it frustrates literary critics and historians. Undisputed is Orwell's extraordinary impact on postwar Anglo-American political and popular culture through sales of his last two novels, which have sold more copies worldwide than any other pair of books by any other literary or popular postwar author.

Selected Bibliography: Crick, Bernard. *George Orwell: A Life.* Boston: Little, Brown, 1980; Norris, Christopher, ed. *Inside the Myth: Orwell, Views from the Left.* London: Lawrence and Wishart, 1984; Patai, Daphne. *The Orwell Mystique: A Study in Male Ideology.* Amherst: U of Massachusetts P, 1984; Rodden, John. *The Politics of Literary Reputation: The Making and Claiming of "St. George" Orwell.* New York: Oxford UP, 1989.

Kristin Bluemel

OSOFISAN, FEMI (1946–). Nigerian writer, cultural analyst, and political commentator. Osofisan has repeatedly defined himself *vis à vis* writers of earlier generations, emerging as a man of the left, committed to writing and producing challenging plays (in English) for, essentially, campus audiences. His work shows his anxiety to encourage an understanding of society and to foster a recognition that it can be changed.

Born at Erunwon, Ogun State, in 1946, Osofisan was brought up by his widowed mother, a teacher. He traced a distinguished path through the elite Government College, Ibadan (1959–1963), to the well-established University of Ibadan (1966–1969). As an undergraduate student of French, he spent some time in Dakar (1968–1969) and, after graduation and some postgraduate work, attended the Université de Paris III (1972–1973) before returning to Nigeria to teach French at the University of Ibadan and to complete a doctorate on "The Origins of Drama in West Africa" (1974). Studies were combined with acting, directing, and writing. These activities, together with an academic career, running a theater group, directing outside Nigeria, establishing a publishing house, and being, for a period, responsible for the Nigerian National Theatre, have occupied much of Osofisan's time during the last thirty years.

Osofisan was a member of the editorial collective responsible for the "nonsectarian and undogmatic" publication *Positive Review* (first published in Ife, 1978). He shares the collective's commitment to "socialism with a human face" and to "the autonomous self-development of Africa." While recognizing the existence of classes and class antagonisms among other divisive forces, the collective was positive and progressive in aspiring to transcend divisions.

Though important as a poet (writing as Okinba Launko), essayist, and teacher, Osofisan most deserves attention as a political playwright who has written for stage, television, and radio. In more than forty plays and in numerous productions he has explored a wide variety of theatrical traditions. While drawing on Yoruba musical, narrative, poetic, and "dilemma" traditions, his work also has elements in common with those of **Bertolt Brecht**, Antonin Artaud, Augusto Boal, and recent advocates of participatory theater for development. Osofisan has written about major African politicians, including **Nkrumah** and Cabral, and has tackled pressing continental issues, such as the massacre in Rwanda, in theatrical terms.

While he sometimes works in traditions familiar to Europe—for example, *Who's Afraid of Tai Solarin?* (after Gorky, 1978), *Midnight Hotel* ("after Feydeau through Brecht," 1986), *The Inspector and the Hero* (a detective drama for television, published in 1990), and *The Engagement* (an adaptation of Chekhov's *Proposal*, 1995), there are also more challenging engagements with Nigerian society and traditions. *Once Upon Four Robbers* (1978), for example, uses folk motifs, incorporates an audience discussion, offers the audience a chance to vote, and provides alternative endings, thus illustrating the playwright's interest in open-ended, interactive conventions. It would be inadequate to assess his contribution without taking into account other major concerns, including his engagement with history (*Morountodun*, 1979) and the issues he has confronted in his many closely argued addresses and papers.

In *No More the Wasted Breed* (1980) and other work, Osofisan has engaged with older Nigerian authors, particularly **Wole Soyinka**. In contrast with Soyinka, he advocates a group response, a class-aware analysis, a focused program promoting social change, an articulate subversion of religion, a radicalization of history, a positive approach to the characterization of the masses and women, and a determination to move plays toward positive conclusions.

Selected Bibliography: Awodiya, Muyiwa P., ed. *Excursions in Drama and Literature: Interviews with Femi Osofisan*. Ibadan: Kraft Books, 1993; Griffiths, Gareth. "Femi Osofisan." *African Writers*. Ed. C. Brian Cox. New York: Scribner's, 1997. 619–29; Richards, Sandra L. *Ancient Songs Set Ablaze: The Theatre of Femi Osofisan*. Washington, DC: Howard UP, 1996.

James Gibbs

OSTROVSKY, NIKOLAI ALEKSEEVICH (1904–1936) was an icon of the socialist literary establishment, both in the Soviet Union and in other socialist countries. To many growing up in a socialist country, his life and his only completed novel—*Kak zakal'als Stal* (**How the Steel Was Tempered**, 1932–1934)—were symbols of the struggles, hardships, and sacrifice people in the Soviet Union had to endure in order to create a socialist society where workers could have decent lives. The largely autobiographical *How the Steel Was Tempered* is one of the best examples of **socialist realism**. Ostrovsky's second novel, *Rozhdennye burei* (*Born of the Storm,* begun in 1936), was left unfinished.

Ostrovsky was born in western Ukraine in a family of laborers. His formal education ended at age twelve, when he was expelled from elementary school by his scriptures teacher. From 1915 to 1919, he worked at various manual jobs, as an assistant stoker, a kitchen aid, a timber-yard worker, an assistant electrician, and so on. During the **Russian Revolution**, he was a courier for the local Bolshevik underground. In 1919, he joined the Komsomol and volunteered for the Red Army, where he served in the famous Kotovsky cavalry brigade. He was twice badly wounded and eventually demobilized on medical grounds. In 1921, he went to work in a railroad workshop in Kiev and focused on political work among the workers.

In 1922, while participating in railroad construction crucial for the region, he contracted typhus and rheumatism. Upon recovery, he was declared an invalid and was unable to do any manual labor. He was then appointed commissar of the Red Army's Battalion "Berezdov" and was sent to the border region to work on political propaganda. He joined the **Communist Party** in 1924. As his health continued to deteriorate, he was sent to a sanatorium in Crimea. From then on, Ostrovsky spent much of his life in hospitals and sanatoriums. In 1926, after a serious attack of polyarthritis, he became almost completely paralyzed; in 1929, his illness affected his vision and he went blind.

Despite such serious health problems, Ostrovsky always remained determined to be a productive member of Soviet society. He put all his energies into political work: he lead Marxist discussion circles, educated young party members, contributed to newspapers and journals, spoke on the radio. In 1929, he finished a correspondence course at the Sverdlov Communist University in Moscow and began working on *How the Steel Was Tempered*, which became one of the most popular Soviet novels of all time. In 1934, he became a member of the Union of Soviet Writers. That same year, he was awarded the Order of Lenin. He was thirty-two when he died in 1936.

Selected Bibliography: Luker, Nicholas. *From Furmanov to Sholokhov.* Ann Arbor, MI: Ardis, 1988; *Sovetskii Entsiklopediiski Slovar.* Moscow: Sovetskaia Entsiklopedia, 1989.

Dubravka Juraga

OWEN, WILFRED (1893–1918). Born in the remote country town of Shrewsbury, England, and raised within a devout Evangelical family, Owen ultimately became one of the best-known and best-loved poets of **World War I**. In October 1915, he enlisted with the Artist's Rifles, but quickly lost faith in the war cause; after months of continual shelling and then experiencing a nervous breakdown, he began to compose highly critical poems of the war and its effects on the human spirit. Written primarily over a period of fourteen months, while Owen recuperated at the Craiglockheart War Hospital in Edinburgh, his poetry is notable for its hallucinatory depictions of trench life and man-to-man combat; it combines horrific details of the experience of battle with a lyrical expressionism and a mastery of poetic devices (alliteration, assonance, half-rhyme, and pararhyme).

Owen's early life was defined by a series of influences and infatuations that, taken together, perhaps explain his initial attraction to war as well as his success as a war poet. First, his domineering mother preached the sins of the flesh and the need for painful acts of purification. As a teenager, Owen discovered the romantic poets and replaced the idea of a suffering Christ with the image of the suffering artist. Finally, from October 1911 to February 1913, Owen worked as a lay assistant to a local vicar, and his duties included visits to the sick and poor. His letters outline a growing infatuation with these figures, an odd blend of pity and fascination with the scarred and maimed lads of the countryside. Throughout, Owen's youth was also shaped by a strong if inchoate homoeroticism. His rather guilty desire was at once encouraged and sustained by a semiliterary cult of suffering and thus readily provided the terms for his intense poetic descriptions of masculine combat.

Owen's complex youth also inspired a budding if vague feeling toward socialism. His political sentiments tended toward the humanistic and the fraternal, an almost simple outrage against hypocrisy, inequality, and oppression. Mostly, though, his politics were shaped by a strong fascination with suffering and a persistently erotic attention to the wounded male body. Ultimately, his best poetry is at once condemnatory and fascinated, attuned to both the horror and the thrill of war. Often, it dwells on hauntingly romantic images of blinded eyes, torn limbs, and dead mouths; he writes best about young lads charged by battle and the lifeless, beautiful corpses strewn across the battlefield.

Owen died only a week before the armistice and remained unknown as a poet until **Siegfried Sassoon** published a volume of his verse in 1920. Since then, he has held a firm place in the British literary canon as a poet of originality, social commitment, and national pride.

Selected Bibliography: Caesar, Adrian Caesar. *Taking It Like a Man: Suffering, Sexuality and the War Poets.* Manchester: Manchester UP, 1993; Fussell, Paul. *The Great War and Modern Memory.* New York: Oxford UP, 1975; Hibberd, Dominic. *Owen the Poet.* Athens: U of Georgia P, 1986; Owen, Harold. *Journey from Obscurity: Memoirs of the Owen Family.* Vol. 1. London: Oxford UP, 1963; Owen, Wilfred. *Collected Letters.* Ed. Harold Owen and John Bell. London: Oxford UP, 1967.

Ed Comentale

P

PADMORE, GEORGE (ca. 1901–1959). One of the most influential and important Pan-African intellectuals of the twentieth century, Padmore was born Malcolm Ivan Meredith Nurse in Trinidad in either 1901 or 1902 (his date of birth is a matter of debate). In 1924, he left Trinidad to study medicine—and later law—at Fisk University in Nashville, Tennessee. He became actively involved in the **Communist Party**, attracted by the resources communism seemed to promise for realizing decolonization in the Caribbean and Africa. After changing his name to George Padmore, he traveled to the Soviet Union in 1929 and became head of the Negro Bureau of the Red International of Labor Unions; in 1930, he was responsible for organizing the first International Conference of Negro Workers. His first book, *The Life and Struggle of Negro Toilers* (1931), would prove inspirational to a growing number of anticolonial intellectuals in the colonized world.

By 1931, Padmore had settled in Hamburg and was editor of the *Negro Worker*, yet his relations with the Communist Party became strained; in 1933, the Soviet Union dissolved the International Trade Union Committee of Negro Workers, much to Padmore's disgust, and his subsequent resignation from his positions of responsibility led to his formal expulsion from the party on February 24, 1934, for "petty bourgeois nationalist deviation." He relocated to London in 1935 and set about continuing his anticolonial activities. Here he met and worked with a number of important African and Caribbean intellectuals and radicals, including **C.L.R. James** (a boyhood friend), Ras Makonnen, Jomo Kenyatta, and I.T.A. Wallace-Johnson. The networks of influence Padmore helped create among these remarkable figures would centrally impact the struggle for political independence in Africa and elsewhere in the colonized world. Following the Italian invasion of Abyssinia in 1935, Padmore joined the International Friends of Abyssinia (renamed in 1937 the International African Service Bureau), where he encountered Kenyatta, Amy Ashwood Garvey, and Sam Manning. Padmore was soon a key figure in the burgeoning Pan-African movement forged in London during the 1930s, writing for a number of radical publications, such as the *New Leader* and the *Socialist Leader*. During this time, he wrote two important texts vital to the cause of Pan-Africanism: *How Britain Rules Africa* (1936) and *Africa and World Peace* (1937). He also worked closely with Britain's Independent Labour Party (ILP).

In 1944, Padmore founded the Pan-African Federation, and in October 1945 was closely involved in the Sixth Pan-African Congress in Manchester, England, which brought together Kenyatta, **W.E.B. Du Bois**, **Kwame Nkrumah**, and Hastings Banda. In 1956, he published *Pan-Africanism or Communism?* a major work in the political evolution of Pan-African politics. Padmore worked closely with Nkrumah and became his personal representative in London leading up to Ghanaian independence in 1957. He later worked as Nkrumah's personal advisor for African affairs. Padmore died of a liver complaint in London in 1959; it is a sign of his centrality to the struggle for decolonization in Africa that Nkrumah requested Padmore's ashes to be scattered in Accra.

Selected Bibliography: Geiss, Imanuel. *The Pan-African Movement.* Trans. Ann Keep. London: Methuen, 1974; Hooker, James T. *Black Revolutionary: George Padmore's Path from Communism to Pan-Africanism.* London: Mall P, 1967; James, C.L.R. "George Padmore: Black Revolutionary." *At the Rendezvous of Victory: Selected Writings.* Vol. 3. London: Allison and Busby, 1984. 251–63; McLeod, John. "A Night at 'the Cosmopolitan': Axes of Transnational Encounter in the 1930s and 1940s." *Interventions: International Journal of Postcolonial Studies* 4.1 (2002): 53–67; Padmore, George. *How Britain Rules Africa.* London: Wishart Books, 1936; Padmore, George. *The Life and Struggles of Negro Toilers.* London: International Council of Trade and Industrial Unions, 1931; Padmore, George. *Pan-Africanism or Communism? The Coming Struggle for Africa.* London: Dennis Dobson, 1956; Schwarz, Bill. "George Padmore." *West Indian Intellectuals in Britain.* Ed. Bill Schwarz. Manchester: Manchester UP, 2004. 132–52.

John McLeod

PAGE, MYRA (1897–1993). Born Dorothy Page Gary in Newport News, Virginia, to middle-class, progressive parents, Myra Page early developed an antiracist consciousness and chafed against the restrictions imposed on her as a southern white woman. In 1925, she initiated her lifelong membership in the **Communist Party**; by the late 1920s, she had married fellow leftist John Markey and obtained M.A. and Ph.D. degrees in sociology. As a journalist, Page wrote for *Southern Workman*, *Working Woman*, the ***Daily Worker***, and *Soviet Russia Today*. She taught classes at the League of American Writers and at the Highlander Folk School in Tennessee. Page is best known for her three novels. *Gathering Storm: A Story of the Black Belt* (1932) chronicles the development of class consciousness among sharecroppers turned proletarian, culminating in the **Gastonia Mill Strike** of 1929. Somewhat mechanical in structure and style, the novel nonetheless testifies to Page's appreciation of the key roles played by women and African Americans in southern class struggles. It is one of very few proletarian novels in which the "black-belt thesis" makes an appearance. *Daughter of the Hills* (1977; first published as *Sun in Our Blood* in 1950) is based on Page's extensive interviews with a coal miner's widow, Dolly Hawkins, whose loyalties and ambivalences are effectively captured in the novel's first-person narrative.

Moscow Yankee (1935), Page's most significant novel, draws on her experiences in the Soviet Union during the first Five-Year Plan. Focusing on Frank Anderson (Andy), an unemployed Detroit autoworker who goes to Moscow for work, the novel follows his gradual abandonment of procapitalist illusions and (partly through his attachment to a winsome young Bolshevik co-worker) his growing commitment to the young Soviet society. The love plot is paralleled by a factory plot in which key issues about socialist production—labor, efficiency, incentives, and wages—are raised. Although Page's pro-Soviet partisanship is unambiguous, *Moscow Yankee* treats the shortcomings and successes of early socialist construction evenhandedly and offers a fascinating window on the appeal that the early-1930s Soviet Union held for U.S. radicals.

Selected Bibliography: Baker, Christina. *In a Generous Spirit: A First-Person Biography of Myra Page.* Urbana: U of Illinois P, 1996; Foley, Barbara. Introduction. *Moscow Yankee.* By Myra Page. Urbana: U of Illinois P, 1995. vii–xxviii; Rosenfelt, Deborah. Afterword. *Daughter of the Hills.* By Myra Page. New York: Feminist P, 1986. 247–68; Sowinska, Suzanne. "Writing across the Color Line: White Women Writers and the 'Negro Question' in the Gastonia Novels." *Radical Revisions: Rereading 1930s Culture.* Ed. Bill Mullen and Sherry Lee Linkon. Urbana: U of Illinois P, 1996. 120–43.

Barbara Foley

PALEY, GRACE (1922–). Grace Paley's commitment to political radicalism has never been much in doubt. Comparatively few contemporary writers have accompanied American POW's home from Hanoi, been arrested on the White House lawn, or been dragged off in shackles to serve time in the Greenwich Village Women's House of Detention. Paley's pacifist, socialist politics are deeply rooted in a family past built on tsarist oppression—one uncle shot dead carrying the red flag, parents who reached America only because the Tsar had a son and amnestied all political prisoners under the age of twenty-one. Her grandmother recalled family arguments around the table among Paley's father (socialist), Uncle Grisha (communist), Aunt Luba (Zionist), and Aunt Mira (also communist). Paley's own streetwise adolescence involved the usual teenage gang fights—between adherents of the Third and Fourth Internationals.

Until recently, critics of Paley's work have tended to focus on gender politics and on the feminist form of her writing, with its communal narration, revisions of conventional genre, and restoration of women's unwritten experience. The 1998 publication of *Just as I Thought*, a collection of Paley's autobiographical pieces, has drawn attention back to politics in the newspaper sense of the term. Although reviewers see Paley as exemplifying an idealistic, romantic, impractical leftism, complacently convinced of its own righteousness, Paley defends the political impetus behind her stories. When interviewed, she complained that Americans are inhibited about writing about people who live and think politically, and that in no other country in the world would readers be surprised by the presence of political themes in literature. Although Paley is also a poet, her greatest impact is through her short stories (*Collected Stories*, nominated in 1994 for the National Book Award), which focus on such questions as the possibility of individual political intervention ("Samuel"), local as opposed to global politics ("Friends," "Politics," "The Story Hearer"), the Holocaust ("In Time Which Made a Monkey of Us All"), Vietnam ("Faith in a Tree"), the American terrorist underground ("The Expensive Moment"), race relations ("The Little Girl," "The Long-Distance Runner," "Zagrowsky Tells"), pacifism ("Listening"), and above all the problem of finding appropriate forms for political protest—in life as in story.

Selected Bibliography: Arcana, Judith. *Grace Paley's Life Stories: A Literary Biography.* Urbana: U of Illinois P, 1993; Heller, Deborah. "Faith, Optimism and the Place of the Personal." *Studies in American Jewish Literature* 22 (2003): 79–91; Meyer, Adam. "Faith and the 'Black Thing': Political Action and Self-Questioning in Grace Paley's Short Fiction." *Studies in Short Fiction* 31 (1994): 79–89; Newman, Judie. "Napalm and After: The Politics of Grace Paley's Short Fiction." *Yearbook of English Studies* 31 (2001): 1–9; Paley, Grace. *Just as I Thought.* New York: Farrar, Straus and Giroux, 1998; Taylor, Jacqueline. *Grace Paley: Illuminating the Dark Lives.* Austin: U of Texas P, 1990.

Judith Newman

PARTISAN REVIEW. Arguably the most influential American literary magazine of the mid-twentieth century, from the 1940s through the 1960s *Partisan Review* served as an arbiter of taste in literature and the arts, and significantly contributed to securing the cultural preeminence of New York City and the United States in the postwar era. Emerging from Jewish ethnic enclaves and the left-wing political milieu of the 1930s, the magazine came to espouse secular, universalist values grounded in a unique marriage of cultural **modernism** and broadly liberal politics.

Founded in 1934 by editors William Phillips and Philip Rahv as the organ of the New York City branch of the **John Reed Club**, *Partisan Review* was originally one of many "little" proletarian magazines under the auspices of the **Communist Party**. After a yearlong hiatus from 1936 to 1937, the magazine was reintroduced with a commitment to independent, anti-Stalinist socialism and to literary modernism. As the unofficial organ of the **New York intellectuals**—the most influential circle of American intellectuals in the post–**World War II** period—*Partisan Review* became the most formidable literary magazine of its day, eventually spawning such influential publications as *Commentary, Dissent,* the *New Criterion,* the *New York Review of Books, Politics,* and *Public Interest.* Employing a distinctively sharp, polemical style, which Irving Howe characterized as "free-lance dash, peacock strut, daring hypothesis, knockabout synthesis," *Partisan Review* waged a series of key cultural battles that continue to influence American cultural and intellectual life. The first of these was the successful campaign to discredit Stalinism and the Communist Party during the late 1930s. On the literary battlefield, *Partisan Review* joined with proponents of the **New Criticism** (whose formalist critical methods it otherwise eschewed) in successfully championing literary modernism. Among contemporary American writers, the magazine enthusiastically endorsed **James Baldwin** and **Ralph Ellison**, and secured the ascendancy of the Jewish American novel by heaping praise on the young Saul Bellow and Philip Roth. In the visual arts, Clement Greenberg, Harold Rosenberg, and Meyer Schapiro exerted enormous influence in gaining a worldwide reputation for the New York school of abstract expressionists.

In the 1950s, the magazine often condemned mass culture and cultural conformism, though its social criticism was tempered by its defense of the West in the face of the Soviet threat. Despite their active support of the civil rights movement and gradual opposition to the Vietnam War, the *Partisan Review* critics, with a few notable exceptions, remained unimpressed with the rebellious **beat** writers of the 1950s or the New Left and counterculture of the 1960s. As elder statesmen or sibling rivals, some of the magazine's writers took the opportunity to attack these emerging cultural and political trends, which included feminism, poststructuralism, and later, in the 1990s, "political correctness." Turning from what its sole surviving editor William Phillips considered America's small-minded, overly politicized culture and academic life, the magazine directed its waning energies toward support of Eastern European writers in their struggle against communism. In 2003, just a year after William Phillips's death, the magazine closed down after a nearly seventy-year run.

Selected Bibliography: Bloom, Alexander. *Prodigal Sons: The New York Intellectuals and Their World.* New York: Oxford UP, 1986; Cooney, Terry A. *The Rise of the New York Intellectuals: "Partisan Review" and Its Circle.* Madison: U of Wisconsin P, 1986; Douglas, Ann. "The Failure of the New York Intellectuals." *Raritan* (Spring 1998): 1–23; Gilbert, James. *Writers and Partisans: A History of Literary Radicalism in America.* 1968. New York: Columbia UP, 1992; Howe, Irving. "The New York Intellectuals." *Selected Writings: 1950–1990.* New York: Harcourt Brace Jovanovich, 1990; Jacoby, Russell. *The Last Intellectuals: American Culture in the Age of Academe.* New York: Basic Books, 1987; Kurzweil, Edith, and William Phillips, eds. *Writers and Politics: A "Partisan Review" Reader.* Boston: Routledge, 1983; Phillips, William. *A Partisan View: Five Decades of the Literary Life.* New York: Stein and Day, 1983; Teres, Harvey M. *Renewing the Left: Politics, Imagination, and the New York Intellectuals.* New York: Oxford UP, 1996; Wald, Alan M. *The New York Intellectuals: The Rise and Decline of the Anti-Stalinist Left from the 1930s to the 1980s.* Chapel Hill: U of North Carolina P, 1987.

Harvey Teres

PASOLINI, PIER PAOLO (1922–1975),

enormously productive and provocative Italian poet, fiction writer, dramatist, cultural theorist, militant public intellectual, screenplay writer, and filmmaker (in which role he is best known internationally). Pasolini was one of the foremost and most controversial cultural personalities in Italy during the third quarter of his century. Fascism and Marxism tangled with Pasolini family romance during Italy's debacle of 1943–1945, and Pasolini combined a visceral, atavistic love for the spontaneous sexuality of the Friulian peasantry and the Rome underclass with a Marxian sense—learned from **Antonio Gramsci**'s *Prison Notebooks*—of the historic destiny of proletarian emancipation. All this was further complicated by his homoeroticism, which led to his murder, with unproven suspicions of political (neofascist) involvement. His poetry (much of which is collected in English translation in the 1982 volume *Poems*), essays, and articles most explicitly track his artistic and cultural endeavor to confront the all-pervasive power transforming all human experience from its mythic authenticity into alienated commodification. Even communism, with which Pasolini was in constant dialogue, appealed to him more as naive mass enthusiasm than as rational project for material betterment or for the appropriation of power. The appalling ultrarealism of his Roman tales of the 1950s, the six ultramodern tragedies of his "verbal theater" (*teatro della parola*) of the late 1960s, and the caustic poetry of the antinovel *Teorema* (1968) are but some examples of the "neo-experimentalism" with which he kept faith—that is, an attempt to keep a mental grip on the artifact and its psychic content. A summation of this is the huge phantasmagoric novel he left unfinished at his death, which was published in 1992 as *Petrolio* (Petroleum). A few days before he was murdered, he had promised in a weekly that he would name names of those at the highest level complicit in systematic political corruption and crime.

Selected Bibliography: Barański, Zygmunt G., ed. *Pasolini Old and New: Surveys and Studies.* Dublin: Four Courts P, 1999; Rumble, Patrick Allen, and Bart Testa. *Pier Paolo Pasolini: Contemporary Perspectives.* Toronto: U of Toronto P, 1996; Van Watson, William. *Pier Paolo Pasolini and the Theatre of the Word.* Ann Arbor, MI: UMI Research P, 1989.

John Gatt-Rutter

PAVESE, CESARE (1908–1950), an important mediator of U.S. writing into fascist Italy, developed first as a poet, courageously conveying workaday realities with mythic intensity in *Lavorare stanca* (*Hard Labor*, 1936). Exiled to a remote village on account of his antifascist associations, Pavese started a daybook of his intellectual and existential concerns (including tantalizingly little on politics), *Il mestiere di vivere* (*The Burning Brand*, 1952). He stayed out of the Resistance but joined the **Communist Party** after the liberation, contributed to postwar debates about literary politics, and wrote several novels and stories that explore both the alienation of individuals not unlike himself (though variously male or female, bourgeois or working class, urban or rural dwellers), and the destructive vices of males unlike himself. Here the personal is political; in other works, the invisible influence of a fascist or postfascist political and social system is felt. Others build up into the history of a political epoch, shadowing Pavese's own experiences—with his equivocations and evasions, typical of many intellectuals—from exile in the south in *Il carcere* (*The Political Prisoner*, 1949), to abstention from the Resistance struggle in *La casa in collina* (*The House on the Hill*, 1949), to anguished perplexity at the renewal of class struggle in postwar Italy torn between Christian Democrats and Communists in *La luna e i falò* (*The Moon and the Bonfires*, 1950). *Il compagno* (*The Comrade*, 1947) less convincingly shows a guitar-playing freewheeler (corresponding to the writer or intellectual) being drawn into the prewar antifascist struggle.

Selected Bibliography: Biasin, Gian-Paulo. *The Smile of the Gods: A Thematic Study of Cesare Pavese's Works.* Ithaca, NY: Cornell UP, 1968; Thompson, Doug. *Cesare Pavese: A Study of the Major Novels and Poems.* Cambridge: Cambridge UP, 1982.

John Gatt-Rutter

PETER THE FIRST (***PETR I,*** **1929–1945)** is a major, though unfinished, historical novel by **Alexei Tolstoy,** one of the key figures of the early Soviet literary and cultural scene. Centering on the figure of the Russian tsar Peter the Great, the novel is an epic portrayal of the Russian society of his time and its arduous move from feudal backwardness and stagnation to the Western concept of bourgeois society. Tolstoy portrays Russian society with a broad brush, offering his readers interesting vignettes of the people living at the end of the seventeenth and beginning of the eighteenth century; the real protagonist of the novel, however, is Russia itself.

The novel begins with the depiction of social and political conditions in Russia in the 1680s. The tsar is dying and there is much uncertainty about the future, while the present is rife with social unrest. Tolstoy depicts the hardships suffered by many Russians, from the landowners constantly asked to supply Moscow with goods and services, to peasants trying to eke out a bare livelihood from the unyielding land while struggling under heavy taxes levied by their feudal owners and the central government. With a keen eye, Tolstoy depicts political conditions in the country through a portrayal of various classes and their conflicting interests. He particularly emphasizes the role played by religion in paralyzing Russia's social and economic development. In particular, his focus is on the religious opposition to progress and any new social developments that could potentially improve the living conditions of the Russian people.

Tsar Peter stands out in sharp contrast to such a background. Tolstoy follows his life from the early days of learning and practicing military skills with a "toy army," to early failures at military conquest (the defeat at Azov), to Peter's realization of the importance of open-sea trade routes in the Baltics for landlocked Russia. Tolstoy then depicts Peter's efforts to make Russia a sea power and his vigorous struggles to modernize Russia. The tsar does so by every possible means he has at his disposal—from force and decrees (as when he orders boyars to shave off their beards, or when he orders a large number of young aristocrats to spend a year in Western Europe learning sciences and crafts), to the individual support and personal encouragement he gives to capable individuals irrespective of their original social status, as to his confidant Alexei Menshikov and to the serf-turned-merchant-tycoon Ivan Brovkin.

Tolstoy's panoramic novel also includes many scenes from the lives of people in various social classes: the runaway serf Tsigan and his robber gang; a visionary inventor trying to design a flying machine; life in the foreign section; the military *streltsy* and aristocratic boyars. But the focus of the novel remains firmly on Peter's attempts to jump-start Russia's stagnant feudal society, on his efforts to bring Russia closer to a Western bourgeois social order he perceived as superior to Russian tradition, and on the strategies he employed in order to bring such change. By showing this historical movement of the Russian society, *Peter the First* remains one of the finest examples of Soviet **socialist realism**.

Selected Bibliography: Alpatov, A. V. *Aleksei Tolstoi—master istoricheskogo romana.* Moscow: Sovetskii pisatel, 1958.

Dubravka Juraga

PILNYAK, BORIS ANDREYEVICH (1894–1938). Pilnyak was the leading modernist prose writer in 1920s postrevolutionary Russia, during a burst of experimental creativity across the arts. His father descended from German settlers named Vogau, but Pilnyak changed his name to avoid anti-German hostility during **World War I**. He was born in Mozhaisk in the Moscow region and spent his childhood in small towns there and in Saratov on the middle Volga, whose rural backwardness and tradition of peasant revolt provided the background to many of Pilnyak's works.

Pilnyak's first major achievement, the novel *Golyi god* (*The Naked Year,* 1921), reflected the impact of the revolution on provincial Russia. The brilliance of Pilnyak's ornamentalist style made the work an instant success. Though not explicitly pro-communist, the influence of Scythianism (an idea influenced by Spengler's thought that as a vigorous young nation, Russia was destined to supplant the moribund West) made the book acceptable to communist sentiment. Pilnyak was given the qualified approval of **Trotsky**, who coined the phrase fellow traveler to refer to young writers who were not anticommunist and worth supporting. Pilnyak's success allowed him to travel to Germany and England, which modified the ideas of his next major novel *Mashiny i volki* (*Machines and Wolves*, 1924), on the impact of industrialization on a backward country.

Pilnyak's concerns were literary: the persistence of history into the present, the nature of consciousness, and the problem of transmuting experience into art. Despite his dogged public insistence that art was different from politics, he was attacked by those who believed literature should be written from a class perspective. These problems became more acute in 1925–1926 as **Stalin** consolidated his power and undermined Trotsky. Pilnyak caused a scandal with the publication of *Povest' nepogashennoi luny* (*The Tale of the Unextinguished Moon,* 1926), which implicitly attacked Stalin for organizing the death of a senior military figure, Frunze. The story was rapidly suppressed, but Pilnyak was a marked man. As leader of the Moscow branch of the independent writers' union, he and his close friend **Evgeny Zamyatin**, who headed the Leningrad branch, were subjected to a vitriolic and mendacious press campaign in 1929. This was the signal for the party to take complete control of literature and impose the style of **socialist realism**.

In the 1930s, Pilnyak stuck to his artistic concerns, seeking to manipulate the conventions of socialist realism despite censorship and regular outbursts of criticism. He was arrested in 1937 and executed in 1938. Though formally rehabilitated in 1956, his works were only patchily available in Russia until after the collapse of the Soviet Union. His dramatic role in Russian literary politics has tended to cloud critical appreciation of his work as literature, but his fiction and travel writing are a significant achievement of early-twentieth-century **modernism**.

Selected Bibliography: Browning, Gary. *Boris Pilniak: Scythian at a Typewriter.* Ann Arbor, MI: Ardis, 1985; Jensen, Peter Alberg. *Nature as Code: The Achievement of Boris Pilnjak, 1915–1924.* Copenhagen: Rosenkilde and Bagger, 1979; Kemp-Welsh, A. *Stalin and the Literary Intelligentsia, 1928–1939.* Hong Kong: Macmillan, 1991.

Doug Martin

PINTER, HAROLD (1935–). British poet, screenwriter, polemicist, and novelist. Pinter is chiefly known and widely acclaimed for his many plays, numbering over thirty and including *The Room* (1957), *The Dumb Waiter* (1957), *The Birthday Party* (1957), and *No Man's Land* (1974)—plays whose political significance has only recently been widely acknowledged. Early labeled "comedies of menace," the plays of the 1950s through the 1970s received widespread critical and scholarly reevaluation after the performance of his short pieces *One for the Road* (1984), *Mountain Language* (1988), and *The New World Order* (1991), which dramatize situations resonant of prison camps, torture chambers, and upper reaches of power as exercised in the globalized world of money and politics. As a result, most now acknowledge that his early domestic plays present investigations and indictments of similar forms of power and domination on the microcosmic level of the home. His work since *Mountain Language*, including *Ashes to Ashes* (1996) and *Celebration* (1999), has returned to a more oblique indictment of atrocity, domination, and social injustice, again in the intimate if menacing domestic settings that marked his early works. Pinter remains an outspoken critic of the injustices of globalized capitalism and neoimperialism, and the West's complicity in them.

Selected Bibliography: Billington, Michael. *The Life and Works of Harold Pinter.* London: Faber and Faber, 1996; Burkman, Katherine H., and John L. Kundert-Gibbs, eds. *Pinter at Sixty.* Bloomington: Indiana UP, 1993; Esslin, Martin. *Pinter: The Playwright.* 5th ed. London: Methuen, 1992; Gillen, Francis, and Stephen H. Gale, eds. *The Pinter Review: Collected Essays 2001 and 2002.* Tampa, FL: U of Tampa P, 2002; Peacock, D. Keith. *Harold Pinter and the New British Theatre.* Westport, CT: Greenwood, 1997; Quigley, Austin E. *The Pinter Problem.* Princeton, NJ: Princeton UP, 1975; Silverstein, Marc. *Harold Pinter and the Language of Cultural Power.* Lewisburg, PA: Bucknell UP, 1993.

Craig N. Owens

PLATONOV, ANDREI PLATONOVICH (1899–1951). Born Andrei Klimentev, the son of a railway worker from the provincial Russian city of Voronezh, Platonov began writing in earnest about the time of the October 1917 **Russian Revolution** and was one of the few genuinely proletarian writers in the early years of the Soviet regime. In the 1920s, he wrote a series of journalistic pieces and short stories expressing the fervent hope that the Bolshevik Revolution would transform not just Russian society but physical existence as well, an aim he had absorbed from the proletarian cultural movement led by Aleksandr Bogdanov.

This utopian combination of existential and political concerns—in essence, the longing to see the Soviet experiment transform what Platonov regarded as humanity's dire existential circumstances—remained a hallmark of his writing throughout his career. From the late 1920s on, however, his ambivalence toward the "construction of socialism" deepened, and his works developed a satirical edge that considerably damaged his relations with the institutions of literary officialdom established under Stalin in the 1930s. His novel *Chevengur* (late 1920s, published in full only in 1988) depicts the eccentric activities of a motley group of figures who attempt to create communism overnight in an isolated steppe town, only to watch their experiment disintegrate and fall prey to marauding Cossacks. *The Foundation Pit* (*Kotlovan*, 1929–1930, but published in Russia only in 1987) portrays an even more lurid series of events attending plans to construct a gigantic housing project for the proletariat, which yields only an enormous foundation pit. *Chevengur* and *Kotlovan* are especially notable for their strange but eerily effective deformations of the Russian language, in particular of the political slogans ubiquitous in the Stalin era.

The 1931 publication of a work entitled *For Future Use: A Poor Peasant's Chronicle* (*Vprok: Bedniatskaia khronika*), a satirical account of collectivization in the Russian countryside, had disastrous consequences for Platonov. Subjected to vicious attack in the central press, he found it impossible to publish anything for more than two years. When sporadically allowed back into print, he had to mute his earlier tendencies toward satire and verbal experimentation. In the mid-thirties, he worked on a novel entitled *Happy Moscow* (*Schastlivaia Moskva*), an ambivalent attempt at the genre of **socialist realism** that persisted in indulging the somber existential themes typical of Platonov's earlier works. Platonov served as a correspondent for the Soviet army newspaper during **World War II**. Ill throughout the later 1940s with tuberculosis, he died on January 5, 1951. In addition to journalism, stories, and two novels, he wrote several plays, poetry, and literary criticism.

Selected Bibliography: Borenstein, Eliot. *Men without Women: Masculinity and Revolution in Russian Fiction, 1917–1929.* Durham, NC: Duke UP, 2000; Brodsky, Joseph. "Catastrophes in the Air." *Less Than One: Selected Essays.* New York: Farrar, Straus and Giroux, 1986. Naiman, Eric. "Andrej Platonov and the Inadmissibility of Desire." *Russian Literature* 23 (1988): 319–66; Seifrid, Thomas. *Andrei Platonov: Uncertainties of Spirit.* Cambridge: Cambridge UP, 1992.

Thomas Seifrid

PLENZDORF, ULRICH (1934–). When the literary scene in East Germany was no longer dominated by **Brecht** and **Seghers**, Plenzdorf became the most visible writer of his country. He was born and grew up in Berlin. In 1954–1955, he studied Marxist philosophy in Leipzig, and from 1955 to 1958, he worked as a stagehand for the East German film studio DEFA. After one year of military service, he was a student at the film academy in Potsdam-Babelsberg for four years; then he worked as a scenarist for DEFA and wrote film scripts. Although it was not until several years later that some of his scripts where used and published—a movie entitled *Karla* was completed but not released by the censors—Plenzdorf continued to write, and he eventually reached enthusiastic audiences on both sides of the Iron Curtain. Thus, he became a freelance, which he has continued to be while living in Berlin since the fall of the wall.

Plenzdorf's first book has remained his best-known work. It is a novel entitled *The New Sufferings of Young W.* (*Die neuen Leiden des jungen W,* English translation 1979), which was first published in the prestigious East German literary journal *Sinn und Form* in 1972. Its fame rests less on its parodic treatment of one of the most famous works in German literature, **Goethe**'s *Die Leiden des jungen Werthers* (1774), or its parallels to other works of world literature, most specifically J. D. Salinger's *The Catcher in the Rye* (1951), than on its controversial attitude toward East Germany's political system. Following its 1973 book publication in both parts of Germany, critics arrived at entirely different conclusions about its political persuasion. Stirred by the work's condemnation by an Eastern critic because of the protagonist's admiration of Western values—expressed in his use of teenage jargon and his liking for jeans and pop music—other Eastern critics tried to save the novel for the socialist system by interpreting it as the story of a young man's struggle for integration into the proletarian workforce. Contrarily, Western critics saw the protagonist as a social outsider and his death as an expression of despair over his inability to find personal happiness under a political dictatorship. The latter interpretation is supported by the novel's manuscript of 1968–1969, in which the protagonist commits suicide, a subject that was unacceptable to the communist authorities. Nevertheless, even in the form in which the work was first published, it serves as an indication of the thawing of restrictions in art and literature effected by the East German Communist Party Convention of 1971. Social nonconformists and downtrodden individuals also stand at the center of Plenzdorf's other works.

Selected Bibliography: Currie, Barbara. "Diverging Attitudes in Literary Criticism: The 'Plenzdorf Debate' in the Early 1970s in East and West Germany." *Neophilologus* 79.2 (April 1995): 283–94; Fickert, Kurt F. "Literature as Documentation: Plenzdorf's *Die neuen Leiden des jungen W.*" *International Fiction Review* 12.1 (Winter 1985): 69–75; Reid, H. J. *Writing without Taboos: The New East German Literature.* NewYork: Oxford UP, 1990; Shaw, Gisela. "Ideal and Reality in the Works of Ulrich Plenzdorf." *GermanLife and Letters* 35.1 (October 1981): 84–97.

Helmut F. Pfanner

LA POESÍA SORPRENDIDA (THE SURPRISED POETRY) was a literary movement and journal that flourished in the Dominican Republic between 1943 and 1947. The editors of the journal—Alberto Baeza Flores, Franklin Mieses Burgos, Mariano Lebrón Saviñón, Freddy Gatón Arce, and Eugenio Granell—defined the movement in terms reminiscent of **surrealism** and **modernism**. The "surprised" and "surprising" poetry was a new poetry, following **Ezra Pound**'s edict to "make it new." It set itself against *la poesía acostumbrada* (the usual poetry); it embraced the "automatic" poetry of the French surrealists; and it meant to shock and awaken *un planeta sordo* (a deaf world). *La poesía sorprendida* published writers as diverse as William Blake, **Johann Wolfgang von Goethe**, the Tang dynasty Chinese poet Tufu ("el Milton chino"), the Spanish poet Jorge Guillén, and the Dominican poet Aída Cartagena Portalatín. It also featured the drawings of Granell, a Spanish surrealist. *La poesía sorprendida* published a total of twenty-one editions (at five hundred copies per edition), as well as fourteen books of poetry. In its time, Latin American and surrealist writers recognized La Poesía Sorprendida as an important literary movement. André Breton, one of the founders of French surrealism, hailed the literary movement's journal as the best produced in Latin America.

La Poesía Sorprendida's appropriation of surrealist themes and forms was linked to the particular political and cultural problems Dominican poets faced under the Trujillo dictatorship. Surrealist language functioned simultaneously to present and to camouflage their criticisms of the dictatorship and, more generally, capitalism. One of the Dominican poets and editors of the journal, Freddy Gatón Arce, wrote in an issue that the "deaf planet" the *sorprendistas* wanted to awaken was none other than the one that ignored the tragedy in the Dominican Republic. The journal's cosmopolitan character and philosophy stood in opposition to the Dominican nationalism promoted by Trujillo. Members of the movement wrote that they "are for a national poetry nourished in the universal" and for "creation without limits, borders, and permanence." Their call for a "universal nationality" was itself a negation of any meaningful sense of "national" difference or chauvinism. Significantly, the journal bore on its masthead "P"—poetry of the universal man.

La Poesía Sorprendida also resisted the dictatorship by promoting poetry concerned with the inner life, including the dream life, in surrealist fashion. Followers argued that the conformity demanded of workers and politicians by the dictatorship laid to waste the inner lives of the people. Their calls for a retreat into inner life thus imply the decadence of public life but, equally, the hope for a creative and critical regeneration of a rebellious mind. La Poesía Sorprendida's introduction of surrealism into the Dominican Republic continues to shape Dominican art and literature.

Selected Bibliography: Alcántara Almánzar, José. *Estudios de poesía dominicana.* Santo Domingo: Editora Alfa y Omega, 1979; Baeza Flores, Alberto. *La poesía dominicana en el siglo XX.* Santiago, Dominican Republic: Universidad Católica Madre y Maestra, 1975–1977; Gatón Arce, Freddy. *Estos días de tíbar—La poesía soprendida.* Santo Domingo: Taller, 1983; Olivera, Otto. "Indices de la poesía soprendida y entre las soledades." *Revista Interamericana de bibliografía* 39.3 (1989): 334–54.

Anthony Dawahare

POLITICAL UNCONSCIOUS. Term introduced by the influential Marxist critic **Fredric Jameson** in his book of that title. Jameson argues that all cultural artifacts contain a "political unconscious": the repressed ideology and material reality out of which the text merges at its particular historical moment. This repression is particularly important to the operation of bourgeois literary texts, because bourgeois ideology consistently seeks to disguise its own nature as a tool of class domination, naturalizing itself as common sense via a deceptive rhetoric of individual liberation. Under capitalism, then, bourgeois literary texts (the only texts that can become canonical under capitalism) are invested in and complicit with bourgeois privilege and class domination. In working with bourgeois texts, then, it is the task of the Marxist critic to seek out the political unconscious of that text, thereby disrupting its effectiveness as a tool of ideological power by pointing out the contradictions between the rhetoric of the text and the dominative ideology on which it is based.

However, for Jameson, all cultural artifacts—even the most degraded of them—also contain unconscious utopian dimensions. That is, the artifacts symbolically resolve, not merely in terms of content but primarily in the artistic process and at the level of form, the unbearable social contradictions that cannot yet be resolved in reality. A key task of the Marxist critic, for Jameson, is to seek out this utopian dimension, which helps to demonstrate that capitalism is historically surmountable, despite its present power. Hence, by seeking out the political unconscious of a text, the critic dialectically unmasks history as the absent cause, revealing cultural artifacts as socially symbolic acts with both positive and negative dimensions.

To identify the political unconscious of a text, we must ask not only *what* it means and *how* it works, but also *why* it works and means as it does, if we are ever to move beyond complicity with and perpetuation of the barbarism of capitalism. In other words, while we should read a text for its immanent meaning, we also need to read a text in terms of the historical environment out of which it emerges and the utopian alternative toward which it yearns. For Jameson, only **Marxism criticism** has the historical vision and interpretive power to perform this dual task of ideological critique and utopian revelation, subsuming all competing (but more limited) interpretive approaches and providing the "absolute horizon" of all reading and interpretation.

Selected Bibliography: Burnham, Clint. *The Jamesonian Unconscious: The Aesthetics of Marxist Theory.* Durham: Duke UP, 1995; Dowling, William C. *Jameson, Althusser, Marx: An Introduction to the Political Unconscious.* Ithaca: Cornell UP, 1984; Jameson, Fredric. *The Political Unconscious: Narrative as a Socially Symbolic Act.* Ithaca, NY: Cornell UP, 1981.

Sandy Rankin

POLONSKY, ABRAHAM (1910–1999). Best remembered as the brilliant screenwriter and director of films like *Body and Soul* (1947) and *Force of Evil* (1948) who courageously stood up to the House Un-American Activities Committee (HUAC), Polonsky was also the author of several remarkable, often overlooked novels. Though the specific challenges presented in his films and books differ, the recurrent narrative of an individual's radicalization and ability to act out of conviction despite the risks within a deterministic, oppressive environment surely evokes Polonsky's own development and commitments.

The son of an immigrant Russian socialist, Polonsky grew up on the East Side of New York City, an experience that later informed his novel *Zenia's Way* (1980). As a student and later teacher at the City College of New York during the 1930s, Polonsky joined an intellectual community of Communists and Socialists deeply engaged with the aesthetics of **proletarian literature**, and he would soon join the **Communist Party** of the United States and work for the Congress of Industrial Organizations. Though he had obtained a law degree from Columbia, his talent with scripts had him authoring many radio programs and led to a contract with Paramount. After serving in the Office of Strategic Services from 1943 to 1945, he returned to Hollywood, where his films dramatized the ways in which money corrupts human relations. His plots characteristically hinged on a character's decision to either compromise values or resist complicity at great cost. After being declared a "dangerous citizen" in the 1951 HUAC hearings and being blacklisted, Polonsky went to Europe for a time, composing *Season of Fear* (1956), a novel that explored one man's inability to withstand the powers of government repression and manipulation. After returning to the United States, he continued to work in the entertainment industry under pseudonyms and, in 1969, was credited as director and screenplay writer for *Tell Them Willie Boy Is Here* (1969). Unlike some of his contemporaries, Polonsky never recanted his political beliefs, saying of the Communist Party in the 1970s that "it's an honor, dubious indeed, but an honor nonetheless to be in it and to be thought well of by the people in it" (Zheutlin 70).

Republished in 1999, Polonsky's *The World Above* (1951) is arguably his greatest novel. In this dynamic study of the politicization of a psychiatrist, Polonsky proposes a materialist psychotherapy that links mental illness to the inequalities inherent in capitalism and accordingly proposes transforming the individual and the larger system as treatment. Called before a HUAC-like board for his radical views, the main character defiantly vows to "devote my life to exposing this society, condemning it and changing it" (464). In all areas of Polonsky's deeply empathic, incisive, and principled work, he affirmed his commitment to this mandate.

Selected Bibliography: Buhle, Paul, and Dave Wagner. *A Very Dangerous Citizen: Abraham Lincoln Polonsky and the Hollywood Left.* Berkeley: U of California P, 2001; McGilligan, Patrick, and Paul Buhle. *Tender Comrades: A Backstory of the Hollywood Blacklist.* New York: St. Martin's, 1997; Shepler, Michael. "Hollywood Red: The Life of Abraham Polonsky." *Political Affairs* 82.8 (2003): 14–17; Zheutlin, Barbara, and David Talbot. *Creative Differences: Profiles of Hollywood Dissidents.* Boston: South End P, 1978.

Rachel Peterson

POPULAR CULTURE. An often confused and confusing term, "popular culture" entertains two main and divergent senses, both intimately linked with the rise of modernity. On the one hand, popular culture has often referred to the objects, rituals, and practices associated with plebeian ways of life and "the people," as opposed to rulers or social elites. This sense is closely intertwined with ideas of "the folk," or "folklore." On the other hand, today, popular culture generally refers to any object or practice that is widespread, crosses class and social boundaries, and originates in the mass culture industry.

The emergence of the idea of the folk begins in the Enlightenment with the collection of stories, songs, and poems from the peasants of Germany, France, and then England and Scotland. The original theoretician of the folk was Johann von Herder, who postulated the origins of a distinctive German national identity in these vernacular materials. Indeed, the earliest anthropological senses of culture begin in Herder's arguments for the value and necessity of studying the folk. Within this strand of thinking, popular culture came to describe a culture that was organic, orally communicated, performance- rather than text-centered, communal rather than individual in production and consumption, and centered on maintaining tradition. For its middle-class and cosmopolitan devotees, popular culture thus served as a counterweight to, and often refuge from, the change and disruptions associated with modernity. As Morag Shiach writes, the term "popular culture" signaled "the attempt to produce . . . an autonomous sphere of authenticity, untouched by changing social and cultural relations" (10). For intellectuals, popular culture often looked backward to preindustrial and precapitalist modes of life and production. Yet despite its conservative implications, it also supplied a critical perspective on capitalism, as its representations of more organic ways of life offered both alternatives to contemporary society and criteria of authenticity—in art and life—by which to judge the injuries and insufficiencies of capitalist society.

This notion of popular culture reached a kind of apogee in late Victorian society—especially in Britain and the United States. William Morris's cultural and political syndicalism, for instance, reflects one especially powerful version. The critical power of popular culture in this sense persisted, however, especially on the left. For instance, the effort among Communists in the 1930s and 1940s, in both the United States and Great Britain, to envision jazz as a "people's art" incorporated many similar assumptions about authenticity, tradition, and performance. "Popular culture" as "people's culture" also nurtured the political and critical visions of a generation of influential British Marxist writers, such as E. P. Thompson, **Raymond Williams**, and Eric Hobsbawm. These writers typically viewed working-class culture as a contemporary type of folk culture, built around values like wholeness, community, immediacy, and tradition.

For these writers and others, the great enemy of this version of popular culture has typically been mass-produced culture because mass culture is seen as replacing popular forms and plebeian values with commercial products and dominant ideologies. Driven by the quest for profit, mass culture transforms participants into consumers. Armed with a vast apparatus to market culture, mass culture exerts tremendous pressures on people not only to consume but to expect and demand the newest and the latest, even as cultural experience must be standardized and commodified. Because this whole enterprise is organized to extract surplus value, Marxist critics have been especially fierce critics of mass culture. For writers like **Theodor Adorno**, Herbert Marcuse, and Dwight Macdonald, to name only a few, mass culture not only commodifies culture but also acts as a kind of ideological conveyor belt, injecting the masses not just with particular messages but also with particular ways of misreading and misunderstanding the world. That is, despite its emphasis on entertainment, fun, and pleasure, mass culture becomes the chief agent of "false consciousness" in contemporary capitalist societies. As Adorno once remarked: "I consider . . . that the average television entertainment is fundamentally far more dangerous politically than any political broadcast has ever been" (Adorno 56). Thus, the "people" become the "masses," a pliant, duped, segmented, and "one-dimensional" (Marcuse) agglomeration of audience markets, and the term "popular" denotes best-selling objects, events, and practices.

This view of contemporary culture is a grim one that oddly recapitulates a rather familiar, bourgeois division of audiences into highbrow and lowbrow, those who mindlessly consume mass culture and those who possess the taste and distinction to appreciate high culture. The ironies of critiques like these being undertaken in the name of Marx or radicalism are obvious.

More recent approaches to popular culture acknowledge its commercial sources and dynamics without surrendering to pessimism about the masses and the people. Key to this approach, associated with the field of cultural studies, has been a recognition that communication within culture is less direct and simple than earlier Marxist critics had assumed. In "Encoding/Decoding" (1980) for instance, the British critic **Stuart Hall** argues that while ideological messages might be encoded in mass culture texts, these same texts required decoding, or reading. And, when readers, viewers, and listeners decoded texts, they brought to bear their own ideologies, knowledges, and interests to make sense of things. As David Morley demonstrated in *The "Nationwide" Audience: Structure and Decoding* (1980), despite efforts by those in power to communicate meanings directly to television viewers, these viewers often read different and sometimes oppositional meanings into the news and information they viewed. Later cultural studies work, like that of Dick Hebdige and John Fiske, elaborated on the ways in which, by reinterpreting received meanings, consumers of mass culture could become creative makers of new meanings. In *Subculture: The Meaning of Style* (1979), Hebdige showed how working-class punk-rock fans recycled dominant images, icons, and meanings to produce oppositional styles and texts that contested both dominant and traditional working-class beliefs and values.

In this view, popular culture is best seen as a process or collection of processes rather than a stable set of texts, objects, audiences, or even venues. As Fiske writes, in a "cultural economy where the circulation is not one of money, but of meanings and pleasures . . . meanings are the only elements in the process that can be neither commodified nor consumed: meanings can be produced, reproduced, and circulated only in that constant process we call culture" (27). Contrary to Adorno and Marcuse, then, the politics of popular culture become something more interesting and complicated. Indeed, as Hall, Hebdige, and Fiske argue, the politics of a popular culture text or object lie in what audiences do with that text rather than the intentions of the text's or object's producers. While there may be tremendous pressures to adopt dominant meanings, there are also counterveiling incentives and desires to refuse and reinterpret these meanings. The cultural politics of popular culture begins, then, with this contest over meaning.

Selected Bibliography: Adorno, Theodor W. *The Culture Industry: Selected Essays on Mass Culture.* Ed. J. M. Bernstein. London: Routledge, 1971; Fiske, John. *Understanding Popular Culture.* London: Routledge, 1991; Hall, Stuart. "Encoding/Decoding." *Culture, Media, Language: Working Papers in Cultural Studies, 1972–79.* London: Hutchinson, 1980. 128–38; Hebdige, Dick. *Subculture: The Meaning of Style.* London: Methuen, 1979; Morley, David. *The "Nationwide" Audience: Structure and Decoding.* London: BFI, 1980; Shiach, Morag. *Discourse on Popular Culture.* Palo Alto, CA: Stanford UP, 1989; Thompson, E. P. *The Making of the English Working Class.* New York: Vintage-Random House, 1966.

Larry Hanley

POPULAR FRONT. As the expansionist designs of the fascist governments in Germany and Italy in the 1930s became clear, many on the left became convinced that the most urgent political problem of the day was resisting fascist aggression rather than working for the immediate overthrow of capitalism. By 1935, the **Third International**, at its congress in Moscow, adopted the official policy of supporting the formation of worldwide popular front organizations, in which various communist parties would work to form alliances with other radical and liberal groups with the common aim of opposing fascism. This strategy, which made official a policy that many leftist groups had been pursuing since Adolf Hitler began his rise to power in Germany in 1932, had a variety of consequences in a variety of places. In France, for example, the Popular Front functioned as an actual political party that went on to win the national elections of 1936, giving France a socialist prime minister, Léon Blum (who had begun his career as a literary critic). In Britain, the Popular Front largely took the form of uneasy cooperation between the **Communist Party** of Great Britain and the Labour Party.

The Communist Party of the United States (CPUSA) had no major political party with which it could directly align itself during the Popular Front (initially referred to as the People's Front in the United States), though the CPUSA dropped its sometimes bitter criticism of the Roosevelt government and instead adopted a conciliatory attitude of supporting the New Deal against its conservative opponents. Initially, rather than attempting any sort of direct alliance with Roosevelt's Democratic Party, the CPUSA pursued the organization of a Farmer-Labor Party that would help to bring communist ideas into the American electoral mainstream. The organization of the Farmer-Labor Party was abandoned in 1938 when it became clear that the new party would be unable to play a major role in U.S. politics. Still, the actual activities of the CPUSA continued to move toward electoral politics and away from street demonstrations and militant labor actions, just as its rhetoric shifted from one of revolution to one of American patriotism. Meanwhile, the party came more and more to support what it saw as the essentially progressive and antifascist nature of the Roosevelt administration in a policy shift that was signaled by a change in designation of the movement from the People's Front to the Democratic Front.

The CPUSA gained considerably in membership and respectability during the Popular Front period, though the policy of conciliation and compromise also meant a diminution of some of the party's more admirable positions. By 1935, the CPUSA had already embarked on a policy of forming alliances with labor and liberal organizations in the interests of causes such as antifascism and opposition to discrimination on the basis of gender and race. These policies can be considered the forerunners of the Popular Front, though the central emphasis on opposition to fascism in the Popular Front era caused the CPUSA to veer away from its formerly militant opposition to social problems such as racism in the United States, thus alienating many African Americans who had seen the CPUSA as the political organization most dedicated to defending their rights.

Meanwhile, the Popular Front policy had a powerful effect on the production of leftist and **proletarian literature**, the themes of which shifted away from support for the revolutionary overthrow of capitalism toward antifacism and support for general social justice. In the United States, for example, the **John Reed Clubs** that had worked to promote the development of revolutionary literature were all but disbanded by the end of 1935, while leading communist cultural journals such as *New Masses* shifted their editorial policies away from emphasis on revolutionary proletarian literature written by worker-writers toward coverage of more mainstream literature and a more general emphasis on freedom and antifascism as literary themes.

The Popular Front organizations in major Western democracies such as France, Great Britain, and the United States ultimately had a certain amount of success in mobilizing progressive forces against fascism, though none of them were successful in what was initially a major aim of the strategy—convincing their nations to provide support to the beleaguered Spanish republican government during the **Spanish Civil War**. Still, while some of the compromises made by the Communist Party during the Popular Front period were highly problematic, the Front has a largely positive legacy worldwide. Thus, any number of liberation movements have adopted Popular Front strategies, or even the name Popular Front (such as the Popular Front for the Liberation of Palestine), to indicate their participation in a legacy of broad-based opposition to tyranny and oppression.

Selected Bibliography: Blaazer, David. *The Popular Front and the Progressive Tradition: Socialists, Liberals, and the Quest for Unity, 1884–1939.* Cambridge: Cambridge UP, 1992; Graham, Helen, and Paul Preston, eds. *The Popular Front in Europe.* New York: St. Martin's, 1987; Jackson, Julian. *The Popular Front in France: Defending Democracy, 1934–38.* Cambridge: Cambridge UP, 1988; McKenzie, Kermit E. *Comintern and World Revolution, 1928–1943.* New York: Columbia UP, 1964; Ottaneli, Fraser M. *The Communist Party of the United States: From the Depression to World War.* New Brunswick, NJ: Rutgers UP, 1991; Pells, Richard H. *Radical Vision and American Dreams: Culture and Social Thought in the Depression Years.* New York: Harper and Row, 1973.

M. Keith Booker

POSTCOLONIAL LITERATURE, the collective term used to indicate the literature produced by writers from nations that were formerly the colonies of European imperial powers. This loose definition encompasses a wide variety of cultures and societies. In the most literal sense, postcolonial literature includes the literature of nations such as Australia, Canada, and even the United States, all of which were formerly British colonies. Indeed, American writers in the nineteenth century, such as Ralph Waldo Emerson, often expressed a conscious desire to contribute to the development of a new postcolonial cultural identity that would move beyond the legacy of the British-dominated past. Thus, one of the pioneering studies of postcolonial literature—*The Empire Writes Back* (1989), by Bill Ashcroft, Gareth Griffiths, and Helen Tiffin—argues that "in many ways the American experience and its attempts to produce a new kind of literature can be seen as the model for all later post-colonial writing" (16). That volume also pays substantial attention to Canadian and Australian literature. However, such cases of postcolonial nations dominated by settlers from Europe after the indigenous peoples have been largely exterminated or displaced clearly represent a different situation than that which prevails in Africa or Asia, where the nations emerging after independence are still dominated by indigenous peoples, and where indigenous cultures make a far more important contribution to the postcolonial cultural identities than in nations formed from settler colonies. **Latin American literature** represents a sort of middle case. When Latin American nations emerged (generally in the nineteenth century) from colonization by Spain and Portugal, the descendants of Spanish and Portuguese settlers continued to play crucial roles, while indigenous cultures typically remained strong influences as well. Ireland, meanwhile, represents another case of a postcolonial society, one that is dominated by the descendants of people who lived there before colonization, but one in which the "indigenous" people are themselves Europeans. Finally, Caribbean literature represents another special situation. Here, the indigenous peoples were essentially exterminated, but the postcolonial societies and cultures tend to be dominated by the descendants not of European settlers but of African slaves (and sometimes East Indian indentured workers), brought to the region to provide labor for sugar plantations and other European colonial enterprises.

As it is most typically used, the term "postcolonial literature" tends to apply to the literature produced by writers from nations that achieved independence from European rule in the major wave of decolonization that occurred after **World War II**, a designation that would apply primarily to African, Caribbean, and certain Asian literatures. The latter have tended to receive less attention as objects of academic study in the West, partly because they are primarily written in Asian languages, while African and Caribbean literature are dominated by works written in English or French, the two dominant colonial languages.

On the other hand, Indian and **South Asian literature** have received much attention as well, especially because the Indian-born **Salman Rushdie** (writing in English) produced what is perhaps the most controversial political novel of the last half century in *The Satanic Verses* (1988), which triggered a violent reaction from Islamic fundamentalists because of its supposedly blasphemous treatment of the prophet Muhammad. It is, however, for his Booker Prize–winning *Midnight's Children* (1981) that Rushdie has exerted the most important influence on postcolonial Indian literature, inspiring an entire generation of Anglophone writers who have collectively come to be known as Rushdie's children, including such varied writers as Vikram Seth, Rohinton Mistry, Nayantara Shagal, Shashi Tharoor, Allan Sealy, Farrukh Dhondy, **Amitav Ghosh**, Bapsy Sidhwa, Shashi Deshpande, and Arundhati Roy (herself a Booker Prize winner).

In the case of the Caribbean, the use of European languages (including Spanish) in the production of literature is a necessity due to the fact that the indigenous populations have essentially been exterminated, so there are no indigenous languages that represent viable choices for writers from the Caribbean. In addition, the colonization of the Caribbean began at the end of the fifteenth century, and the British, French, and Spanish colonies there remained under European rule for nearly five hundred years. As a result, the colonies of the Caribbean were dominated more thoroughly by European cultural paradigms than were the African colonies, even as African culture itself continued to play an important role in the region, despite efforts of Caribbean slaveholders to prevent the continuation of African cultural practices there. The East Indian culture of indentured workers brought in to supplant slave labor after the abolition of slavery in the early nineteenth-century brought in still more cultural influences.

The postcolonial culture of the Caribbean consists of a rich mixture of imported European, African, and East Indian cultural traditions. East Indian culture, itself extremely diverse, remains obviously marginal to the culture of the Caribbean, while white Europeans constitute such a small percentage of the total population that European culture is not fully hegemonic in the region, despite the long history of political and economic domination of the Caribbean by Europe. As a result of this complex heritage, the crucial project of constructing viable postcolonial cultural identities is particularly complex in the Caribbean.

The early evolution of **Caribbean literature (Francophone)** was crucially influenced by the anticolonial politics of the **negritude** movement, with works such as **Aimé Césaire**'s 1939 poem *Cahier d'un retour au pays natal* (*Notebook of a Return to My Native Land*) exerting a strong formative influence. Novelists such as **Edouard Glissant** and **Jacques Roumain**, meanwhile, have written from a particularly radical leftist perspective, often giving Francophone Caribbean literature a much more political tone than its Anglophone counterpart.

Anglophone Caribbean literature has produced radical poets such as **Martin Carter** and **Edward Kamau Brathwaite**, while the less radical but still sometimes politically conscious St. Lucian Derek Walcott reached international prominence as a poet and dramatist when he was awarded the Nobel Prize for literature in 1992. The Anglophone Caribbean novel dates back to the first years of the twentieth century, making it in some ways the forerunner of modern postcolonial literature. On the other hand, the first Caribbean novels, pioneered by the Jamaican Thomas Henry MacDermot (publishing under the anagrammatic pen name "Tom Redcam"), largely attempted to mimic British novels, but with a Caribbean setting.

Claude McKay's participation in the **Harlem Renaissance** led to the publication of three novels—*Home to Harlem* (1928), *Banjo* (1929), and *Banana Bottom* (1933)—which can to an extent be regarded as the founding texts of the black Caribbean novel. However, black literature in the Caribbean—and Caribbean literature as a whole in the sense of being a distinct literary phenomenon—came of age in the 1930s, when economic pressures brought about by the global collapse of capitalist economies in the Great Depression triggered a variety of radical activities in the Caribbean. The most important of these was the growth of a militant trade-union movement throughout the British Caribbean, but this movement was part of a larger growth in awareness that, among other things, greatly spurred the development of a Caribbean culture that began to challenge, rather than emulate, the British (and European) literary tradition. Crucial to this phenomenon was the so-called Beacon Group in Trinidad, whose members were associated with *Beacon* magazine, published in Port of Spain from 1931 to 1934. Three of these members, Alfred Mendes, **C.L.R. James**, and **Ralph de Boissière**, would go on to become important Caribbean novelists, though James would ultimately be far more important as an editor, activist, historian, cultural critic, and political theorist than as a novelist.

The ongoing development of Caribbean literature was slowed by the onset of World War II, though the years following the end of the war saw a second renaissance in Caribbean literature, inspired to some extent by the widespread recognition that Britain's European colonies were rapidly moving toward independence V. S. Reid's *New Day* (1949) can be considered the founding text in this emergent movement. Important for both its casting of Jamaican history as a gradual movement toward inevitable self-rule for Jamaica and its deft use of Jamaican dialect in its narrative voice, Reid's novel would inspire any number of later writers who would draw on both Caribbean history and the rhythms of Caribbean language in their work. Reid continued his interest in the history of anticolonial resistance with the publication of *The Leopard* (1958)—a historical novel set in colonial Kenya, focusing on the Mau Mau rebellion of the early 1950s.

The most important Anglophone Caribbean writers to emerge in the 1950s were three young men who immigrated to England at the beginning of the decade: Sam Selvon and **V. S. Naipaul** of Trinidad and **George Lamming** of Barbados. Lamming has remained one of the most important Caribbean novelists since the 1953 publication of *In the Castle of My Skin*, his first novel, while the Nobel Prize–winning Naipaul is probably the best-known Anglophone Caribbean writer on an international scale. Selvon's first novel, *A Brighter Sun* (1952), became one of the founding texts of the Caribbean literary renaissance of the 1950s and helped to establish trends that would be important in Caribbean literature for years to come. The book makes important use of Trinidadian dialect, especially in the dialogue of the characters, thus helping both to enhance the verisimilitude of the book and to challenge the hegemony of Standard English as a literary language. The novel shows an intense awareness of social and political issues, framing the story of the protagonist within the context of the story of the multicultural society of colonial Trinidad. Selvon quickly followed with other novels set in Trinidad, including *An Island Is a World* (1955) and *Turn Again Tiger* (1958), a direct sequel to *A Brighter Sun*. He also began to publish novels about the expatriate West Indian community in London, including *The Lonely Londoners* (1956) and *The Housing Lark* (1965). Among Selvon's most important works are a pair of sequels to *The Lonely Londoners*, *Moses Ascending* (1975) and *Moses Migrating* (1983).

The charged political climate of the years immediately before and after independence can be seen in the appearance of novels such as Frank Hercules's anticolonial *Where the Hummingbird Flies* (Trinidad, 1961) and Ismith Khan's *The Jumbie Bird* (Trinidad, 1961), which explores the confused cultural identity of Trinidad as it moves toward independence. Also notable is Khan's *The Obeah Man* (1964), a powerful political novel that presents the futility of life in postcolonial Trinidad as a direct consequence of the legacy of colonialism. Namba Roy's *Black Albino* (1961) draws on the legacy of Jamaica's fugitive communities of escaped slaves, or Maroons, in an attempt to help develop a positive historical base for new Jamaican identities, while the protagonist of Denis Williams's *Other Leopards* (Guyana, 1963) goes from

Guyana to Africa in search of his cultural roots. Williams's exploration of cultural and historical links between Africa and the Caribbean is also central to the life and work of the Jamaican novelist and poet Neville Dawes, who spent extensive periods in Ghana, where he was a supporter of **Kwame Nkrumah**, the first president of the postcolonial state there. Dawes's two novels, *The Last Enchantment* (1960) and *Interim* (1978), are interesting for their exploration of Jamaican politics before and after independence.

One of the most important Caribbean novelists to begin his publishing career in the postcolonial era was Trinidad's Earl Lovelace—especially for the novels *The Wine of Astonishment* (1982) and *Salt* (1996), which won the Commonwealth Writers' Prize and is particularly strong in its exploration of political conflicts between Trinidad's East Indian and African populations. Other major postcolonial writers in English include Jamaica's Orlando Patterson and Michael Thelwell, Trinidad's Michael Anthony, Barbados's Austin Clarke, and St. Lucia's Garth St. Omer.

Trinidad's Merle Hodge can be seen as the first of a new generation of Caribbean women writers who built on the work of forerunners such as Jean Rhys and Paule Marshall to initiate a new era in Caribbean women's literature in the 1970s and (especially) the 1980s. Indeed, Hodge's *Crick Crack, Monkey* (1970) in some ways marked the coming of age of the Caribbean women's novel. A **bildungsroman** based partly on Hodge's own childhood experience, this novel also, in a sense, narrates the coming of age of Trinidad and Tobago as an independent nation. The 1980s saw a veritable explosion in production by a new generation of highly skilled, professional Caribbean women novelists with the work of writers such as Erna Brodber, Michelle Cliff, Belize's Zee Edgell, and Grenada's Merle Collins.

Though Caribbean literature, in both the Anglophone and Francophone contexts, to an extent led the way for African literature, African literature has received more attention in **postcolonial theory and criticism**. Still, partly because of the influence of the negritude movement and also because of the important theoretical influence of **Frantz Fanon**, Francophone Caribbean literature has exerted an important influence on modern **Francophone African literature**. Indeed, René Maran's *Batouala* (1921) is sometimes considered the first Francophone African novel, though Maran, like Fanon, was originally from the French colonial island of Martinique in the Caribbean. Maran's distinctive combination of literary techniques derived from the European tradition (such as French symbolism) with important elements of African oral storytelling traditions to produce a vivid depiction of conditions in French colonial Africa would set the tone for many African novels to come, in both French and English.

Several other African novels in French (by Maran and others) were published in the 1920s, 1930s, and 1940s, though many critics consider Camara Laye's *The Dark Child* (*L'Enfant noir*, 1953)—substantially influenced by the negritude movement—to mark the beginning of the modern African novel in French. This work owes relatively little to negritude in a stylistic sense, but its idealized portrayal of conditions in a traditional Malinké society untouched by colonial contamination clearly owes something to the influence of the movement. Subsequent Francophone writers would continue Laye's elaboration of an African cultural identity, but in more explicitly anticolonial and politically engaged ways. For example, the Cameroonian Mongo Beti employed humor and satire to excoriate colonialism (especially as purveyed through Catholic missions) and to contribute to the development of a sense of African identity. In novels such as *The Poor Christ of Bomba* (*Le Pauvre Christ de Bomba*, 1956) and *Mission to Kala* (*Mission terminée*, 1957), Beti provided important early examples of the Francophone satirical novel. Another important early satirist was the Cameroonian Ferdinand Oyono, whose *The Old Man and the Medal* (*Le Vieux Négre et la médaille*, 1956) satirizes French colonialism through the eyes of an old Cameroonian man who has long been loyal to his French masters but then comes to question his earlier attitudes. Oyono's *Houseboy* (*Une Vie de boy*, 1960) is striking for its depiction of the reaction of colonized Africans to the behavior of their French colonizers as bizarre, nonsensical, and even obscene, thus effectively reversing a number of European stereotypes about Africa.

Beginning with the Senegalese Nafissatou Diallo's *A Dakar Childhood* (*De Tilène au plateau: Une enfance dakaroise*, 1975), works by women have been extremely important in the development of the African Francophone novel. In addition to Diallo, prominent Francophone women writers include Ken Bugul of Senegal, Gabriel Ilunga-Kabalu of Zaire, and Werewere Liking of Cameroon, the latter of whom exemplifies a movement from the mid-1970s onward to sophisticated feminist explorations of topics, such as the social construction of gender. Particularly important in a political sense is the work of the Senegalese Aminata Sow Fall, whose intensely engaged political novels combine a feminine perspective with a class-based call for the liberation of Africa's poor and oppressed from economic and political tyranny. Only one of Sow Fall's novels has been translated into English, though she has been extremely influential in Africa. Sow Fall's first novel, *Le Revenant* (The Ghost, 1977) details the experiences of a young man who has just been released from prison, only to find that social conditions in postcolonial Africa constitute a larger kind of prison. Sow Fall's best-known novel (and the only one in English translation) is *The Beggars' Strike* (*La Grève des battu*, 1979), which focuses (like much Western **proletarian literature**) on the motif of a strike to comment on social inequities and the exploitation of workers by unscrupulous bosses. In *L'Áppel des arène* (The Call of the Arena, 1982), *Ex-père de la nation* (Former Father of the Nation, 1987), and *Le Jujubier du patriarche* (The Patriarch's Jujube Tree, 1993), Sow Fall continues this mode of intense political commitment and detailed, realistic representation of the social conditions that inform the lives of Africa's poor and downtrodden.

However, by far the most important Francophone African political novelist is clearly the Senegalese **Ousmane Sembène**, who is also an important pioneer of African cinema. Stylistically, Sembène's fiction derives directly from the tradition of European realism, though Sembène has declared a close relationship between his work and traditional African oral narratives, linking, for example, the role of the modern writer to that of the traditional *griot* in a preface appended to his novel *L'Harmattan* (1963).

Sembène's own working-class background (he began writing after a stint as a dockworker in Marseilles in the 1950s) clearly informs all of his novels, starting with *The Black Docker* (*Le Docker noir*, 1956), which details the travails of a young Senegalese man working on the docks in Marseilles while struggling to become a writer. Sembène moved to the front rank of African Francophone novelists with the publication in

1960 of *God's Bits of Wood* (*Les Bouts de bois de Dieu*), still regarded as one of the masterworks of African literature. The book is a historical novel that dramatizes a 1947–1948 strike against the Dakar-Niger railway in French colonial Africa, paying particular attention to the crucial role played by African women in support of the striking men. While the strikers are black and their bosses are white, Sembène makes clear his socialist orientation by presenting the strike in terms of class struggle rather than racial oppositions.

In 1974, Sembène turned his attention from colonialism to neocolonialism with the short novel *Xala* (1976). Employing a mode of comic satire somewhat in the mode of predecessors like Beti, Sembène explores the ongoing neocolonial exploitation of Senegal through a depiction of a member of the rich, decadent indigenous bourgeoisie who continues to do the bidding of his French masters in order to maintain his wealth and status in postcolonial Senegal. However, vestigial remnants of precolonial social practices (such as polygamy) are satirized as well, and Sembène again makes clear his belief that liberation in Africa must be achieved through socialism rather than through a return to precolonial tradition.

Anglophone African literature, especially in terms of its reception in the West, has to some extent been dominated by novelists. The Nigerian novelist **Chinua Achebe**, for example, is easily the best-known black African writer in the West. But Africa has produced important Anglophone poets such as Nigeria's Christopher Okigbo and dramatists such as Nigeria's Nobel Prize–winning **Wole Soyinka** and South Africa's Athol Fugard. The latter's work illustrates the way in which the special historical phenomenon of **apartheid** inspired an entire body of political writings by authors dedicated to the overthrow of that particularly oppressive political system. Writers such as the Nobel Prize winners J. M. Coetzee and (especially) **Nadine Gordimer** have dedicated much of their writing to criticisms of apartheid from liberal points of view, while **Peter Abrahams** and **Alex La Guma** critiqued apartheid from a particularly radical (communist) perspective.

Marxism has exerted a strong influence on other radical African writers as well. Critics such as Emmanuel Ngara and Georg Gugelberger have rightly called attention to the important influence of Marxism on African literature. Meanwhile, Mudimbe notes that while African thought from the 1930s to the 1950s was informed by a number of important influences, Marxism was clearly the most important of these. Figures such as Césaire, **Léopold Senghor**, Kwame Nkrumah, Julius Nyerere, Patrice Lumumba, Amilcar Cabral, Chris Hani, and Agostinho Neto all made important contributions in the attempt to adapt socialist ideas to an African context.

Fanon was perhaps the most important of those who attempted to adapt Marxist ideas to an African context. His work exerted a strong influence on radical writers such as Sembène, Sow Fall, Abrahams, La Guma, Angola's Pepetela, and Nigeria's **Festus Iyayi**, as well as less radical writers such as Ghana's **Ayi Kwei Armah** and Zimbabwe's Tsitsi Dangarembga. Kenya's **Ngũgĩ wa Thiong'o** is probably the most important Anglophone African writer to have been strongly influenced by Fanon. Drawing also on the long legacy of Kenyan resistance to British colonial rule (especially the Mau Mau rebellion of 1954–1956), Ngũgĩ has produced an impressive body of novels and plays that together constitute a powerful critique of British colonialism as well as the ongoing neocolonialism that continues to dominate postcolonial Kenyan society.

Even his earliest novels, written before his conversion to Marxism, are politically engaged. But it is with *Petals of Blood* (1977) that the full emergence of Ngũgĩ's Marxist consciousness becomes clear. This novel also represents the first unequivocal endorsement in Ngũgĩ's work, in the mode of Fanon, of violent resistance to oppression. His satirical play *Ngaahika Ndeenda* (written in Gikuyu with Ngũgĩ wa Mirii, English translation *I Will Marry When I Want*) was produced by the center's amateur community theater group in October 1977, causing the Kenyatta government to ban the play almost immediately as a danger to "public security," then later to raze the center itself and to detain Ngũgĩ in the Kamiti maximum security prison, the site of mass hangings of Mau Mau guerrillas during the 1950s.

In prison, Ngũgĩ continued his activism as best he could, covertly authoring (on toilet paper smuggled into his cell) a novel in Gikuyu, *Caitaani Mutharaba-ini*. Released from prison after the death of Jomo Kenyatta in late 1978, Ngũgĩ published the novel to brisk sales in 1980, following in 1982 with the publication of his own English translation, *Devil on the Cross*. The book is in many ways Ngugi's most Fanonian novel, filled with echoes of Fanon's warnings in *The Wretched of the Earth* of the corruption and decadence of the native bourgeoisie, who were groomed by Africa's colonial rulers to take power in their stead—and in their image. Ngũgĩ followed with another Gikuyu language novel, *Matigari*, in 1986, and has devoted much of his time since to promoting writing in Gikuyu and other indigenous African languages through his editorship of the Gikuyu-language cultural journal *Mutiiri*.

The works of writers such as Ngũgĩ, Sembène, Sow Fall, Abrahams, La Guma, Pepetela, and Iyayi are among not only the most important postcolonial African novels but the most important works of world literature in the last half century. They provide eloquent testimony to the ongoing importance of socialist ideas in postcolonial culture, providing among other things a counter to the tendency toward poststructuralist readings that has sometimes dominated recent work in postcolonial theory and criticism.

Selected Bibliography: Ashcroft, Bill, Gareth Griffiths, and Helen Tiffin. *The Empire Writes Back: Theory and Practice in Post-Colonial Literatures.* London: Routledge, 1989; Boehmer, Elleke. *Colonial and Postcolonial Literature.* New York: Oxford UP, 1995; Booker, M. Keith. *The African Novel in English.* Portsmouth, NH: Heinemann, 1998; Booker, M. Keith, and Dubravka Juraga. *The Caribbean Novel in English: An Introduction.* Portsmouth, NH: Heinemann, 2001; Fanon, Frantz. *The Wretched of the Earth.* New York: Grove, 1968; Gugelberger, Georg M., ed. *Marxism and African Literature.* London: James Currey, 1985; Ngara, Emmanuel. *Art and Ideology in the African Novel: A Study of the Influence of Marxism on African Writing.* London: Heinemann, 1985; Ngũgĩ wa Thiong'o. *Decolonising the Mind: The Politics of Language in African Literature.* London: James Currey, 1986.

M. Keith Booker

POSTCOLONIAL STUDIES. See POSTCOLONIAL THEORY AND CRITICISM.

POSTCOLONIAL THEORY AND CRITICISM deals with the theoretical issues surrounding the study of **postcolonial literature** and culture. In its broadest application, the discipline includes not only literature but also the history, politics, and culture of all former colonies of European powers. It is, however, not entirely simple to determine which nations truly qualify to be called postcolonial. While countries such as the United States, Canada, and Australia were colonies of England at one time, they were settler colonies that displaced or destroyed the indigenous populations, creating nations with cultural and linguistic identities similar to those of European nations. Thus, most postcolonial scholars prefer to use the term specifically in relation to former colonies in Asia, Africa, and the Caribbean that have achieved independence from Western powers after **World War II** and that still maintain majority indigenous populations.

During the **cold war**, much of what is now termed the postcolonial world came to be known as the third world, in opposition to the first world of the American bloc and the second world of the Soviet bloc. With the collapse of the Soviet Union and Eastern European communism, the term "third world" is no longer strictly relevant, and in any case, not every third-world nation was a European colony—Turkey, for example. In an Anglophone context, the term "commonwealth" to include what is now postcolonial was in wide use in the 1950s and 1960s, and well into the 1970s. It derived from the organization of commonwealth countries, a loose federation of nations that had once been British colonies. "Commonwealth" was discarded because the term implied the centrality of England in the life and culture of commonwealth nations, which was no longer the reality. Moreover, since the project of the postcolonial scholar is presumably to offer a revisionist history of colonization, "commonwealth," because of its imperial associations, opposes this stated goal. On the other hand, some Marxist scholars view postcolonial studies with deep suspicion and would argue that the field typically does little to resist Western capitalist economic and cultural hegemony.

The key founding texts of postcolonial studies were **Frantz Fanon**'s *Black Skin, White Masks* (1952) and *The Wretched of the Earth* (1963), and **Edward Said**'s *Orientalism* (1978). Fanon described the experience of being colonized as well as decolonized in his work, whereas Said, in *Orientalism* and in his subsequent books, focused on the other end of these phenomena—on the culture and politics of the colonizing West and on the continuing Western domination of the Orient and other parts of the world through postcolonial cultural, economic, and military establishments. Said's theory of the Orientalist discourse and the specific conclusions he draws from it have been challenged by several postcolonial and Marxist scholars. On the other hand, the importance of the Marxist Fanon in the development of postcolonial studies is undeniable, while Robert Young's recent *Postcolonialism* (2001), a history of the phenomenon of postcolonialism, details the central role played by international communism in the global anticolonial struggle and the growth of independent cultural identities in the colonial world.

Postcolonial studies emphasizes issues in historiography as well as nationalism. Drawing on recent theoretical works in a variety of disciplines not exclusive to literature, it explores the national and cultural experiences of being postcolonial. Benedict Anderson's *Imagined Communities: Reflections on the Origin and Spread of Nationalism* (1983) deals with the rise of various nationalisms across the globe and has proved to be a groundbreaking work in nationalism studies. So are Tom Nairn's *The Break-up of Britain* (1977), which addresses complexities of nationalism in the United Kingdom, and *Faces of Nationalism: Janus Revisited* (1997), which argues in favor of modern nationalisms to resist imperial formations. Through his illustrations in the latter book, referring to countries such as Ireland, Palestine, and Cambodia, Nairn's insights on nationalism illuminate the postcolonial condition in many regions. Equally useful in studying nationalism are Partha Chatterjee's *Nationalist Thought and the Colonial World: A Derivative Discourse* (1986) and *The Nation and Its Fragments: Colonial and Postcolonial Histories* (1993), and Sunil Khilnani's *The Idea of India* (1997). Gauri Viswanathan's *Masks of Conquest* (1989) studies British colonial education policies, especially in India, exploring the heavy emphasis on English literature in the curricula, and is useful in studying various aspects of colonial culture.

The "post" in *postcolonial* suggests an affinity with other movements with the same prefix, especially as the rise of postcolonial studies was contemporaneous with the rise of poststructuralism and **postmodernism** in Western academia. While Said's theory, strongly influenced by **Michel Foucault**'s idea of discursive formations, leans on poststructuralist modes of thought, Said is hardly a poststructuralist. In fact, he is equally indebted to Marxist analyses of power, in particular to the work of **Antonio Gramsci**; at the same time, he is critical of the Marxist account of colonialism, believing it to be Eurocentric and thus complicit with imperialist ideology.

However, some other postcolonial theorists evince more pronounced poststructuralist tendencies. Drawing on **Jacques Derrida** and Jacques Lacan, as well as Sigmund Freud and Fanon, Homi Bhabha argues that the Orientalist discourse is fraught with ambivalence. He believes that in its attempt to create a stable Orient defined as the "other" of Europe, Orientalism is continually undermined by "alterity and ambivalence." For Orientalism to function effectively, the native subject is to be constructed as the "other"; the colonial project, on the other hand, seeks to tame the subject and recast his identity within the Western mode of thought. This contradictory pressure upsets the status quo Orientalism wants to maintain, creating a split within itself. Mimicry and hybridity are two theoretical concepts Bhabha applies to his examination of the postcolonial subject and culture. Mimicry occurs when the native subject begins to accommodate Western/Orientalist discourse; the colonial power perceives this assimilation as threatening. The colonial encounter, in a similar fashion, results in cultural hybridity, changing both the colonizer and the colonized.

Combining Derridian deconstruction with a Marxism influenced by **Louis Althusser**, **Gayatri Spivak** raises pointed questions regarding women's issues in postcolonial studies. Spivak's essay on Sandra Gilbert and Susan Gubar's *The Madwoman in the Attic* demonstrates Western feminism's inadequacy in dealing with racial and colonial issues. In colonial representations of the subject woman, Spivak seeks to recover the voices of the marginalized. Additionally, she questions first-world women's ability to speak for third-world women, noting as well that she is not necessarily better suited to represent Indian women just because she herself is an Indian. Another contribution of Spivak is her concern about the methodology in the "subaltern" studies project, an attempt by a group of Indian scholars, influenced by Gramsci and Said, to rewrite colonial history to represent the lesser voices in colonial representations—for example, voices of those who are not the major players in traditional political history.

Said, Bhabha, and Spivak dominate the theoretical realm in postcolonial studies. Robert Young wryly observes in *Colonial Desire: Hybridity in Theory, Culture, and*

Race (1995) that the three "constitute the Holy Trinity of colonial-discourse analysis, and have to be acknowledged as central to the field." Young's *White Mythologies: Writing History and the West* (1990) centers on the colonized subject and offers a sophisticated analysis of Hegel's impact on colonial representations. Bill Ashcroft, Garland Griffiths, and Helen Tiffin's *The Empire Writes Back: Theory and Practice in Post-Colonial Literatures* takes its title from **Salman Rushdie**'s well known "The Empire Strikes Back with a Vengeance," an article in which Rushdie champions the arrival of new literature from former European colonies—a new English, so to speak, that has cleansed itself of colonial reverberations. Dwelling on "hybridization," the process of mingling the traditions of English with those of "english"—the argot of the natives—Ashcroft et al. envision the postcolonial project as a kind of reinvention of identity through resistant use of language. Some postcolonial authors, primarily of Marxist orientation, have serious misgivings about writing in English (or english). **Ngũgĩ wa Thiong'o** rejects English altogether in his later work because he finds English inadequate to express the reality of his people and prefers his native Gikuyu instead. In *Decolonising the Mind* (1992), he argues persuasively that English is ill suited to describe African reality, noting that the language native to a culture has "a suggestive power well beyond the immediate and lexical meaning."

Postcolonial studies has recently come under severe criticism, primarily by Marxist theorists—such as Benita Parry, Arif Dirlik, and **Epifanio San Juan Jr.**—who find postcoloniality symptomatic of the postmodern turn in contemporary culture and who feel that the emphasis on poststructuralist theory in postcolonial studies has resulted in a lack of attention to material political reality. Their chief criticism of postcolonialism is its insensitivity to class issues; a prime target is the critical output of Bhabha, who uses only a watered-down Fanon devoid of Marxism. Growing within a humanist tradition but advocating antihumanism, poststructuralism, Marxists feel, poses a theoretical impasse that the decolonized world can ill afford. After all, it is a world where material needs far outweigh the desire for theoretical sophistication that at its best can suggest indeterminacy as the way out. Marxist critics also point out that centered in Western universities, postcolonialism's popularity has been ushered in by scholars who are keen on promoting their professional agenda. The neocolonial character of postcolonialism, they add, can be hardly ignored because the term implies an end to colonialism whereas conditions in many postcolonial nations, because of their continuing economic dependence on former masters, suggest otherwise. Finally, postcolonialism, according to Marxists, is a new form of cultural hegemony because its spread has been parallel to the global movement of capital. While American popular culture, with its technological powers, overwhelms the world's common way of life, postcolonialism dominates its intellectual front.

A particularly powerful Marxist critique of postcoloniality has come from the Indian scholar Aijaz Ahmad, whose *In Theory: Classes, Nations, Literatures* (1992) launched a major attack on Said's theory of the Orientalist discourse. Through a close reading of *Orientalism*, Ahmad demonstrates several methodological and conceptual flaws in Said's book and vehemently objects to his characterization of Marx as a nineteenth-century Orientalist thinker. *In Theory* also censures **Fredric Jameson**'s controversial essay "Third-World Literature in the Era of Multinational Capitalism," in which Jameson muses on the value of positing that "all third-world texts are necessarily . . . allegorical" and that "they are to be read as . . . *national allegories*."

Ahmad's implication is clear: the Marxist Jameson, a dialectical thinker, has become in this essay a Foucauldian/Saidian Jameson, a poststructuralist/postmodernist.

Some scholars, on the other hand, have attempted to bridge the gap that exists in studies of colonization and its aftermath. Leela Gandhi's *Postcolonial Theory: A Critical Introduction* (1998) gestures toward such a possibility because the book seems to be keen on extracting the Marxist elements in the works of postcolonial scholars, particularly Spivak. An open invitation to reconciliation comes from Crystal Bartolovich in her introduction to *Marxism, Modernity, and Postcolonial Studies* (2002); she writes, "Marxist theorists can and should engage *with* postcolonial studies in mutual sites of concern, and concede to the field the authentic insights and advances that have been generated within it."

Selected Bibliography: Ahmad, Aijaz. *In Theory: Classes, Nations, Literatures.* London: Verso, 1992; Ashcroft, Bill, Gareth Griffiths, and Helen Tiffin. *The Empire Writes Back: Theory and Practice in Post-Colonial Literatures.* London: Routledge, 1989; Bartolovich, Crystal, and Neil Lazarus, eds. *Marxism, Modernity, and Postcolonial Studies.* Cambridge: Cambridge UP, 2002; Bhabha, Homi. *The Location of Culture.* London: Routledge, 1994; Bhabha, Homi, ed. *Nation and Narration.* London: Routledge, 1994; Dirlik, Arif. *The Postcolonial Aura: Third World Criticism in the Age of Global Capitalism.* Boulder, CO: Westview P, 1997; Fanon, Frantz. *Black Skin, White Masks.* New York: Grove, 1982; Fanon, Frantz. *The Wretched of the Earth.* New York: Grove, 1968; Gandhi, Leela. *Postcolonial Theory: A Critical Introduction.* New York: Columbia UP, 1998; López, Alfred. *Posts and Pasts: A Theory of Postcolonialism.* New York: State U of New York P, 2001; Mongia, Padmini, ed. *Contemporary Postcolonial Theory: A Reader.* London: Arnold, 1996; Parry, Benita. *Postcolonial Studies: A Materialist Critique.* London, Routledge, 2004; Said, Edward. *Culture and Imperialism.* New York: Vintage-Random House, 1994; Said, Edward. Orientalism. New York: Vintage-Random House, 1979; San Juan, E., Jr. *Beyond Postcolonial Theory.* New York: St. Martin's, 1998; Spivak, Gayatri Chakravorty. "Can the Subaltern Speak?" *Marxism and the Interpretation of Culture.* Ed. Cary Nelson and Lawrence Grossberg. Urbana: U of Illinois P, 1988. 271–313; Spivak, Gayatri Chakravorty. *A Critique of Postcolonial Reason: Toward a History of the Vanishing Present.* Cambridge, MA: Harvard UP, 1999; Spivak, Gayatri Chakravorty. *In Other Worlds: Essays in Cultural Politics.* London: Methuen, 1987; Young, Robert J. C. *Colonial Desire: Hybridity in Theory, Culture, and Race.* London: Routledge, 1995; Young, Robert J. C. *Postcolonialism: An Historical Introduction.* Oxford: Blackwell, 2001; Young, Robert J. C. *White Mythologies: Writing History and the West.* London: Routledge, 1990.

Farhad B. Idris

POST-MARXISM utilizes the resources of postmodernist and poststructuralist philosophy and social theory to deconstruct, textualize, or supplement the traditional **Marxist criticism** and theory. Post-Marxism no longer accepts class as the fundamental category for explaining social inequality. It rejects the working class as the primary agent of liberation from capitalism in favor of a cross-class hegemony, as perhaps best expressed in Ernesto Laclau and Chantal Mouffe's *Hegemony and Socialist Strategy*, a key post-Marxist manifesto. In this vision, class becomes one category among others, which include most prominently race, gender, and sexuality. These categories are seen as entangled, with no one more important than any other, though critics of post-Marxism often see a marked tendency for class to disappear altogether.

Some post-Marxists reject the category of class interest because it assumes a unity and historical necessity that they replace with contingency and difference. The very idea that there are objective interests is rejected, along with the concepts of ideology as false consciousness and the vanguard party—presumably the agent that reveals this false consciousness to the benighted proletariat. Most post-Marxists reject the Marxist categories of necessity, totality, and dialectics, though some post-Marxists appropriate the latter term as consistent with their ideas of contingent political agency. Post-Marxists usually reject the Marxist revolutionary project as millenarian, though **Slavoj Zizek**, often associated with the movement, has recently deployed the concept of contingency to defend both Leninism and revolution.

Post-Marxism has been associated with the new social movements and with identity politics but usually rejects essentialist versions of the latter in favor of hybridity. Just as race, class, and gender are entangled as explanatory categories, so are they entangled as identity categories, and because identities are discursively constructed and differential, there are no pure identities. While most post-Marxists reject the category of "preconstituted interests" in favor of discursive construction, it would be wrong to say that such critics are constructivists, as this leaves out the post-Marxist emphasis on constitutive exclusion, on the fundamental failure or aporia at the heart of all identity formation. This emphasis on necessary failure, often the only kind of necessity they acknowledge, leads to an optimistic politics. Having cleared away the obstacles posed by class structure, post-Marxists can then view "power" as something to be appropriated, rearticulated, re-signified, recast, both at psychic and institutional levels. Institutions are not a priori functional for capitalism but sites of struggle.

Marxist critics see the critique of class reductionism as itself reductionist, falsely equating the Marxist structural analysis of inequality with some combination of economic determinism and teleology, thereby allowing the Marxist dialectic of class structure and class struggle, structure and agency, to be turned into aporia. In addition, they assert that the textualization of class combined with a misappropriation of **Antonio Gramsci**'s notion of hegemony makes post-Marxism, in its understanding of power, hardly different from liberal pluralism. Their commitment to negativity, the impossibility of the social, openness, flexibility (to be distinguished from the neoliberal meaning), leads to a fantasy of institutionalizing negative capability, and the ceaseless reiteration and contestation of norms, irrespective of content.

Selected Bibliography: Butler, Judith, Slavoj Zizek, and Ernesto Laclau. *Contingency, Hegemony, Universality: Contemporary Dialogues on the Left.* London: Verso, 2000; Ebert, Teresa L. "Left of Desire." *Cultural Logic* 3.1 (Fall 1999–Spring 2000), http://eserver.org/clogic/3-1%262/ebert.html; Laclau, Ernesto, and Chantal Mouffe. *Hegemony and Socialist Strategy: Towards a Radical Democratic Politics.* London: Verso, 1985; Omi, Michael, and Howard Winant. *Racial Formation in the United States.* New York: Routledge, 1986; Sivanandan, A. *Communities of Resistance.* London: Verso, 1990.

Gregory Meyerson

POSTMODERNISM. Used as a derogatory term by critics concerned with the poverty of American mass culture in the 1950s, the term "postmodernism" first came to the forefront of critical discussions of contemporary culture in the late 1960s, when critics such as Ihab Hassan celebrated postmodernism as a radical new emancipatory form of cultural production, congruent with the oppositional political movements of that decade. At about the same time, poststructuralist theorists such as

Jean-François Lyotard began to embrace postmodernism as well, and postmodernism and poststructuralism have been closely associated ever since. In general, however, the most insightful readings of the politics of postmodernism have been performed by Marxist critics such as **Fredric Jameson**, who have been highly suspicious of the subversive and antiauthoritarian energies often attributed to postmodernism, seeing it instead as a cultural phenomenon that, at best, has limited critical potential and, at worst, works in the interests of the global capitalist hegemony.

Postmodernism is a broad cultural phenomenon that responds to a specific historical condition and thus impacts an extremely wide array of cultural products, including literature, where the postmodernist novel has been particularly important. A simple list of the novelists who have been identified as postmodernist indicates the diversity of postmodernist fiction. To an extent, postmodernist fiction, like other forms of postmodernist art, has been dominated by American writers, beginning with the early work of such writers as William Gaddis (*The Recognitions*, 1955) and Joseph Heller (*Catch-22*, 1961), with the Russian emigré **Vladimir Nabokov** often being considered postmodern as well, especially in later, playful works such as *Pale Fire* (1962). As postmodernism moved to the forefront of American culture in the 1960s and 1970s, writers such as Gilbert Sorrentino (*Mulligan Stew*, 1979) produced a radically self-reflexive form of metafiction that often seemed to be concerned with nothing other than itself. However, writers such as Thomas Pynchon (*The Crying of Lot 49*, 1966) produced more substantial work, and Pynchon's *Gravity's Rainbow* (1973) eventually gained the oxymoronic status of a "classic" of postmodernism.

Pynchon's writing is often politically engaged, though his playful, ironic approach sometimes makes it difficult to decode any specific political statement in his work. Other postmodernist writers have also addressed explicitly political themes, such as Robert Coover's skewering of 1950s conformism and **anticommunism** in *The Public Burning* (1977) and **E. L. Doctorow**'s various chronicles of American history, such as his exploration of the beginnings of modern consumer culture in *Ragtime* (1975). More recently, cyberpunk **science fiction** writers such as William Gibson (*Neuromancer*, 1984) have often been regarded as paradigmatic of postmodernism, while writers such as **Salman Rushdie** (*Midnight's Children*, 1981) have produced crucial works that serve as reminders of the global nature of the phenomenon. Meanwhile, though postmodernist fiction has been a largely masculine preserve, writers such as Kathy Acker have introduced feminist perspectives, while writers such as **Toni Morrison** and Maxine Hong Kingston have shown a simultaneous concern with gender and ethnicity in producing complex fictions informed by postmodernist tendencies.

Jameson famously describes postmodernism as the "cultural logic" of "late capitalism," or capitalism in its post–**World War II**, global, postimperial phase, as described in Ernest Mandel's seminal work *Late Capitalism*, first published in German in 1972 (and in English translation in 1975). For Jameson, late capitalism occurs when modernization has swept over the globe and transnational corporations have become the world's most powerful and important entities, accompanied by a number of other phenomena, including

> the new international division of labor, a vertiginous new dynamic in international
> banking and the stock exchanges (including the enormous Second and Third World

debt), new forms of media interrelationship (very much including transportation systems such as containerization), computers and automation, the flight of production to advanced Third World areas, along with all the more familiar social consequences, including the crisis of traditional labor, the emergence of yuppies, and gentrification on a now-global scale. (*Postmodernism* xix)

Jameson argues that the global hegemony of capitalism leads to the global homogenization of culture, with postmodernism as the dominant mode worldwide. This does not, of course, mean that no other cultural forms survive in the postmodern age, only that the postmodern forms are the dominant ones. Thus, for Jameson, "the only authentic cultural production today has seemed to be that which can draw on the collective experience of marginal pockets of the social life in the world system," a category that for him includes such heterogeneous entities as third-world literature, African American literature, British working-class rock, women's literature, gay literature, and the *roman québecois* (*Signatures* 23).

For Jameson, late capitalism is characterized by plurality, fragmentation, and constant innovation, leading among other things to the production of a psychically fragmented postmodern subject that has extreme difficulty with "cognitive mapping," or understanding its own place within the world system. Meanwhile, beginning with his groundbreaking essay "Postmodernism and Consumer Society," Jameson suggests that postmodernist art has two key characteristics: the importance of the practice of pastiche (which suggests an erosion of the sense of each artist as a creator with a unique style) and "schizophrenic" formal fragmentation (which is related to a loss of historical sense and of confidence in the wholeness of the bourgeois subject).

Drawing on the work of Jacques Lacan, Jameson argues that amid the increasing complexity and fragmentation of experience in the postmodern world, the individual subject experiences a loss of temporal continuity that causes him or her to experience the world somewhat in the manner of a schizophrenic. The schizophrenic, Jameson says,

is condemned to live in a perpetual present with which the various moments of his or her past have little connection and for which there is no conceivable future on the horizon. In other words, schizophrenic experience is an experience of isolated, disconnected, discontinuous material signifiers which fail to link into a coherent sequence. The schizophrenic does not know personal identity in our sense, since our feeling of identity depends on our sense of the persistence of the "I" and the "me" over time. ("Postmodernism and Consumer Society" 119)

Not surprisingly, Jameson suggests that this schizophrenic fragmentation in personal identity strongly influences postmodern narratives, in which the characters often experience fragmented, plural, and discontinuous identities. This schizophrenia also, for Jameson, can be seen in the formal fragmentation of the narratives themselves, leading to the production of postmodern "schizophrenic" texts by authors such as **Samuel Beckett.**

Jameson describes the tendency of postmodernist art to reproduce both the style and the content of earlier works from various periods as pastiche, or "blank parody."

For Jameson, "pastiche is, like parody, the imitation of a peculiar or unique, idio-syncratic style, the wearing of a stylistic mask, speech in a dead language. But it is a neutral practice of such mimicry, without any of parody's ulterior motives, ampu-tated of the satiric impulse, devoid of any laughter and of any conviction that along-side the abnormal tongue you have momentarily borrowed, some healthy linguistic normality still exists" (*Postmodernism* 17). For Jameson, pastiche is not only the most representative technique of postmodernist art but also one with profound implica-tions for his understanding of postmodernism. This reliance on the styles of the past serves as an indication of the loss of historical sense that Jameson sees as a crucial characteristic of postmodernist thought. Postmodernist artists draw on the past, but have no real sense of the past as the prehistory of the present. Thus, the cultural ar-tifacts of the past serve as a sort of museum of styles from which postmodernist artists can draw, without any regard to the historical contexts in which those artifacts were produced. This "random cannibalization of all the styles of the past" reduces the past to a series of spectacles, a collection of images disconnected from any genuine sense of historical process.

Postmodernist architecture may be the clearest example of this bricoleur-like rum-maging through the styles of the past for usable images, but Jameson suggests the "nostalgia film" as a particularly telling example of the postmodernist fascination with the past. Jameson is thinking of overtly nostalgic representations of the past in films such as *American Graffiti* (1973), as well as the retooling of past film genres in works such as the neonoir films *The Long Goodbye* (1973), *Chinatown* (1974), and *Body Heat* (1981). However, this practice of generic pastiche is part of a much broader postmodern phenomenon in which artworks increasingly take both their styles and their subject matter from other cultural artifacts rather than from anything in mate-rial reality.

As the cultural logic of late capitalism, postmodernism should be expected to arise in the years after World War II, when the great European colonial empires collapsed and capitalism began to take on its new global form. It is also no accident that this same period saw the rise of television as a dominant cultural form, especially in the United States. Numerous critics have identified commercial television as the ultimate example of postmodernist culture (see Booker, *Strange TV*). For example, Jim Collins (who makes virtually no distinction between television and postmodernism as cul-tural phenomena) argues that what makes television truly postmodern is not so much the content of any particular program as the fact that multiple programs are simul-taneously available via the same multichannel medium. For Collins, the multiple channels of commercial television is thus the central example of the simultaneous presence of multiple styles that for him is characteristic of the "postmodern context": "Post-Modernism departs from its predecessors in that as a textual practice it actu-ally incorporates the heterogeneity of those conflicting styles, rather than simply as-serting itself as the newest radical alternative seeking to render all conflicting modes of representation obsolete" (114–15).

This multiplicity, celebrated by proponents of postmodernism as a democratic characteristic, also contributes to the complexity that has caused so much critical dis-agreement over the exact nature of postmodernism, though numerous critics have developed accounts of the formal and aesthetic strategies of postmodernist works.

While the specifics of these accounts vary, there is a reasonable consensus that post-modernist works tend to be self-conscious, ironic, parodic, and formally fragmented. **Terry Eagleton** summarizes this consensus as a belief that postmodernist art is a "depthless, decentred, ungrounded, self-reflexive, playful, derivative, eclectic, plural-istic art which blurs the boundaries between 'high' and 'popular' culture, as well as between art and everyday experience" (vii).

In addition, Eagleton notes that this vision of postmodernist art has been closely aligned with the notion that such art arose within the context of fundamental shifts in Western thought that occurred in the decades following World War II. This era of "postmodernity" is, in the consensus view, characterized by

> a style of thought which is suspicious of classical notions of truth, reason, identity and objectivity, of the idea of universal progress or emancipation, of single frameworks, grand narratives or ultimate grounds of explanation. Against these Enlightenment norms, it sees the world as contingent, ungrounded, diverse, unstable, indeterminate, a set of disunified cultures or interpretations which breed a degree of skepticism about the objectivity of truth, history and norms, the givenness of natures and the coherence of identities. This way of seeing, so some would claim, has real material conditions: it springs from an historic shift in the West to a new form of capitalism—to the ephemeral, decentralized world of technology, consumerism and the culture industry, in which the service, finance and information industries triumph over traditional manufacture, and classical class politics yield ground to a diffuse range of "identity pol-itics." (vii)

One might compare here a similar characterization by Best and Kellner, who see post-modernism as "organized around a family of concepts, shared methodological as-sumptions, and a general sensibility that attack modern methods and concepts as overly totalizing and reductionistic; that decry utopian and humanistic values as dystopian and dehumanizing; that abandon mechanical and deterministic schemes in favor of new principles of chaos, contingency, spontaneity, and organism; that challenge all beliefs in foundations, absolutes, truth, and objectivity, often to em-brace a radical skepticism, relativism, and nihilism; and that subvert boundaries of all kinds" (19).

Eagleton's own concern in *The Illusions of Postmodernism* is not with postmodernist culture but with postmodernity, with the complex of ideas that have informed post-modern—and, to a large extent, poststructuralist—thought. And his critique of the diffuse, confused, and contradictory nature of those ideas goes a long way toward ex-plaining why it has been so difficult to reach a critical consensus concerning the true nature and historical implications of postmodernism and postmodernity. In any case, however, Eagleton reminds us that postmodern plurality and boundary crossing are hardly subversive of capitalist authority, given that "capitalism is the most pluralistic order history has ever known, restlessly transgressing boundaries and dismantling op-positions, pitching together diverse life-forms and continually overflowing the mea-sure" (133).

However contradictory, critical attempts to characterize postmodernism have often been tied together by a common attempt to characterize postmodernism in contrast with **modernism**. Many accounts of postmodernism, in fact, have simply argued that postmodernist works are informed by essentially the same aesthetic impulses as modernist ones, but that these impulses take more radical forms in postmodernism. For example, Brian McHale, in an influential survey of postmodernist fiction, notes the epistemological skepticism that is crucial to both modernism and postmodernism. However, McHale argues that modernist fiction is informed by a belief in the existence of a fundamental reality about which basic truths exist, however difficult those truths might be to determine. Postmodernist fiction, on the other hand, is, for McHale, informed by a basic skepticism toward the very existence of such truths, reality itself being unstable, multiple, and socially determined.

This notion of the skepticism of postmodernism has often translated into a vision of postmodernist works as fundamentally opposed to authoritarian versions of truth and reality, often in contrast to a basic desire for order and authority that informs modernist works. Hassan, one of the critics most responsible for initially promoting the idea of postmodernism in the 1960s, characterizes postmodernism in a crucial article by listing the major rubrics of modernism, then explaining the ways in which postmodernism moves beyond modernism through subversive challenges to modernist ideas of order and authority. For Hassan, "whereas Modernism created its own forms of Authority, precisely because the center no longer held, Postmodernism has tended toward Anarchy, in deeper complicity with things falling apart" (29).

Critics such as Hassan tend to see postmodernism as an irreverent, rule-breaking, populist challenge to the received conventions of the Western aesthetic tradition, somewhat along the lines of the oppositional political movements of the 1960s. Linda Hutcheon, one of the most effective apologists for postmodernist fiction, implicitly takes this tack when she argues that such fiction is centrally informed by a subversive challenge to authority, and especially to authoritative, official narratives of history. Thus, for Hutcheon, the paradigmatic form of postmodernist narrative is what she calls "historiographic metafiction," a special form of the **historical novel** that reflexively calls attention to its own construction but also, at the same time, calls attention to the assumptions on which official accounts of history have been constructed by those in authority.

Arguing that "critique" is "crucial to the definition of the postmodern," Hutcheon acknowledges that this political element of postmodernism can be seen as part of "the unfinished project of the 1960s, for, at the very least, those years left in their wake a specific and historically determined distrust of ideologies of power and a more general suspicion of the power of ideology" (*Politics* 10). Of course, by the 1960s, when such visions of postmodernism as somehow anti-ideological began to arise, more than a decade of incessant **cold-war** propaganda had made "ideology" almost synonymous with "communism." It is perhaps not surprising, then, that what coherence Eagleton does find in postmodernity has to do with a widespread suspicion toward the traditional ideas of the left and with a sense that the rise of postmodernism has a great deal to do with the perception (accurate or not) of a historical experience of defeat of the left in the West in the decades following World War II.

Perry Anderson, in his investigation of the historical roots of the idea of postmodernism, finds a fundamental antisocialism at the base of most postmodernist thought. Discussing the well-known suggestion by Lyotard that postmodernism is informed by a basic "incredulity toward metanarratives," Anderson offers a convincing argument that by "metanarratives," Lyotard really means only one metanarrative—that of classical Marxism. Further, Anderson argues that Lyotard's rejection of Marxism is part of a thoroughgoing rejection of all utopian alternatives to the existing capitalist order. Indeed, Anderson concludes that the various versions of postmodernism, as they developed in the work of thinkers as otherwise various as Lyotard, Hassan, Charles Jencks, and **Jürgen Habermas**, were united by a consistent antipathy toward the traditional utopian values of socialism and the Left: "Common to all was a subscription to the principles of what Lyotard—once the most radical—called liberal democracy, as the unsurpassable horizon of the time. There could be nothing but capitalism. The postmodern was a sentence on alternative illusions" (46).

Anderson's suggestion that postmodernism is rooted in pessimism and resignation contrasts dramatically with the vision of postmodernism as subversive, which informs the work of critics such as Hassan and Hutcheon. Indeed, as a whole, the rich body of Marxist commentary on postmodernism, epitomized by the work of Jameson, tends to see the rise of postmodernist culture as aligned with (rather than opposed to) the expansion and transformation of capitalism after World War II. For example, David Harvey associates the rise of postmodernism with a fundamental transformation of capitalism into a post-Fordist mode of production after World War II. For Harvey, this new, more subtle and flexible form of capitalism extends the control of the economic system into areas (including culture) that had previously been relatively autonomous. Postmodernism, then, "signals nothing more than a logical extension of the power of the market over the whole range of cultural production" (62).

Other Marxist critics have warned against exaggerating the extent to which capitalism has changed in the postwar years, fearing that an emphasis on such changes might obscure fundamental continuities in the basic form of capitalist production. Even Harvey, for example, reminds us that, whatever changes capitalism has undergone in the postwar era, "we still live, in the West, in a society where production for profit remains the basic organizing principle of economic life" (121). Consequently, Harvey also concludes that while postmodernist art may be a distinct phenomenon, "there is much more continuity than difference between the broad history of modernism and the movement called postmodernism" (116). Alex Callinicos is even more insistent on this continuity, doubting that postmodernism exists at all except in the minds of certain theorists—largely because he doubts the reality of postmodernity as a genuinely new historical stage. For Callinicos, meanwhile, postmodernism is again antisocialist, and the invention of postmodernity is intimately linked to a "rejection of socialist revolution as either feasible or desirable" (9). That is, he sees the idea of the postmodern as the invention of theorists who would seek to argue that history has entered a radical new stage, in which the long tradition of Marxist critique—rooted as it is in the prior, modern stage—has been rendered ineffectual if not entirely irrelevant.

Teresa Ebert also worries that postmodern theory obscures the economic realities of the contemporary world. She grants that capitalism has undergone changes since World War II but insists that "the most important point to be made about the shifting patterns of production and employment is that they are still grounded on the basic structural relations of capitalism—*the expropriation and exploitation of living*

labor (surplus labor) for profit" (112, Ebert's emphasis). In light of this basic continuity, Ebert suggests that there are two separate strains in postmodernist thought,
which she labels "ludic" postmodernism and "resistance" postmodernism. The ludic
strain, for Ebert, is complicit with capitalism, while the resistance strain retains the
ability effectively to critique capitalism. In addition, Ebert argues that the two strains
can be distinguished by their different views of the recent history of capitalism. Ludic
postmodernism, she argues, envisions postmodernism as the product of a break in
the evolution of capitalism so radical that all previous history (including the history
of Marxist critique) is rendered irrelevant. Resistance postmodernism, with which
Ebert aligns her own work, emphasizes the historical continuity in the development
of capitalism, seeing the postmodern era as the product not of a radical break in history but of the historical evolution of capitalism, which constantly finds "new articulations of the relations of production. The extraordinary superstructural changes
that we mark as postmodernism are simply new mediations of the fundamental social contradictions resulting from the division and exploitation of labor" (133).

Many analysts of postmodernism have detected competing tendencies of the kind
Ebert indicates. Perhaps the most sophisticated discussion of competing impulses
within postmodernism remains that of Andreas Huyssen, who produces his own account of a contrast between a purely affirmative postmodernism and a postmodernism that maintains an effective critical dimension. Huyssen's best known and most
widely cited argument is that postmodernism is informed by a democratic challenge
to received notions of a "great divide" between high and low culture, notions that
for Huyssen most modernist artists not only accepted but sought to maintain. Further, Huyssen sees modernism as centrally informed by an attempt to "ward off" the
threat posed to "genuine" art by mass culture, which he also sees as symbolically associated (for the modernists) with the threat of the feminine.

However, Huyssen's analysis is anything but a simple celebration of the liberating
democratic impulses of postmodernism. On the one hand, Huyssen locates the rise
of postmodernist art amid the pop-art movement of the 1960s, concluding that "from
the beginning . . . the most significant trends within postmodernism have challenged
modernism's relentless hostility to mass culture" (188). At the same time, this alignment of postmodernism with pop always threatens to reduce postmodernist art to
the status of mere commodity, especially in the United States, where the cultural rebellion entailed in the experimental art of the 1960s, while reacting against the conformity of the 1950s, was not accompanied by any coherent program of radical social
and political transformation (169). Indeed, Huyssen notes the rapidity with which
the Western culture industry began to exploit new marketing opportunities produced
by the pop-art explosion of the 1960s (141–42).

Nevertheless, Huyssen believes that postmodernism cannot be regarded simply as
a representative symptom of capitalism. One of his central ideas is that the direct
predecessor to postmodernism in Western cultural history is not modernism but the
avant-garde. As such, postmodernism inherits many of the critical and oppositional
energies of the avant-garde. In the 1960s in particular, these energies were aimed at
the entrenched visions of modernism (such as in the American **New Criticism**) that
had been institutionalized in the 1950s. Huyssen is careful to distinguish between

modernism itself (as it was practiced and experienced by the modernists of the early twentieth century) and these institutionalized visions of modernism from the 1950s, which, for Huyssen, are profoundly reactionary, based on a cultural elitism that reinforces inequalities on the basis of class, race, and gender, which have long informed the capitalist culture of the West. In addition, Huyssen argues that this conservative, institutionalized version of modernism cannot be separated from the climate of the cold war, in which modernism became enshrined as the official example of the superiority of Western high culture to both Western mass culture and Soviet **socialist realism** (which was itself always intended as mass culture, not high art). For Huyssen, postmodernism in the 1960s "was never a rejection of modernism per se, but rather a revolt against that version of modernism which had been domesticated in the 1950s, become part of the liberal-conservative consensus of the times, and which had even been turned into a propaganda weapon in the cultural-political arsenal of Cold War anticommunism" (190).

However, following the important analysis of Peter Bürger, Huyssen notes that by the time of the rise of postmodernism, the political energies of the avant-garde had largely been spent because the once-shocking techniques of avant-garde art had already been absorbed and appropriated by advertising and other forms of commodified culture. For Huyssen, then, the postmodernist culture of the 1960s had in turn exhausted much of its critical energies by the 1970s, leading to the rise of a "largely affirmative postmodernism which had abandoned any claim to critique, transgression or negation" (189). At the same time, Huyssen also argues that a new, potentially critical form of postmodernism also arose in the 1970s, differing substantially from the avant-garde and basing its oppositional strategies on a "new creative relationship between high art and certain forms of mass culture" (194). Thus, while Huyssen does not entirely dismiss the notion that postmodernism might develop in genuinely oppositional ways in the future, he characterizes the explosion of postmodernist art in the 1960s as "the closing chapter in the tradition of avantgardism," as "the endgame of the avantgarde and not as the radical breakthrough it often claimed to be" (164, 168).

Huyssen's recognition of the two-sided nature of so many aspects of postmodernism represents an attempt at a genuine dialectical analysis of the phenomenon. Indeed, he specifically places his work in the Marxist dialectical tradition: "Just as Marx analyzed the culture of modernity dialectically as bringing both progress and destruction, the culture of postmodernity, too, must be grasped in its gains as well as in its losses, in its promises as well as in its depravations" (200). Huyssen believes that Jameson's vision of postmodernism as directly aligned with late capitalism is an exaggeration. However, Huyssen himself probably overstates the case for anticapitalist tendencies in postmodernism that derive from the avant-garde tradition and that are closely associated with the youth and pop-art movements of the 1960s. For example, Matei Calinescu is much more skeptical than Huyssen about the subversive power of avant-garde art, even at its height, and he is far more negative than Huyssen himself about the remaining political threat posed by the avant-garde by the 1960s. In particular, he argues that by the 1960s, avant-garde art had been thoroughly appropriated as popular entertainment with little or no critical power.

In addition, if neither the avant-garde nor the counterculture of the 1960s is necessarily anticapitalist, it is also the case that capitalism itself contains extremely complex and contradictory impulses. Indeed, one of Marx's central arguments was that capitalism was powerful enough as a historical force to overwhelm every competing system with which it came into contact, but that capitalism contained the seeds of its own destruction and would ultimately produce its own downfall. In short, Jameson's totalizing vision of postmodernism as the cultural logic of late capitalism is not necessarily simplistic, defeatist, or nondialectical. Instead, this vision still allows for a variety of competing impulses (including anticapitalist ones) within postmodernism because capitalism itself contains such impulses.

Critics continue to debate the exact nature and implications of postmodernism in the early years of the twenty-first century, partly because it is such a complex and plural phenomenon but also for the simple reason that postmodernism is still underway and still developing. The Marxist consensus that postmodernist culture is part of the capitalist problem rather than part of the solution seems at this point the most compelling characterization. However, it may well be that genuinely oppositional forms of postmodernist culture may yet arise. Indeed, there are currently signs of such potential in the recent science fiction of such writers as Ken MacLeod (*The Star Fraction*, 1995) and Don Sakers (*Dance for the Ivory Madonna*, 2002), which often has much in common with cyberpunk, but lacks the skepticism and cynicism that have often marked cyberpunk visions of the technological future, instead envisioning a future world in which technological innovation can lead to genuine and progressive change in human societies—and even human beings themselves. Meanwhile, the cyberspace that informs such fiction is becoming increasingly important in the real world as well, and it remains to be seen how the growing importance of internet culture will ultimately affect the historical course of postmodernism.

Selected Bibliography: Anderson, Perry. *The Origins of Postmodernity.* London: Verso, 1998; Best, Steven, and Douglas Kellner. *The Postmodern Turn.* New York: Guilford P, 1997; Booker, M. Keith. *Strange TV: Innovative Television Series from "The Twilight Zone" to "The X-Files."* Westport, CT: Greenwood, 2002; Calinescu, Matei. *Five Faces of Modernity.* Durham, NC: Duke UP, 1987; Callinicos, Alex. *Against Postmodernism: A Marxist Critique.* New York: St. Martin's, 1989; Collins, Jim. *Uncommon Cultures: Popular Culture and Post-Modernism.* New York: Routledge, 1989; Connor, Steven. *Postmodernist Culture: An Introduction to Theories of the Contemporary.* 2nd ed. Oxford: Blackwell, 1997; Eagleton, Terry. *The Illusions of Postmodernism.* Oxford: Blackwell, 1996; Ebert, Teresa L. *Ludic Feminism and After.* Ann Arbor: U of Michigan P, 1996; Harvey, David. *The Condition of Postmodernity: An Inquiry into the Origins of Cultural Change.* Cambridge, MA: Blackwell, 1990; Hassan, Ihab. "POSTmodernISM." *New Literary History* 3 (1971): 5–30; Hutcheon, Linda. *A Poetics of Postmodernism: History, Theory, Fiction.* New York: Routledge, 1988; Hutcheon, Linda. *The Politics of Postmodernism.* New York: Routledge, 1989; Huyssen, Andreis. *After the Great Divide: Modernism, Mass Culture, Postmodernism.* Bloomington: Indiana UP, 1986; Jameson, Fredric. *Postmodernism; or, The Cultural Logic of Late Capitalism.* Durham, NC: Duke UP, 1991; Jameson, Fredric. "Postmodernism and Consumer Society." *The Anti-Aesthetic: Essays on Postmodern Culture.* Ed. Hal Foster. Port Townshend, WA: Bay P, 1983. 111–26; Jameson, Fredric. *Signatures of the Visible.* New York: Routledge, 1992; Lyotard, Jean-François. *The Postmodern Condition: A Report on Knowledge.* Trans. Geoff Bennington and Brian Massumi. Minneapolis: U of Minnesota P, 1984; Mandel, Ernest. *Late Capitalism.* Trans. Joris De Bres. London: NLB, 1975; McCaffery, Larry, ed. *Storming the Reality Studio: A Casebook of Cyberpunk and Postmodern Fic-

tion. Durham, NC: Duke UP, 1991; McHale, Brian. *Constructing Postmodernism.* London: Routledge, 1992; McHale, Brian. *Postmodernist Fiction.* New York: Methuen, 1987.

M. Keith Booker

POUND, EZRA (1885–1972), one of the major modernist poets of the twentieth century. However, Pound's reputation for poetic brilliance has been clouded by his anti-Semitism and his political allegiance to fascism. After leaving America in 1908 to live in London (1908–1920), Paris (1921–1924), and Rapallo, Italy (1924–1945, 1958–1972), Pound energetically promoted not only his own work but also that of his fellow artists. In his view, economic liberalism favored salable mediocrity over artistic excellence, the old literary recipes over modernist artistic invention. Pound's first political goal was to find and maintain a basis for the subsistence of the modernist cultural project.

This goal made him especially receptive to Major C. H. Douglas's economic theory known as social credit. Douglas started from the premise that due to the interest charges that industry has to pay for new production, the prices in an economy were much higher than the purchasing power of the consumer. Douglas argued that the wealth of the nation consisted in a national heritage composed of natural wealth, accumulation of mechanical inventions, and new production. Every citizen had a birthright to this wealth and therefore a claim to a national dividend from it. In Douglas's vision, the gold standard would be abolished, credit would be issued by the state on the basis of the national heritage, and the banks would lose the right to issue money. The dividend would enable the citizens to refuse exploitative employment and give them leisure to be creative. Pound believed that artists could thus live and contribute meaningfully to the spiritual wealth of a nation without degrading their work.

After moving to Rapallo in 1924, Pound observed and increasingly admired Mussolini's fascist experiment. In his opinion, the dictator was totally dedicated to the welfare of the nation, shaping his policies to serve the general interest. Pound believed that the fascist government came closest to putting Douglas's economic vision into practice. After meeting Mussolini personally on January 30, 1933, Pound became confident that Italy was distributing work and benefits in a similar manner to social credit. This made him condone Mussolini's war in Abyssinia in 1935, the military involvement in the **Spanish Civil War** in 1936, and the alliance with Hitler leading to Italy's participation in **World War II**. When anti-Semitic legislation took effect in Italy in 1938, Pound became overtly anti-Semitic in his articles for fascist periodicals. Between 1941 and 1943, he contributed to Italian war propaganda with a series of broadcasts directed at the United States and Britain. These speeches triggered an indictment for treason by a grand jury in Washington, D.C. Pound was arrested in May 1945 and incarcerated first in a disciplinary training camp at Pisa. In November he was brought to Washington for trial but was judged mentally unfit to cooperate meaningfully in his defense. He was interned at St. Elizabeth's Hospital for the Criminally Insane, from which he was released as incurable in 1958. He spent his remaining years in Italy and died in Venice in 1972.

Selected Bibliography: Marsh, Alec. *Money and Modernity: Pound, Williams, and the Spirit of Jefferson.* Tuscaloosa: U of Alabama P, 1998; Nadel, Ira, ed. *The Cambridge Companion to Ezra Pound.* Cambridge: Cambridge UP, 1999; Preda, Roxana. *Ezra Pound's (Post)modern Poetics and Politics*. New York: Peter Lang, 2001; Redman, Tim. *Ezra Pound and Italian Fascism*. Cambridge: Cambridge UP, 1991; Surette, Leon. *Pound in Purgatory: From Economic Radicalism to Fascism and Anti-Semitism*. Urbana: U of Illinois P, 1999.

Roxana Preda

PRICHARD, KATHARINE SUSANNAH (1883–1969). A founding member of the Australian **Communist Party** (ACP), Katharine Prichard's radicalism was clearly inspired by her own early struggles with poverty as well as the momentous international events she lived through during the early twentieth century. The declining health of her journalist father, who eventually committed suicide, meant that she was unable to attend university but had to earn her living as a governess in country New South Wales. Periods spent as a journalist in London before **World War I** put her in touch with international radical thought and gave her further experience of workers' struggles. In 1919, she married the war hero Hugo Throssell and moved to Perth, Western Australia, becoming a member of the central committee of the ACP in 1920. While she was away on a visit to Russia in 1933, her husband committed suicide because of financial difficulties.

Prichard wrote poems, plays, and short stories, as well as nonfictional works—including an autobiography—but is best known for her novels, where her aim was to "represent the Australian people to themselves." *Working Bullocks* (1926) traces the lives of timber getters and mill workers in Western Australia, and their failed attempt at strike action for better wages and conditions. *Coonardoo* (1928), also set in Western Australia, focuses on the doomed love between an Aboriginal woman and a white station owner. *Intimate Strangers* (1937), the only one of Prichard's novels with a contemporary city setting, looks at the tensions in a marriage. Prichard's most thoroughgoing attempt to write in the socialist realist manner, a trilogy of historical novels set on the Western Australian goldfields—*The Roaring Nineties* (1946), *Golden Miles* (1948), and *Winged Seeds* (1950)—has generally been judged inferior to her earlier fiction.

Selected Bibliography: Bird, Delys, ed. *Katharine Susannah Prichard: Stories, Journalism and Essays*. St. Lucia: U of Queensland P, 2000; Buckridge, Pat. "Katharine Susannah Prichard and the Literary Dynamics of Political Commitment." *Gender, Politics and Fiction: Twentieth Century Australian Women's Novels*. Ed. Carole Ferrier. St. Lucia: U of Queensland P, 1986. 85–100; Hay, John, and Brenda Walker, eds. *Katharine Susannah Prichard: Centenary Essays*. Nedlands, Western Australia: U of Western Australia Centre for Studies in Australian Literature, 1984; Throssell, Ric. *Wild Weeds and Wind Flowers: The Life and Letters of Katharine Susannah Prichard*. Sydney: Angus and Robertson, 1975.

Elizabeth Webby

PRISON LITERATURE. An important area for social and cultural critique that has only begun to come into focus as an area of academic study beginning in the last decades of the twentieth century. Despite the lack of scholarly focus, imprisoned writers have been producing texts for centuries. Such diverse authors as **Miguel de Cervantes**, the Marquis de Sade, **Henry David Thoreau**, and E. E. Cummings have dealt with themes of imprisonment—the captive's tale contained within *Don Quixote* and *Los baños de Argel*, based on Cervantes' five-year captivity in Algeria and Morocco; de Sade's letters from prison as well as his novel *Justine*, which was written there; Thoreau's "Resistance to Civil Government," inspired by his night in jail for not paying what he considered to be an unjust tax; and Cummings's **World War I** experience evoked in *The enormous room* all fall within this genre. A difference between these works and later texts that also belong to this category is that the newer works have had to face a much greater struggle to become widely read.

Prison literature in its various forms (memoirs, letters, confessions, denouncements, manifestoes, novels, plays, poetry) has difficulty gaining readers because of censorship and the difficulty of getting a manuscript out of a prison. To make matters worse, finding materials and means to physically produce a text is difficult. Martin Luther King Jr. was forced to write his "Letter from Birmingham Jail" on the margins of a newspaper, continued on scraps of writing paper provided by an African American trusty, and finally concluded "on a pad my attorneys were eventually permitted to leave me." The Kenyan novelist **Ngũgĩ wa Thiong'o** wrote his novel *Devil on the Cross* (1980) on toilet paper while in detention. Beyond these material problems is the stigma attached to any writing coming out of a prison. Its goal is often criticism of the society that has imprisoned its writer—often a socially difficult task coming from the margins of imprisonment. H. Bruce Franklin writes of the public discomfort with prison literature in his introduction to *Prison Writing in Twentieth-Century America*: "The public is not supposed to know of or be concerned with any degradation or abuse going on inside the prison nor with the prisoners' responses to their punishment" (2). Such an attitude has helped to contribute to the scarcity of public interest in and academic studies done on prison literature and the cultural resistance and critique that it produces.

Several typical characteristics of prison literature—especially in the more radical twentieth-century texts—include genre fluidity, linkage of political and patriarchal oppression, cultural criticism, microcosmic symbolism, resistance to totalizing norms, and psychosocial transformation in relation to questions of identity and self-definition. Multiple genres and multiple narrative points of view often appear in a single text, which might mix stream-of-consciousness, epistolary, journal writing, testimonial, and journalistic and autobiographical formats. The linkage of resistance, identity, and patriarchal oppression can be found where female, alternative, and non-patriarchally approved sexualities are foregrounded as a form of political critique, especially when characters resist the traditional roles that patriarchal societies would impose on them.

African literature has produced prison-literature texts in the twentieth century from writers such as Ngũgĩ wa Thiong'o and **Wole Soyinka,** who write against cultural and governmental oppression. African American writers such as Dr. Martin Luther King Jr., Malcolm X, Piri Thomas, and Mumia Abu-Jamal have written texts from and about prison that focus the same sort of cultural critique on white/Anglo cultural, economic, and sociopolitical oppression within the United States. Europe has seen texts from authors such as Cummings, **Aleksander Solzhenitsyn,** and **Antonio Gramsci** in that same period, as well as the finest philosophical consideration of the prison from French thinker **Michel Foucault** in his *Discipline and Pun-*

ish: The Birth of the Prison (1975). This text examines how the transfer of older forms of immediate punishment practiced on the physical body moved toward a delayed punishment on the mind/liberty, with the final result being a "docile body," as well as the growing control that structures of power (governments, prisons, mental hospitals) hold over the people held within. For Foucault, the concept of the "panopticon"—a circular prison where the guard stationed in the middle can see all the prisoners' activities while isolating them from each other—is a model equally useful for defining how traditional societies perform the same function on their citizens.

Writers from Latin America have produced a vast range of texts that deal with the effects of imprisonment under various governments during the twentieth century, particularly novels, memoirs, and novel-like *testimonios*. While some texts have been written from within prisons, the vast majority have been written after-the-fact from a position of exile, such as Ariel Dorfman's play *Death and the Maiden* (*La muerte y la doncella*, 1990) and Manuel Puig's novel *Kiss of the Spiderwoman* (*El beso de la mujer araña*, 1976). Others, such as Brazilian author Graciliano Ramos's *Memórias do cárcere* (Memoirs of Prison), were written from a position of *insilio*—a position of internal exile, in which an author has survived prison and must later live in silence for fear of further governmental oppression.

Kiss of the Spiderwoman (adapted to film in 1985) is one of the earliest and best-known works of prison literature from Latin America. It explores the relationship between two cell mates—one a homosexual arrested for statutory rape and the other a revolutionary arrested for activities against the state. The two tell each other stories based on films they have seen, each slowly becoming infused with the social concerns of the other. The controversial sexual relationship that develops between them is an example of the confluence of personal and political difference practiced in prison literature as a means to critique a dictatorial government (in this case, the military junta that controlled Puig's home country of Argentina from 1976 to 1983).

Selected Bibliography: Davies, Ioan. *Writers in Prison*. Oxford: Basil Blackwell, 1990; Foucault, Michel. *Discipline and Punish: The Birth of the Prison*. Trans. Alan Sheridan. New York: Vintage-Random House, 1979; Franklin, H. Bruce. Introduction. *Prison Writing in Twentieth-Century America*. Ed. H. Bruce Franklin. New York: Penguin, 1998; Franklin, H. Bruce. *Prison Literature in America: The Victim as Criminal and Artist*. Exp. edition. New York: Oxford UP, 1989; Gelfand, Elissa D. *Imagination in Confinement: Women's Writings from French Prisons*. Ithaca, NY: Cornell UP, 1983; Harlow, Barbara. *Barred: Women, Writing and Political Detention*. Hanover, NH: Wesleyan UP, 1992; Tierney-Tello, Mary Beth. *Allegories of Transgression and Transformation: Experimental Fiction by Women Writing under Dictatorship*. Albany: State U of New York P, 1996.

Jason G. Summers

PROCHAIN EPISODE (NEXT EPISODE, 1965). This major neonationalist Québécois novel is the first and best known of the four that Hubert Aquin produced over a nine-year period. This brilliant, troubled writer took his life in 1977 following a series of political/personal setbacks and especially his inability to complete a new work in progress, "Obombre." The narrator is an anonymous revolutionary under police guard in a Montreal mental institution. Having failed to assassinate a

Canadian secret-service agent in Switzerland, he is awaiting trial and writing a novel about a similarly failed plot to eliminate the elusive triple-identity "Mountie," H. de Heutz. The narrator of the novel-within-the-novel also misses a rendezvous with his lover, designated only as "K" (Quebec?), who seems to be a double agent and likely the cause of the primary narrator's arrest on his return to Canada. A third failure is the inability of the main narrator to complete the novel-in-progress, a microcosm of the first. The two narrations project a final episode in which revolutionary action will lead to Quebec's independence, and the novel-within-the-novel will simultaneously be brought to a successful conclusion.

The two strands of the work are constantly intertwined in what is also a reflection on the relationship between art and political violence. In the novel-within-the-novel, one of the main reasons for the narrator's failure to eliminte de Heutz is the former's fascination with the wealth and objets d'art found in the castle of the latter, his "enemy-brother" (Smart). The central theme of failure flashes back to the revolutionary period of 1837–1838, when crushed uprisings for independence from Britain occurred in both Lower Canada—today's Quebec—and Upper Canada (Ontario), the latter unmentioned here as in most Francophone fiction on that period. The secondary narrator opines that Louis-Joseph Papineau, leader of the revolts in Quebec, would have done better to blow his brains out, perhaps an understandable view for a writer who penned a celebrated essay entitled "Ecrivain faute d'être banquier" ("A writer, for want of becoming a banker").

Prochain episode is the best-known example of the *texte national* (Jacques Godbout) that emerged during Quebec's "Quiet Revolution" of the 1960s, treating the sociopolitical tensions between Quebec and Canada. It has been analyzed in numerous books and articles, most of which deal with its experimentation and self-reflexive form, including its combination of baroque, erotic, and even burlesque elements. It was (poorly) translated by Penny Williams (1967) under the original title and (far better) by Sheila Fischman in 2001 as *Next Episode*.

Selected Bibliography: Aquin, Hubert. *Prochain episode*. Critical edition. Ed. Jacques Allard et al. Montreal: Bibliothèque québécoise, 1995; Shek, Ben-Z. *French-Canadian and Québécois Novels*. Toronto: Oxford UP, 1991; Smart, Patricia. "*Prochain episode*" and "Hubert Aquin." *Oxford Companion to Canadian Literature*. 2nd ed. Ed. Eugene Benson and William Toye. Toronto: Oxford UP, 1997. 58–60, 970–71.

Ben-Z. Shek

PROLETARIAN FICTION, AMERICAN. Term generally applied to a Depression-era (1929–1941) movement to produce a homegrown American radical literature that featured novels and short fiction of oppressed, rebellious working-class life. In this golden age of leftist literature, left-wing U.S. authors, including those from working-class backgrounds, viewed themselves as cultural workers, attended writers' congresses to map out manifestoes, and doubled as reporters or activists in the labor struggles and poor people's protests that often formed the narrative backbone of these writers' fictive accounts. Although critical battles still rage on the form and mission of proletarian literature, some of its characteristic themes are revolutionary awareness of class struggle; opposition to capitalism and competitive individualism; and the value of collective action in combating oppression and reshaping government.

As a formidable contribution to the body of leftist texts, proletarian novels and stories—empowered by the economic crisis of the American 1930s—looked confidently to a workers' world. As a cultural product, proletarian literature—and, to a lesser extent, literature with proletarian elements—remained focused on the diverse values, vernaculars, and daily lives of laboring and jobless people; the work floor, strike hall, and picket line; the life of the road; the sharecropping or farm tenantry district; the after-hours ethnic tenement street; and the myriad comradeships, families, social networks, and living arrangements particular to people who worked with their hands.

Precursors of this fiction, though marked by patrician attitudes, range from mid-nineteenth-century novels deploring factory conditions—such as **Rebecca Harding Davis**'s *Life in the Iron Mills* and Elizabeth Stuart Phelps's *The Silent Partner*—to **Upton Sinclair**'s avowedly socialist *The Jungle* and *King Coal* as well as **Jack London**'s *The Iron Heel*. In fact, London, writing in the socialist journal the *Comrade*, had employed the term "proletarian fiction" as early as 1901. But for two and a half more decades, the term largely referred to pro-labor novelists and storytellers with some allegiance to the middle class or to authors of more ephemeral pieces.

According to preeminent explicator Barbara Foley, by 1917, the term "proletarian literature" was commonly used to define prewar fiction in leftist magazines such as the *International Socialist Review* and the *Comrade*. Certainly American literature was presciently proletarian in the **World War I** era's fragmentary writings of troubadour agitators allied to the **Industrial Workers of the World (IWW)**. As an inclusively syndicalist organization preceding the formation of the American **Communist Party** in 1919, IWW, or "Wobbly," narratives included Joe Hill's songs, T-Bone Slim's stories, and the lore surrounding Big Bill Haywood and Elizabeth Gurley Flynn. The itinerant and casual labor experiences of the IWW generated short but eloquent testaments to the migrant, lumber mill, dockside, free-speech movement, and pacifist trials, especially in the Pacific Northwest. As such, the Wobblies laid the groundwork for the extended and ideologically specific fiction of the early 1930s.

By the end of the 1920s, the fledgling American Communist Party had developed sufficiently to advance worker-writers in forms of revolutionary art. Abroad, international congresses debated the application of postrevolution Soviet models—especially that of Proletkult, or agitprop through literary studios—to American conditions. Neither in the Soviet Union nor in the United States was Proletkult ever "scientifically" applicable to imaginative literature, but the notion of literary activity as an arm of class struggle underlay the cultural radicalism at the heart of American proletarian authorship.

Early on, such precepts were filtered through cultural organs such as the **John Reed Clubs** (1929–1935) and the journal *New Masses* (founded in 1926 in Greenwich Village), as well as a host of literary magazines including the *Anvil* and *Blast* ("A Magazine of Proletarian Short Stories"). **Mike Gold** was chief among those *New Masses* definers who sought to transform the pieces by textile mill worker Martin Russak, peppermill veteran Joseph Kalar, miner Ed Falkowski, and other "worker correspondents"—either reporting back from the Soviet Union or affiliated with the Communist Party of the United States—into proletarian art. A very different spokesman for literary proletarianism, one soon to break with the *New Masses* group, was the Missouri-born **Jack Conroy**. He too envisioned a literary forum for "the working men, women, and children in America." Soon there arose a division between admirers of the Soviet model, those "Union Square Easterners" like Gold, and Conroy's midwestern radicals, who spoke for more indigenous traditions of protest. This division would soon join many other debates—among critics, between critics and authors, between former and still-committed party members—generated by the elusiveness of the form for American writers.

Despite such disagreements, in the early 1930s, the most publicized proletarian literature, balancing themes of comradeship and struggle with detailed descriptions of work, celebrated the masculine experience in the basic industrial trades. Excellent examples abound: Pietro di Donato's *Christ in Concrete*, Louis Colman's *Lumber*, Tom Tippett's *Horse Shoe Bottoms*, Catherine Brody's *Nobody Starves*, **Tillie Olsen**'s unfinished *Yonnondio*, H. T. Tsiang's *And China Has Hands*. Yet there were challenges as well to this white-male focus by women writers and those of color; by authors with middle-class backgrounds; and by those who simply pointed to blue-collar individualism, conservatism, and even bigotry to justify the critic Malcolm Cowley's complaint as the proletarian novel faded from view that "it has been praised, reviled and more recently buried in potter's field; but the interesting point is that it has rarely been written." What did Cowley mean?

What Proletarian Fiction Is and Is Not

From its inception as a term, critics disagreed over the definition of proletarian fiction, an argument that modern explicators have inherited. Then and now, such debates encompass authorship, working-class origins and experience, political content, and literary traditionalism. One school of thought, for instance, maintains that defeatist, or "bottom dog," fiction—a mainstay of worker-writers like Edward Anderson (*Hungry Men*), Tom Kromer (*Waiting for Nothing*), and Nelson Algren (*Somebody in Boots*)—cannot be truly proletarian. Another equally persuasive argument finds in this fiction not only true proletarian sympathies for the downtrodden but an implicit (if unstated) radical message.

It is certainly the case that the "bottom dog" narratives of such writers shared many sympathies with proletarian literature. For example, in a fashion characteristic of the subgenre, *Hungry Men* (1935) opens with the 1930s "forgotten man," in this case Acel Stecker. A sensitive register of Stecker's financial and emotional deprivation in the pre–New Deal years, Anderson uses economy of language to tell much about a society still wedded to private—or absent—philanthropy.

> The weak bubble of the mission's water fountain and its flat, swimming-hole taste washed away the dull satisfaction that had been Acel Stecker's on reaching the free shelter. He straightened slowly, wiping his mouth on the shoulder of his corduroy jacket. . . . The afternoon shade was lengthening into the baking side street. Bums sat on the curb, their backbones arched like drawn bows squatted against the mission's scaly walls, dragged aimlessly around in that calloused weariness that men of the road know. (1)

World-weary but expressive, the passage shares the fierce anger to reform social structures that animates virtually all proletarian fiction.

Part of the problem in defining this literary school is that the term has often been seen as loosely synonymous with radical, social realist, and social protest novels and stories. While these forms and proletarian fiction do intersect in places, there are important distinctions among them. "Radical," when applied to the fiction of the early 1930s, is an umbrella term for a novel's implicit or explicit leftist orientation and commitment to revolutionary rather than evolutionary political change. As critic Edmund Wilson realized early on, a radical call for a new literary movement need not be restricted to proletarian fiction. Other literary radicals who called for and often dramatized strikes and marches as crucial to laborers' self-activity backgrounded workers as winners—or, more often, losers—in a historical drama written by powerful capitalists. "Social realism" or "**socialist realism**," a Soviet-influenced form, became the official technique in Soviet literature under the aegis of the Union of Soviet Writers. (Both Russian and American writers had a shifting relationship to art fashioned as a class weapon, and the term seemed to migrate to the graphic propaganda of the visual arts.) "Social protest" fiction, though it sometimes offers a class analysis, is unlike more radical literature in that it often resists clearly political solutions to workers' problems.

Proletarian literature draws on radical, social realist, and social protest art, but with a difference. In their clearest form, proletarian novels, novellas, and short stories emanate from the life and consciousness of working people, typically laborers in the mass-industrial world, whether or not such people overcome their lived oppression. From **Clara Weatherwax**'s *Marching, Marching*, a Pacific Coast novel that features Filipino organizing, to Albert Halper's *The Chute*, about a mail-order sweatshop in New York City, such works typically narrate the political insight or odyssey of a figure dedicated to participation in collective struggle. The denouement provides or predicts for its ensemble cast a full consciousness of working-class oppression and a readiness to challenge capitalist structures through the use of force if need be. Conversely, many novels with few or largely silenced worker figures—as Edwin Seaver wrote approvingly in the January 1935 *New Masses*, one of the chief journals dedicated to advancing proletarian fiction—could be proletarian novels, for they "accelerate the destruction of capitalism and the establishment of a workers' government."

These were brave words, particularly as the American literary left was dominated by middle-class authors, and proletarian fiction itself appealed to a basically non-blue-collar readership. Mike Gold realized that to forestall literary gentility in the midst of radicalism, U.S. authors could find inspiration in classics of socialist realism like Fyodor Gladkov's *Cement*. Issued serially in Russian in 1925 and available in translation a few years later, *Cement* brought deadly earnestness and Proletkult energy to the story of a 1920s workers' takeover of a cement factory. Gold published a number of worker authors serially in the ***Daily Worker*** to foster a more homegrown early model for a literary-political proletarian art. Such an author was Mike Pell, whose *S.S. Utah* was published in 1933 by the party-controlled International Press. Set aboard a cargo ship bound for the Soviet Union, it employed a cast of characters familiar to the form: an anti-Red delegate of the more conservative International Seaman's Union; a Red with the generic Wobbly name of Slim, who "converts" the crew to socialism; and slangy veteran seamen from Denmark to Alaska. Slim's speeches, so dated today, soon rouse the men to strike:

> When . . . the *Daily Worker* says "Defend the Soviet Union" they're not just appealing to you as an American, but especially as a worker. As an exploited American worker you, all of us here, together with the workers all over the world, will take the rifles that the boss-class shoves into our hands and use them, not against our Russian fellow workers, but to set up Soviet governments of our own. (27)

Despite Slim's many such speeches, Pell's novel also breaks free of party-line language, as do a wide range of such long-forgotten works. He cannot avoid injecting American high-spiritedness into his crew, just as the Eisenstein film *Battleship Potemkin*, also concerning a shipboard strike, reflected Russian melancholy and gravitas. Furthermore, Pell takes care to register regional characteristics and dialects, job-induced attitudes, and able seamen hierarchies aboard ship. By novel's end, the differences among various crew members are erased in their embrace of the "fellow workers" ideology.

Not surprisingly, Pell's novel soon seemed too conventionally proletarian to provide talented young authors with viable models. Furthermore, despite the international cultural leftism emanating from the Soviet Union, the John Reed Clubs, and the *New Masses,* the radical, social realist, and proletarian novel's revolutionary enterprise itself kept changing shape. In 1935, there was a party shift—both abroad and at home—away from revolution and toward the **Popular Front**, with its slogans like "Communism is twentieth-century Americanism." More and more, as worker subjects became less fashionable, left-wing novels were grounded in subjects such as "bourgeois decay"; the history of the more established trade unions; discontented clerical workers; and downwardly mobile middle-class narrators who hoped, however unrealistically, to return to their former lives.

To many critics, the proletarian novel of economic dispossession and comradely solutions faded as the 1930s wore on, Hitler rose to power, **Stalin** conducted Moscow show trials, and antifascist fiction tried to cement U.S. relations with the Soviet bloc. Worker-fueled and underdog plots simply became less fashionable. Previously friendly literary critics such as those connected to the ***Partisan Review*** now opined that proletarian novels were Soviet paint-by-number exercises that distorted rather than balanced both doctrine and artistry.

The negative judgment that the rigidity with which proletarian art stressed the deadened life of the working class before its necessary enlightenment in the face of "historical necessity" has proved to have considerable staying power. Yet it ignores the better proletarian writers of the early 1930s, whose work involves considerable complexity: radical "conversions" are often redefined, the "collective novel" can include eyewitness narrative, and a working-class allegiance is enhanced by psychological insights. Far from producing formulaic didactic prose, many proletarian writers found ways not only to animate the new ideology of collective goals, pragmatic militancy, and the growth of working-class consciousness but (as importantly) to Americanize it as well.

American Proletarians

The project of forging an American radical voice largely began with the attempts of Gold and Conroy to transform the worker sketch into the proletarian **bildungsroman**, at the same time seeking to solve the formidable problem of dispensing with a bourgeois narrator and his upwardly mobile belief system. Activists as well as writers, Gold and Conroy quickly amassed impressive Communist Party militant, or third period (1928–1934), credentials. By 1930, Gold had participated in the important Charkov Conference, whose purpose was to form a program for a proletarian cultural movement in the United States. He himself had been published under **Comintern** auspices. Conroy's "Hoover City" (1935) would soon be published by the English-language magazine of the International Union of Revolutionary Writers' (IURW), *International Literature*.

Gold's novel *Jews without Money*, parts of which Gold, heeding his own call, had published in the *New Masses* in the late 1920s, seemed in many ways ideal as a model for proletarian fiction. Though not so stated, the literary issue was how to write oneself into the narrative without sacrificing what Gold called "rebel things" and the "hard facts of proletarian life." Autobiography may not require or engender sentimentality, but its focus on the vicissitudes of the self can be at odds with a more revolutionary agenda. Gold's *Jews without Money* and Conroy's *The Disinherited* soon became models for pieces by actual working-class writers in U.S. Proletkult circles, such as the John Reed Clubs and ancillary networks of worker-writers from New York to Chicago to San Francisco. *The Disinherited*, one of the most critically successful leftist responses to Gold's call for worker art, was partly published in *New Masses* in the early 1930s. Published in book form in 1933, Conroy's novel was hailed as "one of the first memorable proletarian novel[s] of the decade," even though its sales were modest.

Jews without Money tells the story of the growth to maturity (and radical consciousness) on the part of its protagonist, Mikey Gold. In the course of telling this story—by constant shifts from son's to father's perspective, punctuated by vignettes of the saintly mother—the novel demonstrates both the continuity of class affiliation and the ideological shifts from one generation to the next. One major way Gold argued for a new order of things was to lament for the overworked father who played by capitalist rules and failed. As the fictional Herman Gold, a sympathetic and vocal stand-in for Gold's own parent, realizes late in the book, he was "twenty years in America and poorer than when I came" (301).

Conroy based much of his novel on his own working-class experience as the son of a coal miner martyred in an industrial accident. As the protagonist, Larry Donovan, moves from the paternalistic experience of a pre–World War I Missouri mining camp to the strike-torn Midwest rail yards of 1922 to a Fordist factory in Detroit, he gradually learns to understand the importance of his childhood promise to his father "to be a thief, a murderer, anything, but [never] a scab!" (190–91). Elsewhere in the multi-industrial narrative, Conroy's ethnography generates a small army of flat labor characters who constitute an industrial choir of worker voices. In so doing, he produces a novelistic compendium of the industrial folklore enriching factory life. His tall tales, accounts of workplace feats, eccentrics, and poverty-crazed characters all escape agitprop classification. In an experimental spirit, Conroy combines aspects of the previous century's novels of gentlemen workers thrust into real-life industrial strife with a series of work and road stories, Wobblylike travelers, and mining-camp fixtures. At the end of the search for salvation at the heart of so much 1930s fiction, Larry learns to stand with his fellow workers rather than seek individual success. He utters the memorable phrase that he will "rise with [his] class" (265).

In other works long out of print, a working-class ethic underscores political solutions to labor exploitation. For example, Robert Cantwell's pulp-factory novel *Land of Plenty* (1934), using observations culled from his own years in a Washington State plywood factory, delves beneath the speedups, pay cuts, and work-site dangers that provoke a failed strike. Cantwell adds texture to the work culture not only by frankly detailing the fears of workers caught up in violence that they have planned but had not envisioned fully but by taking time and care to point out the bittersweetness of sexual tensions between male and female factory workers.

Also neglected in **cold-war** and post–cold war assessments of proletarian authorship is the innovative approach to form that often informed proletarian fiction. Gold's own *Jews without Money* is a linguistic experiment: ghetto profanity intertwines with tenement prose poems utterance. **Meridel LeSueur**'s *The Girl* dispenses with conventional narrative to plunge the reader into identification with her unwed mother heroine and the supportive, penniless women's community of Minneapolis in the early Depression years. Considerable formal experimentation can also be found in the fantasies and hallucinatory sections of **James T. Farrell**'s Irish American Chicago *Studs Lonigan* trilogy (1932–1935); African American "black belt" articulator **Richard Wright**'s rhetorical experiments in *Native Son*'s (1940) deliberately repetitive Chicago courtroom scenes; **John Dos Passos**'s mixed-prose-style historical trilogy *U.S.A.* (1930–1936); and Edwin Rollins's recounting of the **Gastonia Mill Strike**, *The Shadow Before* (1934).

Whether in its pre-1935 heyday or later, there were creative tensions, conventional Marxist attitudes, and a vernacular Americanism that embraced an individualist ethic of upward mobility, which had been so central to pre-proletarian literature from Benjamin Franklin to F. Scott Fitzgerald. Proletarian fiction did not dispense with so much as reenvision the American success ethic. Which side were mass-industrial workers on, that of employers or those bottom dogs whose fall could soon be their own? In short, how could one working American be content to achieve success at another's expense?

The Other "Others" of American Proletarian Fiction

Paul Lauter's astute observation that proletarianism takes a different form when it intersects with race and gender is amply born out by writers of color and women authors who came to the fore in the later 1930s. Like their white male counterparts, their relations with Marxist orthodoxy were often ambivalent and even volatile, and their fiction finds a kind of solace in the minority laborer untouched or unaided by party pronouncements on the dictatorship of the proletariat. A cleaning woman in *Native Son* cries, "All I do is work [she cried], work like a dog! From morning to night. I ain't got no happiness. I ain't ever had none. I just work! . . . I just work. I'm black and I work and don't bother anybody." This proletarian speech functions in this preeminent Depression-era novel of black America as a dramatically ironic prophecy of the woman's own death: she is soon murdered by another desperate character, the protagonist Bigger Thomas, who is unable to question his motives or the terms of his own life. Bigger never has the opportunity of a Mikey Gold or a Larry Donovan to take hold of his life, much less make it an activist one. He is an alternative proletarian, an antihero of a disturbing kind.

In the literary recovery of working-class history, for novelists of men's militancy, the struggle was to contextualize workingmen's diversity within a critique of capitalism. The relationship between feminism and the proletarian novel was more complex. Much of the important leftist fiction by and about women told the story of the oppressed mother. Neither adulatory nor denigrating, Tillie Olsen (*Yonnondio*), Meridel LeSueur (*The Girl*), and **Agnes Smedley** (*Daughter of Earth*) rewrote, from women's perspectives, what male texts argued were the aspirations and ambitions of proletarian mothers and their worker-daughters.

Olsen, Le Sueur, and Smedley, with their visceral understanding of women's paid and domestic toil, joined the radical female storytellers of the Gastonia Strike to crystallize the struggle of the working-class woman writer as well as her subjects. In addition, these writers—including **Myra Page** (*Moscow Yankee*), **Fielding Burke** (*Call Home the Heart*), and Mary Heaton Vorse (*Strike!*)—dramatized their belief that women's proletarian experience was not adequately accounted for by party ideology, with its focus on class. Rather than defining a gendered work group with common work experiences and values, writers from Olsen to Page struggled to be faithful to women's less orthodox labor experiences, including the labor of childbirth, while advocating the collective ascension at the heart of the era's most radical fiction.

Proletarian and other radical women writers engaged in dialogue with not only their party's expectations of women's subordinate roles but the culture's as well. All too often in the male proletarian novel women are left behind in manless communities to endure and to survive. It is difficult for them to redefine rising with their class if they are left behind the lines of the class struggle. It is similarly difficult to reconcile the motherly ideal with women on the barricades, a task undertaken by female radical novels. Like their male colleagues, radical women writers refer to a labor past, engaged in an ethnographic present, and experiment with decentering the narrator. Whether telling the oppressed parents' story or creating a liberating mentor figure, as did their male colleagues, they refigure the collective envisioned in the male proletarian novel.

The Proletarian Aesthetic

In its day as in our own, defenders rejected the charge that leftist fiction in general and proletarian fiction in particular are eviscerated by doctrine; that they bypass race, gender, and ethnicity; or that they are at odds with literary experimentation. Thus, the best explicators of 1930s proletarian literature steer clear of both pre- and post-McCarthyism denunciations on the one hand, and exaggerated claims for proletarian authenticity on the other. Yet there remains a need to widen their discussion of the worker characters of 1930s labor fiction. For one thing, proletarian fiction engaged in a variety of appropriations of earlier plots, devices, and labor events with a new awareness that novels must no longer neglect or suppress the voices of the workers themselves. At its best, proletarian fiction combines a belief in the common man (and woman) with a freshness of observation and an openness to formal and stylistic experimentation. Inherent in this body of literature is a desire for the classless society so often mythically associated with the United States but so little in evidence in its economic reality.

The Legacy of Proletarian Fiction

The crushing effects of the McCarthy era soon pushed proletarian authors into the shadows. A determined group of writers associated with the *New Masses'* successor, *Masses and Mainstream*, including Philip Bonosky and the proletarian "noir" novelist Thomas McGrath, joined others like Alexander Saxton, **Abraham Polonsky**, and Ira Wolfert in continuing the proletarian literary tradition. Moreover, central insights of the proletarian literature movement have continued to influence any number of American cultural productions. Some historians continue to believe that the 1930s saw the opening of a class war in literature, the first act in a larger renaissance that stamped an indelible working-class imprint on American culture. Worker-writers and their allies will continue to establish workshops, fund small presses, and occasionally make the best-seller lists. The proletarian literary moment may be gone, but variants on the proletarian novel no doubt will continue to exist, set everywhere from migrant fruit fields in New Jersey to crack dens in the inner city to Nike sweatshops in Chinatown and Indonesia.

Selected Bibliography: Anderson, Edward. *Hungry Men.* 1935. Norman: U of Oklahoma P, 1993; Booker, M. Keith. *The Modern American Novel of the Left: A Research Guide.* Westport, CT: Greenwood, 1999; Conroy, Jack. *The Disinherited.* 1933. Columbia: U of Missouri P, 1991; Denning, Michael, *The Cultural Front. The Laboring of American Culture in the Twentieth Century.* New York: Verso, 1996; Foley, Barbara. *Radical Representations: Politics and Form in U.S. Proletarian Fiction, 1929–1941.* Durham, NC: Duke UP, 1993; Gold, Michael. *Jews without Money.* 1930. New York: Carroll and Graf, 1984; Hapke, Laura. *Labor's Text: The Worker in American Fiction.* Rutgers UP, 2001; Lauter, Paul. "American Proletarianism." *The Columbia History of the American Novel.* Ed. Emory Elliott et al. New York: Columbia UP, 1991. 331–56; Pell, Mike. *S.S. Utah.* New York: International P, 1933; Rideout, Walter B. *The Radical Novel in the United States, 1900–1954.* Cambridge: Harvard UP, 1956; Suggs, Jon-Christian. "The Proletarian Novel." *Dictionary of Literary Biography.* Vol. 9, pt. 3. Ed. James J. Martine. Detroit: Gale Research, 1981. 231–45; Wald, Alan M. *Exiles from a Future Time: The Forging of the Mid-Twentieth-Century Literary Left.* Chapel Hill: U of North Carolina P, 2002; Wright, Richard. *Native Son.* 1940. New York: Harper and Row, 1989.

Laura Hapke

PROLETARIAN LITERATURE. *See* PROLETARIAN FICTION, AMERICAN.

PUSHKIN, ALEKSANDR SERGEEVICH (1799–1837), pioneering Russian author of poetry, prose, drama, history, and essays, deemed by many the equal of **Shakespeare** and **Goethe**. Pushkin and his works were more often politicized by others than political themselves: both during his lifetime and after his death in a duel, radical Russian critics hailed Pushkin as an opponent of social and political stagnation, and Soviet critics later transformed him into a herald of revolution. In fact, while Pushkin celebrated individual and artistic liberty, and recurrently chafed against political restraints, he articulated no broad vision of social or political change.

Born in Moscow to aristocratic if impoverished parents and educated in St. Petersburg, Pushkin was sentenced in 1820 to internal exile in the Caucasus for writing allegedly seditious poems, such as "Freedom: An Ode" ("Vol'nost': Oda," 1817). Even after being allowed to return to his family's rural estate in 1824, Pushkin was kept under surveillance by government agents and denied permission to travel. In subsequent years, tsarist authorities repeatedly interrogated Pushkin about his writings, notably "André Chenier" ("Andrei Shen'e," 1825), a poem praising this French revolutionary as "a singer of freedom." Censors deemed the poem a veiled tribute to the failed December revolt of 1825, in which Pushkin himself did not participate, although it was launched by acquaintances of his seeking liberal social reforms and a constitutional monarchy. The authorities also feared the popularity Pushkin had achieved through such works as the serially published narrative poem *Eugene Onegin* (*Evgenii Onegin*, 1823–1831), a dazzling verbal performance depicting Onegin as a self-centered, aimless "superfluous man," spawned by a dilettantish Russian upper class.

Over time, Pushkin turned increasing attention to Russian history and its political and moral ambiguities. In the play *Boris Godunov* (1825), Pushkin explored the murky circumstances of early-seventeenth-century Russia that brought forth questionable sovereigns; in the narrative poem *The Bronze Horseman* (*Mednyi vsadnik*, 1833), he suggested that the founding of St. Petersburg in the early eighteenth century set at odds the legitimate interests of individuals and the state; and in the historical novel *The Captain's Daughter* (*Kapitanskaia dochka*, 1836), he attributed both unmitigated cruelty and exceptional beneficence to the mid-eighteenth-century populist rebel Pugachev. Pushkin also proposed reforms for Russia's educational system and sought permission to found a political journal, but both projects were rejected. Although sympathetic to liberal causes and dedicated to artistic independence, Pushkin signaled no desire to overthrow the Russian political establishment. Nevertheless, for many, he became Russia's "national poet," whose works presaged the revolutionary political and social struggles to come.

Selected Bibliography: Binyon, T. J. *Pushkin: A Biography.* New York: Knopf, 2003; Levitt, Marcus C. *Russian Literary Politics and the Pushkin Celebration of 1880.* Ithaca, NY: Cornell UP, 1989; Sandler, Stephanie. *Commemorating Pushkin: Russia's Myth of a National Poet.* Stanford, CA: Stanford UP, 2004; Todd, William Mills, III. *Fiction and Society in the Age of Pushkin: Ideology, Institutions, and Narrative.* Cambridge, MA: Harvard UP, 1986.

Elizabeth Cheresh Allen

·R·

RACE AND ETHNICITY STUDIES. The field of race and ethnicity studies encompasses a series of histories, a discourse, and a relatively recent academic institution. An interdisciplinary, multidisciplinary, and comparative study of racial and ethnic groups and their interrelations, the field often emphasizes groups that have historically been neglected. It constitutes a general rubric—related to cultural studies—under which researchers investigate and track intragroup phenomena by direct observation (or field research) interviews, public records, and so on. Pertinent phenomena include festivals, rites, foods, modes of dress, and internal changes resulting from interaction with (and sometimes isolation from) other groups. Other work studies interaction between groups or with amalgamated society in general, such as exogamy, job competition, mutual representation, and how specific groups exist as knowable quantities within larger mainstreams. A more fluid approach between these two observes and critiques the racial or ethnic elements at play in social events. Rather than inserting "race" or "ethnicity" into public consciousness, as some detractors claim, such an approach instead maps how race and ethnicity as concepts underlie many social and historical phenomena.

Race and ethnicity were already the objects of studies of various sorts long before they were cemented into the academic and greater public consciousness by university institutions. In Europe, much current institutional concern with race and ethnicity came about in the wake of the dissolution of the British and French empires and the influx of former subject populations back to the erstwhile imperial centers in the 1960s and 1970s. Analogous interests arose in the United States in response to various black liberation movements and military and commercial involvement in Vietnam and elsewhere. Race and ethnicity studies, in the sense of both early individual efforts toward racist justification and later academically institutionalized antiracist curricula, are therefore products of and responses to the histories of colonialism and expanding capital.

For much of their histories, "race" and "ethnicity" were used interchangeably and maintained an ambivalent relation. "Ethnic," from the Greek *ethnikos*, indicates a people or nation, usually in the religious sense. It also denotes ties of common culture, language, and geographical area. "Ethnicity" was first used in G. Vacher de la

Pouge's *Les sélections sociales* (1896) to designate the cultural, psychological, and social characteristics of a population, whereas "race" then implied only a series of physical characteristics. **Max Weber**'s *Wirtschaft und Gesellschaft* (1922) further distinguished race (country of origin), ethnicity (subjective belief in shared origins), and nation (intense political "passion") (Bolaffi et al. 94). "Ethnicity" often maintains its religious designation, as in the "triple melting pot" thesis of Will Herberg's *Protestant, Catholic, Jew* (1955). Much later studies, such as Omi and Winant's *Racial Formation in the United States: From the 1960s to the 1990s* (1994), finally insist that theories of ethnicity do not fit problems of race because the two remain distinct experiences.

While also connoting provenance and progeny, "race" has historically been taken as a more presumable and absolute category than ethnicity, based on visible somatic markers such as skin color. The ancient world immediately translated such physical differences through social color symbolism into arbitrary hierarchies of human superiority or value. Often used in biblical exegesis to explain the differences among peoples of the world, the French *race* or *rasse* (Italian *razza*, Spanish *raza*) entered English in the early sixteenth century and indicated features derived from shared descent through the nineteenth century (Cashmore 332). Diderot's *Encyclopédie* maintained the term as a genealogical category. "Race" has also denoted species and subspecies simultaneously, and works such as slave owner Edward Long's three-volume *History of Jamaica* (1774) proposed whites and blacks as different species. Whether the different races were only variations of a common ancestry (monogenesis, supported variously by the Bible and Darwinism) or were the result of distinct genetic origins (polygenesis, often invoked by white supremacists) obsessed the late 1800s and 1900s. Considerations of race as a marker of genetics (biological determinism) or environment, or as a divine intervention as described in the Bible and minor Talmudic traditions (the "sons of Ham") also clouded matters. Eventually, Sir Julian Huxley and A. C. Haddon's *We Europeans* (1935) averred the designation "ethnic groups" over "races" for European groups, given the influence of language, custom, and geographic area on identity formation.

While writers such as Kwame Anthony Appiah in his "The Uncompleted Argument" (1985) declare that "race" as such never existed, others equally insist that, despite the problems that plague thinking about race as a social construct, those on the object end of such discourses often find such a construct indispensable to formulating political action (Bolaffi et al. x–xi). Through the advent of genetic sciences, race now appears endlessly divisible by genetic variation, so that the number of assignable races is limited by only the ideological predilection of the observer. Approaches such as the "new ethnicity" maintain the distinctions between race and ethnicity while noting their shared and fluid influences, and emphasis has shifted from race and ethnicity as sets of essential or adopted traits to sets of lived experiences.

The most unlikely texts from early in modern colonial history constitute race and ethnic studies. Spanish missionary Juan Rogel's 1572 letter reporting skirmishes with Caribbean natives reads Spanish and native identities as cultural, specifically in terms of language retention. Benjamin Franklin's "Letter to Those Who Would Remove to America" (1782), however problematically, constructed and projected a black vernacular speech within his argument against the supposed genetic disposition of American settlers to industriousness.

Many race studies of the 1800s fomented supposedly anthropologically based racist and essentialist concepts that reflected developing paranoia about race in an increasingly colonial world. Early race theorist Joseph Arthur de Gobineau's four-volume *Essai sur l'inégalité des races humaines* (1853–1855) proposed the thesis of racial degeneration, whereby initially necessary admixtures of bloodlines that compensate each respective line's essential deficiencies amount, eventually, to pollution. This schema not only perpetuated a hierarchy of racial ability and worth, but also established the standard essentialist "types" on which much racist thought still depends today. The ambiguities that riddled such theories guaranteed their use by U.S. white supremacists who pored over English translations of the first volume of Gobineau's *Essai*. Such subsequent studies include Madison Grant's *The Passing of the Great Race* (1916) and Lothrop Stoddard's *The Rising Tide of Color* (1920), each of which "scientifically" claimed not only the (simultaneous and contradictory) inferiority of blacks and the threat they posed to white American society, but also the dangers of miscegenation and the necessity of maintaining racial "purity" (the "race instinct" defense). Racist groups in 1930s and 1940s Germany publicized and promoted Gobineau's studies, culminating in the adoption of his works, adjusted under Hitler's approval, as primary school texts (Cashmore 172). Selections from Grant found their way, with little alteration, into Hitler's *Mein Kampf*. "Ethnology" became synonymous with eugenics on both sides of the Atlantic.

Writing very much against this grain, **W.E.B. Du Bois**'s "double consciousness" in *The Souls of Black Folk* (1903) posited the internal and external phenomenology of race. Anthropologist and ethnologist Franz Boas's *Race, Language and Culture* (1912) critiqued ethnology from within while further espousing race and ethnicity as lived experiences. Between the two, playwright Israel Zangwill's *The Melting Pot* (1909) offered one of America's most enduring and contested metaphors for race and ethnicity. Meanwhile, increased immigration to the United States in the early 1900s directed the emerging field toward groups' respective success or failure to assimilate into a centralized culture erroneously considered homogeneous.

The Anglo-American sociology of race originated with the Chicago School's urban studies of blacks who had moved from the rural South to the industrialized North. This school's approach shifted race discourse from ascribing identity based on "fixed ontological characteristics" to identity based on lived experience (Osborne and Sandford 5). Post–**World War II** Britain later adopted this methodology to address the labor situation created by immigrants from the former British colonies. **Frantz Fanon** similarly addressed French colonialism in his highly influential *Peau noir, masques blancs* (*Black Skin, White Masks*, 1954), bringing psychoanalysis to bear on a field increasingly influenced by phenomenology.

In 1963, Nathan Glazer and Daniel Patrick Moynihan's *Beyond the Melting Pot* refuted earlier assimilation theories, while Thomas F. Gossett's *Race: The History of An Idea in America* provided one of the first full historical treatments of race discourse through U.S. history. British discourses on race relations further modified the Chicago School approach toward considerations of culture (Osborne and Sandford 5–6). Stephen Castles and Godula Kosak's *Immigrant Workers and the Class Structure of Western Europe* (1973), however, would point out that American-style race relations did not fit the situation of ethnic-worker populations in Europe; Britain and Europe needed their own models. In this contentious environment, the Birmingham Centre for Contemporary Cultural Studies—formed in 1964 under **Stuart Hall** and others—reconfigured discourses about race and ethnicity within rubrics of "culture." Hall and the Birmingham School turned away from the customary work of **Raymond Williams**, Edward Thompson, and Richard Hoggart, and toward the work of **Antonio Gramsci** and **Louis Althusser**. Birmingham's greatest contribution was its theorizing of race, tracing its existence to the heart of modern philosophy.

Birmingham's methodologies translated back across the Atlantic to the United States in time for the racially charged late 1960s and early 1970s. The journal *Ethnicity* signaled more consolidated public awareness of the field. Student-organized action groups in 1968, developed around increasing U.S. race and ethnic awareness, culminated in ethnic studies programs and departments at San Francisco State University and the University of California at Berkeley. Under mounting social pressures by black, Latino, and Asian students and populations, other U.S. universities soon followed their lead. By the 1970s, such programs also encouraged reevaluation of previously accepted and mainstreamed ethnicities, such as the Irish and Italians (as Catholics), Poles and other eastern Europeans, "other Britons" (Welsh, Scots), Germans (including religious groups such as the Amish), and Jews (Yang 5). Michael Novak's *The Unmeltable Ethnics* (1972) and Perry Weed's *The White Ethnic Movement and Ethnic Politics* (1973) posited even ostensibly unified mainstream groups as indeed ethnically diverse.

University financial hardships often provided excuses, in the late 1970s, for closing such programs and departments. Successive Republican administrations in the 1980s further diminished the role of such departments and their academic and social concerns, as well as their public financial standing. Nevertheless, **Edward Said**'s 1978 watershed ***Orientalism*** resituated race and ethnicity debates on global and transhistorical scales in its critique of the creation and maintenance of the racial and ethnic "other." The Birmingham School's *The Empire Writes Back* (1989) literally gave voice to those disenfranchised by increasing both postimperial global capitalism and resulting nationalist reactionism. In 1983, Eric Hobsbawm and Terence Ranger's *The Invention of Tradition* and Benedict Anderson's *Imagined Communities* exposed the centrality of a constructed "origin myth" not only to nationalist groups but often within the history of race and ethnicity studies themselves.

The late 1980s and 1990s indicated an ongoing need for such detailed theorizations of race and ethnicity in the wake of the dissolution of the Soviet empire, "ethnic cleansing" regimes in the Balkans and Africa, and the plight of groups such as the Kurds in Iraq before and after the first Gulf War. The growing commercial selling power of race-oriented music and culture contrasted Republican invocations of Willy Horton during the 1988 presidential campaign and the Rodney King riots in Los Angeles. Latino markets also gained public exposure. By the 1990s, a race- and ethnicity-conscious academic *zeitgeist* in general contributed to the reinstitution of race and ethnicity studies programs and the application of many of their theories across curricula.

Race and ethnicity studies remain largely institutionalized academic discussions, now focused more often through postmodernist, postcolonial, and deconstructive attention to the philosophies and ideologies of race. Such texts as Cornell West's *Keeping Faith: Philosophy and Race in America* (1993) and Kwame Anthony Appiah and Amy Gutman's *Color Consciousness: The Political Morality of Race* (1996) indicate the field's current path of both theorizing and concretizing experience as a self-reflexive praxis. Race and ethnicity studies now equally covers the history of its own discourse as well as its traditional concerns. It has become so ingrained as a multidisciplinary and interdisciplinary field that in the 2000s, it seems on the brink of another identity crisis—does it still warrant its own department, or must it disseminate as an interdepartmental discipline?

Selected Bibliography: Bolaffi, Guido, Raffaele Bracalenti, Peter Braham, and Sandro Gindro, eds. *Dictionary of Race, Ethnicity and Culture.* London: Sage, 2003; Cashmore, Ellis, ed. *Encyclopedia of Race and Ethnic Studies.* New York: Routledge, 2004; Gossett, Thomas F. *Race: The History of an Idea in America.* Dallas: Southern Methodist UP, 1963; Hannaford, Ivan. *Race: The History of an Idea in the West.* Baltimore: Johns Hopkins UP, 1996; Osborne, Peter, and Stella Standford. *Philosophies of Race and Ethnicity.* London: Continuum, 2002; Yang, Philip Q. *Ethnic Studies: Issues and Approaches.* New York: State U of New York P, 2000.

Nick Melczarek

THE RAGGED TROUSERED PHILANTHROPISTS. First published in condensed form in 1914 (three years after its author's death), *The Ragged Trousered Philanthropists* is one of the founding texts of modern British working-class fiction and one of the most important and influential examples of the genre, even though the full text was not published until 1955. Authored by Robert Tressell, an Irish-born house painter whose real name was Robert Noonan, the novel is particularly striking for its vivid depiction of British working-class life. Tressell's own working-class perspective comes through not only at the level of content but also in the form and style of his book. As **Raymond Williams** argues, "there is no finer representation, anywhere in English writing, of a certain rough-edged, mocking, give-and-take conversation between workmen and mates" (254). Moreover, as Wim Neetens points out, *The Ragged Trousered Philanthropists* engages in an extended subversive dialogue with the tradition of bourgeois fiction, succeeding in negating "the dictates of the literary market place by being intelligent without being trivial, oppositional without being marginal, instructive without being patronising or dull" (88).

Tressell's most important violation of the accepted decorum of the bourgeois novel is to make his book an unapologetic work of socialist propaganda. Tressell's preface begins by stating that his intention in writing the book was "to present, in the form of an interesting story, a faithful picture of working-class life—more especially of those engaged in the Building trades—in a small town in the south of England" (11). *The Ragged Trousered Philanthropists* succeeds admirably in this task. It relates in great detail the lives of building-trades workers, especially house painters, in the fictional town of Mugsborough, including their experiences on the job, in their private homes with their families, and in various public activities in their community. But the book goes beyond mere representation of everyday life among workers to develop a detailed and systematic theoretical explanation for why their lives are the way they are. The protagonist, Frank Owen, is a highly intelligent, self-educated sign painter who provides the central point of view from which Tressell observes the complex workings of the capitalist system. Owen observes abundance of production all around him, while he and his fellow workers live in abysmal poverty. Such observations run throughout the book and are reinforced with detailed introductory explications of socialist theory.

Much of *The Ragged Trousered Philanthropists* is devoted to a depiction of the cultural practices by which the capitalist system maintains its hegemony by blinding the workers to their own exploitation. Religion comes in for particular criticism as an opiate of the masses in a way that recalls **Marx**'s famous observation, but that also resembles the diagnoses of religion as a mind-numbing force that appear in the works of Tressell contemporaries such as **James Joyce** and Arnold Bennett. Where Tressell differs from these writers in his clear understanding of the participation of religion in a class-oriented economic system. One working-class character, for example, observes, "As for all this religious business, it's just a money-making dodge. It's the parson's trade, just the same as painting is ours, only there's no work attached to it and the pay's a bloody sight better than ours is" (153). Similarly, in a way that anticipates later Marxist thinkers such as Max Horkheimer and **Theodor Adorno**, Tressell identifies **popular culture**, in the form of devices such as the *Daily Obscurer* newspaper, as a major factor in the workers' lack of understanding of the true nature of the capitalist system and of their antagonism toward socialism as an alien force supposedly contrary to their interests.

Tressell's book attempts to engage these cultural forces head-on and to provide an alternative cultural voice, both as a cultural artifact in its own right and in the ways Owen and his fellow socialist, Barrington, attempt to counter the hegemony of bourgeois ideology by winning their fellow workers over to their ideas through extended rational argumentation. The difficulty of these efforts is indicated in the title itself, which refers to the way that most of the workers in the book, despite their own conditions of poverty and deprivation, are willing to work so diligently in order to support their rich bosses, who do little or no real work at all.

However, Tressell successfully negotiates this pitfall by building into his book a profound respect for workers and their work. He also lightens his criticism of them with a liberal dose of humor. Meanwhile, despite its sometimes pessimistic-sounding presentation of the difficulty of convincing workers of the value of socialism, *The Ragged Trousered Philanthropists* maintains a strong utopian dimension and a consistent underlying tone of optimism. As the book ends, Owen, sick with tuberculosis and in desperate need of money, is suddenly saved when Barrington (who turns out to be a rich man who has been working just to observe working-class conditions) supplies him with the needed cash. Sudden changes for the better, this motif seems to say, are possible. The book then ends on a note of utopian optimism, anticipating the coming triumph of socialism as "the light that will shine upon the world wide Fatherland and illumine the gilded domes and glittering pinnacles of the beautiful cities of the future, where men shall dwell together in true brotherhood and goodwill and joy. The Golden Light that will be diffused throughout all the happy world from the rays of the risen sun of Socialism" (630).

Selected Bibliography: Ball, Gordon. "Ginsberg and Revolution." *Selected Essays: West Georgia College International Conference on Representing Revolution 1989.* West Georgia International Conference, 1991: 137–50; Fox, Pamela. *Class Fictions.* Durham: Duke UP, 1994; Miles, Peter. "The Painter's Bible and the British Workman: Robert Tressell's Literary Activism." *The British Working-Class Novel in the Twentieth Century.* Ed. Jeremy Hawthorn. London: Edward Arnold, 1984. 1–18; Neetens, Wim. "Politics, Poetics, and the Popular Text: *The Ragged Trousered Philanthropists.*" *Literature and History* 14.1 (1988): 81–90; Smith, David. *Socialist Propaganda in the Twentieth-Century British Novel.* Totowa, NJ: Rowman and Littlefield, 1979; Williams, Raymond. *Writing in Society.* London: Verso, 1983.

M. Keith Booker

REALISM. The presentation of credible experiences and happenings in literature, realism resembles the Aristotelian notion of literature as "mimesis," or imitation of reality, because it suggests a mode of representation that portrays true life. However, works of realist literature do not necessarily represent reality accurately in any absolute sense; rather, they function through an elaborate and ideologically conditioned constellation of conventions and assumptions about the nature of reality and the transparency of representation. In particular, realism as a literary movement came to prominence in Europe in the eighteenth century, concurrent with the rise to power of the bourgeoisie, a class whose point of view the genre well expressed. Indeed, the prominent Marxist critic **Fredric Jameson** has argued that "realism is to be grasped as a component in a vaster process that can be identified as none other than the *capitalist* (or the *bourgeois*) cultural revolution itself" (164, Jameson's emphasis). Realism rose to the peak of its dominance as a literary mode in the nineteenth century and now continues to inform many of our basic assumptions about literature, even after the phenomena of **modernism** and **postmodernism** have challenged so many of the tenets of realism.

Realism sharply contrasts with romance—the genre of the medieval period in which tales of ideal love and chivalric adventures were written, largely in verse. The distinction between realism and romance, however, is not absolute, and works of romance continued to be produced (in prose) in the modern era. Distinctive qualities that place a work in the mode of realism, on the other hand, do exist. Ian Watt distinguishes several such qualities in *The Rise of the Novel.* Watt postulates that the growth of realism in the eighteenth and nineteenth centuries was closely connected with the rise of the novel at that time. He points out that it was no accident that Daniel Defoe, Henry Fielding, and Samuel Richardson started writing at about the same time, and that even though they did not constitute a literary school, they adhered to certain principles and obeyed certain conventions in writing (many driven by market forces amid the emergent capitalism of the era) that represented the spirit of the age. For Watt, it is precisely realism as a mode of representation that defines the works of these authors as novels and precisely the rise of the bourgeoisie and their distinctive worldview that conditions the rise of realism. The theories of philosophers such as Descartes and Locke also helped to shape the aesthetics of this new genre. Descartes emphasized the truth of felt experience, that nothing can be taken on trust, while Locke developed the theory of association, that ideas and sensation can come in succession.

Watt identifies six conventions of realist fiction:

· *Plot* is based on actual experience, something that could happen in reality.

· *Names* suggest greater individual identity because they are proper names.

- *A new concept of time* suggests that past experience is the cause of present action, that time proceeds in a linear fashion; thus, details of everyday life can be made more vivid if they are linked to historical time.

- *Place* is another feature of the new mode of realism. Characters inhabit an actual identifiable world whose conventions obey the natural laws; events occur in an actual physical environment, often locatable on a real map.

- *Greater denotative use of language* replaces the old style, which was more rhetorical and was not concerned with the correspondence of words to things.

- *Individual experience* replaces collective tradition or communal experience on which the romance mode primarily relied.

Watt discusses key eighteenth-century texts to demonstrate how aspects of realism facilitated their growth as novels. It is pertinent to mention that Watt's theory of the rise of the novel, in particular the role realism plays in its growth, has been questioned, or at least supplemented, by later scholars. For example, Lennard Davis's *Factual Fictions* explores the relationship between the novel and nonfiction forms such as journalism and views the novel as a consolidation of journalism, history, and literature that arose out of anxieties over fictionality and as a response to censorship. Jane Spencer's *The Rise of the Woman Novelist* goes beyond Watt to consider the important role played by women novelists in the rise of the genre. And Firdous Azim's *The Colonial Rise of the Novel* usefully extends Watt's analysis to discuss the important role played by colonialism in providing material for novels and in stimulating the novelistic imaginations of both writers and readers.

Michael McKeon's more dialectical *The Origins of the English Novel, 1600–1740* extends Watt's discussion by paying more attention to the roots of the novel before the eighteenth century and to the persistence of prior forms in the eighteenth century. Margaret Anne Doody's *The True Story of the Novel* traces the origins of the novel back even further than McKeon to ancient literary sources, including such early texts as the *Satyricon* of Petronius. In this long view of the history of the novel, Doody recalls the work of **Mikhail Bakhtin**, whom she draws on. Indeed, Bakhtin's vision of the novel as an infinitely flexible, highly dialogical, ever-evolving genre that remains in close contact with contemporary reality has been the most influential theoretical elaboration of the novel in the past century.

Georg Lukács's Kantian *The Theory of the Novel* has also been influential, though Lukács is more important for his later (Marxist) studies of realism. Lukács largely focuses on the nineteenth century and illustrates his observations from European novels. Lukács approaches realism from a dialectical perspective in insightful essays on the topic, which appeared in *The Historical Novel* (1937), *Essays on Realism* (1948), *Studies in European Realism* (1950), and *Realism in Our Time* (1958). These scholarly works define not only realism but also naturalism, formalism, and modernism and go on to make valuable contributions to the development of Marxist aesthetics and cultural study.

According to Lukács, realism in its proper form links everything with everything else, presenting human societies as complexly interconnected totalities. This interconnectedness makes realism a fluid, vibrant medium of transaction between different spheres of life: the private and the public, the individual and the social, the mental and the physical. The realist assumes his or her position at the center of the world.

True realism—or "classical realism," as Lukács calls it—creates "typical" characters in the most profound sense of the term because they embody the fundamental social and historical forces of their time. The **historical novel**, especially those of Walter Scott and James Fenimore Cooper, provide the perfect genre for typical characters. Located in a specific time and place and acting at crucial junctures of history, these characters are who they are as a result of historical forces; they represent the spirit of the age in their ability to inhabit the whole world in its totality, moving in and out of its different spheres.

The hero to a historical novelist like Scott is a mediocre person, an individual with average intelligence. The strategy enables Scott to guide the actions in many directions. The mediocrity of his heroes, Lukács argues, precludes Scott from being a romantic writer. Besides, Scott's heroes are not at all like the epic heroes who tend to be all embracing because their actions reflect the fates of nations. In showing heroism in common individuals, Scott suggests the possibility that it is a quality not exclusive to a select group of people and can be exhibited even by those who are not elites. Popular culture and individual destiny, thus, find an expression in fiction—though Scott never loses sight of the fact that larger social and historical events govern people's lives.

Lukács believes that realism presents a complete picture of the world it depicts, including the social components of that world; detailed focus on any one aspect is not necessary in this scheme. Lukács also thinks that this totality of vision depends on what Hegel called the "totality of objects," which are those essential elements that are integrally linked to the lives of the characters. In contrast, in the work of a naturalist such as **Émile Zola**, the objects themselves have an autonomous existence. Characters are not animated by the objects, which instead serve merely the purpose of providing a lifeless background to the actions. This diminishment of humanity is the hallmark of **naturalism**, which, Lukács maintains, slowly replaces realism after the 1848 revolutions, in which the conservative stance of the bourgeoisie marked the end of their historical career as a revolutionary class. Writers after these unsuccessful revolutions failed to display a proletarian class consciousness; instead of being participants, they became mere spectators of social development. The result was a failure to see life in its totality, leading to the deterioration of realism into naturalism. Lukács notices several traits in European realism after 1848: "private" characters replace dramatic and epic characters and are drawn with a few sketches; unknown social forces govern human action; shallow emotions replace deep ones; and details of social reality obtain high significance, even if they do not combine to form a social totality.

Two other distinctions that can be made within realism are "critical realism" and "**socialist realism**." Critical realism is the realism of those authors who show an awareness of the social process, including the role of the working class, though critical realists do not necessarily promote the cause of the proletariat; Scott, Balzac, **Leo Tolstoy**, and the other major realists Lukács discusses are primarily critical realists. Socialist realism, on the other hand, is the narrative mode of authors possessing a strong commitment to the cause of the proletariat and displaying an equally strong sense of historical movement toward the revolutionary victory of the working class.

Socialist realism became the official aesthetic doctrine of the former Soviet Union and was aggressively promoted by **Joseph Stalin**, **Maxim Gorky**, and Andrei Zhadanov.

Interestingly, Lukács ran afoul of both nondoctrinaire Marxists and Stalinists because of his views on realism. On the one hand, Soviet cultural officials condemned Lukács for his admiration for bourgeois realist writers such as Balzac. On the other hand, **Bertolt Brecht** felt that Lukács was too supportive of socialist realism, though it should be noted that Jameson has argued in his introduction to *The Historical Novel* that Lukács's strong aversion to naturalism is, in fact, a veiled attempt to critique the dogmatic form of socialist realism. In any case, in the so-called **Brecht-Lukács debate**, Brecht disagreed with Lukács's view of realism in general as the most effective mode of revolutionary writing, feeling instead that the experimental forms of modernism could better support revolutionary social change.

According to Lukács, realism degrades into naturalism, then further dissipates into formalism and modernism in the twentieth century. The depiction of totality in nineteenth-century realism collapses when fragmentation becomes the dominant aesthetic mode in the early twentieth century, a trend further exaggerated with the advent of postmodernism. However, the twentieth century has witnessed a good deal of well-known realist works, many of which were written by non-Western authors or by authors who write about the non-Western world, such as **Chinua Achebe**, **V. S. Naipaul**, or J. G. Farrell.

It would be a huge mistake, however, to think that in the genre of non-Western fiction, realism is the only mode. **Magical realism** often becomes the defining characteristic of this literature. As a twentieth-century variant of traditional realism, magical realism allows fantastic events to occur in a narrative that is otherwise realistic and pedestrian. The absurdity in such a depiction often leads to comic effects and can have satiric implications. The handling of the genre varies a great deal from writer to writer. While a fairy-tale-like atmosphere can be found in some magical realist works, grim reality, condemning the corruption in the third world, exists in many of them—**Ousmane Sembène**'s *Xala*, for example. Magical realism has been particularly important in **Latin American literature**, as in the works of Jorge Luis Borges and **Gabriel García Márquez**; it has also been important to other non-Western writers, such as the Indo-Anglian **Salman Rushdie** or Nigeria's Ben Okri. Some Western authors also use the mode of magical realism, such as John Fowles and **Günter Grass**.

Selected Bibliography: Azim, Firdous. *The Colonial Rise of the Novel.* London: Routledge, 1993; Davis, Lennard. *Factual Fictions: The Origins of the English Novel.* New York: Columbia UP, 1983; Doody, Margaret Anne. *The True Story of the Novel.* New Brunswick, NJ: Rutgers UP, 1996; Jameson, Fredric. *Signatures of the Visible.* New York: Routledge, 1992; Lukács, Georg. *Essays on Realism.* Ed. Rodney Livingstone. Cambridge, MA: MIT P, 1981; Lukács, Georg. *The Historical Novel.* Trans. Hannah Mitchell and Stanley Mitchell. Lincoln: U of Nebraska P, 1983; Lukács, Georg. *Realism in Our Time: Literature and the Class Struggle.* Trans. John Mander and Necke Mander. New York: Harper and Row, 1964; Lukács, Georg. *Studies in European Realism: A Sociological Survey of the Writings of Balzac, Stendhal, Tolstoy, Gorky, and Others.* Trans. Edith Bone. New York: Fertig Howard, 2002; Lukács, Georg. *The Theory of the Novel.* 1920. Trans. Anna Bostock. Cambridge, MA: MIT P, 1971; Lunn, Eugene. *Marxism and Modernism: An Historical Study of Lukács, Brecht, Benjamin, and Adorno.* Berkeley: U of California P, 1982; McKeon, Michael. *The Origins of the English Novel, 1600–1740.* Baltimore: Johns Hopkins

UP, 1987; Spencer, Jane. *The Rise of the Woman Novelist: From Aphra Behn to Jane Austen*. Oxford: Blackwell, 1986; Taylor, Ronald, ed. *Aesthetics and Politics*. London: NLB, 1977; Watt, Ian. *The Rise of the Novel: Studies in Defoe, Richardson, and Fielding*. Berkeley: U of California P, 1957.

Farhad B. Idris

RED LETTERS. Founded in 1976 by the Literature Group of the **Communist Party** of Great Britain, *Red Letters* was designed to provide a forum for people who were working on literary problems using a Marxist approach. It was informed by the heritage of 1968 and, following the precepts of **Antonio Gramsci** and **Louis Althusser**, found in culture an area of political struggle. Its initial subtitle, "Communist Party Literature Journal," was dropped from issue 11 (when it turned out that only two of the seven editors at the time were CP members). Nominally appearing three times a year but often delayed by uncertain finances (there was never any financial support from the CPGB), *Red Letters* published twenty-nine issues in its sixteen years until it closed in 1991. It reached an international audience, at its high point had some six hundred subscribers, and published some of the leading writers on culture of the day as well as many who have since gained academic reputations. At a time when English departments offered little scope for discussion of literary theory let alone cultural theory, people working in these areas were looking for a platform, which *Red Letters* provided. It played a major role in establishing cultural politics as an area of serious investigation, and photocopies of its innovative articles for many years circulated as handouts in university courses.

The initial format of *Red Letters* was popular in character, calculated to attract a general student audience. It then changed for eighteen issues to a journal style, with a more scholarly air and a mid-range price. The gradual change of direction from theoretically dense articles to material of more popular interest was signaled in issue 16 (1984) with the reintroduction of a subtitle, "A Journal of Cultural Politics." In 1989, with issue 24, there was a complete redesign, which shook off the fusty academic image with a visually stunning tabloid design, and the subtitle's "journal" was changed to "review."

Despite an enlivened content and design, *Red Letters* folded six issues later. Unlike so many little magazines of the Left, its demise was not from lack of funds; rather, the environment had changed by the 1990s. The collapse of the socialist world had a negative impact on leftist politics in general, and the rise of Thatcherite individualism devalued collective work. Both Marxist theory and cultural studies had come in from the margins and gained a place in academe, and authors who once found in *Red Letters* their only platform could now seek respectability in academic journals. The time of the project had ended, but in bringing together outstanding radical critics of an earlier generation, writers of current academic distinction, cultural theorists, creators of literature and art (e.g., Michelene Wandor, Maud Sulter, John Arden, Margaretta D'Arcy, and Conrad Atkinson), and others engaged in actual revolutionary struggle (e.g., Albie Sachs), *Red Letters* developed an important perspective and helped to legitimize the political interpretation of culture.

David Margolies

RED LOVE (VASILISA MALYGINA, **1926)** is **Alexandra Kollontai**'s best-known fictional work. This novella of ideas was originally published in the trilogy *Love of Worker Bees (Liubov' pchel trudovykh).* In the foreward to the English translation, Kollontai writes that she wanted to write not a "study in morals," but a "purely psychological study of sex-relations in the post-war period" in the Soviet Union. The **Russian Revolution** brought fundamental social and political changes, and they were influential in restructuring the position of women in Russian society. Kollontai explores these changes, points out the difficulties they created, and suggests the direction gender relations should take in the future.

Red Love is partly based on Kollontai's own life, in particular on her love and (free) marriage to a revolutionary, Pavel Dybenko, and on the eventual dissolution of their relationship. The novel depicts Vasilisa Malygina and Vladimir Ivanovich, who fall in love during the heady days of the October Revolution. Both dedicated revolutionaries, they become close working for the revolution together, eventually falling in love and living together. However, their relationship is not a traditional bourgeois marriage: both Vladimir and Vasilisa are independent, politically active, with not much thought or time to devote to personal life. Kollontai emphasizes the need for each individual to contribute to the development of socialism as a prerequisite for successful lives of individuals.

When Vladimir is transferred to a distant town, Vasilisa cannot join him. Her work in Moscow is too important to be abandoned for personal reasons. Eventually she goes to visit him, only to discover that he has changed. The New Economic Program (NEP) of compromise is underway and, much to Vasilisa's chagrin, Vladimir is a thriving entrepreneur espousing many bourgeois values. He also has a lover, Nina. Realizing that the love between Vladimir and Nina is genuine, Vasilisa wishes them well, only to discover upon return to Moscow that she is pregnant. She plans to raise the child on her own, with the help of her community and friends. Kollontai thus gestures toward the idea of motherhood as a communal/social concept and that the birth of a child outside wedlock is a happy and positive event for the society.

The novel is brimming with new ideas of gender relations that Kollontai wants to introduce into the Soviet society, such as the concept of a marriage as a union of free people, which should be dissolved when mutual love disappears. But she also notes the difficulties in making such a decision due to traditional patriarchal upbringing and values. The novel also examines women's changed role in the new society and is a critique of the NEP and its detrimental influence on socialist values, which were being so painstakingly introduced into Soviet society.

Kollontai does not paint a rosy picture of contemporary life, but her belief that the socialist direction is the right one is unwavering. The difficulties faced by the new society are legion, both from individuals who do not accept socialist ideals and in the psychological makeup of some individuals who, even when accepting values of the new society, cannot overcome their own background and inherited values. Thus, *Red Love* is a fine example of **socialist realism**, depicting the present situation and gesturing toward the socialist future.

Selected Bibliography: Farnsworth, Beatrice. *Aleksandra Kollontai: Socialism, Feminism, and the Bolshevik Revolution.* Stanford, CA: Stanford UP, 1980.

Dubravka Juraga

REED, JOHN (1887–1920). Although he was not a major force in the American literary scene of the first two decades of the twentieth century, Reed's legacy nevertheless is an enduring one. His best-known work, *Ten Days That Shook the World* (1919), is an unqualifiedly sympathetic firsthand account of the Bolsheviks' rise to power in the **Russian Revolution** in 1917. Ultimately, though, Reed's lasting influence owes as much to his near-mythic reputation as a bohemian revolutionary as it does to his writing, a reputation that was revived to some extent via the 1981 film *Reds*, based on his life.

Reed was born to a well-off family in Portland, Oregon. After a mercurial and uneven undergraduate career at Harvard, Reed moved to New York in 1911 at the urging of journalist Lincoln Steffens. He began publishing sketches, poems, and articles and was invited by **Max Eastman** to join the editorial board of the *Masses* late in 1912. Reed's work with the *Masses* put him into direct contact with such leftist intellectuals as Walter Lippmann, Carl Van Vechten, Gertrude Stein, and Mabel Dodge. In 1913, Reed became involved with "Big Bill" Haywood's **Industrial Workers of the World (IWW)**. Reed was briefly jailed in April 1913 after participating in an IWW strike in Paterson, New Jersey, an experience he soon chronicled in the *Masses*. In this piece, his authorial perspective changed from simply reporting events to actively participating in them, an evolution that marked most of his subsequent work. Reed was commissioned late in 1913 to cover the ongoing Mexican Revolution. He gained the confidence of the revolutionary Pancho Villa, and Reed's well-received dispatches—expanded in 1914 into his first book, *Insurgent Mexico*—served as much to promote Villa's politics as they did to establish Villa's romanticized legend.

When **World War I** broke out, Reed was quickly engaged as a war correspondent, but lacked commitment to either side in the conflict. As a result, he returned to the United States in 1916 after several picaresque exploits on both major fronts. After getting married and briefly working with the groundbreaking Provincetown Players theater group, Reed actively opposed U.S. entry into the war. In August 1917, Reed traveled to Russia to report on life after the coup that had toppled the Romanov dynasty. He was unimpressed with the provisional government and allied himself, both ideologically and personally, with the Bolsheviks, especially **Leon Trotsky**. He witnessed many of the events that unfolded as the Bolsheviks seized power in November 1917, which he later chronicled in *Ten Days That Shook the World*. Upon returning home in 1918, Reed found himself ostracized for his involvement with communism. The editors of *The Masses*—Reed included—were indicted under the newly passed Espionage Act, and the magazine was banned, thus depriving Reed of his main vehicle for publication. Nevertheless, he spent the last two years of his life vigorously advocating communism, both through his actions—such as helping to found the American Communist Labor party and attending communist congresses in the Soviet Union—and his copious journalistic work, mostly confined to pro-communist publications. He died of typhus in Moscow on October 17, 1920, and was buried with honor beside the walls of the Kremlin.

Selected Bibliography: Aaron, Daniel. *Writers on the Left: Episodes in American Literary Communism.* New York: Harcourt, Brace and World, 1961; Duke, David C. *John Reed.* Boston: Twayne, 1987; Hicks, Granville. *John Reed: The Making of a Revolutionary.* New York: Macmillan, 1937; Reed, John. *Ten Days That Shook the World.* New York: Penguin, 1977; Rosenstone, Robert A. *Crusade of the Left: The Lincoln Battalion in the Spanish Civil War.* New York: Pegasus, 1969.

Derek C. Maus

REIFICATION is a Marxist concept used to describe the way in which social relations under capitalism appear as natural, static, and thinglike; the concept is translated from the German word *Verdinglichung*, "thingification." **Karl Marx** was the first theorist to use the concept of reification. In *Capital*, Marx applies the concept in his seminal analysis of **commodification**, wherein he argues that the commodity form of the products of human labor produces a mystification of capitalist social relations. He terms this mystification "commodity fetishism," since the products of human labor produced within historically specific social relations appear in commodity society as "autonomous" and "endowed with a life of their own" (165). The reification of social relations, however, is not simply a misperception but rather inheres within capitalist society. Labor is treated as a thing to be abstracted and quantified in the labor process to produce exchange values; the alienated products of labor are not in the workers' control. Marx suggests that the problem of reification cannot be overcome until commodity society is abolished and production is consciously planned and controlled by the working class to produce use-values for the fulfillment of its needs.

In the twentieth century, **Georg Lukács**, a Hungarian Marxist, made the most significant contribution to the theory of reification in his essay "Reification and the Consciousness of the Proletariat" in *History and Class Consciousness* (1922). Basing his argument largely on Marx's analysis of commodity fetishism as well as **Max Weber**'s analysis of rationalization, Lukács argues that capitalist reification is a structural and cognitive problem that penetrates all aspects of society, from bourgeois philosophy to working-class consciousness. Reification makes the social world appear as if it is regulated by unchanging natural laws; the market economy appears as a brute fact to which the individual must conform. Alienated from their work and products under the system of private property, workers, for Lukács, take a contemplative attitude toward the seemingly fast and fixed world that they in fact re-create daily. Lukács specifically identifies this reified consciousness as an ideological problem that naturalizes and legitimizes capitalist social relations.

The concept of reification has important implications for theories of ideology. Since reification emanates from the commodity structure of capitalism, it is not simply a set of ideas imposed on subjects by ruling classes interested in preserving the capitalist mode of production. Moreover, in Lukács's terms, it is the opposite of and an obstacle to the production of class consciousness and hinders the conceptualization of society as a totality always in dialectical process, and not a "fact" or "thing." Hence, as Marx implies and Lukács theorizes, reification is a cognitive-ideological problem to be overcome if the working class is to understand itself as the only subject capable of making history, of having the power to free itself from the oppressive and exploitative social relations of capitalism. For Lukács, only the working class has the need and the capacity to end reification by revolting against its own commodity status and by abolishing capitalism.

Selected Bibliography: Bewes, Timothy. *Reification, or the Anxiety of Late Capitalism.* London: Verso, 2002; Lukács, Georg. *History and Class Consciousness: Studies in Marxist Dialectics.* Trans. Rodney Livingstone. Cambridge, MA: MIT P, 1971; Marx, Karl. *Capital: A Critique of Political Economy.* Vol. 1. Trans. Samuel Moore and Edward Aveling. Ed. Friedrich Engels. New York: International Publishers, 1967.

Anthony Dawahare

***THE REPUBLIC* (380–370 B.C.E.),** the greatest work of Plato (427–347 B.C.E.) and the first work of systematic philosophy in the Western tradition. Among the most important and influential works of philosophy ever written, *The Republic* is written in the form of a dialogue, with Socrates as the main character. Socrates was Plato's teacher, though to what extent *The Republic* accurately reports his thought is unknown. *The Republic* is primarily concerned with issues of morality and politics. The main question it sets out to answer is: What is justice? In answering this question, the work deals with many other areas of philosophy, including the philosophy of education, the theory of knowledge, metaphysics, and the philosophy of art.

The book answers its central question by constructing an ideal society, making it one of the first works of **utopian fiction.** The resulting society is rigidly hierarchical, divided into three classes: an elite of Guardians (or rulers), aided by Auxiliaries (or soldiers), and finally a class of workers. It is not clear whether there are slaves as well, as was common in Greece in Plato's time. For Plato, just as an organism thrives when its parts fulfill their specific tasks, so too is society well functioning and "just" when each class carries out its allotted role in the context of the whole. Plato thus equates justice with social harmony, health, and happiness.

Justice is a quality of individuals as well as communities, and an elaborate analogy between society and the individual self runs throughout the book. The self is divided into three parts—reason, spirit, appetites—which correspond to the three basic social classes. The self is just and happy when these parts work together harmoniously. Injustice is discord in the self, a form of mental illness. Justice in the self is achieved when reason is in command and the appetites kept under strict control. Likewise, the just society is one in which philosophers—the rational Guardians—are rulers. These philosopher-rulers are to be selected and trained through a lengthy educational process. To explain the nature of their philosophical training, Plato puts forward his "theory of Forms." The highest reality is not immediately present to the senses but can be grasped only through the use of reason. The mind must free itself from the influence of the senses and grasp the higher reality of the Forms. Only thus can the ruling Guardians have true knowledge of what is just and guide society correctly. In one of the most celebrated passages in the book, Plato portrays human beings as confined in a dark cave, shackled in illusion. Only a few escape and make their way out and into the sunlight, where they eventually gain true knowledge. This image suggests a bleak picture of the human condition. On the other hand, it involves a radiant comparison of knowledge with illumination and sunlight, which has had an impact on generations of subsequent thinkers.

Plato takes a very negative view of poetry and art; they deal in illusions and are to be banished from his ideal Republic. This is ironic given that *The Republic* and Plato's other dialogues are such great works of literature. *The Republic* in particular puts forward a systematic, rationalist, dualistic outlook with extraordinary clarity and persuasiveness.

Selected Bibliography: Annas, Julia. *An Introduction to Plato's Republic.* Oxford: Clarendon, 1981; Plato. *The Republic.* Trans. H.D.P. Lee. 2nd rev. ed. Harmondsworth: Penguin, 1987; Sayers, Sean. *Plato's Republic: An Introduction.* Edinburgh: Edinburgh UP, 1999; White, N. P. *A Companion to Plato's Republic.* Oxford: Blackwell, 1979.

Sean Sayers

THE REVENGE FOR LOVE (1937) is a novel of pre–civil war Spain by **Wyndham Lewis** that is increasingly regarded as one of the most significant political novels of the 1930s. The novel is less concerned with public politics than with states of mind, and explores the ways public ideas are received and adapted to personal need. In it, some are true Communists, others are bourgeois pretenders. The true Communist is Percy Hardcaster, his politics based on those of **Ralph Bates**, whom Lewis knew. The bourgeois Communists are a group of failed artists and writers whose "communism" is a cover for sexual and economic self-interest. The novel is set in 1932 (1991 edn., 302) and derives its impetus from the British Communists in Bates's *Lean Men* (1934). When it opens, Hardcaster is in a Spanish prison, from which he escapes, losing a leg when he is shot. In London, Communists such as Tristram Phipps enlarge their self-importance by their devotion to him. Phipps's wife, Gillian, appears in a memorable chapter, "Gillian Communist," in which her self-deceiving "mental communism" (177ff.) is ground down by the seducer and political ignoramus Jack Cruze. In Cruze, Lewis scathingly exposes the thought processes of sexual vulgarity.

The tragedy of the novel focuses on Margot Stamp, whose partner, Victor, is a failed painter forced to forge Van Goghs for "bourgeois communists" smuggling guns into Spain. Victor is recruited to drive a car with a false bottom full of guns (actually bricks) across the Pyrenees, but he is a decoy. The novel was originally entitled *False Bottoms*, and false walls and forgery parallel the falsely held politics. Margot has a false and sentimental mental landscape made up of scraps from **Woolf** and Ruskin, but Lewis values her for being undeceivable. When Margot and Victor die in Spain, Hardcaster's communism breaks into compassion: "And down the front of the mask rolled a sudden tear, which fell upon the dirty floor of the prison" (336). **Fredric Jameson** has called this "the realest tear in all literature" (177).

Lewis's publishers obliged him to alter his manuscript to suit the demands of a circulating library. Dasenbrock's 1991 edition is a masterly reconstruction of Lewis's intentions, and the 2004 edition is the first to reprint this version. The growing reputation of this novel may seem surprising, given Lewis's actual and alleged right-wing politics at the time, which went largely against the leftist tide of the decade.

Selected Bibliography: Jameson, Fredric. *Fables of Aggression: Wyndham Lewis, the Modernist as Fascist.* Berkeley: U of California P, 1979; Lewis, Wyndham. *Left Wings over Europe.* London: Cape, 1936; Lewis, Wyndham. *The Revenge for Love.* Ed. Reed Way Dasenbrock. Santa Rosa, CA: Black Sparrow P, 1991; Lewis, Wyndham. *The Revenge for Love.* Intro. Paul Edwards. London: Penguin, 2004.

Alan Munton

REVUELTAS, JOSÉ (1914–1976). Novelist, activist, and heterodox Marxist critical thinker, Revueltas ranks as one of the most compelling figures in twentieth-century Mexican literary politics. His work was relentless in its analyses of the historical shortcomings of the Mexican Revolution, in its exposure of the contradictions within the Mexican Left, as well as in its own self-criticism. Though little known outside of Mexico, Revueltas's influence inside Mexico has been considerable, and increased dramatically with his participation in the massive student and worker demonstrations in Mexico City, which culminated on October 2, 1968, in the infamous massacre of hundreds of demonstrators by government troops, known as

Tlatelolco. For his role in the protests, Revueltas was imprisoned at the "black palace" of Lecumberri from 1968 to 1971, and his martyrdom inspired the political engagement of a whole generation of young Mexican writers.

Revueltas was born into a modest but remarkable family from Durango, which gave Mexico the actress Rosaura, the avant-garde composer Silvestre, and the muralist painter Fermín, all siblings. After the family moved to Mexico City, Revueltas immersed himself in political philosophy and soon joined the youth brigades of the fledgling Mexican **Communist Party**. He was first imprisoned for clandestine political activities at the age of fifteen, then again in 1931 and between 1933 and 1935. Revueltas's relations with his fellow militants were also dramatic and conflictive; he was banished from the Communist Party, first in 1943 and again in 1959. In 1960, he founded an independent party, the Liga Leninista Espartaco, which was short-lived. Often struggling to make ends meet, Revueltas variously worked as a journalist, a teacher, and a screenwriter for the Mexican film industry.

Revueltas's posthumous collected works (*Obras completas*, 1978–1987) span some twenty-seven volumes and encompass short stories and plays, many iconoclast essays in sociohistorical analysis and political theory, and two fascinating volumes of memoirs, but his seven completed novels constitute his principle legacy. Critics have pointed out certain infelicities and extensive moral and philosophical digressions in Revueltas's novels, but these are also part of the authenticity that makes him such an intriguing figure: his denunciations of alienation and exploitation can verge on an almost perverse fascination with the eschatological. All the novels are far removed from the optimism prescribed by **socialist realism**, and embody Revueltas's own version of a common Latin American melding of Christian-like sacrifice with Marxist passion. *Human Mourning* (*El luto humano*, 1943) brought Revueltas early critical acclaim; through interior monologues and flashbacks, it excavates Mexico's recent and distant pasts in search of redemption. Revueltas's third novel, *Los días terrenales* (Earthly Days, 1949), which many consider his best, is representative in its juxtaposition of Fidel's cold and inflexible orthodox militancy with Gregorio's perhaps imperfect but absolute empathy. In response to public criticisms of the novel's "pessimism" by fellow militants, Revueltas once went door-to-door pulling it from bookstore shelves. *Los errores* (Mistakes, 1964) and *El apando* (Solitary, 1969), both noteworthy, round out his novelistic production.

Selected Bibliography: Durán, Javier. *José Revueltas: una poética de la disidencia.* Xalapa: Universidad Veracruzana, 2002; Escalante, Evodio. *José Revueltas: una literatura del "lado moridor."* Mexico City: Era, 1979; Negrín, Edith, ed. *Nocturno en que todo se oye: José Revueltas ante la crítica.* Mexico City: Era/UNAM, 1999.

Steven M. Bell

RICKWORD, EDGELL (1898–1982). War poet, essayist, and influential editor, Rickword represents the internationalist strand in British Marxism. He was already an established literary figure when he joined the **Communist Party** of Great Britain (CPGB) in 1934, under the influence of **Nancy Cunard**, with whom he had worked on the anthology *Negro* (1934), though the immediate stimulus was the fascist riots in Paris on February 6 that year. Paris was for him the center of civilization, and there would always be a strong cultural impulse in his Marxism. Rickword edited the CPGB's literary and political journal *Left Review* between January 1936 and June 1937. From November 1944 to July 1947, he edited another party journal, *Our Time*. Neither was sufficiently valued by the party hierarchy, which contrived the closure of both—stories told in Charles Hobday's excellent biography of Rickword and in Andy Croft's life of **Randall Swingler**. In the 1970s, Rickword's reputation revived when two volumes of his collected essays and his selected poems were published.

Born in Colchester, Essex, UK, Rickword went straight from school into the war in 1916, losing an eye and being awarded the Military Cross. Rejecting Oxford after four terms, he set up the *Calendar of Modern Letters* (1925–1927) with Douglas Garman. From their *Scrutinies* series, Leavis took the name of his own journal, *Scrutiny*. Rickword was one of the finest British reviewers and essayists of the 1920s, arguably second only to **T. S. Eliot**. In fact, the *Calendar* was intended as an alternative to Eliot's *Criterion*. It is unfortunate that Rickword's best-known poem is the striding "Winter Warfare" because he wrote much love poetry of great subtlety before turning to satire in *Twittingpan* (1931). The satire on power, "To the Wife of Any Non-Intervention Statesman" (1938), is a memorable response to **Spanish Civil War** policy. A careful reader of published documents, Rickword was skeptical about the Moscow trials, but held on in the CPGB until 1956, when he quietly failed to renew his membership.

Rickword explored the English radical tradition in politics and literature, recovering a forgotten history reaching from the medieval period down to **Milton**, Cobbett, Hazlitt, and Cruikshank. *A Handbook of Freedom: A Record of English Democracy through Twelve Centuries*, edited with **Jack Lindsay** (1939), is a masterpiece of research that found its way into many a knapsack during **World War II**. In a 1979 tribute, William Empson said of the soft-spoken Rickword, "he was the real one, if you happened to know."

Selected Bibliography: Hobday, Charles. *Edgell Rickword: A Poet at War*. Manchester: Carcanet, 1989; Munton, Alan, ed. "Edgell Rickword: A Celebration." *PN Review* 6.1 (1979): i–xxxii. Contributions by William Empson, E. P. Thompson, and C. Hill.

Alan Munton

RIDGE, LOLA (1873–1941). Born in Dublin, Ireland, and raised in Australia and New Zealand, Ridge came to the United States in 1907 and remade herself into an American poet, anarchist, and feminist. In 1908, Ridge settled into New York City's radical bohemia and became active in the Francisco Ferrer Association, where she founded and edited its journal, *Modern School*. Through her connection to the Ferrer Association, Ridge came in contact with **Emma Goldman** and Alexander Berkman and contributed poems to their journal *Mother Earth*. Ridge also traveled in avant-garde literary circles and helped edit two influential modernist journals— *Others*, founded by Alfred Kreymborg, and *Broom*, founded by Wall Street heir Harold Loeb. For a short period, she was also a contributing editor of the *New Masses*. Ridge's first critical acclaim as a poet occurred when she published excerpts of her long poem "The Ghetto" in the *New Republic*. "The Ghetto" was the first English language modernist poem published in America on the subject of ghetto life.

Following shortly was her first collection, *The Ghetto and Other Poems* (1918). The book's publication helped establish Ridge's reputation as a poet of social conviction. Poems such as "Lullaby," written in response to the East St. Louis riots; "Frank Little at Calvary," about the torture and lynching of an **International Workers of the World** organizer; as well as "Electrocution," a sonnet condemning the death penalty, and "Morning Ride," about the Leo Frank lynching—both from her third book *Red Flag* (1927)—are bold examples of Ridge's belief that feelings of social outrage should be expressed rather than suppressed in poetic composition.

In 1927, Ridge joined fellow artists and intellectuals around the world to protest the executions of Italian anarchists Nicola Sacco and Bartolomeo Vanzetti. Her activism resulted in the publication of *Firehead* (1929), a book-length verse poem about Christ's crucifixion, with allegorical references to the Sacco and Vanzetti case. Her interest in the ancient history of the Americas and the Middle East led Ridge to travel to Beirut and Baghdad in the early 1930s, and to Mexico in the latter part of the decade. Inspired by these travels, Ridge had planned to write a five-volume poem cycle, *Lightwheel,* which remained unfinished at her death.

Selected Bibliography: Berke, Nancy. *Women Poets on the Left: Lola Ridge, Genevieve Taggard, Margaret Walker.* Gainesville: UP of Florida, 2001; Daly, Catherine, et al. "Readings: Lola Ridge." *How2* 1.7 (Fall 2002). http://www.scc.rutgers.edu/however/v1_8_2002/current/index.shtm; Drake, William. *The First Wave: Women Poets in America, 1915–1945.* New York: Macmillan, 1987.

Nancy Berke

ROBINSON, KIM STANLEY (1952–). Easily the most important of the left-leaning U.S. **science-fiction** novelists since **Philip K. Dick** and **Ursula Le Guin**, Robinson is also a greatly admired writer of "hard" science within his many novels. Winner of Nebula, Asimov, Campbell, Locus, World Fantasy, and Hugo awards, he has earned himself more than a niche. He constitutes, perhaps, a trend all by himself.

Robinson, raised in Orange County with a keen awareness of damaged and disappearing ecosystems (but also of environmental remnants bearing great beauty), earned a Ph.D. in English on the subject of Philip K. Dick, guided in part by the prominent Marxist critic **Fredric Jameson**. It was, on publication, the outstanding study of Dick, but perhaps also a way for would-be novelist Robinson to distance himself from Dick's approach. Teaching college courses briefly, Robinson shifted to Davis, California, with his wife, an environmental chemist; worked for several years in a local bookstore; and rewrote the dissertation into a book. He then began his prodigious production of science fiction (SF), not more in quantity than other SF writers of the last several generations but with vastly higher literary quality than the norm.

Best known are the volumes of the *Mars* trilogy—*Red Mars* (1993), *Green Mars* (1994), and *Blue Mars* (1996)—plus a sort of addendum of related material, *The Martians* (1999). Altogether, these lengthy novels relate the story that begins with Mars colonization in the twenty-first century, when the dire condition of planet Earth prompts an international effort to find a way out. Among the small group of scientifically qualified figures chosen, one bloc looks to create a new civilization, while a second bloc plans to assist megacorporations in mining the resources of the colonized planet. They cooperate in the initial project of "terraforming," making islands of livable air for humans, earthen animals, and plants between Martian deserts. Among the radicals, success brings a further division: Greens, who want to keep going with the transformation, and Reds, who want to preserve as much of the natural Martian environment as possible. Against this backdrop, with anarchist communes and corporate cityscapes, comes invasion (by the corporate backers) and war. By the time centuries have passed, colonization reaches even the most seemingly uninhabitable planets—such as Mercury—with entire enclosed cities sliding across the planetary axes to escape the solar inferno.

Jameson has called the *Mars* trilogy "the great political novel of the 1990s" (*Seeds* 65). This series can be seen as a work of **utopian fiction** in its vision of the possibilities of genuine social and political change. This utopian theme is a hallmark of Robinson's work, which includes much of importance beyond the Mars books. The California trilogy (*The Wild Shore*, 1984; *The Gold Coast*, 1988; *Pacific Edge*, 1990) portrays alternative visions of the future of U.S. civilization (especially in California). The first volume depicts struggles to survive and recover civilization after a nuclear holocaust; the second projects the current course of U.S. capitalism to a dystopian extreme; the third presents an alternative future in which socialists and environmentalists have succeeded in achieving radical social and political change. *Antarctica* (1997) follows Robinson's own travel to the ice continent and projects "rules" there as an ecological model; *Icehenge* (1984) has a similar theme of frozen possibilities but projected to outer space and the distant future; *The Memory of Whiteness* (1985) is a remarkable evocation of an ultra-modern physics based on the principles of music; and *The Years of Rice and Salt* (2002) is a richly detailed alternative history that imagines the possible social and political evolution of a world in which the Black Death has virtually wiped out European populations and removed Europe from the historical scene. Robinson currently lives and works in a semicommunal settlement in California.

Selected Bibliography: Franko, Carol. "Working the 'In-Between': Kim Stanley Robinson's Utopian Fiction." *Science-Fiction Studies* 21.2 (1994): 191–211; Jameson, Fredric. "'If I find one good city I will spare the man': Realism and Utopia in Kim Stanley Robinson's *Mars* Trilogy." *Learning from Other Worlds: Estrangement, Cognition, and the Politics of Science Fiction and Utopia*. Durham, NC: Duke UP, 2001. 208–32; Jameson, Fredric. *The Seeds of Time*. New York: Columbia UP, 1994; Michaels, Walter Benn. "The Shape of the Signifier." *Critical Inquiry* 27.2 (2001): 266–83.

Paul Buhle

ROBINSON, LILLIAN S. (1941–). A trailblazer in second-wave **feminist criticism and theory**, Lillian [Sara] Robinson has remained an important voice in cultural studies and **Marxist-feminism** for more than three decades. Born in New York City, she studied at Brown University, where she eventually wrote a master's thesis on **Ezra Pound**'s poetic theory (1962), and had further training at the Sorbonne, New York University, and Columbia University. The latter institution awarded her a Ph.D. in comparative literature in 1974. During these years, she participated in protest activities—for which she was jailed—and became an important voice for working-class women and issues of race in the burgeoning women's movement. Her doctoral thesis was later published as a book, *Monstrous Regiment: The Lady Knight in Sixteenth-Century Epic* (1985). For nearly two decades from the late 1970s on, she taught at a dizzying number of institutions of higher education (often visiting for only a semester or two), an experience that one critic described as that of an "academic vagabond" (Richter 152). During the periods in which she did not hold such positions, Robinson scraped by on speaking fees, unemployment, and food stamps. She eventually found a permanent position as professor of English at East Carolina University and is currently principal of the Simone de Beauvoir Institute at Concordia University in Montreal.

Robinson is the author and editor of many groundbreaking books. Perhaps as a result of the constraints of her uncertain employment, she became an accomplished essayist; her most significant early books collected these essays. *Sex, Class, and Culture* (1978, reissued 1986) explains that her use of the term "essay" means to call up "forays into critical territory where social reality and cultural production share a common unguarded border" (xi), not "the last word" (xxix). Considering socialist feminist issues in radical criticism, modernism, **Virginia Woolf**, Jane Austen, and soap operas, among other subjects, the collection is stunning in its wide-ranging, fearless, progressive scope. *In the Canon's Mouth* (1997) includes essays reprinted and revised from the *Nation* and from academic periodicals, featuring a conversational and often sardonic tone on the topic of "the culture wars." Throughout, Robinson ruminates on health, the job market, and academic power and privilege, as well as on great books and political correctness.

An invitation to deliver a keynote lecture at a conference in Bangkok led to the coauthored book (with Ryan Bishop) *Night Market* (1998). It examines the Thai sex industry in its historical, political, gendered, and economic complexity. That book was followed by *Wonder Women: Feminisms and Superheroes* (2004), a fascinating study of adventure comics that Robinson calls "probably as close as I'll ever get to a memoir" (x). Her next scholarly project considers mythologies of interracial rape. Robinson has also published poetry and a novel. Two collections of feminist confessional poems, *Robinson on the Woman Question* (1975) and *The Old Life: Five Reactionary Poems for Dick* (1976), eloquently express justified social and personal anger. Her novel, *Murder Most Puzzling* (1998), is an engaging literary mystery, featuring a female detective with a Ph.D., who has never held a regular academic job.

Selected Bibliography: Richter, David H. *Falling into Theory: Conflicting Views on Reading Literature.* 2nd ed. New York: Bedford–St. Martin's, 2000; Robinson, Lillian S. *In the Canon's Mouth: Dispatches from the Culture Wars.* Bloomington: Indiana UP, 1997; Robinson, Lillian S. *Sex, Class, and Culture.* Bloomington: Indiana UP, 1978.

Devoney Looser

ROLLAND, ROMAIN (1866–1944).

ROLLAND, ROMAIN (1866–1944). Of Burgundian legal stock, Rolland trained in the Ecole normale supérieure in Paris as a historian. A sickly child, traumatized by the death of a younger sister, he sought consolation in music, literature, and a neo-Spinozan pantheism, which led him to react against Parisian materialism and decadence. After some years studying in Rome, he took his doctorate in musicology and unenthusiastically developed an academic career, while struggling to establish himself as a dramatist and flirting with both Catholicism and socialism. The Dreyfus affair inspired him to begin a cycle of plays on the **French Revolution** and take an interest in popular theater. He finally achieved fame through a series of heroic biographies and *Jean-Christophe* (1904–1912), a novel cycle based on the life of a German composer, expressing wide internationalist sympathies as well as a love of France, for which he was awarded the 1915 Nobel Prize. Convinced of the dynamic value of faith rather than any specific political creed, he opposed **World War I** in *Au-dessus de la mêlée* (1915), a work based less on pacifist principle than on a sense that the idealism of European youth was being abused. Vilified for his stance and drawn reluctantly into political activism, he spent the war in Switzerland trying to bring together an international elite of intellectuals to stimulate postwar reconciliation. Returning to Paris after the war, he was disappointed by his reception and took up permanent residence in Switzerland. Fascinated by Indian culture, he became an early advocate of Gandhi, wrote studies of Indian religious leaders, and strove to reconcile Gandhian pacifism with Soviet Russia. His highly qualified initial welcome of Bolshevism turned to active support after the mid-1920s, once he became convinced that it was a dynamic revolutionary faith and the most effective means of checking the drift toward fascism and war. He devoted more time to political writing and visited Russia in 1935, but maintained his lifelong principle of independence from any political party. He formed growing doubts about **Stalin**, but silenced them partially due to fears for his Russian wife's family. Disillusioned by the Nazi-Soviet pact, he withdrew from political writing in **World War II**. Having returned to his native roots in Burgundy in 1938, he spent the war years—relatively unmolested by the occupying authorities—on studies of Beethoven and his former associate and publisher Charles Péguy, and died shortly after the liberation. Having always regarded himself as more of a religious than a political writer, he adopted a more sympathetic view of the Catholicism of his family but avoided conversion. He was a prolific writer of novels, plays, biographies, and political writing, but may be best remembered for his prolific correspondence with his family and a wide range of prominent personalities, still only partially published.

Selected Bibliography: Duchatelet, B. *Romain Rolland tel qu'en lui-même.* Paris: Albin Michel, 2002; Fisher, D. J. *Romain Rolland and the Politics of Intellectual Engagement.* Berkeley: California UP, 1979; Francis, R. A. *Romain Rolland.* Oxford: Berg, 1999.

Richard Francis

ROMANTICISM is the term used to describe a literary movement and profound shift in sensibility that took place in Britain and throughout Europe roughly between 1770 and 1848. Intellectually, it can be seen as a reaction against the Enlightenment emphasis on reason, order, and rationality, preferring instead the personal, the spontaneous, the eccentric, and the irrational. Aesthetically, romanticism turns to an expression of the power of the individual imagination while deemphasizing technique and convention. Politically, especially in England, romanticism was something of a demand for the actual enactment of the democratic and individualist rhetoric of the Enlightenment, energized by the revolutions in

America and France, as well as popular wars of independence in Poland, Spain, Greece, and elsewhere. Thus, romanticism was both a reaction against and a product of the central tendencies of the Enlightenment.

A similar doubleness underlies many of the characteristics of romanticism. For example, many romantic works are informed by an air of joyous liberation and freedom from constraints, though an air of torment is common to much romantic literature as well. This doubleness is central to romantic aesthetics as well. As formalized in the philosophy of Immanuel Kant, romantic art is informed by a dual impulse toward the expression of the sublime (which awes and humbles the individual who encounters it) and the beautiful (which inspires and emboldens the individual). Romantic art thus encourages individualism, while also reminding the individual that he or she is not the final authority but must come to terms with more powerful forces. In this sense, the political orientation of romanticism is much like that of capitalism itself, even as the romantic emphasis on nature and the irrational would appear to be opposed to the modernizing impulses of capitalism.

Romanticism had an important impact on virtually all literary genres, though its greatest impact was in poetry, the genre best suited to the romantic emphasis on emotional intensity, creativity, and sincerity. The romantic poet is an almost priestly figure, able to experience and appreciate the beauties of nature and the power of human passion in ways that go beyond the abilities of ordinary mortals, then able in addition to express that experience in a way that makes it available to others. Indeed, M. H. Abrams, a leading theorist of romanticism, has argued that a central goal of the movement was the "secularization of the sublime," an attempt to recapture the emotional and spiritual power of religion but within a secular humanist framework, endowing the natural with a supernatural air.

Romanticism was very much an international phenomenon. The term "romantic" as a designation for a specific school of literature that was opposed to the classical emphasis on form and structure was first used by the German critic Karl Wilhelm Friedrich von Schlegel at the beginning of the nineteenth century. An especially crucial early source of romantic energy was **Johann Wolfgang von Goethe**'s novel *The Sorrows of Young Werther* (1774), though Goethe's later relationship with romanticism was complex and problematic. French thinkers such as Jean-Jacques Rousseau, with his celebration of nature and belief in the natural goodness of man (in both novels and philosophical writings), provided an important inspiration, and writers associated with the **French Revolution**, such as the Viscount de Chateaubriand and Madame de Staël, made important contributions to the growth of romanticism as well.

Retrospectively, English romantic poetry can be seen to begin with the work of William Blake, though a coherent romantic tendency in English poetry can be dated specifically to the publication of *Lyrical Ballads* (1798) by William Wordsworth and **Samuel Taylor Coleridge**. This volume announced the coming of a new poetry, informed by a turn toward the authentic expression of individual passion while tending to value straightforward, ordinary language, eschewing the ornamentation of much eighteenth-century neoclassical poetry. This linguistic decision was not merely aesthetic; it also showed the influence of the democratic values of the recent French Revolution. Wordsworth's preface to the second edition of *Lyrical Ballads* in 1800 formalized the project of romantic poetry, arguing that "all good poetry is the spontaneous overflow of powerful feelings." Wordsworth and Coleridge were soon joined by **Percy Bysshe Shelley**, Lord Byron, and John Keats as the major figures in English romantic poetry, and though the movement was at the height of its power only in the first half of the nineteenth century, it has continued to exert a powerful influence on Western art and aesthetics since that time, especially through its belief in the value of innovation and individual creativity.

Shelley's often-quoted notion that poets serve as the "unacknowledged legislators of the world" indicates the extent to which the English romantic poets saw their project as political, even if that project did not necessarily produce a coherent political alternative to the growing power of capitalism and bourgeois ideology. Meanwhile, both romantic poetry and romantic fiction contributed to the development of a distinctive kind of hero (sometimes referred to as a "Byronic" hero): a dark, defiant outcast figure, who rejects the values of conformist society in favor of his own personal system of values. This vision often led to a radically individualist form of politics. Meanwhile, the romantic emphasis on individual liberation also led to the rise of a number of women writers, including Mary Shelley and the Brontë sisters. Romanticism also exerted a strong influence on the development of the individualist ideology of postrevolutionary American culture and society; the American transcendentalists were particularly closely aligned with romanticism.

Selected Bibliography: Abrams, M. H. *The Mirror and the Lamp: Romantic Theory and the Critical Tradition.* New York: Norton, 1953; Abrams, M. H. *Natural Supernaturalism: Tradition and Revolution in Romantic Literature.* New York: Norton, 1971; Cronin, Richard. *The Politics of Romantic Poetry: In Search of the Pure Commonwealth.* London: Palgrave Macmillan, 2000; Curran, Stewart, ed. *The Cambridge Companion to British Romanticism.* Cambridge: Cambridge UP, 1993; Day, Aidan. *Romanticism.* London: Routledge, 1996; Duff, David. *Romance and Revolution: Shelley and the Politics of a Genre.* Cambridge: Cambridge UP, 1994; Keach, William. *Arbitrary Power: Romanticism, Language, Politics.* Princeton, NJ: Princeton UP, 2004; Redfield, Marc. *The Politics of Aesthetics: Nationalism, Gender, Romanticism.* Stanford, CA: Stanford UP, 2003.

M. Keith Booker

ROUMAIN, JACQUES (1907–1944). One of Haiti's most important and influential writers, Roumain was born into the Haitian elite and educated in Switzerland. After a year in Spain, where he briefly studied agronomy, he returned to Haiti in 1927 where, with Philippe Thoby-Marcelin, he cofounded the literary journal *La Revue indigène* (1927–1928). This journal gave birth to the movement of *indigénisme.* Influenced by Jean Price-Mars' classic Haitian peasant novel *So Spoke the Uncle* (*Ainsi parla l'oncle*, 1928), the *indigénistes* advocated the rejection of European values embraced by the Haitian elite, and a celebration, instead, of indigenous Haitian culture, the Vaudou religion, and the Creole language.

Roumain was also a prominent political activist, and emerged as such during the nationalist opposition to the 1915–1934 U.S. occupation of Haiti. He founded the Haitian **Communist Party** in 1934. As a result of such political activities, he was sent to prison four times between 1928 and 1936, spending approximately thirty-two months in jail before finally going into exile in Brussels, Paris, and New York. During his years in exile, he met and forged links with international left-wing writers, such as **Pablo Neruda**, **Nicolás Guillén**, and **Langston Hughes**. In 1941, Élie Lescot was elected president of Haiti, and Roumain was able to end his six-year exile and return to Haiti. Despite having opposed the Catholic clergy's anti-Vaudou campaign of 1942, which was supported by the president, Roumain was appointed chargé d'affaires in Mexico by Lescot in 1943, and this gave him the creative freedom to write his two most influential works, the novel *Masters of the Dew* (*Gouverneurs de la Rosée*, 1944) and the poetry collection *Ebony Wood* (*Bois d'ébène*, 1945).

Roumain's earliest prose works, *Les Fantoches* (The Puppets, 1931) and *La Proie et l'ombre* (The Prey and the Shadow, 1930) are satires of the Haitian elite, while *La Montagne ensorcelée* (The Bewitched Mountain, 1931) is a pessimistic depiction of the passivity and fatalism of the peasantry. These themes are also evident in *Gouverneurs de la Rosée*, although this novel is much more optimistic than his earlier texts and is a testament to Roumain's Marxist and nationalist convictions. Its protagonist, Manuel, is at once a Christlike figure who must die for the redemption of his community and a Marxist hero committed to his people and his country. It is his most famous work and has been translated into fifteen languages, filmed, and produced as theater.

Roumain was also an ethnographer and directed Haiti's *Bureau d'Ethnologie*, founded in 1941. He published *Contribution à l'étude de l'ethnobotanique précolombienne des Grandes Antilles* (Contribution to the Study of the Ethnobotany of the Greater Antilles) in 1942. At the age of only thirty-seven, Roumain died on August 18, 1944, having returned to Haiti only a month earlier.

Selected Bibliography: Cobb, Martha. *Harlem, Haiti and Havana: A Comparative Critical Study of Langston Hughes, Jacques Roumain and Nicolás Guillén.* Washington, DC: Three Continents P, 1979; Fowler, Carolyn. *A Knot in the Thread: The Life and Work of Jacques Roumain.* Washington, DC: Howard UP, 1976; Ormerod, Beverley. *An Introduction to the French Caribbean Novel.* London: Heinemann, 1985; Thadal, Roland. *Jacques Roumain: l'unité d'une oeuvre.* Port-au-Prince: Editions des Antilles, 1997.

Sam Haigh

ROUTINIZATION. Also known as rationalization, routinization is the term used by social theorists to describe the way in which the historical evolution of Enlightenment rationality and capitalist economic organization has led to a thoroughly secular view of the world. Drawing on the work of **Max Weber**, especially in *The Protestant Ethic and the Spirit of Capitalism* (1904–1905), Marxist theorists have particularly focused on the way in which, under modern capitalist society, every aspect of life becomes regimented, scheduled, standardized, and controlled for maximum economic efficiency, leaving little room for elements of life that might lie outside the realm of the economic. In particular, the routinized world of modern capitalism is a world bereft of magic and supernatural elements, which cannot be organized and controlled by rational administration.

Fredric Jameson, in *The Political Unconscious*, suggests that routinization is very much the same phenomenon as **reification** as described in the work of **Georg Lukács** (226). For Jameson, the ongoing popularity of romance and other nonrealist literary modes (from the oral tales of traditional tribal societies to nineteenth-century adventure tales to contemporary popular genres and forms, such as magical realism, science fiction, and crime fiction) reflects an unconscious utopian yearning for precisely the elements that have been stripped from life by the modern capitalist process of routinization. Meanwhile, Jameson's more recent work on **postmodernism** has identified the increasing cultural and economic homogenization associated with late capitalism as an extension of routinization to a global scale.

Weber's notion of routinization came to particular prominence in American cultural criticism in the 1950s, when important non-Marxist American sociologists such as David Riesman and William Whyte repeatedly drew from Weber in their own discussions of the increasing conformism and bureaucratization of American society in that decade. For example, Whyte declares that the phenomena he associates with the rise of the "organization man" in 1950s America "stem from a bureaucratization of society" that was described in the work of Weber (4). And Daniel Bell, looking back from the perspective of the mid-1970s, declares *The Protestant Ethic and the Spirit of Capitalism* to be "probably the most important sociological work of the twentieth century" (287).

Selected Bibliography: Bell, Daniel. *The Cultural Contradictions of Capitalism.* 1976. New York: Basic Books, 1996; Jameson, Fredric. *The Political Unconscious: Narrative as a Socially Symbolic Act.* Ithaca, NY: Cornell UP, 1981; Weber, Max. *The Protestant Ethic and the Spirit of Capitalism.* 1904–1905. Trans. Talcott Parsons. New York: Scribner's, 1958; Whyte, William. *The Organization Man.* New York: Simon and Schuster, 1956.

M. Keith Booker

RUSHDIE, SALMAN (1947–). Rushdie prominently illustrates the diasporic condition that characterizes the lives of many contemporary authors. He was born in India; completed his education in Cambridge, England; went to Pakistan, where his family had moved; returned to England when he began his writing career; and now lives in the United States. Rushdie grew immensely famous when he published his second novel, *Midnight's Children*, in 1981. This massive work tells the stories of Saleem Sinai—its narrator/protagonist—and his Indian Muslim family, using the political history of modern India as a backdrop. Rushdie's third novel, *Shame*, is also a political allegory but is set in Pakistan. It added to Rushdie's reputation as a consummate writer of South Asian fiction—one who handles the English language in a unique South Asian way and draws on his native roots and Western literary conventions with equal facility.

His next major fiction, ***The Satanic Verses*** (1988), created a huge uproar. *Verses* describes the birth of Islam in seventh-century Arabia and tells the story of, among others, the Prophet Muhammad. Rushdie's account of his life disparagingly portrays his polygamy; it is also extremely critical of the claim Islam lays to its divine origin. Muslims all over the world began to condemn Rushdie, which led to the banning of the book in many Islamic countries. Protest marches against *Verses* often grew violent, and Iran's Ayatollah Khomeini declared a fatwa calling for Rushdie's head and offering a bounty of millions to his assassin. Rushdie went into hiding immediately and remained in safe houses protected by lawmen until recently. Though the government of Iran has distanced itself from the fatwa, the threat against Rushdie's life will probably continue as long as the author is alive.

The fatwa seemed to have little effect on Rushdie's creative output. The 1990s saw the appearance of such works as *Haroun and the Sea of Stories* (1990), *The Moor's Last Sigh* (1995), and *The Ground beneath Her Feet* (1999). Many critical essays appeared at about the same time; nearly all of them were collected in *Imaginary Homelands: Essays and Criticism, 1981–1991* (1991) and later in *Step across This Line: Collected Nonfiction, 1992–2002* (2002). These critical works, however, do not include "The Empire Writes Back with a Vengeance," a short article that Rushdie published in the London *Times* in 1982. It deserves particular mention because in it, Rushdie sought to explain many theoretical issues in postcolonial literature. He argued that a new writing in English about non-English societies and by authors from non-English backgrounds was emerging in Britain and that the phenomenon would create a fresh cultural identity for Britain as well as for its former colonies. What the piece purports to achieve in terms of revamping the English literary canon suggests a left bias. However, Rushdie's views on politics and the role of literature have suffered a shift in the opposite direction since the 1980s, generating acute controversies in its wake. Take, for example, his introduction to *The Vintage Book of Indian Writing: 1947–1997* (1998). Here, Rushdie quite blatantly proclaims that literature written in English in India is far superior to literature written in its sixteen local languages. The comment inflamed many Indian authors (some of whom write in English) to censure Rushdie for his Anglophilia and ignorance. More inflammatory have been some of his recent writings since the September 11 tragedy. In "November 2001: Not about Islam?" republished in *Step across the Line*, Rushdie vilifies Islam and justifies his extreme outlook with a sampling of rabid Muslim opinions on the event, which Western media routinely use to stereotype Islam. In other essays in *Step,* he trashes Western intellectuals who tried to understand anti-American feelings in the Islamic world following September 11 to determine if U.S. foreign policy had unwittingly contributed to such a virulent brand of Islam.

It goes without saying that Rushdie will continue to give rise to disputes and anger. Not surprisingly, he draws a phenomenal amount of critical attention. Books of criticism on him exceed a score; dissertations and theses that treat him singly or view him in relation to other authors exceed two score; and news items, interviews, and short critical pieces are in the thousands.

Selected Bibliography: Booker, M. Keith, ed. *Critical Essays on Salman Rushdie.* New York: G. K. Hall, 1999; Brennan, Timothy. *Salman Rushdie and the Third World: Myths of the Nation.* London: Macmillan, 1989; Cundy, Catherine. *Salman Rushdie.* Manchester: Manchester UP, 1996; Fletcher, M. D., ed. *Reading Rushdie: Perspectives on the Fiction of Salman Rushdie.* Amsterdam, Netherlands: Rodopi, 1995; Harrison, J. *Salman Rushdie.* New York: Twayne, 1992; Rushdie, Salman. *Imaginary Homelands: Essays and Criticism, 1981–1991.* London: Granta, 1991.

Farhad B. Idris

RUSS, JOANNA (1937–). U.S. academic, essayist, and **science-fiction** writer. Russ is the author of some of the most radically politicized science fiction of the 1970s, a decade during which women entered the field in unprecedented numbers. Her work has gained particular attention among critics working in the areas of feminism and **gay and lesbian studies.** She began publishing science fiction (SF) in 1959; in 1972, her brilliant story "When It Changed" propelled her to the forefront of feminist challenges to the genre. Russ later expanded this story into a highly original work of **postmodernism**, *The Female Man* (1976)—a stingingly funny novel that satirizes gender construction and is a classic of lesbian-feminist **utopian fiction**. *The Female Man* is a formally postmodernist metafiction that uses the SF trope of parallel worlds to fragment its single female subject—"J"—into four diverse personalities: Joanna (the "author" of the novel), Jeannine (her extreme "feminine" version), Jael (murderous agent in an ongoing battle between Manland and Womanland), and Janet (envoy from the utopian all-woman planet of Whileaway). Russ is also the creator of one of SF's earliest and most memorable female action heroes, Alyx—protagonist of several short stories and of the novel *Picnic on Paradise* (1968). Much of Russ's short fiction has been collected in *(Extra)ordinary People* (1983) and *The Hidden Side of the Moon* (1987). Her one non-SF novel is *On Strike against God* (1980), an autobiographical lesbian coming-out story.

Like the SF writers **Ursula K. Le Guin** and Samuel R. Delany, Russ has published a series of important critical statements about science fiction in particular and literature in general. Many have been collected in *To Write Like a Woman* (1995), including "Towards an Aesthetic of Science Fiction," an argument for the particular nature of SF as a narrative genre; "*Amor Vincit Foeminam:* The Battle of the Sexes in Science Fiction," a survey of misogynist stories to which "When It Changed" is a direct response; and "Recent Feminist Utopias" (1980), still one of the most incisive analyses of the resurgence of utopian writing by women in the 1970s. Her full-length study *How to Suppress Women's Writing* (1983) is a witty examination of the many kinds of social and political pressures that have been used to keep women's writing out of the literary canon. More than any other writer, Russ has demonstrated the potential in science fiction for feminist opposition and critique, and for lesbian and queer challenges to the unthinking and oppressive heterosexism of contemporary culture. In 1996 she won a retrospective Tiptree Award for *The Female Man*.

Selected Bibliography: Cortiel, Jeanne. *Demand My Writing: Joanna Russ/Feminism/Science Fiction.* Liverpool: Liverpool UP, 1999; Larbalestier, Justine. *The Battle of the Sexes in Science Fiction.* Middletown, CT: Wesleyan UP, 2002; Lefanu, Sarah. *In the Chinks of the World Machine: Feminism and Science Fiction.* London: Women's P, 1988. 173–99; Moylan, Tom. *Demand the Impossible: Science Fiction and the Utopian Imagination.* New York: Methuen, 1986; Russ, Joanna. *To Write Like a Woman: Essays in Feminism and Science Fiction.* Bloomington: Indiana UP, 1995.

Veronica Hollinger

RUSSIAN LITERATURE (NINETEENTH CENTURY). In the period stretching from the late eighteenth century through the first half of the nineteenth, the specter of a serious Russian menace was perceived to arise over Europe. It is surely not entirely coincidental that this was precisely the period in which Russian literature first began to assert itself as a seriously recognized European cultural force. It was the career of **Aleksandr Pushkin** that launched Russian literature on its golden age. This may be dated either (narrowly) to the poetic achievements of the 1820s and 1830s or (more broadly) to the half century of major literary creativity extending to the 1880s, taking in the major novels of **Turgenev**, **Dostoevsky**, and **Tolstoy**. A number of commentators have dated the beginning of Russia's new cultural role to the climax of the Napoleonic wars. Dostoevsky, for instance, saw this period as "the very inception of our true self-consciousness," at the exact moment when "Pushkin appeared." An equally significant, and indeed traumatic, landmark was the (failed) Decembrist uprising, which greeted the accession to the throne of Nicholas I in 1825.

Russia's growing convergence with the West was driven by its own mutations of the key European trends of Enlightenment and **romanticism**. These included the dualities of realism and romanticism in literature; Westernism (or "progress") and Slavophilism (or navel-gazing into "the Russian soul") in thought; and positivism and symbolism, with the approach of the *fin de siècle* silver age.

Dante, **Shakespeare**, and **Cervantes** all left their mark on Russian literature, as did Rousseau, Schiller, **Goethe**, and Byron; Hoffmann, Poe, and **Dickens**; the English romantic poets; and the French symbolists. As Martin Malia puts it, on the European scale, "What France had done for secular rationalism and political radicalism in the previous century, Germany now did for aesthetic Romanticism and philosophical Idealism." Accordingly, just as France had been the main cultural influence on eighteenth-century Russia, German thought and culture—from the romantic philosophical systems of Schelling and Hegel to the materialism of Marx—provided the main ideological thrust for Russia in the nineteenth century. Later still Dostoevsky and Nietzsche occasioned a kind of posthumous symbiotic impact on each other's national cultures. Along with Baudelaire and Wagner, these two figures indeed became what Malia calls "the four evangels" of European culture as it moved into the twentieth century.

The eighteenth century, with the opening of Peter the Great's "window on the West," had seen a rapid influx of Western models and influences, especially of neoclassical literary forms imported from France. French became the court language, while the next significant monarch, Catherine the Great, was herself a German (and a usurper) and a correspondent of the French Enlightenment's *philosophes*. In this period, the Russian literary language (in something approaching its modern form) was struggling to establish itself. The poetic oeuvre of Derzhavin and the pre-romantic prose of Karamzin (first as story writer, then as court historian) supplied the most significant literary landmarks until the advent of the first towering figure of Russian literature and master of many genres, Pushkin.

Literary styles were evolving in Russia in the wake of various strands of European romanticism, with native forms beginning to push out the translations and imitations (initially from the French, but increasingly also from the English and German) that had long dominated the reading habits of the Russian gentility. Historical novels, narrative poems, travel literature, adventure stories, society tales, and gothic stories all featured in the process that established Russian literature—in the second quarter of the nineteenth century—as the newly emerging and most vibrant national literature of Europe. This was soon evident in the lyric and narrative poetry of the golden age (composed by Pushkin, **Lermontov**, Tiutchev, and others), and in at least a few isolated works of drama. Above all, though, it came in the impressive prose forms of the short story, the novella, and—finally and most famously—the novel itself.

At first the "classical" Russian novel came in hybrid forms. Pushkin's *Eugene Onegin* (a "novel in verse") was followed by Lermontov's *A Hero of Our Time* (structurally a cycle of stories), **Gogol**'s *Dead Souls* (an uncompleted trilogy, subtitled "a poem"), Odoevsky's *Russian Nights* (a fictional-cum-philosophical frame tale), and Dostoevsky's *Poor Folk* (an epistolary novel). However, all of these were engaged, in one fashion or another, with the Russia of their time, in mid-century, the Russian novel as we know it was taking serious shape, fashioned by Goncharov (*Oblomov*), Turgenev (*Fathers and Sons*), and Dostoevsky (*Crime and Punishment*). Tolstoy's epic *War and Peace* (1863–1869) can be seen to encompass all the prose ingredients mentioned above, including more than a trace of the macaronic linguistic mélange still functioning in Russian aristocratic circles, while *Anna Karenina* springs forth as the "society-tale" novel *par excellence*. In the course of these same decades, such types as "superfluous men," "repentant noblemen," strong heroines, and figures of mixed rank or origin (the *raznochintsy*) not only were reflected fictionally but were making their presence felt in the formation of what was becoming recognizable as the Russian intelligentsia. In this period, the heyday of autocracy, Orthodoxy, and nationality (*narodnost'*—at this stage a sort of crude "kvass," or, as Nabokov might say, "birch-stump" patriotism), the so-called accursed questions were being widely broached (the tsarist censorship notwithstanding). The now unstoppable rise of the Russian novel soon led it into renowned and unprecedented areas of psychological realism, accompanied by the "great reforms" of the 1860s, which produced too little too late under Alexander II.

This epoch of major literary and political events gave way, as the last quarter of the century wore on, to a temporarily quieter period, amid political reaction (under Alexander III and Nicholas II) and a dominance of minor literary forms. The turn of the century, however, brought an artistic resurgence credited as the silver age, in which a strong neoromantic Russian symbolist movement (of which Blok and **Bely** are commonly adjudged the leading exponents) embraced various strands of European modernism, while realism acquired a more naturalist hue. Russian theater (graced with the innovations of Chekhov and Stanislavsky), music, and painting came to world notice as a Pan-European *avant-gardism* gathered pace. Again a generic and stylistic mix held sway as symbolism yielded to the acmeist and futurist reactions in poetry and revolutionary realism, or neorealism (a synthesis of materialist and idealist aesthetics), in prose. In the "nightmarish atmosphere" of the interlude between the 1905 and the 1917 revolutions, many writers and thinkers (as Aileen Kelly has put it) "devoid of a sense of history . . . lived in eschatological time."

Selected Bibliography: Cornwell, Neil, ed. *The Gothic-Fantastic in Nineteenth-Century Russian Literature.* Amsterdam: Rodopi, 1999; Cornwell, Neil, ed. *Reference Guide to Russian Literature.* Chicago: Fitzroy Dearborn, 1998; Cornwell, Neil, ed. *The Routledge Companion to Russian Literature.* London: Routledge, 2001; Cornwell, Neil, ed. *The Society Tale in Russian Literature: From Odoevskii to Tolstoi.* Amsterdam: Rodopi, 1998; Hingley, Ronald. *Russian Writers and Society in the Nineteenth Century.* 2nd rev. ed. London: Weidenfeld and Nicolson, 1977; Kelly, Aileen M. *Toward Another Shore: Russian Thinkers between Necessity and Chance.* New Haven: Yale UP, 1998; Layton, Susan. *Russian Literature and Empire: Conquest of the Caucasus from Pushkin to Tolstoy.* Cambridge: Cambridge UP, 1994; Malia, Martin. *Russia under Western Eyes: From the Bronze Horseman to the Lenin Mausoleum.* Cambridge, MA: Belknap-Harvard UP, 2000; Nabokov, Vladimir. *Lectures on Russian Literature.* London: Weidenfeld and Nicolson, 1982; Pyman, Avril. *A History of Russian Symbolism.* Cambridge: Cambridge UP, 1994; Reid, Robert, ed. *Problems of Russian Romanticism.* Brookfield, VT: Gower, 1986; Terras, Victor. *A History of*

Russian Literature. New Haven: Yale UP, 1991; Thompson, Ewa M. *Imperial Knowledge: Russian Literature and Colonialism*. Westport, CT: Greenwood, 2000; Todd, William Mills, ed. *Literature and Society in Imperial Russia, 1800–1914*. Stanford: Stanford UP, 1978.

Neil Cornwell

RUSSIAN REVOLUTION. Although the Bolshevik *coup d'état* of November 1917 (which took place in October according to the old Russian calendar still in use at the time, and is thus sometimes called the October Revolution) is the event most widely meant by the term "Russian Revolution," the political transformation of Russia from a hereditary monarchy into a communist state is more accurately perceived as a process that began with the failed revolution of 1905 and continued until the establishment of the Soviet Union in 1922. Several important political and literary figures associated with the Bolsheviks' rise to power were involved with the 1905 revolution. For example, **Vladimir Lenin** and **Leon Trotsky** were both involved in the abortive establishment of a soviet in St. Petersburg in that year and both were forced into exile when this attempt failed. **Maxim Gorky** had helped found *New Life*, the first Bolshevik newspaper in Russia, and his support of the revolution forced him to flee the country in 1906. **Fyodor Gladkov**, whose 1925 novel *Cement* became one of the classics of Soviet **socialist realism**, was also punished for his support of the 1905 insurrection.

Although it failed in its attempt to overthrow the tsars, the 1905 revolution did win some liberalizing concessions from the monarchy, including a relaxation of censorship laws. Partly as a result of these reforms, the years between 1905 and 1917 witnessed a flourishing in avant-garde literature in Russia. Young writers like Ilya Ehrenburg, **Vladimir Mayakovsky**, and **Evgeny Zamyatin** began producing literature during this period that echoed and expanded on the revolutionary sentiments expressed by such works as **Nikolai Chernyshevsky**'s 1863 novel *What Is to Be Done?* (the title of which Lenin had appropriated for a political tract in 1902) or Gorky's *Mother*, which was published in exile in 1907. Symbolists such as Alexander Blok and **Andrei Bely** (whose 1916 novel *Petersburg* is set in 1905) and some of the more abstract cubo-futurists such as Velimir Khlebnikov resisted the inherently political **ideology** of the Bolsheviks but were nevertheless sympathetic to the mood of innovation that swept Russia as a result of the 1905 revolution.

The twin revolutions of 1917 and the civil war that followed set in motion a process of hardening loyalties that laid the groundwork for the rigid and restrictive policies that defined official Soviet literature from the late 1920s onward. The first revolution in early March (late February according to the old calendar) overthrew the tsars and established a liberal "provisional government" under the leadership of Alexander Kerensky. Most Russian intellectuals welcomed the end of the oppressive monarchy that had ruled Russia for centuries. However, divisions quickly arose between Bolsheviks like Lenin and Trotsky (both of whom returned from exile in the spring of 1917), who saw this as only the first step toward a communist world revolution, and more moderate Mensheviks like Kerensky, who believed that Russia needed a transitional period between monarchy and communism. The Bolsheviks and Mensheviks were factions that had separated from a single revolutionary party even before the 1905 revolution, and the revolutions of 1917 simply continued the power struggle between them over the nature of the government that would replace the tsars. Led by Lenin and Trotsky, the Bolsheviks seized power from Kerensky's Menshevik government in November and declared a "dictatorship of the proletariat." Civil war quickly broke out between those supporting the Bolsheviks (the "Reds") and a broad alliance (the "Whites") of anticommunist liberals, Mensheviks, anarchists, and even former monarchists, and lasted for four years before the Bolsheviks managed to finally consolidate their power.

Discussing the political affinities of individual writers during this period is made difficult not only by the conflicting revolutionary impulses represented by the Bolsheviks and the Mensheviks, but also by the official pronouncements made by Lenin and Trotsky about the relationship between revolution and the arts. For every writer like **Valentin Kataev,** Mayakovsky, or Yuri Olesha (each of whom were unambiguously pro-Bolshevik during the civil war), there were many others whose commitment to the revolution was less clear-cut. Lenin was extremely scornful of "soft-headed" intellectuals who supported the Menshevik notion of revolution and even criticized Gorky for wanting to preserve elements of bourgeois literary culture. In his 1923 book *Literature and Revolution*, Trotsky lambasted the wave of writers and intellectuals who abandoned the country after the Bolshevik Revolution as irrelevant holdovers from a dead age. He condemned most of the literature written between 1905 and 1917 as the product of a "decadent . . . individualism . . . [that was] loudly destroyed by" the October revolution. However, Trotsky exempted a number of writers he called "fellow-travelers" from this judgment, claiming that their lack of direct involvement with the Bolshevik cause was offset by the fact that "their literary and spiritual front has been made by the Revolution . . . and they have all accepted the Revolution, each in his own way." Trotsky included writers such as Sergei Esenin, Boris Pilnyak, and the avant-garde collective called the Serapion Brothers among this group. Though initially intended as a form of qualified praise, the "fellow-traveler" label became a condemnation, as unquestioned "party spirit" (*partiinost*) became a requirement for all literary works under **Stalin**'s rule. After the leaders of the revolution began displaying more authoritarian tendencies, many of Trotsky's fellow-travelers distanced themselves from it. This was especially true of Zamyatin, whose novel *We*, a founding text of **dystopian literature**, was published outside the Soviet Union in 1924.

Trotsky explicitly defined revolutionary literature as that "which promotes the consolidation of the workers in their struggle against the exploiters," and a number of different groups tried to take up this mantle. The Proletkult movement was established in the wake of the first 1917 revolution and quickly garnered 80,000 members, whose goal was to create genuinely proletarian art. Both Lenin and Trotsky felt this was impossible, though, and transformed Proletkult into the party-controlled VAPP (All-Russian Association of Proletarian Writers). During the early 1920s, VAPP and other groups—such as Oktyabr' (an association of writers who advocated absolute adherence to the party line) and Mayakovsky's avant-gardist LEF (Left Front)— vied to define revolutionary literature in their own image. All of these groups were subsumed within RAPP (Russian Association of Proletarian Writers) in 1928, which became the Soviet Writers' Union—the sole arbiter of official literature—in 1932.

Selected Bibliography: Erlich, Victor. *Modernism and Revolution: Russian Literature in Transition.* Cambridge, MA: Harvard UP, 1994; Fitzpatrick, Sheila. *The Russian Revolution: 1917–1932.* Oxford: Oxford UP, 1984; Maguire, Robert A. *Red Virgin Soil: Soviet Literature in the 1920s.* Princeton, NJ: Princeton UP, 1968; John. *Ten Days That Shook the World.* New York: Penguin, 1977; Trotsky, Leon. *Literature and Revolution.* Trans. Rose Strunsky. Ann Arbor: U of Michigan P, 1960.

Derek C. Maus